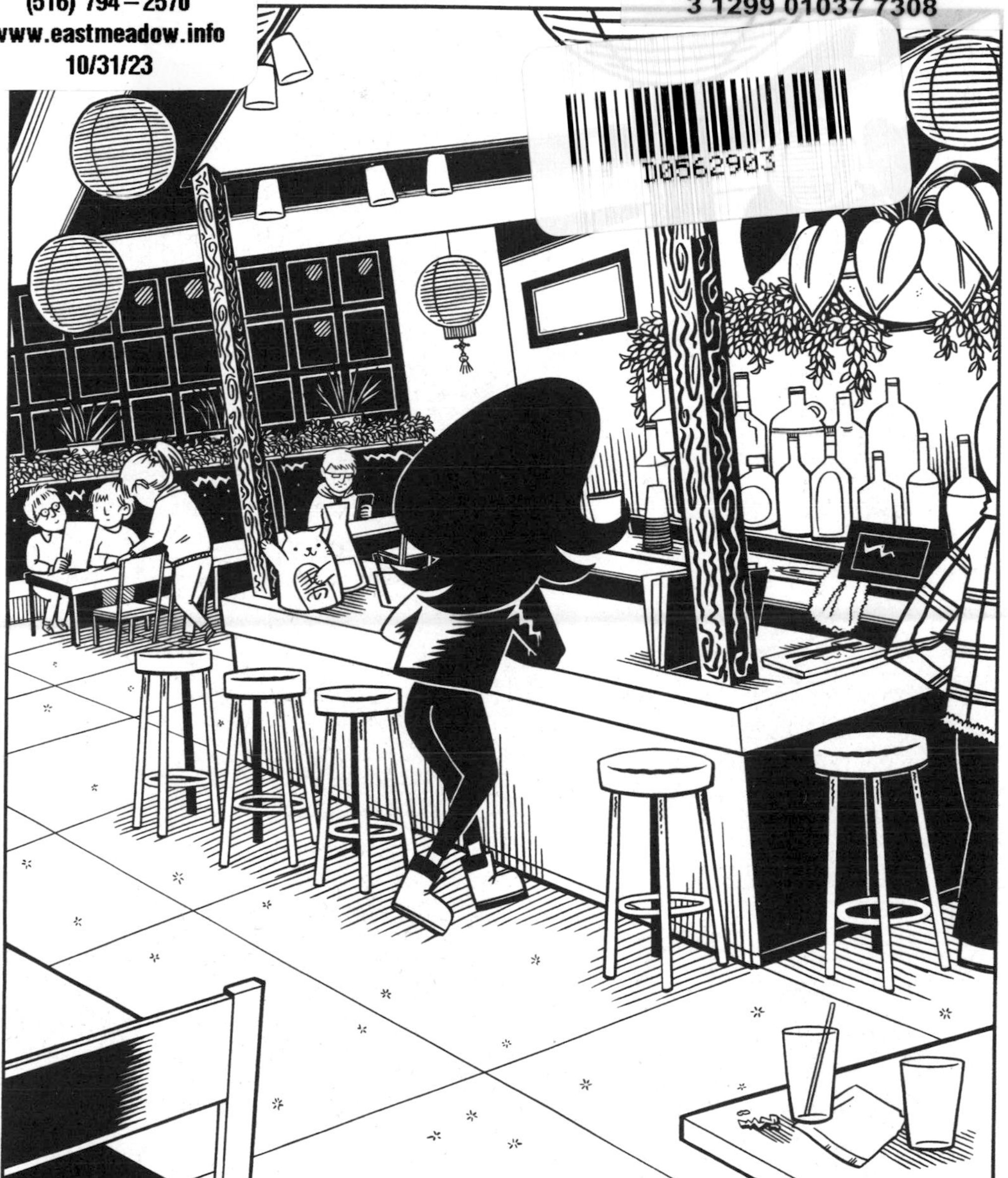

WERE YOU THINKING OF SOMETHING?
YEAH, I'LL DO A VODKA SODA.
SINGLE?
YEAH, AND CLOSE IT OUT.
FIZZ

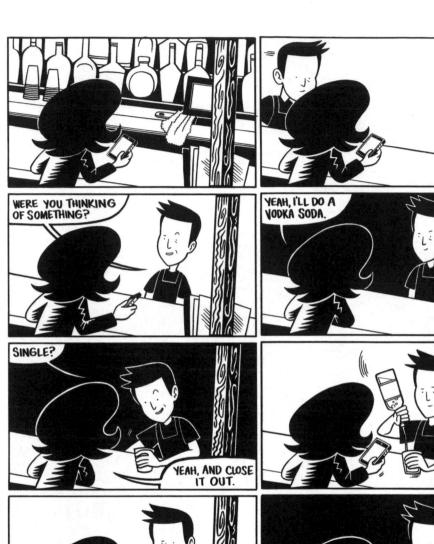

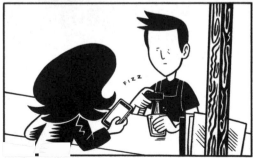

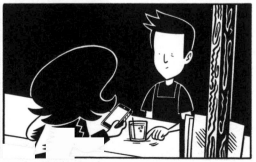

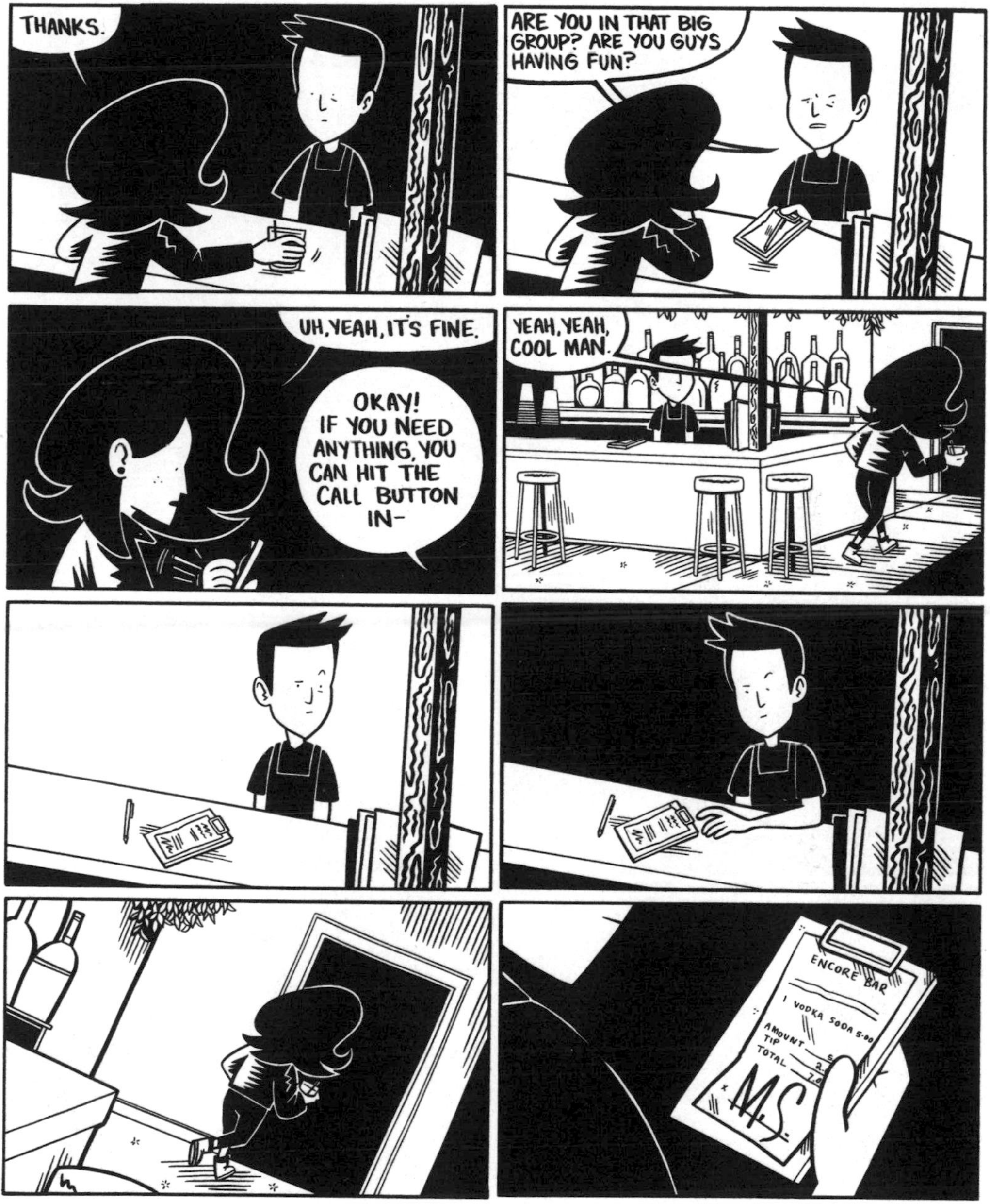
THANKS.
ARE YOU IN THAT BIG GROUP? ARE YOU GUYS HAVING FUN?
UH, YEAH, IT'S FINE.
OKAY! IF YOU NEED ANYTHING, YOU CAN HIT THE CALL BUTTON IN-
YEAH, YEAH, COOL MAN.
ENCORE BAR
1 VODKA SODA 5.00
AMOUNT
TIP
TOTAL
M.S.

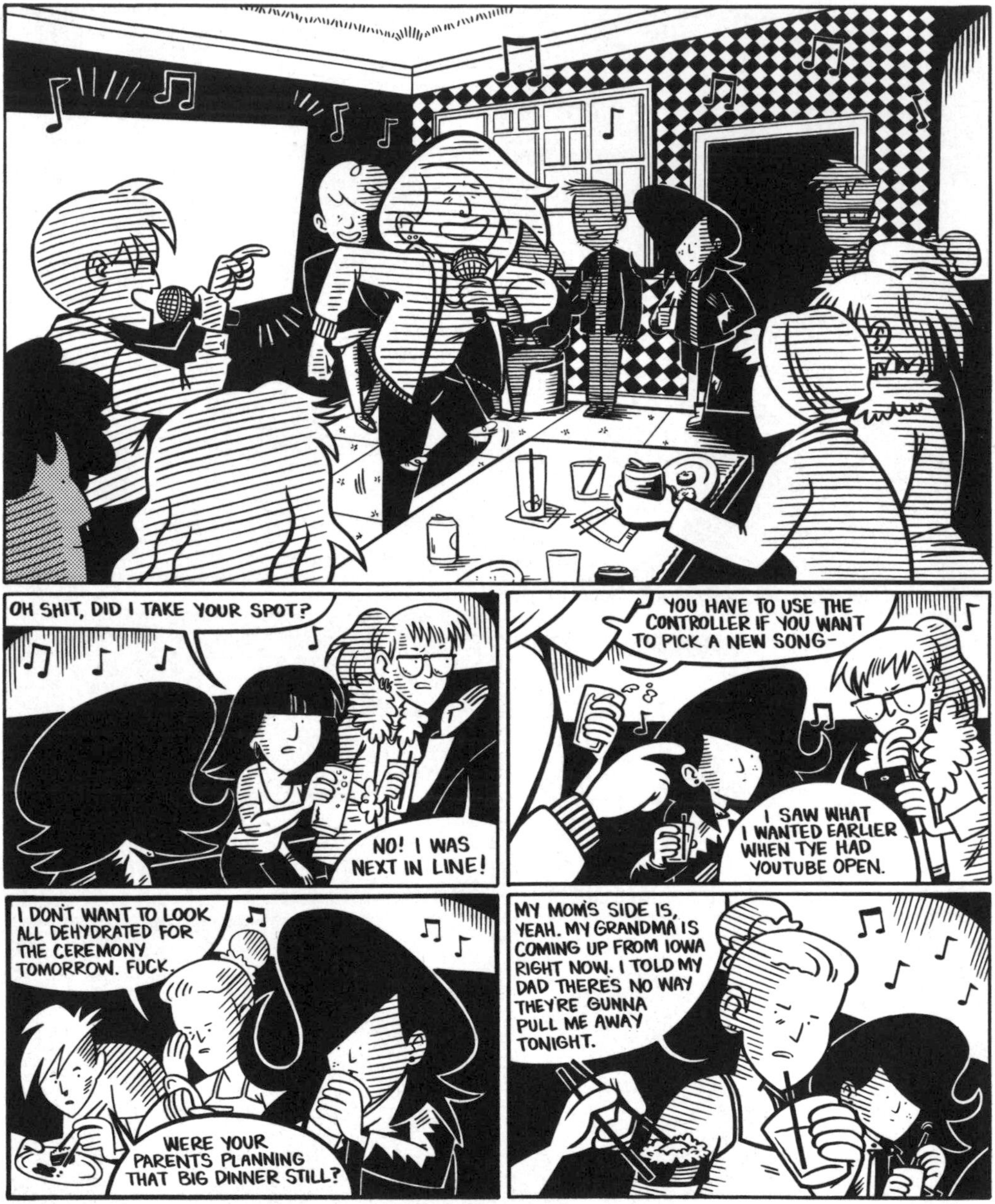

OH SHIT, DID I TAKE YOUR SPOT?
NO! I WAS NEXT IN LINE!
YOU HAVE TO USE THE CONTROLLER IF YOU WANT TO PICK A NEW SONG-
I SAW WHAT I WANTED EARLIER WHEN TYE HAD YOUTUBE OPEN.
I DON'T WANT TO LOOK ALL DEHYDRATED FOR THE CEREMONY TOMORROW. FUCK.
WERE YOUR PARENTS PLANNING THAT BIG DINNER STILL?
MY MOM'S SIDE IS, YEAH. MY GRANDMA IS COMING UP FROM IOWA RIGHT NOW. I TOLD MY DAD THERE'S NO WAY THEY'RE GUNNA PULL ME AWAY TONIGHT.

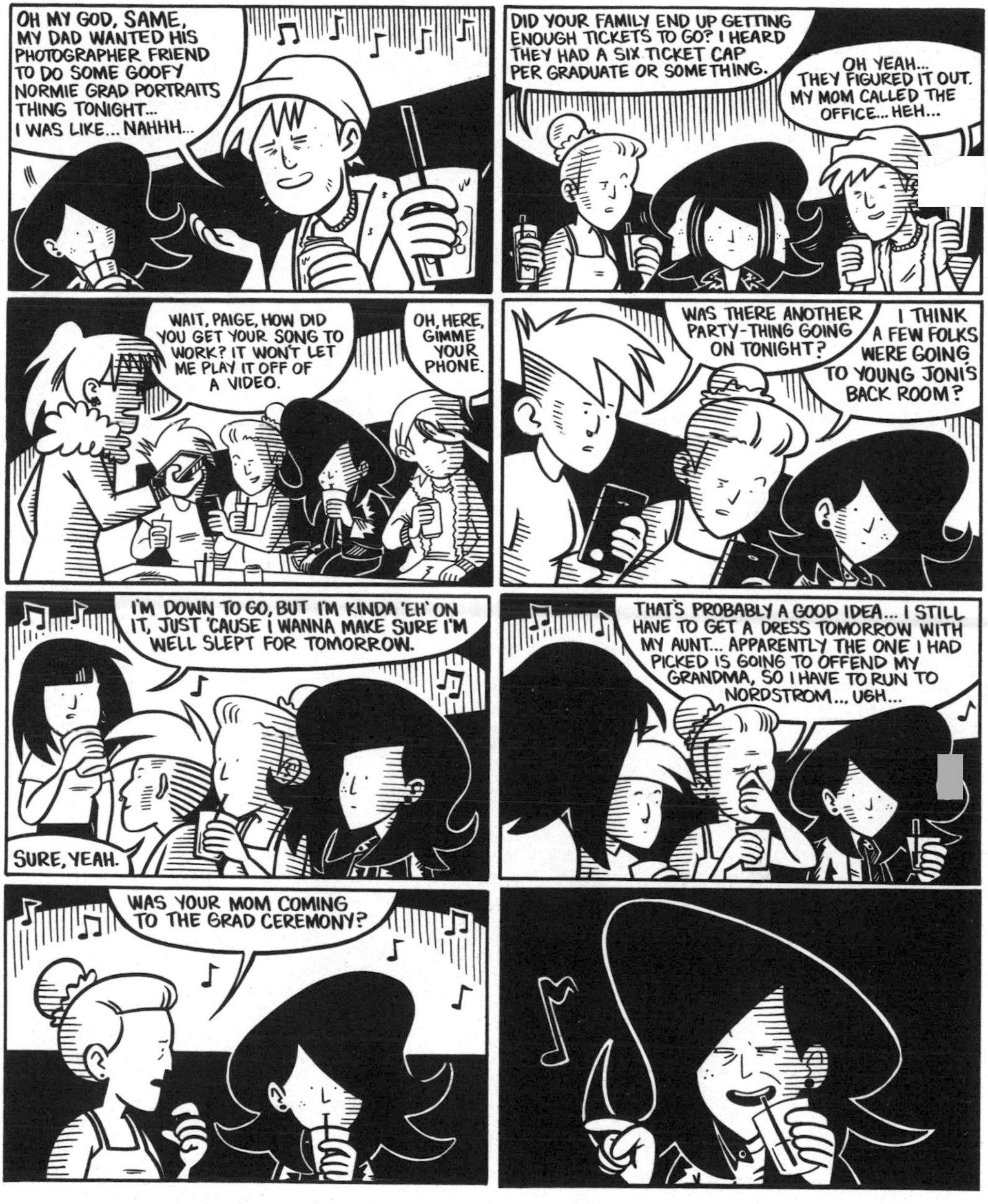
OH MY GOD, SAME, MY DAD WANTED HIS PHOTOGRAPHER FRIEND TO DO SOME GOOFY NORMIE GRAD PORTRAITS THING TONIGHT... I WAS LIKE... NAHHH...
DID YOUR FAMILY END UP GETTING ENOUGH TICKETS TO GO? I HEARD THEY HAD A SIX TICKET CAP PER GRADUATE OR SOMETHING.
OH YEAH... THEY FIGURED IT OUT. MY MOM CALLED THE OFFICE... HEH...
WAIT, PAIGE, HOW DID YOU GET YOUR SONG TO WORK? IT WON'T LET ME PLAY IT OFF OF A VIDEO.
OH, HERE, GIMME YOUR PHONE.
WAS THERE ANOTHER PARTY-THING GOING ON TONIGHT?
I THINK A FEW FOLKS WERE GOING TO YOUNG JONI'S BACK ROOM?
I'M DOWN TO GO, BUT I'M KINDA 'EH' ON IT, JUST 'CAUSE I WANNA MAKE SURE I'M WELL SLEPT FOR TOMORROW.
SURE, YEAH.
THAT'S PROBABLY A GOOD IDEA... I STILL HAVE TO GET A DRESS TOMORROW WITH MY AUNT... APPARENTLY THE ONE I HAD PICKED IS GOING TO OFFEND MY GRANDMA, SO I HAVE TO RUN TO NORDSTROM... UGH...
WAS YOUR MOM COMING TO THE GRAD CEREMONY?

TWO WEEKS PRIOR.

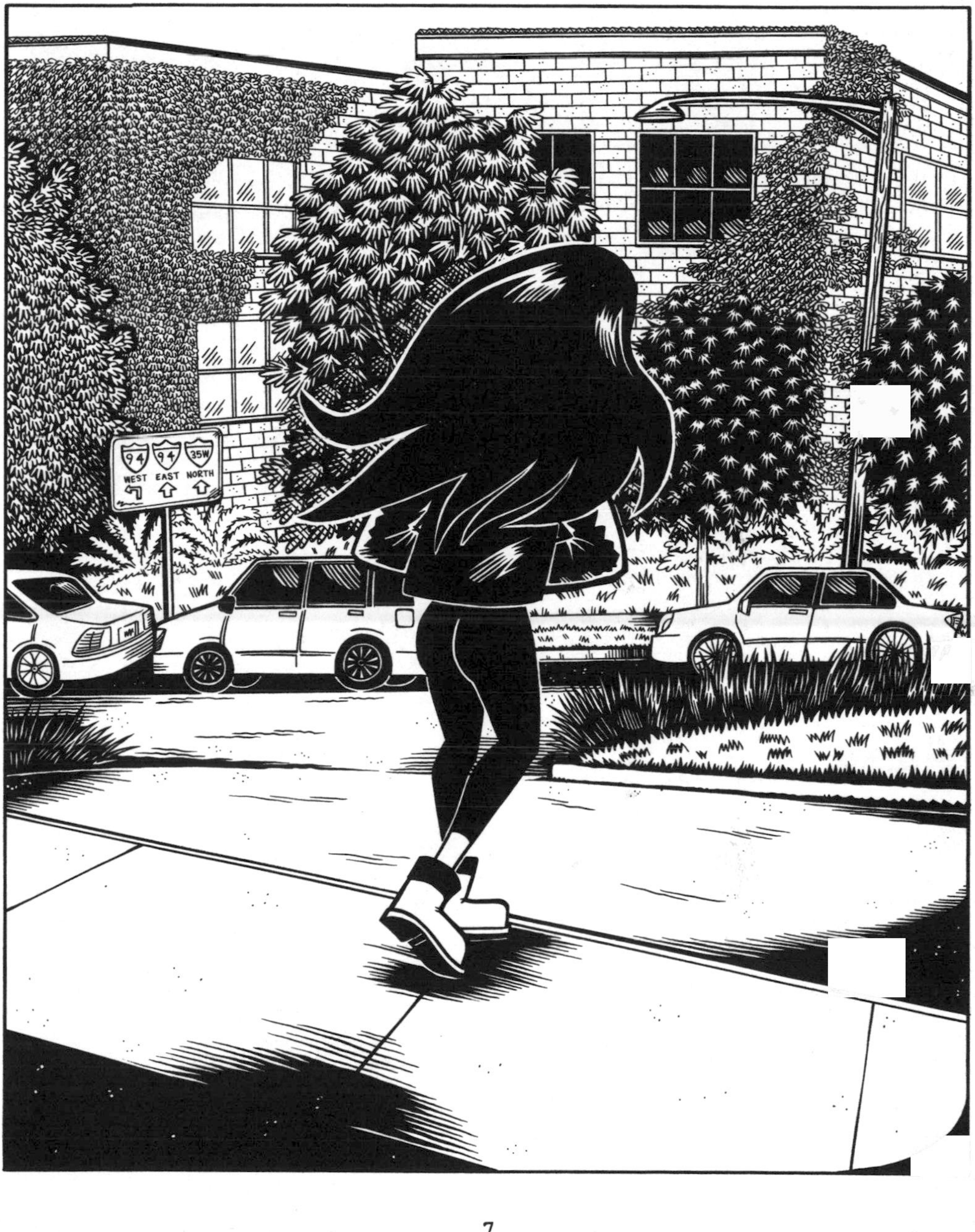
94 94 35W
WEST EAST NORTH

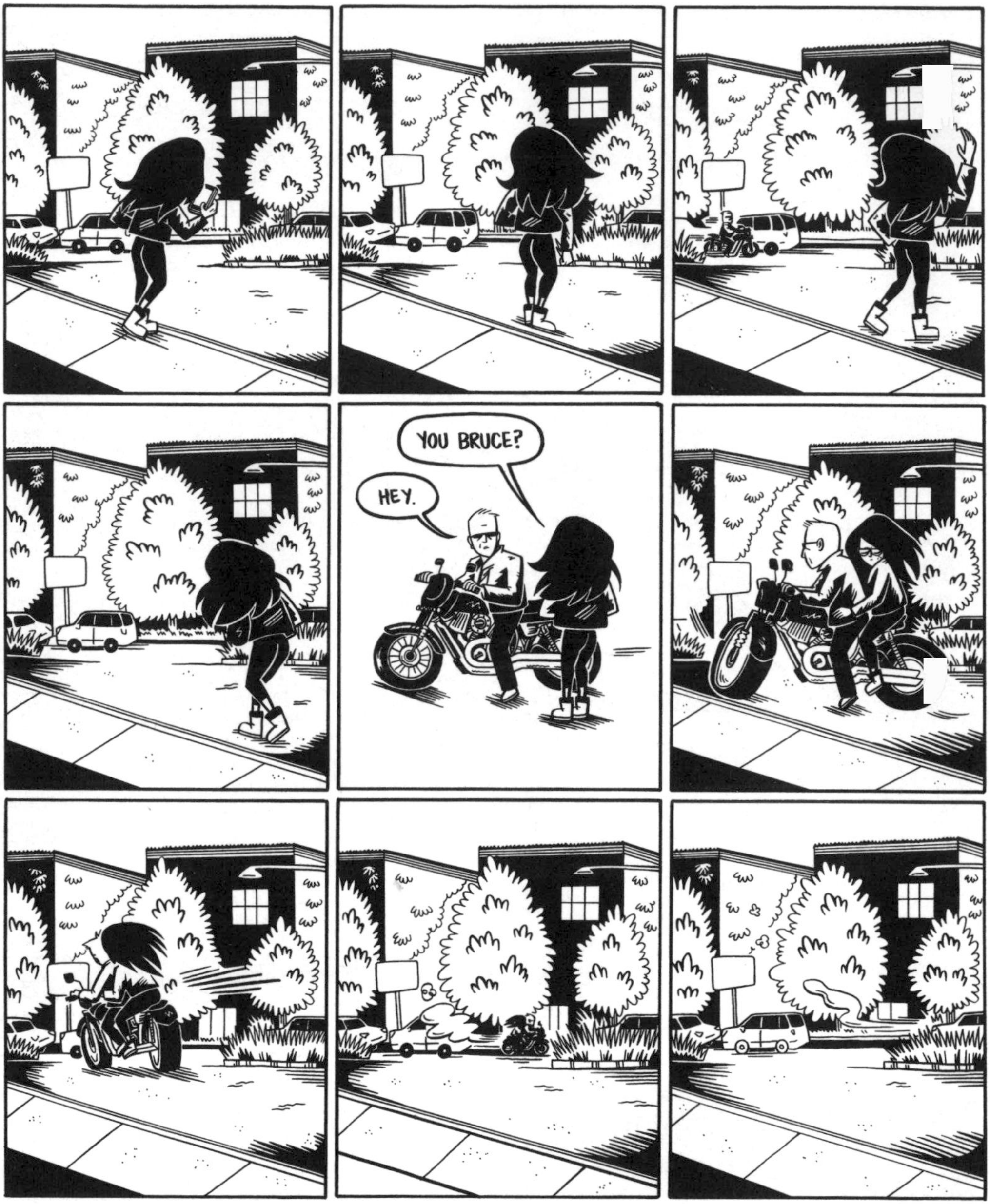
YOU BRUCE?
HEY.

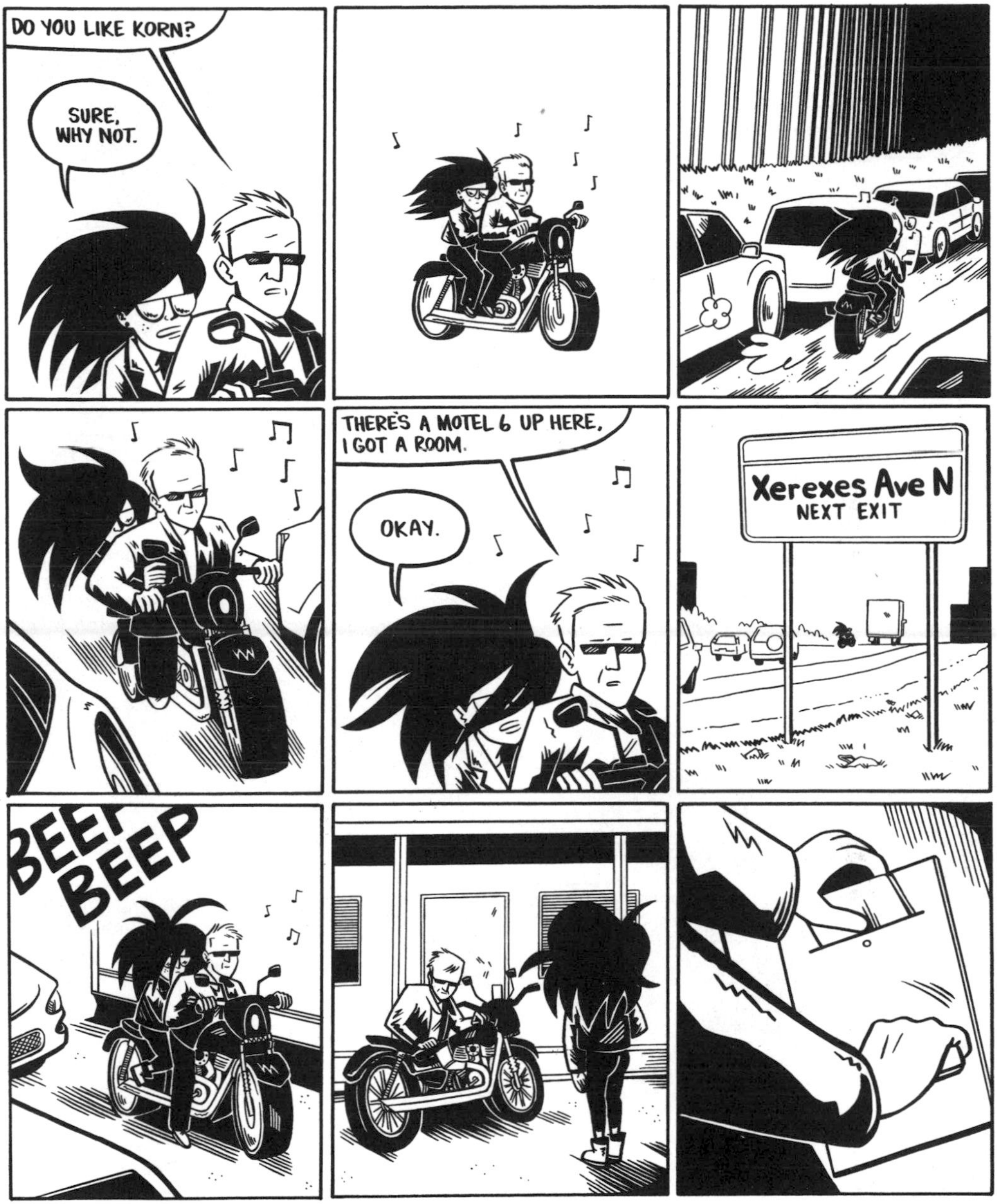
DO YOU LIKE KORN?
SURE, WHY NOT.
THERE'S A MOTEL 6 UP HERE, I GOT A ROOM.
OKAY.
Xerexes Ave N
NEXT EXIT
BEEP BEEP

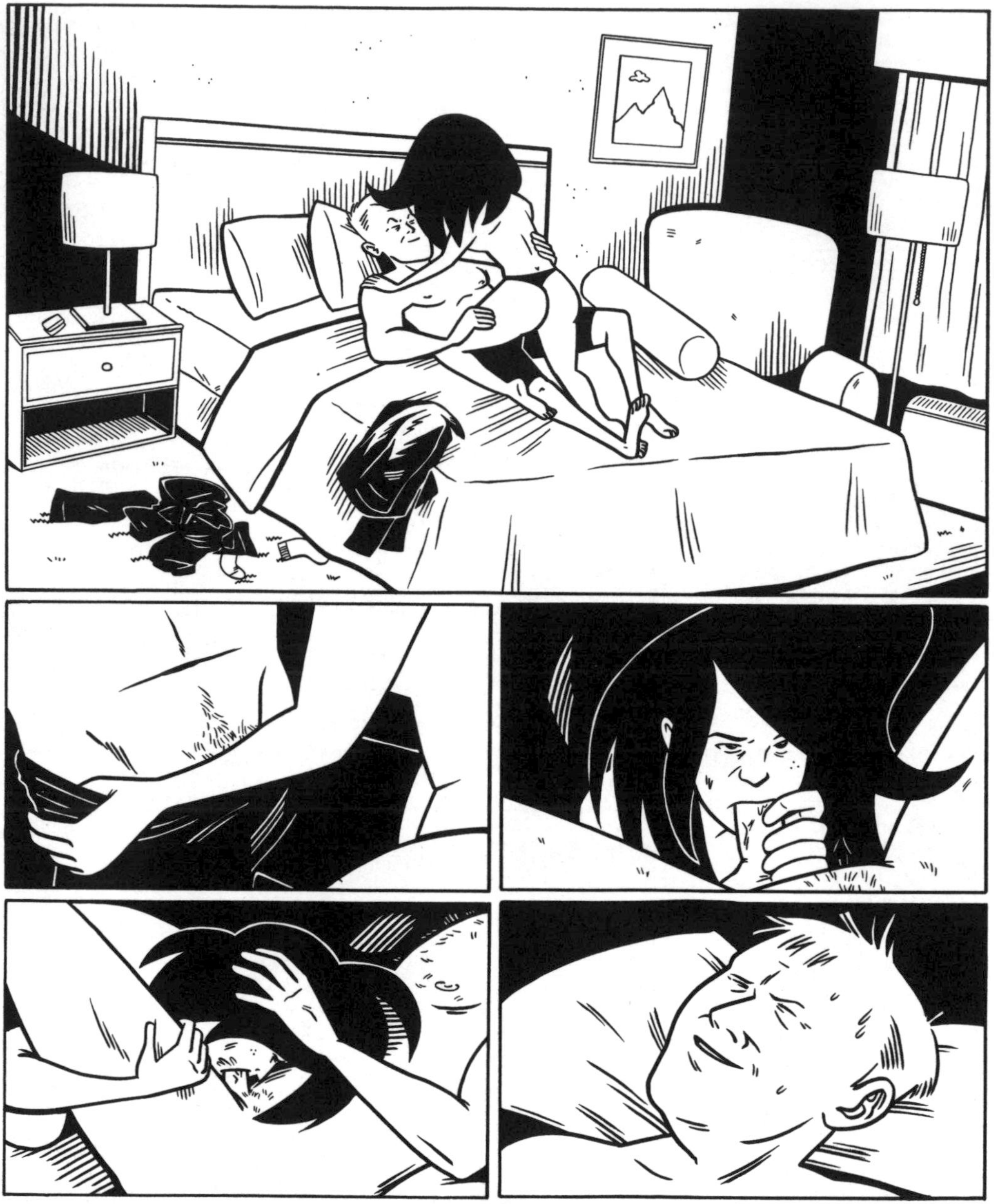

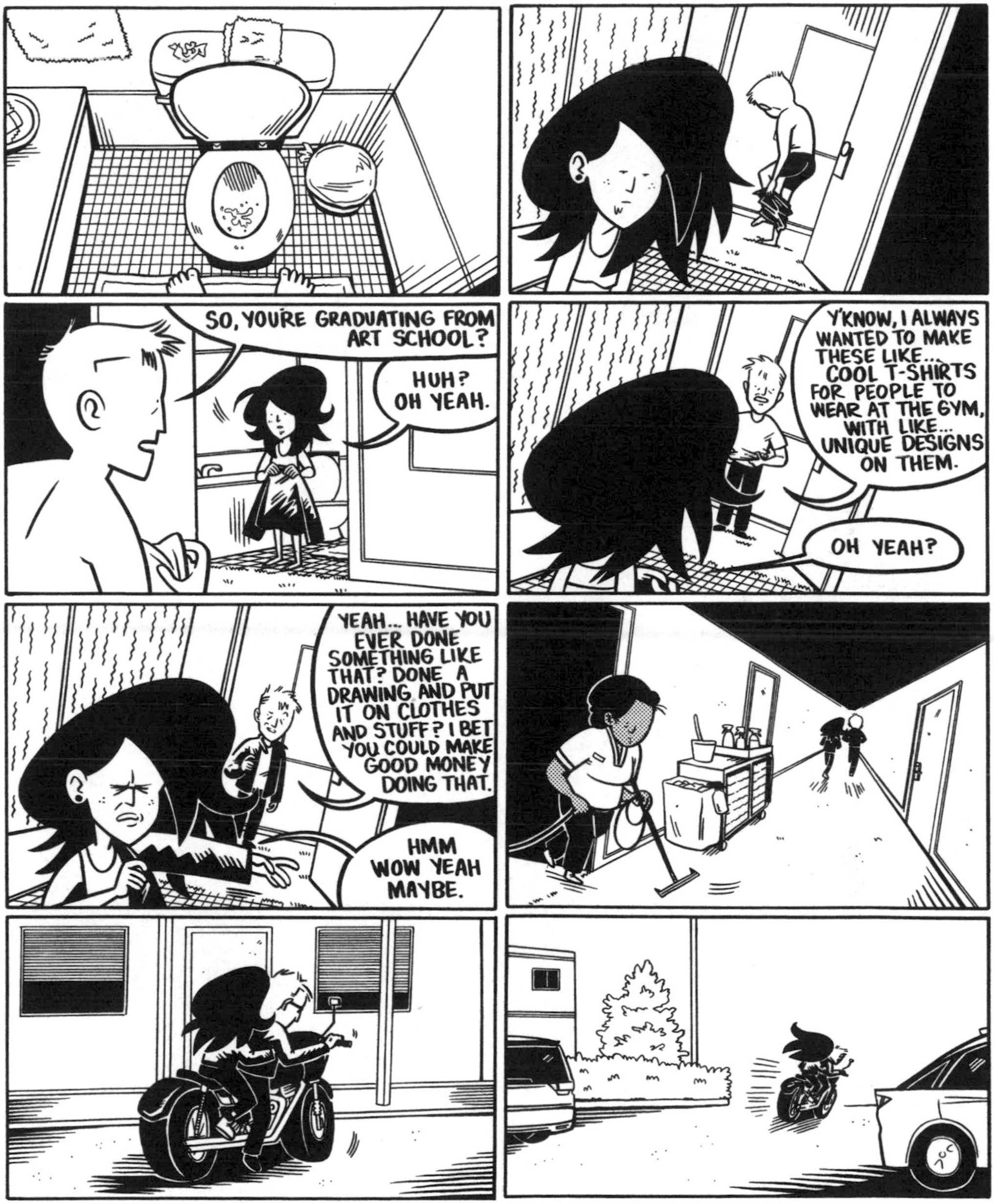
SO, YOU'RE GRADUATING FROM ART SCHOOL?
HUH? OH YEAH.
Y'KNOW, I ALWAYS WANTED TO MAKE THESE LIKE... COOL T-SHIRTS FOR PEOPLE TO WEAR AT THE GYM, WITH LIKE... UNIQUE DESIGNS ON THEM.
OH YEAH?
YEAH... HAVE YOU EVER DONE SOMETHING LIKE THAT? DONE A DRAWING AND PUT IT ON CLOTHES AND STUFF? I BET YOU COULD MAKE GOOD MONEY DOING THAT.
HMM WOW YEAH MAYBE.

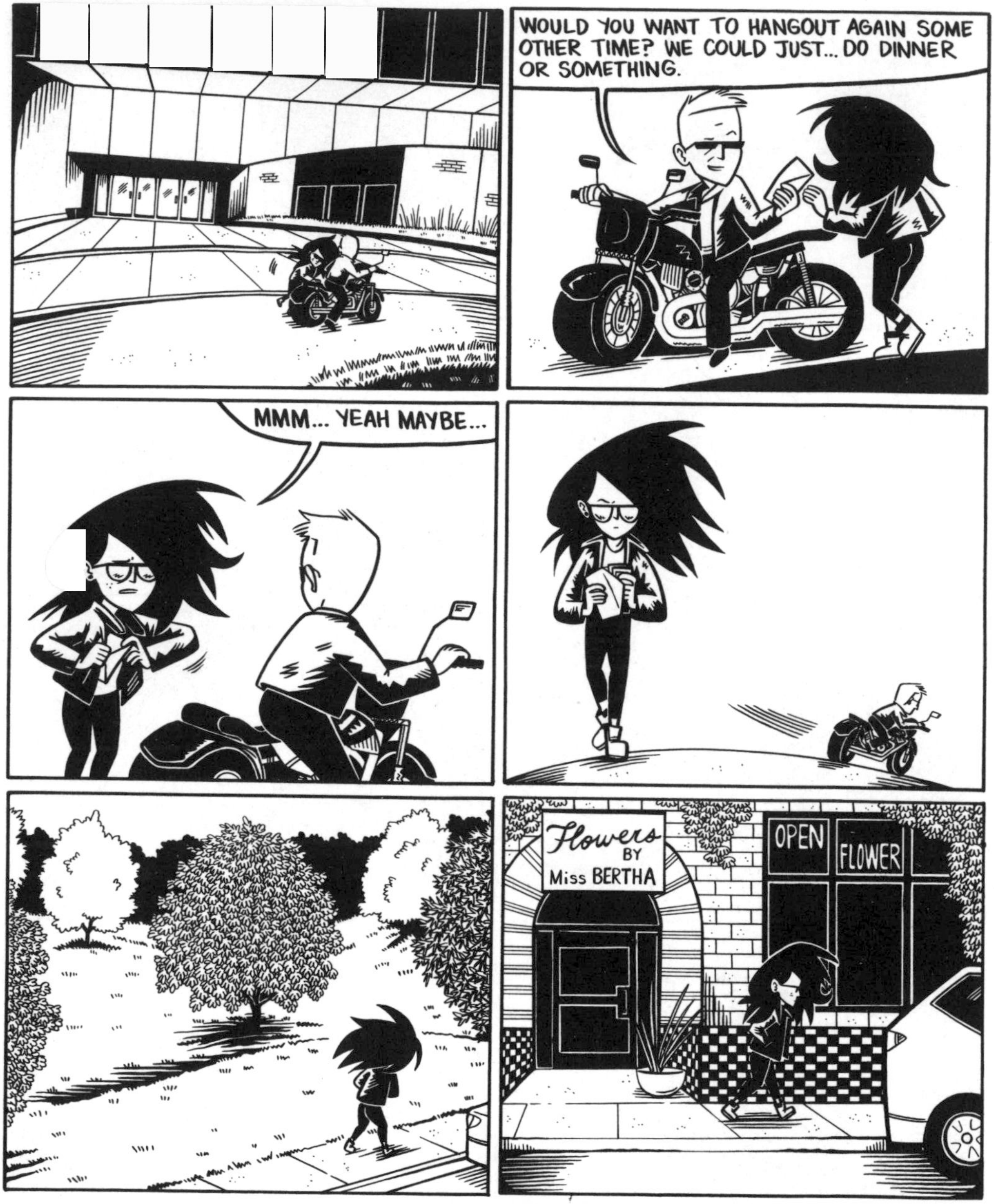
WOULD YOU WANT TO HANGOUT AGAIN SOME OTHER TIME? WE COULD JUST... DO DINNER OR SOMETHING.
MMM... YEAH MAYBE...
Flowers BY Miss BERTHA
OPEN
FLOWER

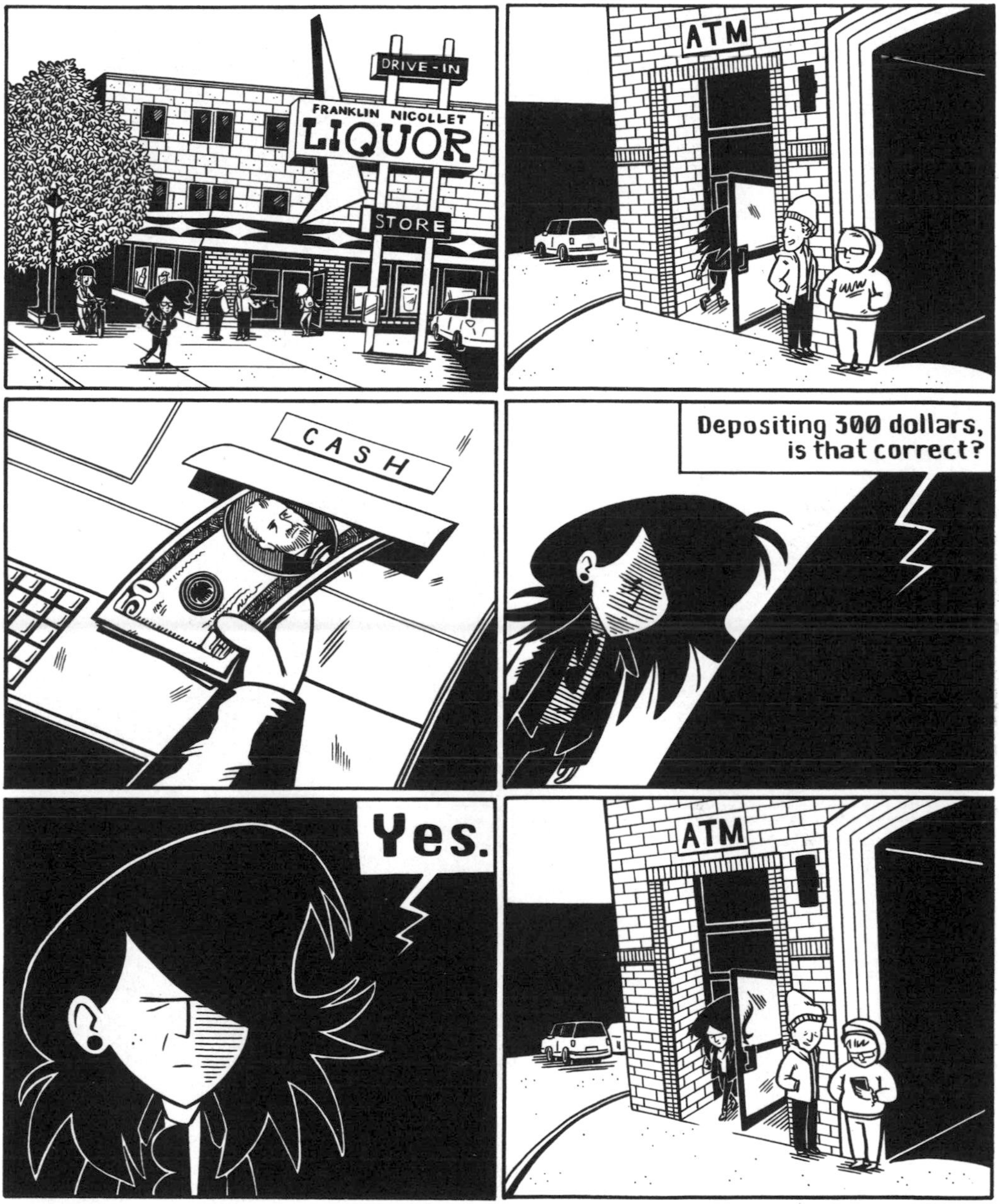
DRIVE-IN
FRANKLIN NICOLLET
LIQUOR
STORE
ATM
CASH
Depositing 300 dollars, is that correct?
Yes.
ATM

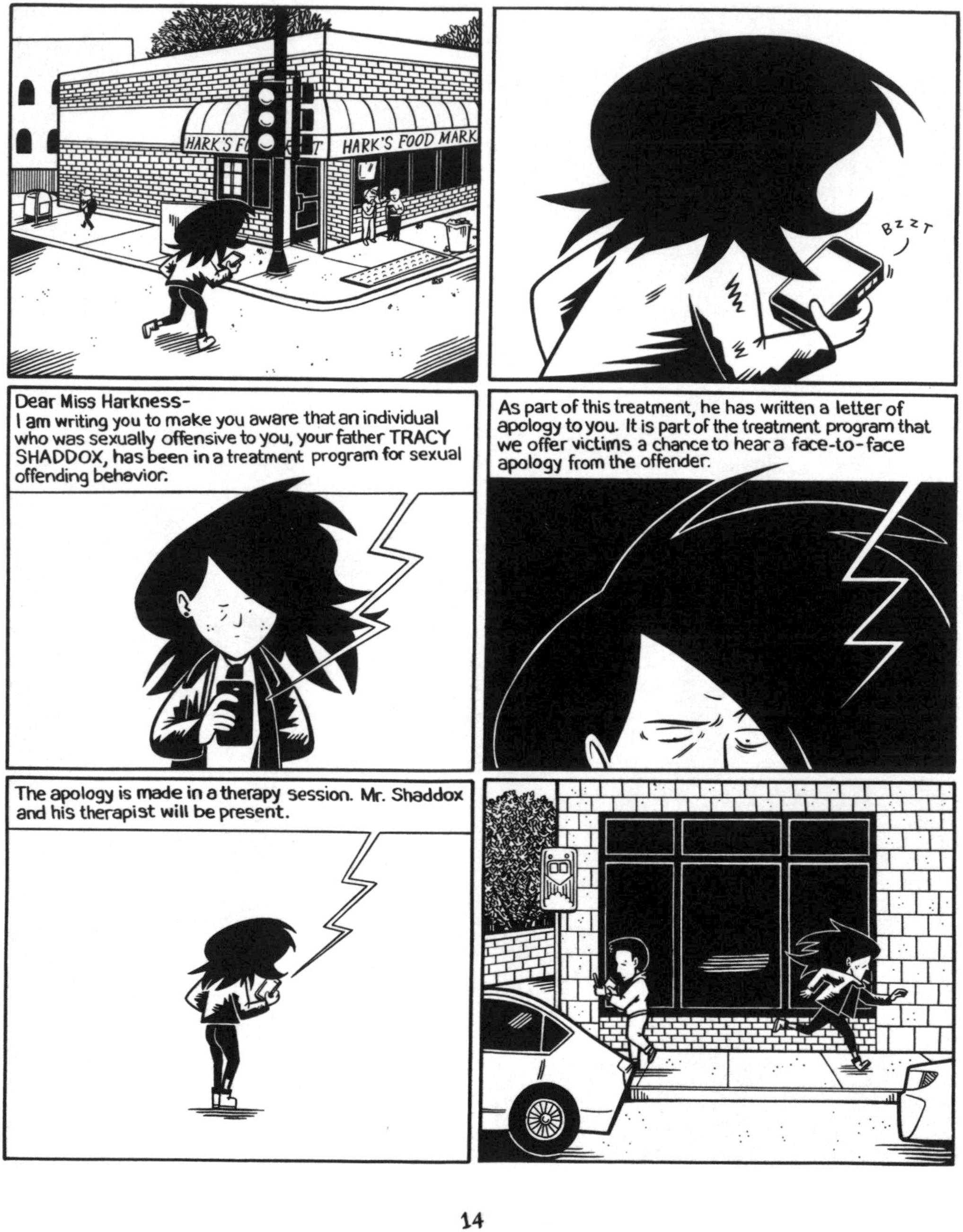
HARK'S FO
ET
HARK'S FOOD MARK
BZZT
Dear Miss Harkness-
I am writing you to make you aware that an individual who was sexually offensive to you, your father TRACY SHADDOX, has been in a treatment program for sexual offending behavior.
As part of this treatment, he has written a letter of apology to you. It is part of the treatment program that we offer victims a chance to hear a face-to-face apology from the offender.
The apology is made in a therapy session. Mr. Shaddox and his therapist will be present.

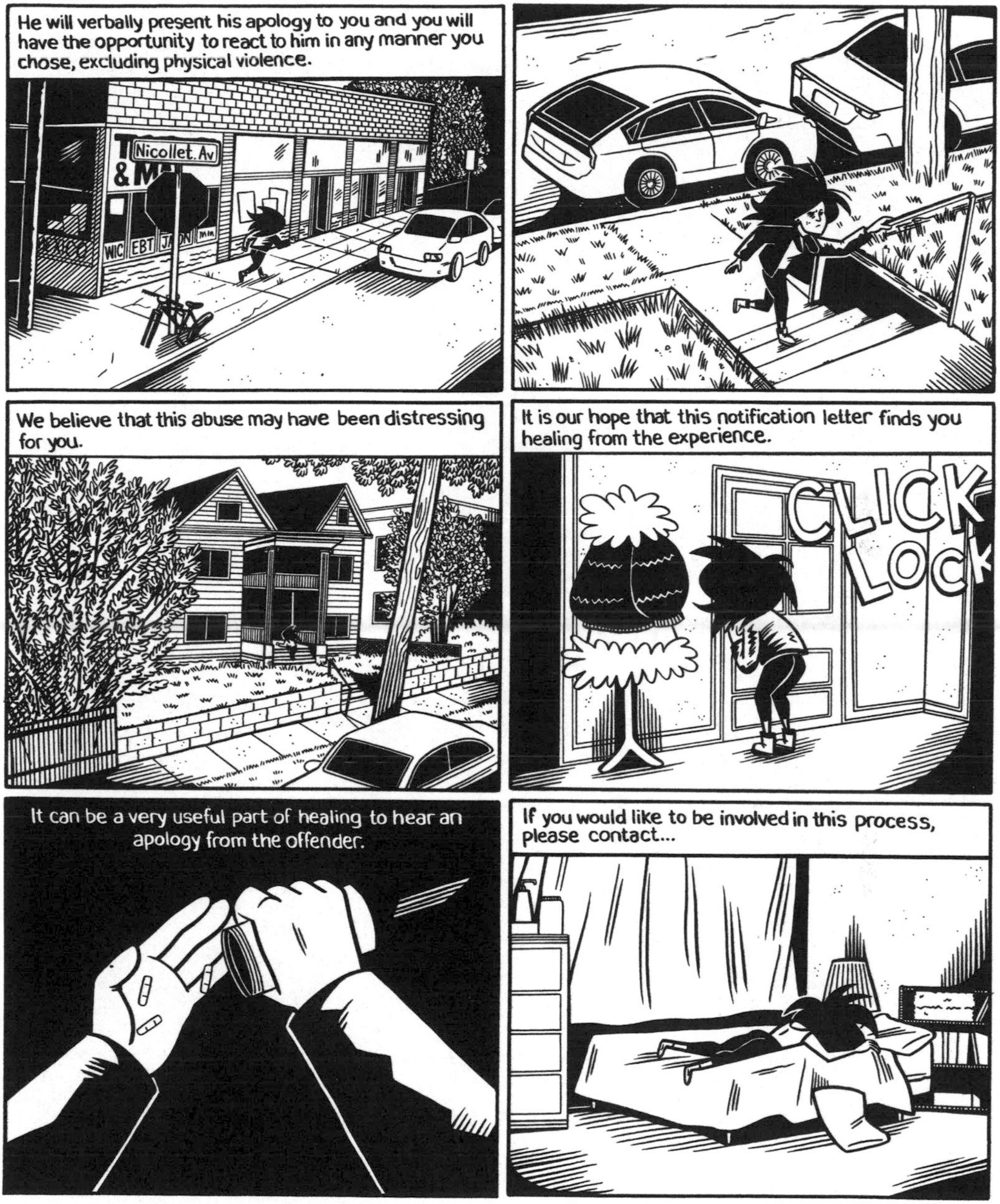
He will verbally present his apology to you and you will have the opportunity to react to him in any manner you chose, excluding physical violence.
Nicollet.Av
WIC
EBT
We believe that this abuse may have been distressing for you.
It is our hope that this notification letter finds you healing from the experience.
CLICK
LOCK
It can be a very useful part of healing to hear an apology from the offender.
If you would like to be involved in this process, please contact...

ONE WEEK BEFORE THAT.

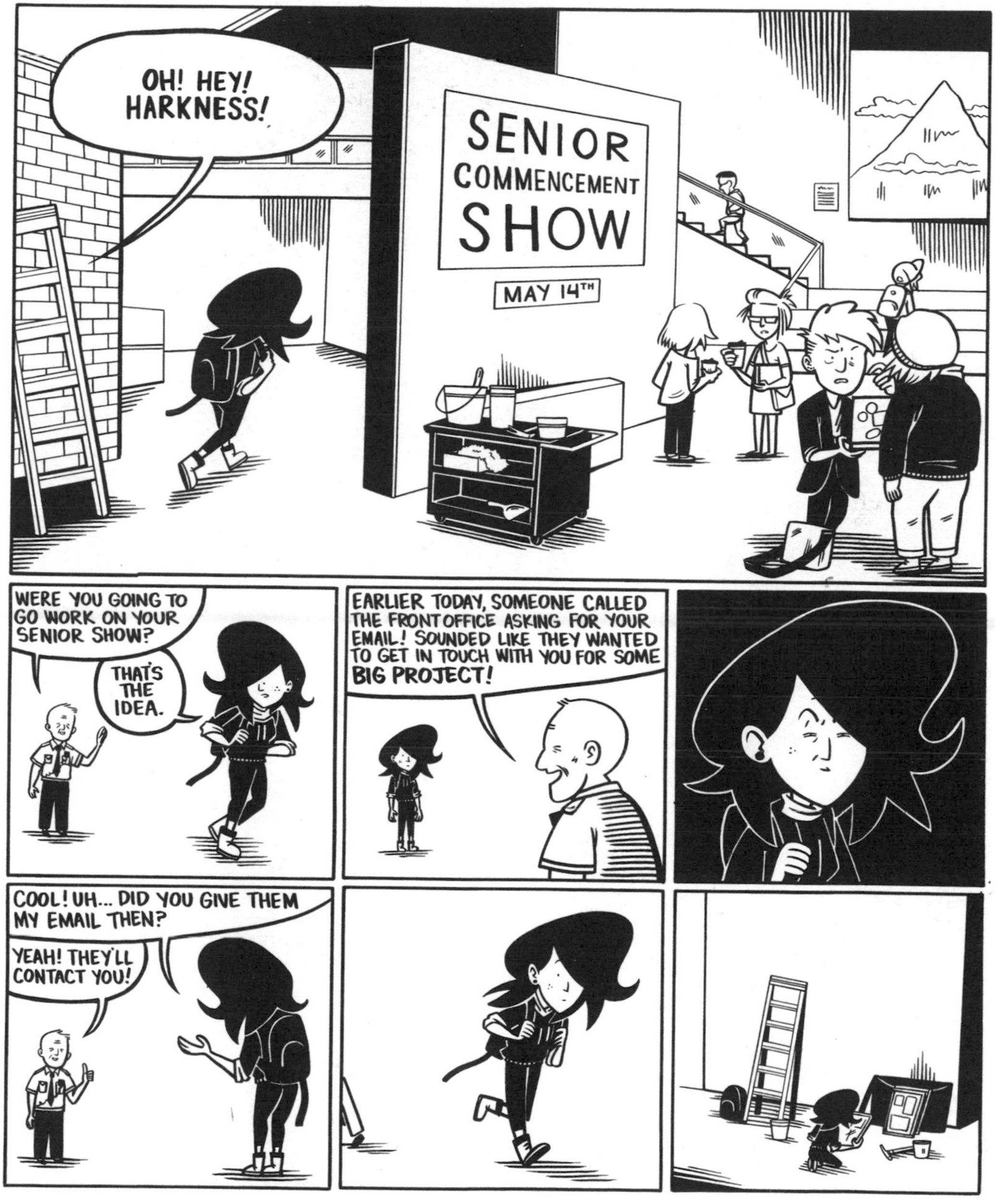
OH! HEY! HARKNESS!
SENIOR COMMENCEMENT SHOW
MAY 14TH
WERE YOU GOING TO GO WORK ON YOUR SENIOR SHOW?
THAT'S THE IDEA.
EARLIER TODAY, SOMEONE CALLED THE FRONT OFFICE ASKING FOR YOUR EMAIL! SOUNDED LIKE THEY WANTED TO GET IN TOUCH WITH YOU FOR SOME BIG PROJECT!
COOL! UH... DID YOU GIVE THEM MY EMAIL THEN?
YEAH! THEY'LL CONTACT YOU!

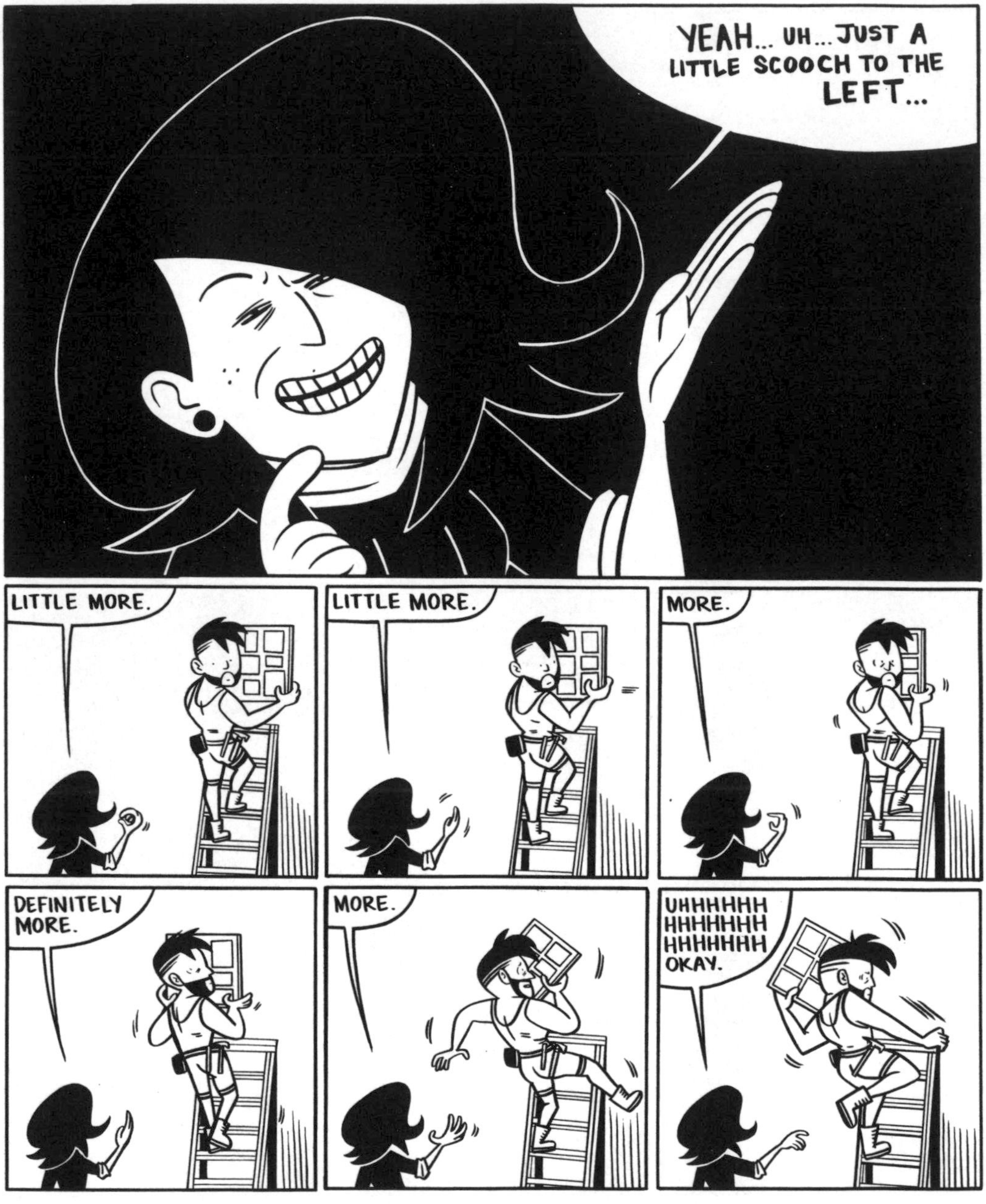
YEAH... UH... JUST A LITTLE SCOOCH TO THE LEFT...
LITTLE MORE.
LITTLE MORE.
MORE.
DEFINITELY MORE.
MORE.
UHHHHHH HHHHHHH HHHHHHH OKAY.

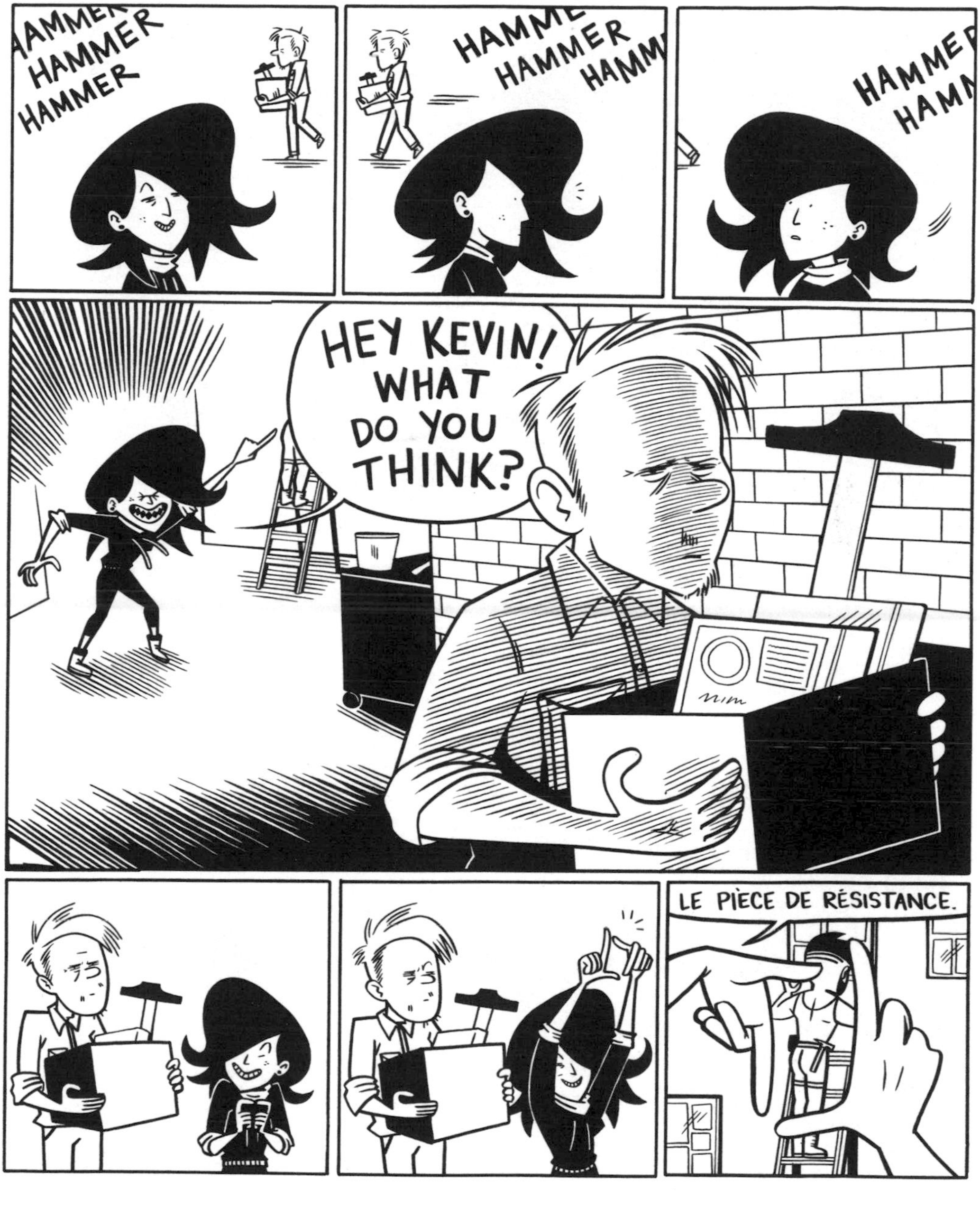
HAMMER HAMMER HAMMER
HAMMER HAMMER HAMM
HAMMER HAMM
HEY KEVIN! WHAT DO YOU THINK?
LE PIÈCE DE RÉSISTANCE.

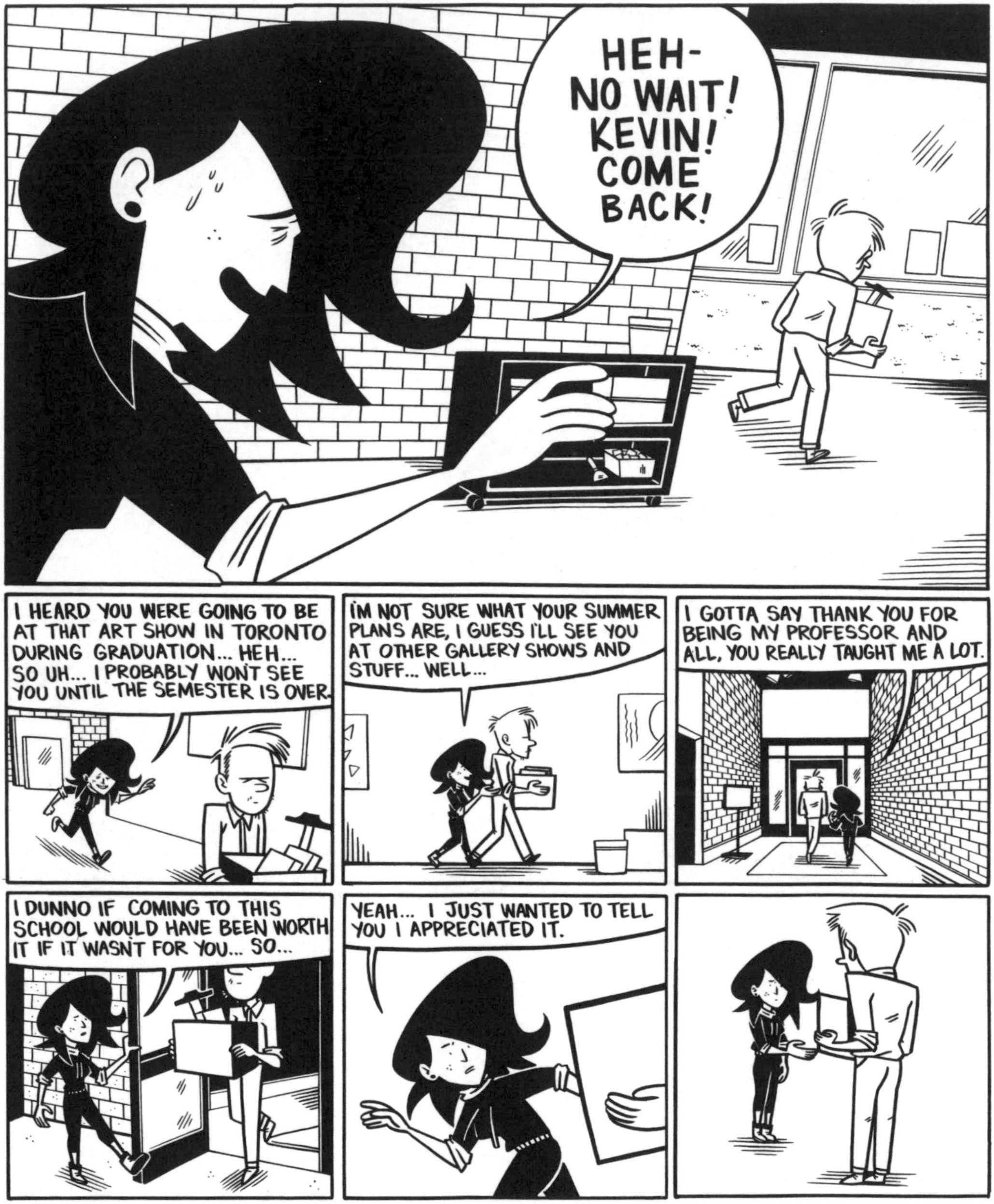
HEH- NO WAIT! KEVIN! COME BACK!
I HEARD YOU WERE GOING TO BE AT THAT ART SHOW IN TORONTO DURING GRADUATION... HEH... SO UH... I PROBABLY WON'T SEE YOU UNTIL THE SEMESTER IS OVER.
I'M NOT SURE WHAT YOUR SUMMER PLANS ARE, I GUESS I'LL SEE YOU AT OTHER GALLERY SHOWS AND STUFF... WELL...
I GOTTA SAY THANK YOU FOR BEING MY PROFESSOR AND ALL, YOU REALLY TAUGHT ME A LOT.
I DUNNO IF COMING TO THIS SCHOOL WOULD HAVE BEEN WORTH IT IF IT WASN'T FOR YOU... SO...
YEAH... I JUST WANTED TO TELL YOU I APPRECIATED IT.

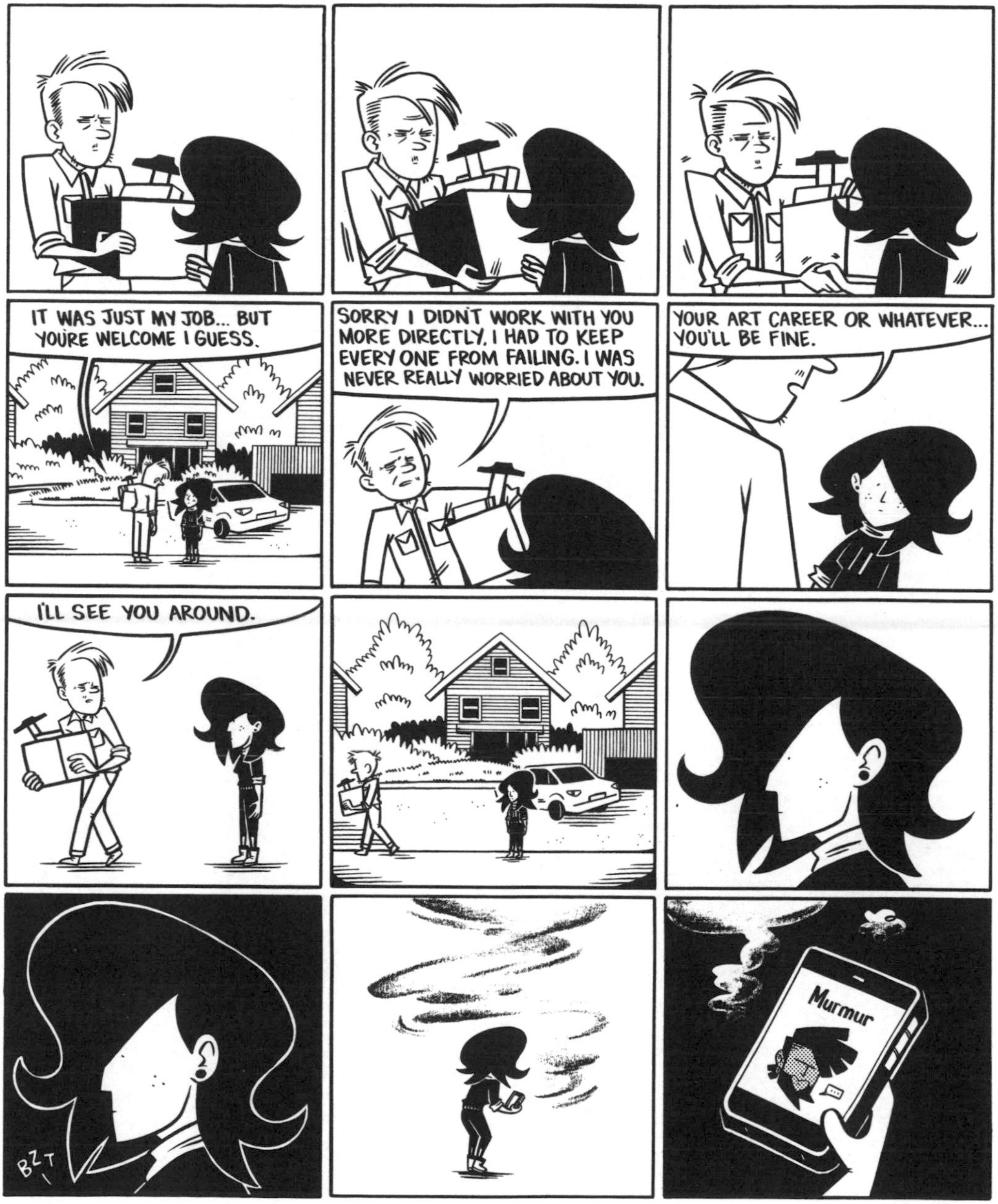
IT WAS JUST MY JOB... BUT YOU'RE WELCOME I GUESS.
SORRY I DIDN'T WORK WITH YOU MORE DIRECTLY. I HAD TO KEEP EVERY ONE FROM FAILING. I WAS NEVER REALLY WORRIED ABOUT YOU.
YOUR ART CAREER OR WHATEVER... YOU'LL BE FINE.
I'LL SEE YOU AROUND.
BZT
Murmur

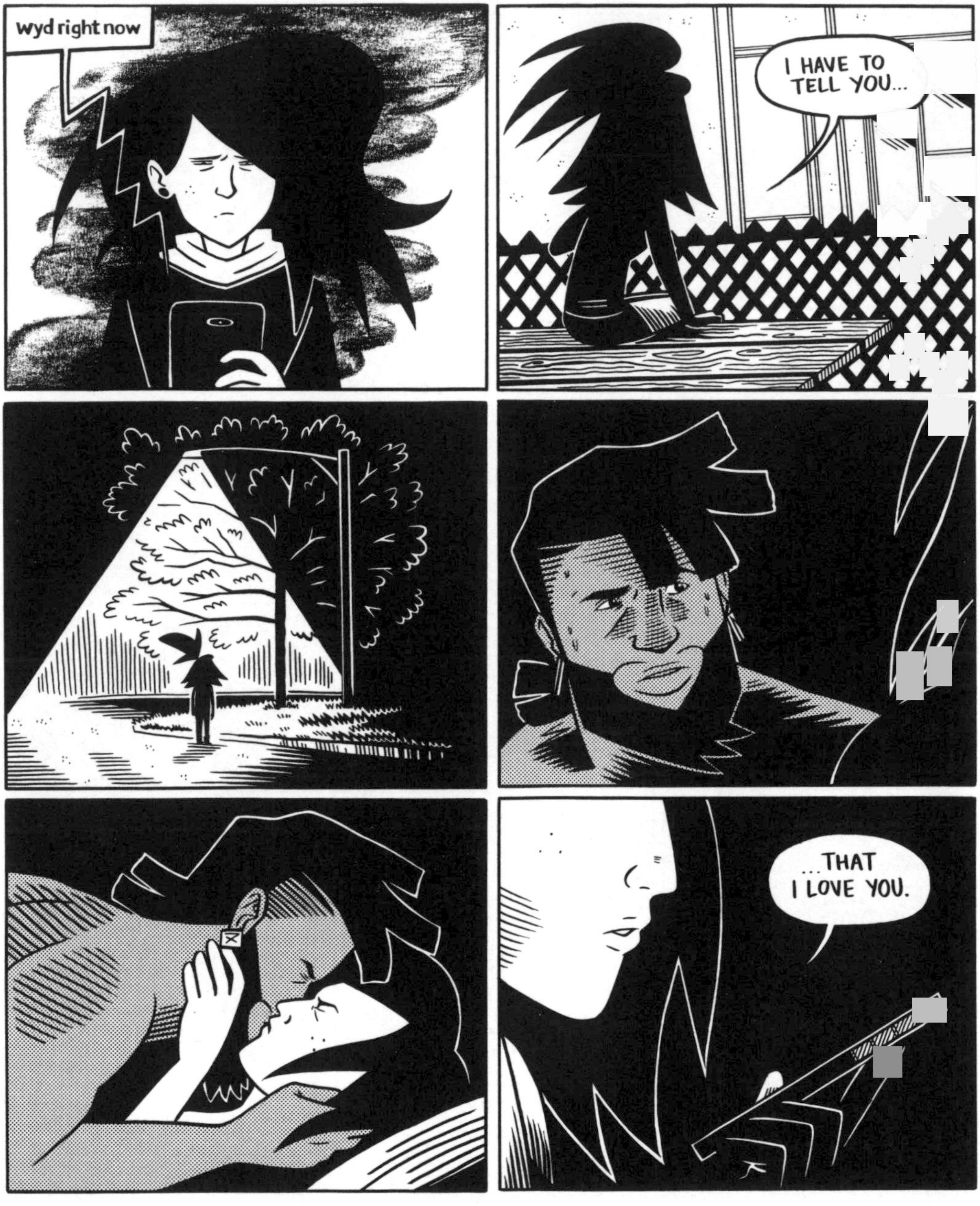
wyd right now
I HAVE TO TELL YOU...
...THAT I LOVE YOU.

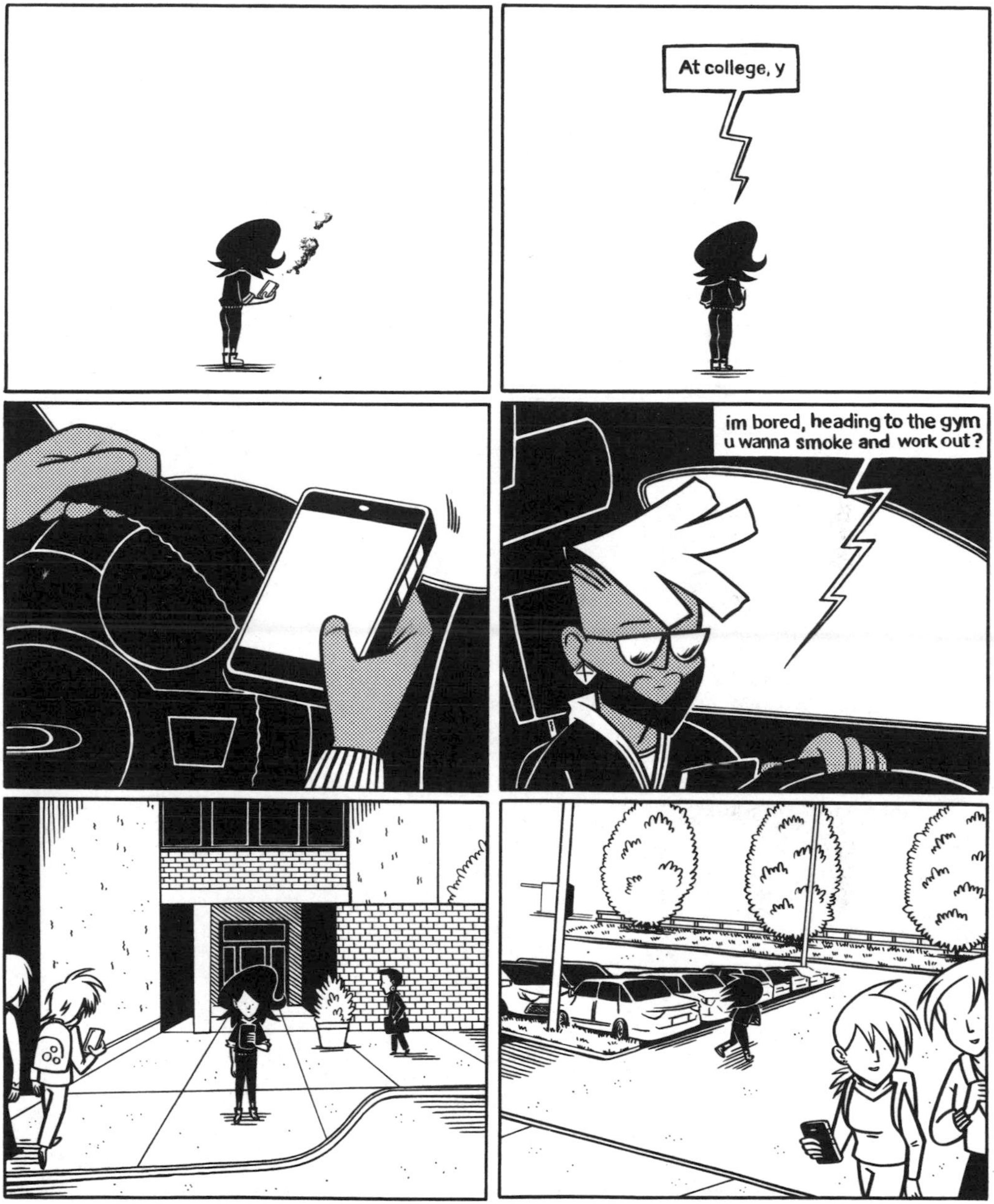
At college, y
im bored, heading to the gym
u wanna smoke and work out?

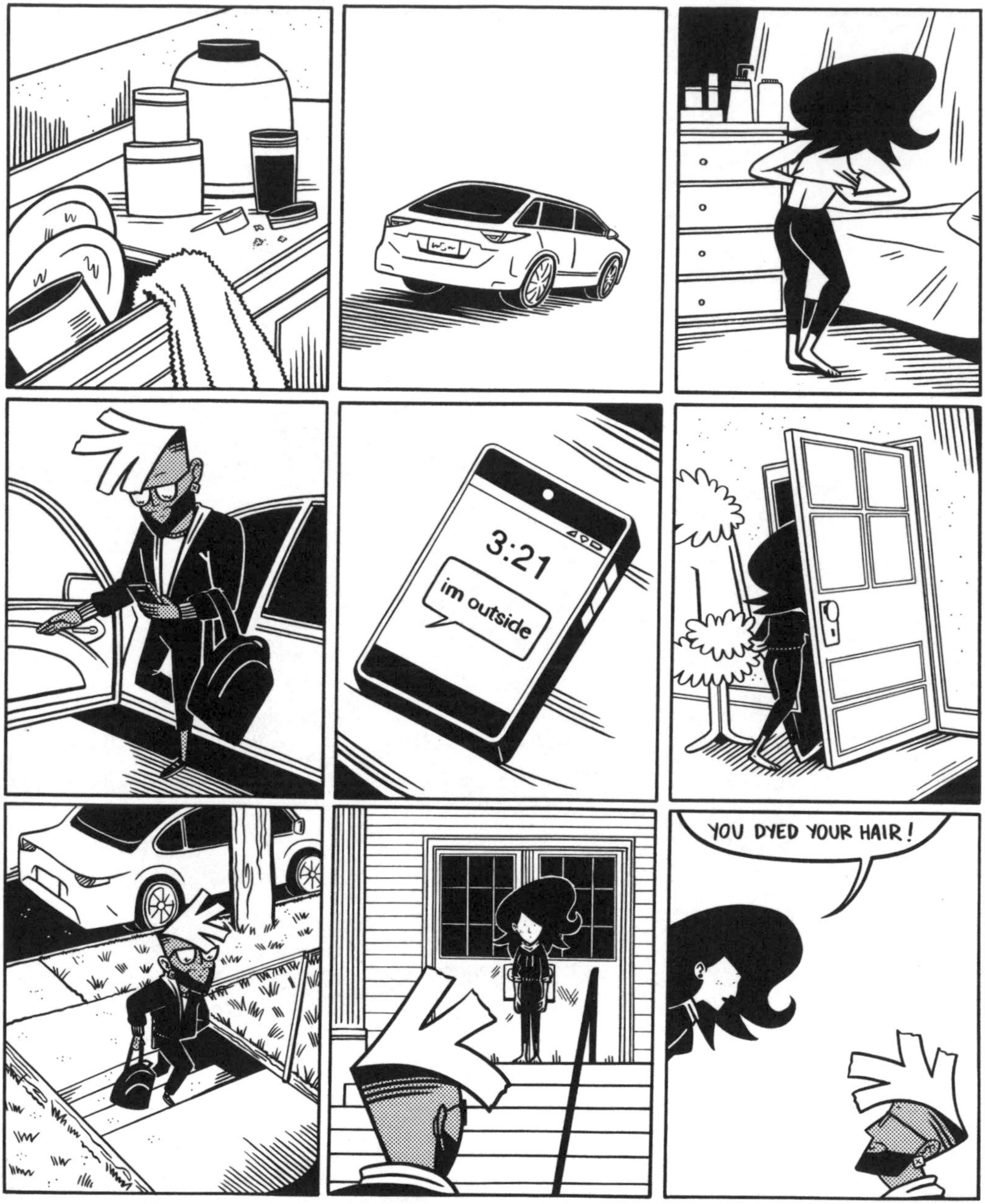
3:21
im outside
YOU DYED YOUR HAIR!

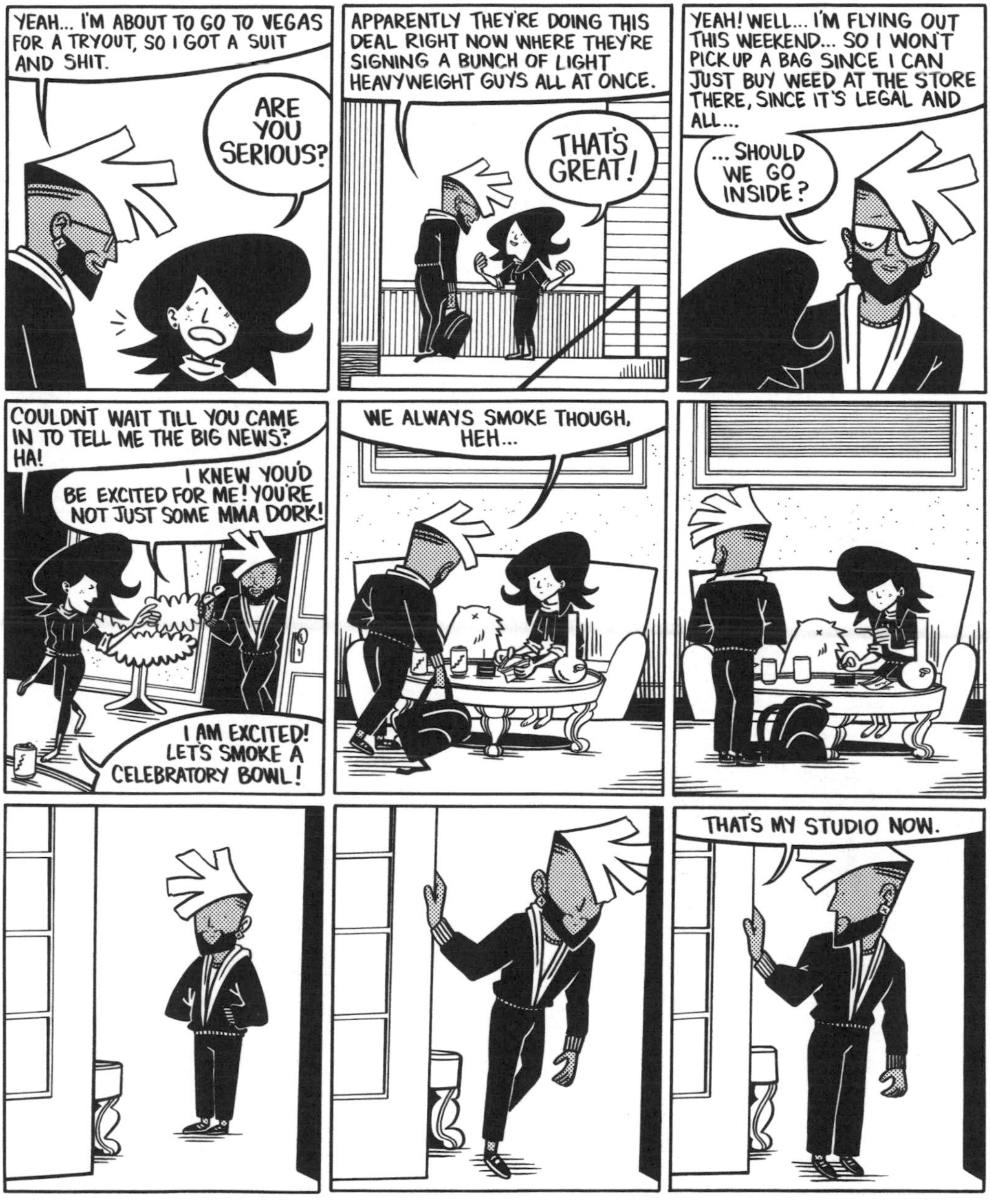
YEAH... I'M ABOUT TO GO TO VEGAS FOR A TRYOUT, SO I GOT A SUIT AND SHIT.
ARE YOU SERIOUS?
APPARENTLY THEY'RE DOING THIS DEAL RIGHT NOW WHERE THEY'RE SIGNING A BUNCH OF LIGHT HEAVYWEIGHT GUYS ALL AT ONCE.
THAT'S GREAT!
YEAH! WELL... I'M FLYING OUT THIS WEEKEND... SO I WON'T PICK UP A BAG SINCE I CAN JUST BUY WEED AT THE STORE THERE, SINCE IT'S LEGAL AND ALL...
... SHOULD WE GO INSIDE?
COULDN'T WAIT TILL YOU CAME IN TO TELL ME THE BIG NEWS? HA!
I KNEW YOU'D BE EXCITED FOR ME! YOU'RE NOT JUST SOME MMA DORK!
I AM EXCITED! LET'S SMOKE A CELEBRATORY BOWL!
WE ALWAYS SMOKE THOUGH, HEH...
THAT'S MY STUDIO NOW.

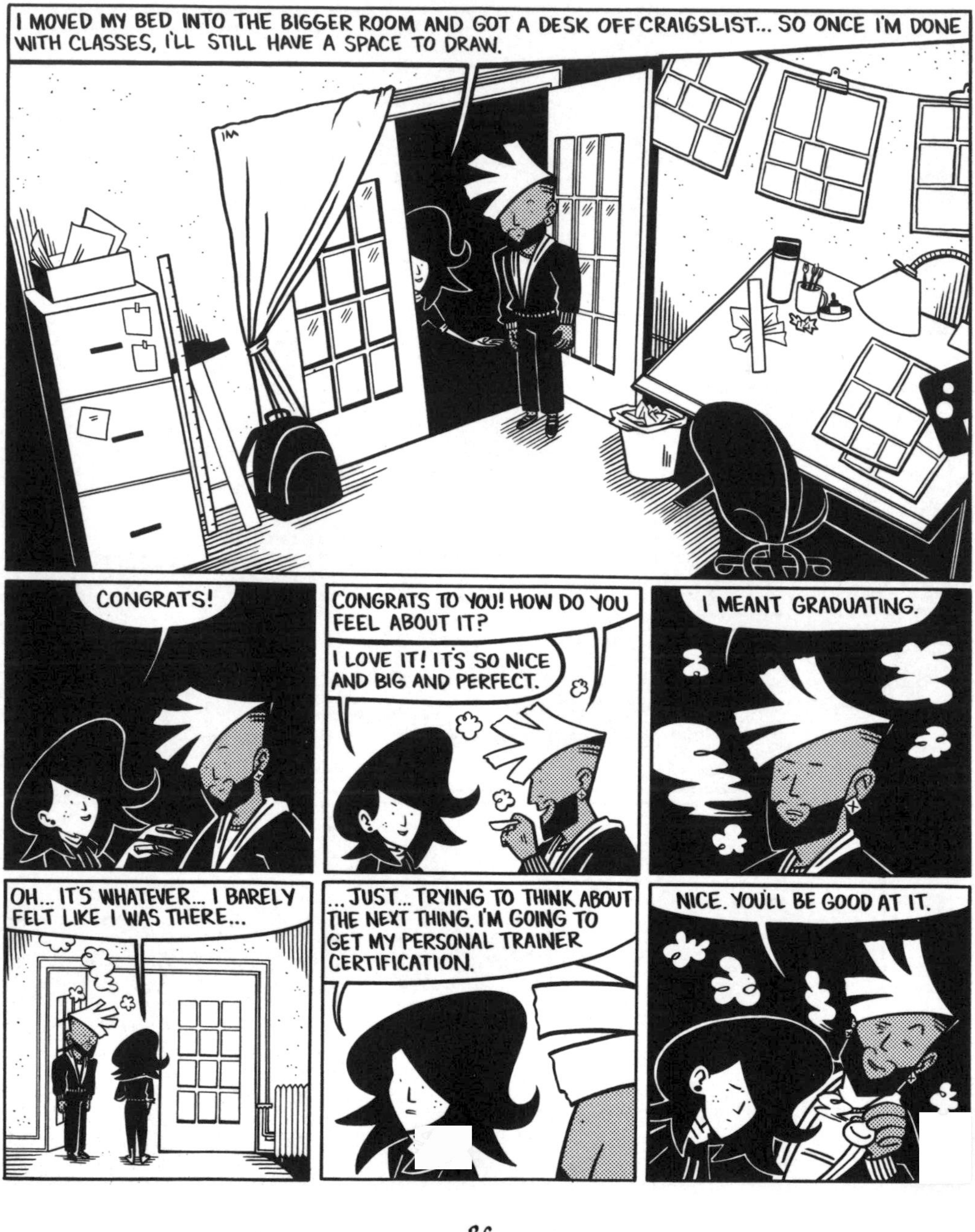
I MOVED MY BED INTO THE BIGGER ROOM AND GOT A DESK OFF CRAIGSLIST... SO ONCE I'M DONE WITH CLASSES, I'LL STILL HAVE A SPACE TO DRAW.
CONGRATS!
CONGRATS TO YOU! HOW DO YOU FEEL ABOUT IT?
I LOVE IT! IT'S SO NICE AND BIG AND PERFECT.
I MEANT GRADUATING.
OH... IT'S WHATEVER... I BARELY FELT LIKE I WAS THERE...
...JUST... TRYING TO THINK ABOUT THE NEXT THING. I'M GOING TO GET MY PERSONAL TRAINER CERTIFICATION.
NICE. YOU'LL BE GOOD AT IT.

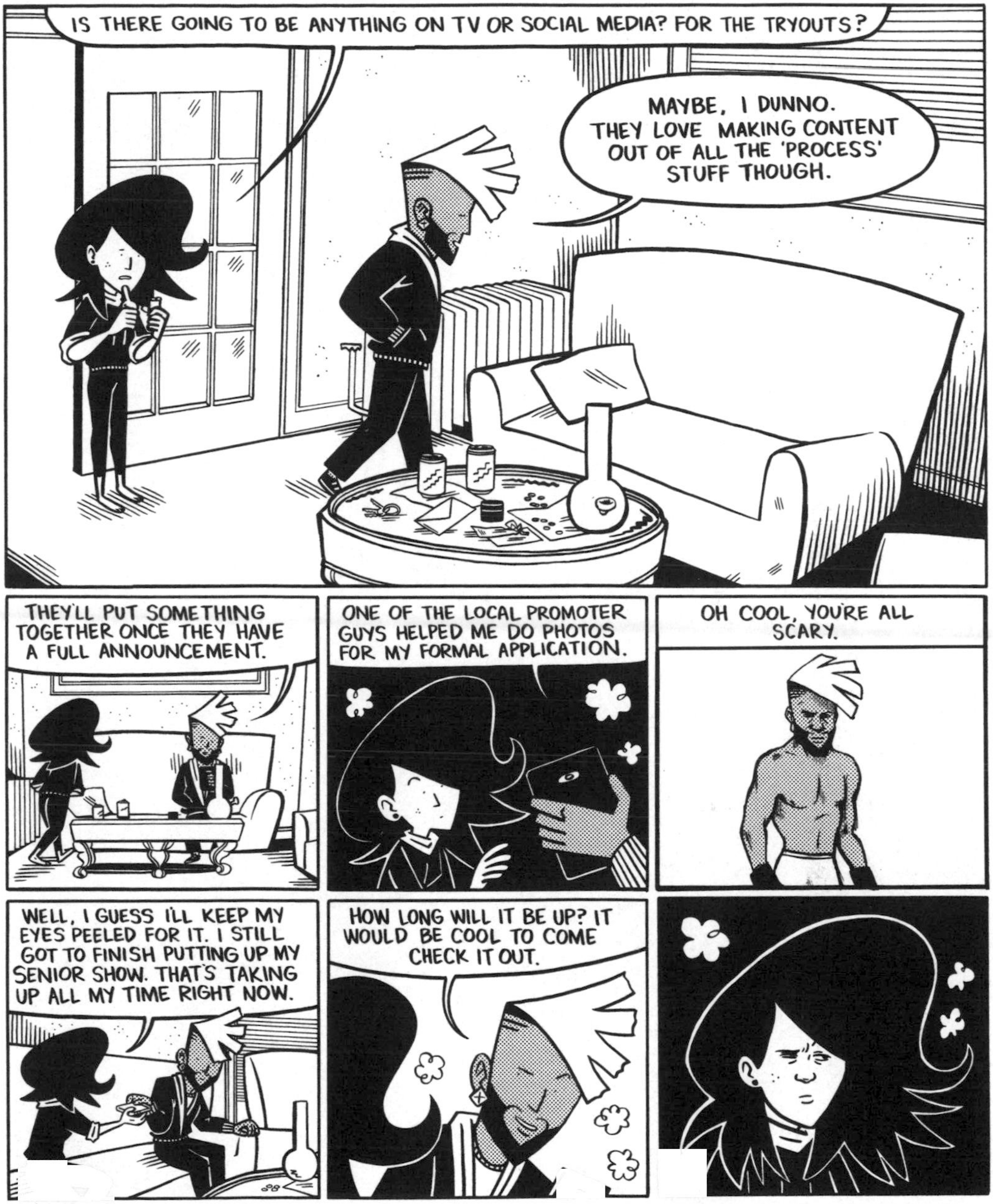
IS THERE GOING TO BE ANYTHING ON TV OR SOCIAL MEDIA? FOR THE TRYOUTS?
MAYBE, I DUNNO. THEY LOVE MAKING CONTENT OUT OF ALL THE 'PROCESS' STUFF THOUGH.
THEY'LL PUT SOMETHING TOGETHER ONCE THEY HAVE A FULL ANNOUNCEMENT.
ONE OF THE LOCAL PROMOTER GUYS HELPED ME DO PHOTOS FOR MY FORMAL APPLICATION.
OH COOL, YOU'RE ALL SCARY.
WELL, I GUESS I'LL KEEP MY EYES PEELED FOR IT. I STILL GOT TO FINISH PUTTING UP MY SENIOR SHOW. THAT'S TAKING UP ALL MY TIME RIGHT NOW.
HOW LONG WILL IT BE UP? IT WOULD BE COOL TO COME CHECK IT OUT.

TWO WEEKS AFTER THAT.

CHICAGO-LAKE LIQUORS
WE FEATURE ALL NATIONAL BRANDS AT DISCOUNT PRICES

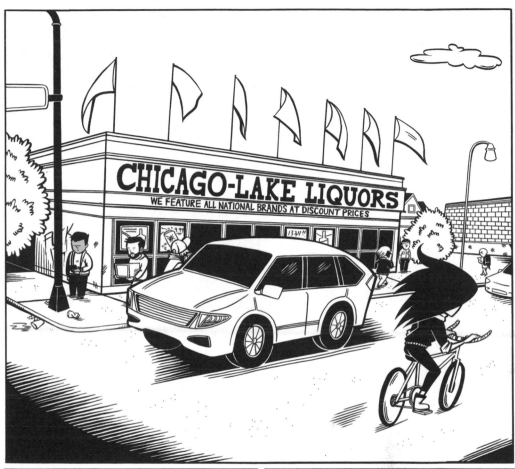

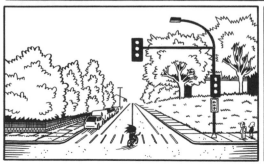

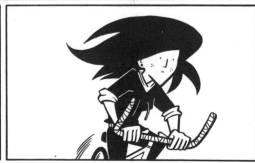

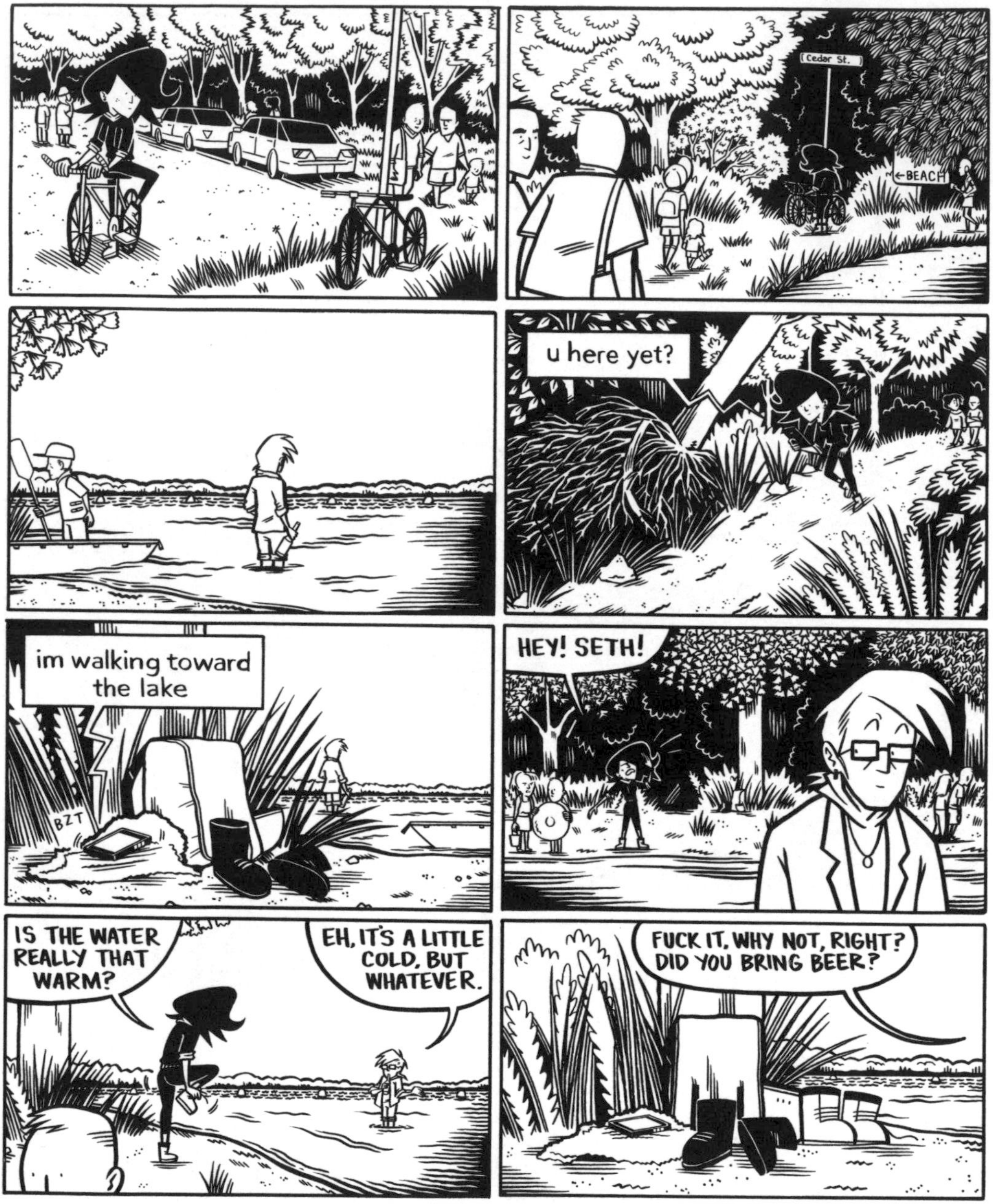
Cedar St.
←BEACH
u here yet?
im walking toward the lake
BZT
HEY! SETH!
IS THE WATER REALLY THAT WARM?
EH, IT'S A LITTLE COLD, BUT WHATEVER.
FUCK IT, WHY NOT, RIGHT? DID YOU BRING BEER?

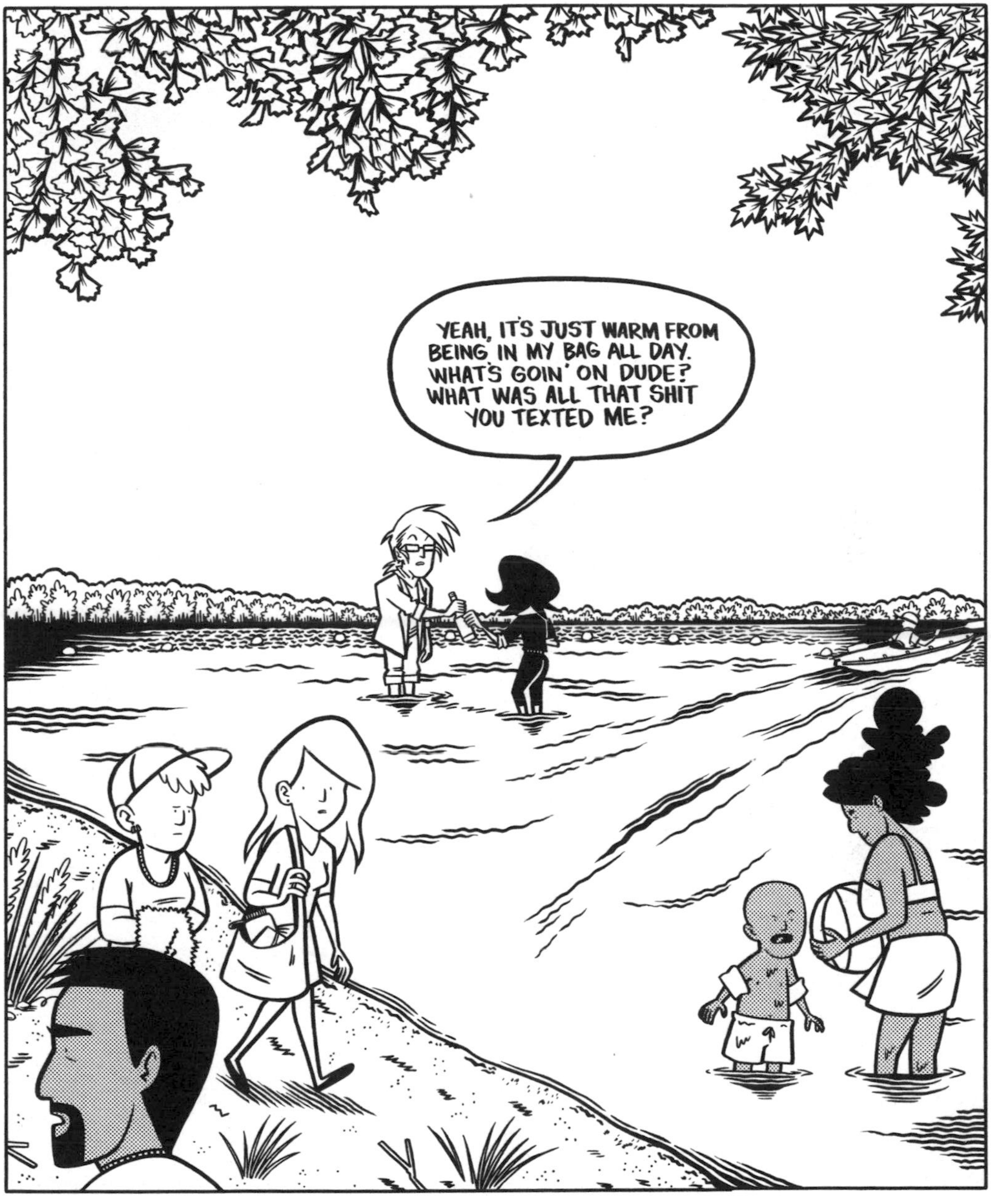
YEAH, IT'S JUST WARM FROM BEING IN MY BAG ALL DAY. WHAT'S GOIN' ON DUDE? WHAT WAS ALL THAT SHIT YOU TEXTED ME?

MY DAD WANTS TO VIOLATE HIS PAROLE TO "APOLOGIZE" TO ME.

YIKES.

FIVE YEARS IN PRISON AND HE HAS SOME "SPIRITUAL AWAKENING" TO STOP BEING A NARCISSISTIC JACKASS I GUESS.

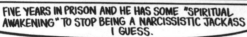

GROSS.

AND SO, BECAUSE OF THAT, MY MOM IS TRYING TO INTERFERE AND CALL THE ATTORNEY'S OFFICE ON HIM.

COULD YOU SUE HIM OR SOMETHING? FOR VIOLATING PAROLE?

DAMN... MAYBE? GET MY STUDENT LOANS PAID... HIT A HOMER...

PLOP!

WELL... WHAT'RE YOU THINKIN' THEN? HOW DO YOU FEEL?

I DUNNO. ANNOYED? HOW ARE YOU AND COLE DOIN?

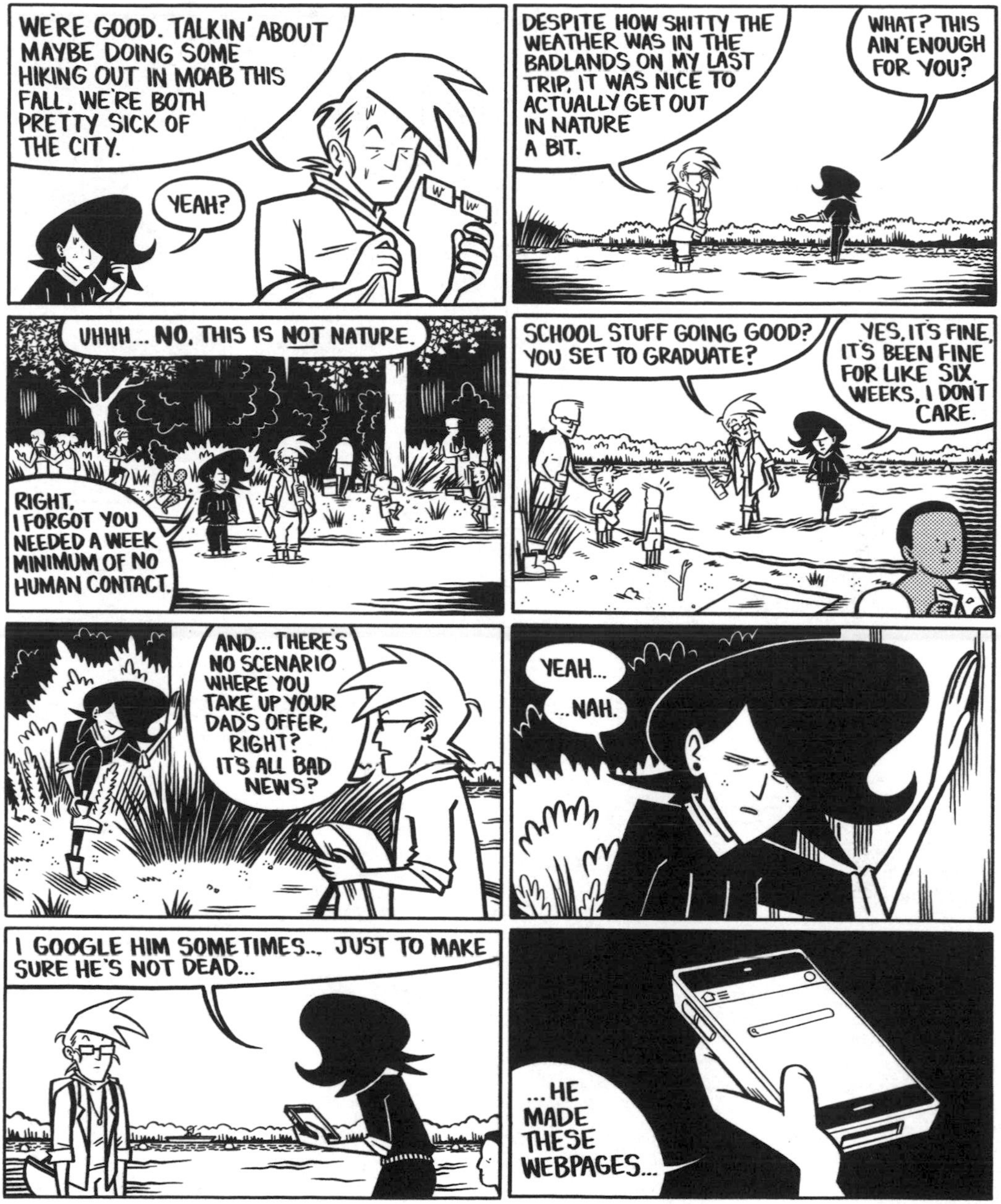
WE'RE GOOD. TALKIN' ABOUT MAYBE DOING SOME HIKING OUT IN MOAB THIS FALL. WE'RE BOTH PRETTY SICK OF THE CITY.
YEAH?
DESPITE HOW SHITTY THE WEATHER WAS IN THE BADLANDS ON MY LAST TRIP, IT WAS NICE TO ACTUALLY GET OUT IN NATURE A BIT.
WHAT? THIS AIN' ENOUGH FOR YOU?
UHHH... NO, THIS IS NOT NATURE.
RIGHT, I FORGOT YOU NEEDED A WEEK MINIMUM OF NO HUMAN CONTACT.
SCHOOL STUFF GOING GOOD? YOU SET TO GRADUATE?
YES, IT'S FINE, IT'S BEEN FINE FOR LIKE SIX WEEKS, I DON'T CARE.
AND... THERE'S NO SCENARIO WHERE YOU TAKE UP YOUR DAD'S OFFER, RIGHT? IT'S ALL BAD NEWS?
YEAH...
...NAH.
I GOOGLE HIM SOMETIMES... JUST TO MAKE SURE HE'S NOT DEAD...
...HE MADE THESE WEBPAGES...

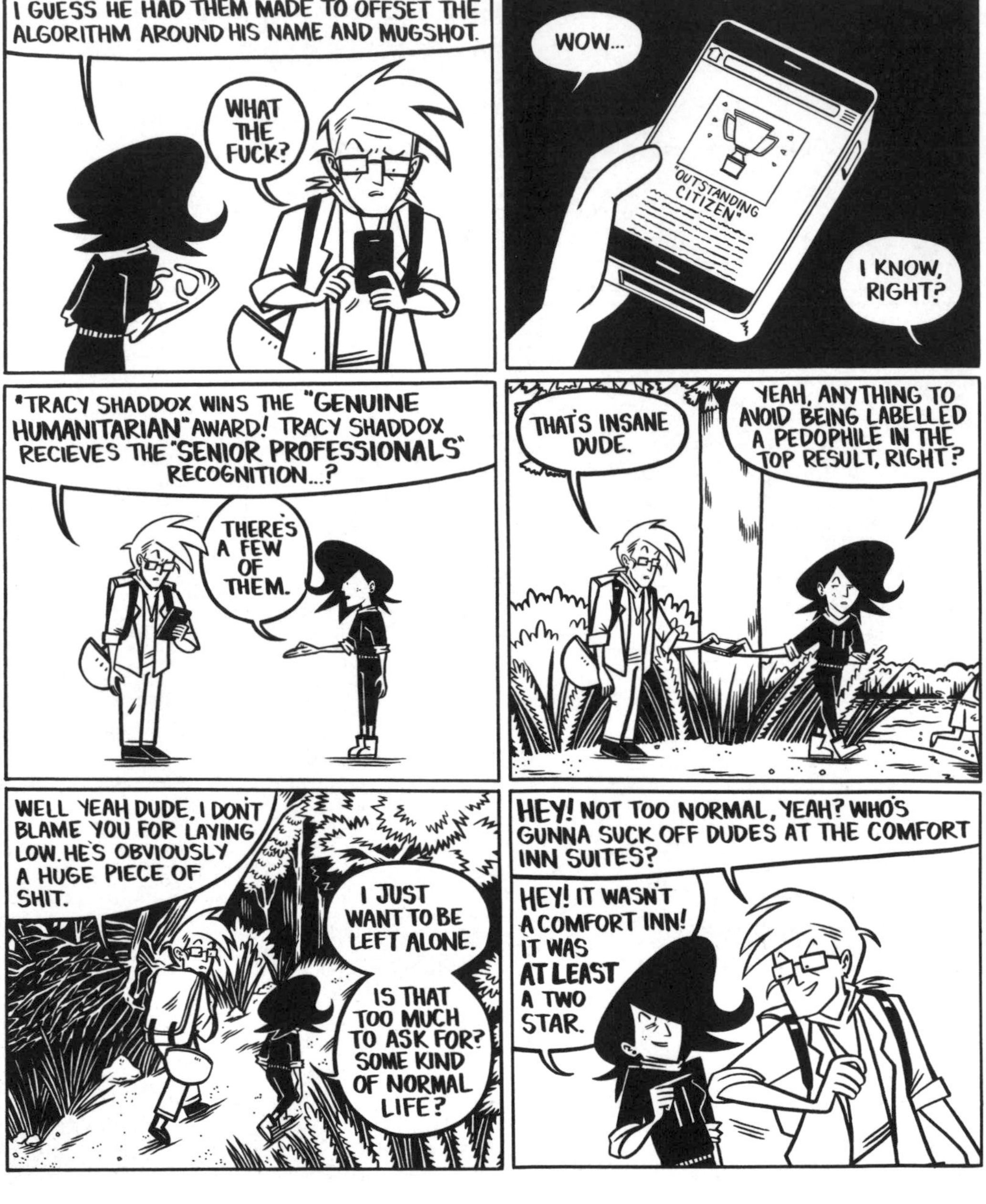
I GUESS HE HAD THEM MADE TO OFFSET THE ALGORITHM AROUND HIS NAME AND MUGSHOT.
WHAT THE FUCK?
WOW...
"OUTSTANDING CITIZEN"
I KNOW, RIGHT?
"TRACY SHADDOX WINS THE "GENUINE HUMANITARIAN" AWARD! TRACY SHADDOX RECIEVES THE "SENIOR PROFESSIONALS" RECOGNITION...?
THERE'S A FEW OF THEM.
THAT'S INSANE DUDE.
YEAH, ANYTHING TO AVOID BEING LABELLED A PEDOPHILE IN THE TOP RESULT, RIGHT?
WELL YEAH DUDE, I DON'T BLAME YOU FOR LAYING LOW. HE'S OBVIOUSLY A HUGE PIECE OF SHIT.
I JUST WANT TO BE LEFT ALONE.
IS THAT TOO MUCH TO ASK FOR? SOME KIND OF NORMAL LIFE?
HEY! NOT TOO NORMAL, YEAH? WHO'S GUNNA SUCK OFF DUDES AT THE COMFORT INN SUITES?
HEY! IT WASN'T A COMFORT INN! IT WAS **AT LEAST** A TWO STAR.

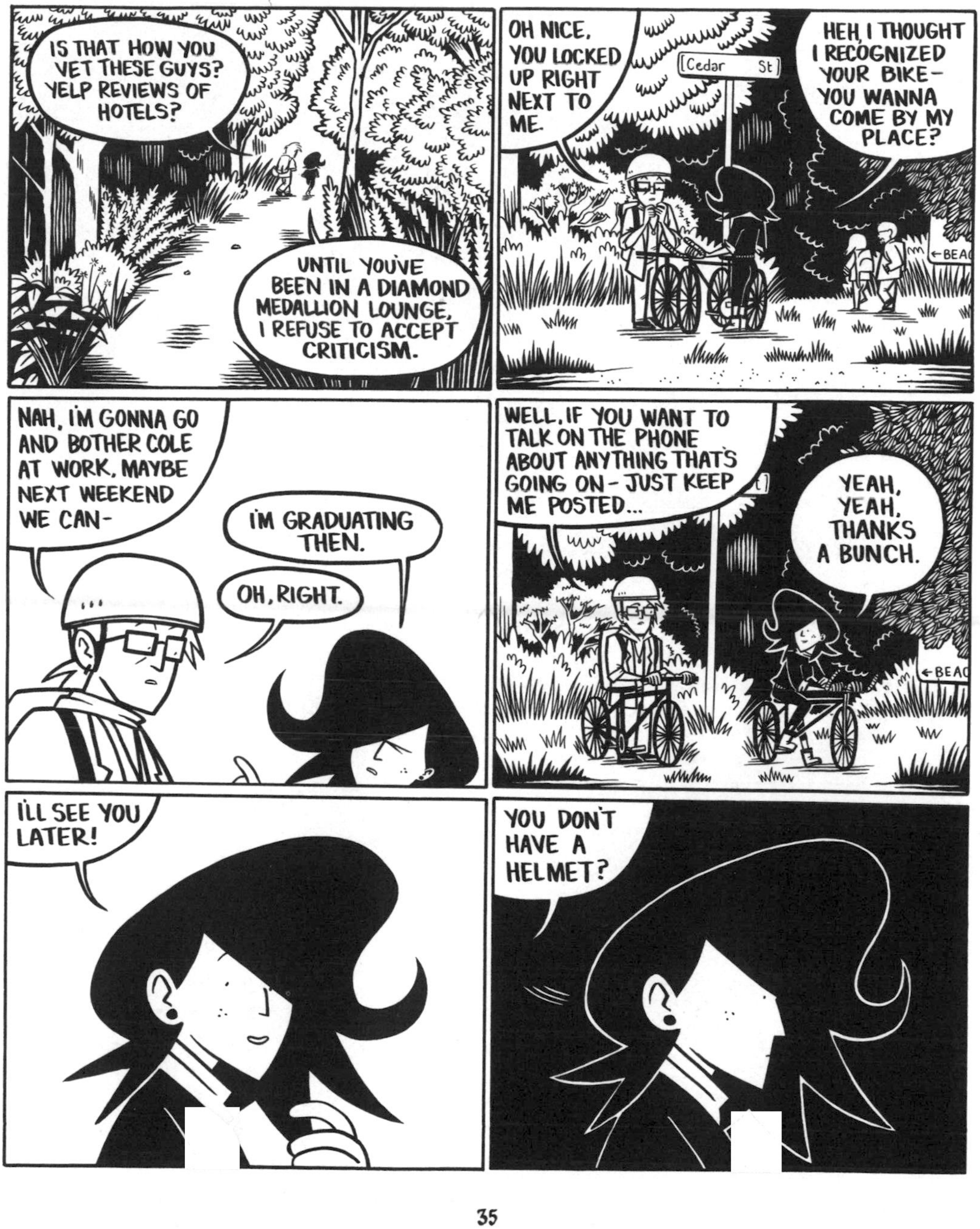
IS THAT HOW YOU VET THESE GUYS? YELP REVIEWS OF HOTELS?
UNTIL YOU'VE BEEN IN A DIAMOND MEDALLION LOUNGE, I REFUSE TO ACCEPT CRITICISM.
OH NICE, YOU LOCKED UP RIGHT NEXT TO ME.
Cedar St
HEH, I THOUGHT I RECOGNIZED YOUR BIKE- YOU WANNA COME BY MY PLACE?
←BEAC
NAH, I'M GONNA GO AND BOTHER COLE AT WORK, MAYBE NEXT WEEKEND WE CAN-
I'M GRADUATING THEN.
OH, RIGHT.
WELL, IF YOU WANT TO TALK ON THE PHONE ABOUT ANYTHING THAT'S GOING ON- JUST KEEP ME POSTED...
YEAH, YEAH, THANKS A BUNCH.
←BEAC
I'LL SEE YOU LATER!
YOU DON'T HAVE A HELMET?

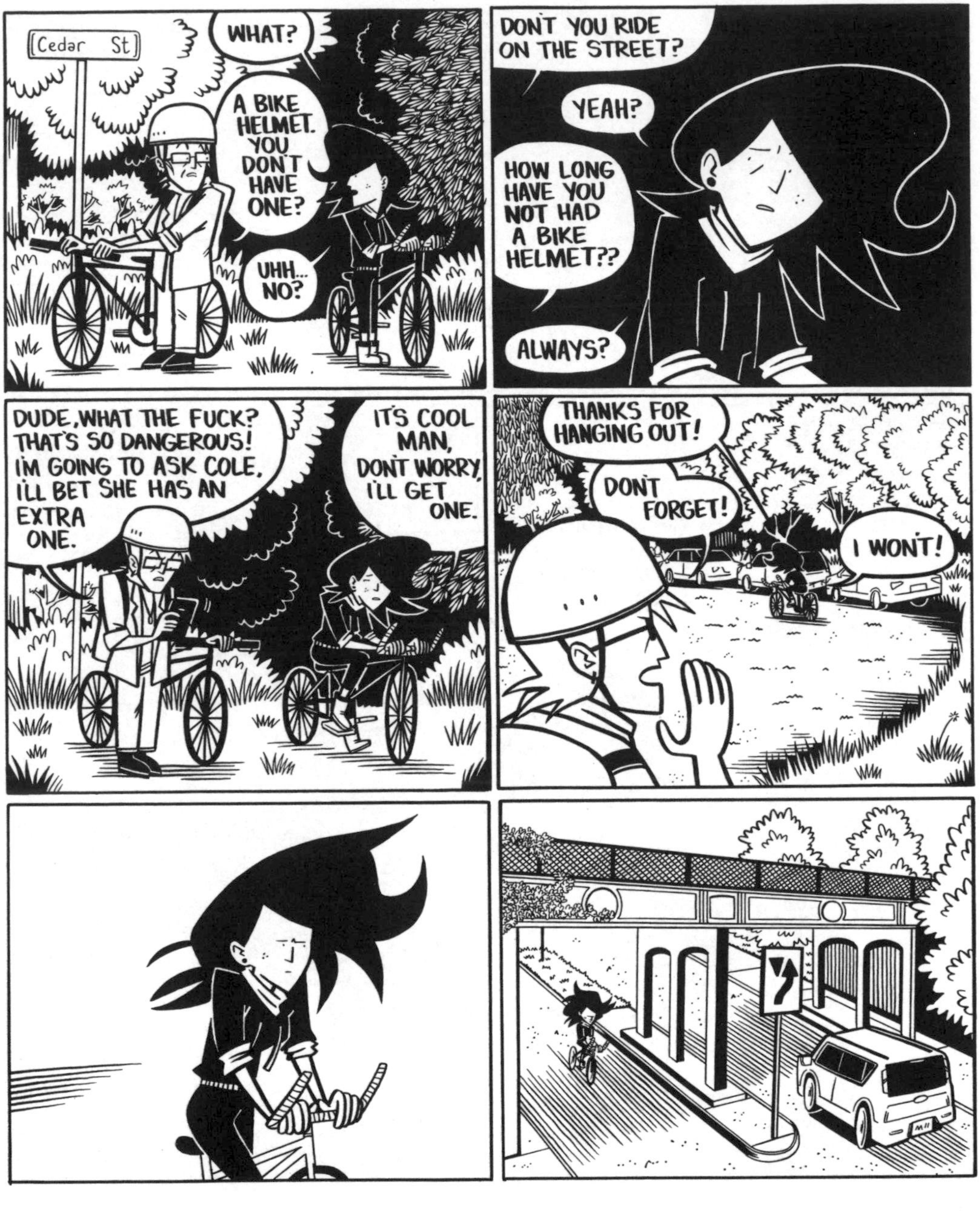
Cedar St
WHAT?
A BIKE HELMET. YOU DON'T HAVE ONE?
UHH... NO?
DON'T YOU RIDE ON THE STREET?
YEAH?
HOW LONG HAVE YOU NOT HAD A BIKE HELMET??
ALWAYS?
DUDE, WHAT THE FUCK? THAT'S SO DANGEROUS! I'M GOING TO ASK COLE, I'LL BET SHE HAS AN EXTRA ONE.
IT'S COOL MAN, DON'T WORRY, I'LL GET ONE.
THANKS FOR HANGING OUT!
DON'T FORGET!
I WON'T!

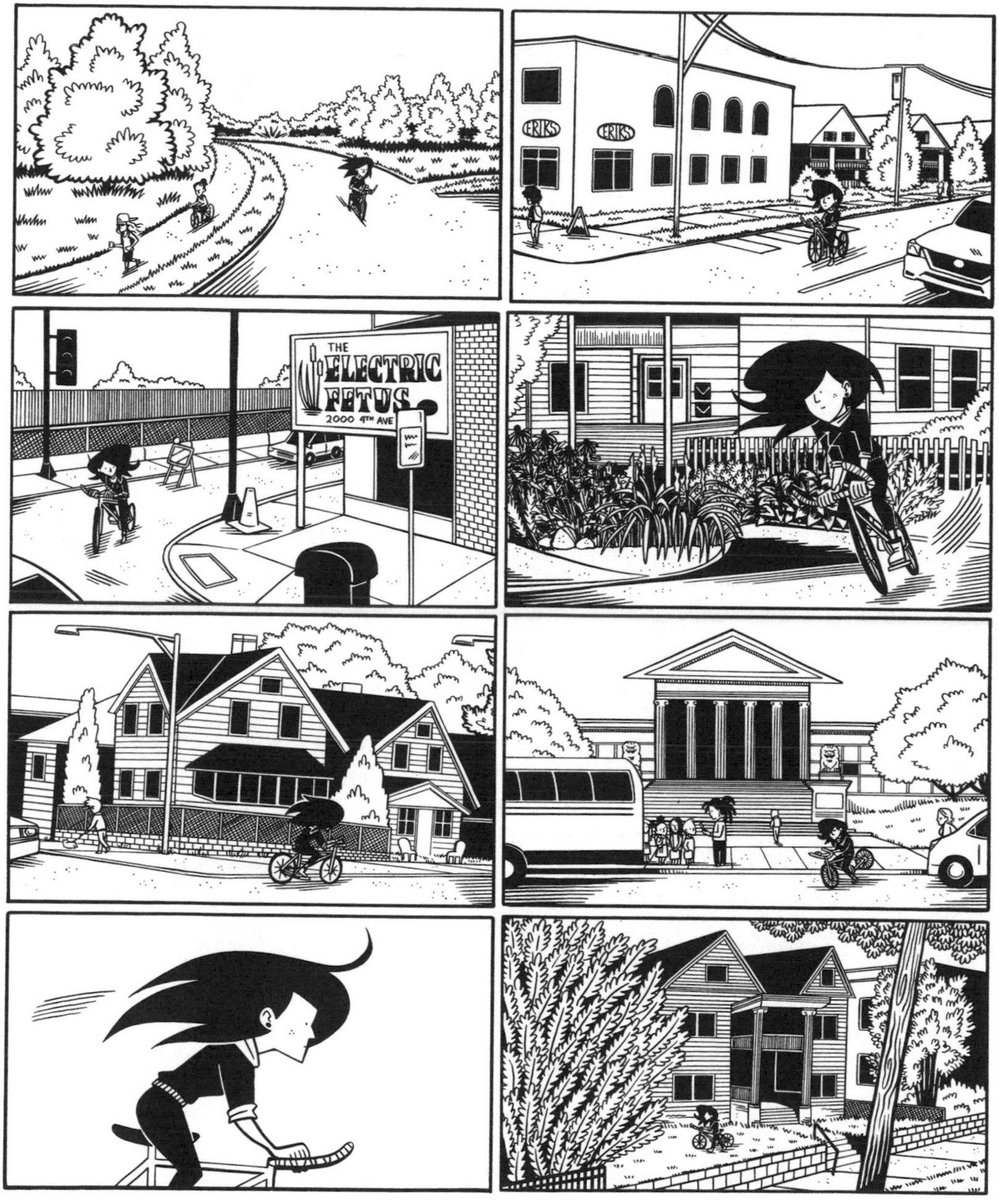
ERIKS
ERIKS
THE ELECTRIC FETUS
2000 4TH AVE

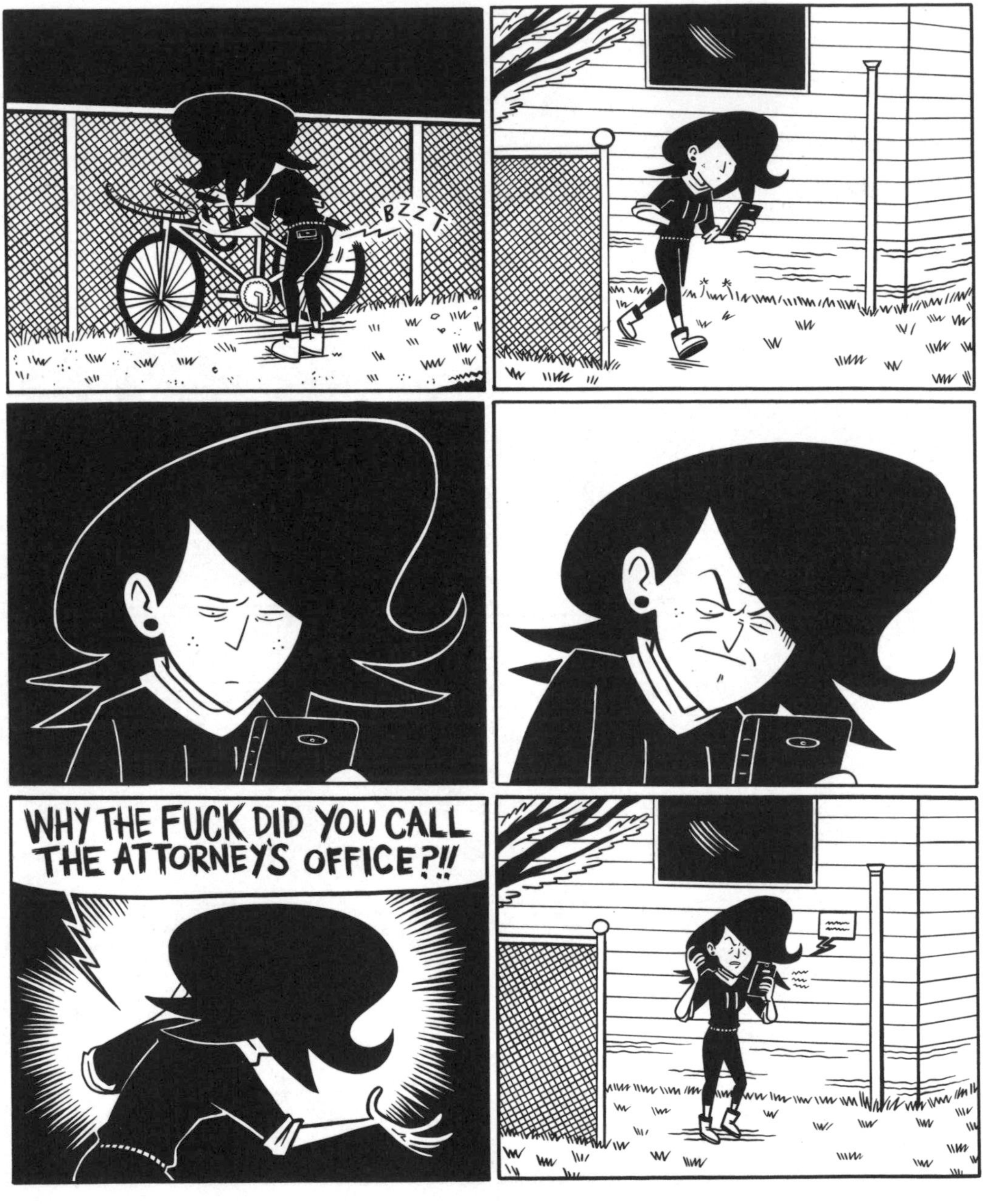
BZZT
WHY THE FUCK DID YOU CALL THE ATTORNEY'S OFFICE?!!

MOM, I EXPLICITLY TOLD YOU NOT TO FUCKING DO THAT!!!
THIS IS BETWEEN ME AND HIM! DO YOU HEAR ME? WHATEVER SHIT YOU'RE FEELING? THAT'S ON YOU!
CLICK

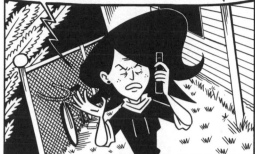

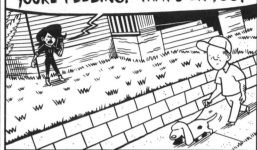

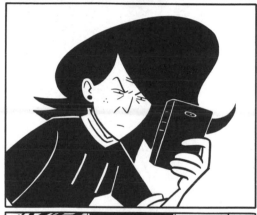

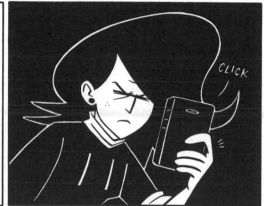

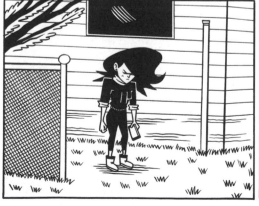

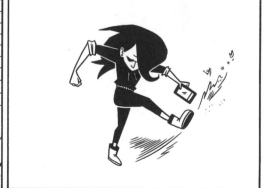

ONE MONTH BEFORE GRADUATION.

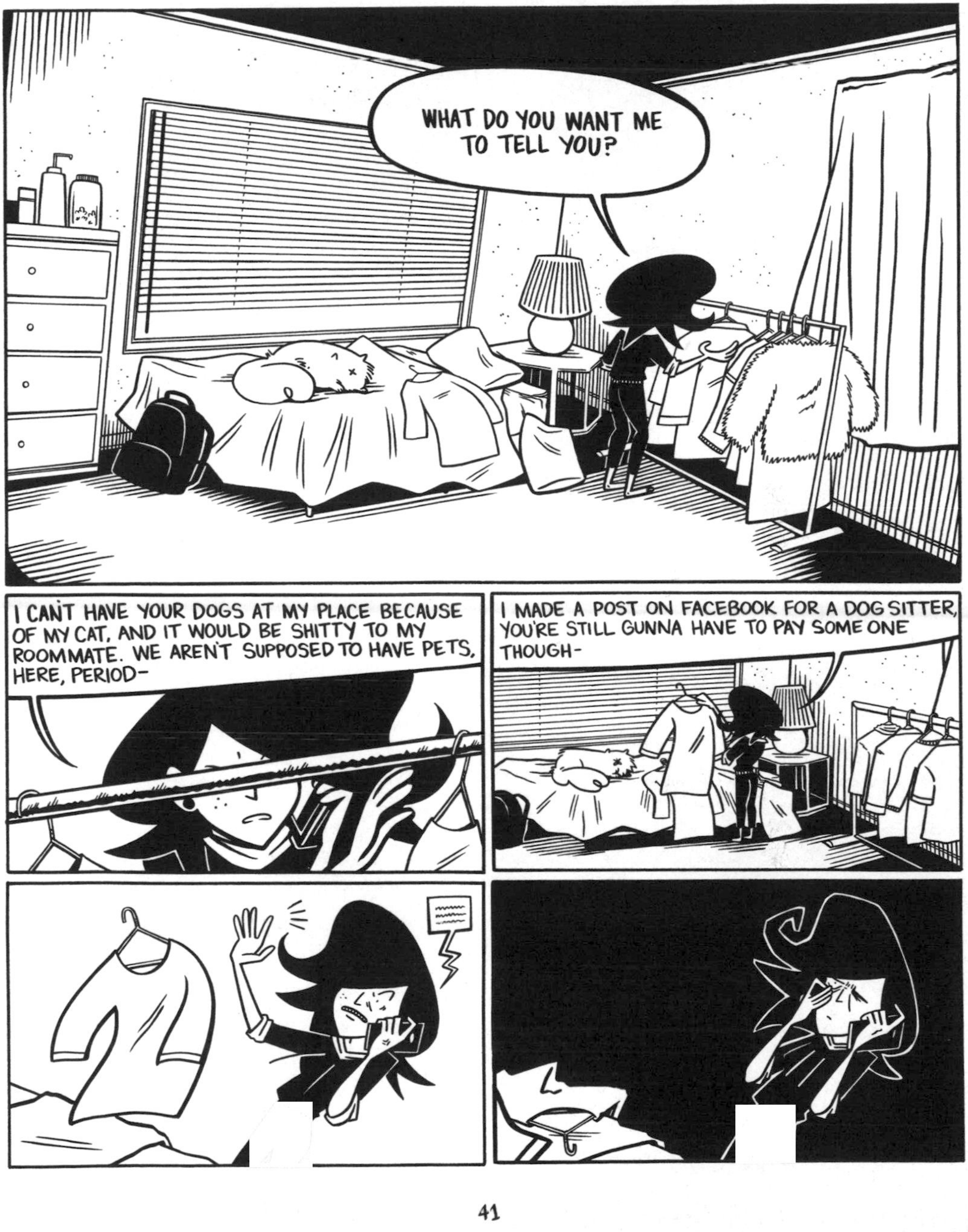
WHAT DO YOU WANT ME TO TELL YOU?
I CAN'T HAVE YOUR DOGS AT MY PLACE BECAUSE OF MY CAT, AND IT WOULD BE SHITTY TO MY ROOMMATE. WE AREN'T SUPPOSED TO HAVE PETS, HERE, PERIOD-
I MADE A POST ON FACEBOOK FOR A DOG SITTER, YOU'RE STILL GUNNA HAVE TO PAY SOME ONE THOUGH-

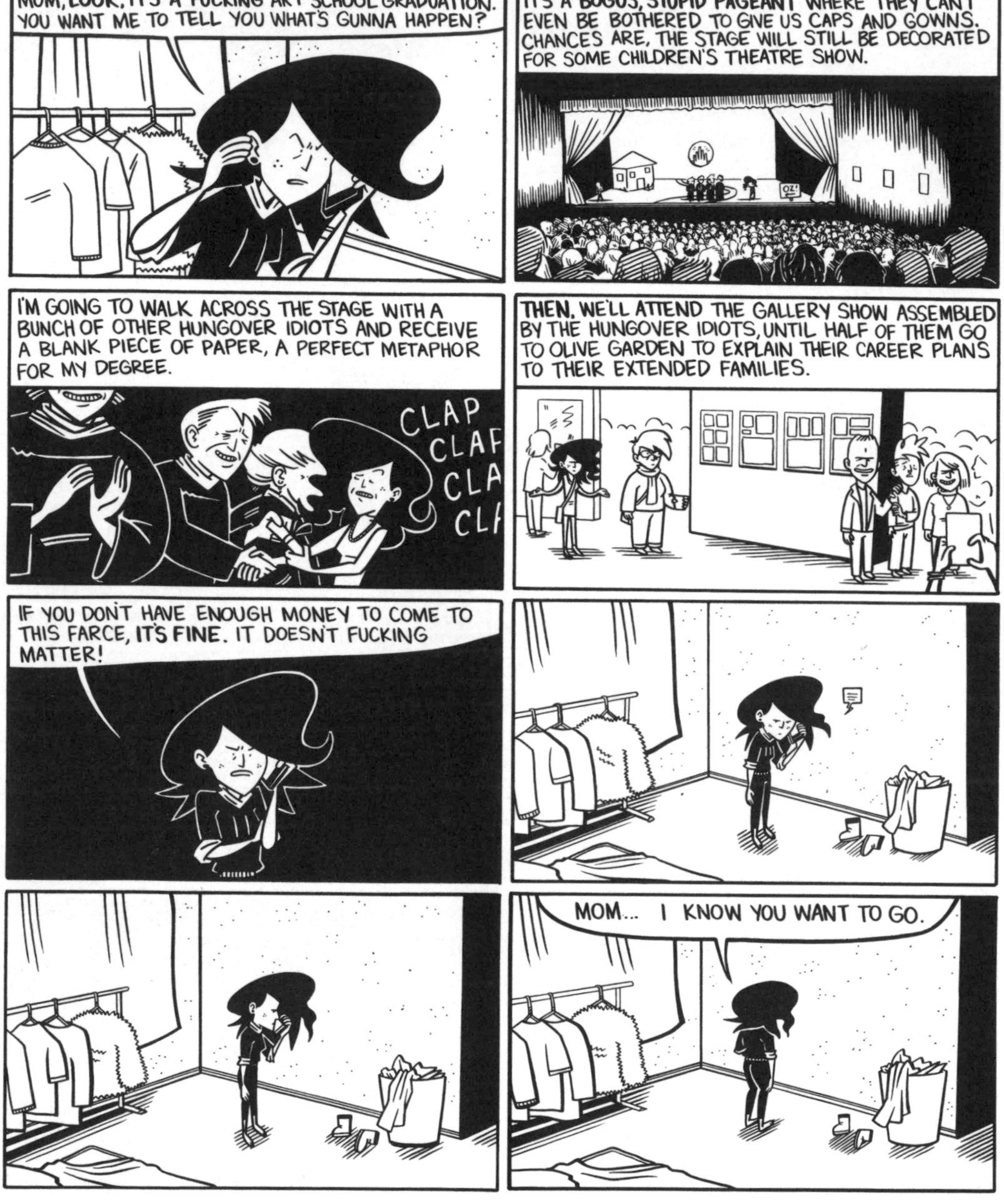
MOM, LOOK. IT'S A FUCKING ART SCHOOL GRADUATION. YOU WANT ME TO TELL YOU WHAT'S GUNNA HAPPEN?
IT'S A BOGUS, STUPID PAGEANT WHERE THEY CAN'T EVEN BE BOTHERED TO GIVE US CAPS AND GOWNS. CHANCES ARE, THE STAGE WILL STILL BE DECORATED FOR SOME CHILDREN'S THEATRE SHOW.
OZ!
I'M GOING TO WALK ACROSS THE STAGE WITH A BUNCH OF OTHER HUNGOVER IDIOTS AND RECEIVE A BLANK PIECE OF PAPER, A PERFECT METAPHOR FOR MY DEGREE.
CLAP
CLAP
CLA
CL
THEN, WE'LL ATTEND THE GALLERY SHOW ASSEMBLED BY THE HUNGOVER IDIOTS, UNTIL HALF OF THEM GO TO OLIVE GARDEN TO EXPLAIN THEIR CAREER PLANS TO THEIR EXTENDED FAMILIES.
IF YOU DON'T HAVE ENOUGH MONEY TO COME TO THIS FARCE, IT'S FINE. IT DOESN'T FUCKING MATTER!
MOM... I KNOW YOU WANT TO GO.

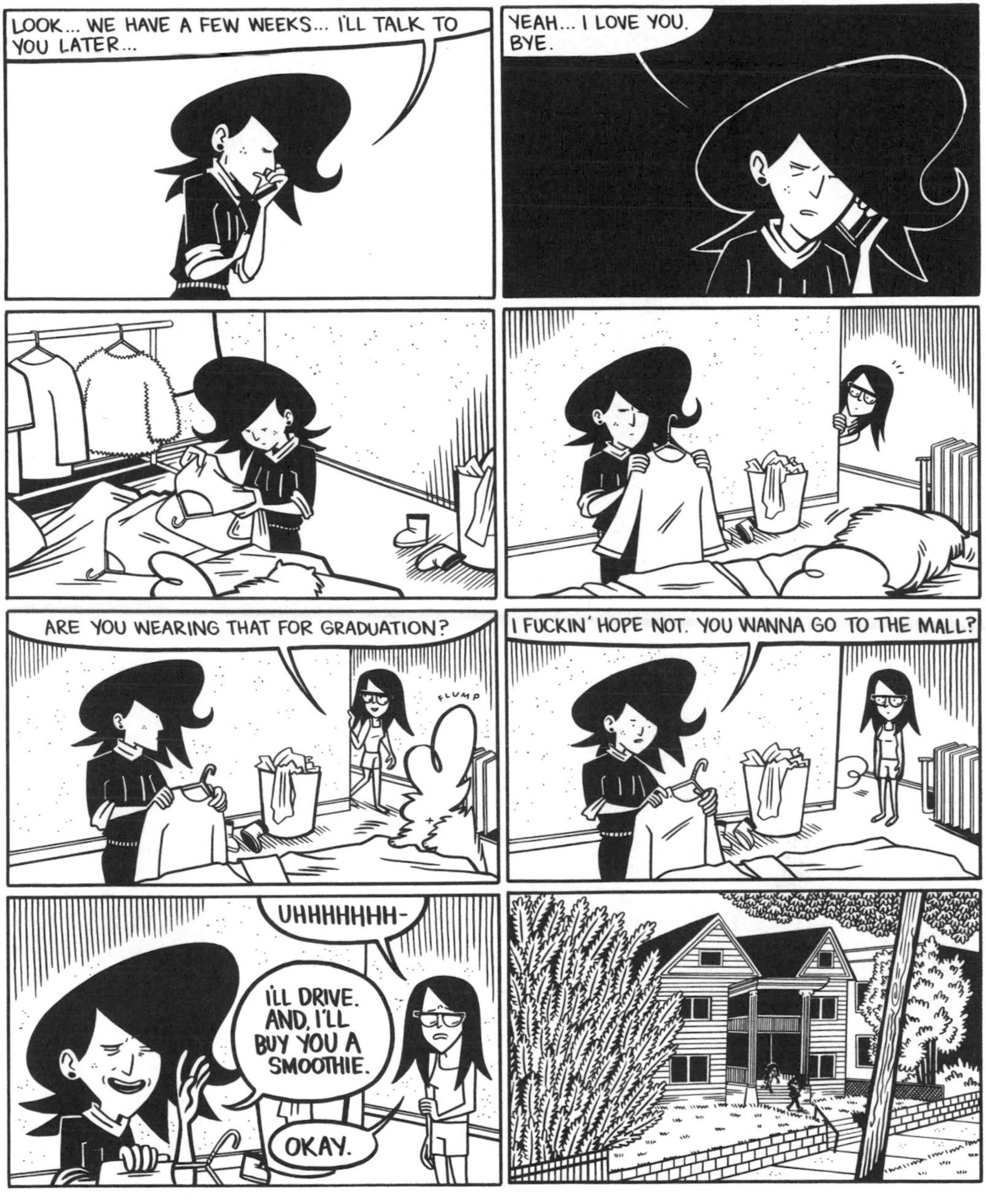
LOOK... WE HAVE A FEW WEEKS... I'LL TALK TO YOU LATER...
YEAH... I LOVE YOU. BYE.
ARE YOU WEARING THAT FOR GRADUATION?
FLUMP
I FUCKIN' HOPE NOT. YOU WANNA GO TO THE MALL?
UHHHHHHH-
I'LL DRIVE. AND, I'LL BUY YOU A SMOOTHIE.
OKAY.

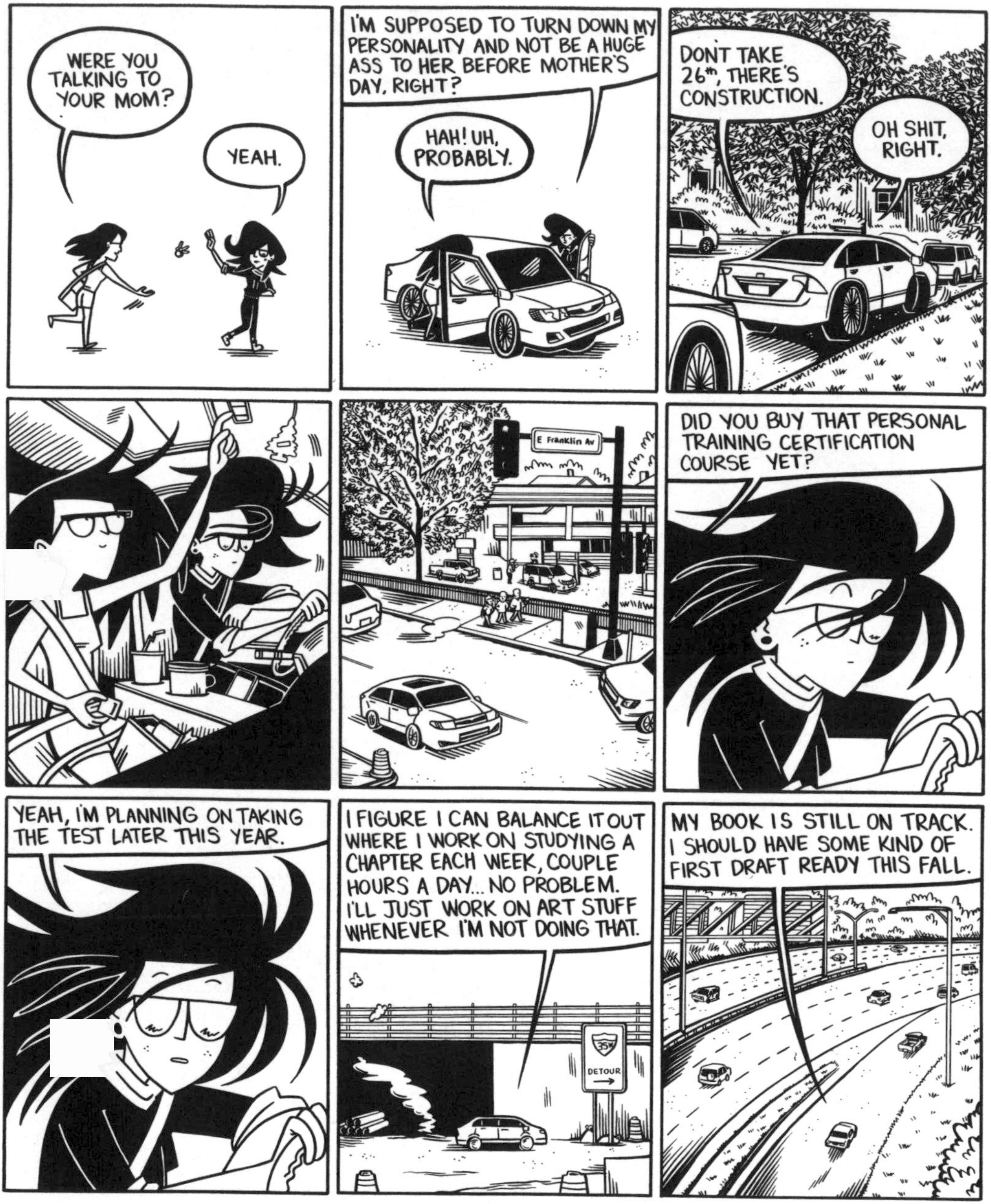
WERE YOU TALKING TO YOUR MOM?
YEAH.
I'M SUPPOSED TO TURN DOWN MY PERSONALITY AND NOT BE A HUGE ASS TO HER BEFORE MOTHER'S DAY, RIGHT?
HAH! UH, PROBABLY.
DON'T TAKE 26th, THERE'S CONSTRUCTION.
OH SHIT, RIGHT.
E Franklin Av
DID YOU BUY THAT PERSONAL TRAINING CERTIFICATION COURSE YET?
YEAH, I'M PLANNING ON TAKING THE TEST LATER THIS YEAR.
I FIGURE I CAN BALANCE IT OUT WHERE I WORK ON STUDYING A CHAPTER EACH WEEK, COUPLE HOURS A DAY... NO PROBLEM. I'LL JUST WORK ON ART STUFF WHENEVER I'M NOT DOING THAT.
35W
DETOUR
MY BOOK IS STILL ON TRACK. I SHOULD HAVE SOME KIND OF FIRST DRAFT READY THIS FALL.

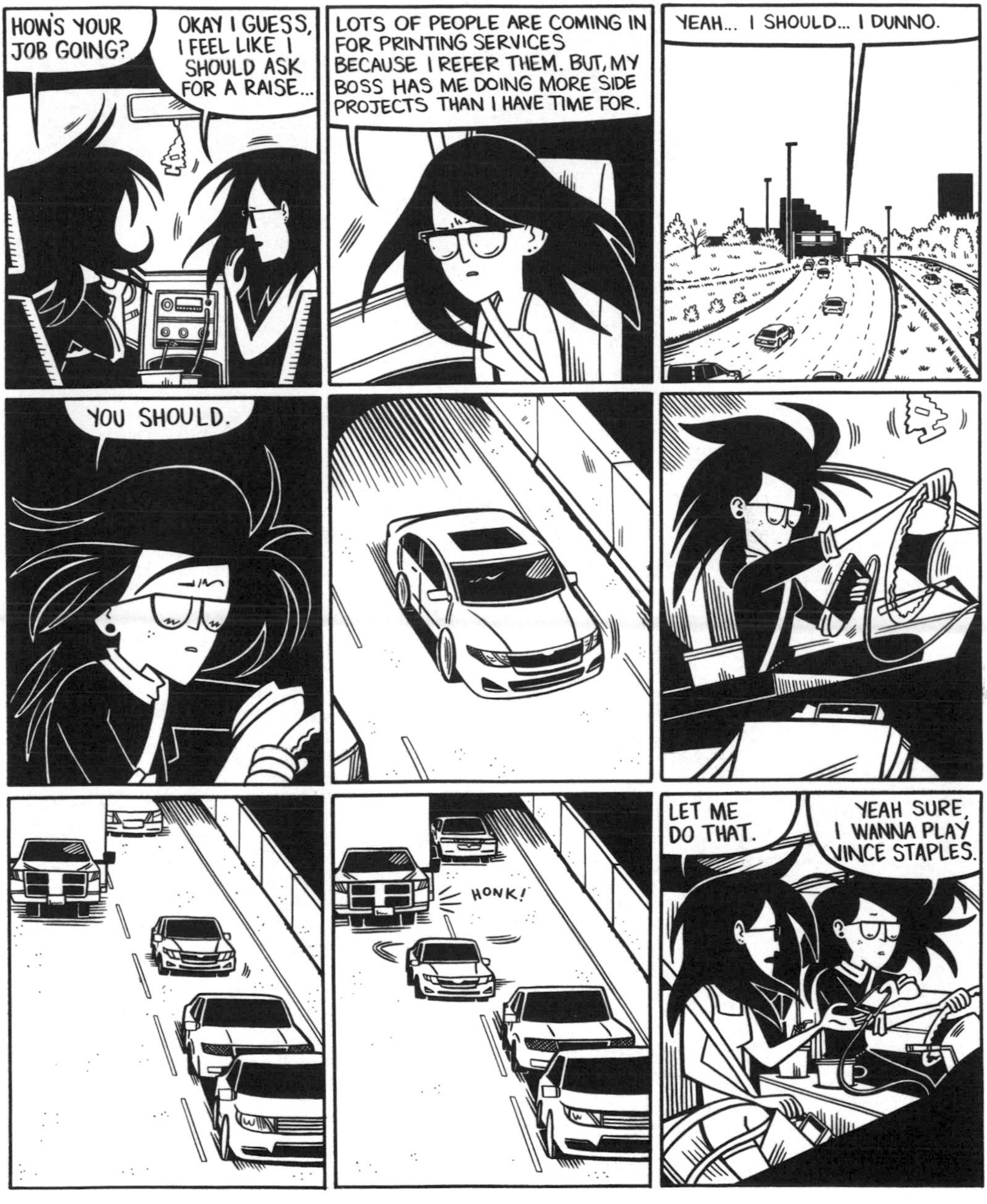
HOW'S YOUR JOB GOING?
OKAY I GUESS, I FEEL LIKE I SHOULD ASK FOR A RAISE...
LOTS OF PEOPLE ARE COMING IN FOR PRINTING SERVICES BECAUSE I REFER THEM. BUT, MY BOSS HAS ME DOING MORE SIDE PROJECTS THAN I HAVE TIME FOR.
YEAH... I SHOULD... I DUNNO.
YOU SHOULD.
HONK!
LET ME DO THAT.
YEAH SURE, I WANNA PLAY VINCE STAPLES.

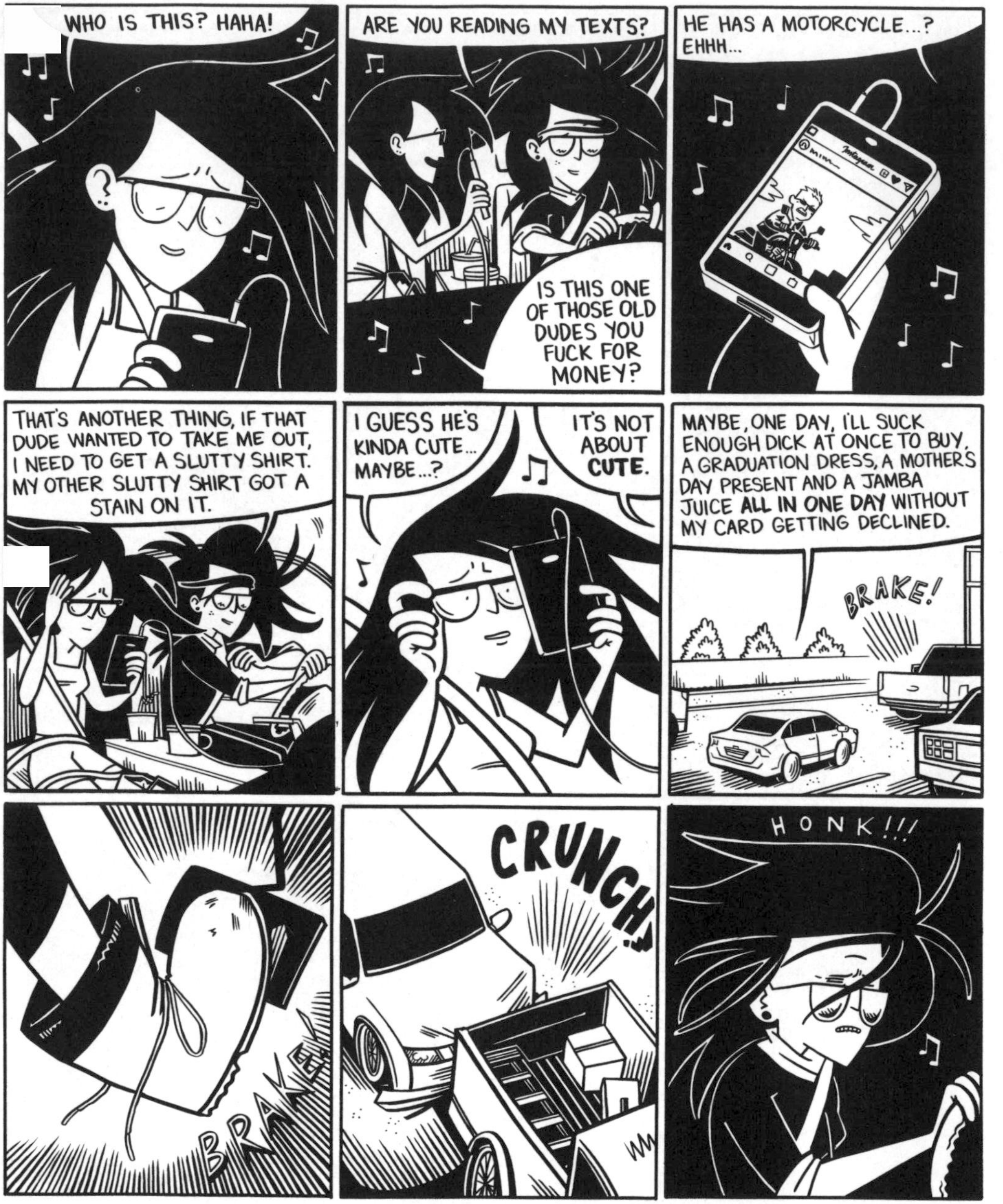
WHO IS THIS? HAHA!
ARE YOU READING MY TEXTS?
IS THIS ONE OF THOSE OLD DUDES YOU FUCK FOR MONEY?
HE HAS A MOTORCYCLE...? EHHH...
THAT'S ANOTHER THING, IF THAT DUDE WANTED TO TAKE ME OUT, I NEED TO GET A SLUTTY SHIRT. MY OTHER SLUTTY SHIRT GOT A STAIN ON IT.
I GUESS HE'S KINDA CUTE... MAYBE...?
IT'S NOT ABOUT **CUTE**.
MAYBE, ONE DAY, I'LL SUCK ENOUGH DICK AT ONCE TO BUY, A GRADUATION DRESS, A MOTHER'S DAY PRESENT AND A JAMBA JUICE **ALL IN ONE DAY** WITHOUT MY CARD GETTING DECLINED.
BRAKE!
BRAKE!
CRUNCH!
HONK!!!

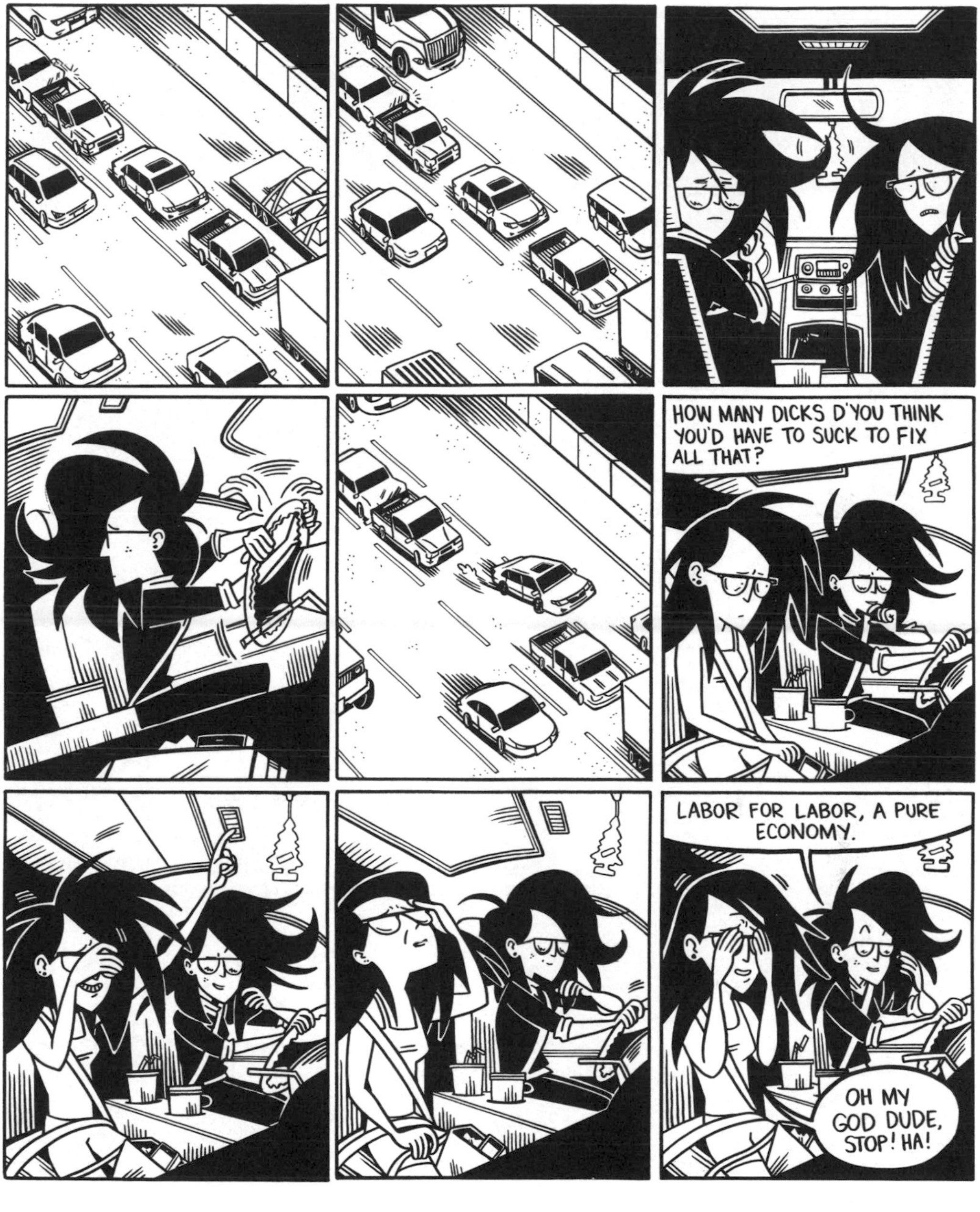
HOW MANY DICKS D'YOU THINK YOU'D HAVE TO SUCK TO FIX ALL THAT?
LABOR FOR LABOR, A PURE ECONOMY.
OH MY GOD DUDE, STOP! HA!

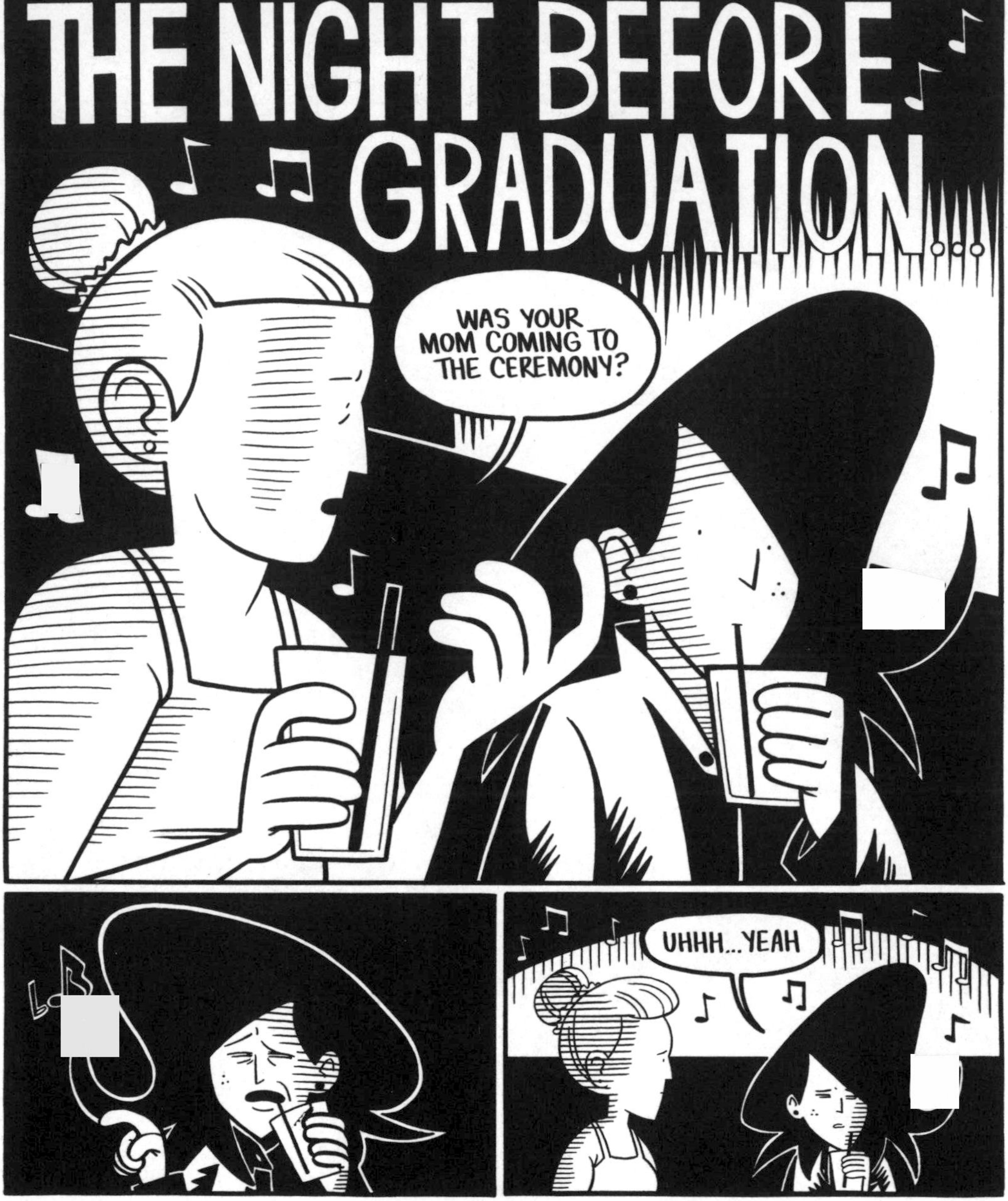
THE NIGHT BEFORE GRADUATION...
WAS YOUR MOM COMING TO THE CEREMONY?
UHHH...YEAH

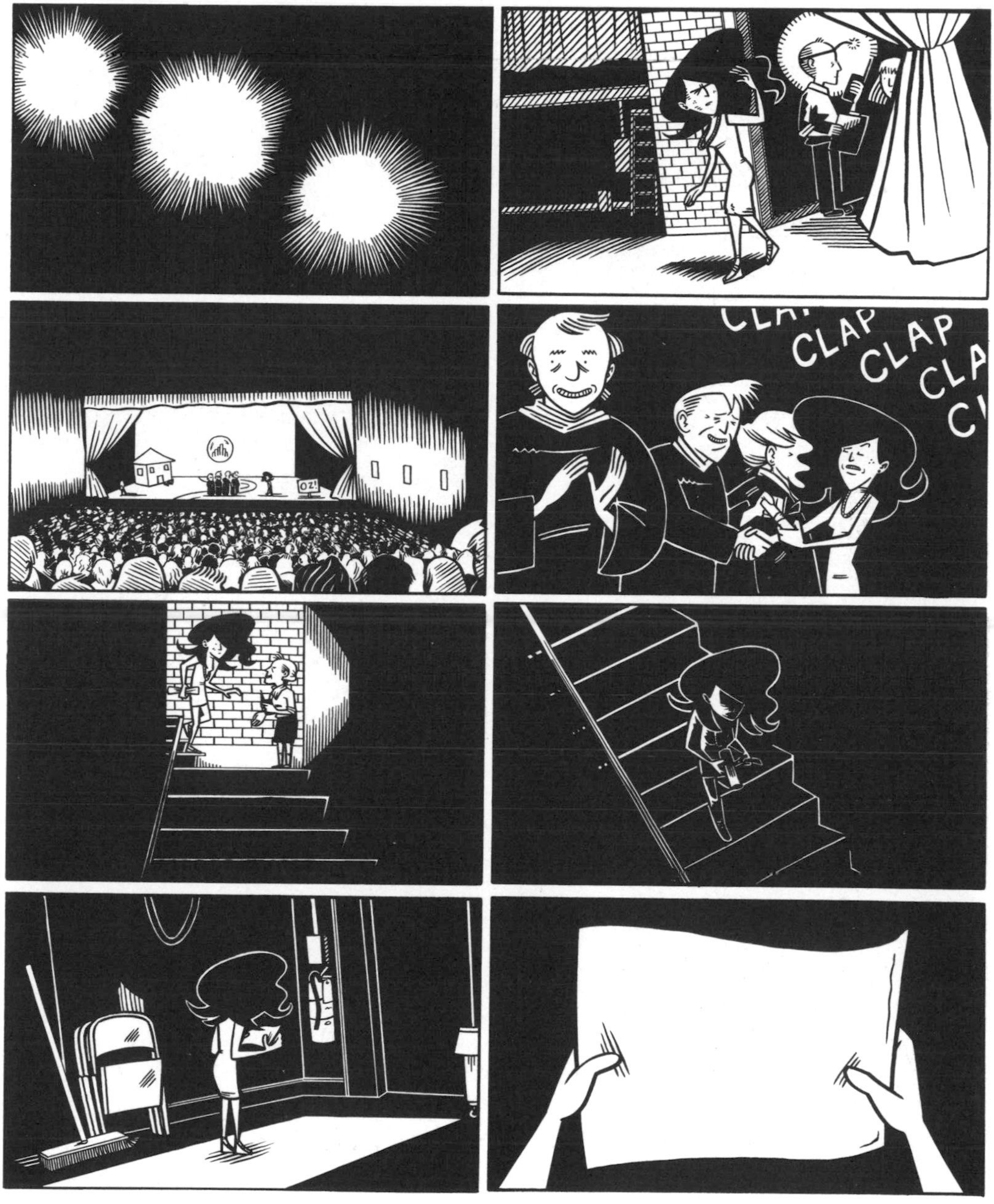
CLAP
CLAP
CLAP
CLAP
CLA
C

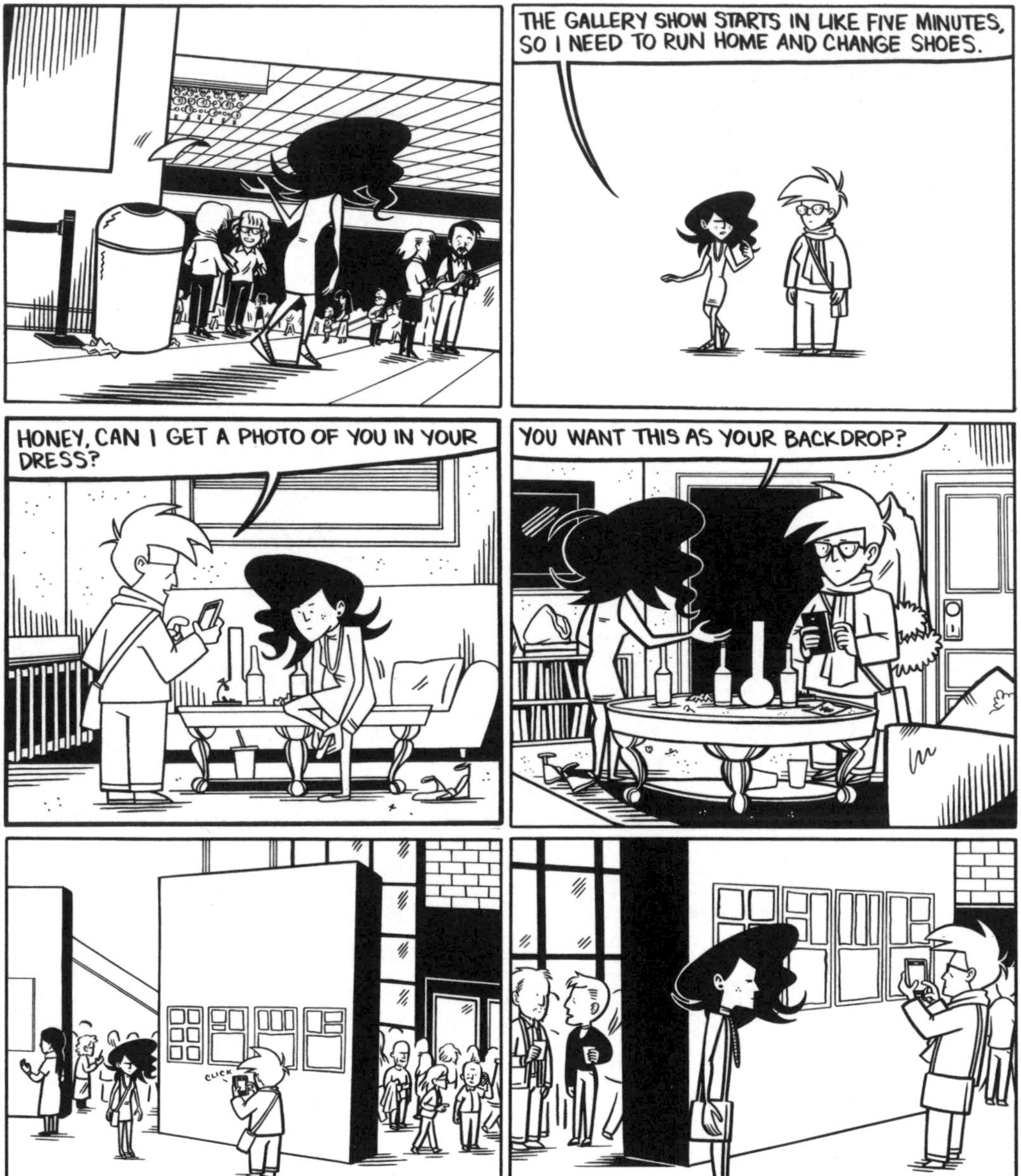
THE GALLERY SHOW STARTS IN LIKE FIVE MINUTES, SO I NEED TO RUN HOME AND CHANGE SHOES.
HONEY, CAN I GET A PHOTO OF YOU IN YOUR DRESS?
YOU WANT THIS AS YOUR BACKDROP?
CLICK

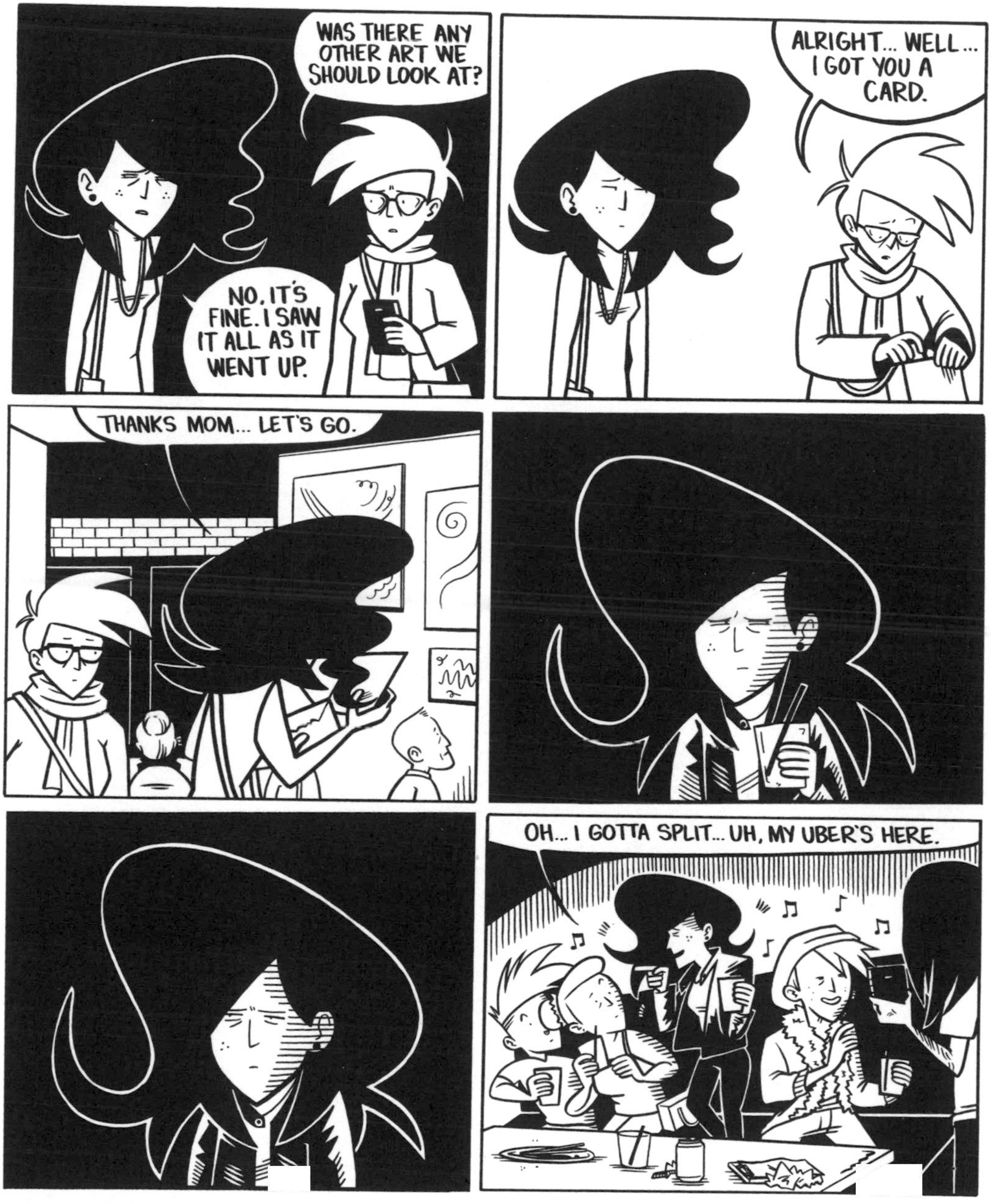
WAS THERE ANY OTHER ART WE SHOULD LOOK AT?
NO, IT'S FINE. I SAW IT ALL AS IT WENT UP.
ALRIGHT... WELL... I GOT YOU A CARD.
THANKS MOM... LET'S GO.
OH... I GOTTA SPLIT... UH, MY UBER'S HERE.

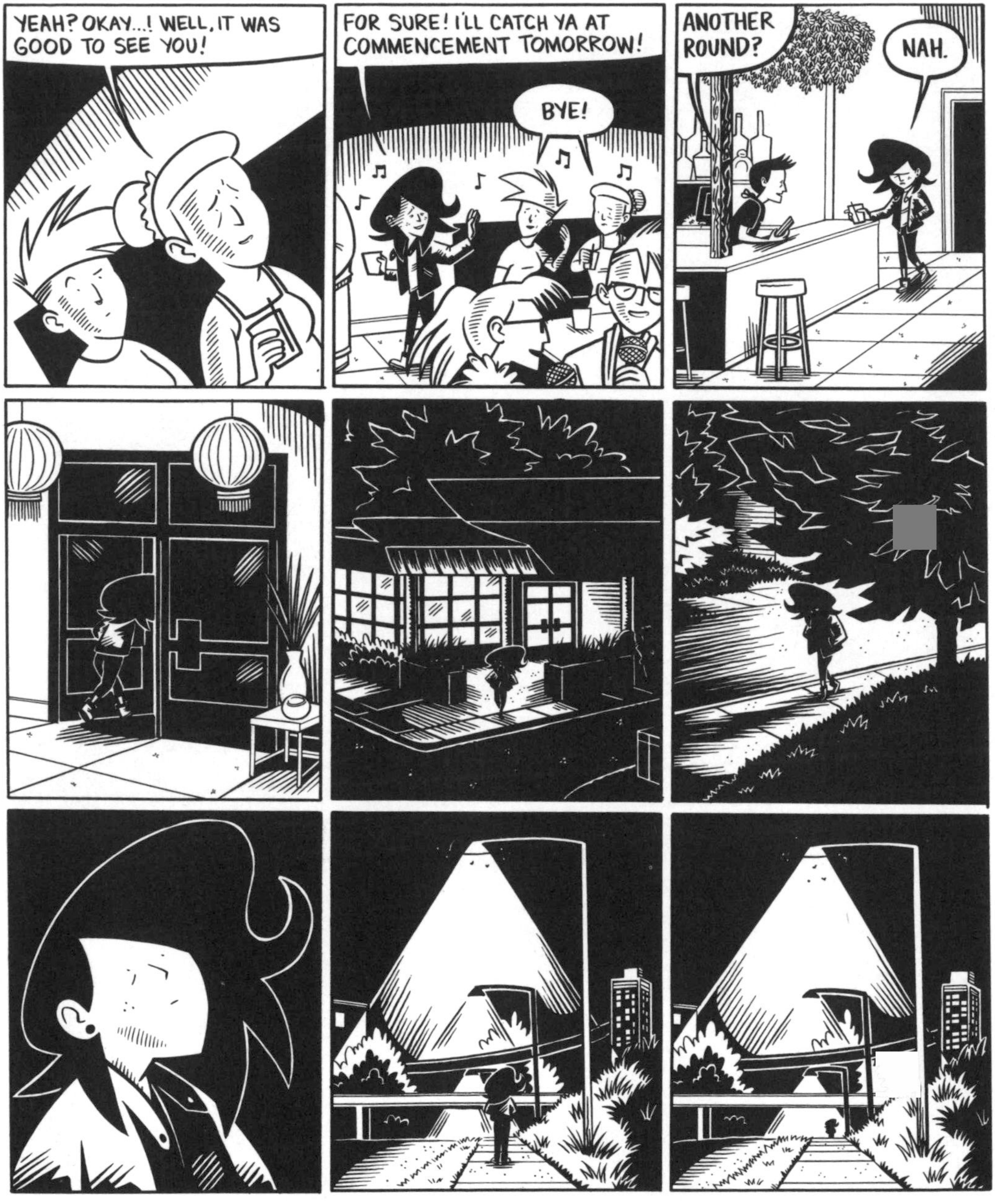
YEAH? OKAY...! WELL, IT WAS GOOD TO SEE YOU!
FOR SURE! I'LL CATCH YA AT COMMENCEMENT TOMORROW!
BYE!
ANOTHER ROUND?
NAH.

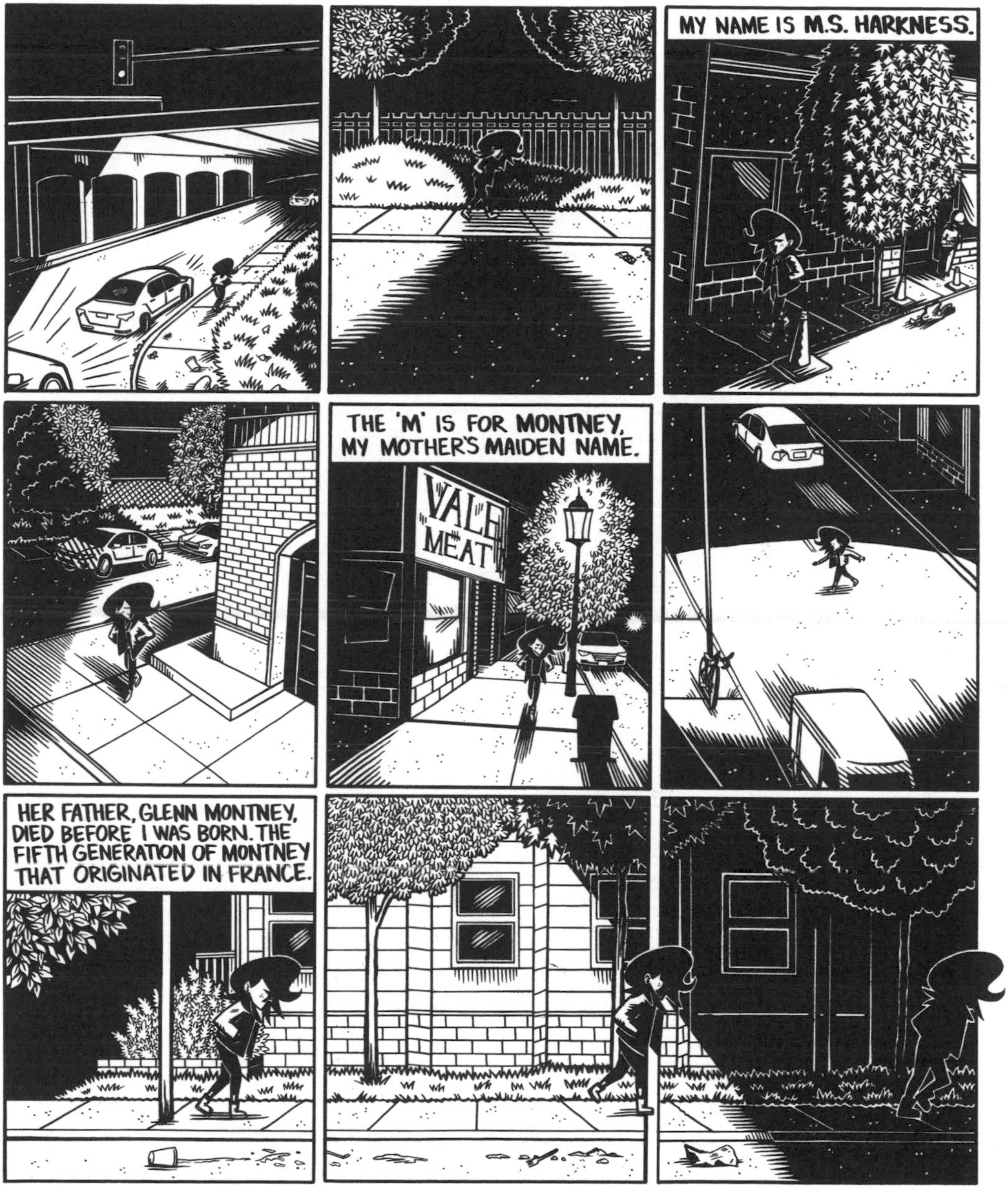
MY NAME IS M.S. HARKNESS.
THE 'M' IS FOR MONTNEY, MY MOTHER'S MAIDEN NAME.
VALE MEAT
HER FATHER, GLENN MONTNEY, DIED BEFORE I WAS BORN. THE FIFTH GENERATION OF MONTNEY THAT ORIGINATED IN FRANCE.

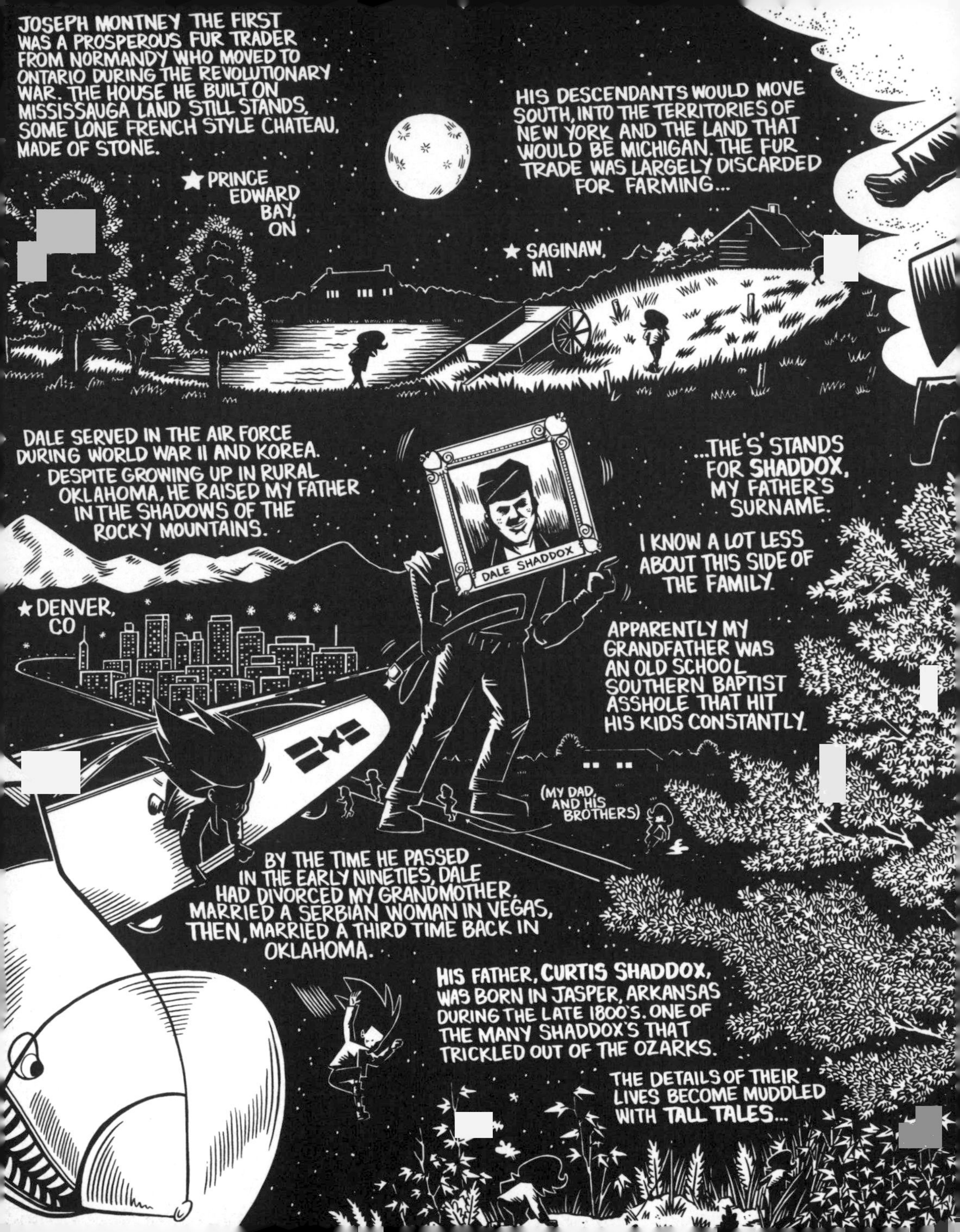
JOSEPH MONTNEY THE FIRST WAS A PROSPEROUS FUR TRADER FROM NORMANDY WHO MOVED TO ONTARIO DURING THE REVOLUTIONARY WAR. THE HOUSE HE BUILT ON MISSISSAUGA LAND STILL STANDS, SOME LONE FRENCH STYLE CHATEAU, MADE OF STONE.
★ PRINCE EDWARD BAY, ON
HIS DESCENDANTS WOULD MOVE SOUTH, INTO THE TERRITORIES OF NEW YORK AND THE LAND THAT WOULD BE MICHIGAN. THE FUR TRADE WAS LARGELY DISCARDED FOR FARMING...
★ SAGINAW, MI
DALE SERVED IN THE AIR FORCE DURING WORLD WAR II AND KOREA. DESPITE GROWING UP IN RURAL OKLAHOMA, HE RAISED MY FATHER IN THE SHADOWS OF THE ROCKY MOUNTAINS.
DALE SHADDOX
...THE 'S' STANDS FOR SHADDOX, MY FATHER'S SURNAME.
I KNOW A LOT LESS ABOUT THIS SIDE OF THE FAMILY.
★ DENVER, CO
APPARENTLY MY GRANDFATHER WAS AN OLD SCHOOL SOUTHERN BAPTIST ASSHOLE THAT HIT HIS KIDS CONSTANTLY.
(MY DAD, AND HIS BROTHERS)
BY THE TIME HE PASSED IN THE EARLY NINETIES, DALE HAD DIVORCED MY GRANDMOTHER, MARRIED A SERBIAN WOMAN IN VEGAS, THEN, MARRIED A THIRD TIME BACK IN OKLAHOMA.
HIS FATHER, CURTIS SHADDOX, WAS BORN IN JASPER, ARKANSAS DURING THE LATE 1800'S. ONE OF THE MANY SHADDOX'S THAT TRICKLED OUT OF THE OZARKS.
THE DETAILS OF THEIR LIVES BECOME MUDDLED WITH TALL TALES...

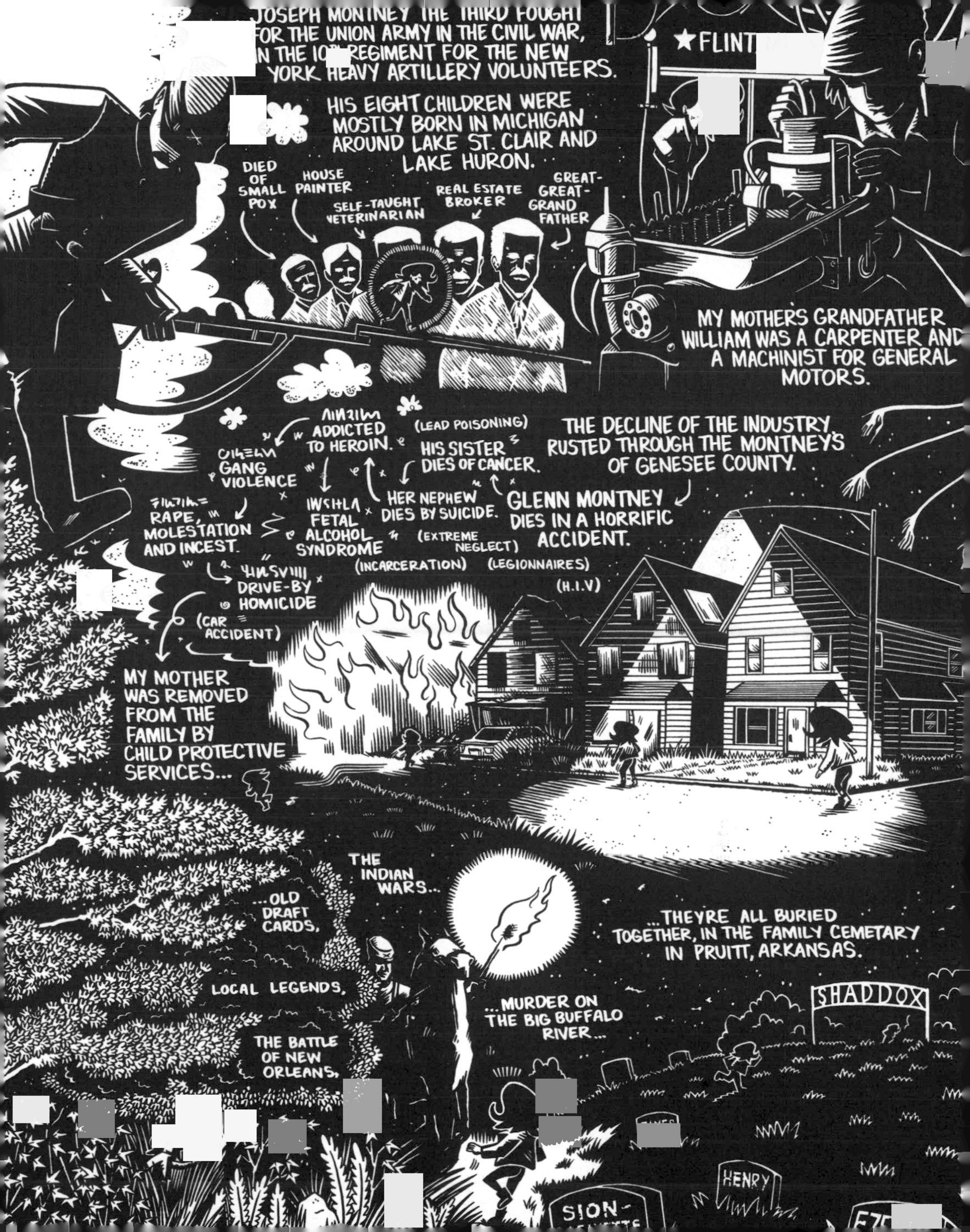

JOSEPH MONTNEY THE THIRD FOUGHT FOR THE UNION ARMY IN THE CIVIL WAR, IN THE 10 REGIMENT FOR THE NEW YORK HEAVY ARTILLERY VOLUNTEERS.
★FLINT
HIS EIGHT CHILDREN WERE MOSTLY BORN IN MICHIGAN AROUND LAKE ST. CLAIR AND LAKE HURON.
DIED OF SMALL POX
HOUSE PAINTER
SELF-TAUGHT VETERINARIAN
REAL ESTATE BROKER
GREAT-GREAT-GRAND FATHER
MY MOTHER'S GRANDFATHER WILLIAM WAS A CARPENTER AND A MACHINIST FOR GENERAL MOTORS.
ADDICTED TO HEROIN.
(LEAD POISONING)
HIS SISTER DIES OF CANCER.
THE DECLINE OF THE INDUSTRY RUSTED THROUGH THE MONTNEY'S OF GENESEE COUNTY.
GANG VIOLENCE
HER NEPHEW DIES BY SUICIDE.
GLENN MONTNEY DIES IN A HORRIFIC ACCIDENT.
RAPE, MOLESTATION AND INCEST.
FETAL ALCOHOL SYNDROME
(EXTREME NEGLECT)
(INCARCERATION)
(LEGIONNAIRES)
(H.I.V)
DRIVE-BY HOMICIDE
(CAR ACCIDENT)
MY MOTHER WAS REMOVED FROM THE FAMILY BY CHILD PROTECTIVE SERVICES...
THE INDIAN WARS...
...OLD DRAFT CARDS,
...THEY'RE ALL BURIED TOGETHER, IN THE FAMILY CEMETARY IN PRUITT, ARKANSAS.
LOCAL LEGENDS,
...MURDER ON THE BIG BUFFALO RIVER...
SHADDOX
THE BATTLE OF NEW ORLEANS,
HENRY
SION-

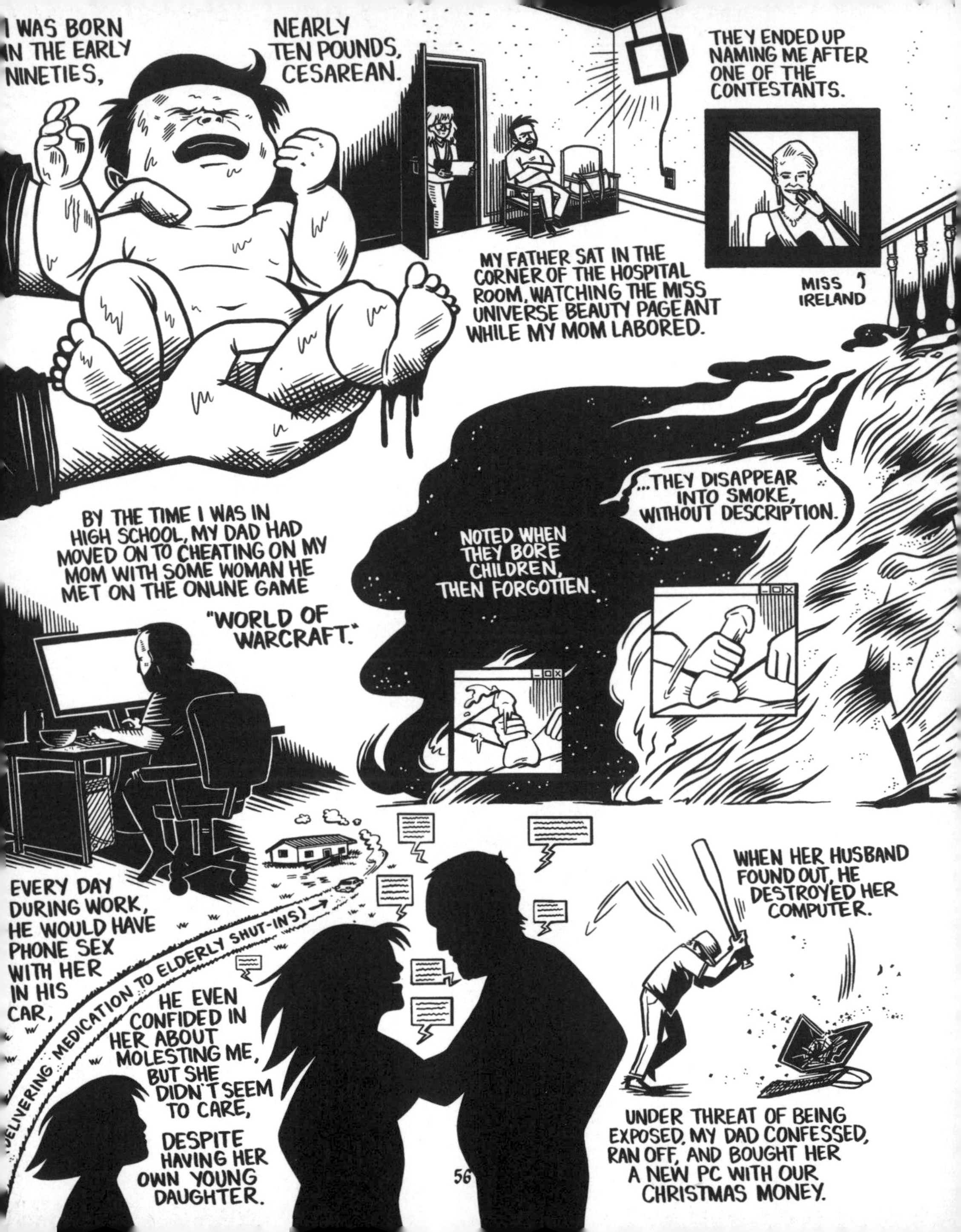
I WAS BORN IN THE EARLY NINETIES,
NEARLY TEN POUNDS, CESAREAN.
MY FATHER SAT IN THE CORNER OF THE HOSPITAL ROOM, WATCHING THE MISS UNIVERSE BEAUTY PAGEANT WHILE MY MOM LABORED.
THEY ENDED UP NAMING ME AFTER ONE OF THE CONTESTANTS.
MISS IRELAND
BY THE TIME I WAS IN HIGH SCHOOL, MY DAD HAD MOVED ON TO CHEATING ON MY MOM WITH SOME WOMAN HE MET ON THE ONLINE GAME
"WORLD OF WARCRAFT."
NOTED WHEN THEY BORE CHILDREN, THEN FORGOTTEN.
...THEY DISAPPEAR INTO SMOKE, WITHOUT DESCRIPTION.
EVERY DAY DURING WORK, HE WOULD HAVE PHONE SEX WITH HER IN HIS CAR,
(DELIVERING MEDICATION TO ELDERLY SHUT-INS)
HE EVEN CONFIDED IN HER ABOUT MOLESTING ME, BUT SHE DIDN'T SEEM TO CARE,
DESPITE HAVING HER OWN YOUNG DAUGHTER.
WHEN HER HUSBAND FOUND OUT, HE DESTROYED HER COMPUTER.
UNDER THREAT OF BEING EXPOSED, MY DAD CONFESSED, RAN OFF, AND BOUGHT HER A NEW PC WITH OUR CHRISTMAS MONEY.

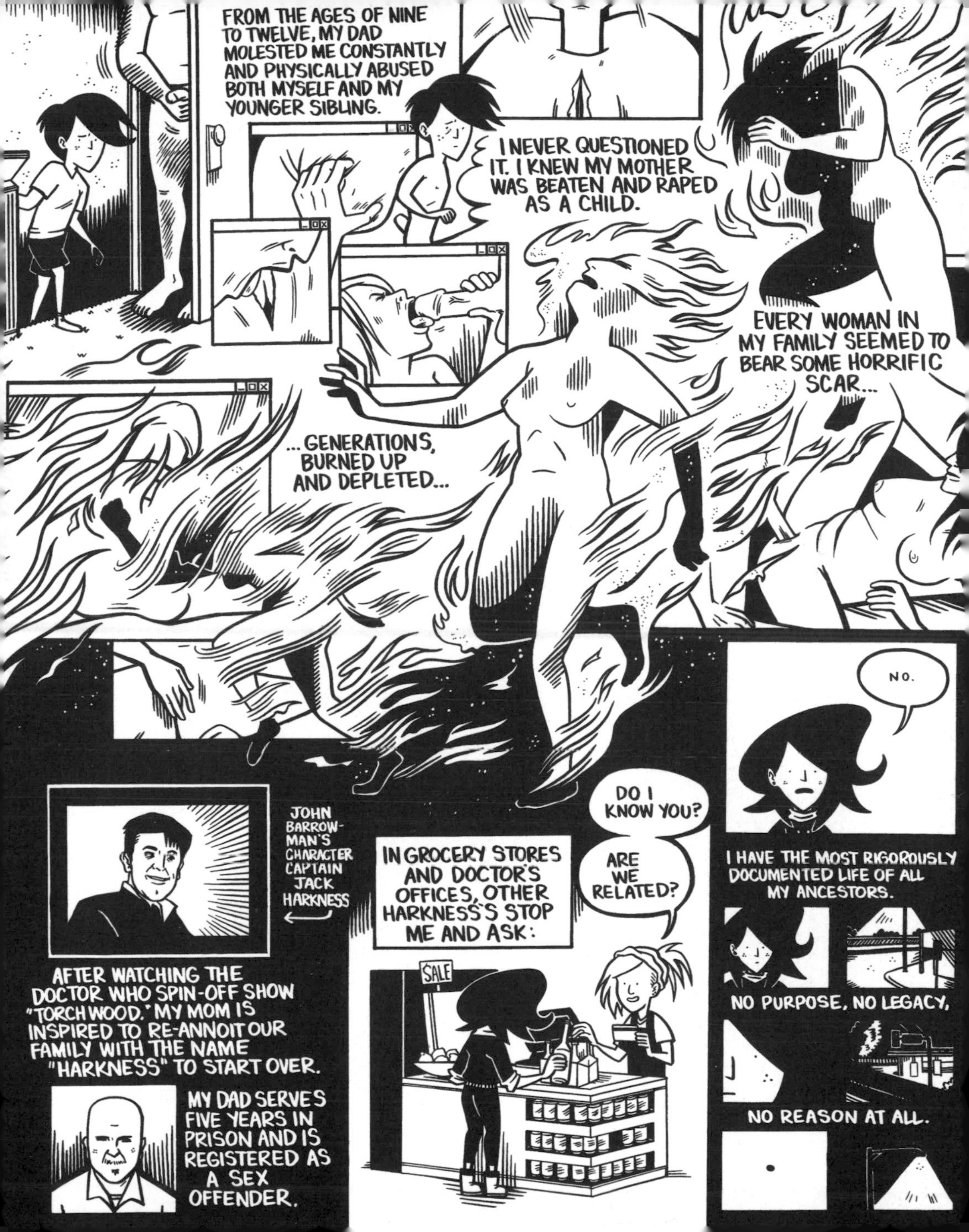
FROM THE AGES OF NINE TO TWELVE, MY DAD MOLESTED ME CONSTANTLY AND PHYSICALLY ABUSED BOTH MYSELF AND MY YOUNGER SIBLING.
I NEVER QUESTIONED IT. I KNEW MY MOTHER WAS BEATEN AND RAPED AS A CHILD.
EVERY WOMAN IN MY FAMILY SEEMED TO BEAR SOME HORRIFIC SCAR...
...GENERATIONS, BURNED UP AND DEPLETED...
JOHN BARROWMAN'S CHARACTER CAPTAIN JACK HARKNESS
AFTER WATCHING THE DOCTOR WHO SPIN-OFF SHOW "TORCHWOOD," MY MOM IS INSPIRED TO RE-ANNOIT OUR FAMILY WITH THE NAME "HARKNESS" TO START OVER.
MY DAD SERVES FIVE YEARS IN PRISON AND IS REGISTERED AS A SEX OFFENDER.
IN GROCERY STORES AND DOCTOR'S OFFICES, OTHER HARKNESS'S STOP ME AND ASK:
DO I KNOW YOU?
ARE WE RELATED?
SALE
NO.
I HAVE THE MOST RIGOROUSLY DOCUMENTED LIFE OF ALL MY ANCESTORS.
NO PURPOSE, NO LEGACY.
NO REASON AT ALL.

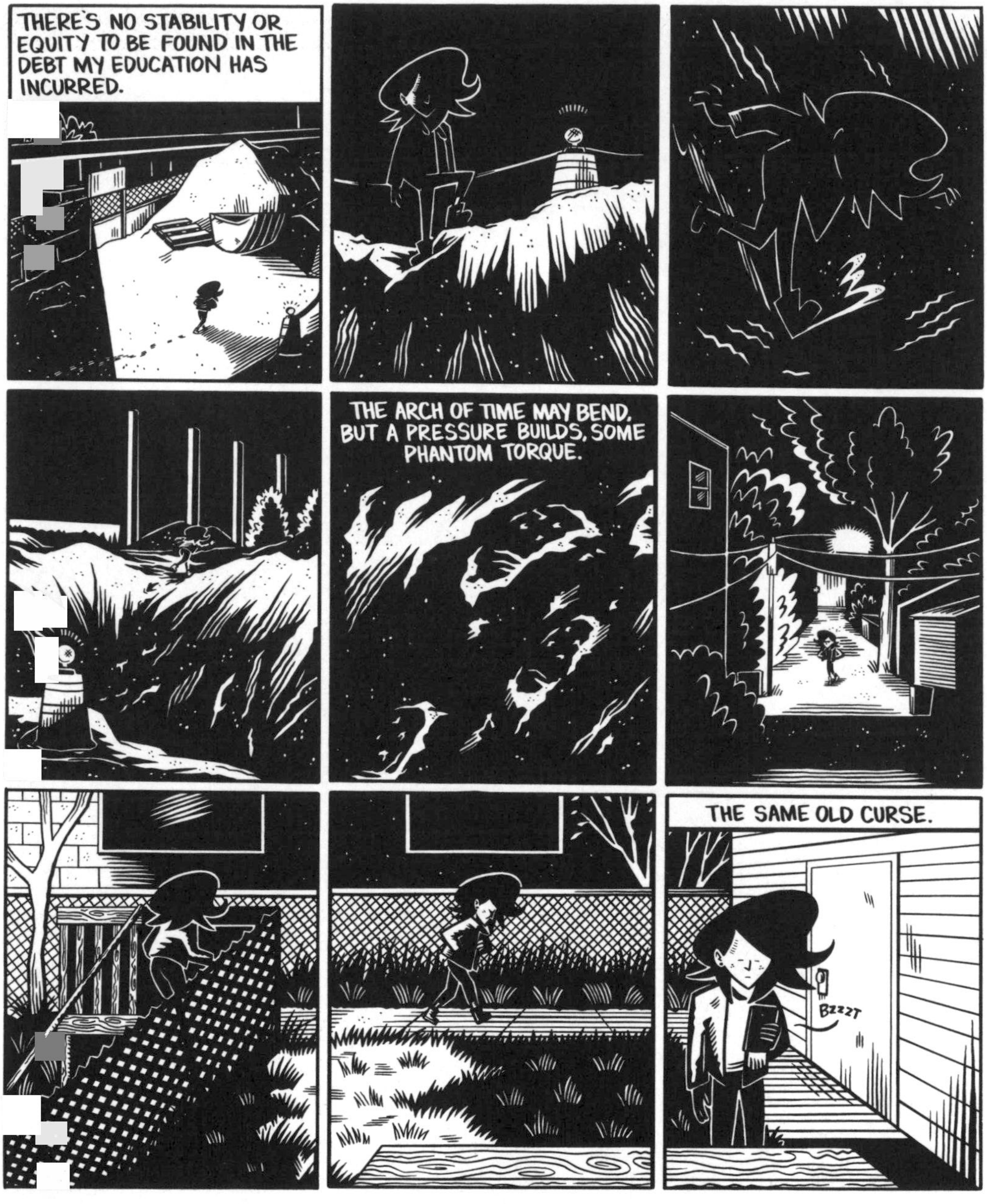
THERE'S NO STABILITY OR EQUITY TO BE FOUND IN THE DEBT MY EDUCATION HAS INCURRED.
THE ARCH OF TIME MAY BEND, BUT A PRESSURE BUILDS, SOME PHANTOM TORQUE.
THE SAME OLD CURSE.
BZZZT

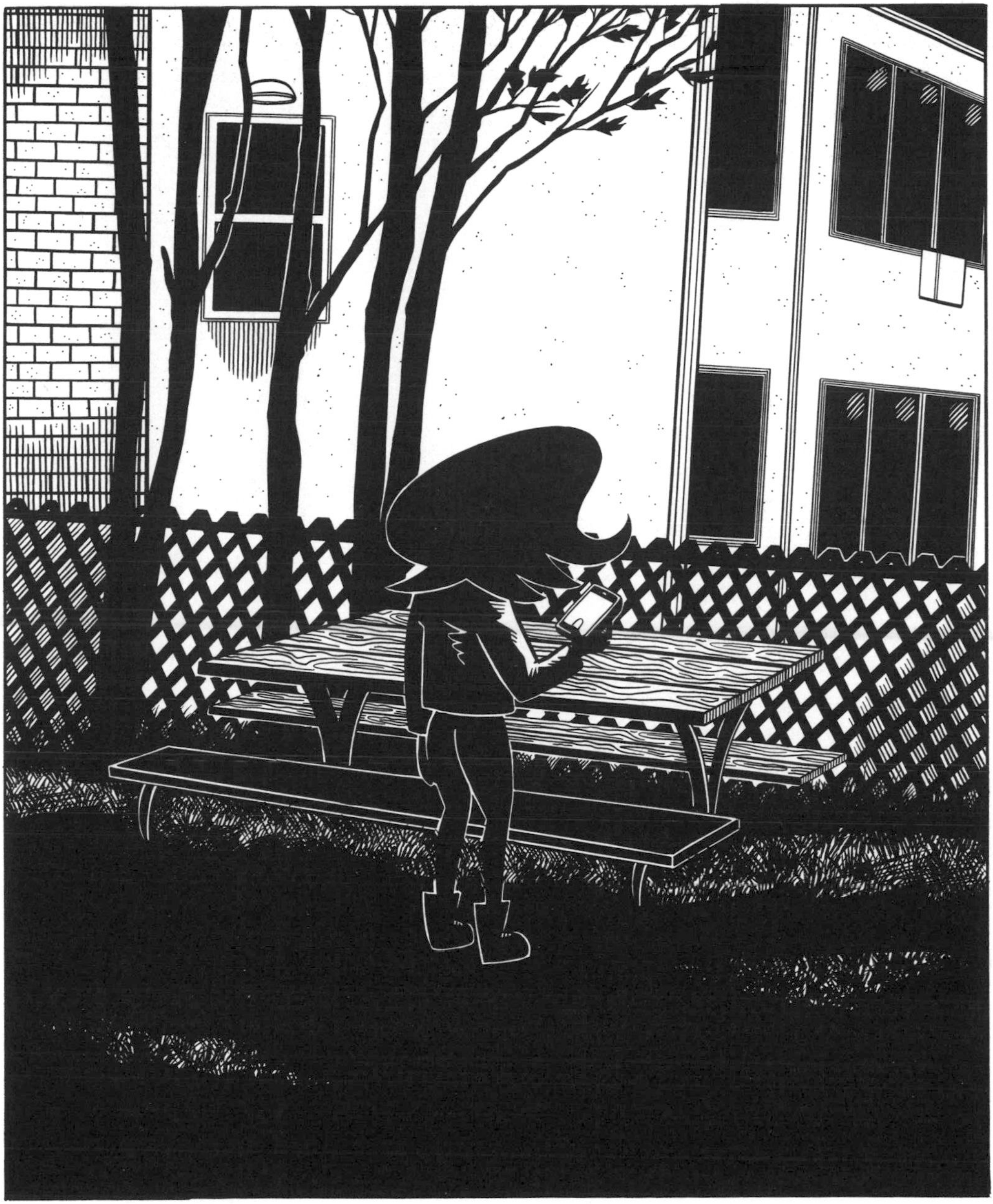

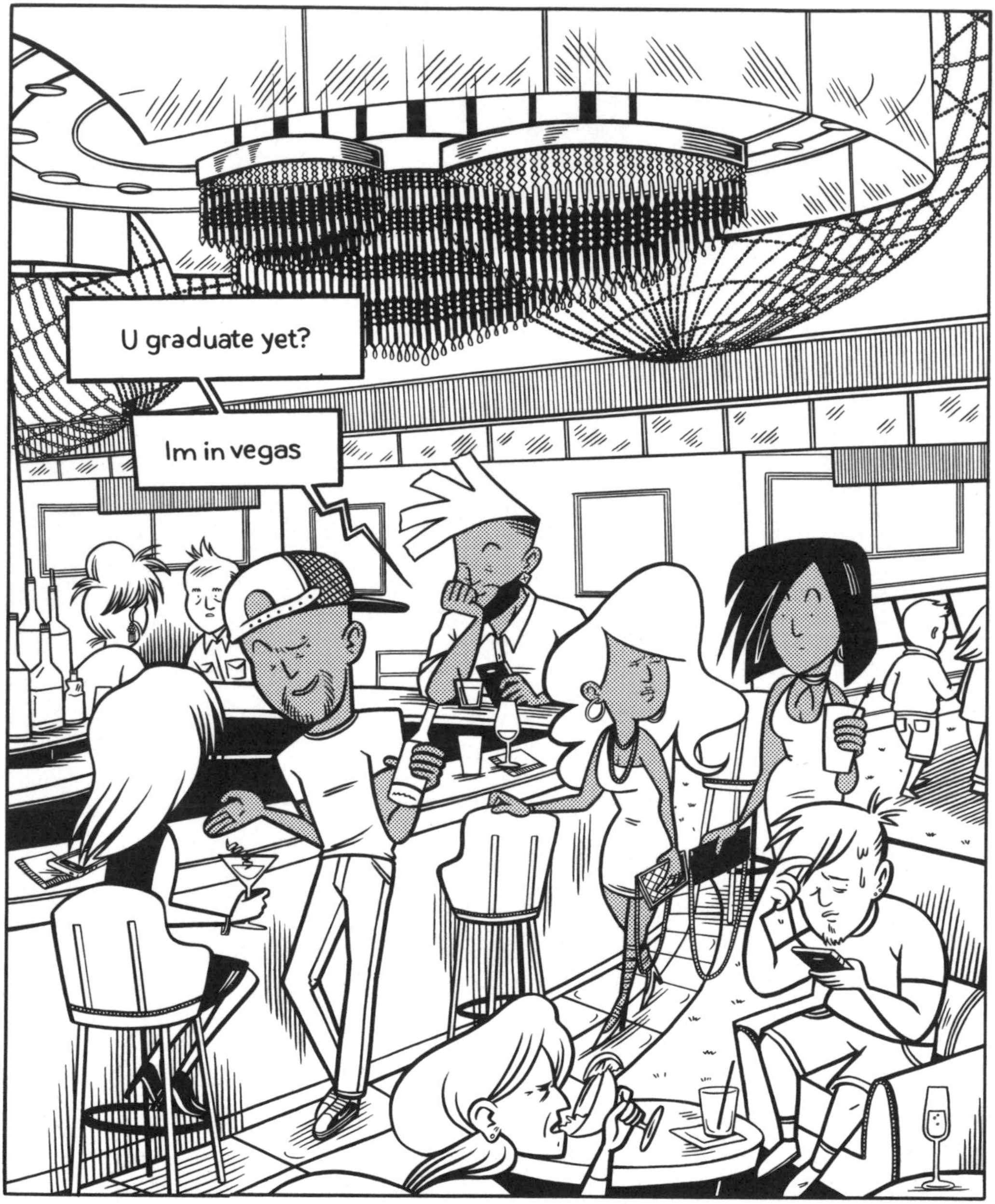
U graduate yet?
Im in vegas

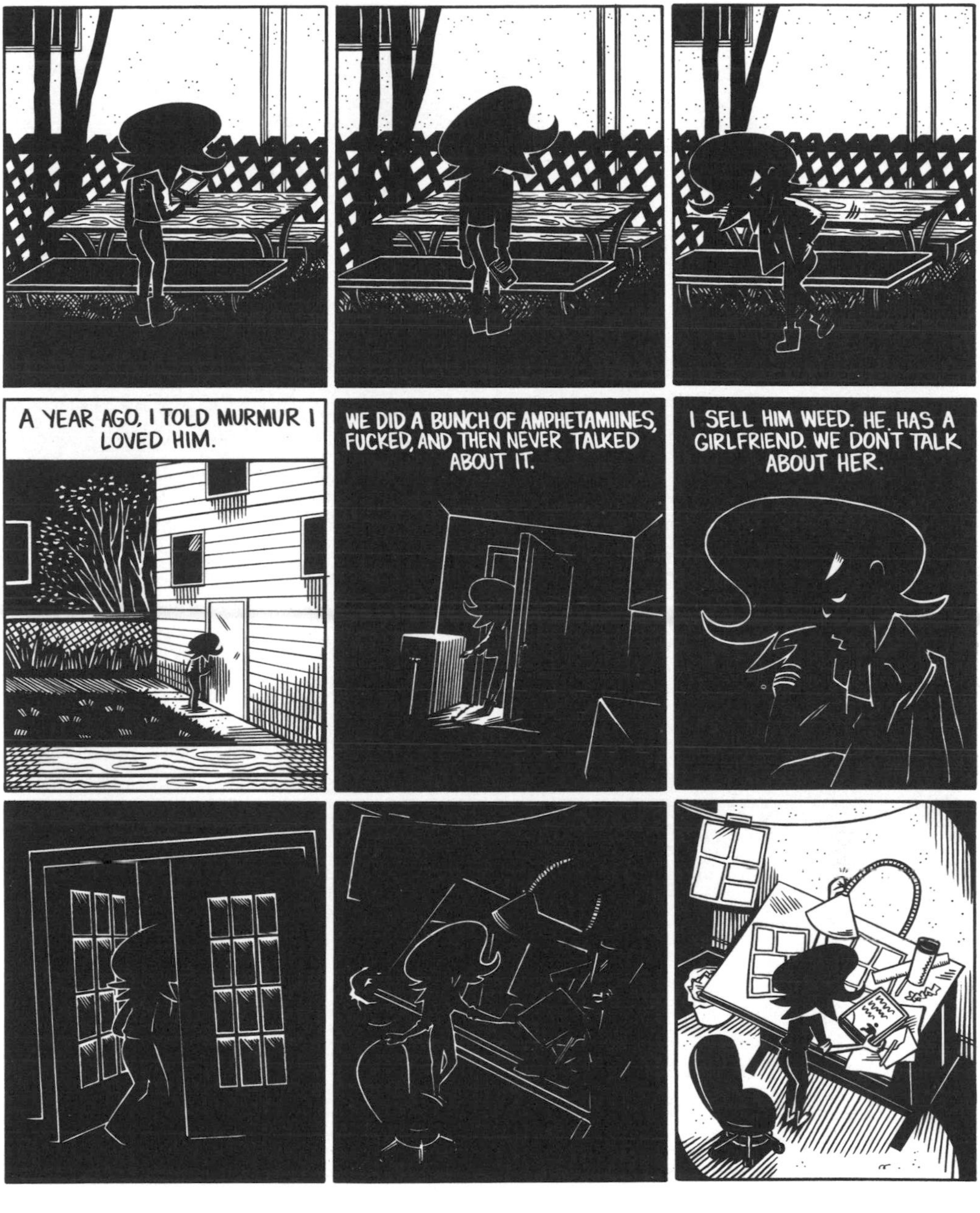
A YEAR AGO, I TOLD MURMUR I LOVED HIM.
WE DID A BUNCH OF AMPHETAMIINES, FUCKED, AND THEN NEVER TALKED ABOUT IT.
I SELL HIM WEED. HE HAS A GIRLFRIEND. WE DON'T TALK ABOUT HER.

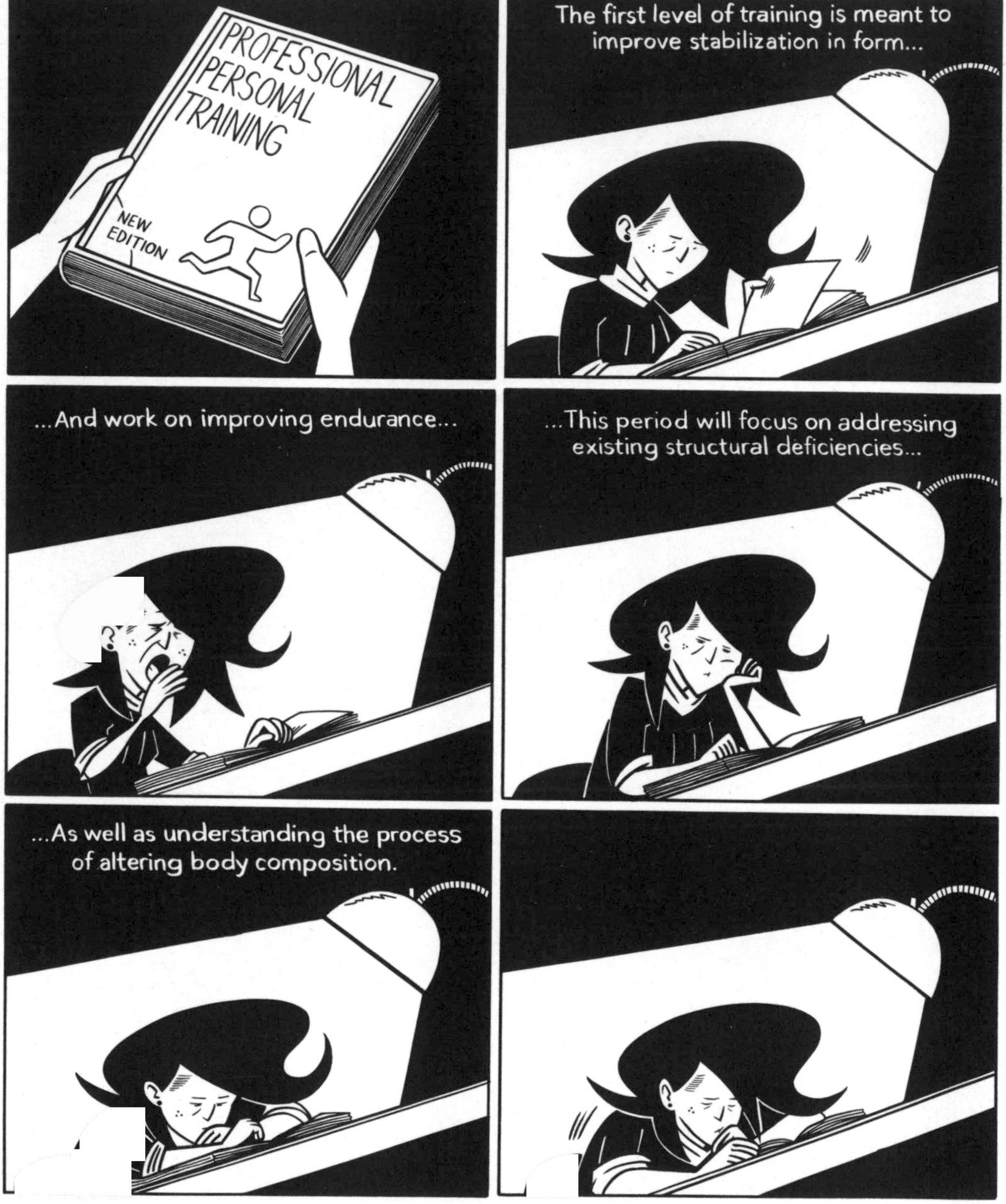
PROFESSIONAL PERSONAL TRAINING
NEW EDITION
The first level of training is meant to improve stabilization in form...
...And work on improving endurance...
...This period will focus on addressing existing structural deficiencies...
...As well as understanding the process of altering body composition.

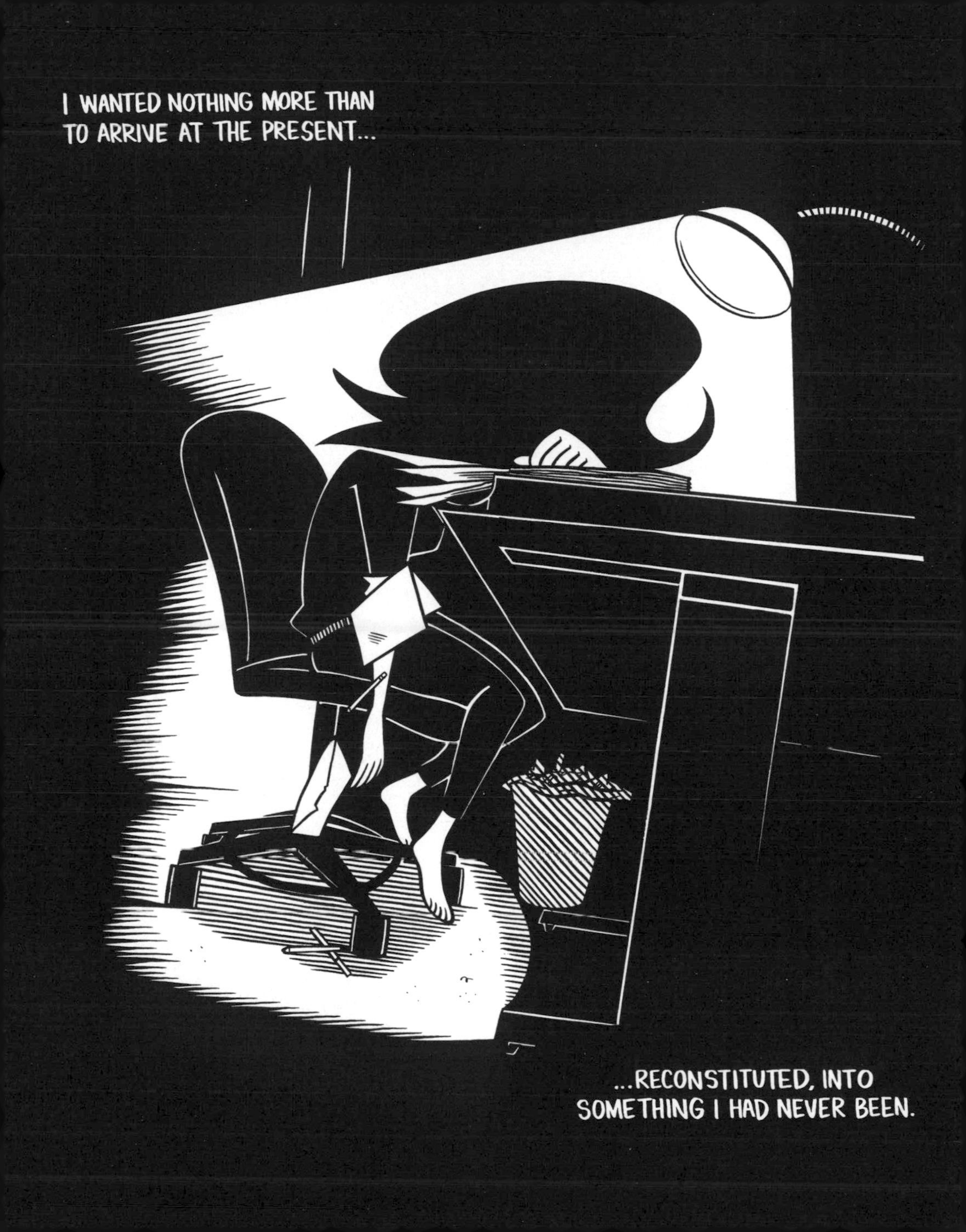
I WANTED NOTHING MORE THAN TO ARRIVE AT THE PRESENT...
...RECONSTITUTED, INTO SOMETHING I HAD NEVER BEEN.

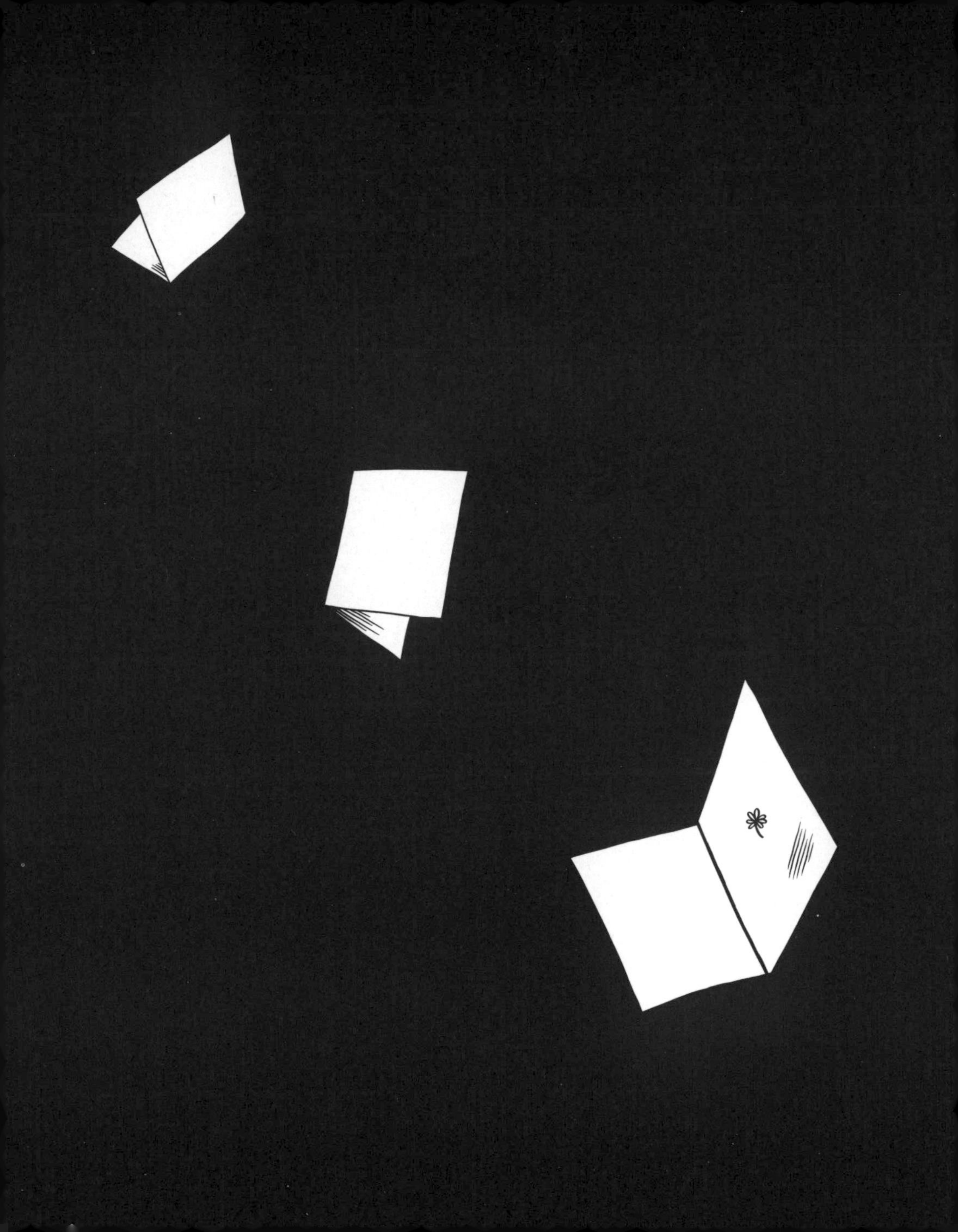

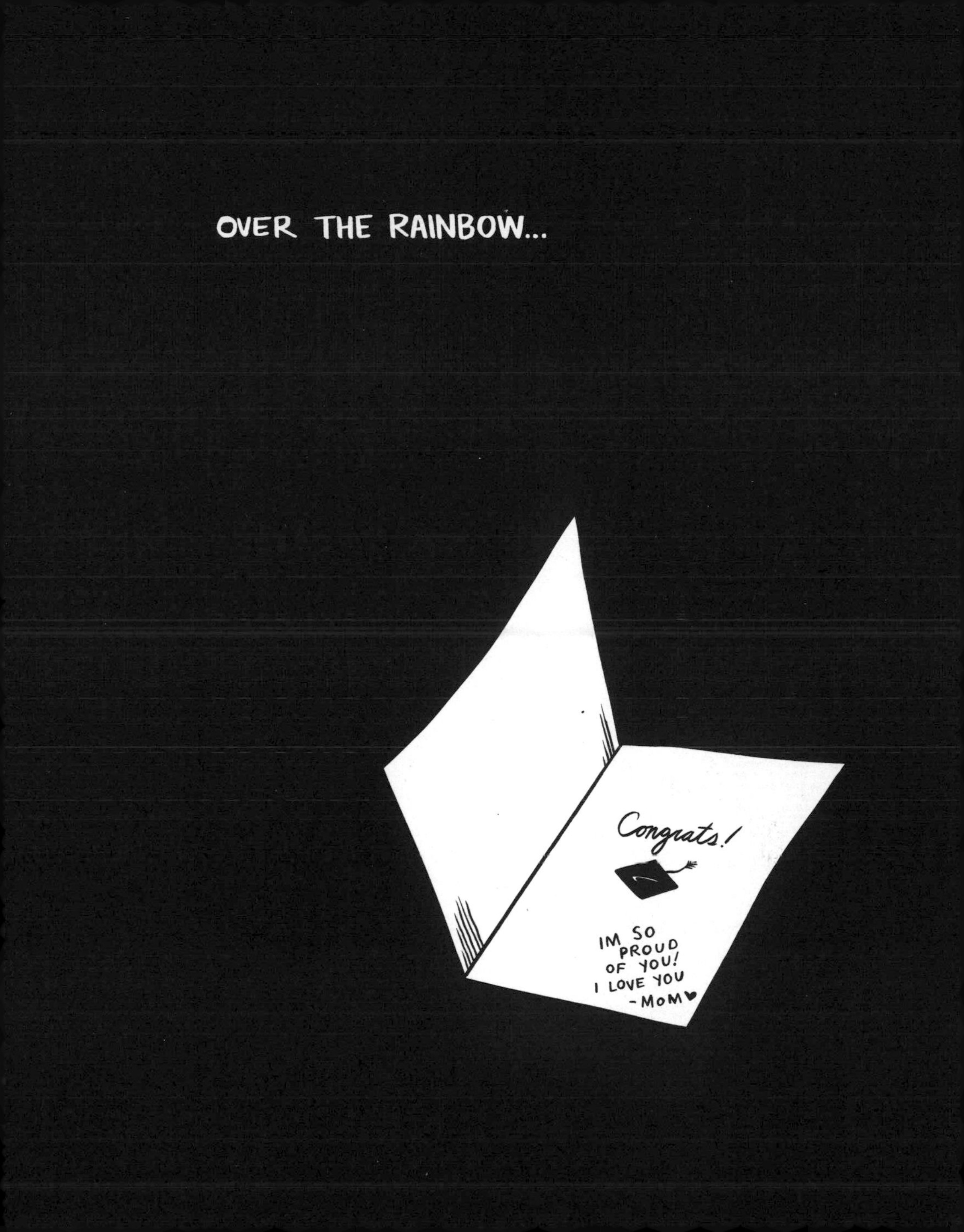
OVER THE RAINBOW...
Congrats!
IM SO PROUD OF YOU! I LOVE YOU -MOM

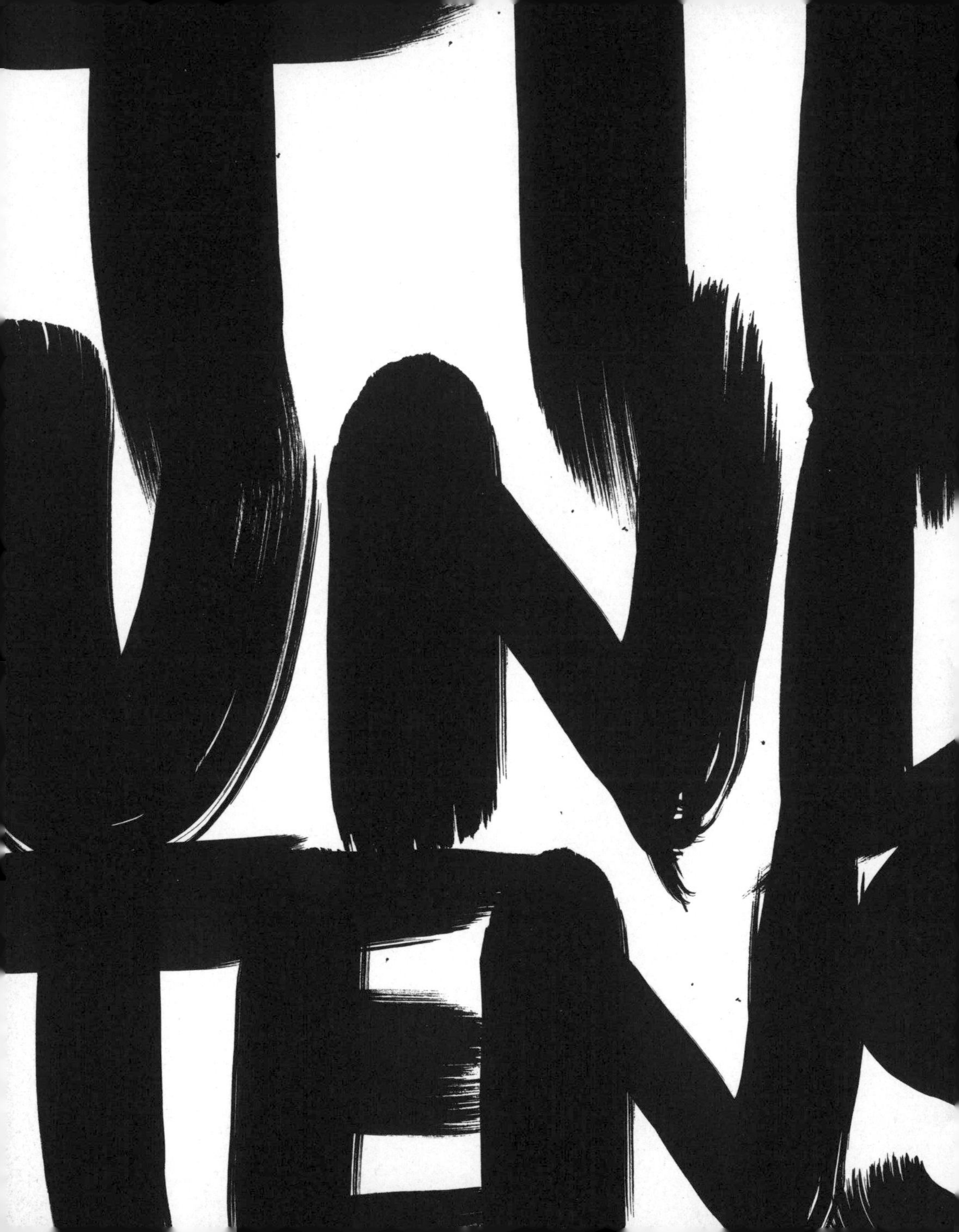

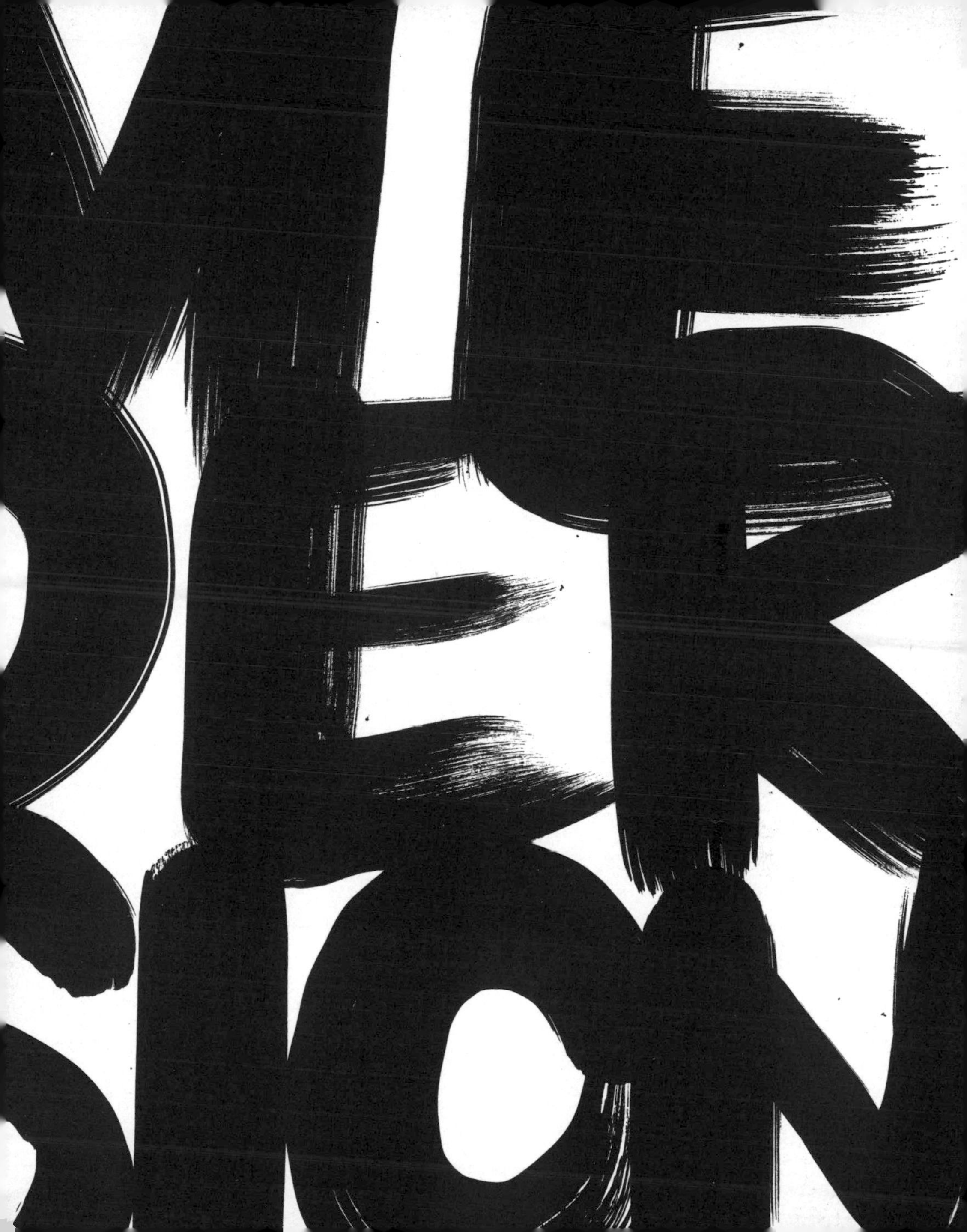

FANTAGRAPHICS BOOKS INC.

7563 LAKE CITY WAY NE

SEATTLE, WASHINGTON, 98115

WWW.FANTAGRAPHICS.COM

DESIGNER: M.S. HARKNESS & KAYLA E.

PRODUCTION: PAUL BARESH

PROMOTION: JACQUELENE COHEN

VP / ASSOCIATE PUBLISHER / EDITOR: ERIC REYNOLDS

PRESIDENT / PUBLISHER: GARY GROTH

ISBN 978-1-68396-896-2

LIBRARY OF CONGRESS CONTROL NUMBER 2023935361

FIRST PRINTING: OCTOBER 2023

PRINTED IN CHINA

"FOR BBA"

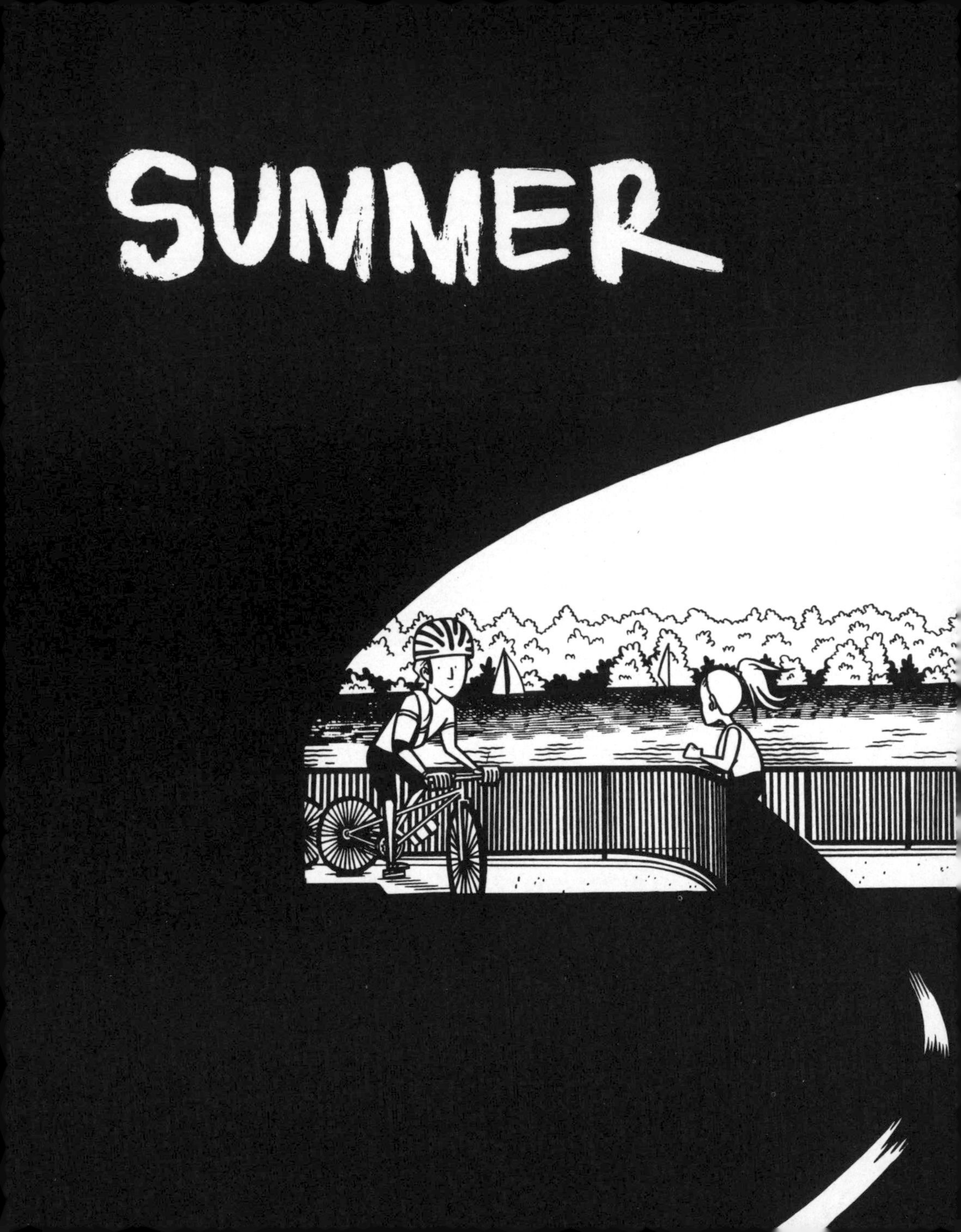
SUMMER

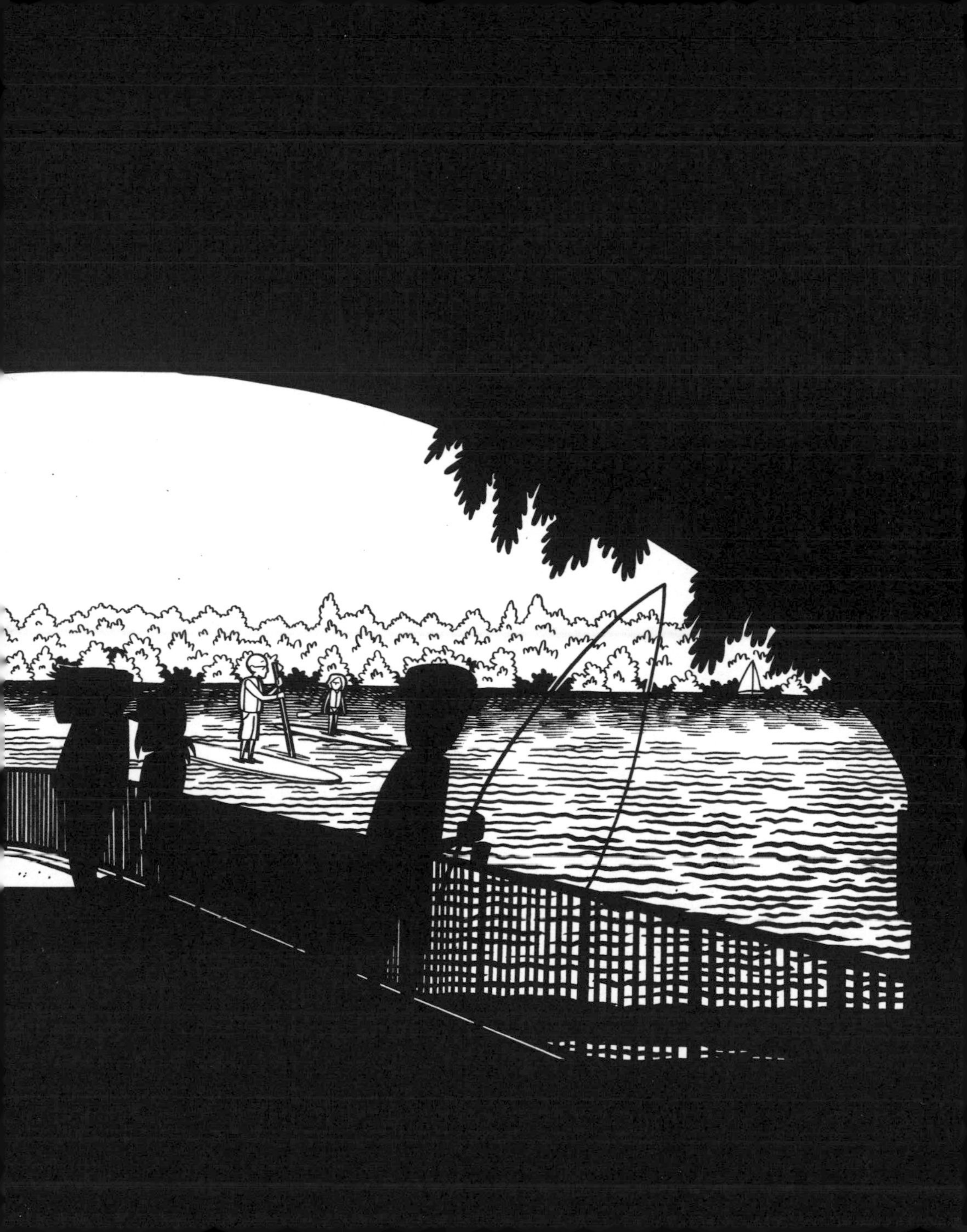

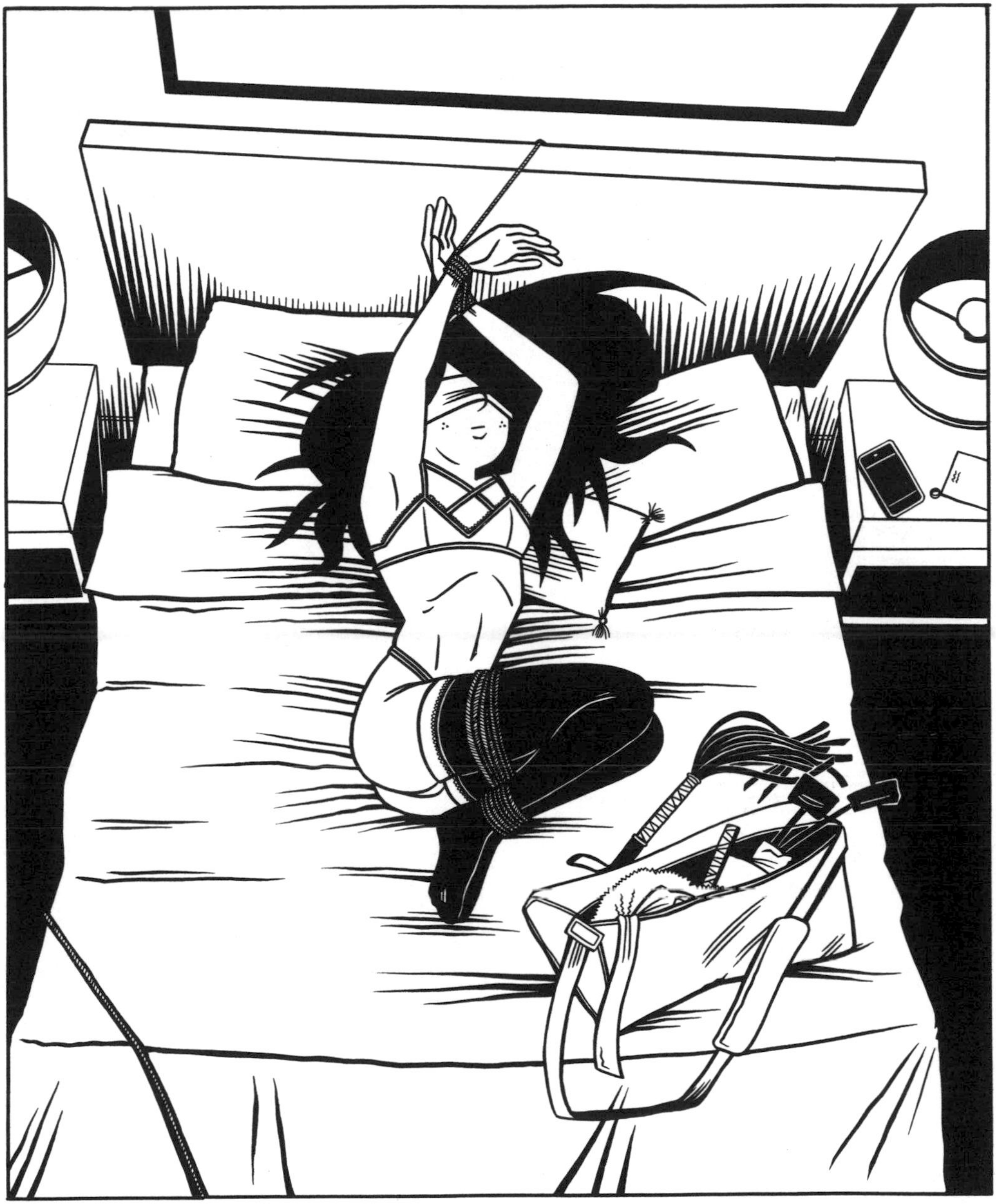

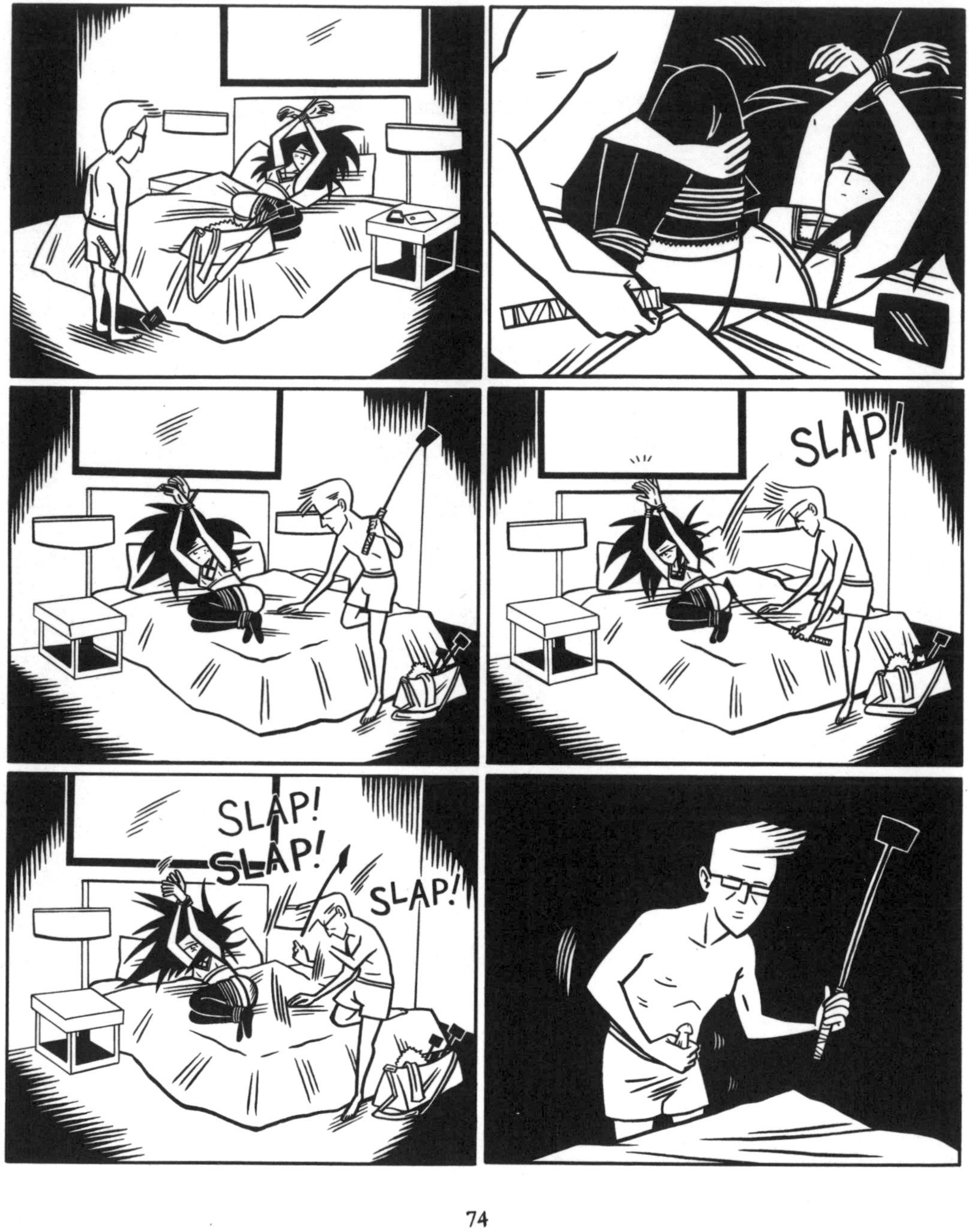
SLAP!
SLAP!
SLAP!
SLAP!

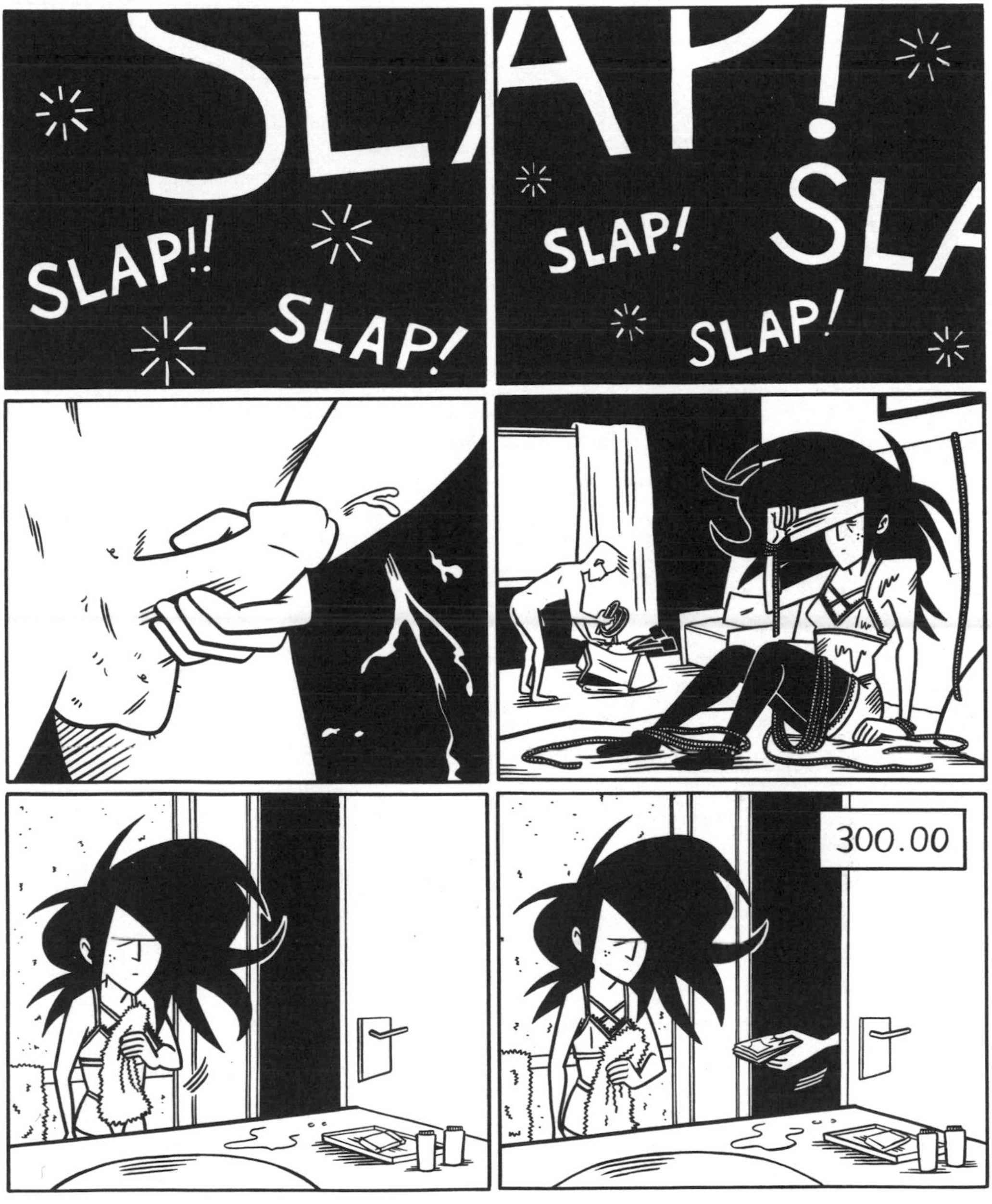
SLAP!
SLAP!!
SLAP!
SLAP!
SLA
SLAP!
300.00

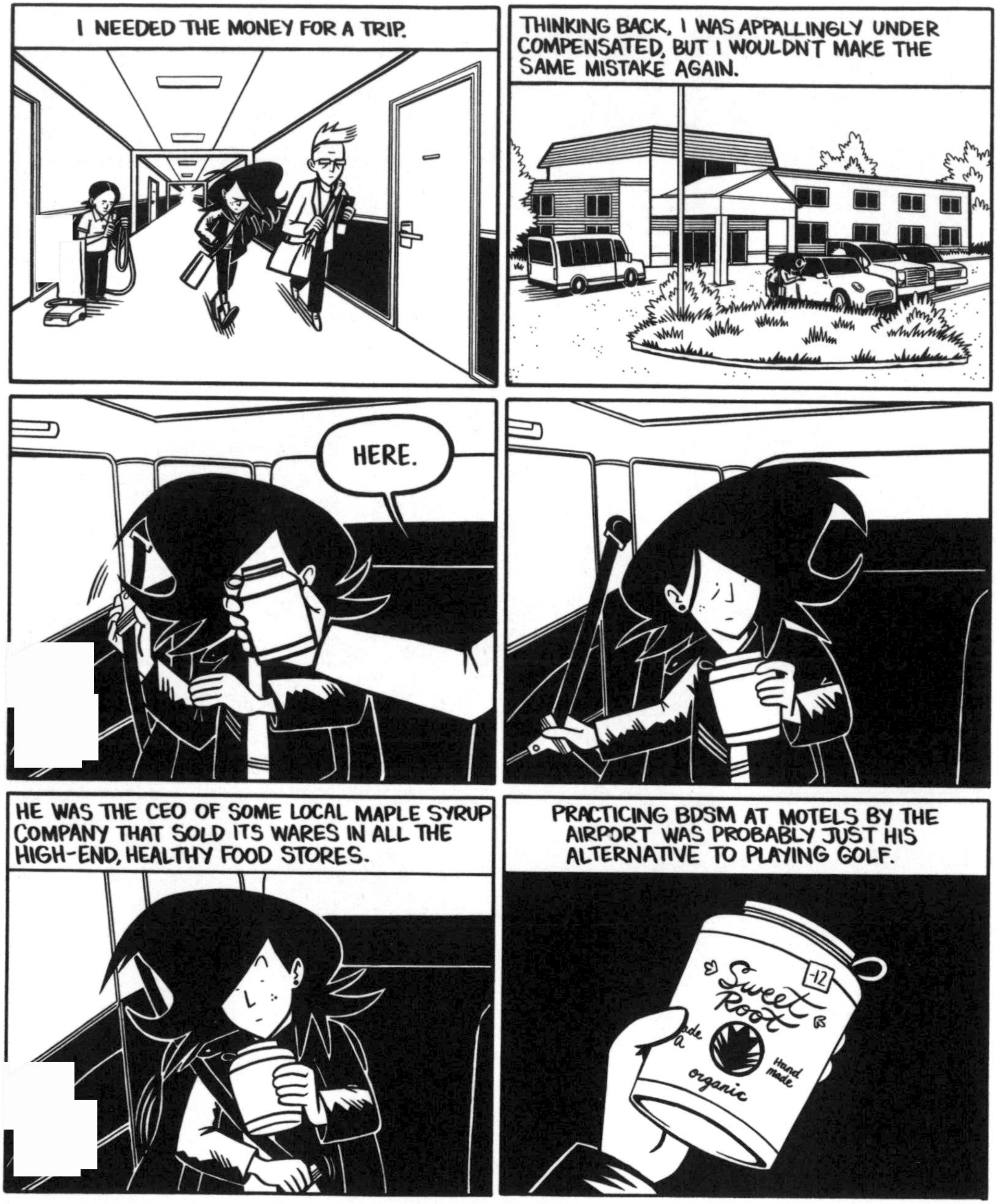
I NEEDED THE MONEY FOR A TRIP.
THINKING BACK, I WAS APPALLINGLY UNDER COMPENSATED, BUT I WOULDN'T MAKE THE SAME MISTAKE AGAIN.
HERE.
HE WAS THE CEO OF SOME LOCAL MAPLE SYRUP COMPANY THAT SOLD ITS WARES IN ALL THE HIGH-END, HEALTHY FOOD STORES.
PRACTICING BDSM AT MOTELS BY THE AIRPORT WAS PROBABLY JUST HIS ALTERNATIVE TO PLAYING GOLF.
Sweet Root
organic
Hand made

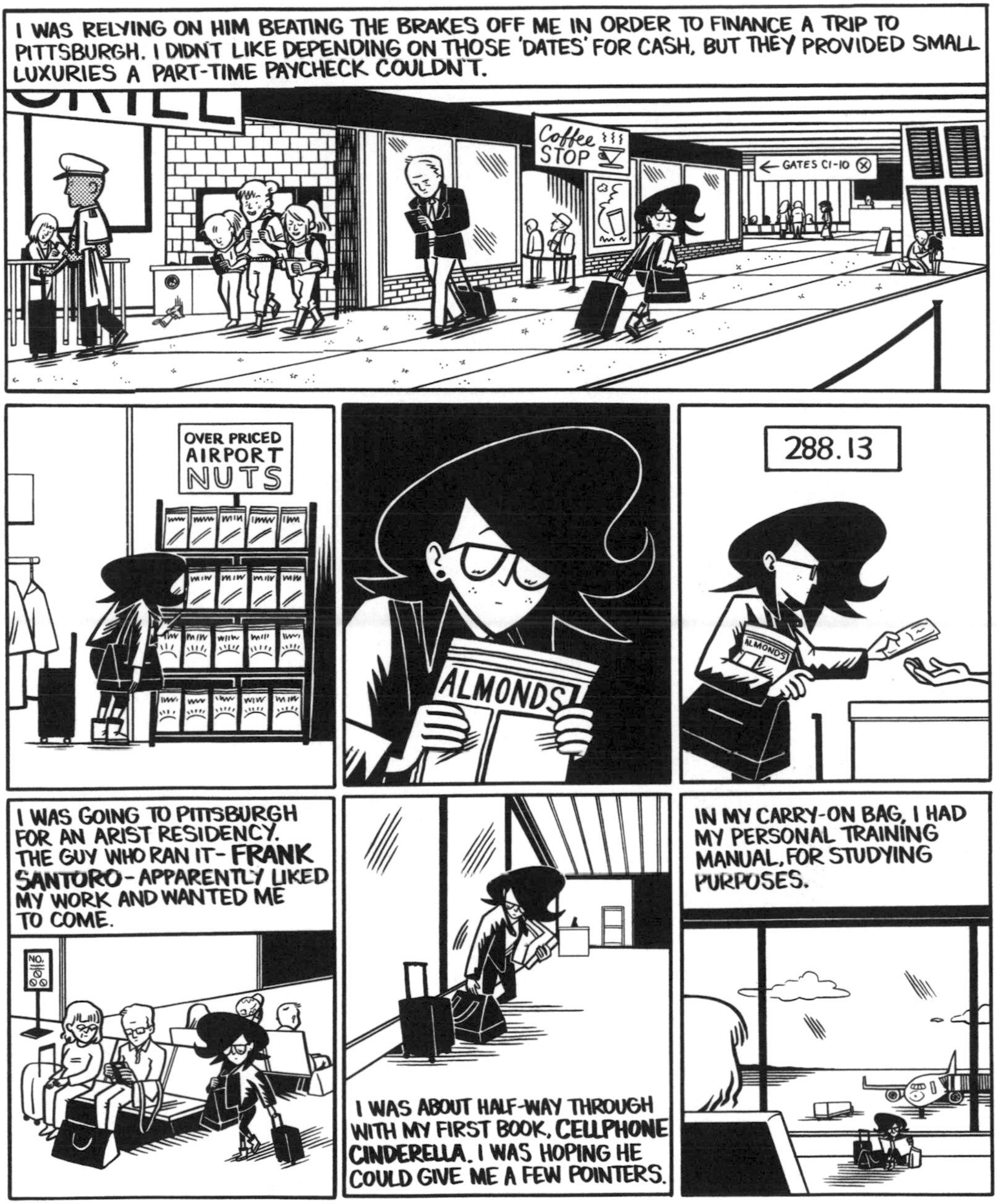
I WAS RELYING ON HIM BEATING THE BRAKES OFF ME IN ORDER TO FINANCE A TRIP TO PITTSBURGH. I DIDN'T LIKE DEPENDING ON THOSE 'DATES' FOR CASH, BUT THEY PROVIDED SMALL LUXURIES A PART-TIME PAYCHECK COULDN'T.
Coffee STOP
← GATES C1-10
OVER PRICED AIRPORT NUTS
ALMONDS
288.13
ALMONDS
I WAS GOING TO PITTSBURGH FOR AN ARIST RESIDENCY. THE GUY WHO RAN IT- FRANK SANTORO- APPARENTLY LIKED MY WORK AND WANTED ME TO COME.
NO.
I WAS ABOUT HALF-WAY THROUGH WITH MY FIRST BOOK, CELLPHONE CINDERELLA. I WAS HOPING HE COULD GIVE ME A FEW POINTERS.
IN MY CARRY-ON BAG, I HAD MY PERSONAL TRAINING MANUAL, FOR STUDYING PURPOSES.

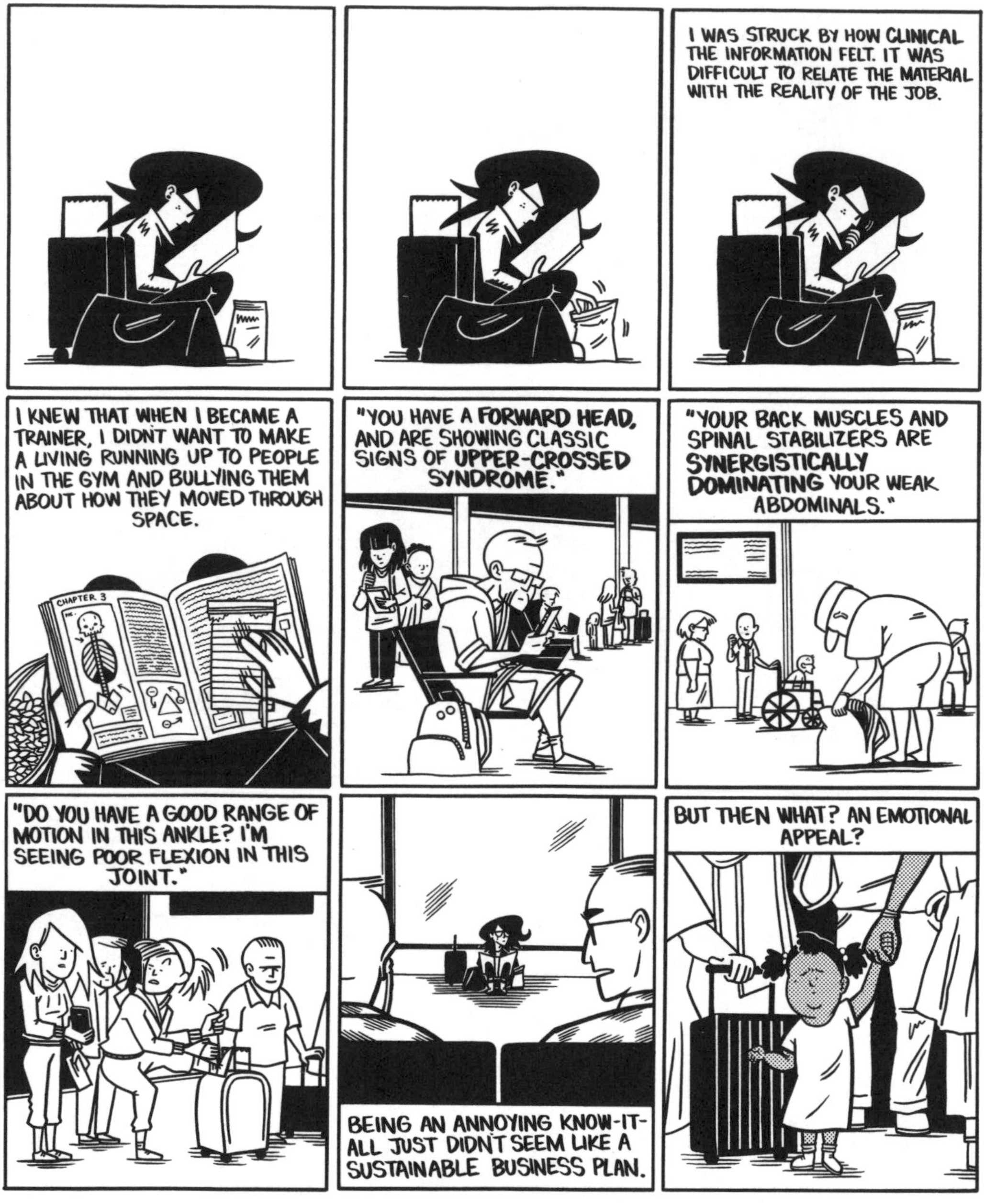
I WAS STRUCK BY HOW CLINICAL THE INFORMATION FELT. IT WAS DIFFICULT TO RELATE THE MATERIAL WITH THE REALITY OF THE JOB.
I KNEW THAT WHEN I BECAME A TRAINER, I DIDN'T WANT TO MAKE A LIVING RUNNING UP TO PEOPLE IN THE GYM AND BULLYING THEM ABOUT HOW THEY MOVED THROUGH SPACE.
CHAPTER 3
"YOU HAVE A FORWARD HEAD, AND ARE SHOWING CLASSIC SIGNS OF UPPER-CROSSED SYNDROME."
"YOUR BACK MUSCLES AND SPINAL STABILIZERS ARE SYNERGISTICALLY DOMINATING YOUR WEAK ABDOMINALS."
"DO YOU HAVE A GOOD RANGE OF MOTION IN THIS ANKLE? I'M SEEING POOR FLEXION IN THIS JOINT."
BEING AN ANNOYING KNOW-IT-ALL JUST DIDN'T SEEM LIKE A SUSTAINABLE BUSINESS PLAN.
BUT THEN WHAT? AN EMOTIONAL APPEAL?

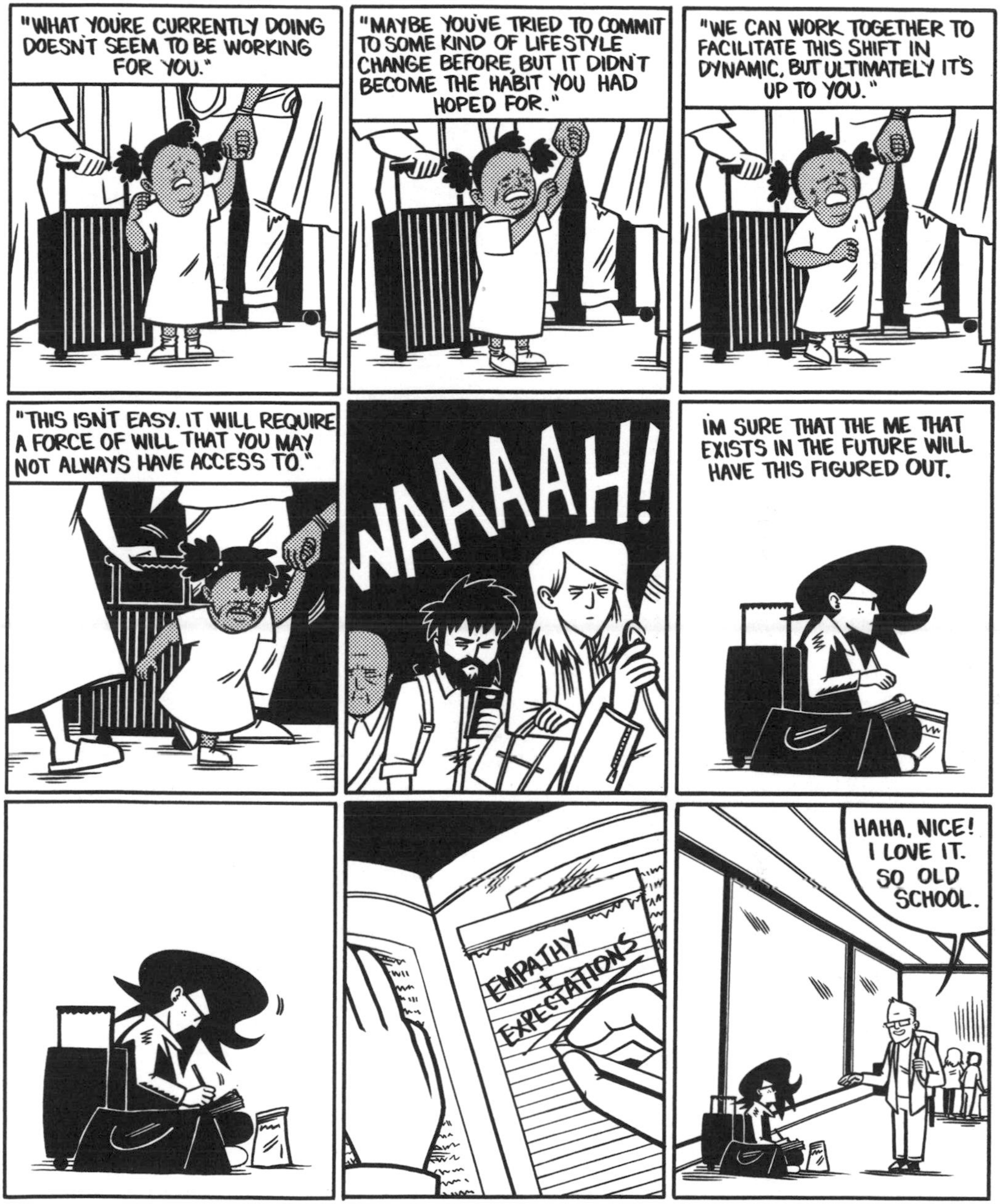
"WHAT YOU'RE CURRENTLY DOING DOESN'T SEEM TO BE WORKING FOR YOU."
"MAYBE YOU'VE TRIED TO COMMIT TO SOME KIND OF LIFESTYLE CHANGE BEFORE, BUT IT DIDN'T BECOME THE HABIT YOU HAD HOPED FOR."
"WE CAN WORK TOGETHER TO FACILITATE THIS SHIFT IN DYNAMIC, BUT ULTIMATELY IT'S UP TO YOU."
"THIS ISN'T EASY. IT WILL REQUIRE A FORCE OF WILL THAT YOU MAY NOT ALWAYS HAVE ACCESS TO."
WAAAAAH!
I'M SURE THAT THE ME THAT EXISTS IN THE FUTURE WILL HAVE THIS FIGURED OUT.
EMPATHY + EXPECTATIONS
HAHA, NICE! I LOVE IT. SO OLD SCHOOL.

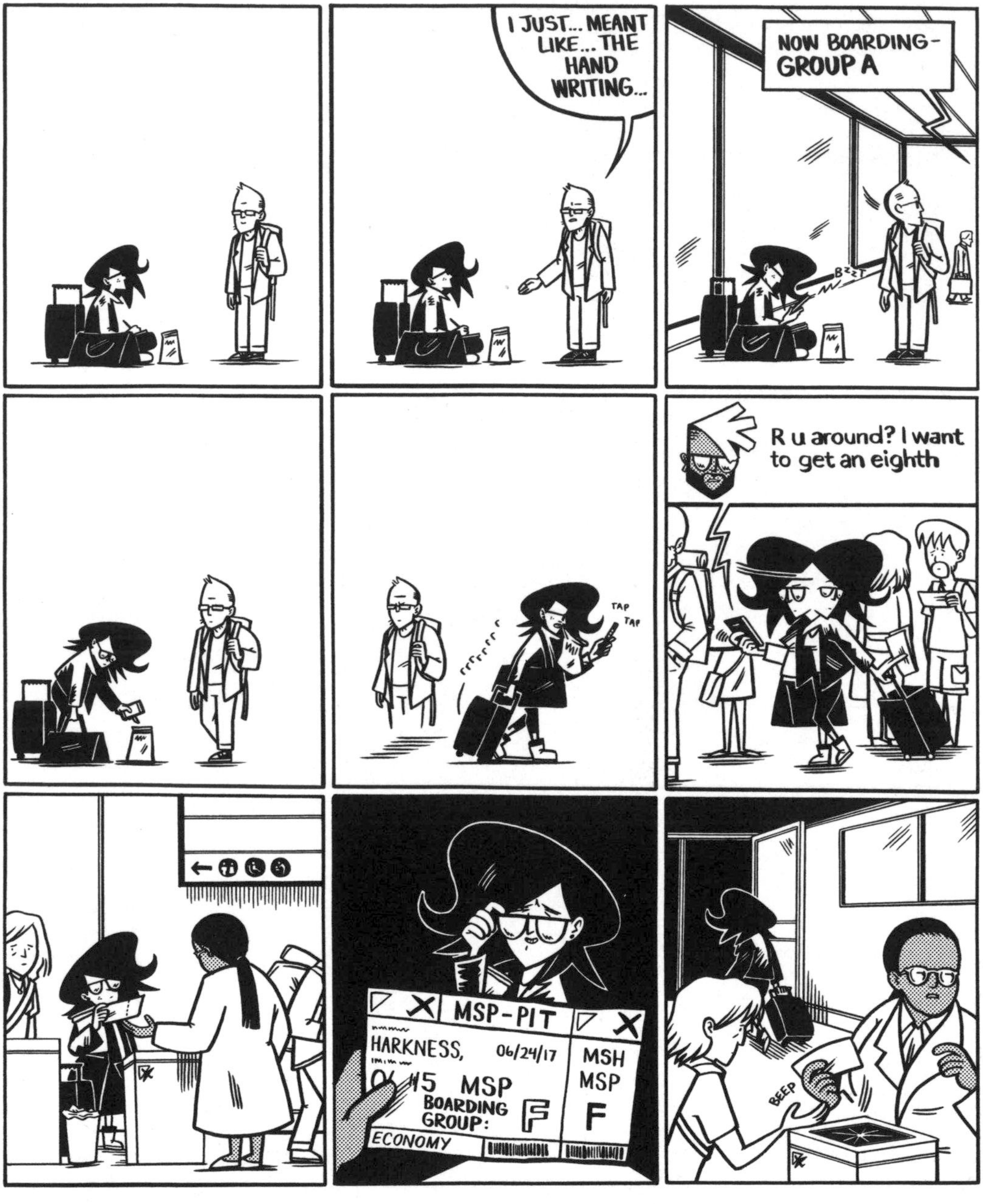
I JUST... MEANT LIKE... THE HAND WRITING...
NOW BOARDING-
GROUP A
BZZT
TAP
TAP
R u around? I want to get an eighth
MSP-PIT
HARKNESS, 06/24/17
MSH
MSP
MSP
BOARDING GROUP:
F
F
ECONOMY
BEEP

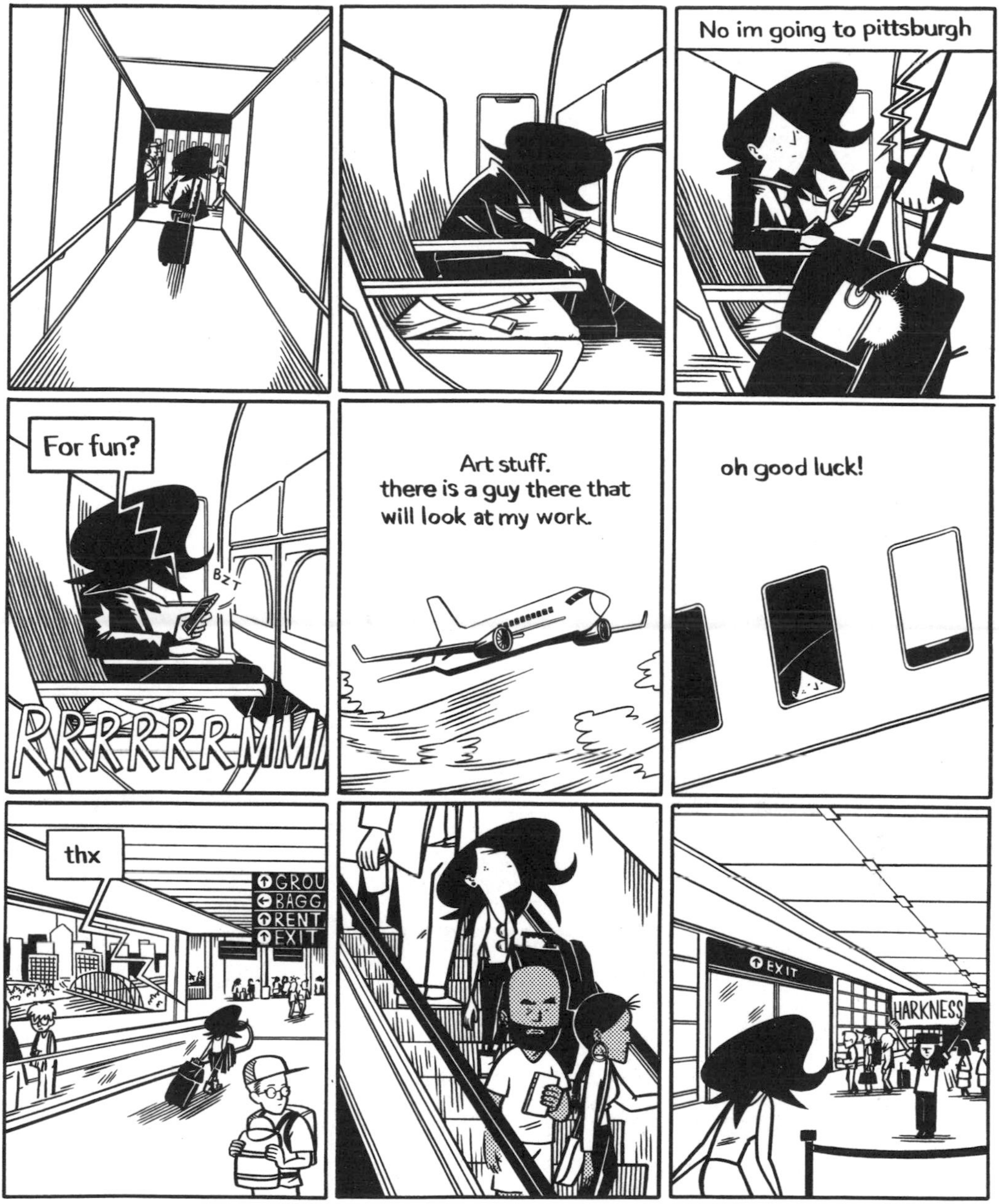
No im going to pittsburgh
For fun?
BZT
RRRRRRRMMM
Art stuff.
there is a guy there that
will look at my work.
oh good luck!
thx
GROU
BAGG
RENT
EXIT
EXIT
HARKNESS

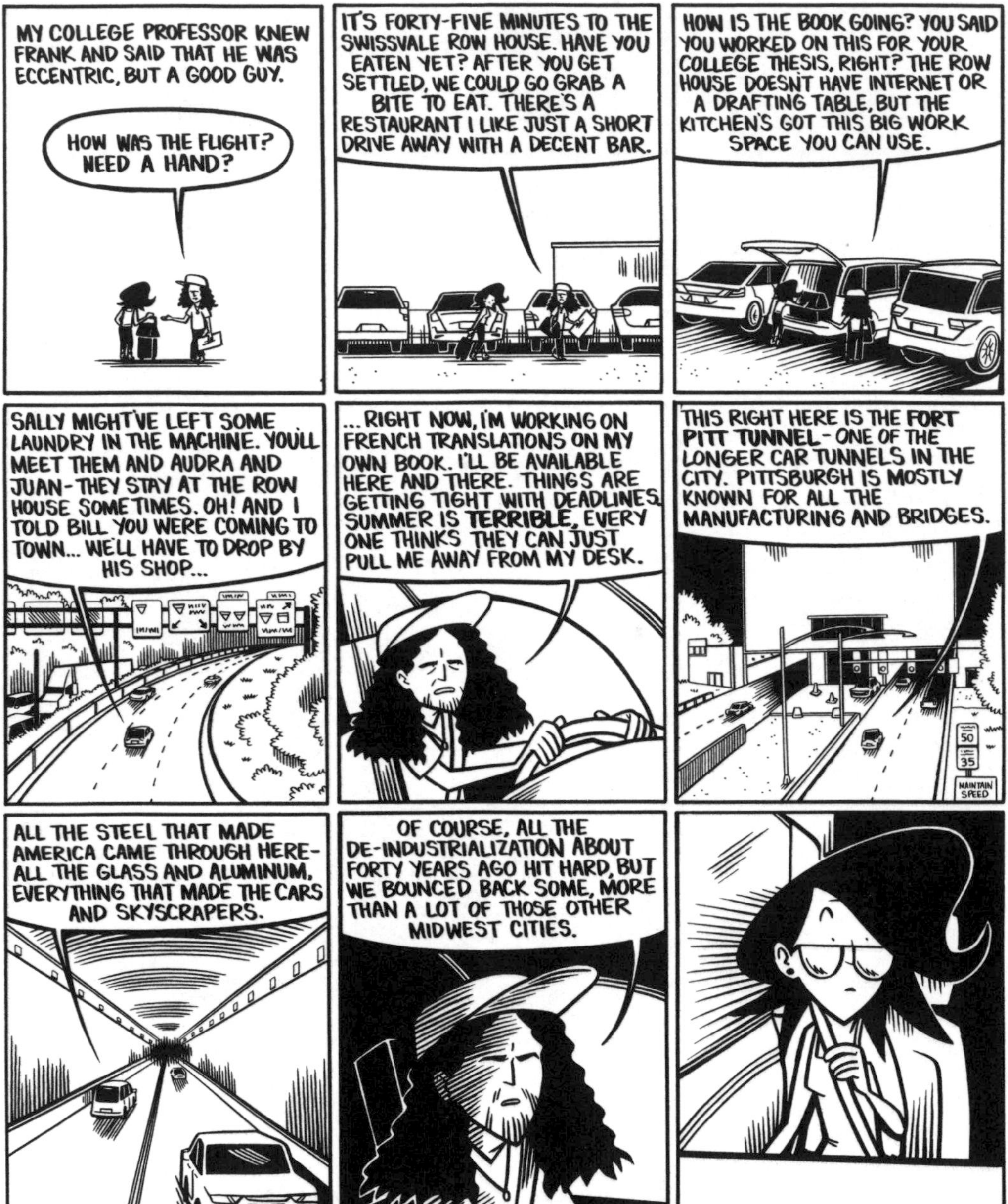
MY COLLEGE PROFESSOR KNEW FRANK AND SAID THAT HE WAS ECCENTRIC, BUT A GOOD GUY.
HOW WAS THE FLIGHT? NEED A HAND?
IT'S FORTY-FIVE MINUTES TO THE SWISSVALE ROW HOUSE. HAVE YOU EATEN YET? AFTER YOU GET SETTLED, WE COULD GO GRAB A BITE TO EAT. THERE'S A RESTAURANT I LIKE JUST A SHORT DRIVE AWAY WITH A DECENT BAR.
HOW IS THE BOOK GOING? YOU SAID YOU WORKED ON THIS FOR YOUR COLLEGE THESIS, RIGHT? THE ROW HOUSE DOESN'T HAVE INTERNET OR A DRAFTING TABLE, BUT THE KITCHEN'S GOT THIS BIG WORK SPACE YOU CAN USE.
SALLY MIGHT'VE LEFT SOME LAUNDRY IN THE MACHINE. YOU'LL MEET THEM AND AUDRA AND JUAN- THEY STAY AT THE ROW HOUSE SOMETIMES. OH! AND I TOLD BILL YOU WERE COMING TO TOWN... WE'LL HAVE TO DROP BY HIS SHOP...
...RIGHT NOW, I'M WORKING ON FRENCH TRANSLATIONS ON MY OWN BOOK. I'LL BE AVAILABLE HERE AND THERE. THINGS ARE GETTING TIGHT WITH DEADLINES. SUMMER IS TERRIBLE, EVERY ONE THINKS THEY CAN JUST PULL ME AWAY FROM MY DESK.
THIS RIGHT HERE IS THE FORT PITT TUNNEL- ONE OF THE LONGER CAR TUNNELS IN THE CITY. PITTSBURGH IS MOSTLY KNOWN FOR ALL THE MANUFACTURING AND BRIDGES.
50
35
MAINTAIN SPEED
ALL THE STEEL THAT MADE AMERICA CAME THROUGH HERE- ALL THE GLASS AND ALUMINUM, EVERYTHING THAT MADE THE CARS AND SKYSCRAPERS.
OF COURSE, ALL THE DE-INDUSTRIALIZATION ABOUT FORTY YEARS AGO HIT HARD, BUT WE BOUNCED BACK SOME, MORE THAN A LOT OF THOSE OTHER MIDWEST CITIES.

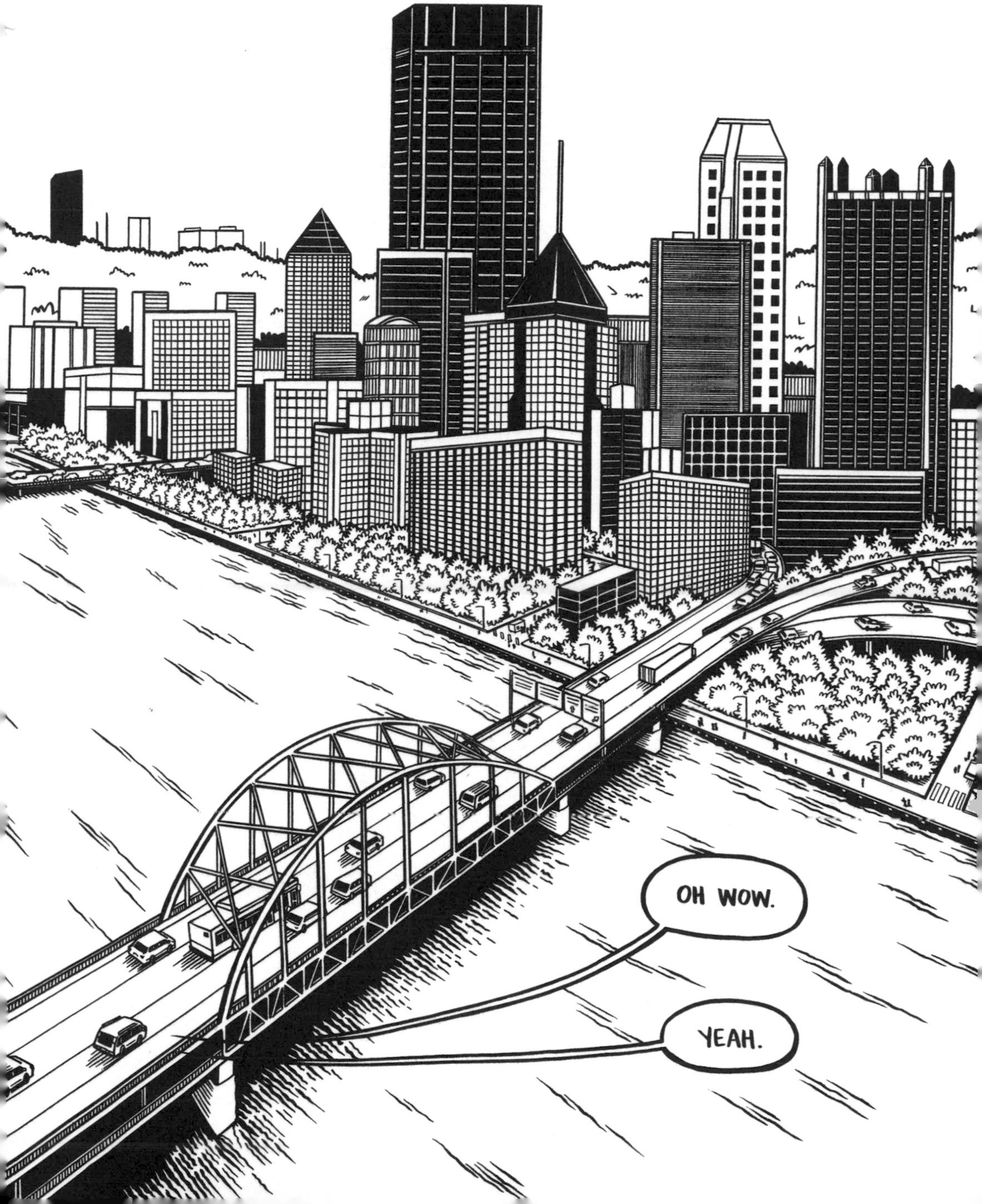
OH WOW.
YEAH.

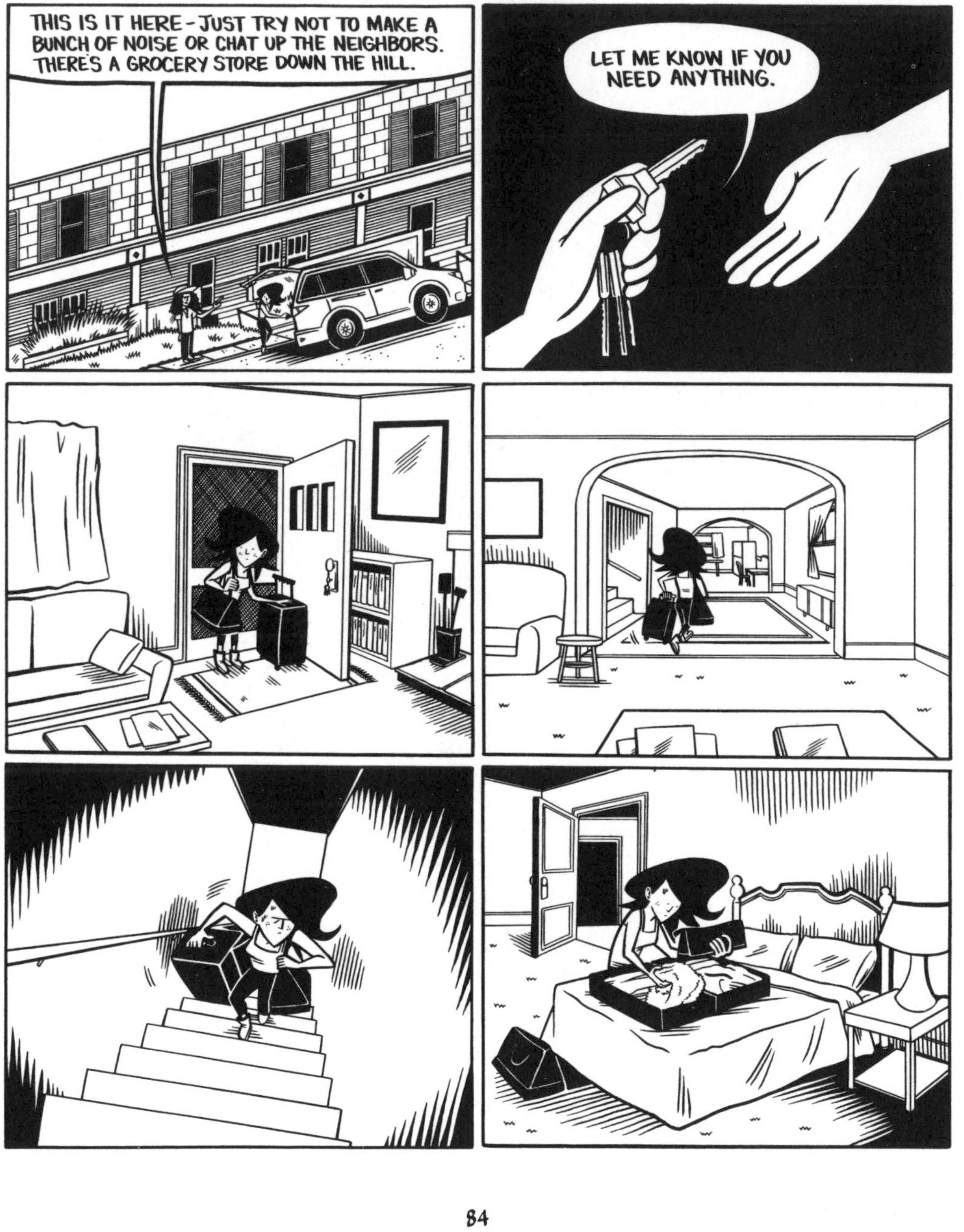
THIS IS IT HERE - JUST TRY NOT TO MAKE A BUNCH OF NOISE OR CHAT UP THE NEIGHBORS. THERE'S A GROCERY STORE DOWN THE HILL.
LET ME KNOW IF YOU NEED ANYTHING.

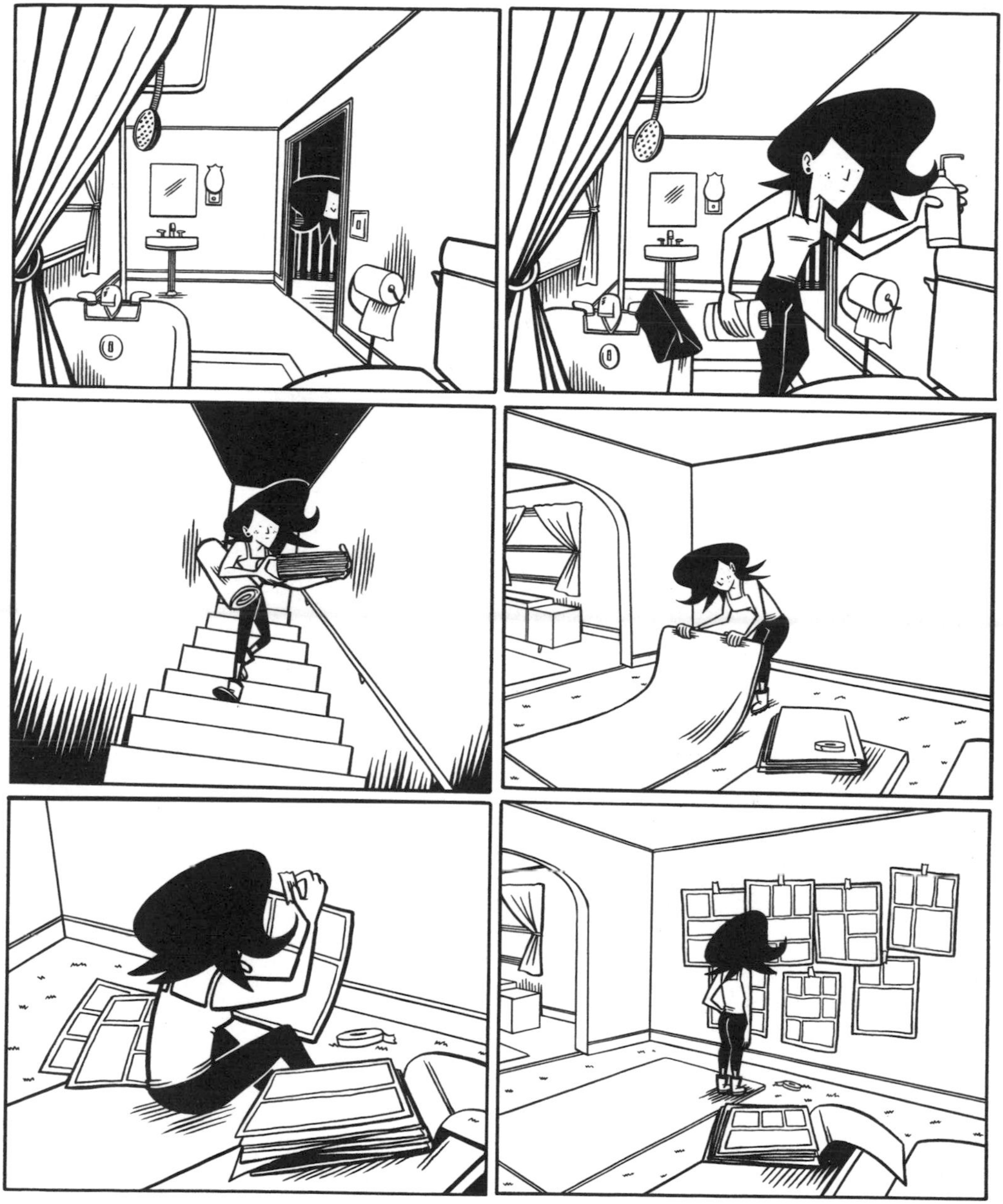

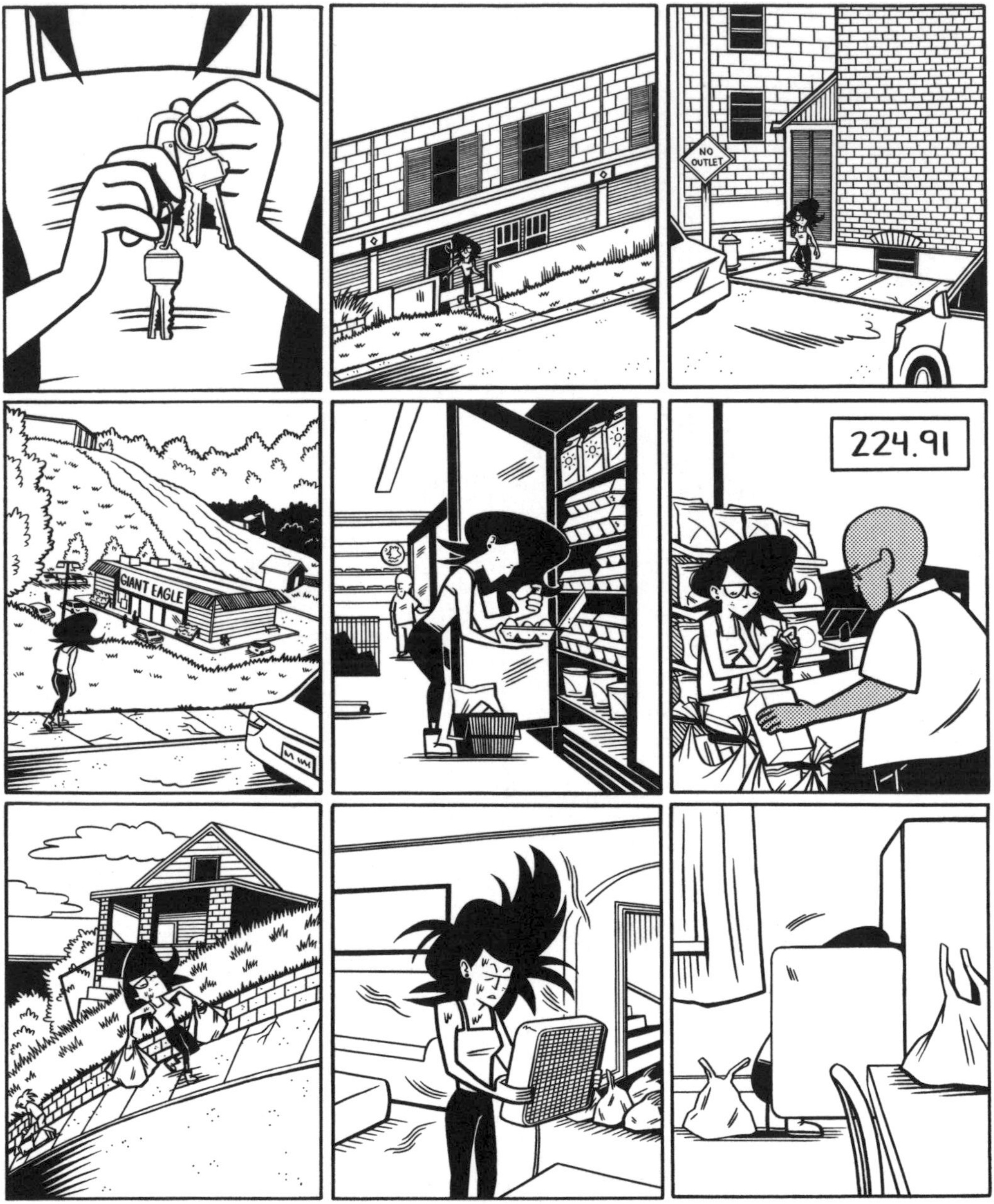
NO OUTLET
GIANT EAGLE
224.91

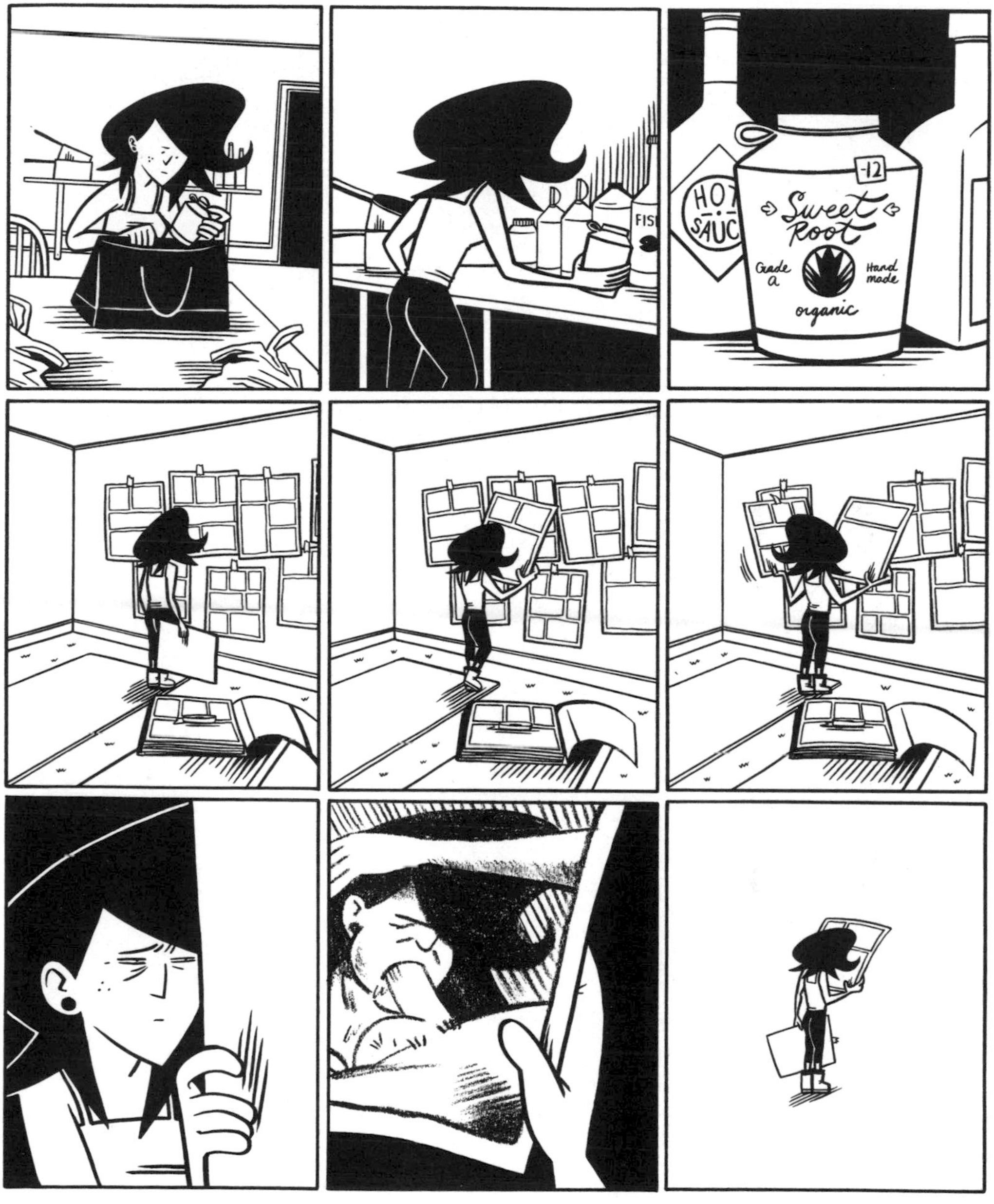
-12
Sweet Root
Grade a
Hand made
organic

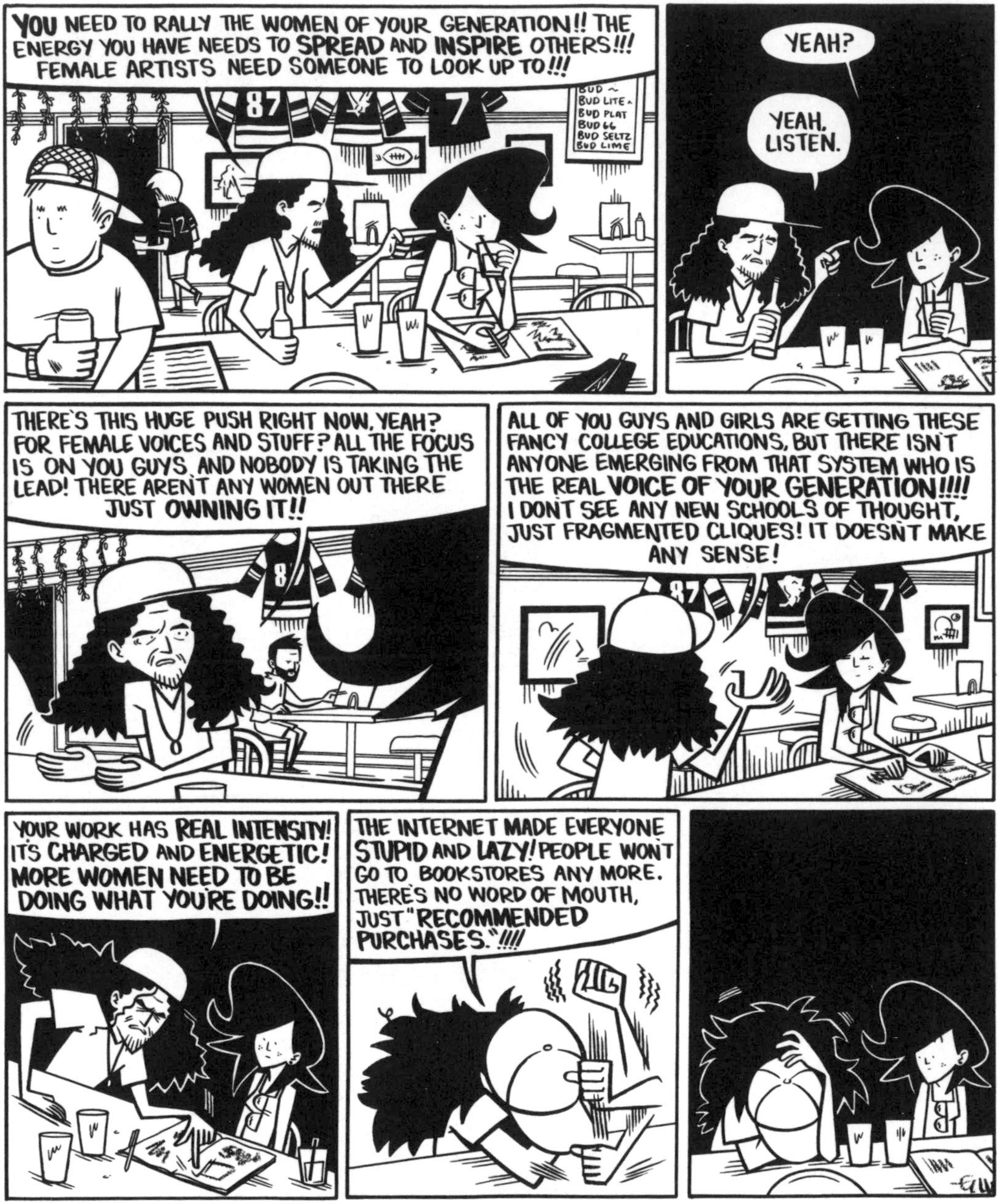
YOU NEED TO RALLY THE WOMEN OF YOUR GENERATION!! THE ENERGY YOU HAVE NEEDS TO SPREAD AND INSPIRE OTHERS!!! FEMALE ARTISTS NEED SOMEONE TO LOOK UP TO!!!
BUD ~ BUD LITE BUD PLAT BUD 66 BUD SELTZ BUD LIME
YEAH?
YEAH, LISTEN.
THERE'S THIS HUGE PUSH RIGHT NOW, YEAH? FOR FEMALE VOICES AND STUFF? ALL THE FOCUS IS ON YOU GUYS, AND NOBODY IS TAKING THE LEAD! THERE AREN'T ANY WOMEN OUT THERE JUST OWNING IT!!
ALL OF YOU GUYS AND GIRLS ARE GETTING THESE FANCY COLLEGE EDUCATIONS, BUT THERE ISN'T ANYONE EMERGING FROM THAT SYSTEM WHO IS THE REAL VOICE OF YOUR GENERATION!!!! I DON'T SEE ANY NEW SCHOOLS OF THOUGHT, JUST FRAGMENTED CLIQUES! IT DOESN'T MAKE ANY SENSE!
YOUR WORK HAS REAL INTENSITY! IT'S CHARGED AND ENERGETIC! MORE WOMEN NEED TO BE DOING WHAT YOU'RE DOING!!
THE INTERNET MADE EVERYONE STUPID AND LAZY! PEOPLE WON'T GO TO BOOKSTORES ANY MORE. THERE'S NO WORD OF MOUTH, JUST "RECOMMENDED PURCHASES."!!!!

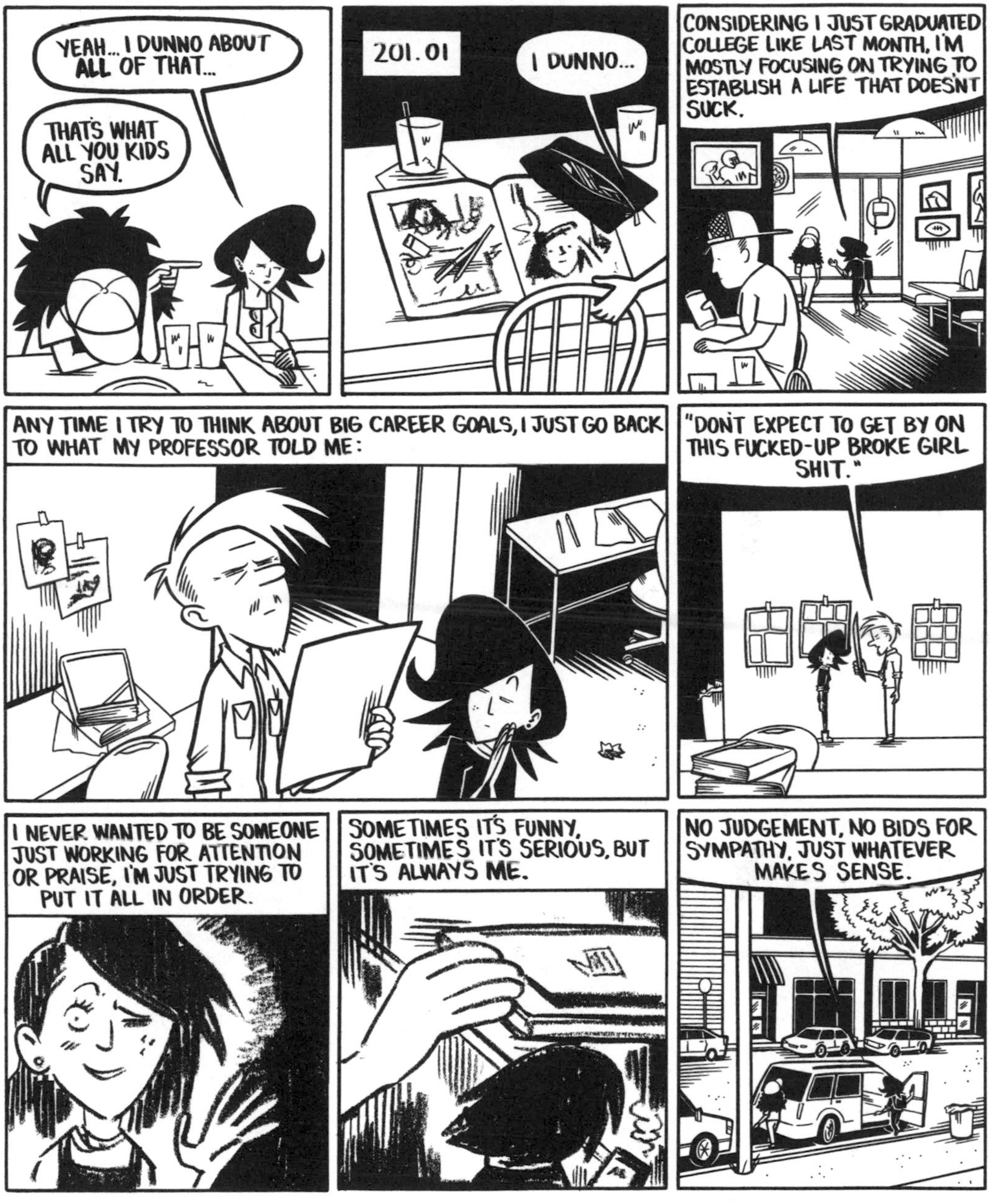
YEAH... I DUNNO ABOUT ALL OF THAT...
THAT'S WHAT ALL YOU KIDS SAY.
201.01
I DUNNO...
CONSIDERING I JUST GRADUATED COLLEGE LIKE LAST MONTH, I'M MOSTLY FOCUSING ON TRYING TO ESTABLISH A LIFE THAT DOESN'T SUCK.
ANY TIME I TRY TO THINK ABOUT BIG CAREER GOALS, I JUST GO BACK TO WHAT MY PROFESSOR TOLD ME:
"DON'T EXPECT TO GET BY ON THIS FUCKED-UP BROKE GIRL SHIT."
I NEVER WANTED TO BE SOMEONE JUST WORKING FOR ATTENTION OR PRAISE, I'M JUST TRYING TO PUT IT ALL IN ORDER.
SOMETIMES IT'S FUNNY, SOMETIMES IT'S SERIOUS, BUT IT'S ALWAYS ME.
NO JUDGEMENT, NO BIDS FOR SYMPATHY, JUST WHATEVER MAKES SENSE.

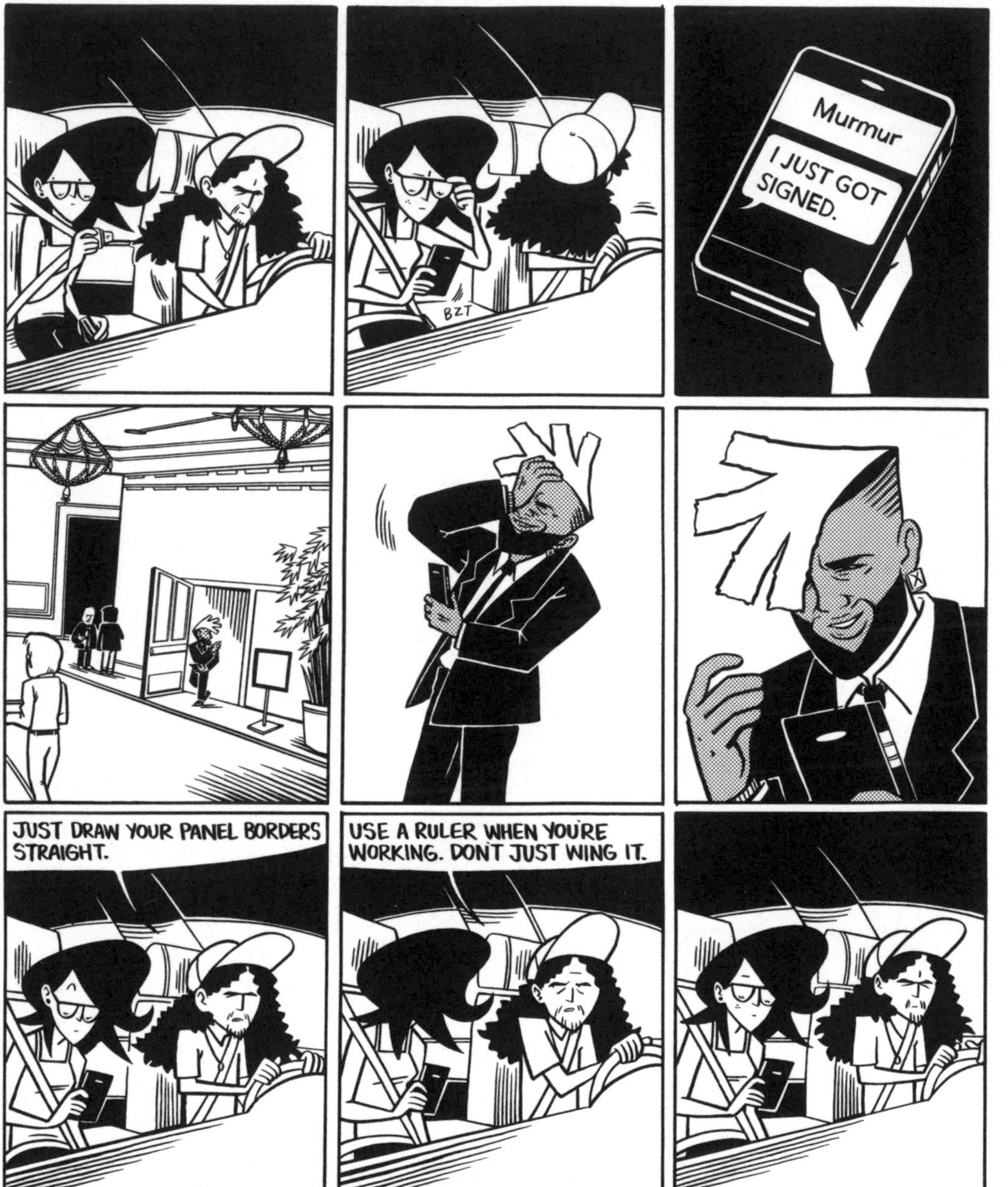
BZT
Murmur
I JUST GOT SIGNED.
JUST DRAW YOUR PANEL BORDERS STRAIGHT.
USE A RULER WHEN YOU'RE WORKING. DON'T JUST WING IT.

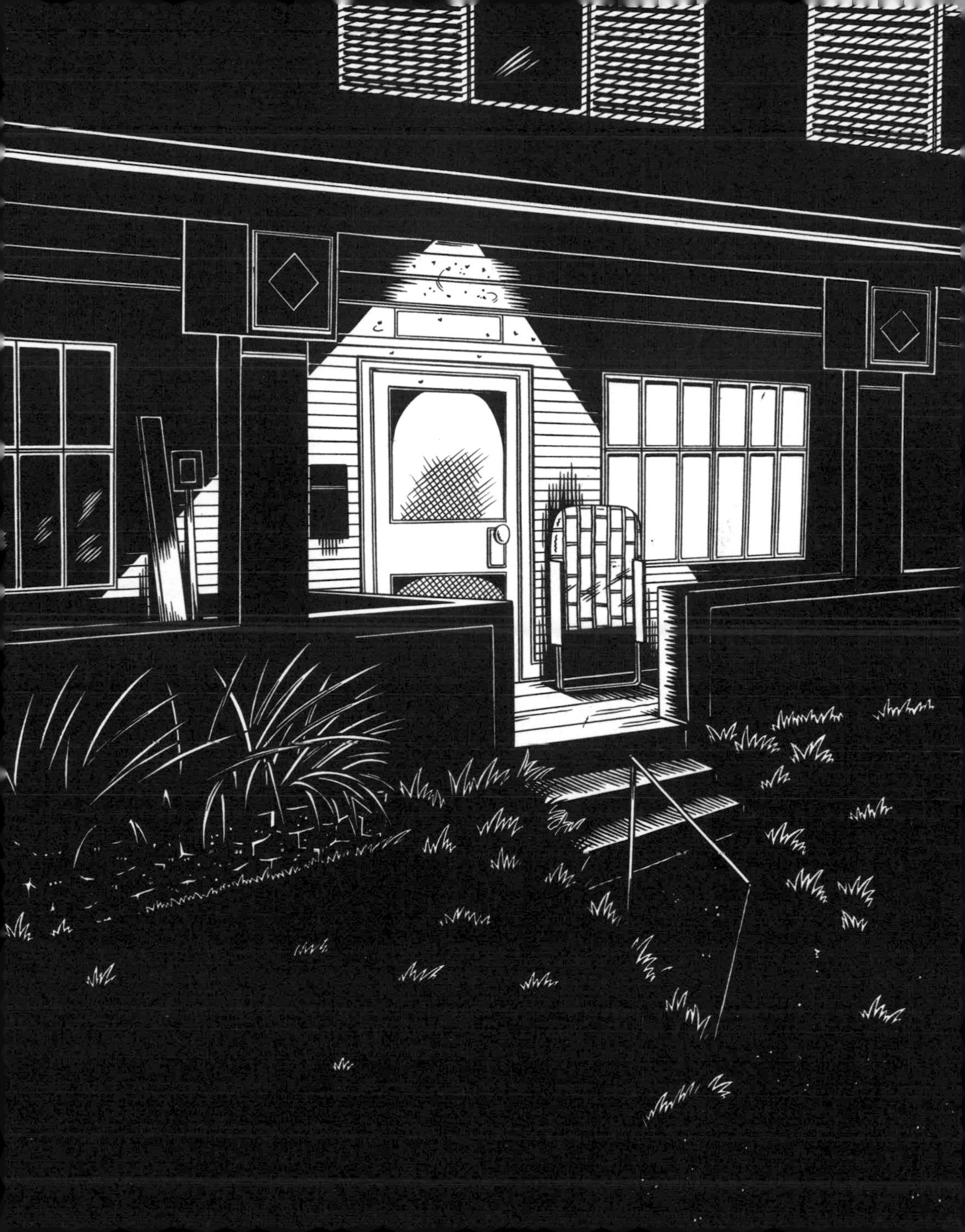

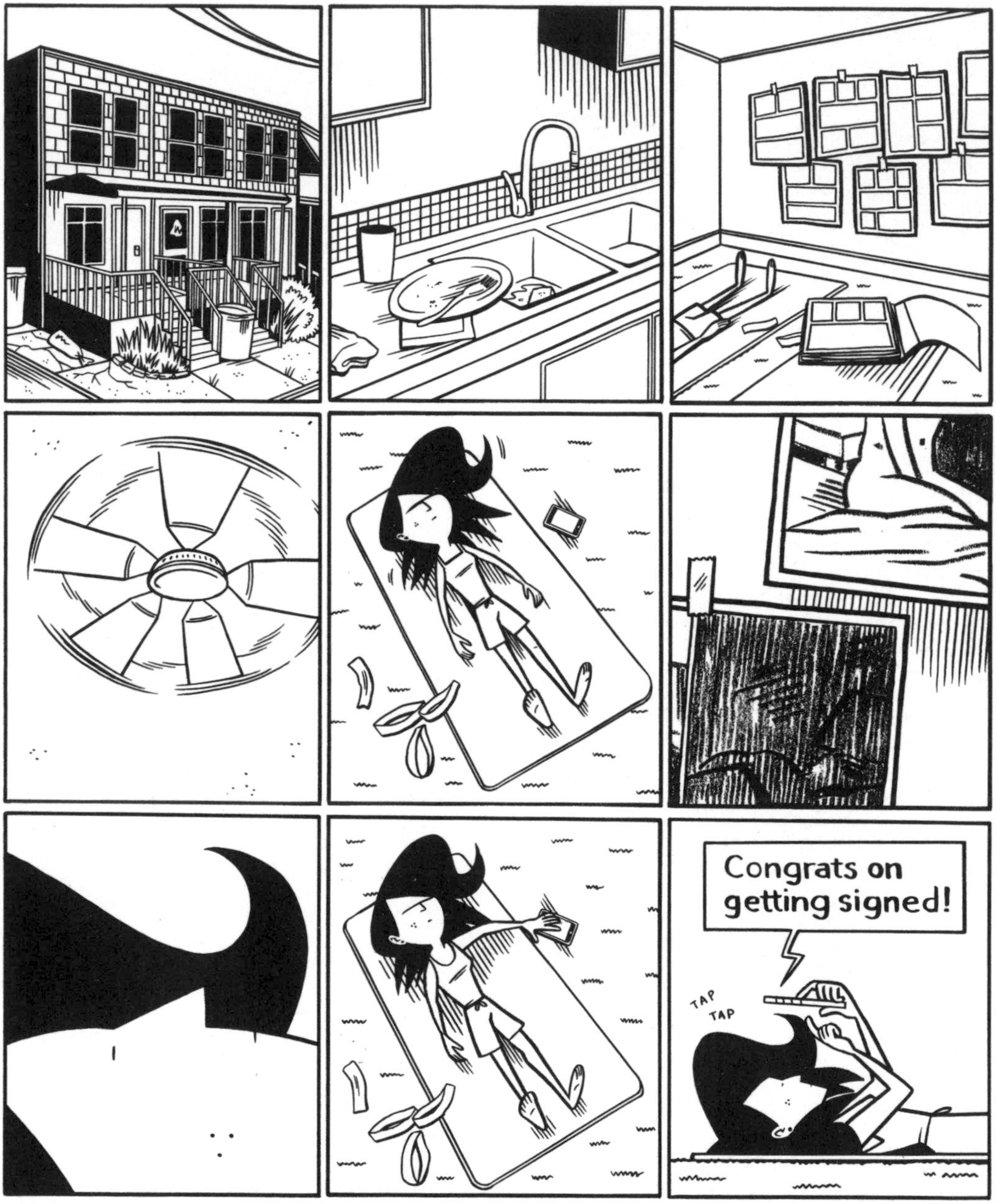
Congrats on getting signed!
TAP TAP

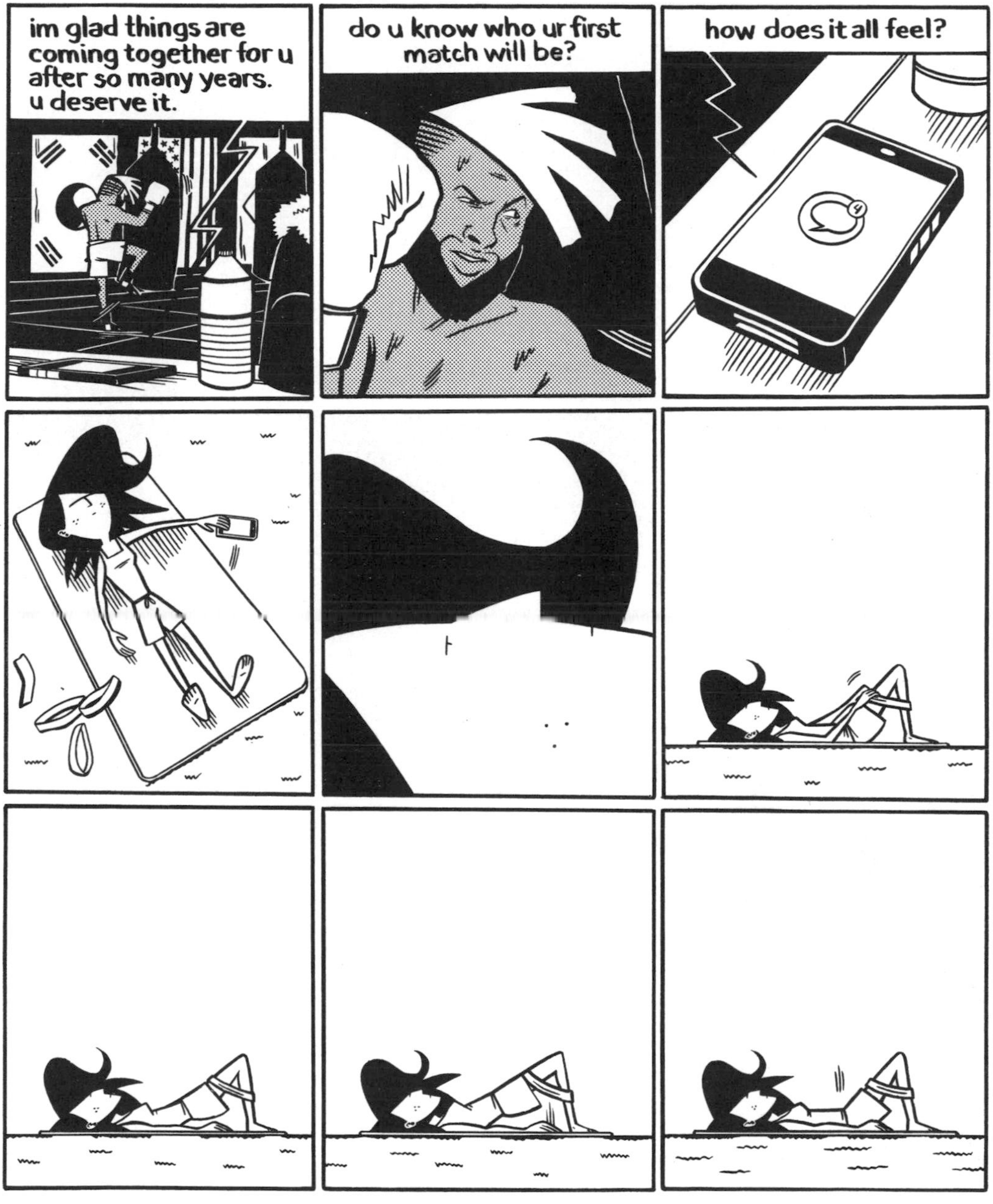
im glad things are coming together for u after so many years. u deserve it.
do u know who ur first match will be?
how does it all feel?

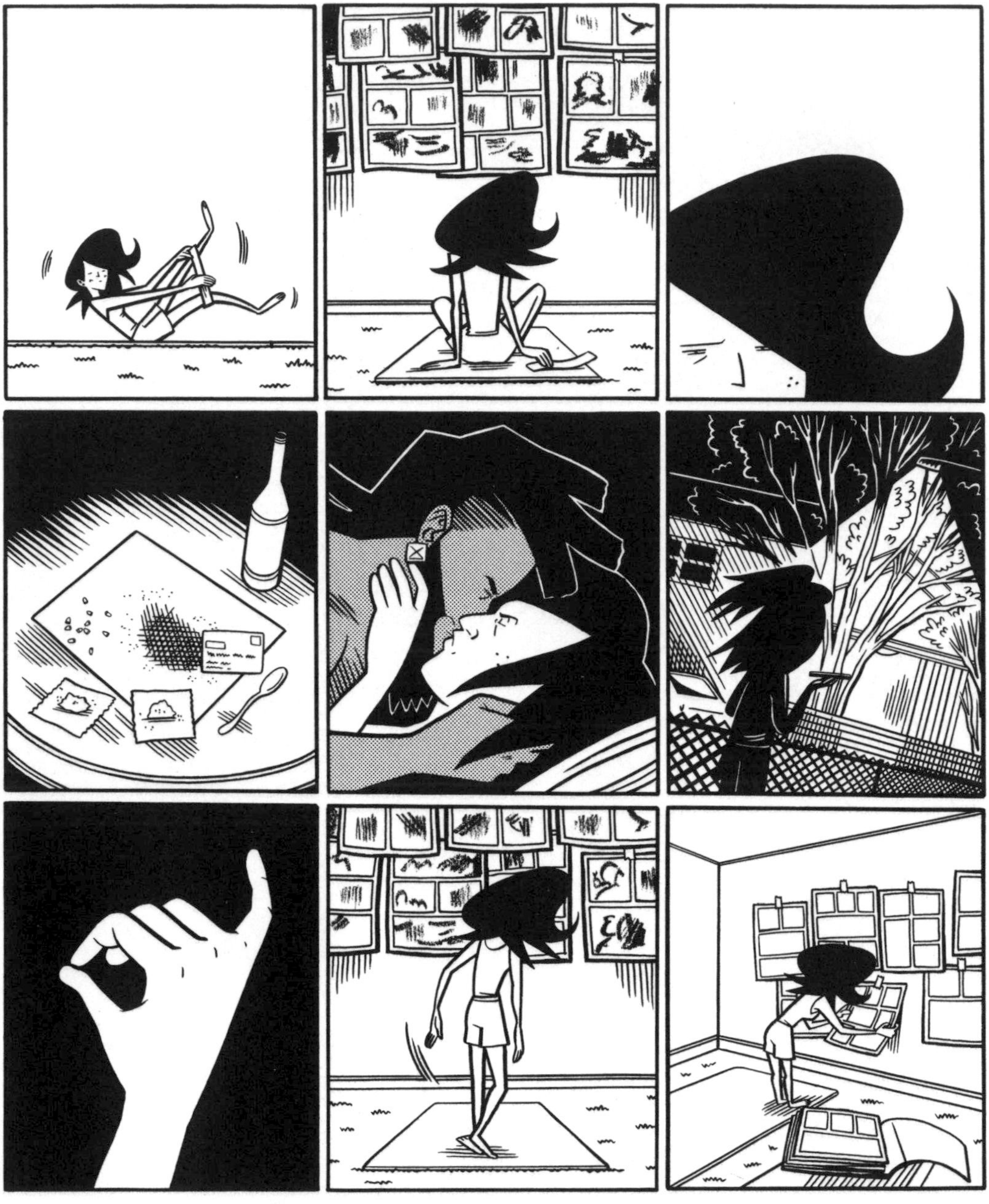

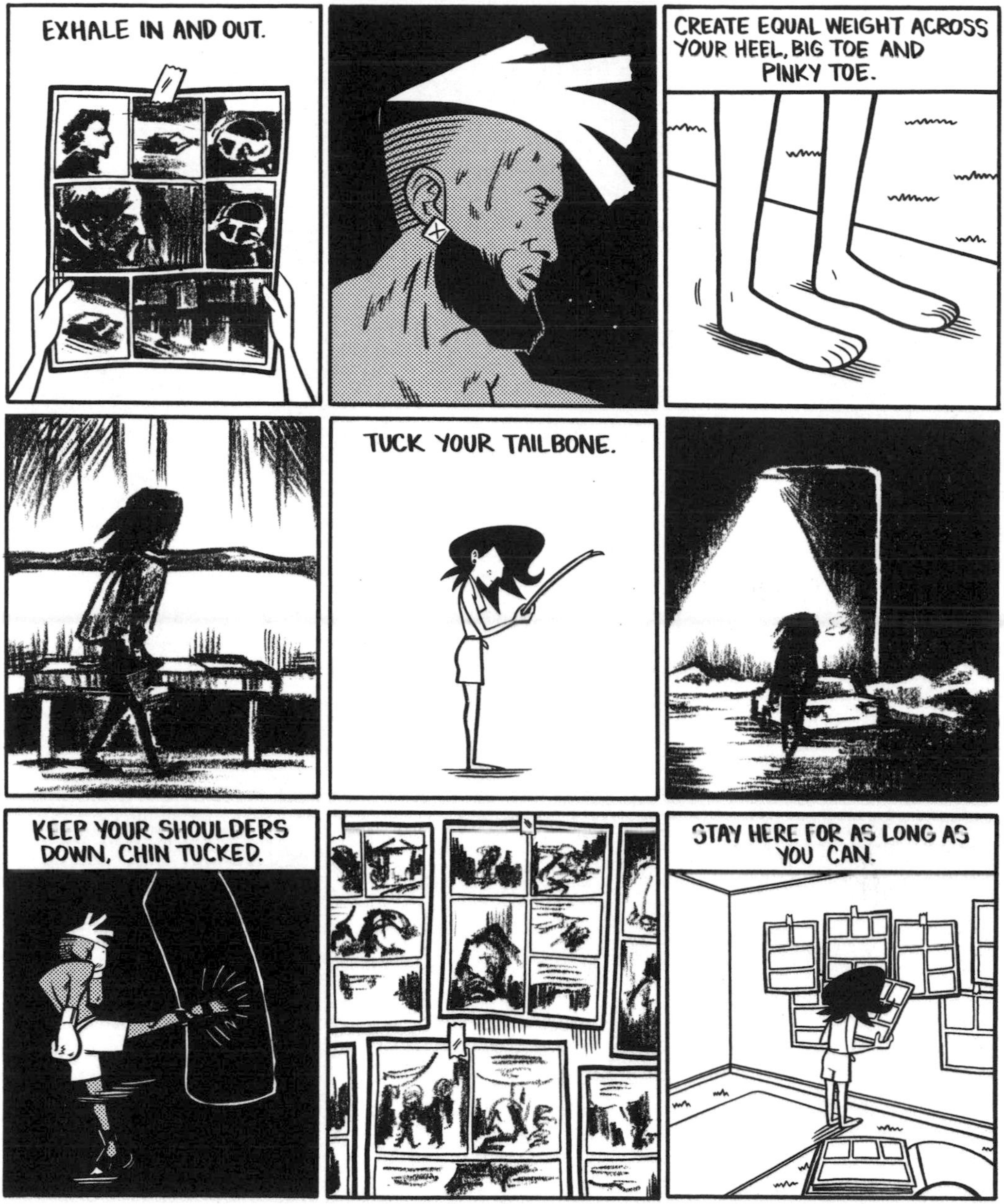
EXHALE IN AND OUT.
CREATE EQUAL WEIGHT ACROSS YOUR HEEL, BIG TOE AND PINKY TOE.
TUCK YOUR TAILBONE.
KEEP YOUR SHOULDERS DOWN, CHIN TUCKED.
STAY HERE FOR AS LONG AS YOU CAN.

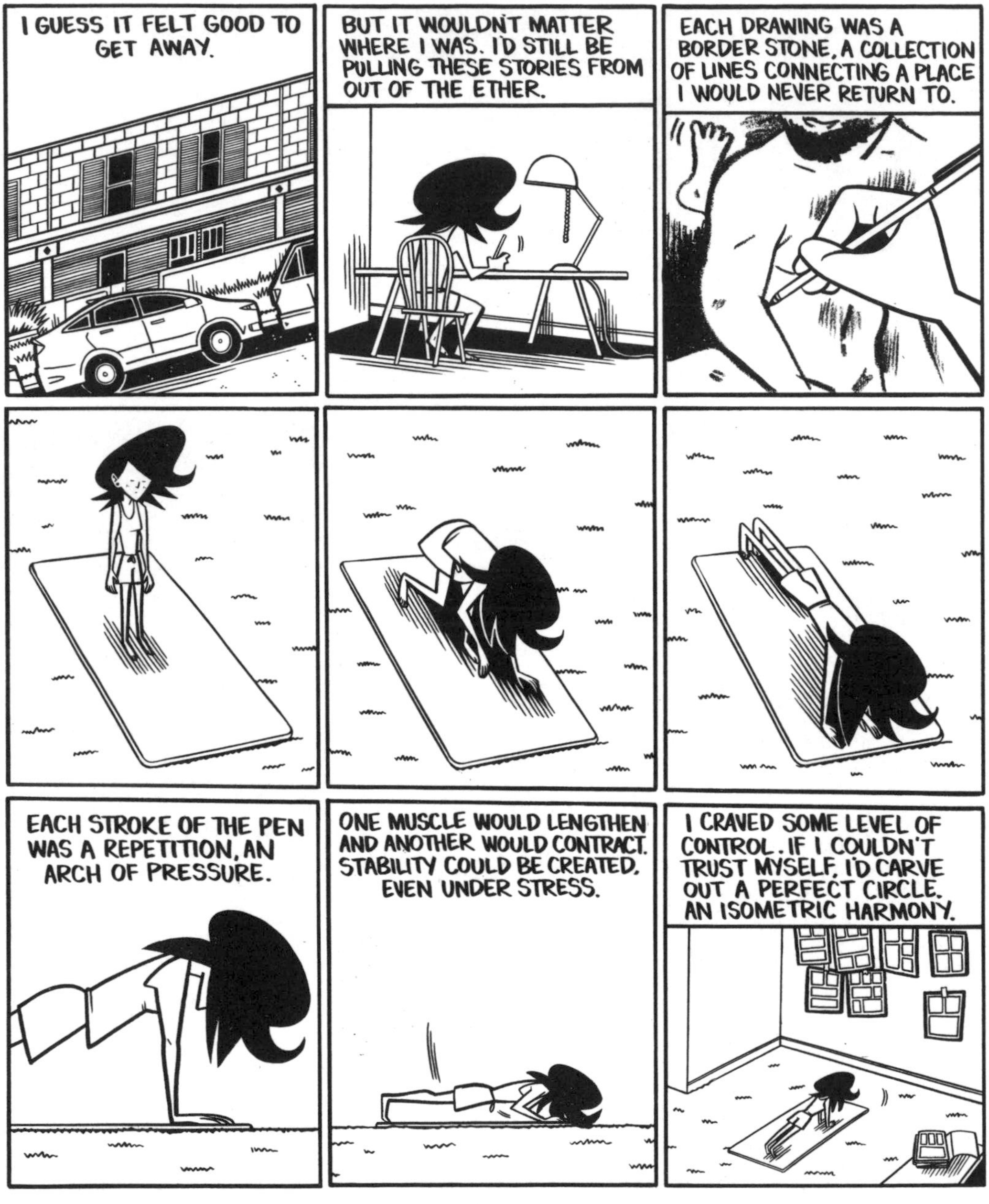
I GUESS IT FELT GOOD TO GET AWAY.
BUT IT WOULDN'T MATTER WHERE I WAS. I'D STILL BE PULLING THESE STORIES FROM OUT OF THE ETHER.
EACH DRAWING WAS A BORDER STONE, A COLLECTION OF LINES CONNECTING A PLACE I WOULD NEVER RETURN TO.
EACH STROKE OF THE PEN WAS A REPETITION, AN ARCH OF PRESSURE.
ONE MUSCLE WOULD LENGTHEN AND ANOTHER WOULD CONTRACT. STABILITY COULD BE CREATED, EVEN UNDER STRESS.
I CRAVED SOME LEVEL OF CONTROL. IF I COULDN'T TRUST MYSELF, I'D CARVE OUT A PERFECT CIRCLE. AN ISOMETRIC HARMONY.

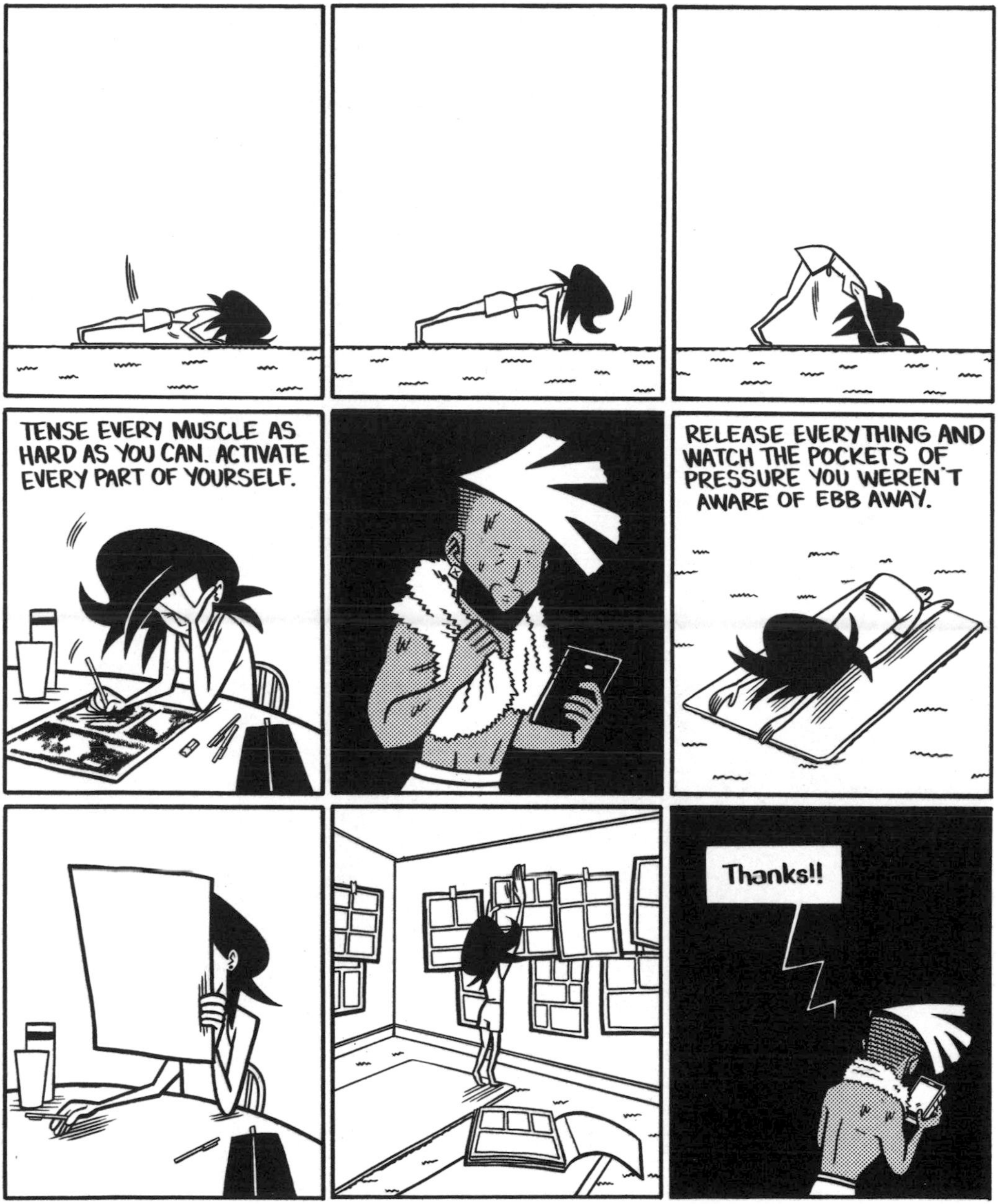
TENSE EVERY MUSCLE AS HARD AS YOU CAN. ACTIVATE EVERY PART OF YOURSELF.
RELEASE EVERYTHING AND WATCH THE POCKETS OF PRESSURE YOU WEREN'T AWARE OF EBB AWAY.
Thanks!!

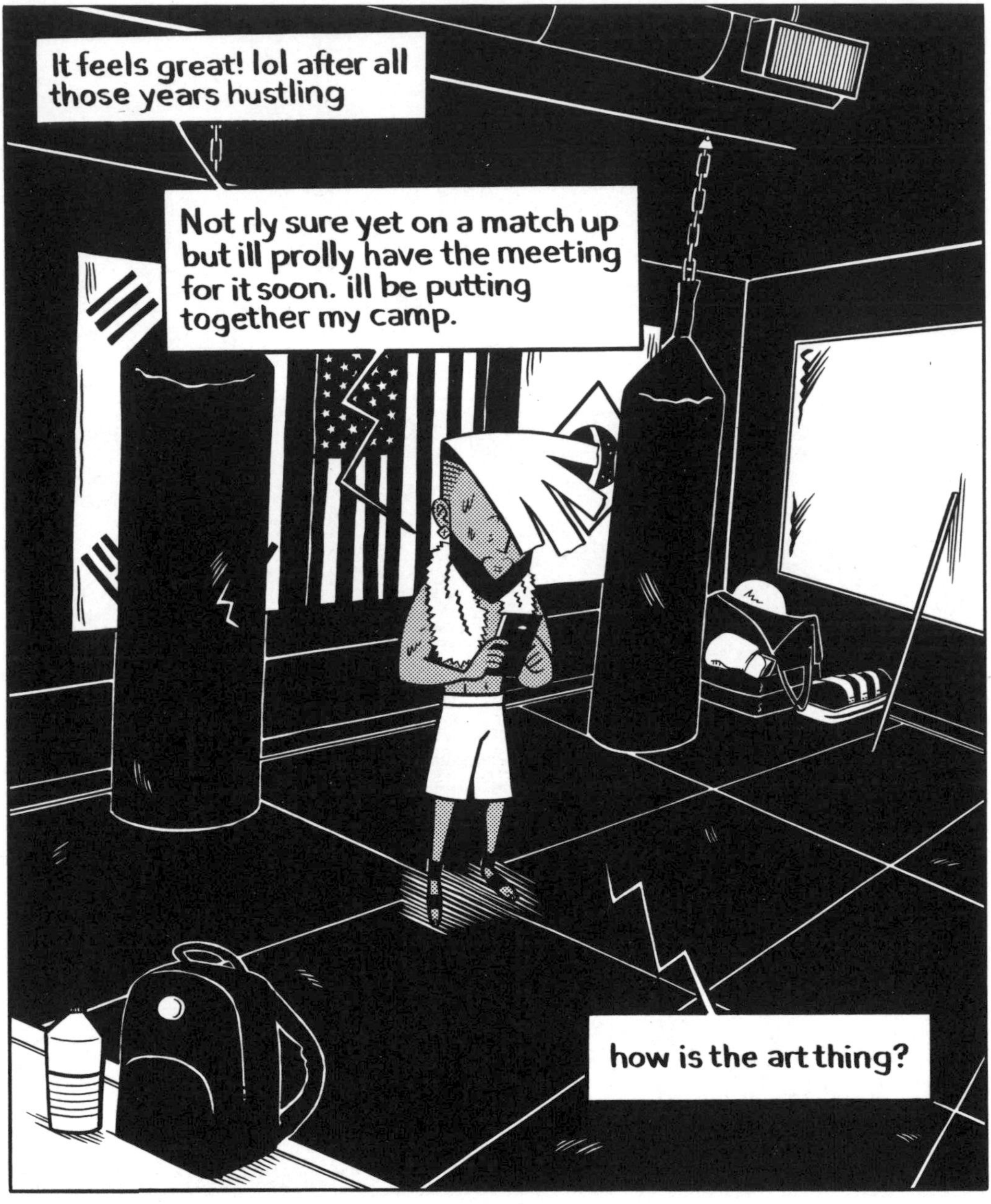
It feels great! lol after all those years hustling
Not rly sure yet on a match up but ill prolly have the meeting for it soon. ill be putting together my camp.
how is the art thing?

PITTSBURGH IS PRETTY COOL.

ALL OF THE OLD INDUSTRIAL STUFF REMINDS ME OF WHERE I GREW UP IN MINNESOTA.

FOR SURE!

ITS A GREAT PLACE IF YOU'RE LOOKING FOR SOME GOOD COMMUNITY. THE RENT COULD ALWAYS BE LOWER, BUT I LIKE BEING JUST A DAY'S DRIVE AWAY FROM ALL THE BIG COASTAL CITIES.

WOULD YOU EVER LEAVE MINNEAPOLIS?

HMM...

I DUNNO... I'M NOT REALLY MARRIED TO ANY ONE PLACE. I JUST NEED SOMEWHERE TO DRAW AND A GYM TO WORK AT.

AND WHY FITNESS? WHY NOT BE AN ILLUSTRATOR OR SOMETHING?

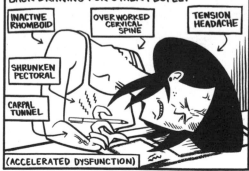

MONEY, MONEY AND I'D RATHER WEAR MY BODY DOWN EVENLY. I DON'T WANT TO MESS UP MY BACK DRAWING FOR OTHER PEOPLE.

INACTIVE RHOMBOID

OVERWORKED CERVICAL SPINE

TENSION HEADACHE

SHRUNKEN PECTORAL

CARPAL TUNNEL

(ACCELERATED DYSFUNCTION)

HEH, YEAH.

BZZZT

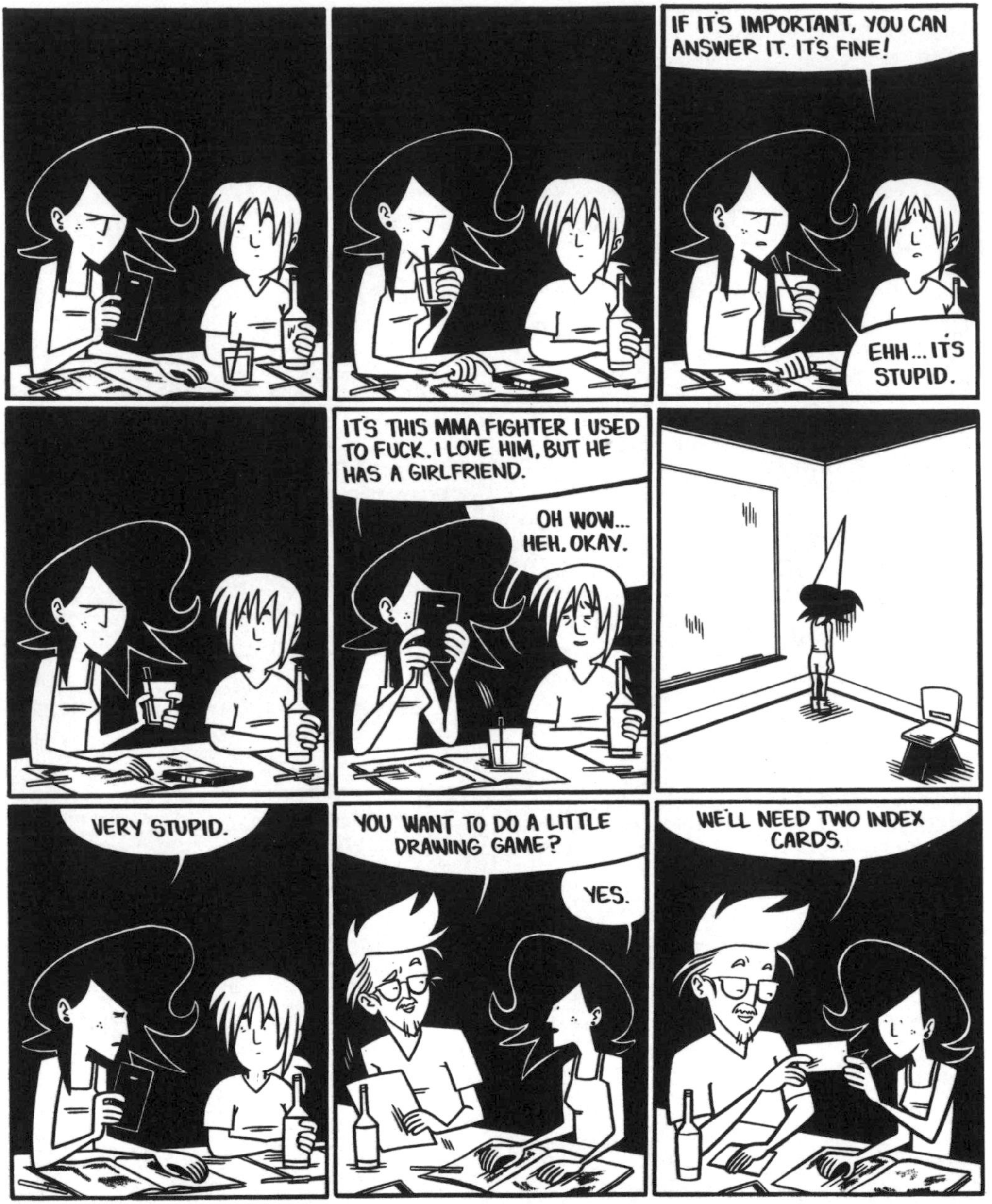
IF IT'S IMPORTANT, YOU CAN ANSWER IT. IT'S FINE!
EHH... IT'S STUPID.
IT'S THIS MMA FIGHTER I USED TO FUCK. I LOVE HIM, BUT HE HAS A GIRLFRIEND.
OH WOW... HEH, OKAY.
VERY STUPID.
YOU WANT TO DO A LITTLE DRAWING GAME?
YES.
WE'LL NEED TWO INDEX CARDS.

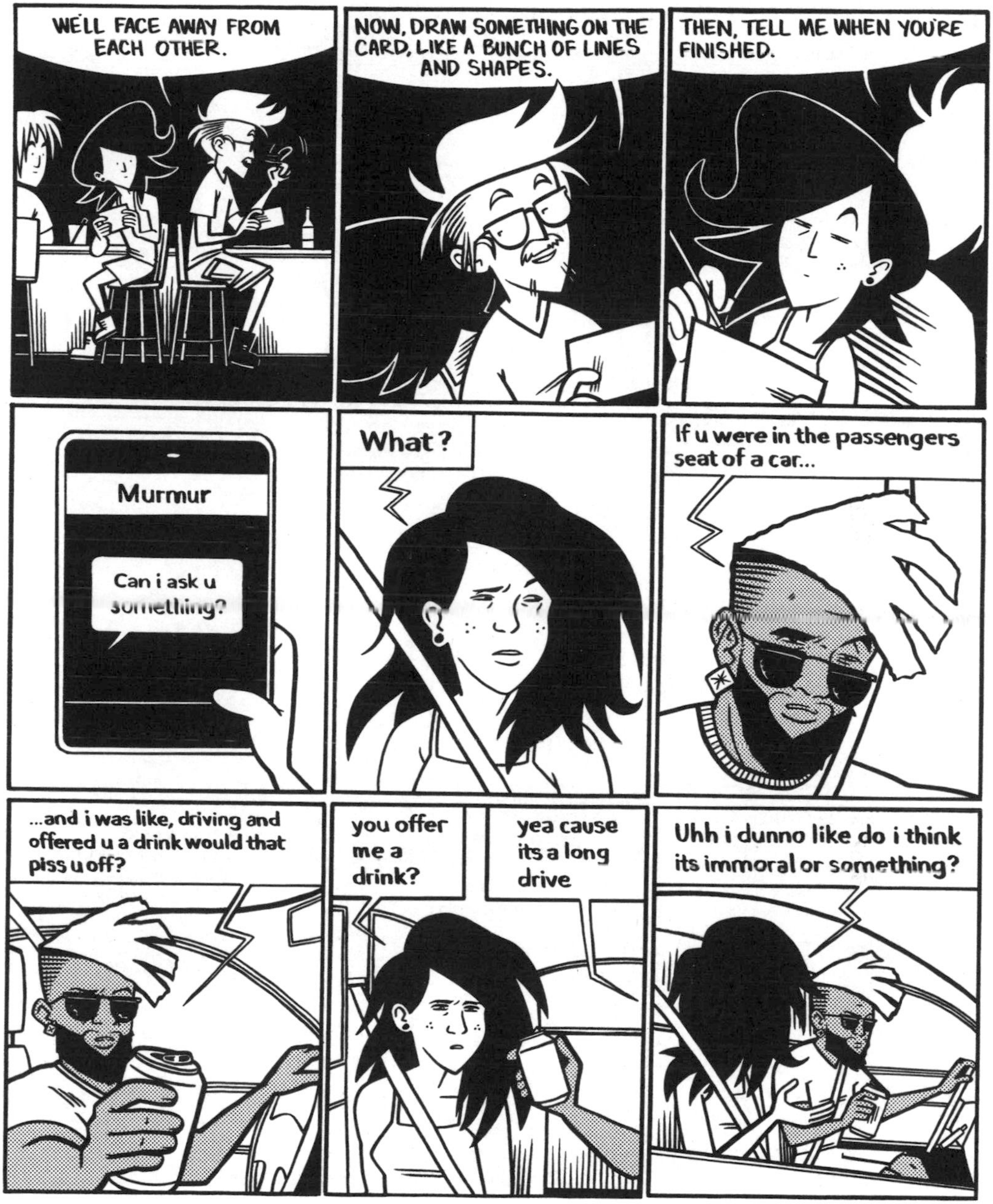

WE'LL FACE AWAY FROM EACH OTHER.
NOW, DRAW SOMETHING ON THE CARD, LIKE A BUNCH OF LINES AND SHAPES.
THEN, TELL ME WHEN YOU'RE FINISHED.
Murmur
Can i ask u something?
What?
If u were in the passengers seat of a car...
...and i was like, driving and offered u a drink would that piss u off?
you offer me a drink?
yea cause its a long drive
Uhh i dunno like do i think its immoral or something?

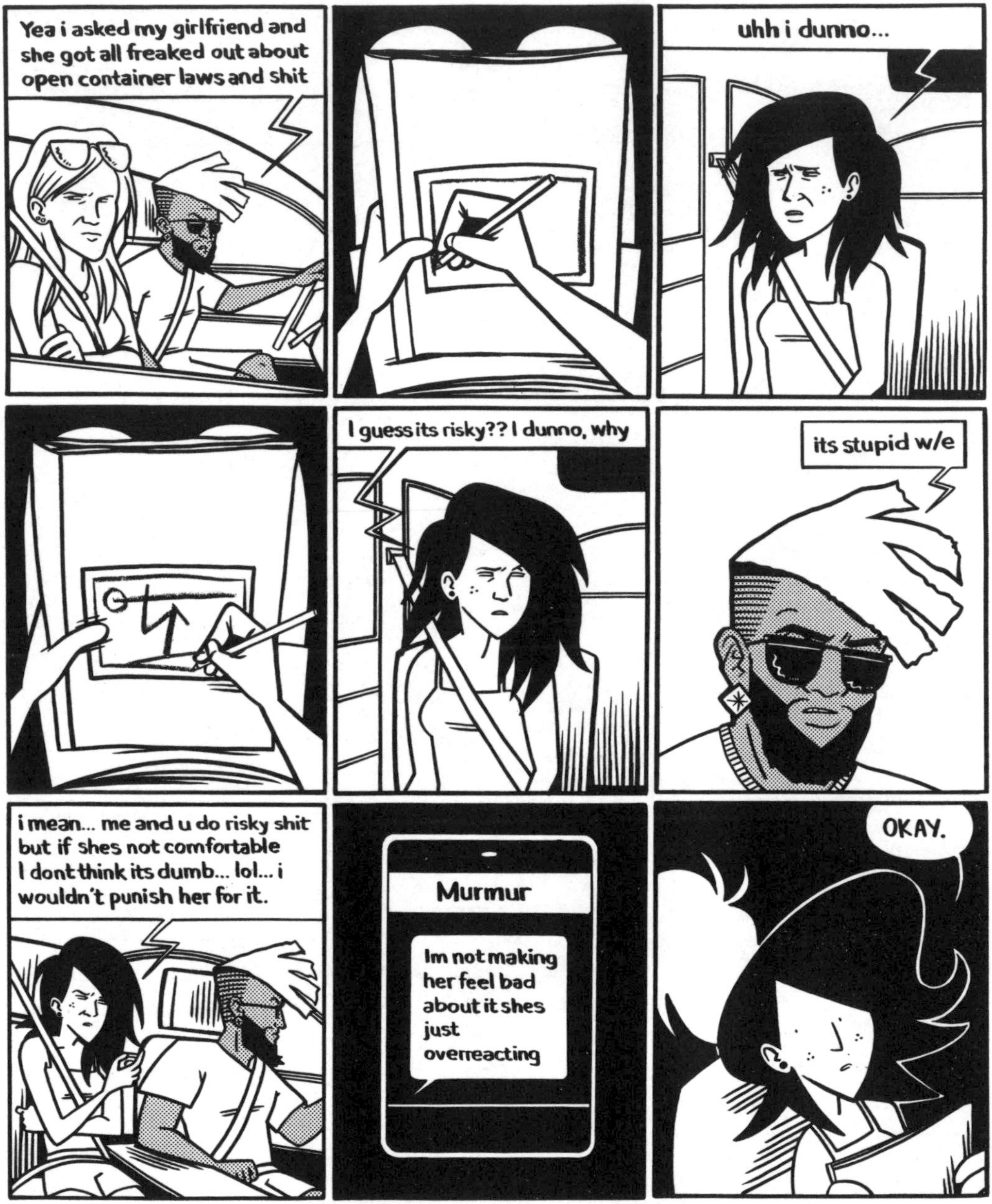
Yea i asked my girlfriend and she got all freaked out about open container laws and shit
uhh i dunno...
I guess its risky?? I dunno, why
its stupid w/e
i mean... me and u do risky shit but if shes not comfortable I dont think its dumb... lol... i wouldn't punish her for it.
Murmur
Im not making her feel bad about it shes just overreacting
OKAY.

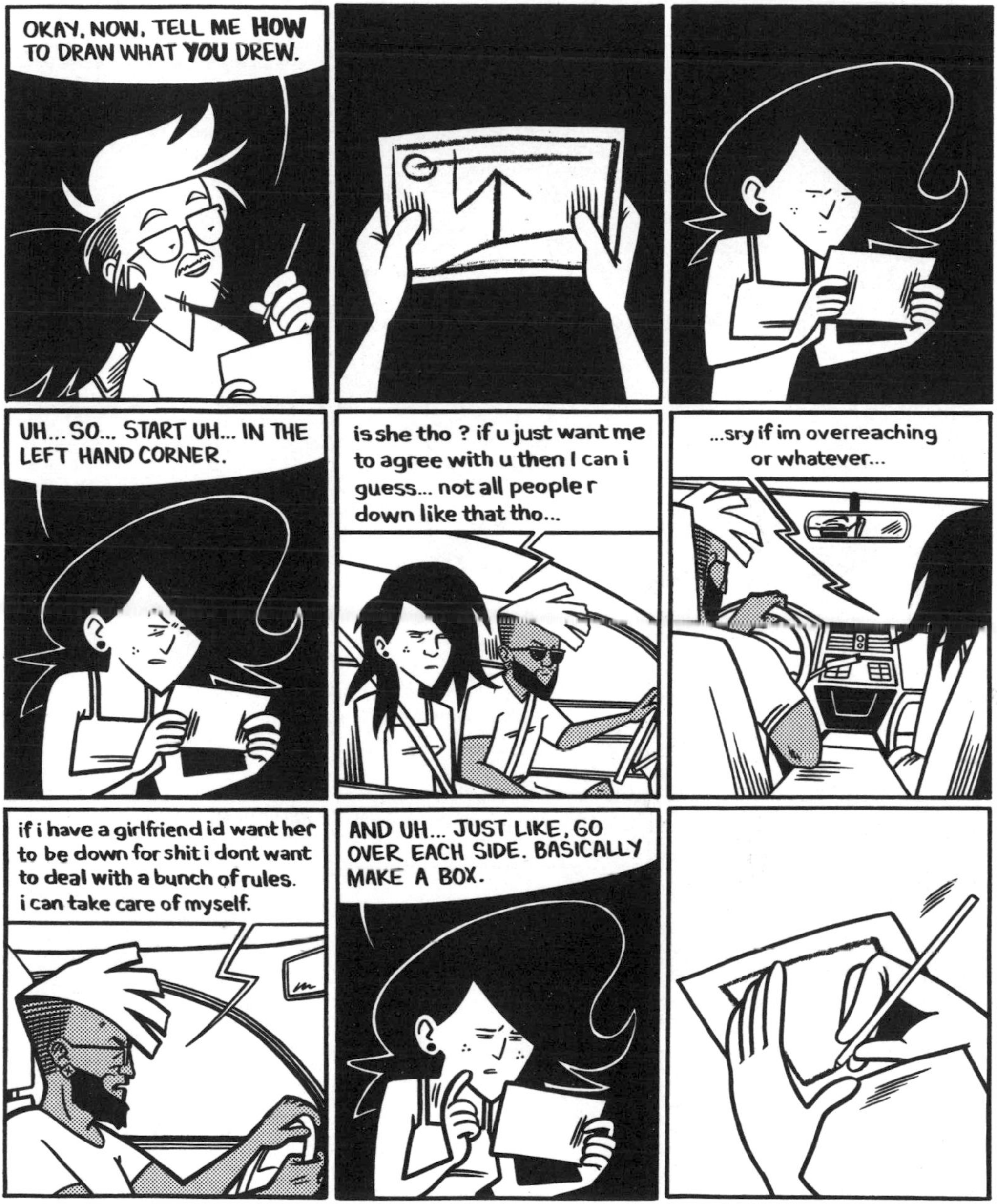
OKAY, NOW, TELL ME HOW TO DRAW WHAT YOU DREW.
UH... SO... START UH... IN THE LEFT HAND CORNER.
is she tho ? if u just want me to agree with u then I can i guess... not all people r down like that tho...
...sry if im overreaching or whatever...
if i have a girlfriend id want her to be down for shit i dont want to deal with a bunch of rules. i can take care of myself.
AND UH... JUST LIKE, GO OVER EACH SIDE. BASICALLY MAKE A BOX.

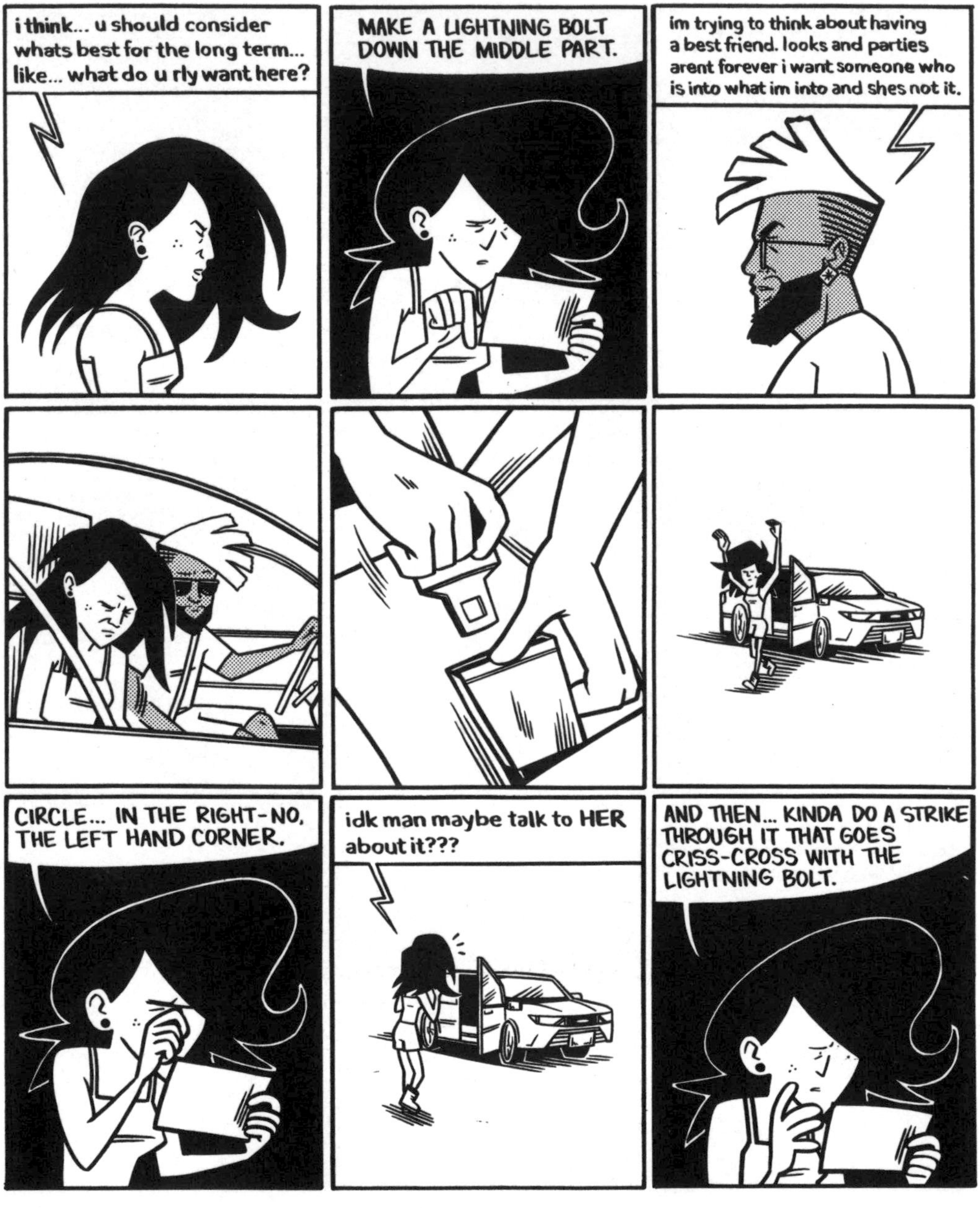
i think... u should consider whats best for the long term... like... what do u rly want here?
MAKE A LIGHTNING BOLT DOWN THE MIDDLE PART.
im trying to think about having a best friend. looks and parties arent forever i want someone who is into what im into and shes not it.
CIRCLE... IN THE RIGHT-NO, THE LEFT HAND CORNER.
idk man maybe talk to HER about it???
AND THEN... KINDA DO A STRIKE THROUGH IT THAT GOES CRISS-CROSS WITH THE LIGHTNING BOLT.

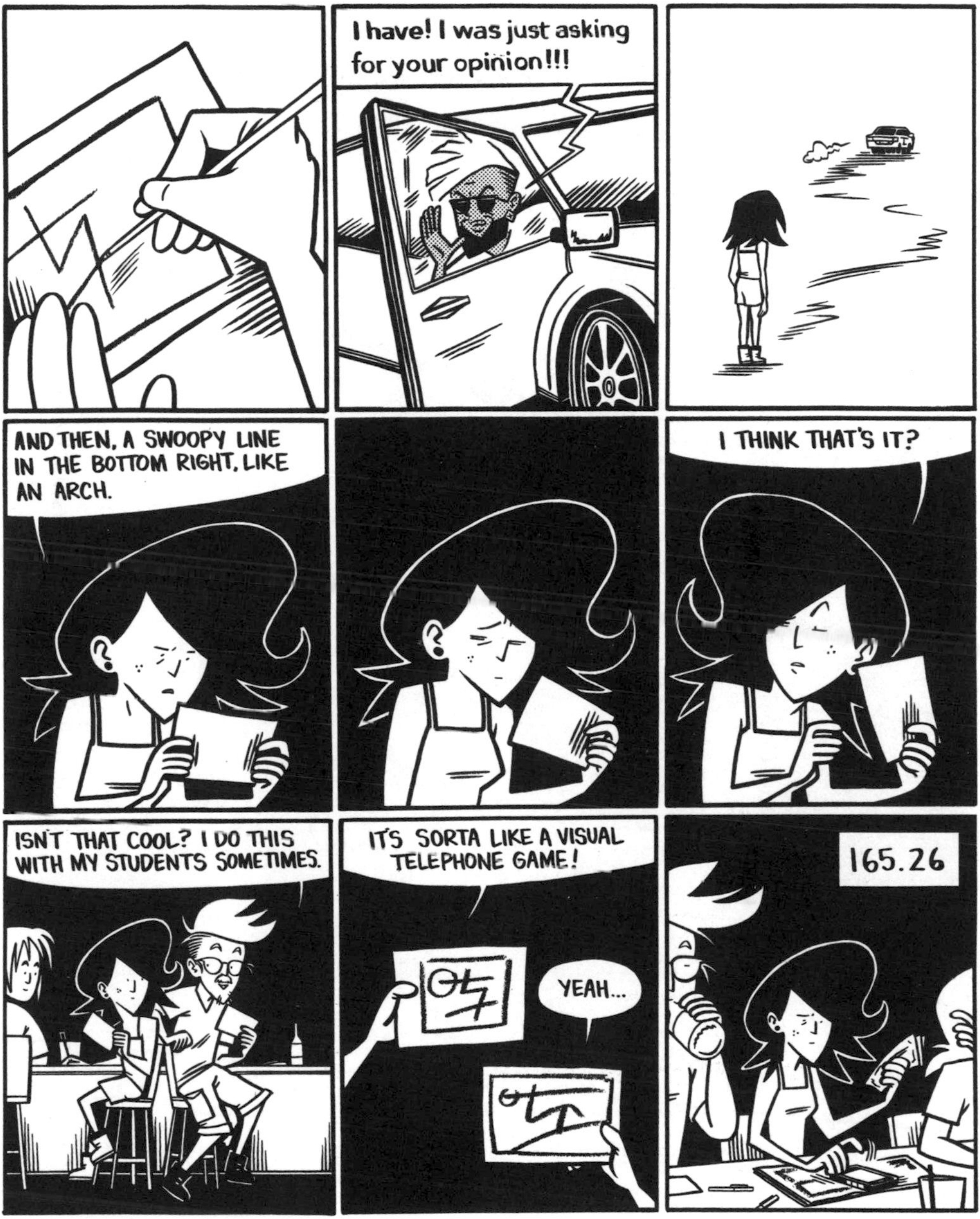
I have! I was just asking for your opinion!!!
AND THEN, A SWOOPY LINE IN THE BOTTOM RIGHT, LIKE AN ARCH.
I THINK THAT'S IT?
ISN'T THAT COOL? I DO THIS WITH MY STUDENTS SOMETIMES.
IT'S SORTA LIKE A VISUAL TELEPHONE GAME!
YEAH...
165.26

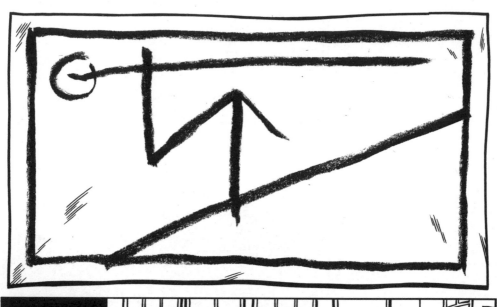

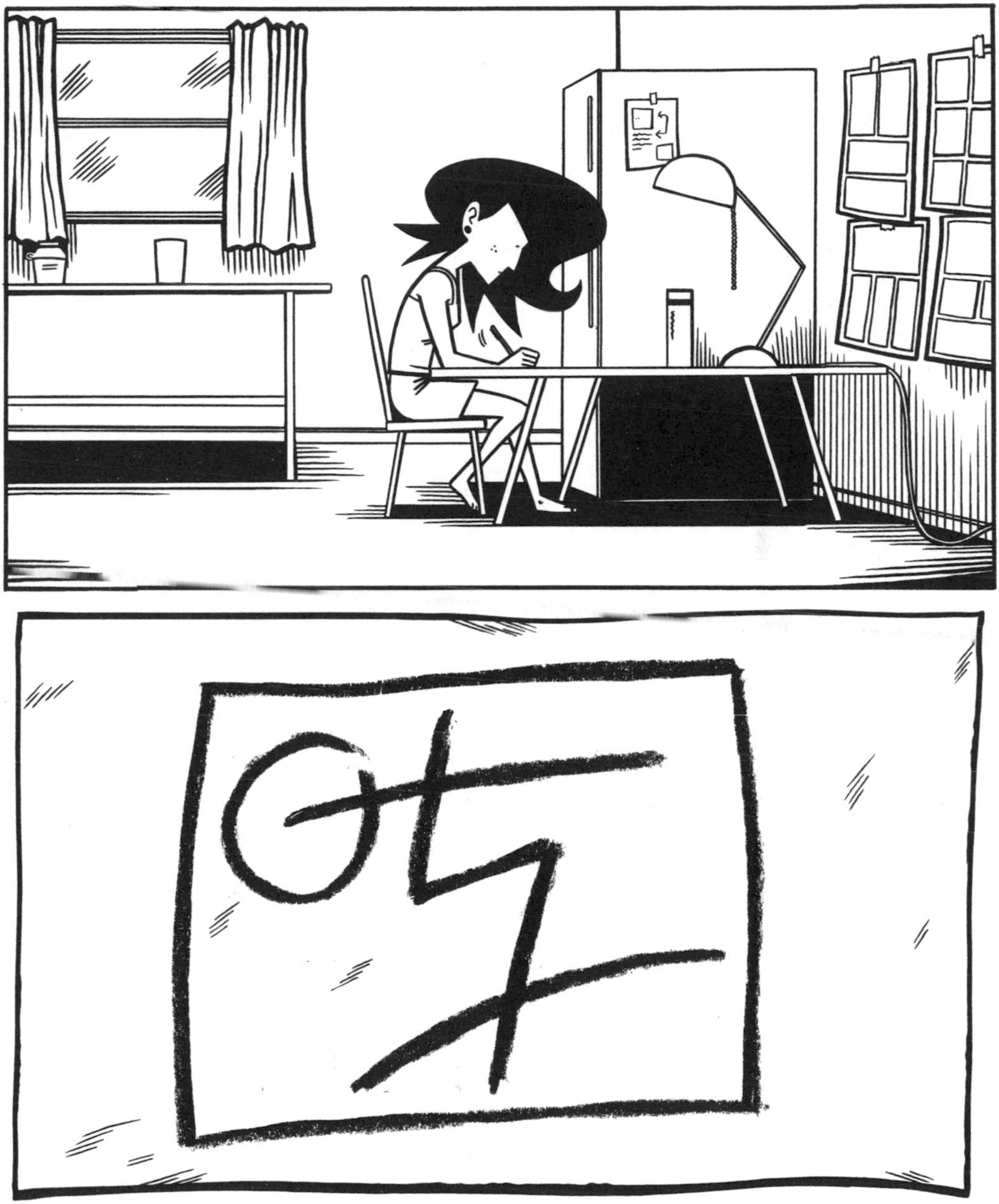

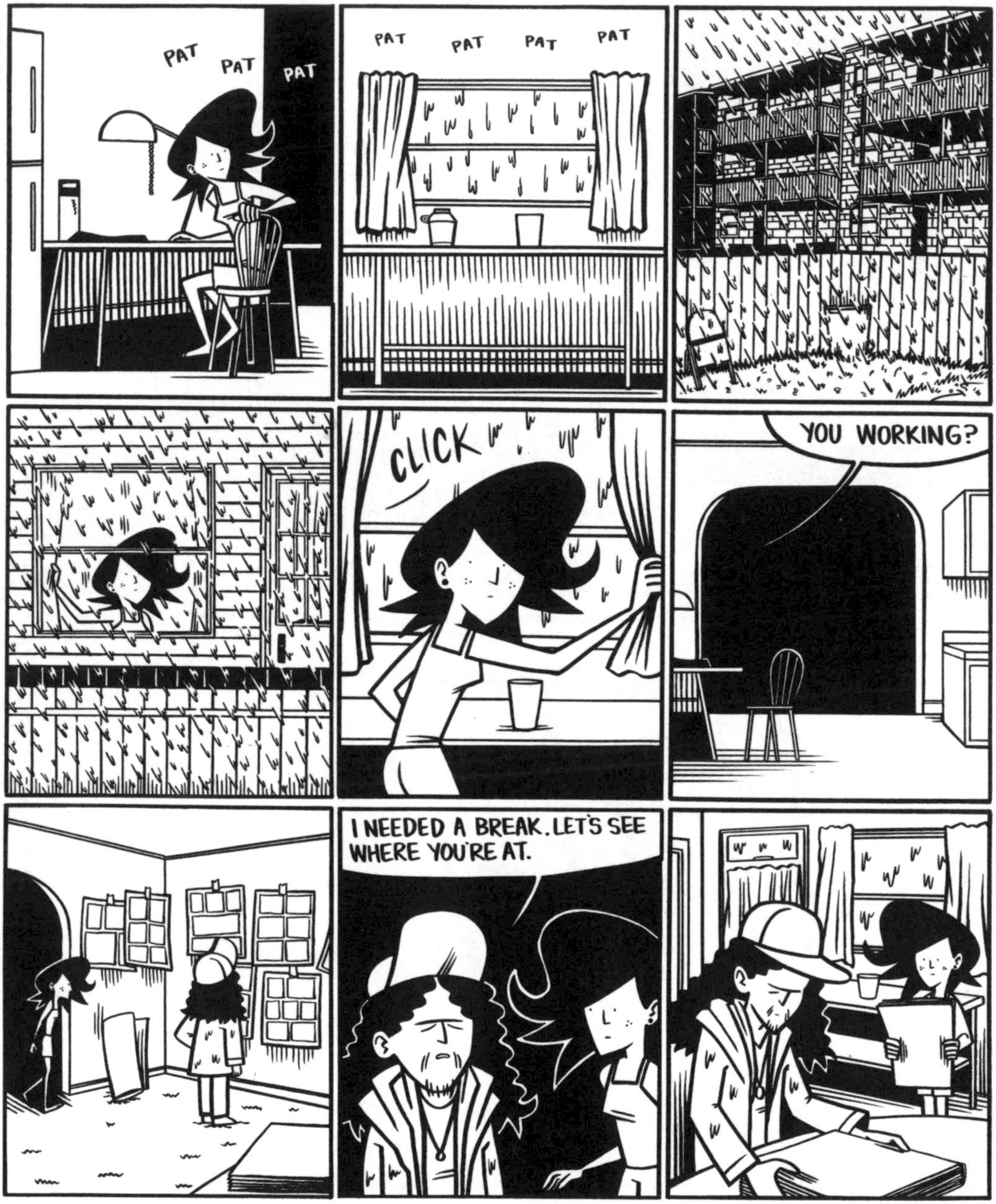
PAT
PAT
PAT
PAT
PAT
PAT
PAT
CLICK
YOU WORKING?
I NEEDED A BREAK. LET'S SEE WHERE YOU'RE AT.

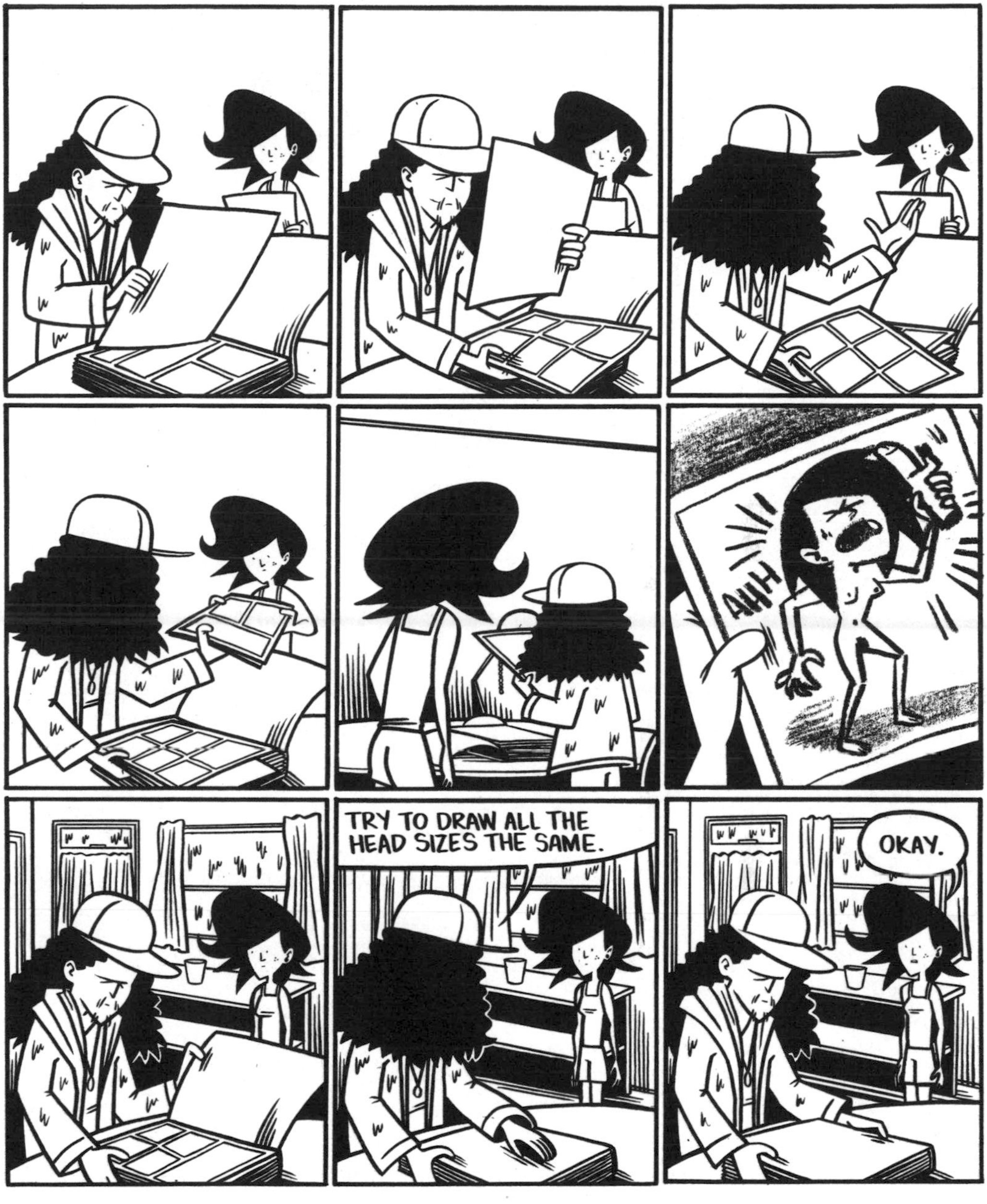
AHH
TRY TO DRAW ALL THE HEAD SIZES THE SAME.
OKAY.

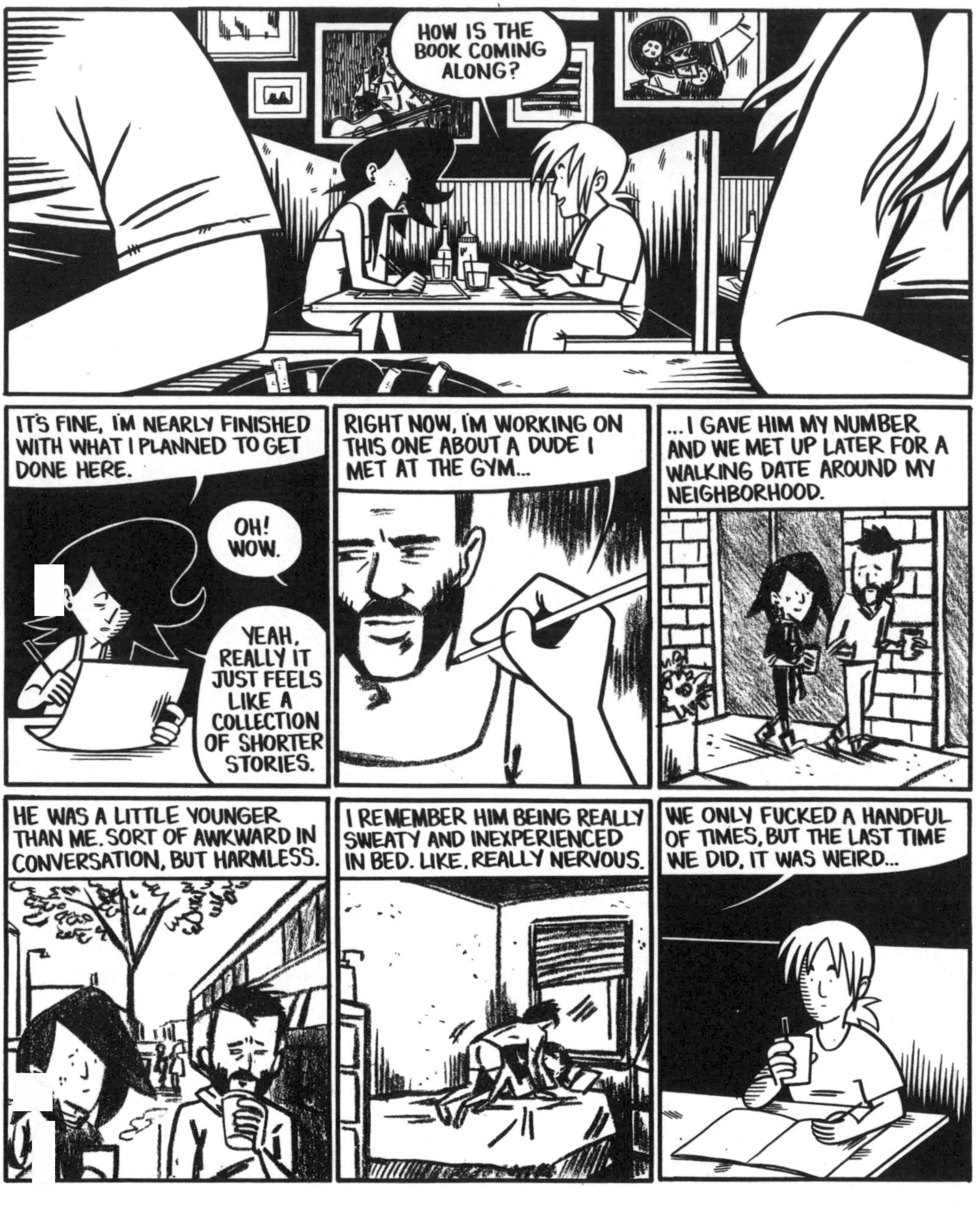
HOW IS THE BOOK COMING ALONG?
IT'S FINE, I'M NEARLY FINISHED WITH WHAT I PLANNED TO GET DONE HERE.
OH! WOW.
YEAH, REALLY IT JUST FEELS LIKE A COLLECTION OF SHORTER STORIES.
RIGHT NOW, I'M WORKING ON THIS ONE ABOUT A DUDE I MET AT THE GYM...
...I GAVE HIM MY NUMBER AND WE MET UP LATER FOR A WALKING DATE AROUND MY NEIGHBORHOOD.
HE WAS A LITTLE YOUNGER THAN ME. SORT OF AWKWARD IN CONVERSATION, BUT HARMLESS.
I REMEMBER HIM BEING REALLY SWEATY AND INEXPERIENCED IN BED. LIKE, REALLY NERVOUS.
WE ONLY FUCKED A HANDFUL OF TIMES, BUT THE LAST TIME WE DID, IT WAS WEIRD...

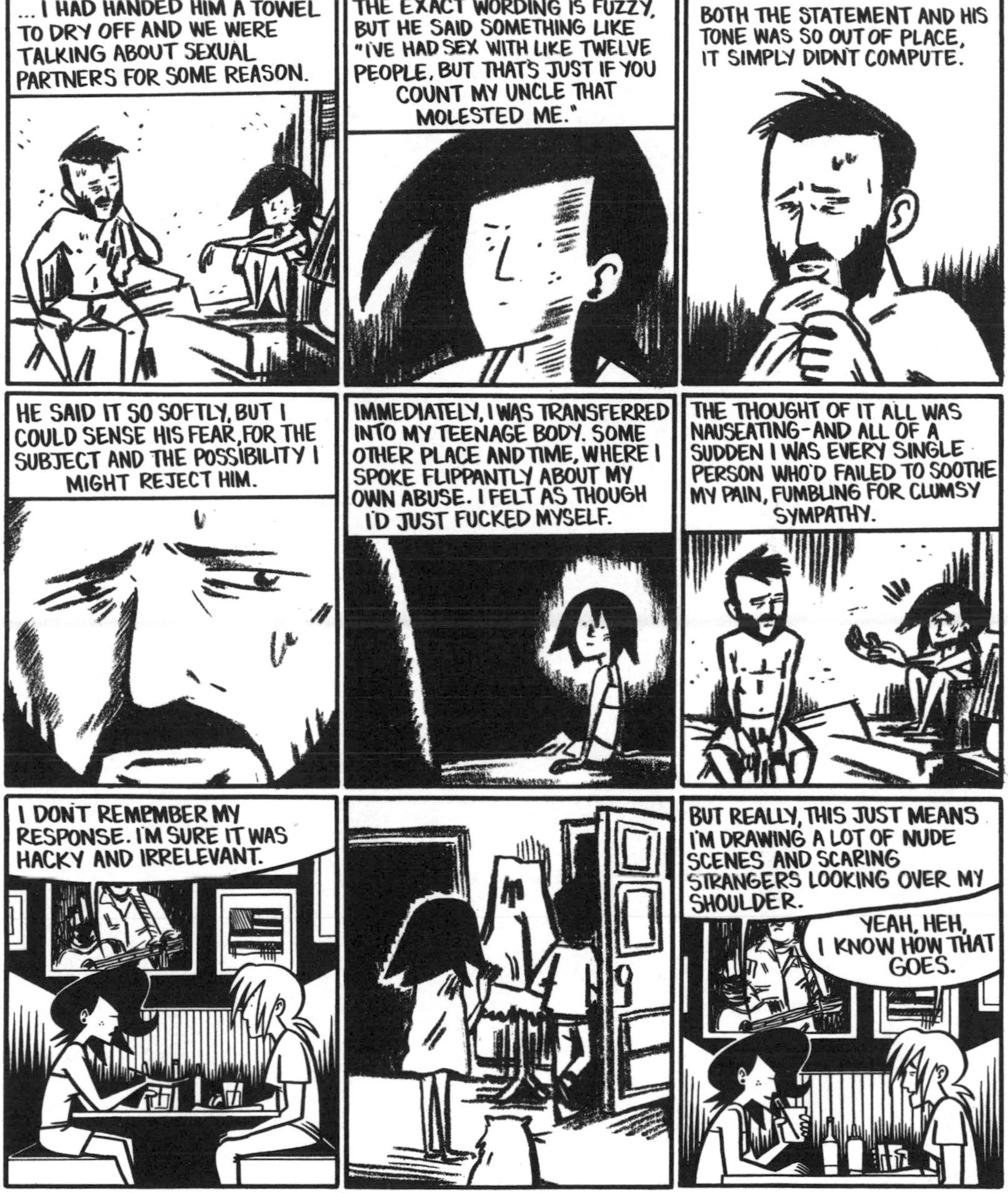
...I HAD HANDED HIM A TOWEL TO DRY OFF AND WE WERE TALKING ABOUT SEXUAL PARTNERS FOR SOME REASON.
THE EXACT WORDING IS FUZZY, BUT HE SAID SOMETHING LIKE "I'VE HAD SEX WITH LIKE TWELVE PEOPLE, BUT THAT'S JUST IF YOU COUNT MY UNCLE THAT MOLESTED ME."
BOTH THE STATEMENT AND HIS TONE WAS SO OUT OF PLACE, IT SIMPLY DIDN'T COMPUTE.
HE SAID IT SO SOFTLY, BUT I COULD SENSE HIS FEAR, FOR THE SUBJECT AND THE POSSIBILITY I MIGHT REJECT HIM.
IMMEDIATELY, I WAS TRANSFERRED INTO MY TEENAGE BODY. SOME OTHER PLACE AND TIME, WHERE I SPOKE FLIPPANTLY ABOUT MY OWN ABUSE. I FELT AS THOUGH I'D JUST FUCKED MYSELF.
THE THOUGHT OF IT ALL WAS NAUSEATING-AND ALL OF A SUDDEN I WAS EVERY SINGLE PERSON WHO'D FAILED TO SOOTHE MY PAIN, FUMBLING FOR CLUMSY SYMPATHY.
I DON'T REMEMBER MY RESPONSE. I'M SURE IT WAS HACKY AND IRRELEVANT.
BUT REALLY, THIS JUST MEANS I'M DRAWING A LOT OF NUDE SCENES AND SCARING STRANGERS LOOKING OVER MY SHOULDER.
YEAH, HEH, I KNOW HOW THAT GOES.

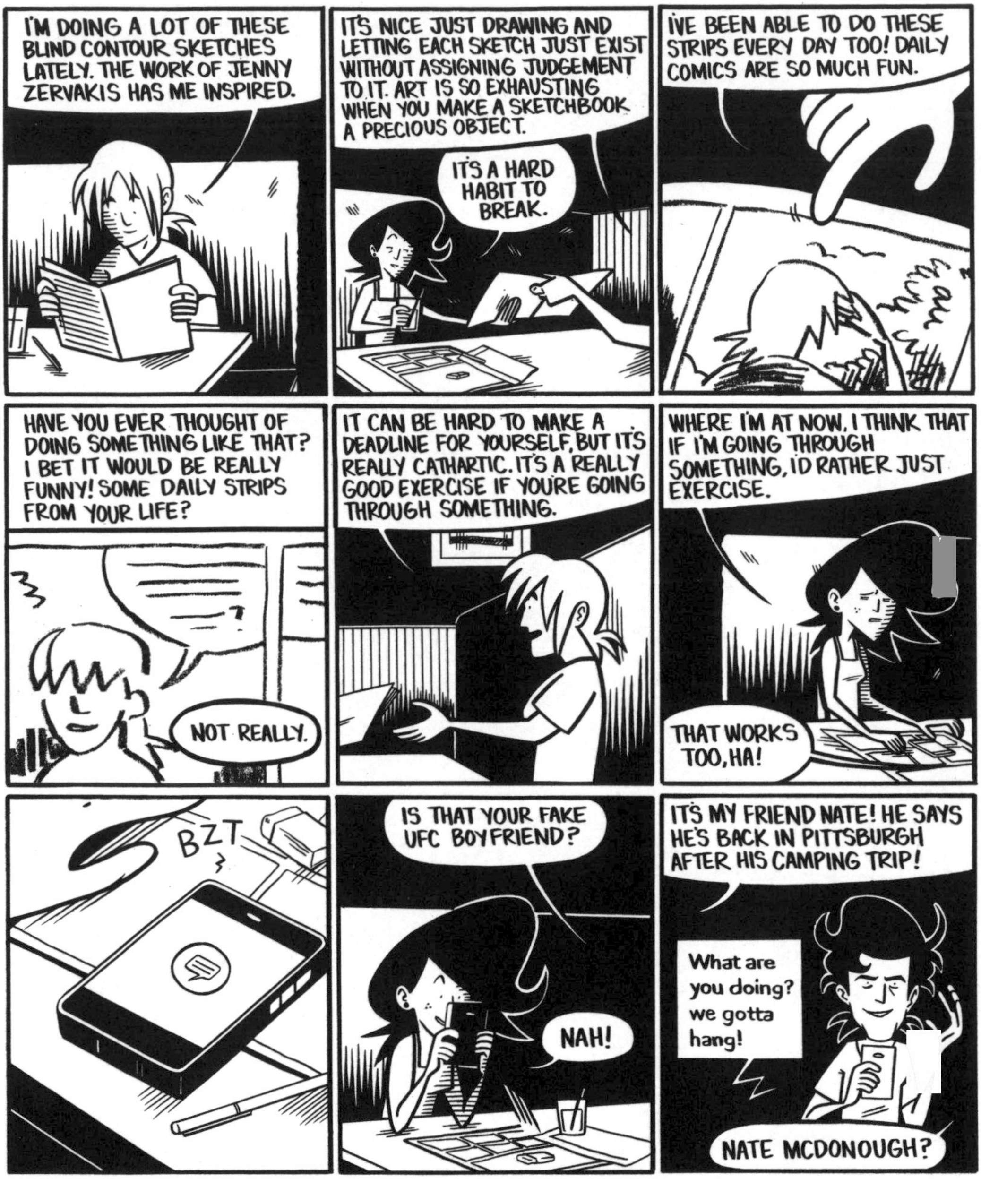
I'M DOING A LOT OF THESE BLIND CONTOUR SKETCHES LATELY. THE WORK OF JENNY ZERVAKIS HAS ME INSPIRED.
IT'S NICE JUST DRAWING AND LETTING EACH SKETCH JUST EXIST WITHOUT ASSIGNING JUDGEMENT TO IT. ART IS SO EXHAUSTING WHEN YOU MAKE A SKETCHBOOK A PRECIOUS OBJECT.
IT'S A HARD HABIT TO BREAK.
I'VE BEEN ABLE TO DO THESE STRIPS EVERY DAY TOO! DAILY COMICS ARE SO MUCH FUN.
HAVE YOU EVER THOUGHT OF DOING SOMETHING LIKE THAT? I BET IT WOULD BE REALLY FUNNY! SOME DAILY STRIPS FROM YOUR LIFE?
NOT REALLY.
IT CAN BE HARD TO MAKE A DEADLINE FOR YOURSELF, BUT IT'S REALLY CATHARTIC. IT'S A REALLY GOOD EXERCISE IF YOU'RE GOING THROUGH SOMETHING.
WHERE I'M AT NOW, I THINK THAT IF I'M GOING THROUGH SOMETHING, I'D RATHER JUST EXERCISE.
THAT WORKS TOO, HA!
BZT
IS THAT YOUR FAKE UFC BOYFRIEND?
NAH!
IT'S MY FRIEND NATE! HE SAYS HE'S BACK IN PITTSBURGH AFTER HIS CAMPING TRIP!
What are you doing? we gotta hang!
NATE MCDONOUGH?

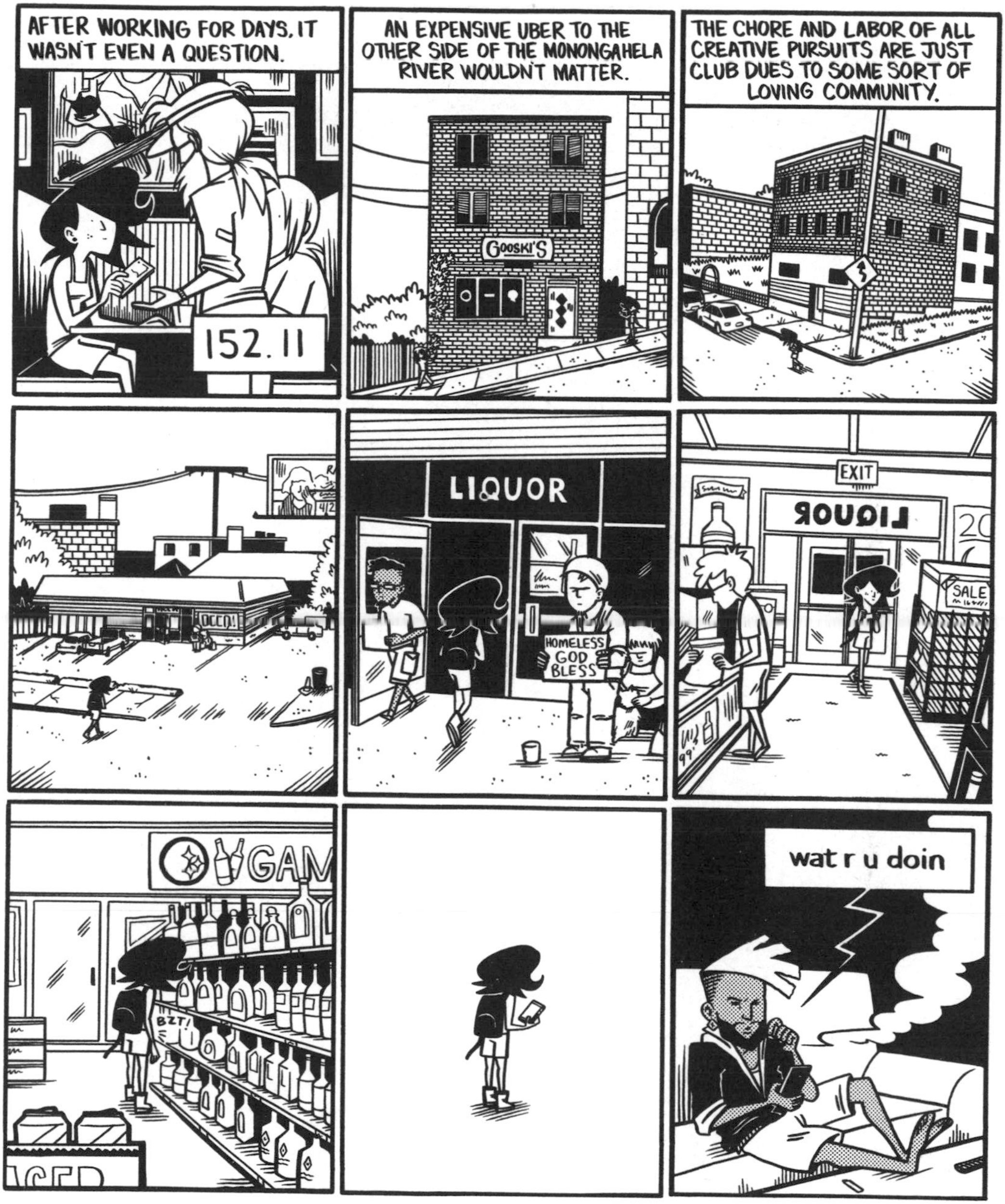
AFTER WORKING FOR DAYS, IT WASN'T EVEN A QUESTION.
152.11
AN EXPENSIVE UBER TO THE OTHER SIDE OF THE MONONGAHELA RIVER WOULDN'T MATTER.
GOOSKI'S
THE CHORE AND LABOR OF ALL CREATIVE PURSUITS ARE JUST CLUB DUES TO SOME SORT OF LOVING COMMUNITY.
LIQUOR
HOMELESS GOD BLESS
EXIT
LIQUOR
SALE
BZT!
wat r u doin

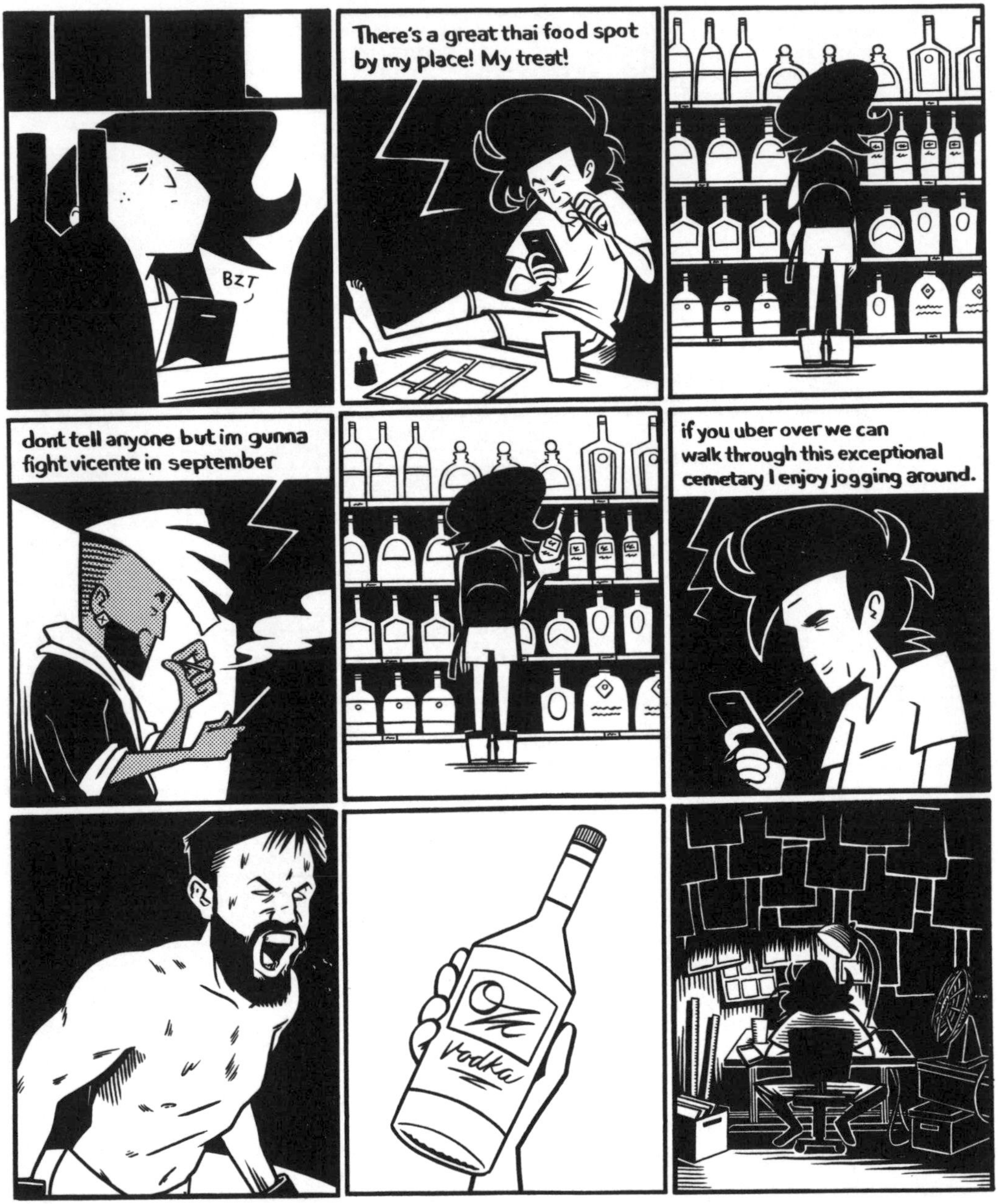
BZT
There's a great thai food spot by my place! My treat!
dont tell anyone but im gunna fight vicente in september
if you uber over we can walk through this exceptional cemetary I enjoy jogging around.
Vodka

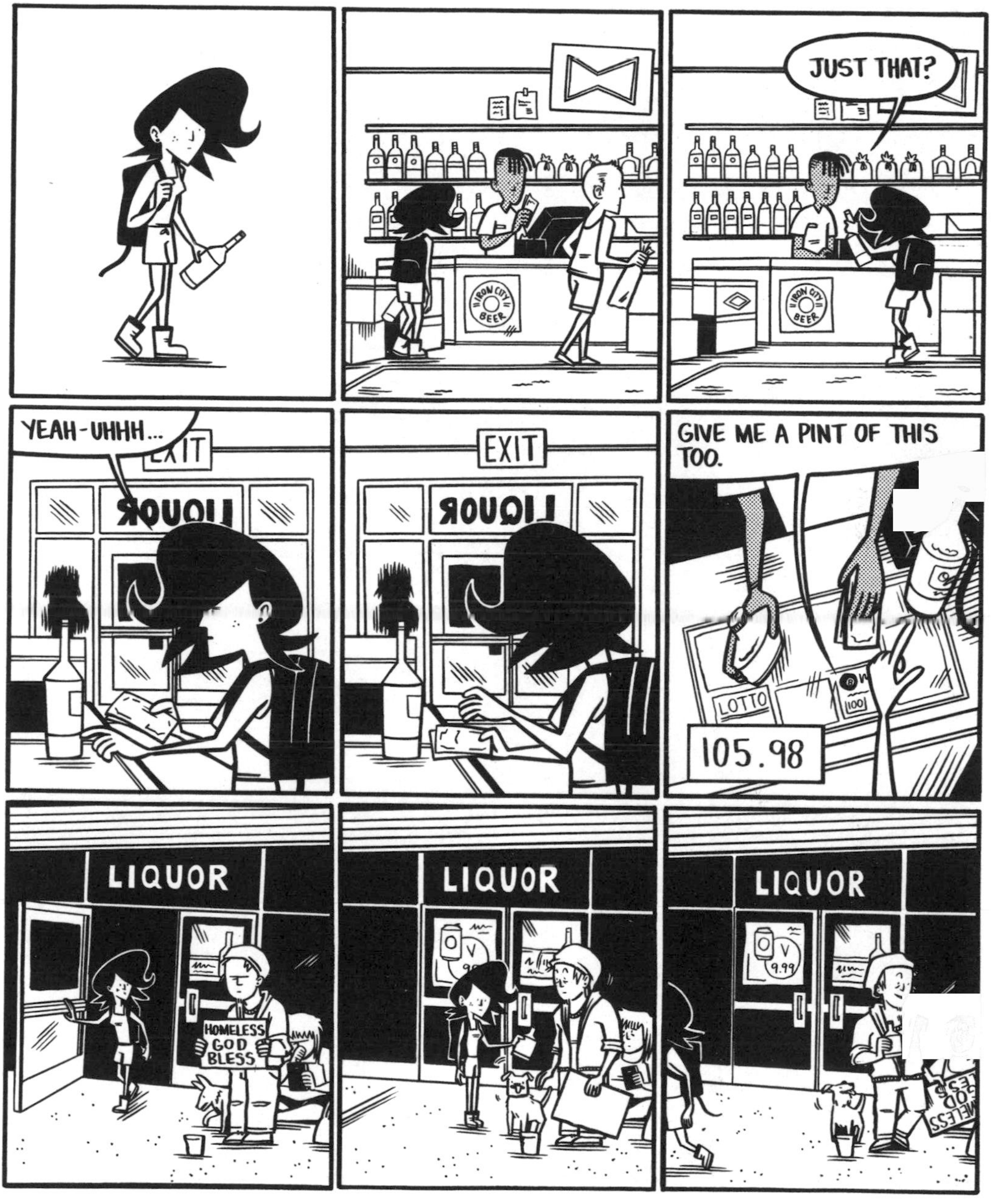
IRON CITY BEER
JUST THAT?
IRON CITY BEER
YEAH-UHHH...
EXIT
EXIT
GIVE ME A PINT OF THIS TOO.
LOTTO
105.98
LIQUOR
HOMELESS GOD BLESS
LIQUOR
LIQUOR
9.99

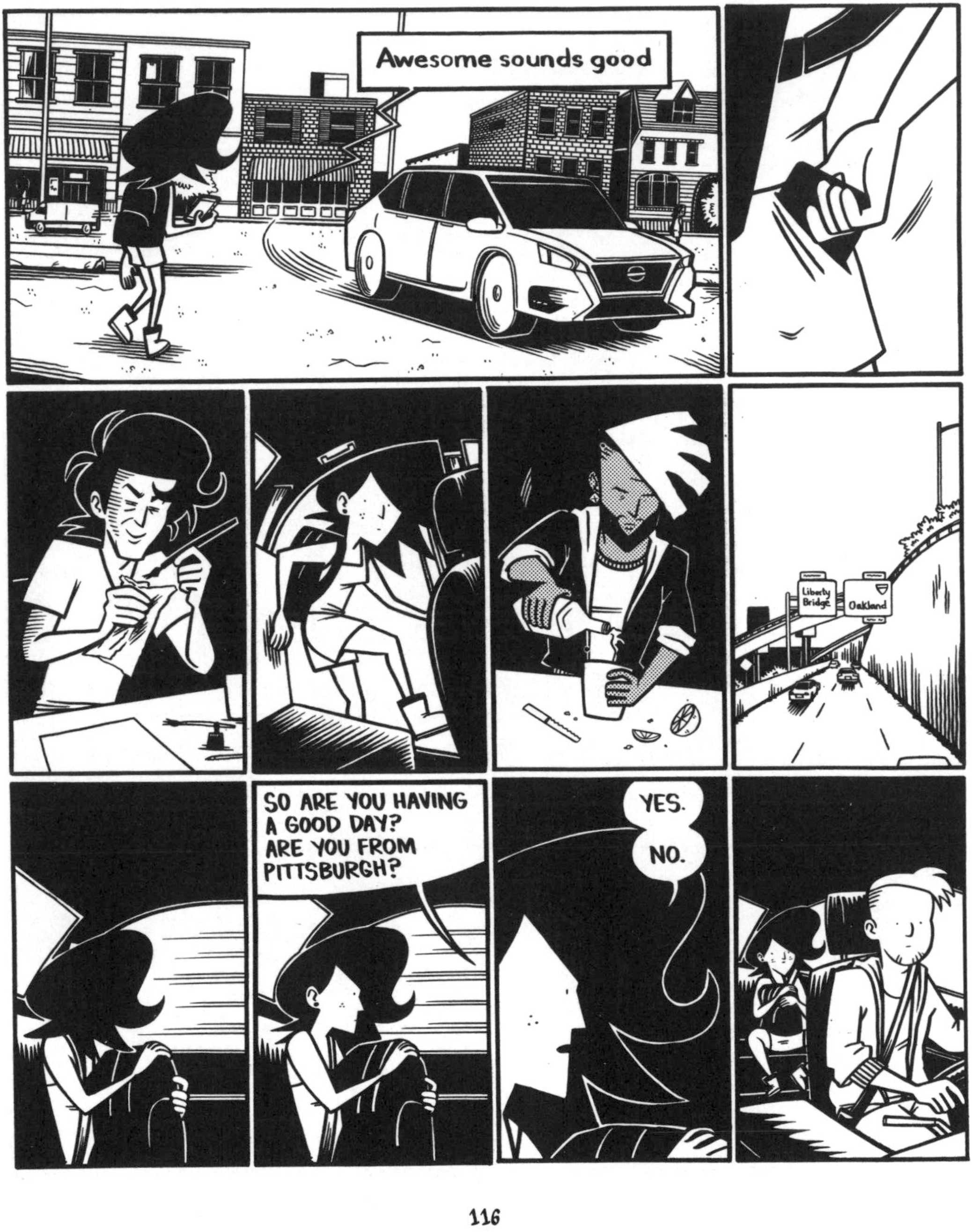
Awesome sounds good
Liberty Bridge
Oakland
SO ARE YOU HAVING A GOOD DAY? ARE YOU FROM PITTSBURGH?
YES.
NO.

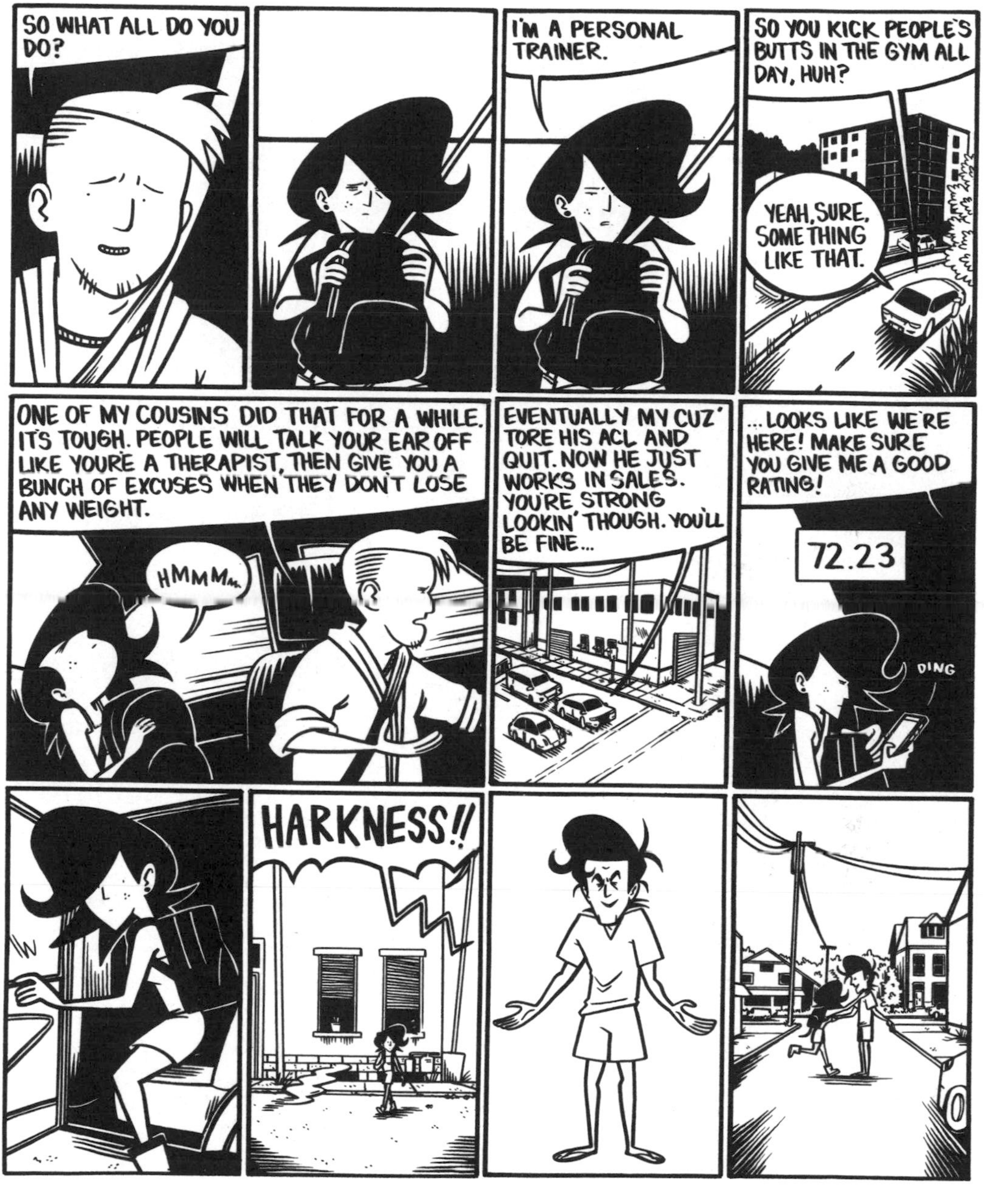
SO WHAT ALL DO YOU DO?
I'M A PERSONAL TRAINER.
SO YOU KICK PEOPLE'S BUTTS IN THE GYM ALL DAY, HUH?
YEAH, SURE, SOMETHING LIKE THAT.
ONE OF MY COUSINS DID THAT FOR A WHILE. IT'S TOUGH. PEOPLE WILL TALK YOUR EAR OFF LIKE YOU'RE A THERAPIST, THEN GIVE YOU A BUNCH OF EXCUSES WHEN THEY DON'T LOSE ANY WEIGHT.
HMMMm
EVENTUALLY MY CUZ' TORE HIS ACL AND QUIT. NOW HE JUST WORKS IN SALES. YOU'RE STRONG LOOKIN' THOUGH. YOU'LL BE FINE...
...LOOKS LIKE WE'RE HERE! MAKE SURE YOU GIVE ME A GOOD RATING!
72.23
DING
HARKNESS!!

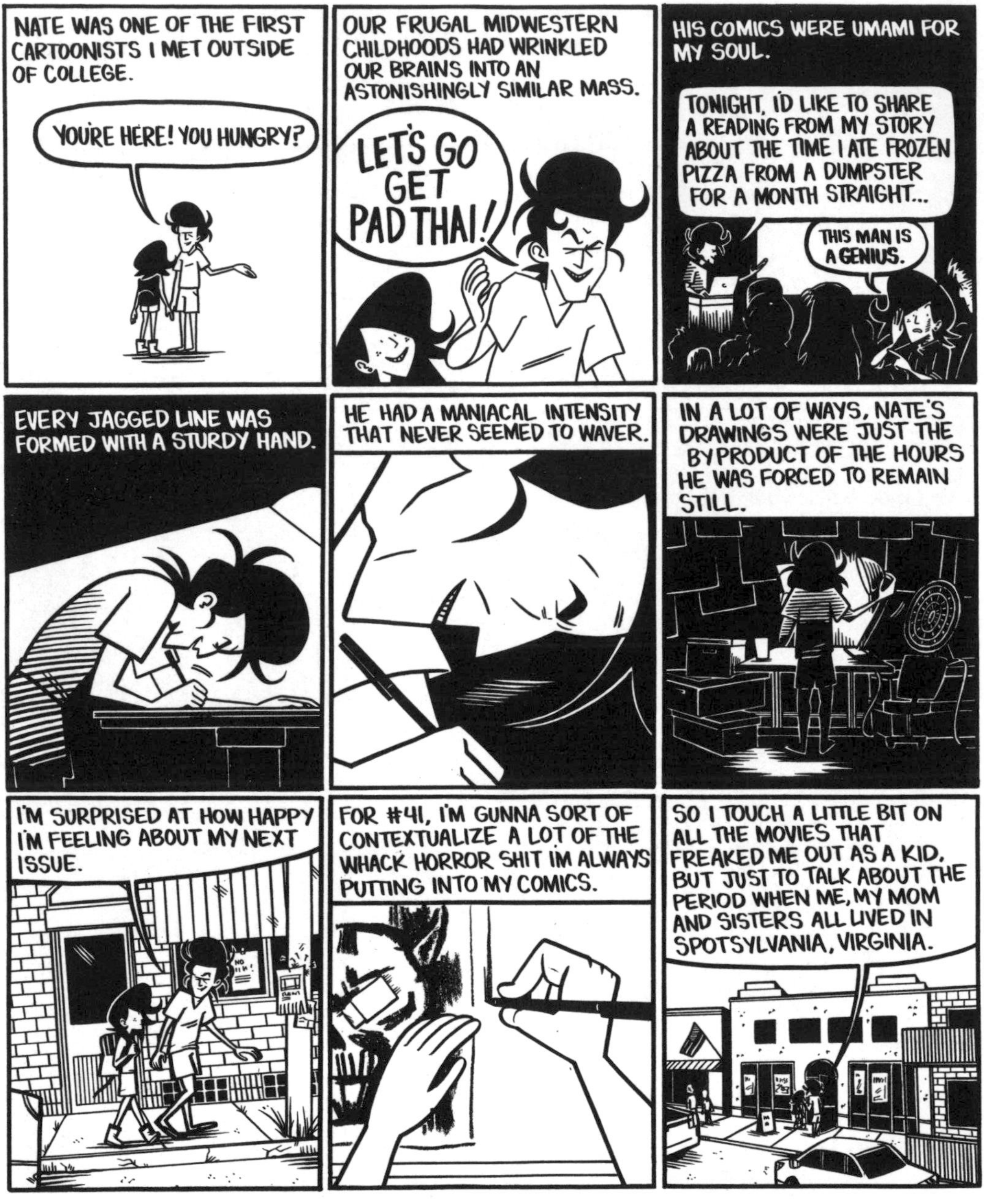
NATE WAS ONE OF THE FIRST CARTOONISTS I MET OUTSIDE OF COLLEGE.
YOU'RE HERE! YOU HUNGRY?
OUR FRUGAL MIDWESTERN CHILDHOODS HAD WRINKLED OUR BRAINS INTO AN ASTONISHINGLY SIMILAR MASS.
LET'S GO GET PAD THAI!
HIS COMICS WERE UMAMI FOR MY SOUL.
TONIGHT, I'D LIKE TO SHARE A READING FROM MY STORY ABOUT THE TIME I ATE FROZEN PIZZA FROM A DUMPSTER FOR A MONTH STRAIGHT...
THIS MAN IS A GENIUS.
EVERY JAGGED LINE WAS FORMED WITH A STURDY HAND.
HE HAD A MANIACAL INTENSITY THAT NEVER SEEMED TO WAVER.
IN A LOT OF WAYS, NATE'S DRAWINGS WERE JUST THE BYPRODUCT OF THE HOURS HE WAS FORCED TO REMAIN STILL.
I'M SURPRISED AT HOW HAPPY I'M FEELING ABOUT MY NEXT ISSUE.
FOR #41, I'M GUNNA SORT OF CONTEXTUALIZE A LOT OF THE WHACK HORROR SHIT I'M ALWAYS PUTTING INTO MY COMICS.
SO I TOUCH A LITTLE BIT ON ALL THE MOVIES THAT FREAKED ME OUT AS A KID, BUT JUST TO TALK ABOUT THE PERIOD WHEN ME, MY MOM AND SISTERS ALL LIVED IN SPOTSYLVANIA, VIRGINIA.

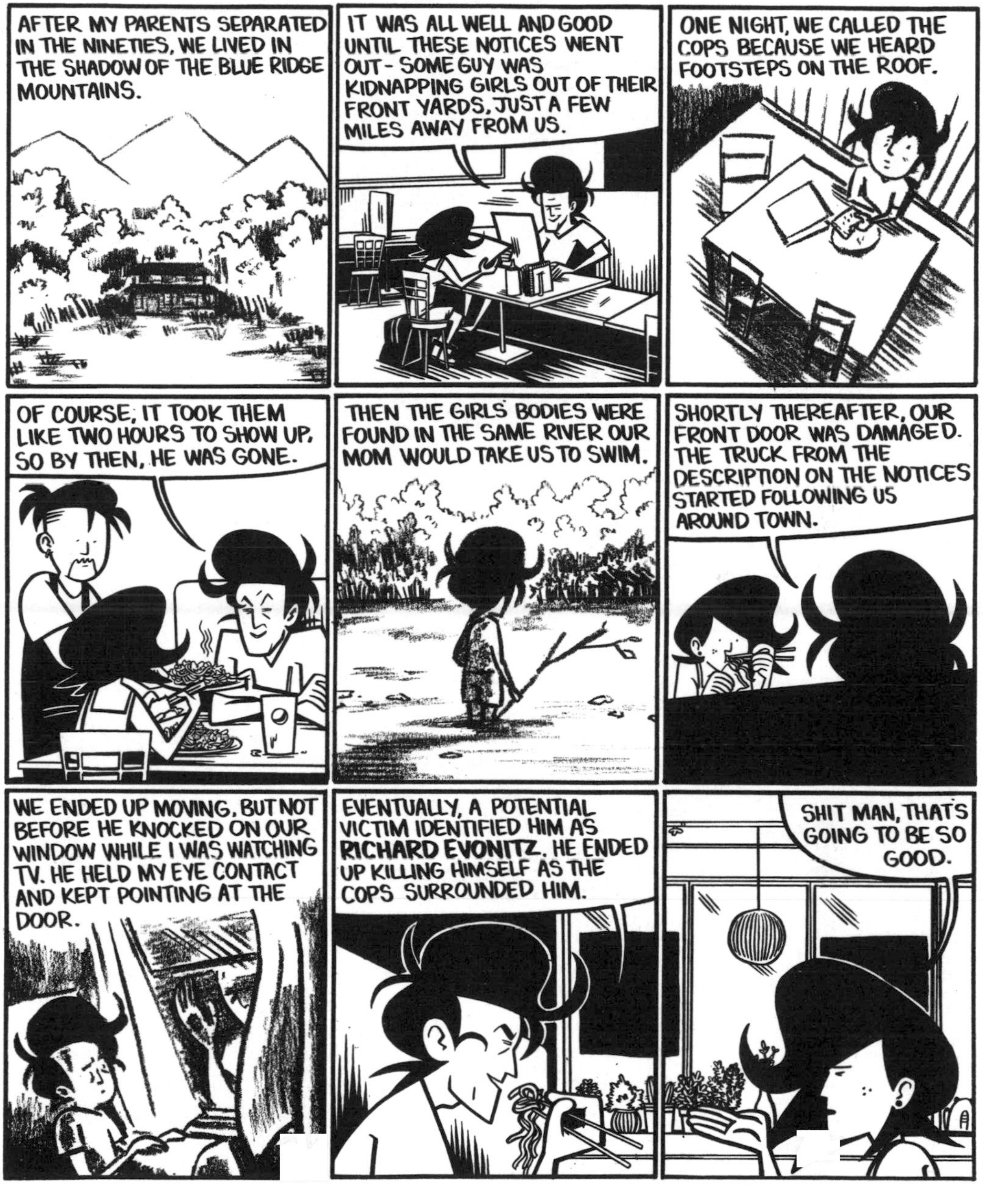
AFTER MY PARENTS SEPARATED IN THE NINETIES, WE LIVED IN THE SHADOW OF THE BLUE RIDGE MOUNTAINS.
IT WAS ALL WELL AND GOOD UNTIL THESE NOTICES WENT OUT - SOME GUY WAS KIDNAPPING GIRLS OUT OF THEIR FRONT YARDS, JUST A FEW MILES AWAY FROM US.
ONE NIGHT, WE CALLED THE COPS BECAUSE WE HEARD FOOTSTEPS ON THE ROOF.
OF COURSE, IT TOOK THEM LIKE TWO HOURS TO SHOW UP, SO BY THEN, HE WAS GONE.
THEN THE GIRLS' BODIES WERE FOUND IN THE SAME RIVER OUR MOM WOULD TAKE US TO SWIM.
SHORTLY THEREAFTER, OUR FRONT DOOR WAS DAMAGED. THE TRUCK FROM THE DESCRIPTION ON THE NOTICES STARTED FOLLOWING US AROUND TOWN.
WE ENDED UP MOVING, BUT NOT BEFORE HE KNOCKED ON OUR WINDOW WHILE I WAS WATCHING TV. HE HELD MY EYE CONTACT AND KEPT POINTING AT THE DOOR.
EVENTUALLY, A POTENTIAL VICTIM IDENTIFIED HIM AS RICHARD EVONITZ. HE ENDED UP KILLING HIMSELF AS THE COPS SURROUNDED HIM.
SHIT MAN, THAT'S GOING TO BE SO GOOD.

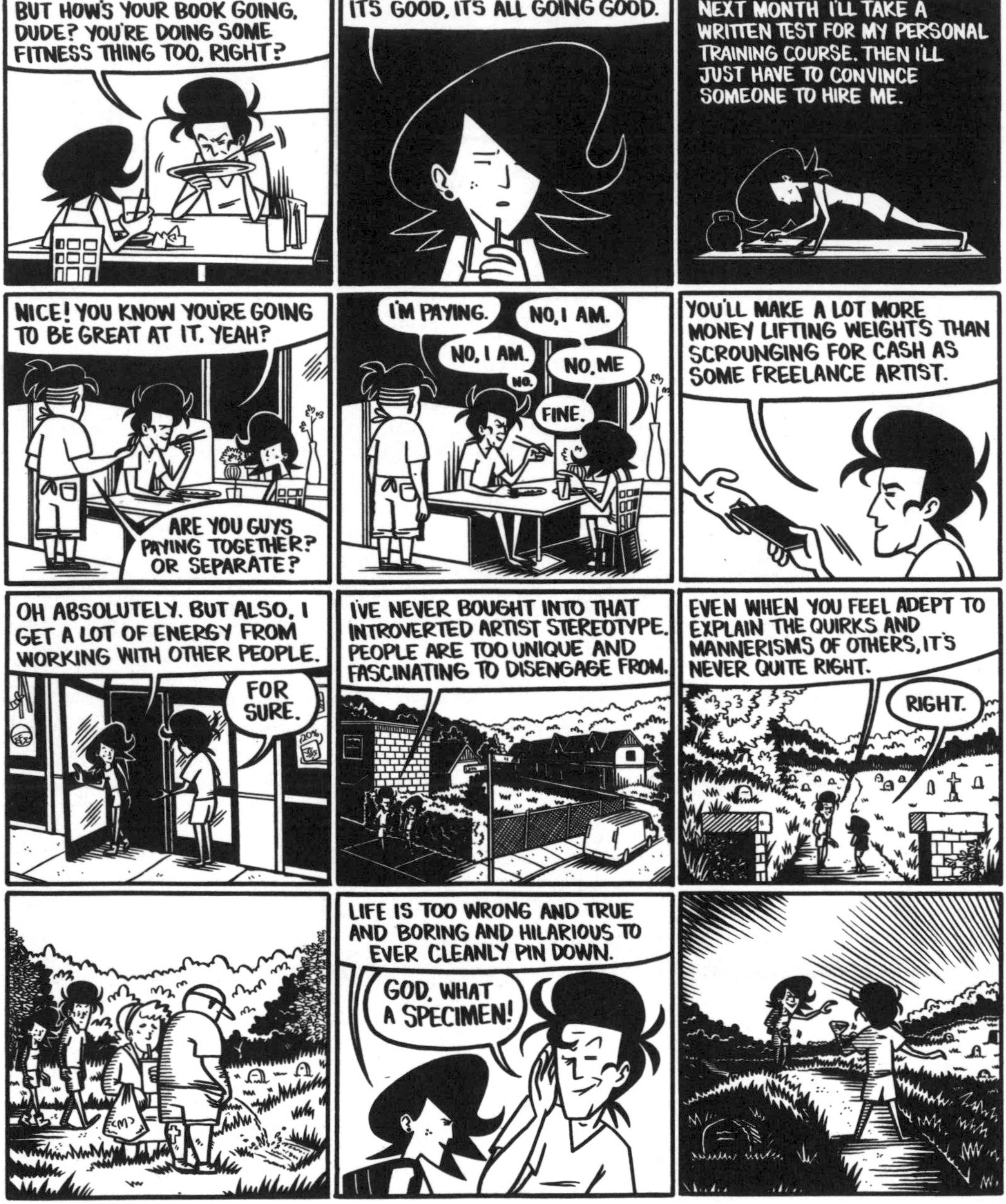
BUT HOW'S YOUR BOOK GOING, DUDE? YOU'RE DOING SOME FITNESS THING TOO, RIGHT?
IT'S GOOD, IT'S ALL GOING GOOD.
NEXT MONTH I'LL TAKE A WRITTEN TEST FOR MY PERSONAL TRAINING COURSE. THEN I'LL JUST HAVE TO CONVINCE SOMEONE TO HIRE ME.
NICE! YOU KNOW YOU'RE GOING TO BE GREAT AT IT, YEAH?
ARE YOU GUYS PAYING TOGETHER? OR SEPARATE?
I'M PAYING.
NO, I AM.
NO, I AM.
NO.
NO, ME
FINE.
YOU'LL MAKE A LOT MORE MONEY LIFTING WEIGHTS THAN SCROUNGING FOR CASH AS SOME FREELANCE ARTIST.
OH ABSOLUTELY. BUT ALSO, I GET A LOT OF ENERGY FROM WORKING WITH OTHER PEOPLE.
FOR SURE.
I'VE NEVER BOUGHT INTO THAT INTROVERTED ARTIST STEREOTYPE. PEOPLE ARE TOO UNIQUE AND FASCINATING TO DISENGAGE FROM.
EVEN WHEN YOU FEEL ADEPT TO EXPLAIN THE QUIRKS AND MANNERISMS OF OTHERS, IT'S NEVER QUITE RIGHT.
RIGHT.
LIFE IS TOO WRONG AND TRUE AND BORING AND HILARIOUS TO EVER CLEANLY PIN DOWN.
GOD, WHAT A SPECIMEN!

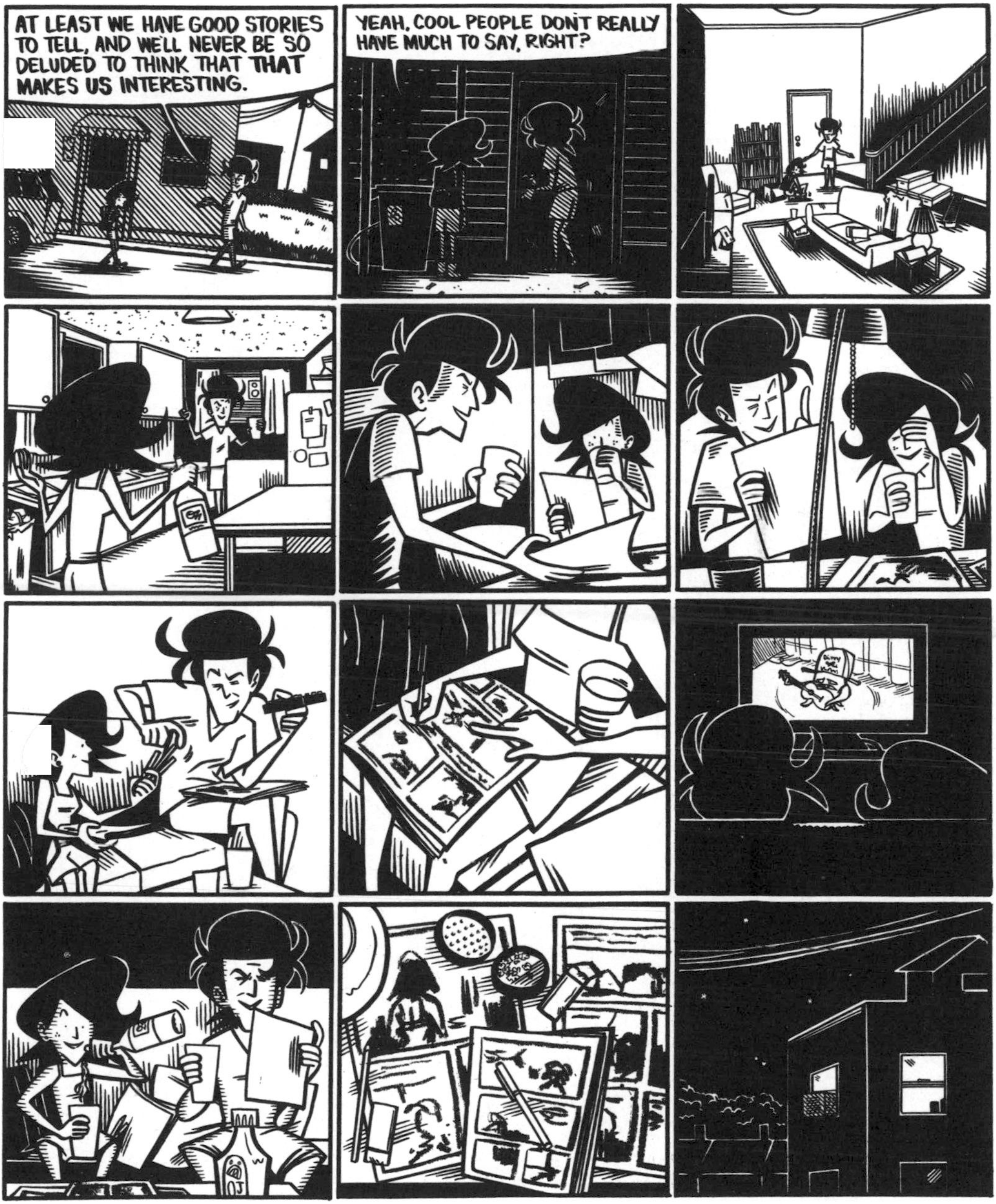
AT LEAST WE HAVE GOOD STORIES TO TELL, AND WE'LL NEVER BE SO DELUDED TO THINK THAT THAT MAKES US INTERESTING.
YEAH, COOL PEOPLE DON'T REALLY HAVE MUCH TO SAY, RIGHT?

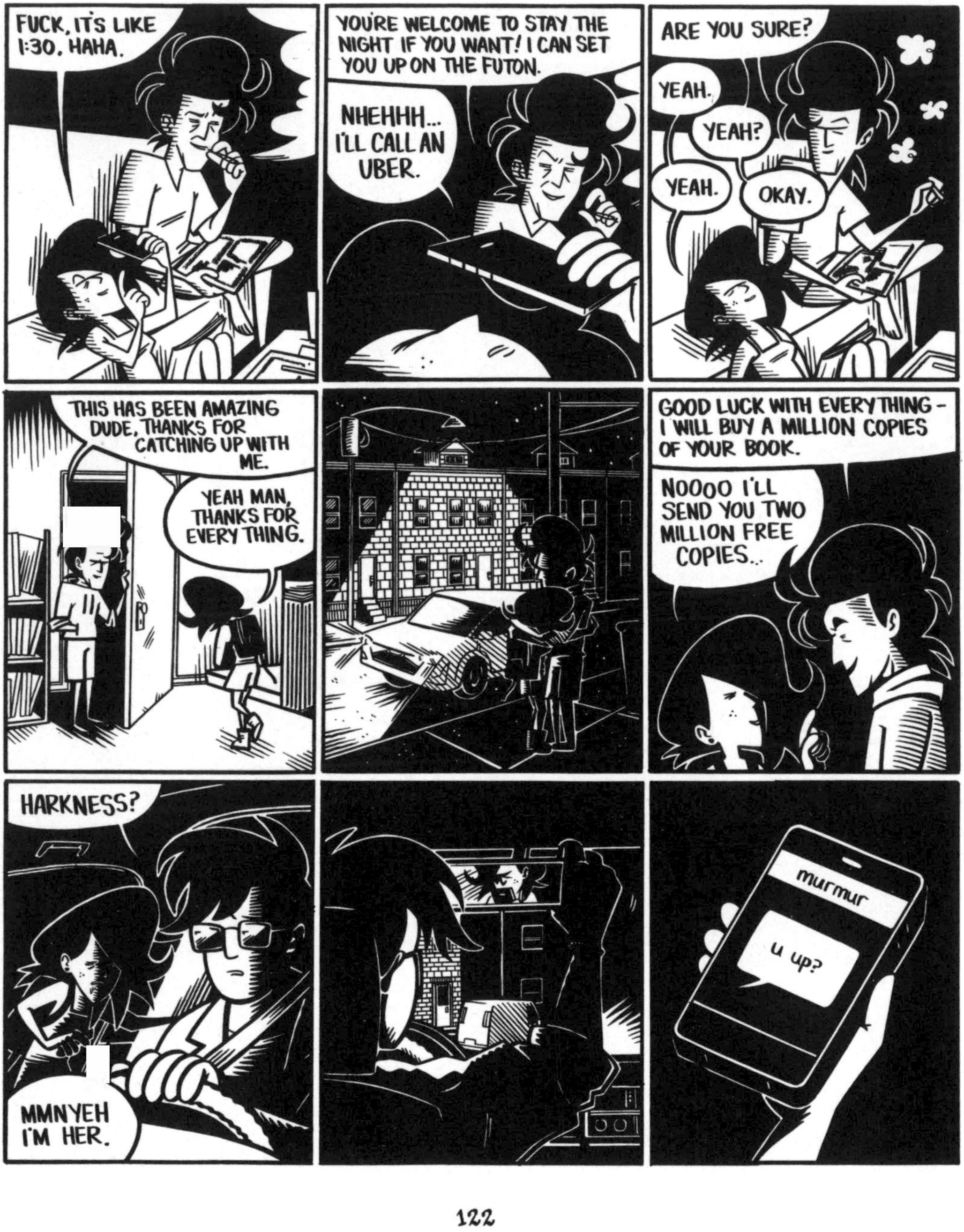
FUCK, IT'S LIKE 1:30, HAHA.
YOU'RE WELCOME TO STAY THE NIGHT IF YOU WANT! I CAN SET YOU UP ON THE FUTON.
NHEHHH... I'LL CALL AN UBER.
ARE YOU SURE?
YEAH.
YEAH?
YEAH.
OKAY.
THIS HAS BEEN AMAZING DUDE, THANKS FOR CATCHING UP WITH ME.
YEAH MAN, THANKS FOR EVERY THING.
GOOD LUCK WITH EVERYTHING - I WILL BUY A MILLION COPIES OF YOUR BOOK.
NOOOO I'LL SEND YOU TWO MILLION FREE COPIES...
HARKNESS?
MMNYEH I'M HER.
murmur
u up?

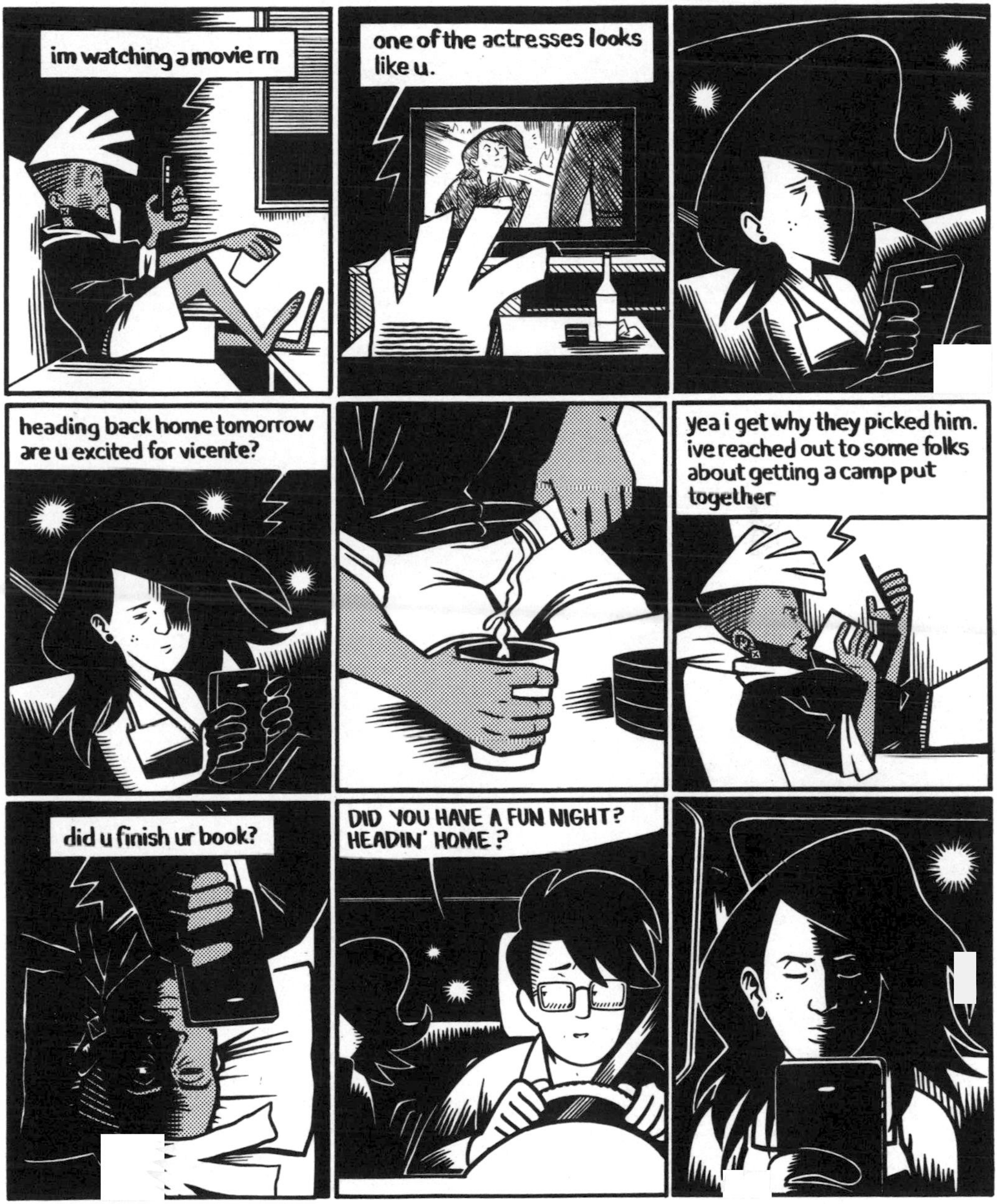
im watching a movie rn
one of the actresses looks like u.
heading back home tomorrow are u excited for vicente?
yea i get why they picked him. ive reached out to some folks about getting a camp put together
did u finish ur book?
DID YOU HAVE A FUN NIGHT? HEADIN' HOME?

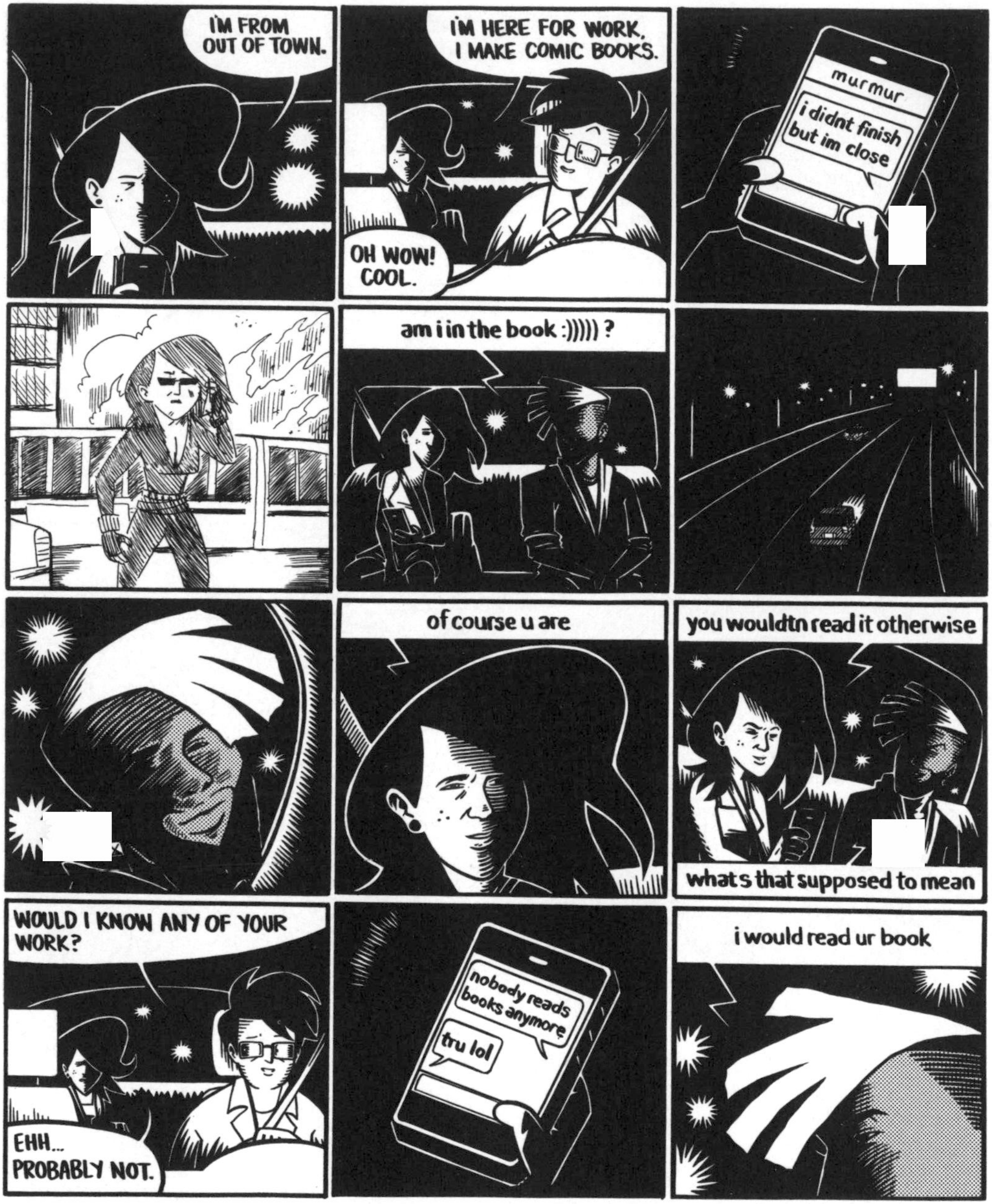
I'M FROM OUT OF TOWN.
I'M HERE FOR WORK. I MAKE COMIC BOOKS.
OH WOW! COOL.
murmur
i didnt finish but im close
am i in the book :))))) ?
of course u are
you wouldtn read it otherwise
whats that supposed to mean
WOULD I KNOW ANY OF YOUR WORK?
EHH... PROBABLY NOT.
nobody reads books anymore
tru lol
i would read ur book

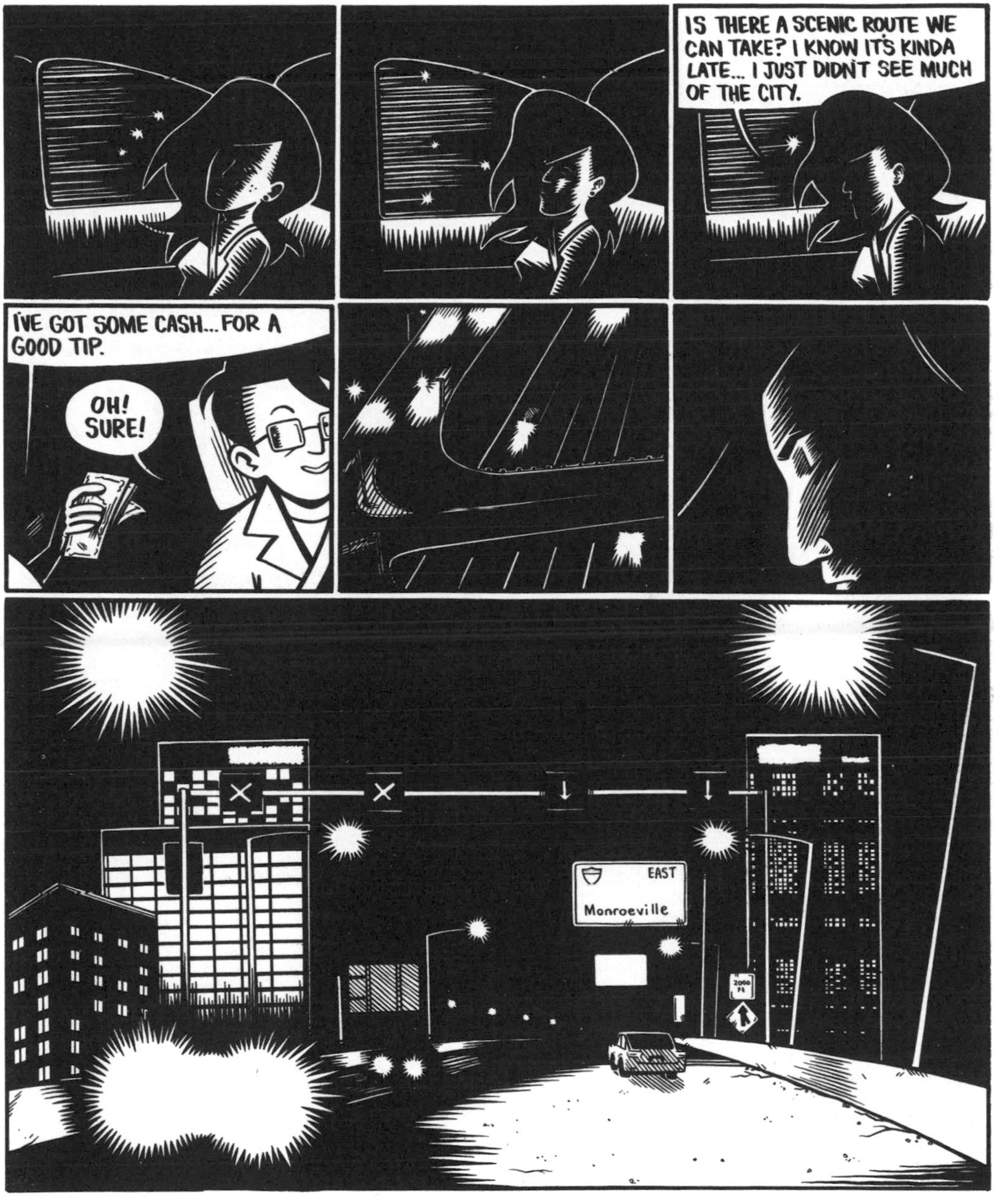
IS THERE A SCENIC ROUTE WE CAN TAKE? I KNOW IT'S KINDA LATE... I JUST DIDN'T SEE MUCH OF THE CITY.
I'VE GOT SOME CASH... FOR A GOOD TIP.
OH! SURE!
EAST
Monroeville

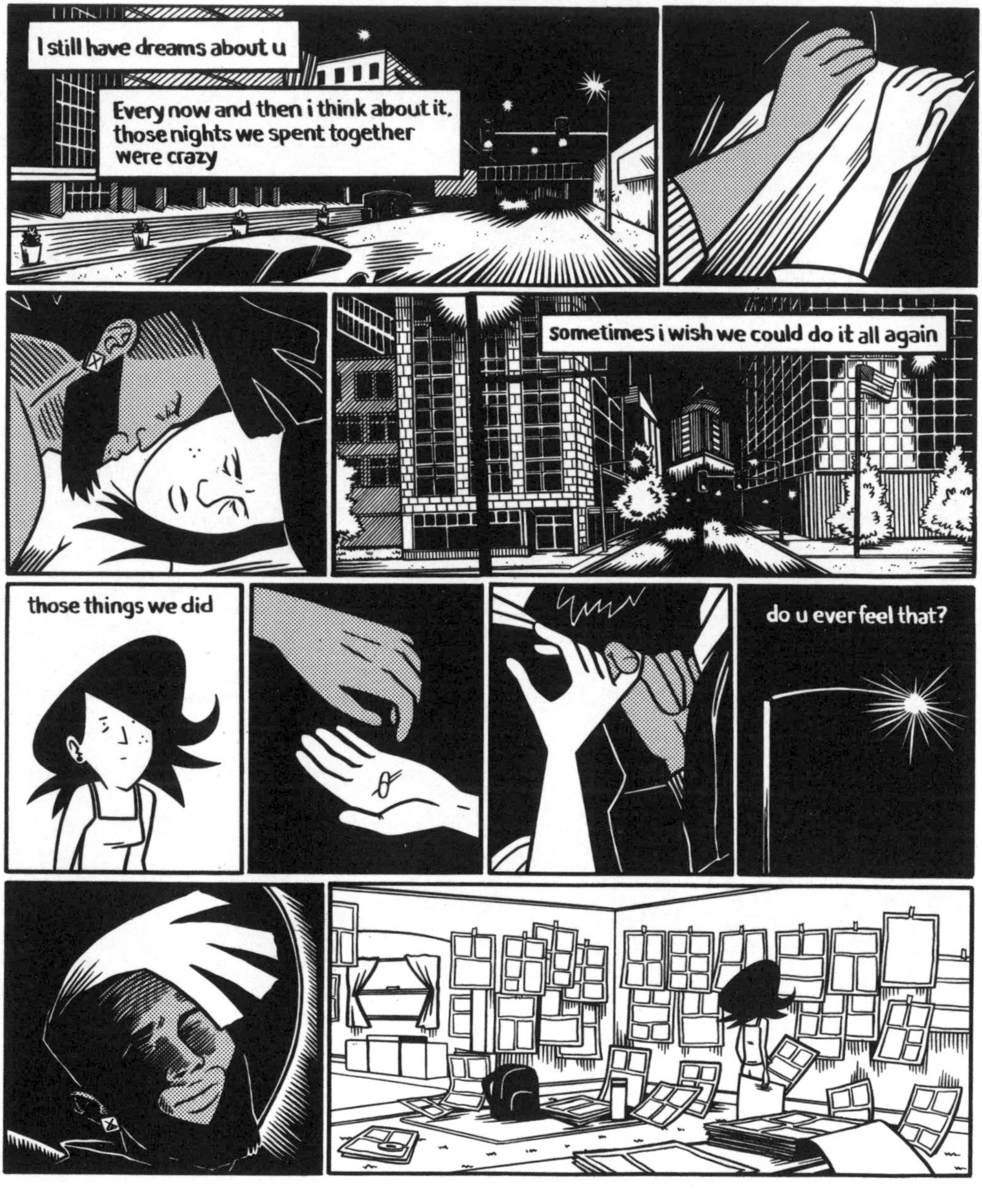
I still have dreams about u
Every now and then i think about it. those nights we spent together were crazy
sometimes i wish we could do it all again
those things we did
do u ever feel that?

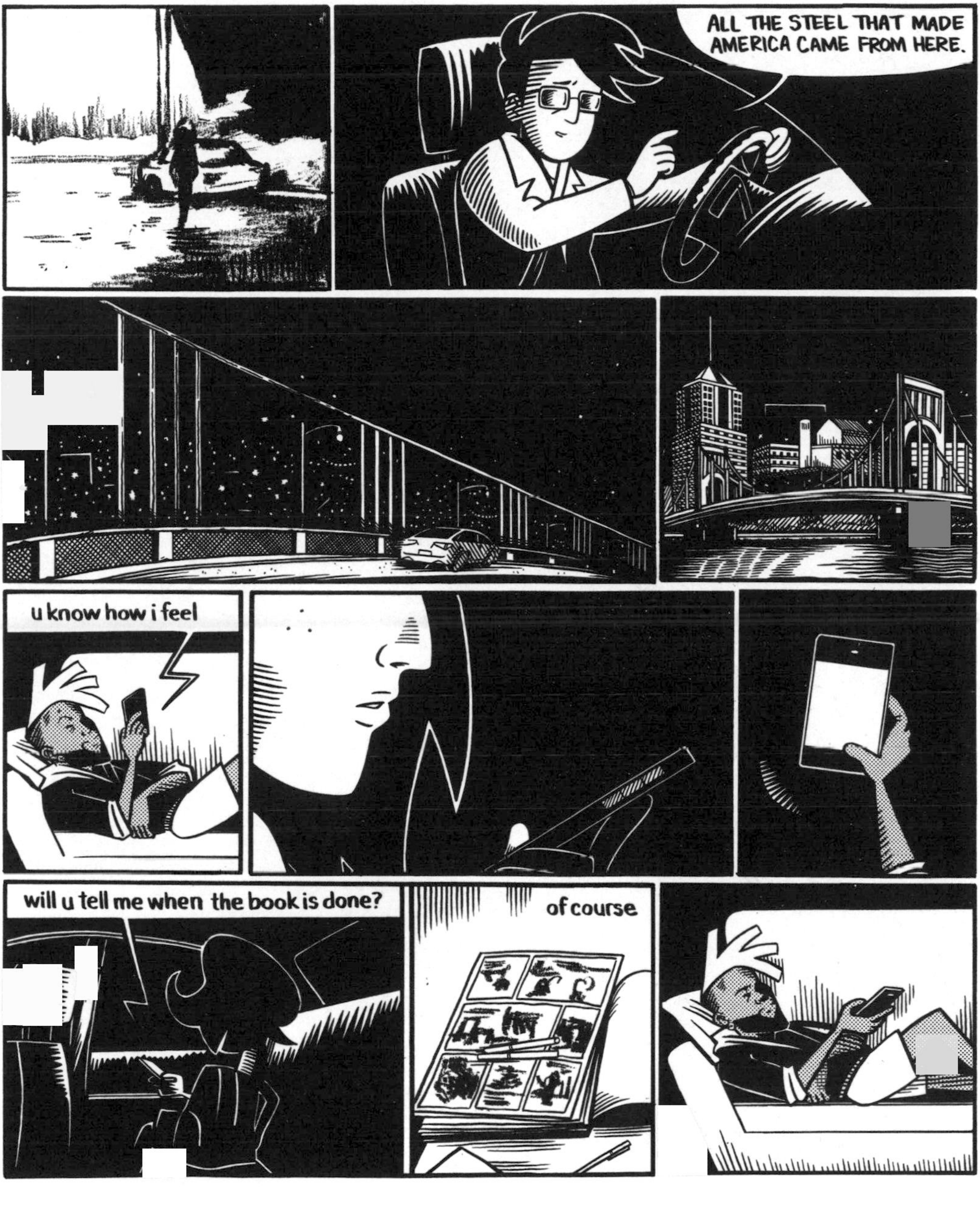
ALL THE STEEL THAT MADE AMERICA CAME FROM HERE.
u know how i feel
will u tell me when the book is done?
of course

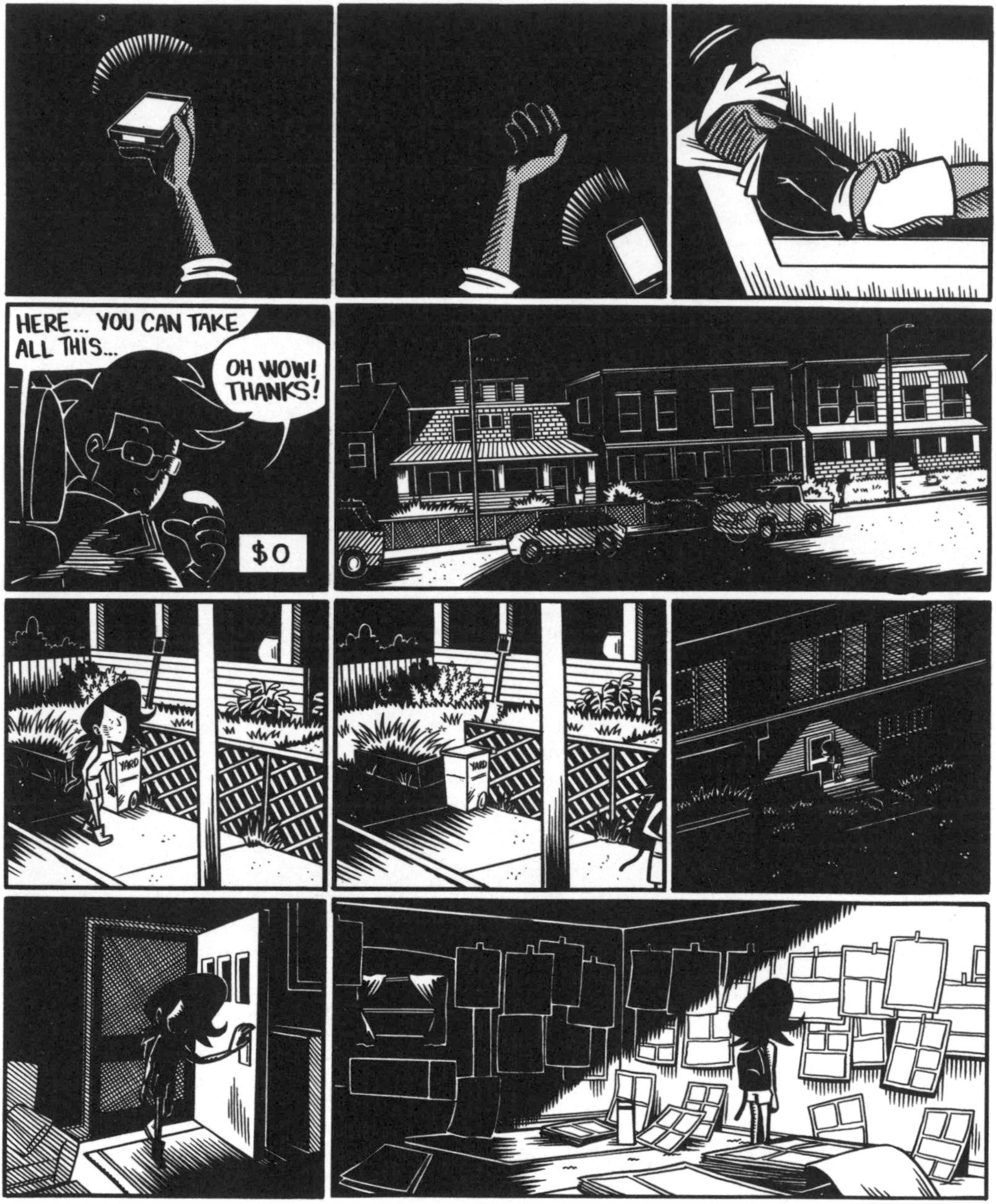
HERE... YOU CAN TAKE ALL THIS...
OH WOW! THANKS!
$0
YARD
YARD

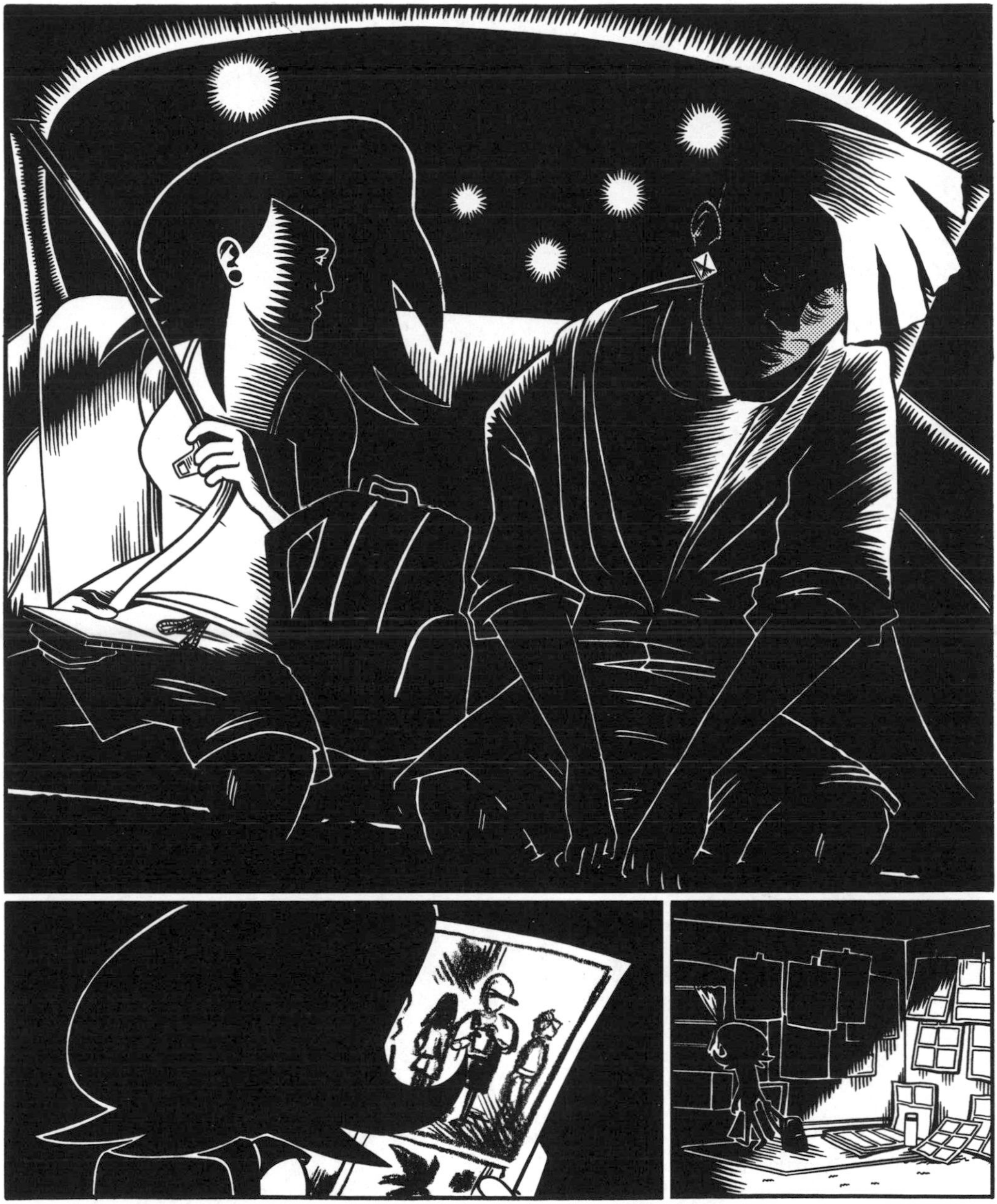

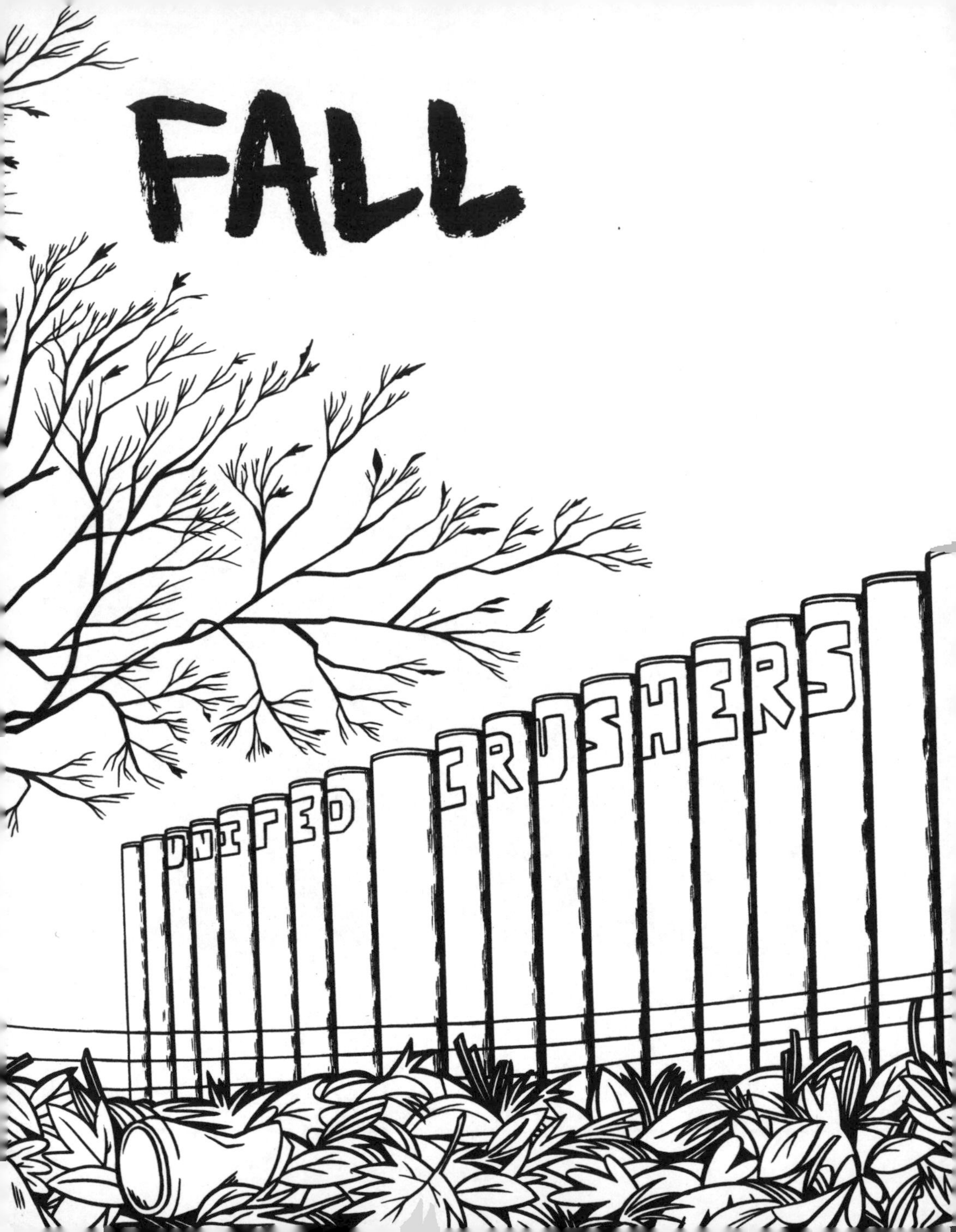
FALL
UNITED
CRUSHERS

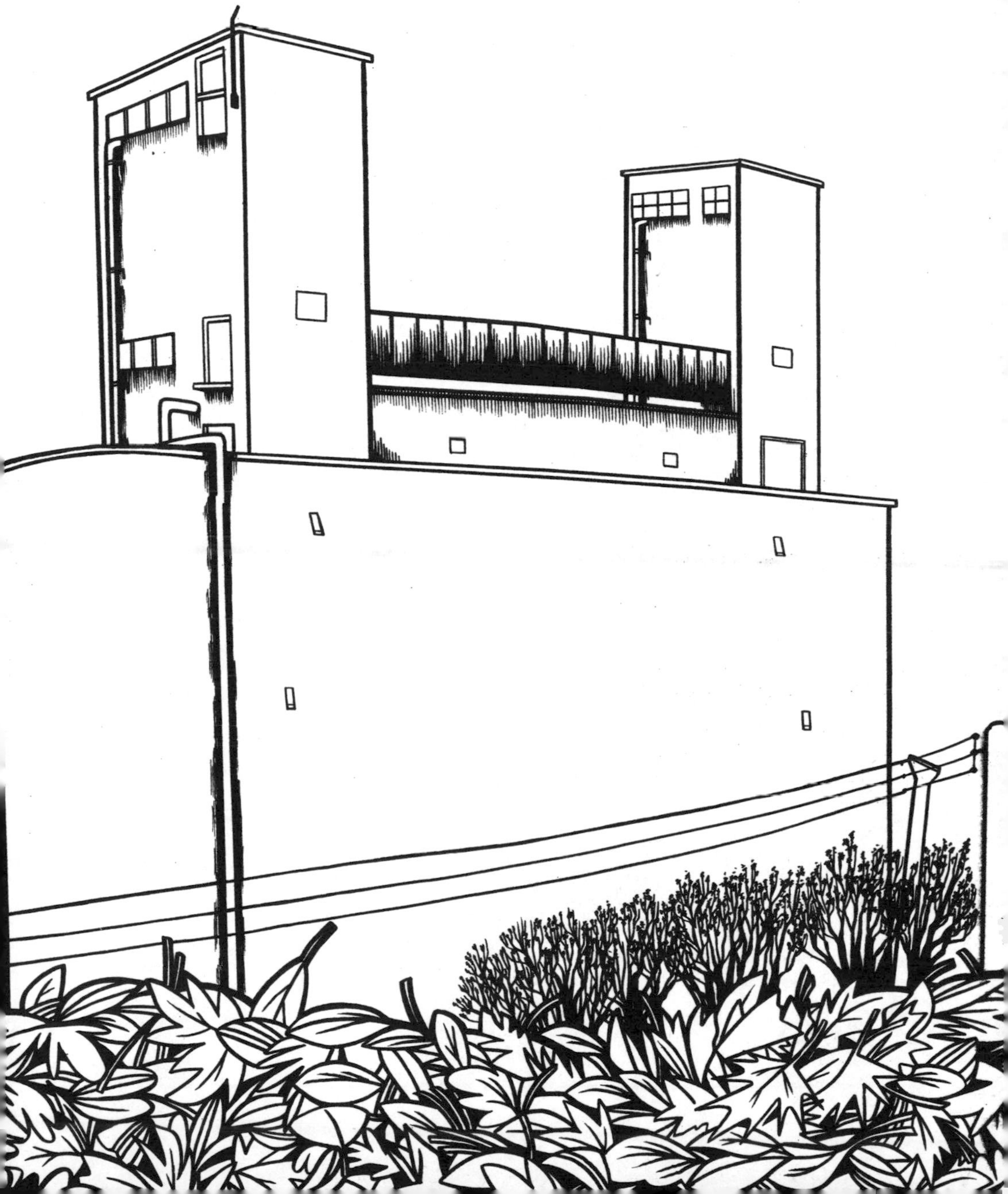

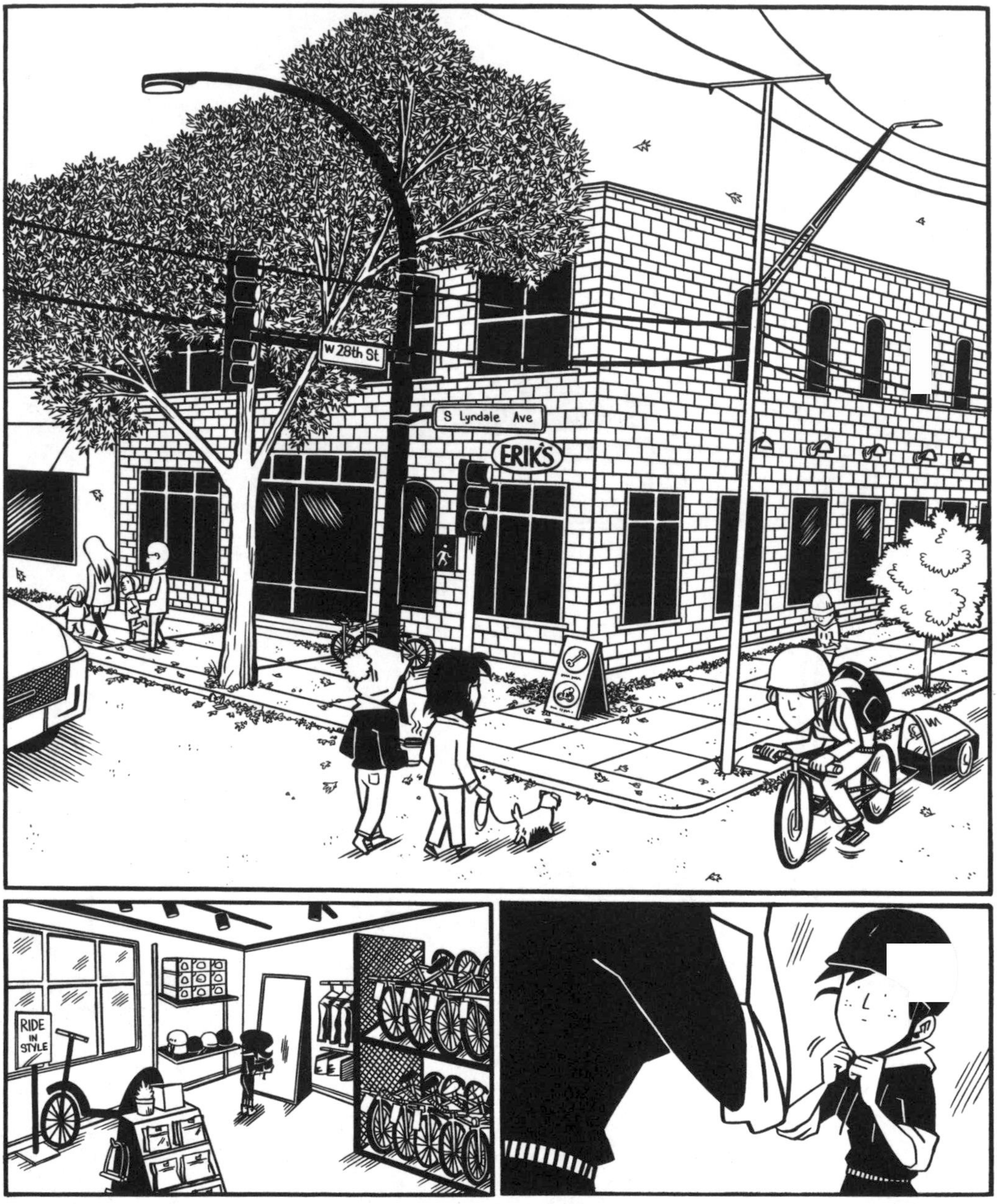
W 28th St
S Lyndale Ave
ERIK'S
RIDE IN STYLE

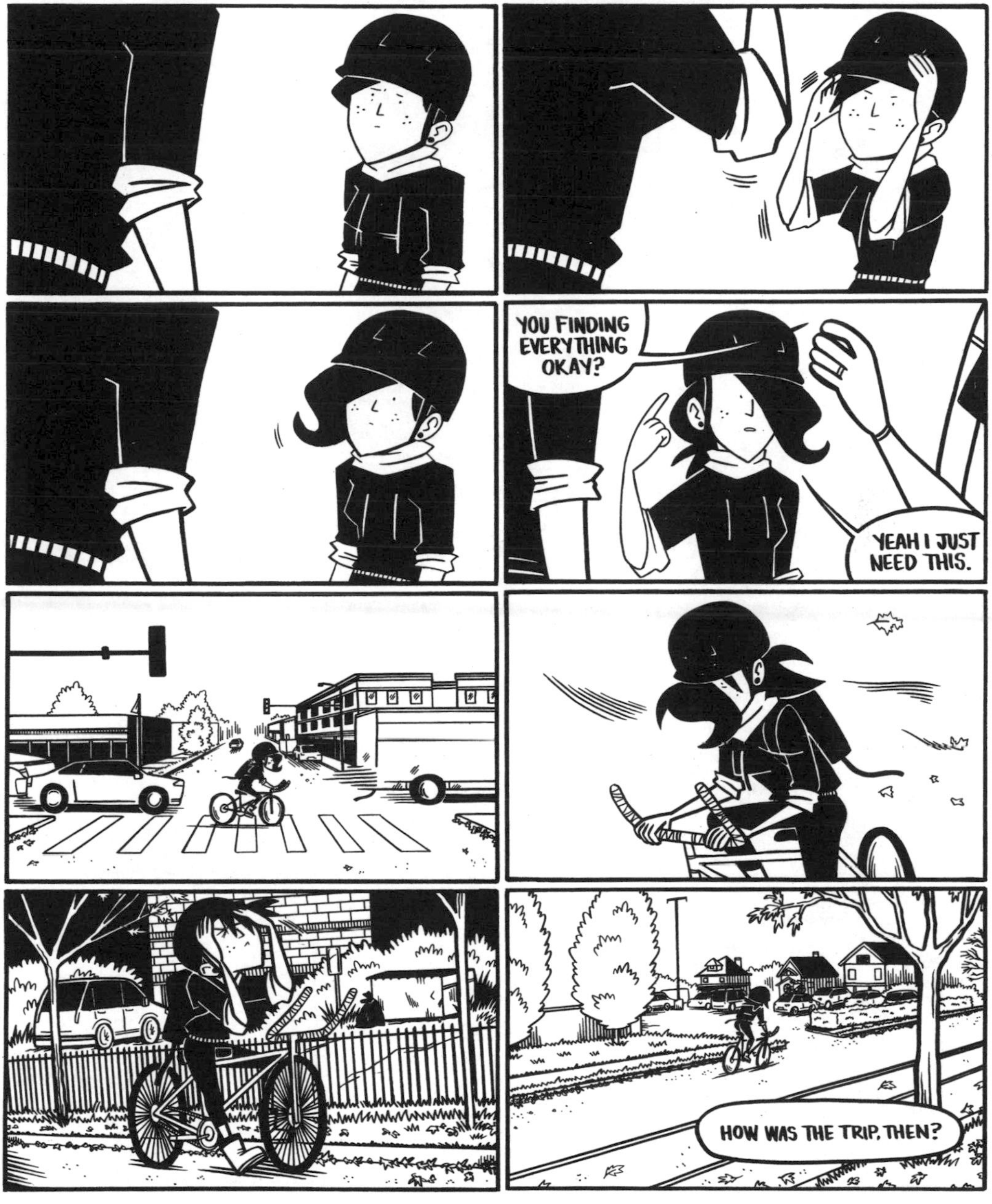
YOU FINDING EVERYTHING OKAY?
YEAH I JUST NEED THIS.
HOW WAS THE TRIP, THEN?

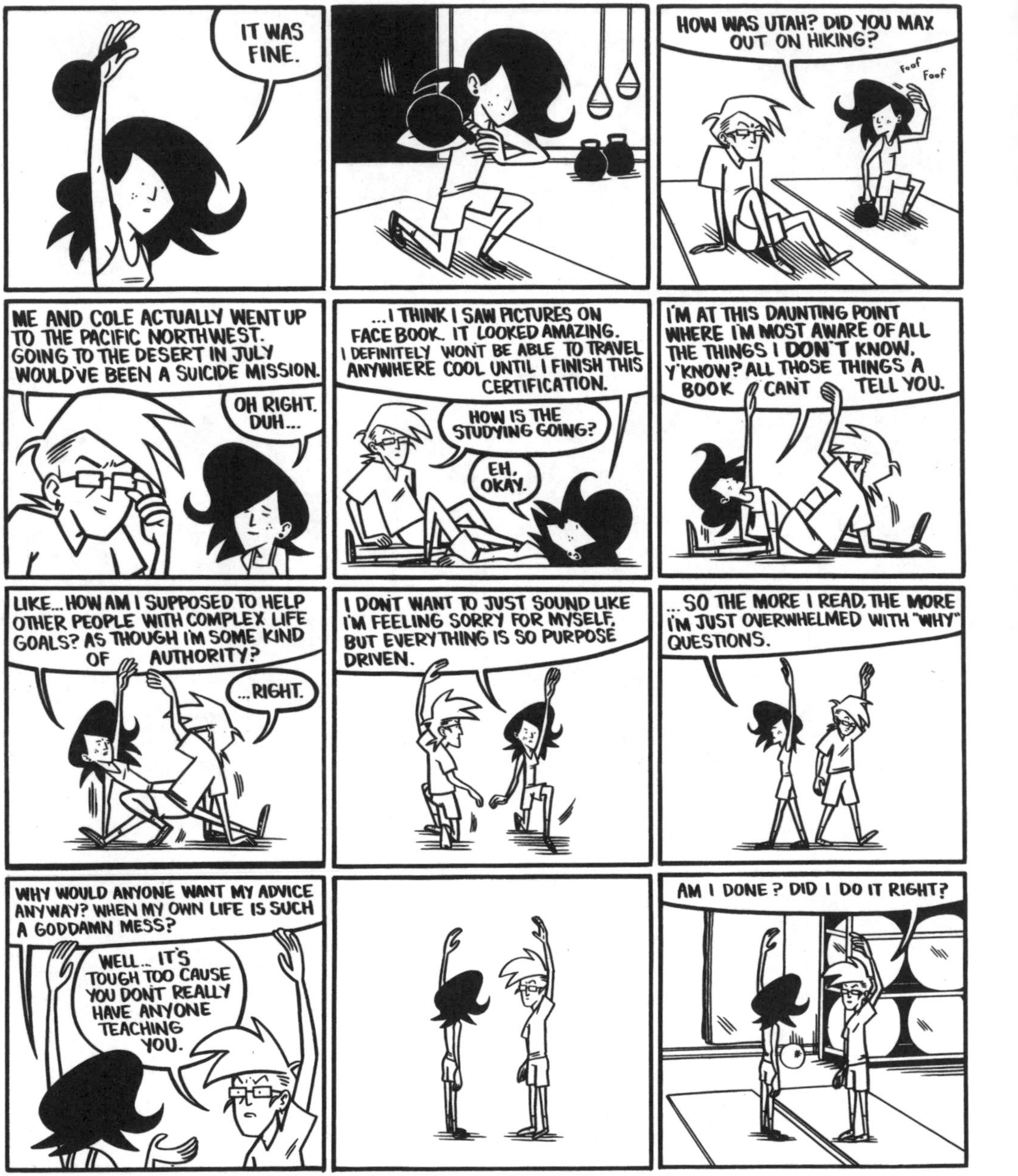
IT WAS FINE.
HOW WAS UTAH? DID YOU MAX OUT ON HIKING?
Foof Foof
ME AND COLE ACTUALLY WENT UP TO THE PACIFIC NORTHWEST. GOING TO THE DESERT IN JULY WOULD'VE BEEN A SUICIDE MISSION.
OH RIGHT. DUH...
...I THINK I SAW PICTURES ON FACEBOOK. IT LOOKED AMAZING.
I DEFINITELY WON'T BE ABLE TO TRAVEL ANYWHERE COOL UNTIL I FINISH THIS CERTIFICATION.
HOW IS THE STUDYING GOING?
EH, OKAY.
I'M AT THIS DAUNTING POINT WHERE I'M MOST AWARE OF ALL THE THINGS I DON'T KNOW, Y'KNOW? ALL THOSE THINGS A BOOK CAN'T TELL YOU.
LIKE... HOW AM I SUPPOSED TO HELP OTHER PEOPLE WITH COMPLEX LIFE GOALS? AS THOUGH I'M SOME KIND OF AUTHORITY?
...RIGHT.
I DON'T WANT TO JUST SOUND LIKE I'M FEELING SORRY FOR MYSELF, BUT EVERYTHING IS SO PURPOSE DRIVEN.
...SO THE MORE I READ, THE MORE I'M JUST OVERWHELMED WITH "WHY" QUESTIONS.
WHY WOULD ANYONE WANT MY ADVICE ANYWAY? WHEN MY OWN LIFE IS SUCH A GODDAMN MESS?
WELL... IT'S TOUGH TOO CAUSE YOU DON'T REALLY HAVE ANYONE TEACHING YOU.
AM I DONE? DID I DO IT RIGHT?

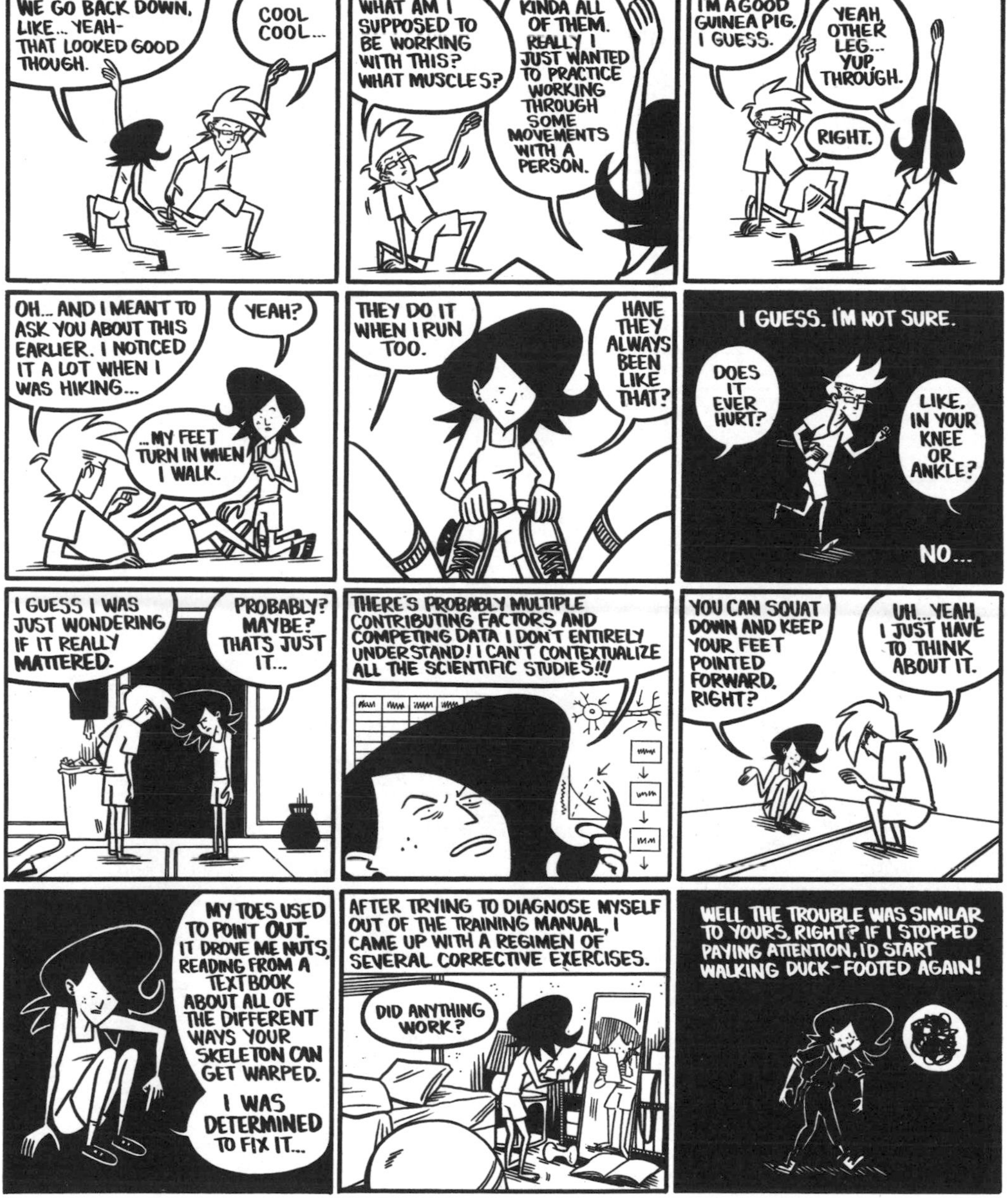
WE GO BACK DOWN, LIKE... YEAH- THAT LOOKED GOOD THOUGH.
COOL COOL...
WHAT AM I SUPPOSED TO BE WORKING WITH THIS? WHAT MUSCLES?
KINDA ALL OF THEM. REALLY I JUST WANTED TO PRACTICE WORKING THROUGH SOME MOVEMENTS WITH A PERSON.
I'M A GOOD GUINEA PIG, I GUESS.
YEAH, OTHER LEG... YUP, THROUGH.
RIGHT.
OH... AND I MEANT TO ASK YOU ABOUT THIS EARLIER. I NOTICED IT A LOT WHEN I WAS HIKING...
YEAH?
...MY FEET TURN IN WHEN I WALK.
THEY DO IT WHEN I RUN TOO.
HAVE THEY ALWAYS BEEN LIKE THAT?
I GUESS. I'M NOT SURE.
DOES IT EVER HURT?
LIKE, IN YOUR KNEE OR ANKLE?
NO...
I GUESS I WAS JUST WONDERING IF IT REALLY MATTERED.
PROBABLY? MAYBE? THAT'S JUST IT...
THERE'S PROBABLY MULTIPLE CONTRIBUTING FACTORS AND COMPETING DATA I DON'T ENTIRELY UNDERSTAND! I CAN'T CONTEXTUALIZE ALL THE SCIENTIFIC STUDIES!!!
YOU CAN SQUAT DOWN AND KEEP YOUR FEET POINTED FORWARD, RIGHT?
UH... YEAH, I JUST HAVE TO THINK ABOUT IT.
MY TOES USED TO POINT OUT. IT DROVE ME NUTS, READING FROM A TEXTBOOK ABOUT ALL OF THE DIFFERENT WAYS YOUR SKELETON CAN GET WARPED.
I WAS DETERMINED TO FIX IT...
AFTER TRYING TO DIAGNOSE MYSELF OUT OF THE TRAINING MANUAL, I CAME UP WITH A REGIMEN OF SEVERAL CORRECTIVE EXERCISES.
DID ANYTHING WORK?
WELL THE TROUBLE WAS SIMILAR TO YOURS, RIGHT? IF I STOPPED PAYING ATTENTION, I'D START WALKING DUCK-FOOTED AGAIN!

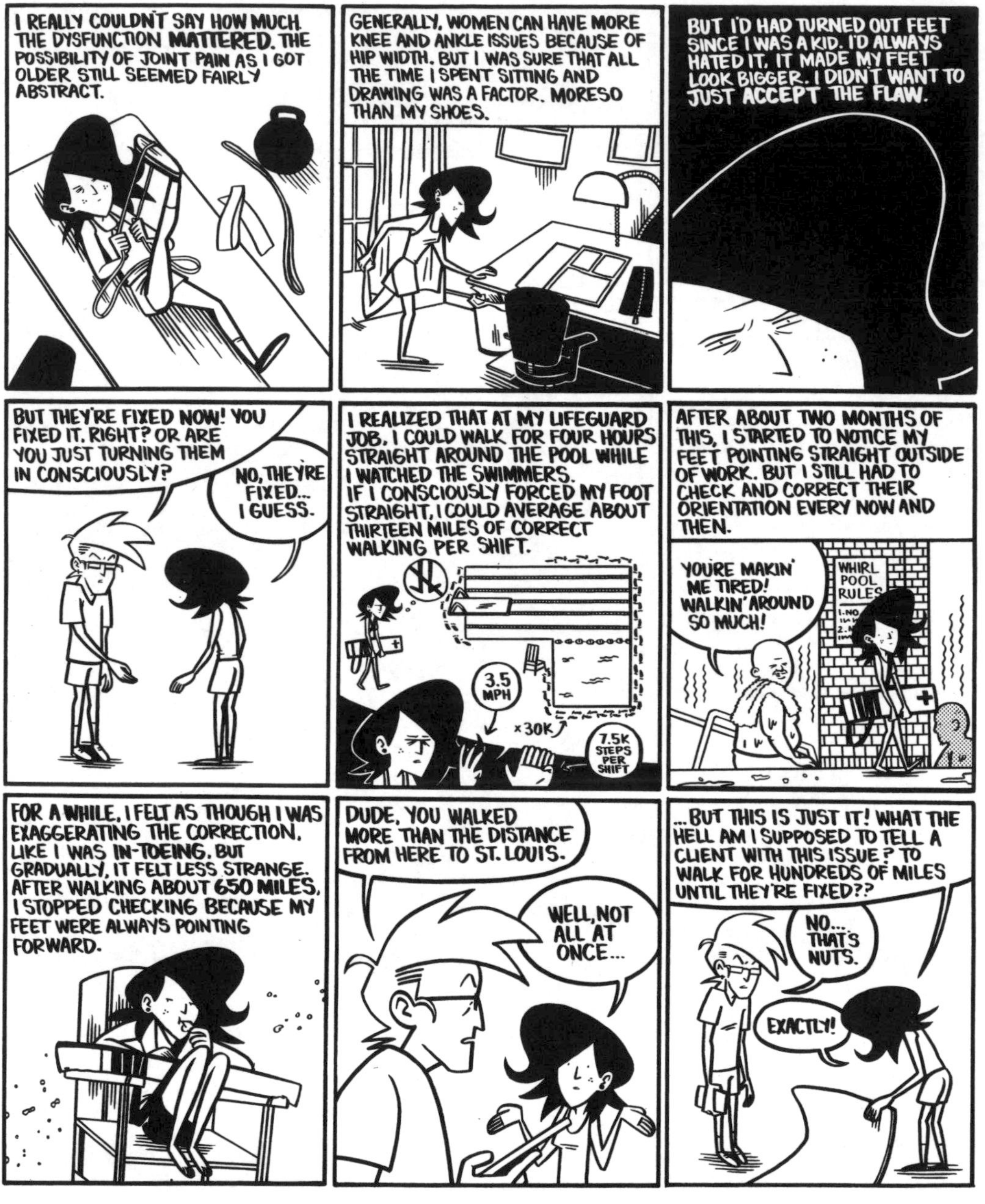
I REALLY COULDN'T SAY HOW MUCH THE DYSFUNCTION MATTERED. THE POSSIBILITY OF JOINT PAIN AS I GOT OLDER STILL SEEMED FAIRLY ABSTRACT.
GENERALLY, WOMEN CAN HAVE MORE KNEE AND ANKLE ISSUES BECAUSE OF HIP WIDTH. BUT I WAS SURE THAT ALL THE TIME I SPENT SITTING AND DRAWING WAS A FACTOR. MORESO THAN MY SHOES.
BUT I'D HAD TURNED OUT FEET SINCE I WAS A KID. I'D ALWAYS HATED IT. IT MADE MY FEET LOOK BIGGER. I DIDN'T WANT TO JUST ACCEPT THE FLAW.
BUT THEY'RE FIXED NOW! YOU FIXED IT, RIGHT? OR ARE YOU JUST TURNING THEM IN CONSCIOUSLY?
NO, THEY'RE FIXED... I GUESS.
I REALIZED THAT AT MY LIFEGUARD JOB, I COULD WALK FOR FOUR HOURS STRAIGHT AROUND THE POOL WHILE I WATCHED THE SWIMMERS.
IF I CONSCIOUSLY FORCED MY FOOT STRAIGHT, I COULD AVERAGE ABOUT THIRTEEN MILES OF CORRECT WALKING PER SHIFT.
3.5 MPH
×30K
7.5K STEPS PER SHIFT
AFTER ABOUT TWO MONTHS OF THIS, I STARTED TO NOTICE MY FEET POINTING STRAIGHT OUTSIDE OF WORK. BUT I STILL HAD TO CHECK AND CORRECT THEIR ORIENTATION EVERY NOW AND THEN.
YOU'RE MAKIN' ME TIRED! WALKIN' AROUND SO MUCH!
WHIRL POOL RULES
FOR A WHILE, I FELT AS THOUGH I WAS EXAGGERATING THE CORRECTION. LIKE I WAS IN-TOEING. BUT GRADUALLY, IT FELT LESS STRANGE. AFTER WALKING ABOUT 650 MILES, I STOPPED CHECKING BECAUSE MY FEET WERE ALWAYS POINTING FORWARD.
DUDE, YOU WALKED MORE THAN THE DISTANCE FROM HERE TO ST. LOUIS.
WELL, NOT ALL AT ONCE...
...BUT THIS IS JUST IT! WHAT THE HELL AM I SUPPOSED TO TELL A CLIENT WITH THIS ISSUE? TO WALK FOR HUNDREDS OF MILES UNTIL THEY'RE FIXED??
NO... THAT'S NUTS.
EXACTLY!

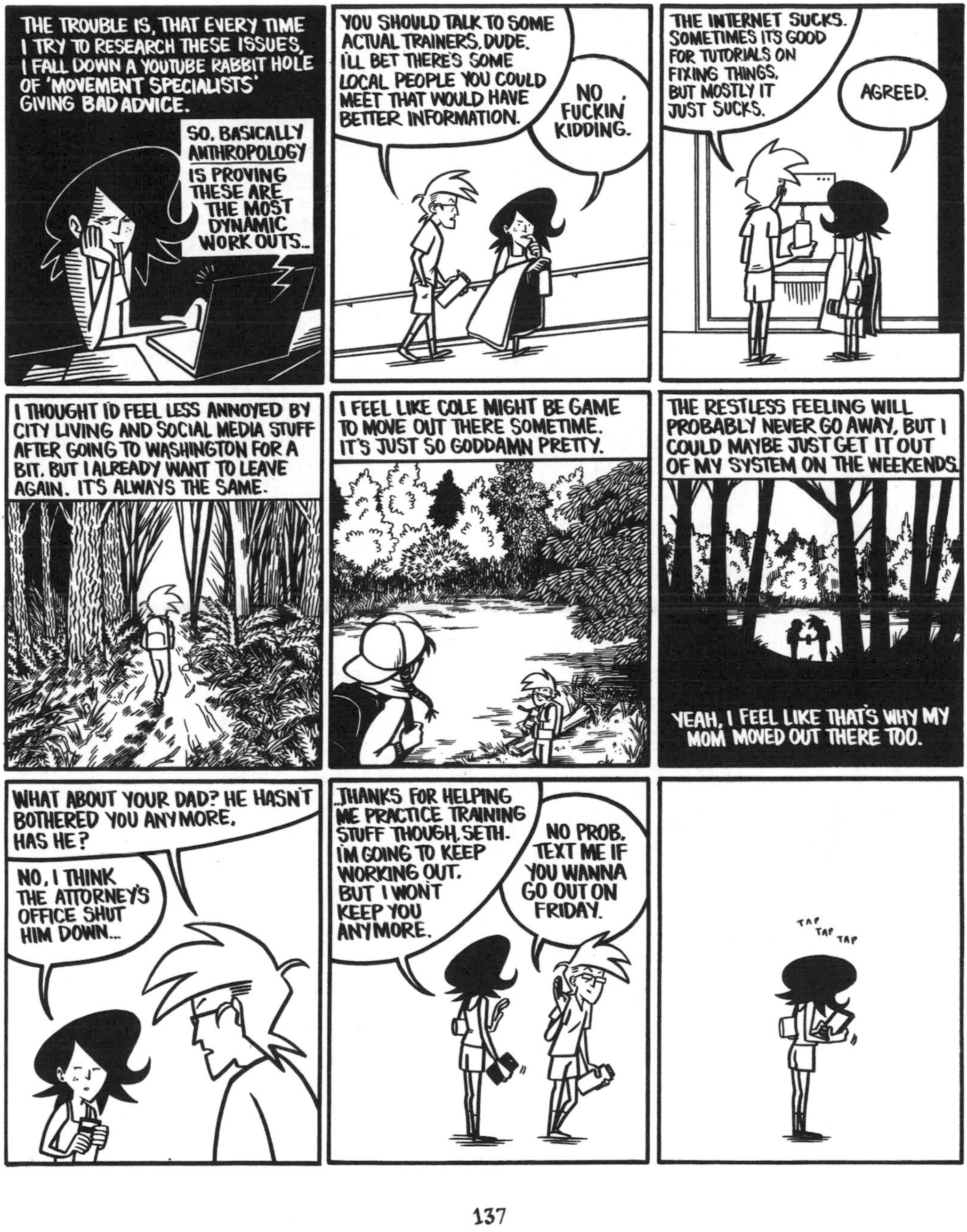
THE TROUBLE IS, THAT EVERY TIME I TRY TO RESEARCH THESE ISSUES, I FALL DOWN A YOUTUBE RABBIT HOLE OF 'MOVEMENT SPECIALISTS' GIVING BAD ADVICE.
SO, BASICALLY ANTHROPOLOGY IS PROVING THESE ARE THE MOST DYNAMIC WORK OUTS...
YOU SHOULD TALK TO SOME ACTUAL TRAINERS, DUDE. I'LL BET THERE'S SOME LOCAL PEOPLE YOU COULD MEET THAT WOULD HAVE BETTER INFORMATION.
NO FUCKIN' KIDDING.
THE INTERNET SUCKS. SOMETIMES IT'S GOOD FOR TUTORIALS ON FIXING THINGS, BUT MOSTLY IT JUST SUCKS.
AGREED.
I THOUGHT I'D FEEL LESS ANNOYED BY CITY LIVING AND SOCIAL MEDIA STUFF AFTER GOING TO WASHINGTON FOR A BIT. BUT I ALREADY WANT TO LEAVE AGAIN. IT'S ALWAYS THE SAME.
I FEEL LIKE COLE MIGHT BE GAME TO MOVE OUT THERE SOMETIME. IT'S JUST SO GODDAMN PRETTY.
THE RESTLESS FEELING WILL PROBABLY NEVER GO AWAY, BUT I COULD MAYBE JUST GET IT OUT OF MY SYSTEM ON THE WEEKENDS.
YEAH, I FEEL LIKE THAT'S WHY MY MOM MOVED OUT THERE TOO.
WHAT ABOUT YOUR DAD? HE HASN'T BOTHERED YOU ANYMORE, HAS HE?
NO, I THINK THE ATTORNEY'S OFFICE SHUT HIM DOWN...
...THANKS FOR HELPING ME PRACTICE TRAINING STUFF THOUGH, SETH. I'M GOING TO KEEP WORKING OUT. BUT I WON'T KEEP YOU ANYMORE.
NO PROB. TEXT ME IF YOU WANNA GO OUT ON FRIDAY.
TAP TAP TAP

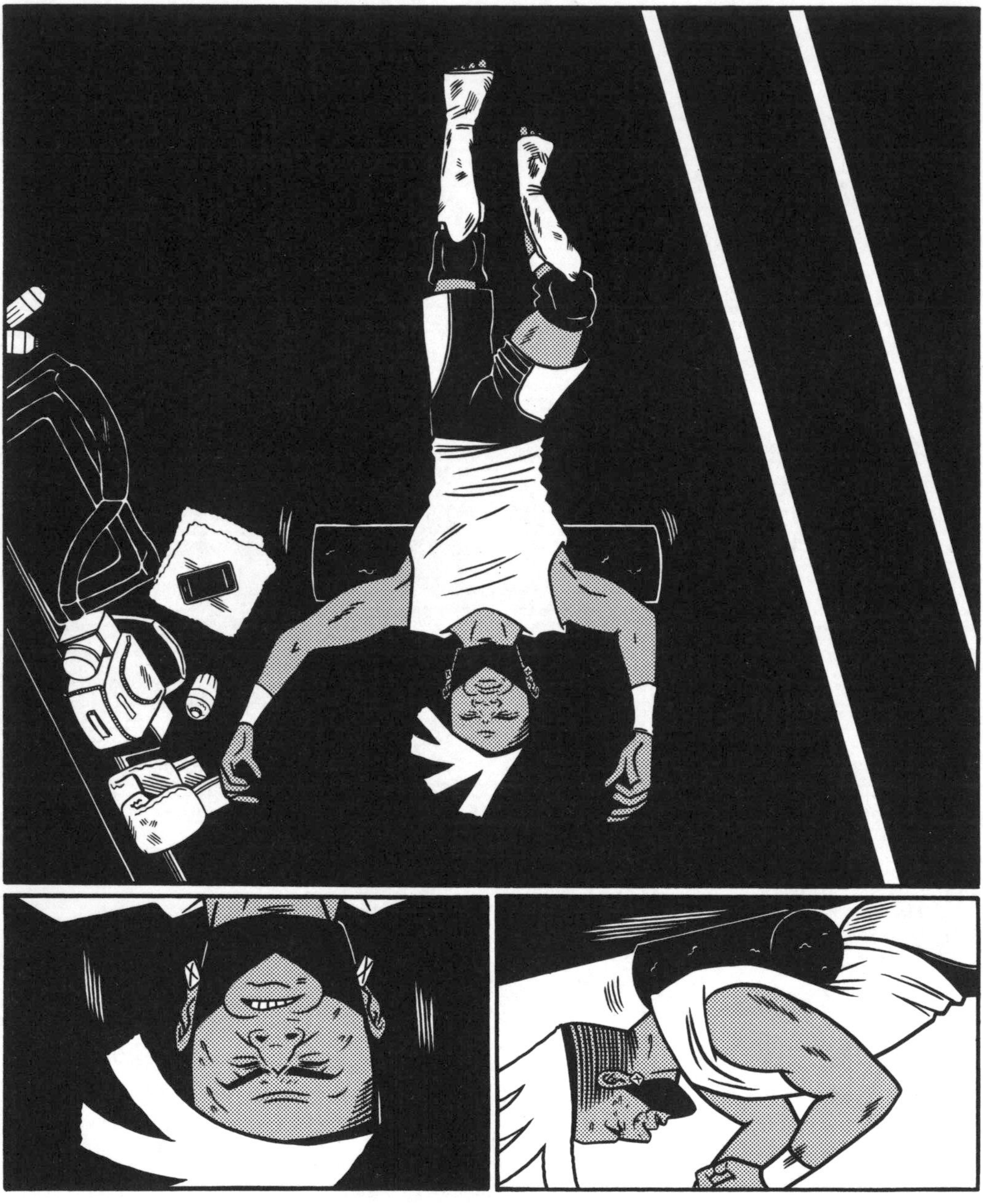

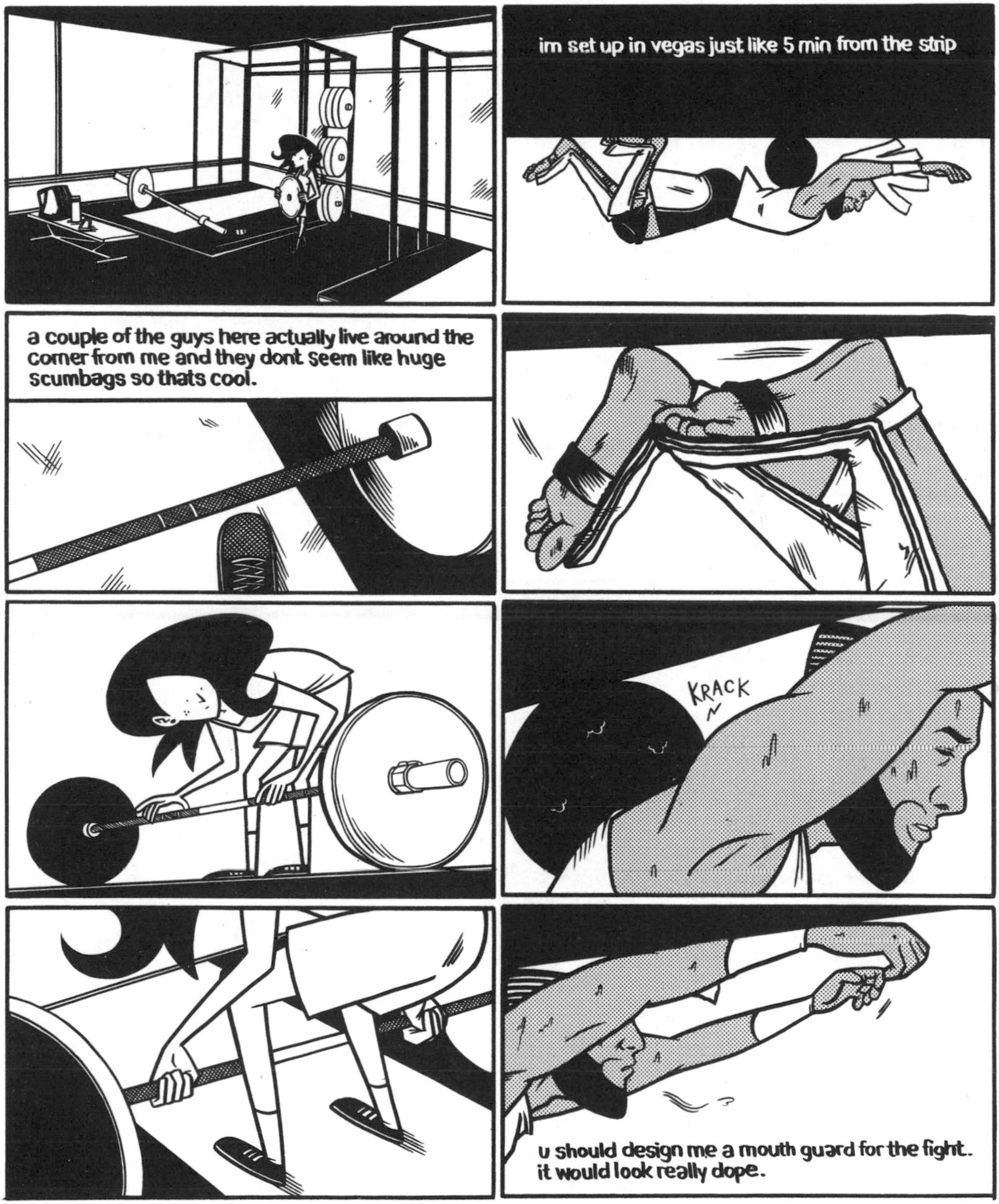
im set up in vegas just like 5 min from the strip
a couple of the guys here actually live around the corner from me and they dont seem like huge scumbags so thats cool.
KRACK
u should design me a mouth guard for the fight. it would look really dope.

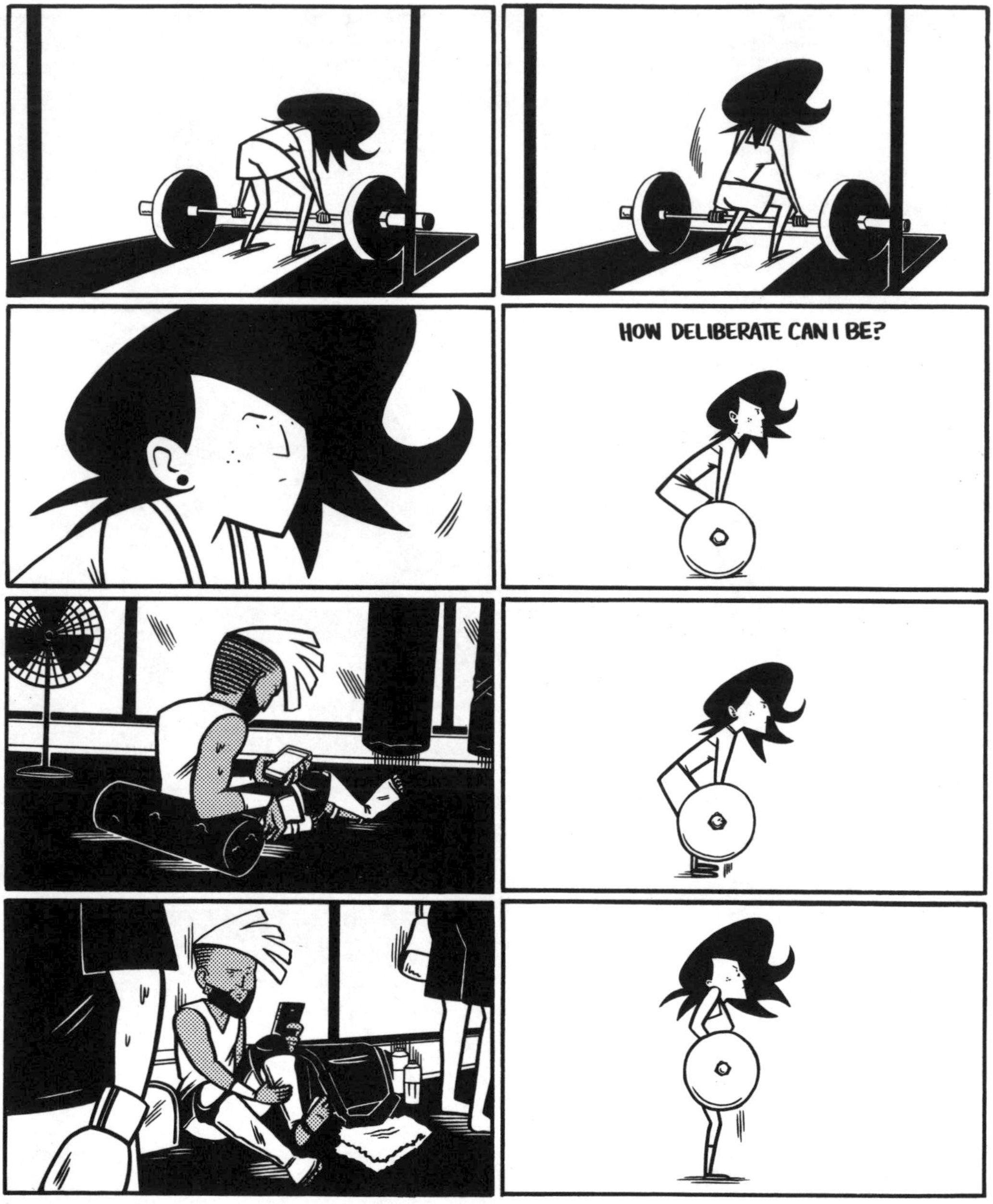
HOW DELIBERATE CAN I BE?

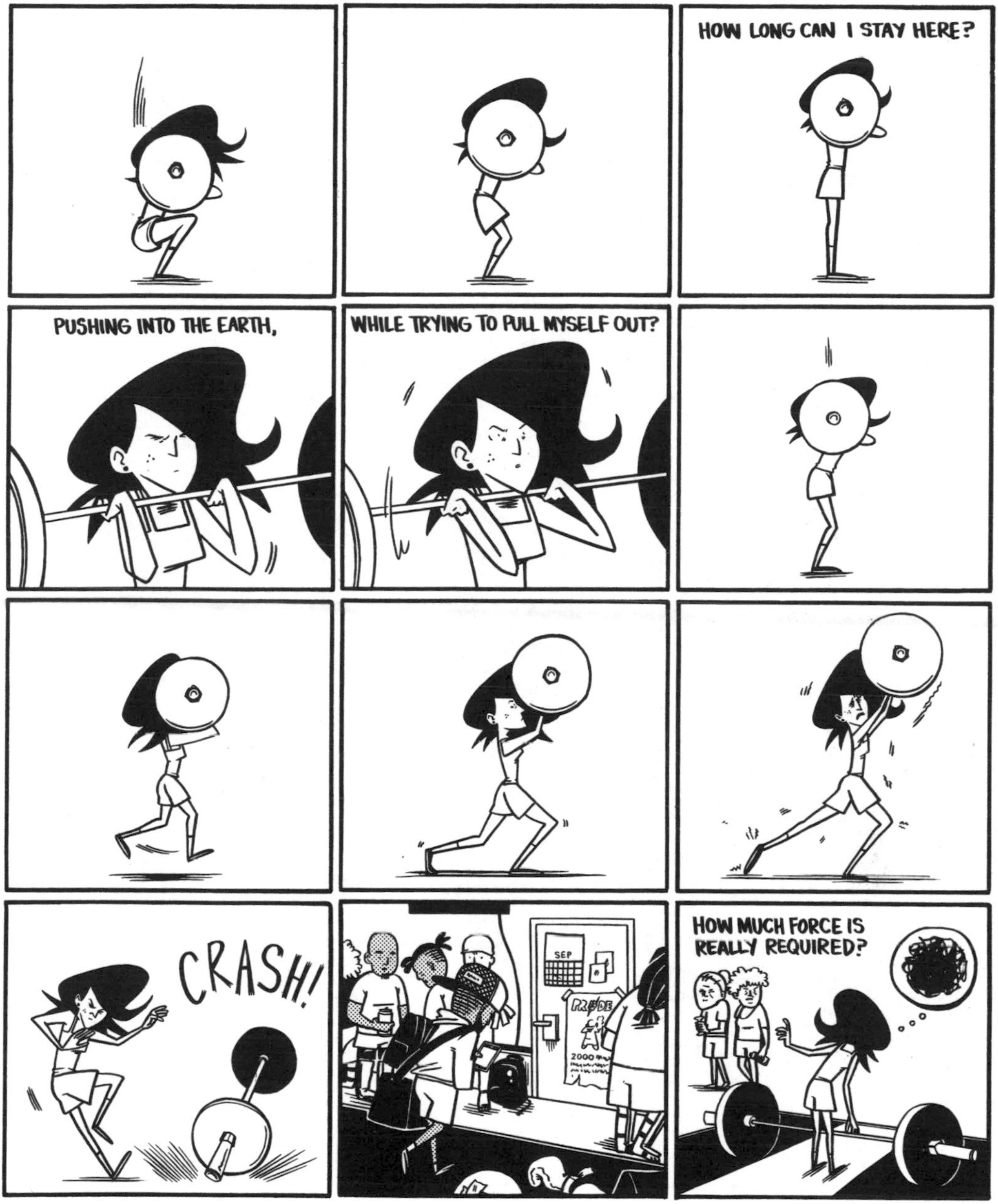
HOW LONG CAN I STAY HERE?
PUSHING INTO THE EARTH,
WHILE TRYING TO PULL MYSELF OUT?
CRASH!
SEP
HOW MUCH FORCE IS REALLY REQUIRED?

I FINISHED MY FIRST BOOK.

RATHER PROMPTLY, I SECURED A PUBLISHER THAT WAS EAGER TO WORK WITH ME.

I SCHEDULED MY PERSONAL TRAINING EXAM DATE FOR THE WINTER.

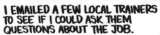

I EMAILED A FEW LOCAL TRAINERS TO SEE IF I COULD ASK THEM QUESTIONS ABOUT THE JOB.

TAP TAP

I TURNED 25.

NONE OF THESE THINGS MADE ME HAPPY OR SATISFIED, SO I SCHEDULED AN APPOINTMENT WITH A THERAPIST.

METRO

PRT PRT PRT

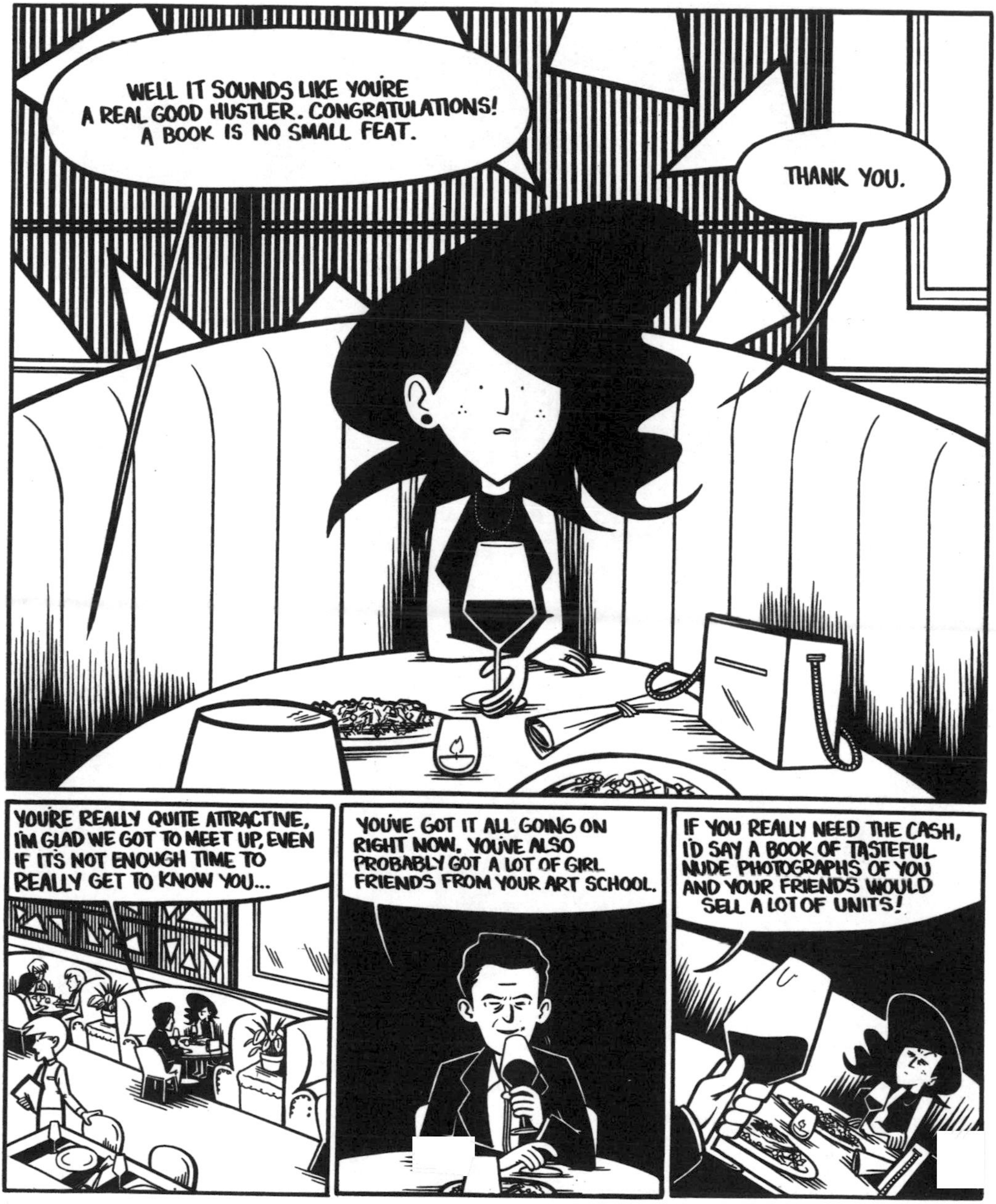
WELL IT SOUNDS LIKE YOU'RE A REAL GOOD HUSTLER. CONGRATULATIONS! A BOOK IS NO SMALL FEAT.
THANK YOU.
YOU'RE REALLY QUITE ATTRACTIVE, I'M GLAD WE GOT TO MEET UP, EVEN IF IT'S NOT ENOUGH TIME TO REALLY GET TO KNOW YOU...
YOU'VE GOT IT ALL GOING ON RIGHT NOW. YOU'VE ALSO PROBABLY GOT A LOT OF GIRL FRIENDS FROM YOUR ART SCHOOL.
IF YOU REALLY NEED THE CASH, I'D SAY A BOOK OF TASTEFUL NUDE PHOTOGRAPHS OF YOU AND YOUR FRIENDS WOULD SELL A LOT OF UNITS!

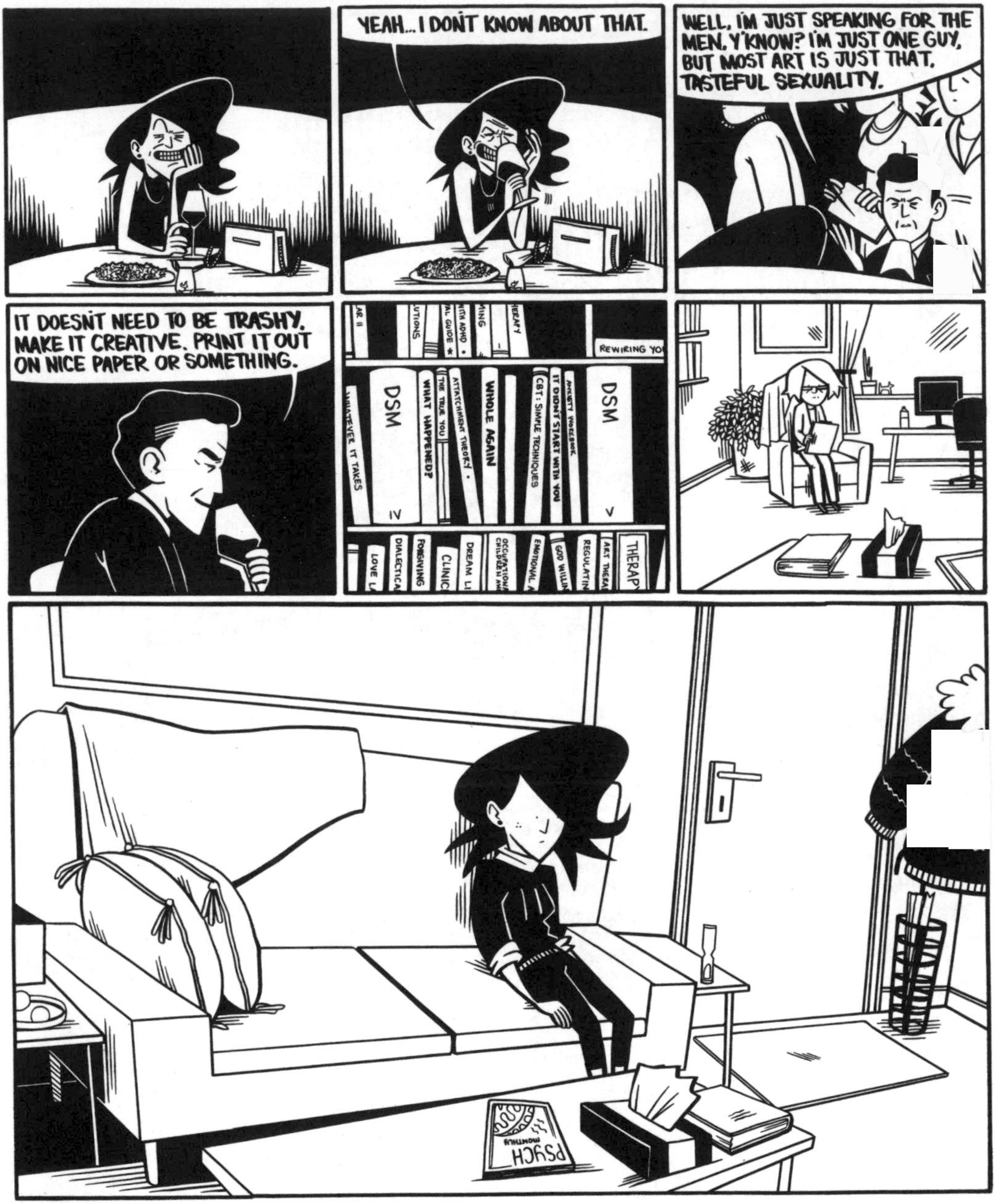
YEAH... I DON'T KNOW ABOUT THAT.
WELL, I'M JUST SPEAKING FOR THE MEN, Y'KNOW? I'M JUST ONE GUY, BUT MOST ART IS JUST THAT. TASTEFUL SEXUALITY.
IT DOESN'T NEED TO BE TRASHY. MAKE IT CREATIVE. PRINT IT OUT ON NICE PAPER OR SOMETHING.
DSM IV
WHAT HAPPENED?
ATTATCHMENT THEORY
WHOLE AGAIN
CBT: SIMPLE TECHNIQUES
IT DIDN'T START WITH YOU
DSM V
THERAPY
PSYCH MONTHLY

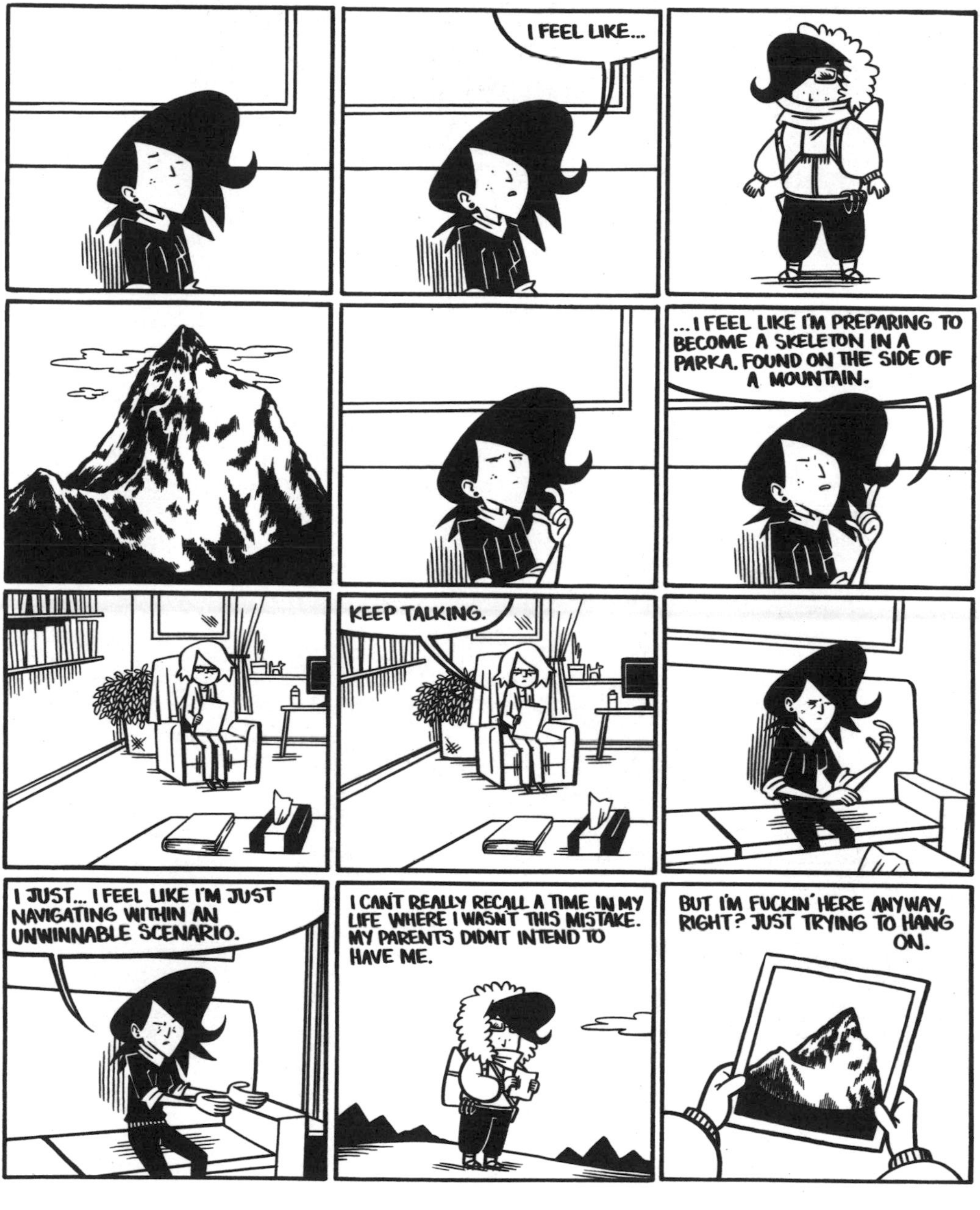
I FEEL LIKE...
...I FEEL LIKE I'M PREPARING TO BECOME A SKELETON IN A PARKA, FOUND ON THE SIDE OF A MOUNTAIN.
KEEP TALKING.
I JUST... I FEEL LIKE I'M JUST NAVIGATING WITHIN AN UNWINNABLE SCENARIO.
I CAN'T REALLY RECALL A TIME IN MY LIFE WHERE I WASN'T THIS MISTAKE. MY PARENTS DIDNT INTEND TO HAVE ME.
BUT I'M FUCKIN' HERE ANYWAY, RIGHT? JUST TRYING TO HANG ON.

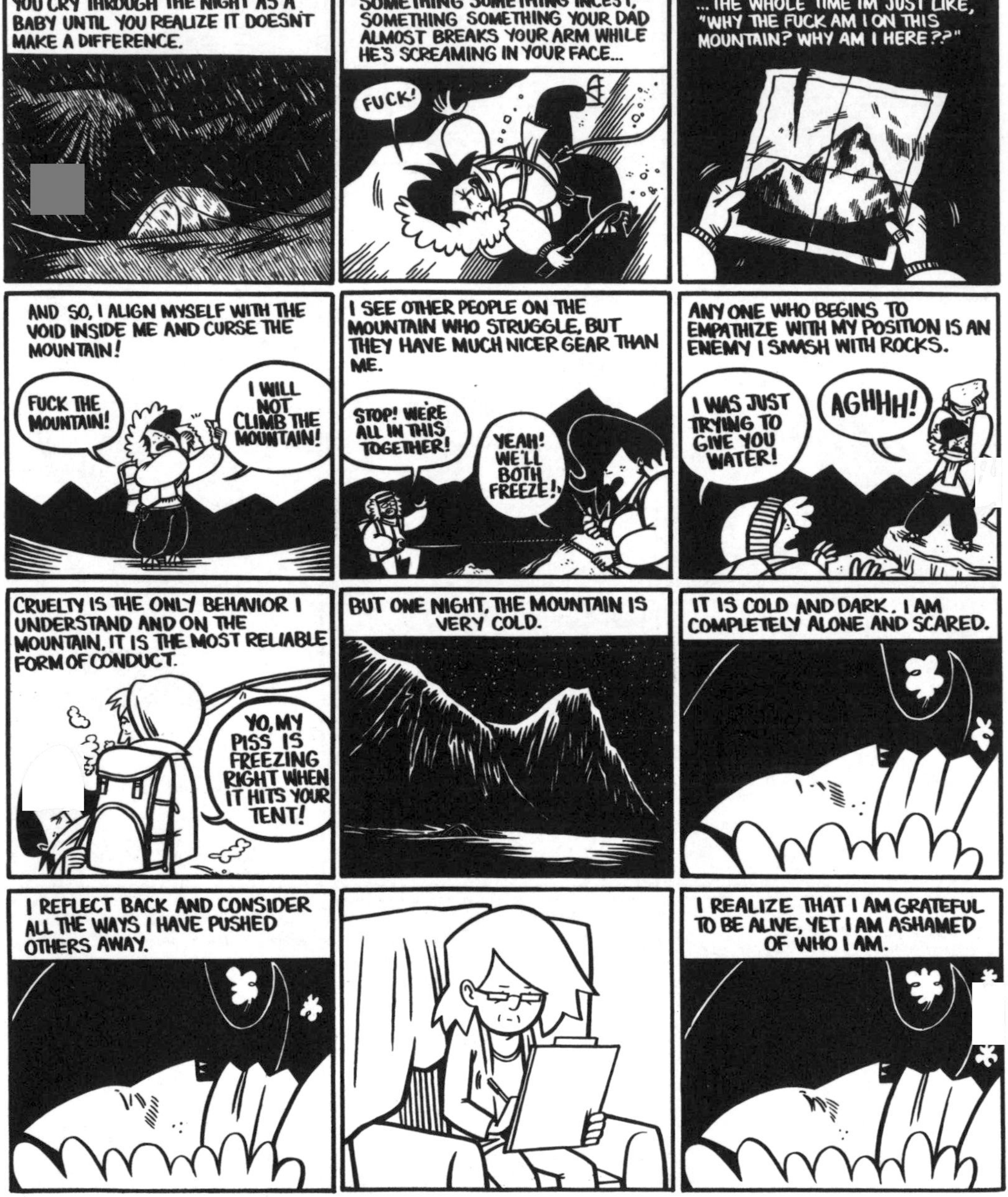
YOU CRY THROUGH THE NIGHT AS A BABY UNTIL YOU REALIZE IT DOESN'T MAKE A DIFFERENCE.
SOMETHING SOMETHING INCEST, SOMETHING SOMETHING YOUR DAD ALMOST BREAKS YOUR ARM WHILE HE'S SCREAMING IN YOUR FACE...
FUCK!
...THE WHOLE TIME I'M JUST LIKE, "WHY THE FUCK AM I ON THIS MOUNTAIN? WHY AM I HERE??"
AND SO, I ALIGN MYSELF WITH THE VOID INSIDE ME AND CURSE THE MOUNTAIN!
FUCK THE MOUNTAIN!
I WILL NOT CLIMB THE MOUNTAIN!
I SEE OTHER PEOPLE ON THE MOUNTAIN WHO STRUGGLE, BUT THEY HAVE MUCH NICER GEAR THAN ME.
STOP! WE'RE ALL IN THIS TOGETHER!
YEAH! WE'LL BOTH FREEZE!
ANY ONE WHO BEGINS TO EMPATHIZE WITH MY POSITION IS AN ENEMY I SMASH WITH ROCKS.
I WAS JUST TRYING TO GIVE YOU WATER!
AGHHH!
CRUELTY IS THE ONLY BEHAVIOR I UNDERSTAND AND ON THE MOUNTAIN, IT IS THE MOST RELIABLE FORM OF CONDUCT.
YO, MY PISS IS FREEZING RIGHT WHEN IT HITS YOUR TENT!
BUT ONE NIGHT, THE MOUNTAIN IS VERY COLD.
IT IS COLD AND DARK. I AM COMPLETELY ALONE AND SCARED.
I REFLECT BACK AND CONSIDER ALL THE WAYS I HAVE PUSHED OTHERS AWAY.
I REALIZE THAT I AM GRATEFUL TO BE ALIVE, YET I AM ASHAMED OF WHO I AM.

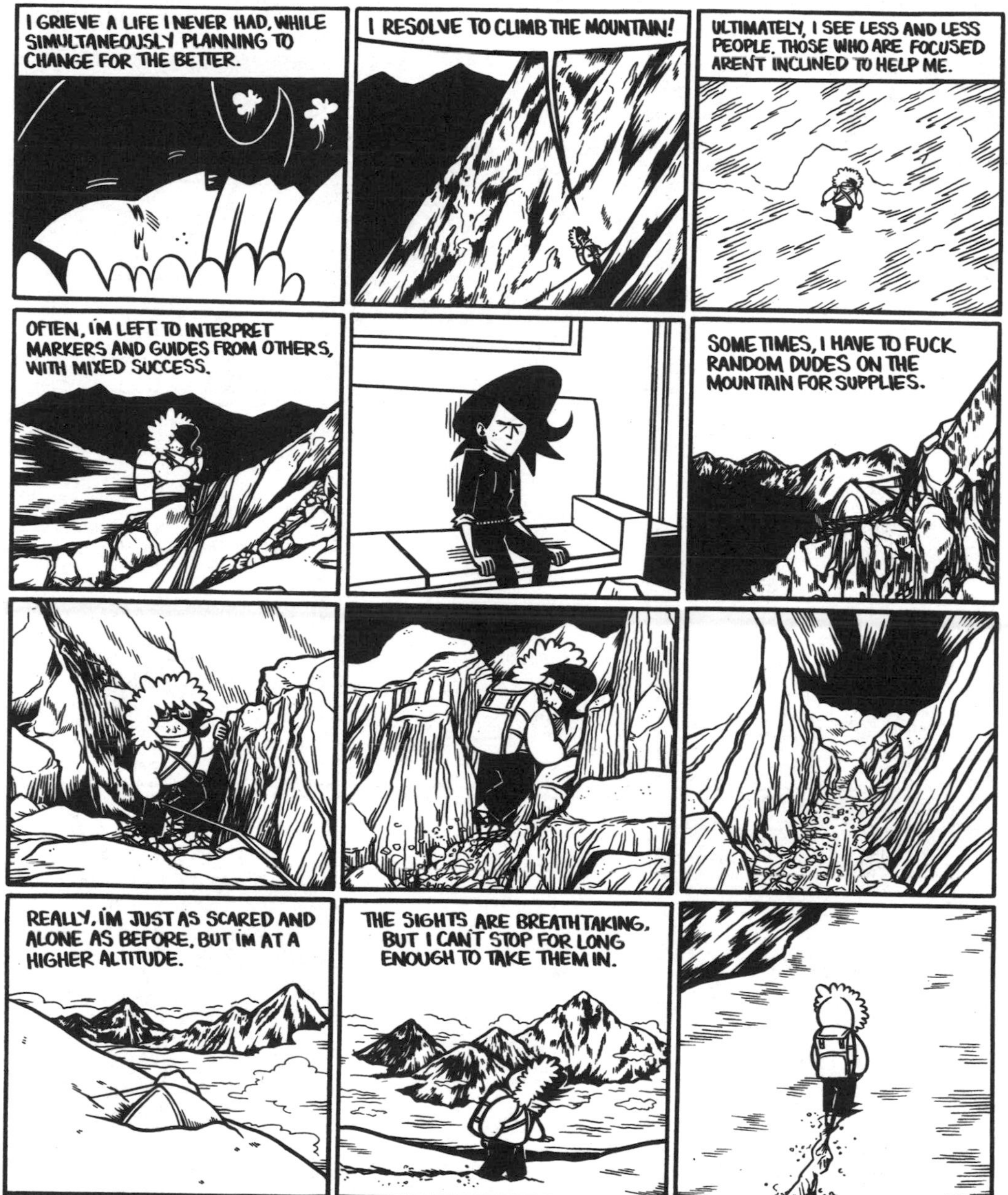
I GRIEVE A LIFE I NEVER HAD, WHILE SIMULTANEOUSLY PLANNING TO CHANGE FOR THE BETTER.
I RESOLVE TO CLIMB THE MOUNTAIN!
ULTIMATELY, I SEE LESS AND LESS PEOPLE. THOSE WHO ARE FOCUSED AREN'T INCLINED TO HELP ME.
OFTEN, I'M LEFT TO INTERPRET MARKERS AND GUIDES FROM OTHERS, WITH MIXED SUCCESS.
SOME TIMES, I HAVE TO FUCK RANDOM DUDES ON THE MOUNTAIN FOR SUPPLIES.
REALLY, I'M JUST AS SCARED AND ALONE AS BEFORE, BUT I'M AT A HIGHER ALTITUDE.
THE SIGHTS ARE BREATHTAKING, BUT I CAN'T STOP FOR LONG ENOUGH TO TAKE THEM IN.

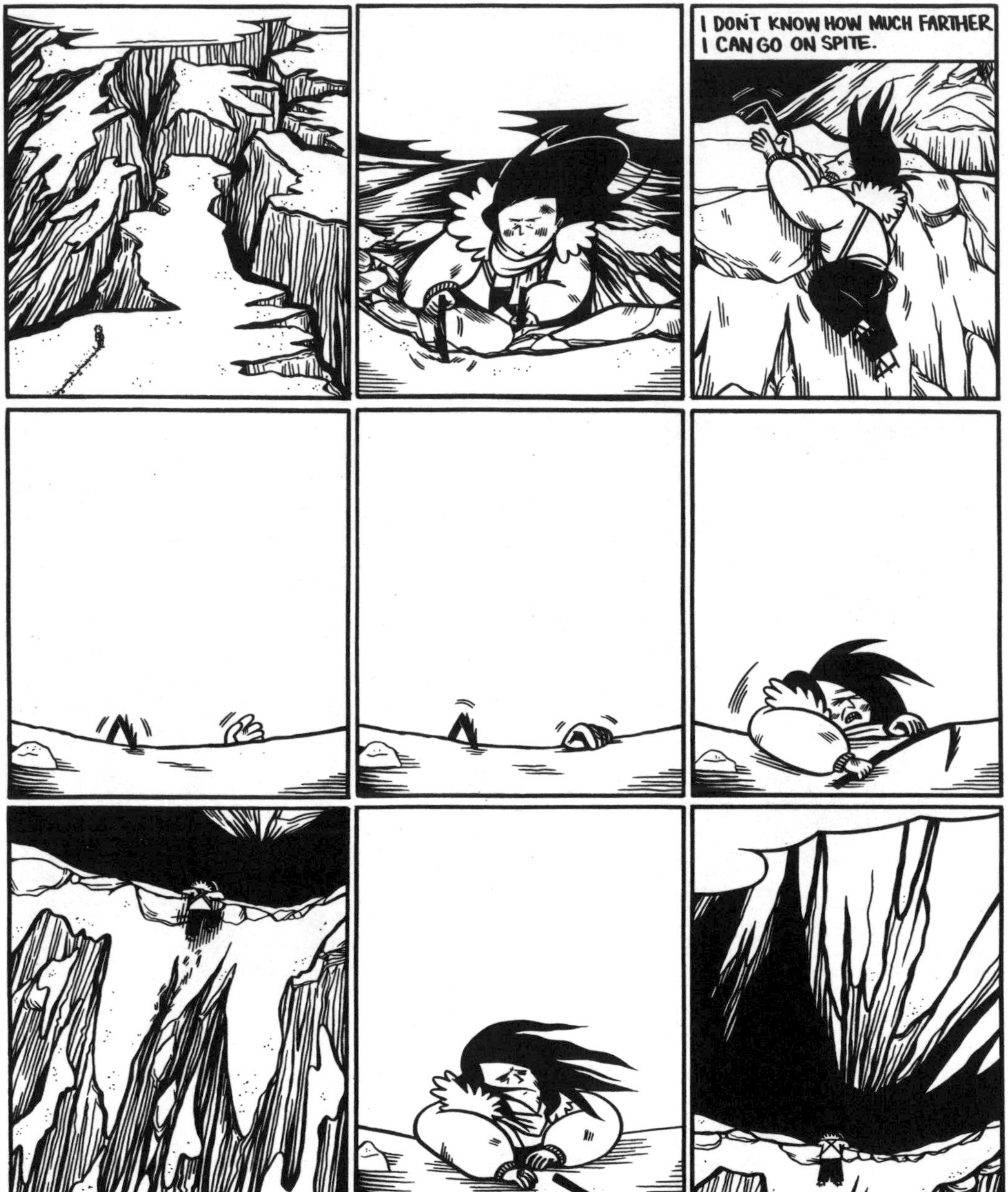
I DON'T KNOW HOW MUCH FARTHER
I CAN GO ON SPITE.

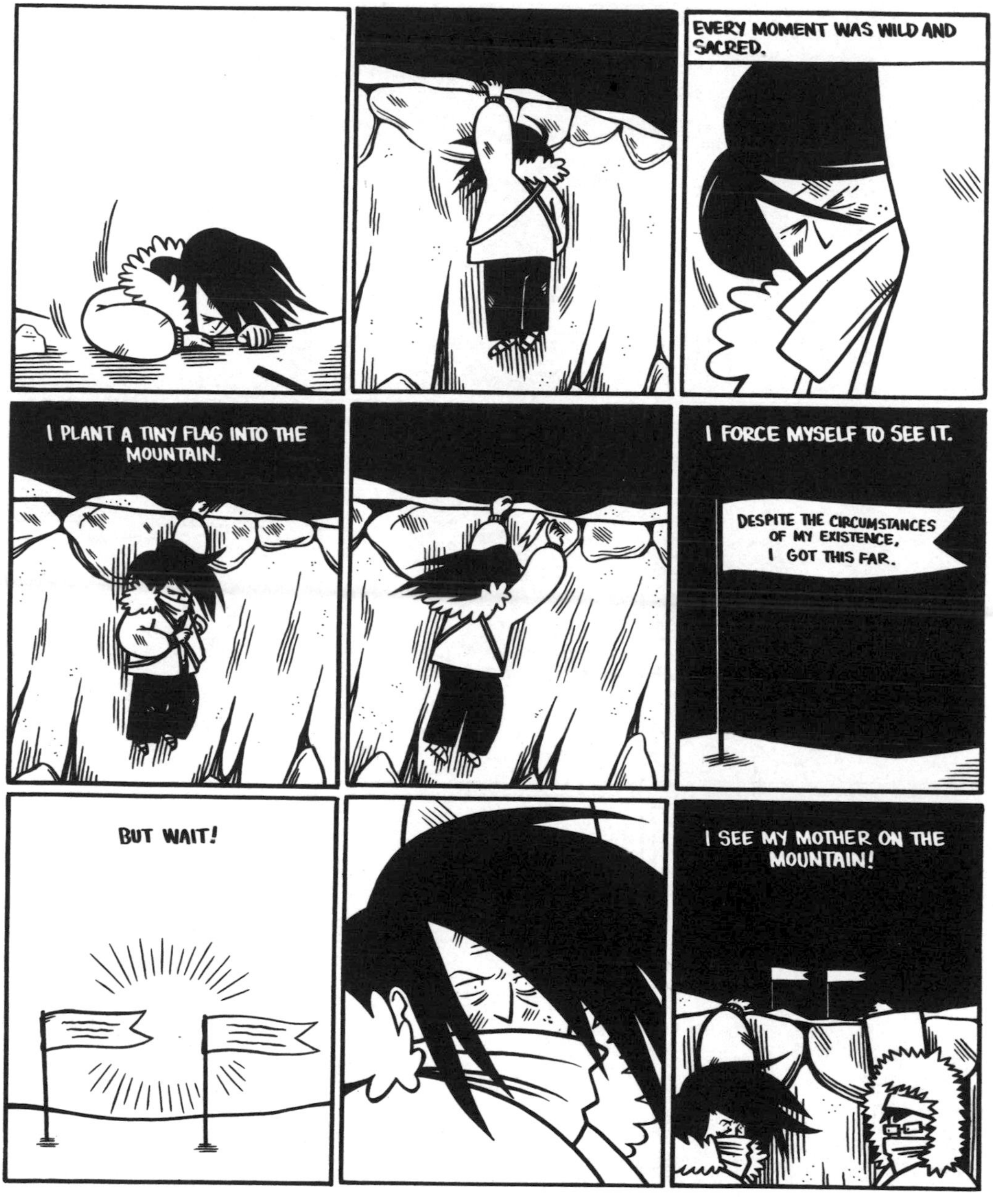
EVERY MOMENT WAS WILD AND SACRED.
I PLANT A TINY FLAG INTO THE MOUNTAIN.
I FORCE MYSELF TO SEE IT.
DESPITE THE CIRCUMSTANCES OF MY EXISTENCE, I GOT THIS FAR.
BUT WAIT!
I SEE MY MOTHER ON THE MOUNTAIN!

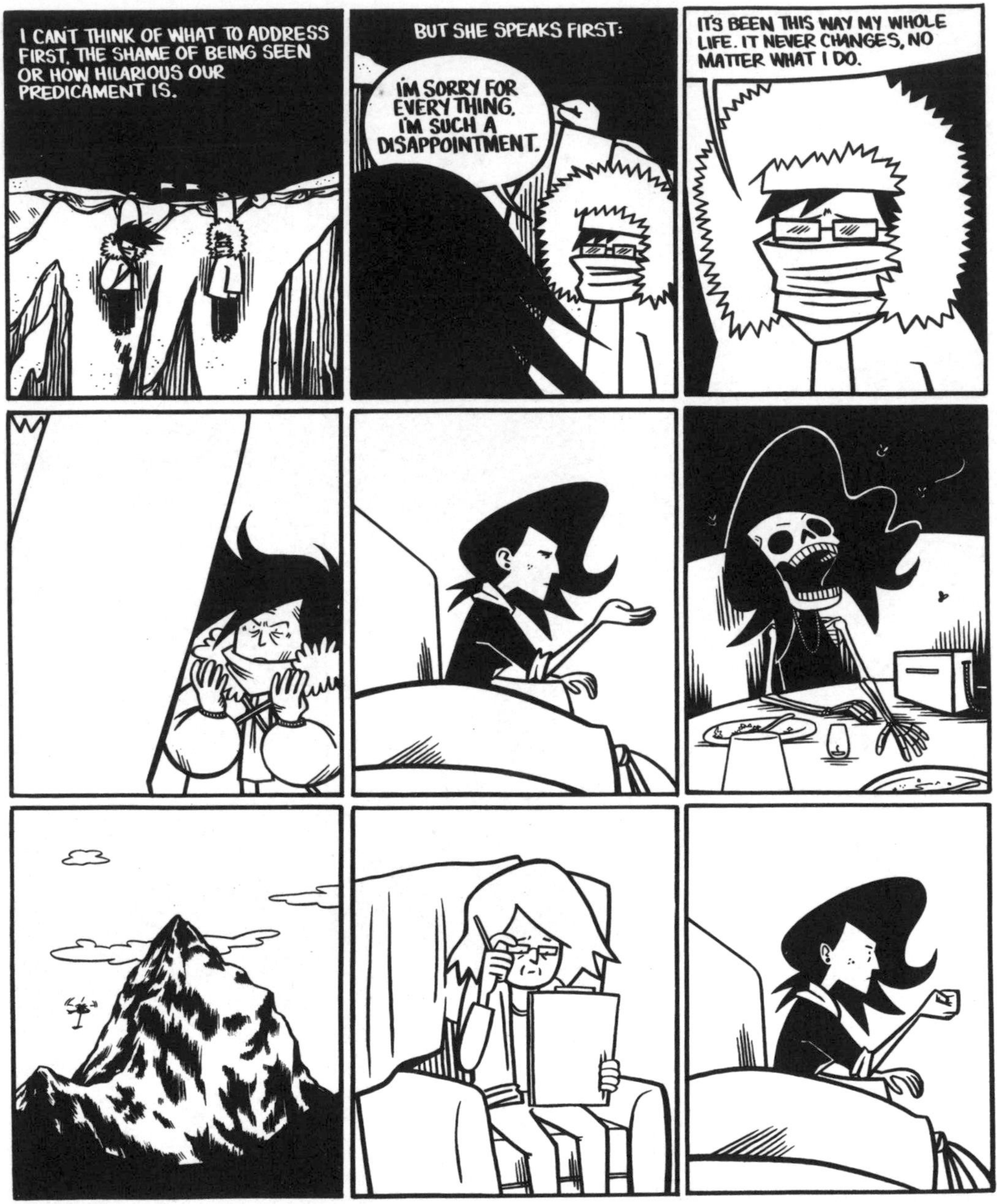
I CAN'T THINK OF WHAT TO ADDRESS FIRST. THE SHAME OF BEING SEEN OR HOW HILARIOUS OUR PREDICAMENT IS.
BUT SHE SPEAKS FIRST:
I'M SORRY FOR EVERYTHING. I'M SUCH A DISAPPOINTMENT.
IT'S BEEN THIS WAY MY WHOLE LIFE. IT NEVER CHANGES, NO MATTER WHAT I DO.

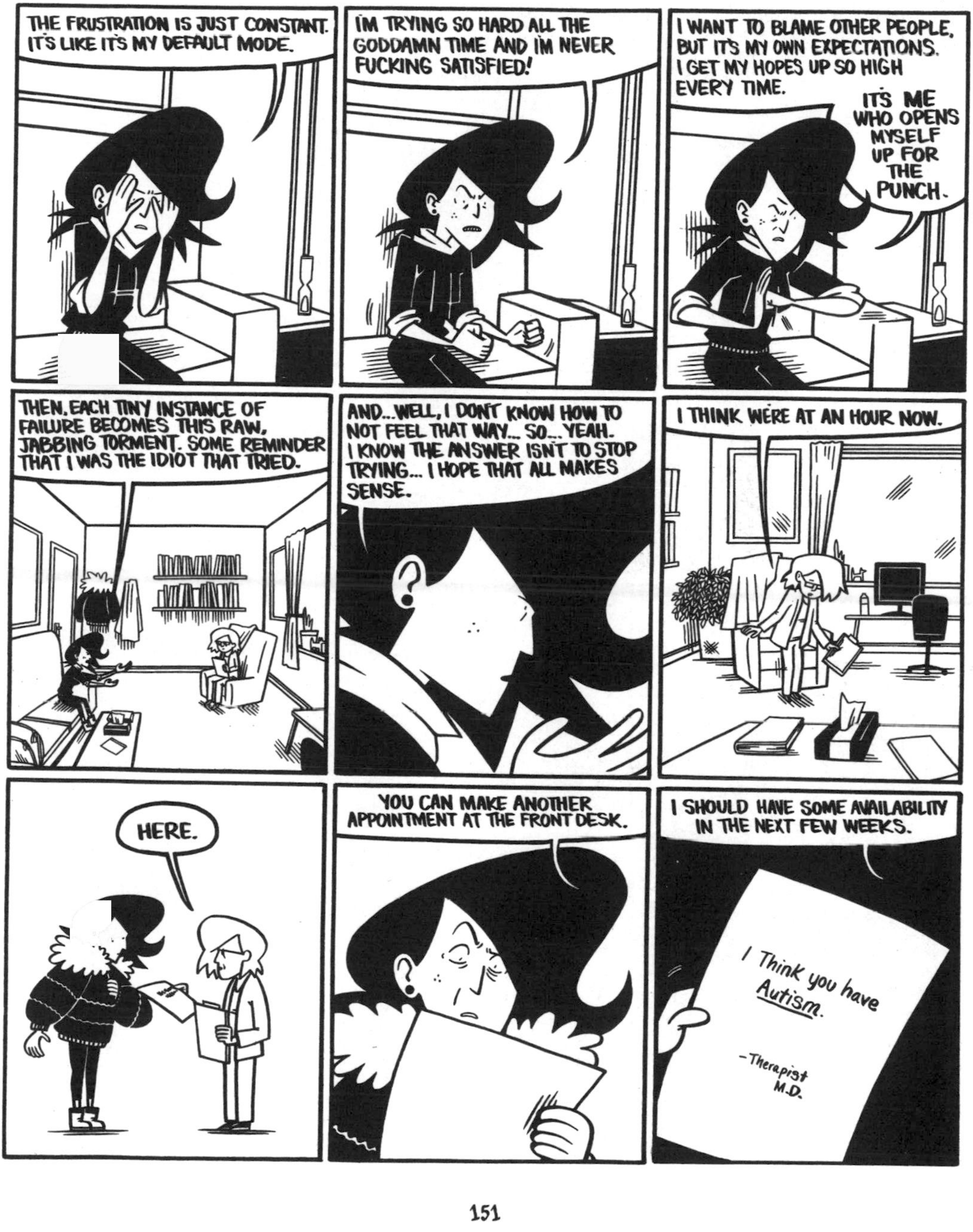
THE FRUSTRATION IS JUST CONSTANT. IT'S LIKE IT'S MY DEFAULT MODE.
I'M TRYING SO HARD ALL THE GODDAMN TIME AND I'M NEVER FUCKING SATISFIED!
I WANT TO BLAME OTHER PEOPLE, BUT IT'S MY OWN EXPECTATIONS. I GET MY HOPES UP SO HIGH EVERY TIME.
IT'S ME WHO OPENS MYSELF UP FOR THE PUNCH.
THEN, EACH TINY INSTANCE OF FAILURE BECOMES THIS RAW, JABBING TORMENT. SOME REMINDER THAT I WAS THE IDIOT THAT TRIED.
AND... WELL, I DON'T KNOW HOW TO NOT FEEL THAT WAY... SO... YEAH. I KNOW THE ANSWER ISN'T TO STOP TRYING... I HOPE THAT ALL MAKES SENSE.
I THINK WE'RE AT AN HOUR NOW.
HERE.
YOU CAN MAKE ANOTHER APPOINTMENT AT THE FRONT DESK.
I SHOULD HAVE SOME AVAILABILITY IN THE NEXT FEW WEEKS.
I Think you have Autism.
-Therapist M.D.

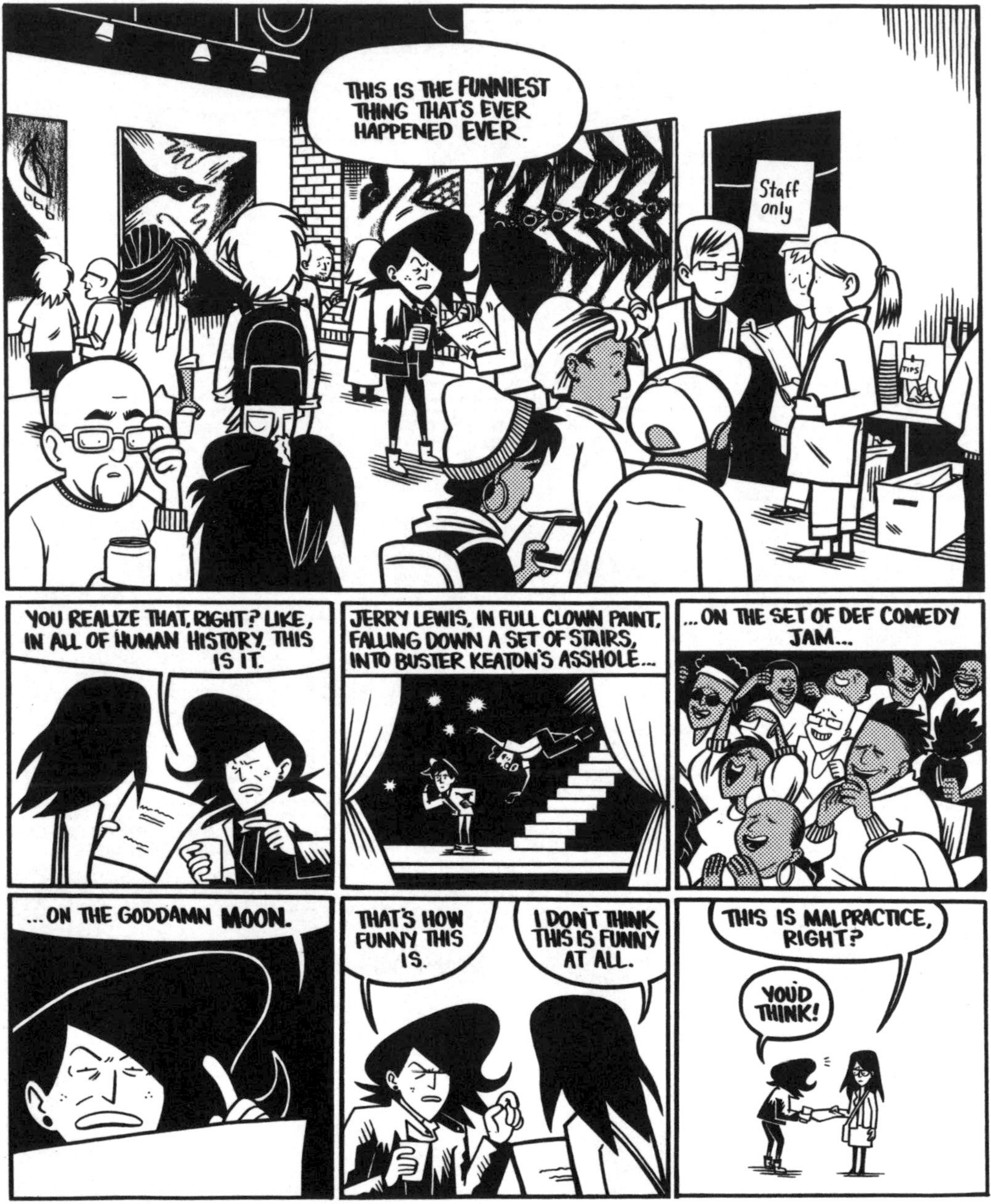

THIS IS THE FUNNIEST THING THAT'S EVER HAPPENED EVER.
Staff only
TIPS
YOU REALIZE THAT, RIGHT? LIKE, IN ALL OF HUMAN HISTORY, THIS IS IT.
JERRY LEWIS, IN FULL CLOWN PAINT, FALLING DOWN A SET OF STAIRS, INTO BUSTER KEATON'S ASSHOLE...
...ON THE SET OF DEF COMEDY JAM...
...ON THE GODDAMN MOON.
THAT'S HOW FUNNY THIS IS.
I DON'T THINK THIS IS FUNNY AT ALL.
THIS IS MALPRACTICE, RIGHT?
YOU'D THINK!

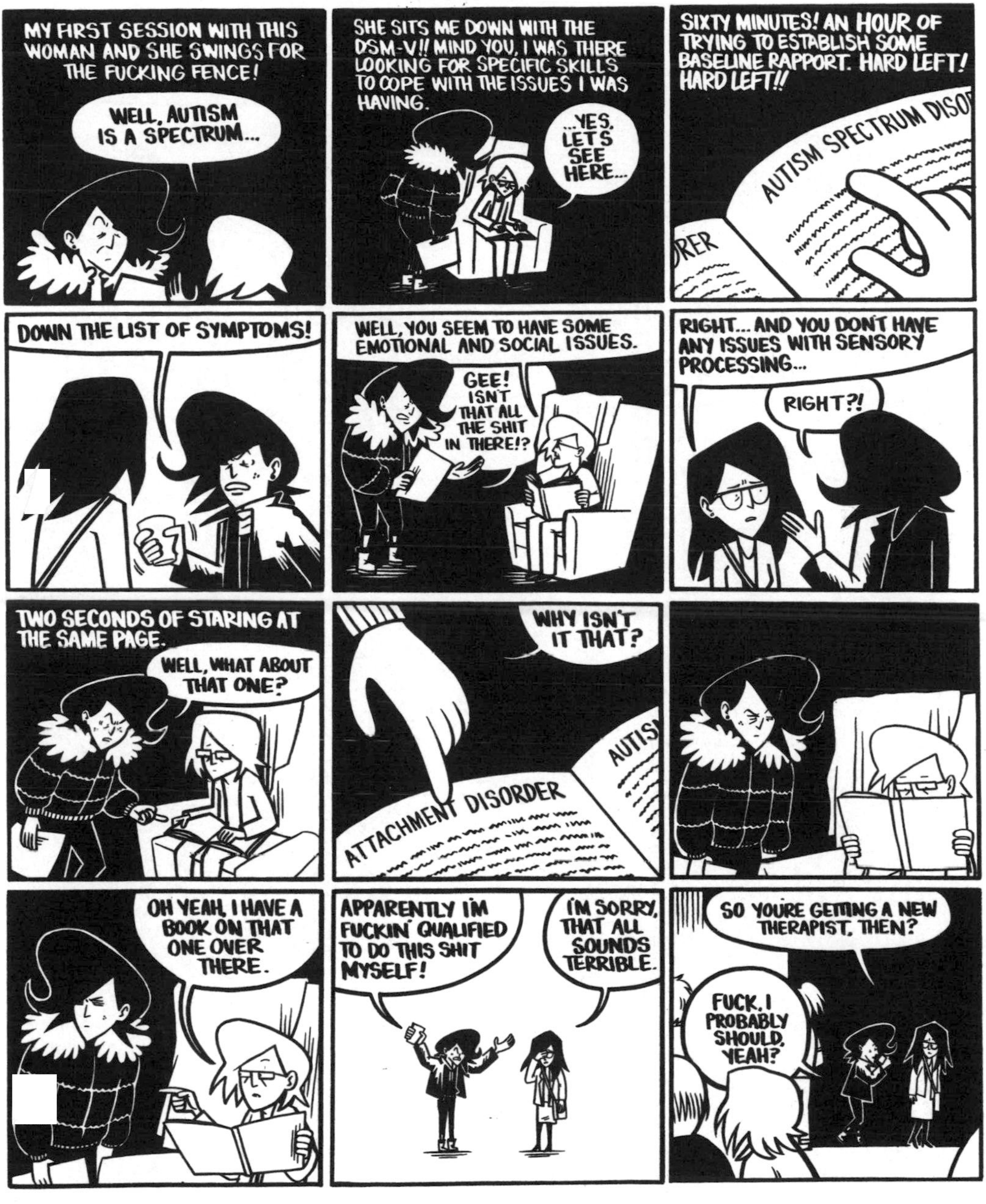
MY FIRST SESSION WITH THIS WOMAN AND SHE SWINGS FOR THE FUCKING FENCE!
WELL, AUTISM IS A SPECTRUM...
SHE SITS ME DOWN WITH THE DSM-V!! MIND YOU, I WAS THERE LOOKING FOR SPECIFIC SKILLS TO COPE WITH THE ISSUES I WAS HAVING.
...YES, LET'S SEE HERE...
SIXTY MINUTES! AN HOUR OF TRYING TO ESTABLISH SOME BASELINE RAPPORT. HARD LEFT! HARD LEFT!!
AUTISM SPECTRUM DISO
DOWN THE LIST OF SYMPTOMS!
WELL, YOU SEEM TO HAVE SOME EMOTIONAL AND SOCIAL ISSUES.
GEE! ISN'T THAT ALL THE SHIT IN THERE!?
RIGHT... AND YOU DON'T HAVE ANY ISSUES WITH SENSORY PROCESSING...
RIGHT?!
TWO SECONDS OF STARING AT THE SAME PAGE.
WELL, WHAT ABOUT THAT ONE?
WHY ISN'T IT THAT?
ATTACHMENT DISORDER
OH YEAH, I HAVE A BOOK ON THAT ONE OVER THERE.
APPARENTLY I'M FUCKIN' QUALIFIED TO DO THIS SHIT MYSELF!
I'M SORRY, THAT ALL SOUNDS TERRIBLE.
SO YOU'RE GETTING A NEW THERAPIST, THEN?
FUCK, I PROBABLY SHOULD, YEAH?

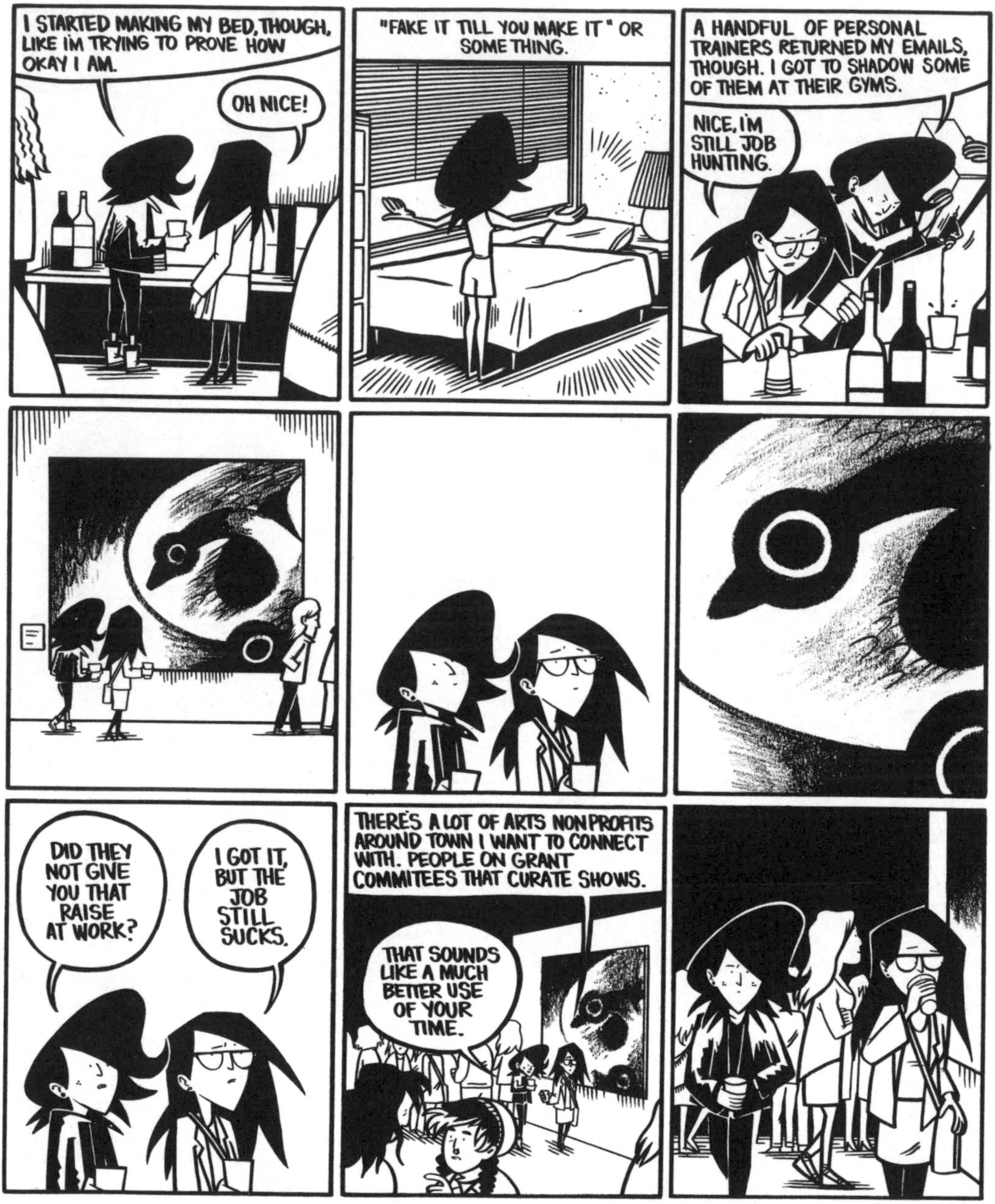
I STARTED MAKING MY BED, THOUGH, LIKE I'M TRYING TO PROVE HOW OKAY I AM.
OH NICE!
"FAKE IT TILL YOU MAKE IT" OR SOME THING.
A HANDFUL OF PERSONAL TRAINERS RETURNED MY EMAILS, THOUGH. I GOT TO SHADOW SOME OF THEM AT THEIR GYMS.
NICE, I'M STILL JOB HUNTING.
DID THEY NOT GIVE YOU THAT RAISE AT WORK?
I GOT IT, BUT THE JOB STILL SUCKS.
THERE'S A LOT OF ARTS NONPROFITS AROUND TOWN I WANT TO CONNECT WITH. PEOPLE ON GRANT COMMITEES THAT CURATE SHOWS.
THAT SOUNDS LIKE A MUCH BETTER USE OF YOUR TIME.

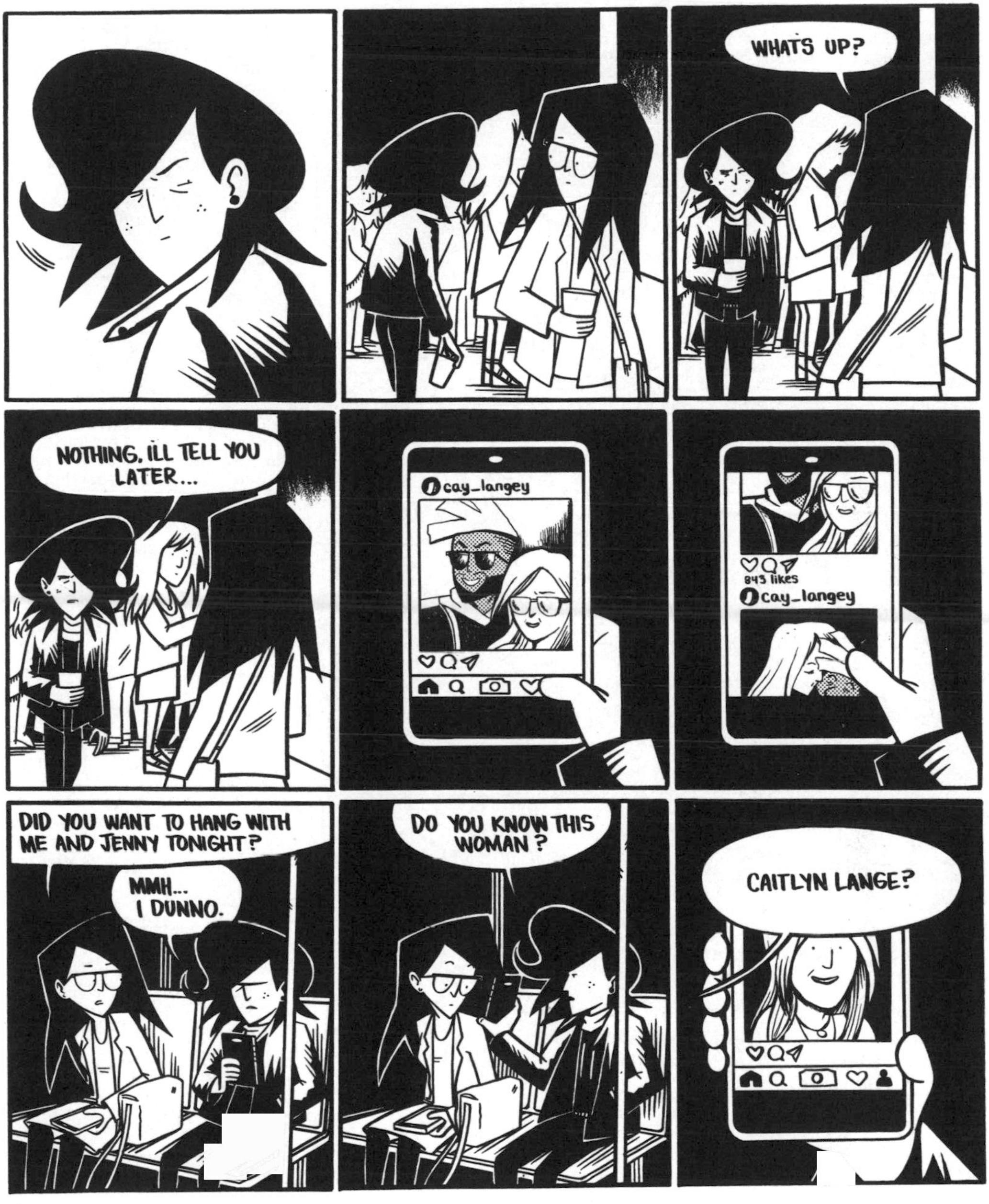
WHAT'S UP?
NOTHING. I'LL TELL YOU LATER...
cay_langey
cay_langey
843 likes
DID YOU WANT TO HANG WITH ME AND JENNY TONIGHT?
MMH... I DUNNO.
DO YOU KNOW THIS WOMAN?
CAITLYN LANGE?

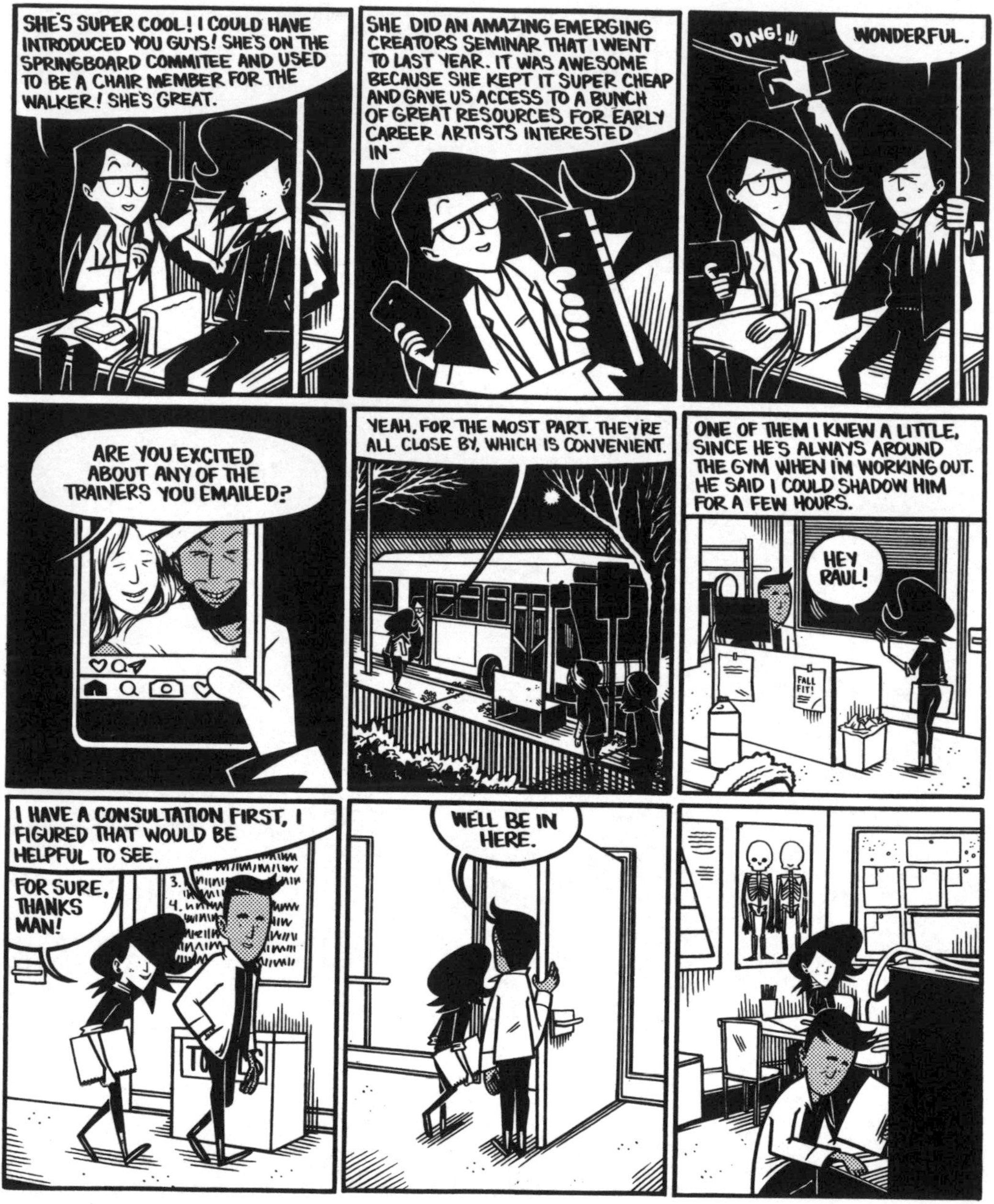
SHE'S SUPER COOL! I COULD HAVE INTRODUCED YOU GUYS! SHE'S ON THE SPRINGBOARD COMMITEE AND USED TO BE A CHAIR MEMBER FOR THE WALKER! SHE'S GREAT.
SHE DID AN AMAZING EMERGING CREATORS SEMINAR THAT I WENT TO LAST YEAR. IT WAS AWESOME BECAUSE SHE KEPT IT SUPER CHEAP AND GAVE US ACCESS TO A BUNCH OF GREAT RESOURCES FOR EARLY CAREER ARTISTS INTERESTED IN-
DING!
WONDERFUL.
ARE YOU EXCITED ABOUT ANY OF THE TRAINERS YOU EMAILED?
YEAH, FOR THE MOST PART. THEY'RE ALL CLOSE BY, WHICH IS CONVENIENT.
ONE OF THEM I KNEW A LITTLE, SINCE HE'S ALWAYS AROUND THE GYM WHEN I'M WORKING OUT. HE SAID I COULD SHADOW HIM FOR A FEW HOURS.
HEY RAUL!
FALL FIT!
I HAVE A CONSULTATION FIRST, I FIGURED THAT WOULD BE HELPFUL TO SEE.
FOR SURE, THANKS MAN!
WE'LL BE IN HERE.

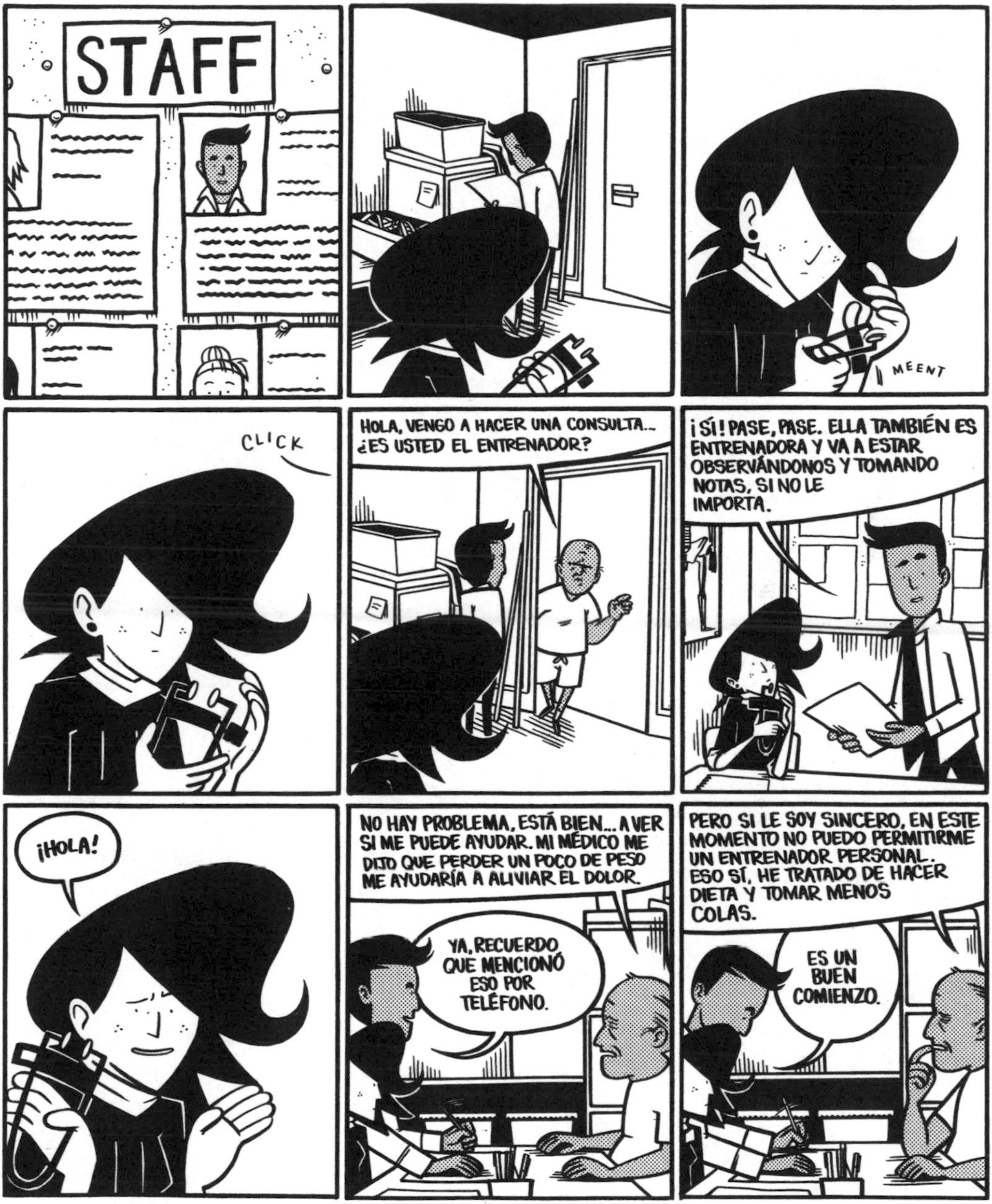
STAFF
MEENT
CLICK
HOLA, VENGO A HACER UNA CONSULTA... ¿ES USTED EL ENTRENADOR?
¡SÍ! PASE, PASE. ELLA TAMBIÉN ES ENTRENADORA Y VA A ESTAR OBSERVÁNDONOS Y TOMANDO NOTAS, SI NO LE IMPORTA.
¡HOLA!
NO HAY PROBLEMA, ESTÁ BIEN... A VER SI ME PUEDE AYUDAR. MI MÉDICO ME DIJO QUE PERDER UN POCO DE PESO ME AYUDARÍA A ALIVIAR EL DOLOR.
YA, RECUERDO QUE MENCIONÓ ESO POR TELÉFONO.
PERO SI LE SOY SINCERO, EN ESTE MOMENTO NO PUEDO PERMITIRME UN ENTRENADOR PERSONAL. ESO SÍ, HE TRATADO DE HACER DIETA Y TOMAR MENOS COLAS.
ES UN BUEN COMIENZO.

YA, PERO MI MUJER SÍ CREE QUE DEBERÍA APUNTARME A UN GIMNASIO A LA LEVANTAR PESAS. LO QUE PASA ES QUE LA ESPALDA ME DUELE DEMASIADO. SOLO EL TRABAJAR YA ME RESULTA COMPLICADO. ME CUESTA UN MONTÓN LEVANTAR CUALQUIER COSA O QUEDARME QUIETO TODO MI TURNO.

CLARO.

HACE POCO, CASI SE ME CAE AL SUELO UNA BANDEJA LLENA, POR UN MAL MOVIMIENTO QUE HICE. FUE GIRARME Y VER LAS ESTRELLAS DE PURO DOLOR. RECUERDO DE NIÑO QUE A MI PADRE LE PASABA LO MISMO... NO QUIERO ACABAR ASÍ YO TAMBIÉN.

¿PODRÍA SOLO ENSEÑARME ALGUNAS RUTINAS? ENTIENDO QUE ES SU TRABAJO, PERO QUIZÁ PUEDA DECIRME SIMPLEMENTE SI LO HAGO BIEN. ESTUVE VIENDO ALGUNOS VIDEOS POR INTERNET.

¿SERÍA MUY MOLESTO PARA USTED COMPROMETERSE A UNA HORA DE ENTRENAMIENTO? LE COSTARÍA SESENTA DÓLARES. SÉ QUE EL DINERO PODRÍA SER UN OBSTÁCULO. PERO ESTO SUPONDRÍA UNA BUENA INVERSIÓN EN SU SALUD.

PUES... BUENO, NO CREO QUE A MI ESPOSA LE MOLESTE.

ASÍ PODRÉ ECHARLE UN OJO A CÓMO REALIZA LOS EJERCICIOS. Y TAMBIÉN PUEDO SUGERIRLE UN PAR MÁS PARA MEJORAR TODOS LOS MÚSCULOS DEL TORSO: LOS ABDOMINALES Y LA ESPALDA.

¡SÍ! ¡ES LO QUE DECÍAN EN LOS VIDEOS!

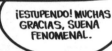

EXACTO. Y SI ESOS EJERCICIOS LE FUNCIONAN, PUEDO ENSEÑARLE MÁS DURANTE NUESTRAS SESIONES. EN SEIS SEMANAS LE HARÍAMOS UN CHEQUEO PARA HACER UN SEGUIMIENTO DE SU PROGRESO. ¿QUÉ LE PARECE?

¡ESTUPENDO! MUCHAS GRACIAS, SUENA FENOMENAL.

EXCELENTE, ENTONCES SOLO NECESITO QUE RELLENE UN FORMULARIO.

HIS BACK HURTS.

OOH.

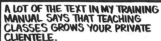
THEN THERE'S THIS OTHER TRAINER THAT DOES SMALL GROUP CLASSES...

A LOT OF THE TEXT IN MY TRAINING MANUAL SAYS THAT TEACHING CLASSES GROWS YOUR PRIVATE CLIENTELE.

ALRIGHT GUYS! ROUND 2! LET'S GO!

90 SECONDS! LET'S PUSH IT!

I TRAIN A LOT OF THESE GUYS INDIVIDUALLY TOO, SOME OF THEM SEE ME THREE TIMES A WEEK.

AM I DOING THIS RIGHT HANNAH?

KEEP YOUR SHOULDERS BACK...

...YEAH, DON'T YOU FEEL TALLER NOW?

AND LET'S NOT BE AFRAID TO MOVE THOSE HIPS!

HEH... I NEVER AM!

THANKS HANNAH! SEE YOU TOMORROW!

DAMN! AND YOU AREN'T EVEN GOOD!

I'M TRYING TO IMAGINE YOU IN A HEADSET TEACHING JAZZERCISE OR SOMETHING.

THERE'S WORSE WAYS TO PAY THE BILLS.

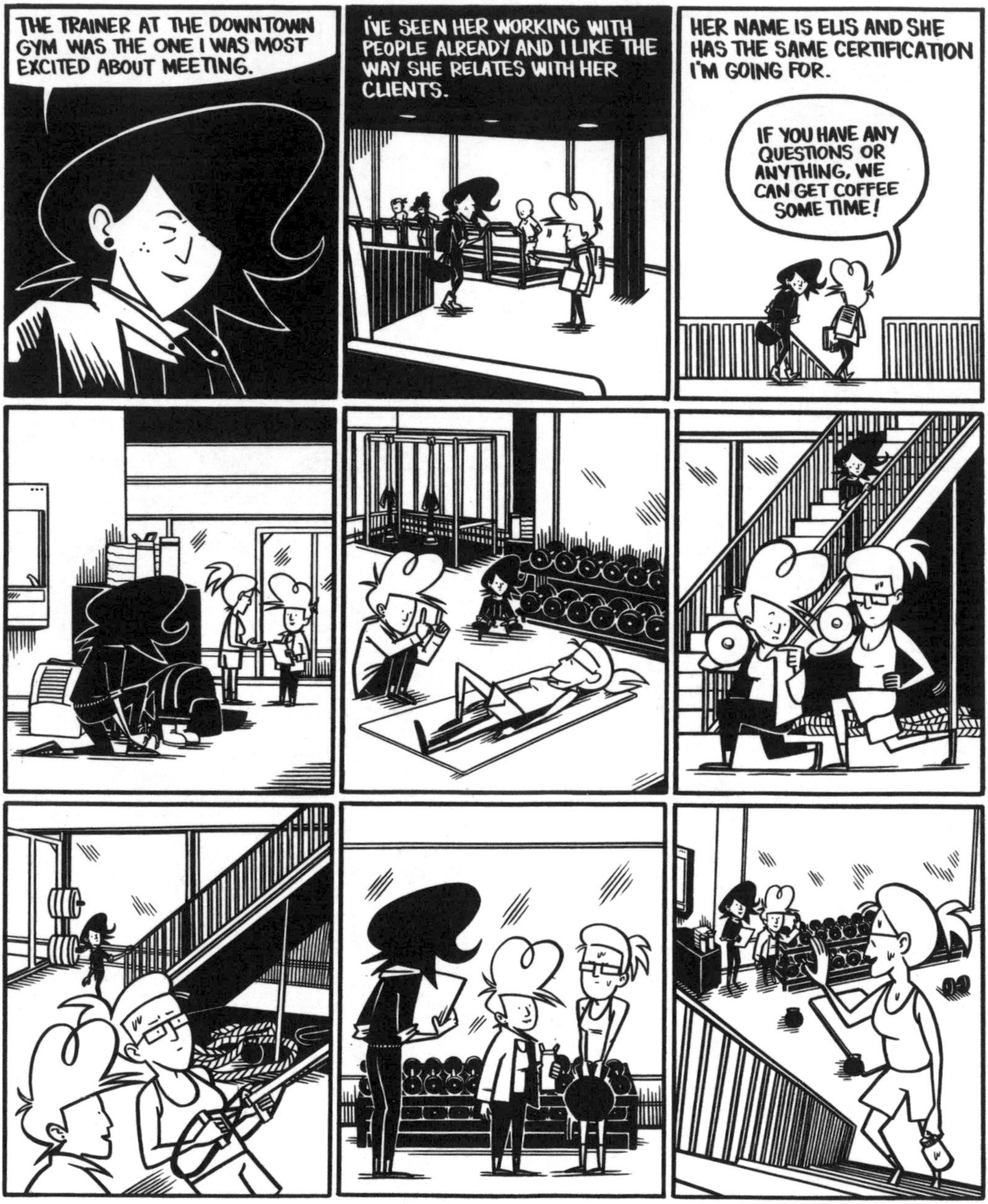
THE TRAINER AT THE DOWNTOWN GYM WAS THE ONE I WAS MOST EXCITED ABOUT MEETING.
I'VE SEEN HER WORKING WITH PEOPLE ALREADY AND I LIKE THE WAY SHE RELATES WITH HER CLIENTS.
HER NAME IS ELIS AND SHE HAS THE SAME CERTIFICATION I'M GOING FOR.
IF YOU HAVE ANY QUESTIONS OR ANYTHING, WE CAN GET COFFEE SOME TIME!

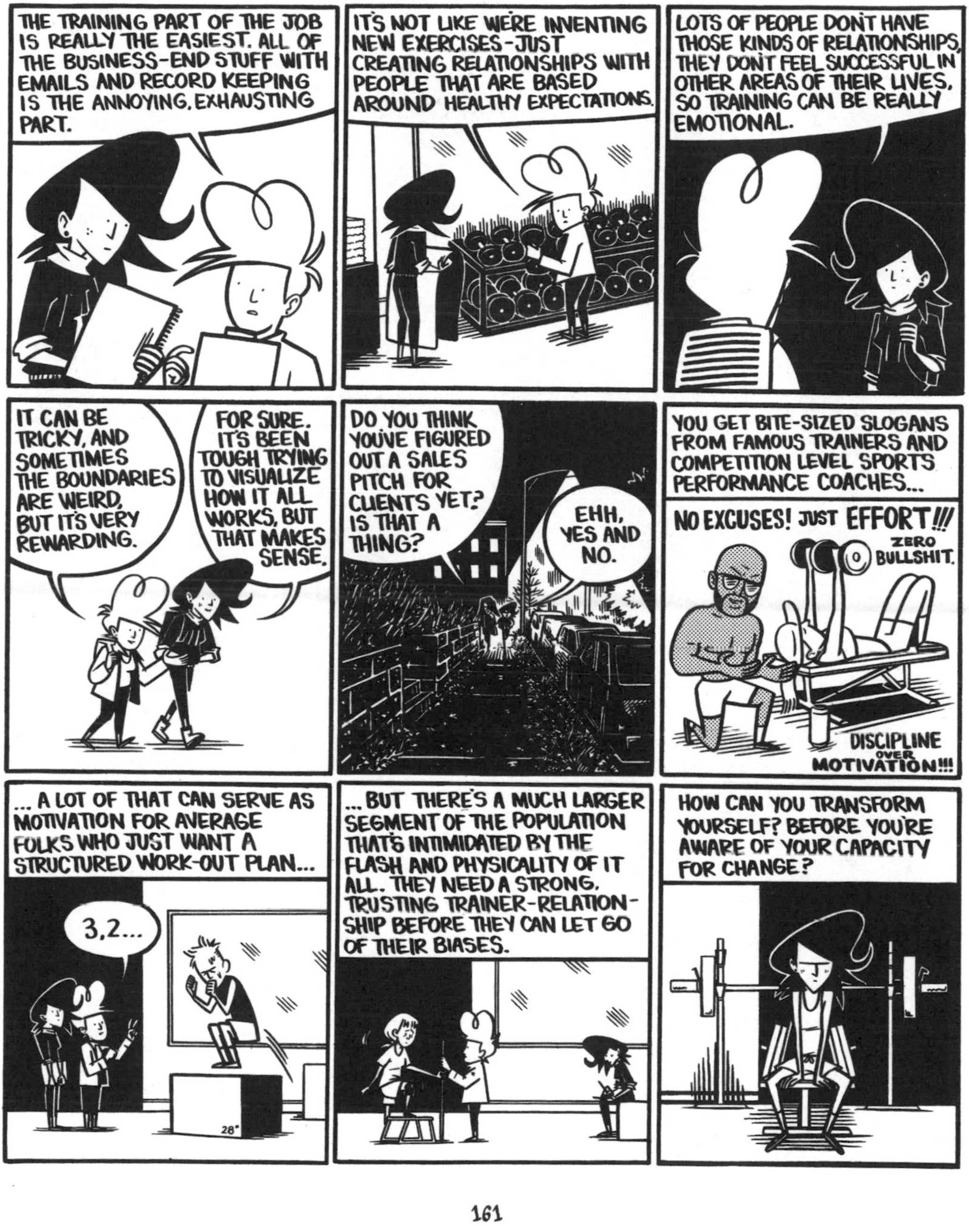
THE TRAINING PART OF THE JOB IS REALLY THE EASIEST. ALL OF THE BUSINESS-END STUFF WITH EMAILS AND RECORD KEEPING IS THE ANNOYING, EXHAUSTING PART.
IT'S NOT LIKE WE'RE INVENTING NEW EXERCISES-JUST CREATING RELATIONSHIPS WITH PEOPLE THAT ARE BASED AROUND HEALTHY EXPECTATIONS.
LOTS OF PEOPLE DON'T HAVE THOSE KINDS OF RELATIONSHIPS, THEY DON'T FEEL SUCCESSFUL IN OTHER AREAS OF THEIR LIVES, SO TRAINING CAN BE REALLY EMOTIONAL.
IT CAN BE TRICKY, AND SOMETIMES THE BOUNDARIES ARE WEIRD, BUT IT'S VERY REWARDING.
FOR SURE. IT'S BEEN TOUGH TRYING TO VISUALIZE HOW IT ALL WORKS, BUT THAT MAKES SENSE.
DO YOU THINK YOU'VE FIGURED OUT A SALES PITCH FOR CLIENTS YET? IS THAT A THING?
EHH, YES AND NO.
YOU GET BITE-SIZED SLOGANS FROM FAMOUS TRAINERS AND COMPETITION LEVEL SPORTS PERFORMANCE COACHES...
NO EXCUSES! JUST EFFORT!!!
ZERO BULLSHIT.
DISCIPLINE OVER MOTIVATION!!!
... A LOT OF THAT CAN SERVE AS MOTIVATION FOR AVERAGE FOLKS WHO JUST WANT A STRUCTURED WORK-OUT PLAN...
3,2...
28"
... BUT THERE'S A MUCH LARGER SEGMENT OF THE POPULATION THAT'S INTIMIDATED BY THE FLASH AND PHYSICALITY OF IT ALL. THEY NEED A STRONG, TRUSTING TRAINER-RELATIONSHIP BEFORE THEY CAN LET GO OF THEIR BIASES.
HOW CAN YOU TRANSFORM YOURSELF? BEFORE YOU'RE AWARE OF YOUR CAPACITY FOR CHANGE?

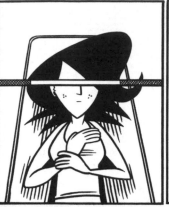

HOW CAN YOU CONVINCE A PERSON OF SOMETHING THEY CAN'T FEEL OR TOUCH?

CAN IT BE DONE? BEFORE YOU UNDERSTAND THE PROCESS? WITH JUST A FEW REASONABLE EXPECTATIONS?

"I CAN PUT THIS BAR IN MY HANDS BECAUSE I KNOW THE BENCH WON'T COLLAPSE UNDER ME."

"THIS IS A SIMILAR WEIGHT TO WHAT I HAVE PRESSED BEFORE."

"EVEN THOUGH I'M LOWERING THIS TO MY CHEST, I WON'T BE PINNED BECAUSE I'M IN CONTROL."

"STRESS IS TO BE EXPECTED. BUT I AM PREPARED."

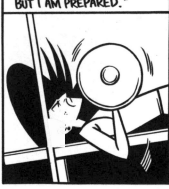

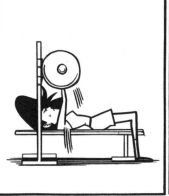

CLACK

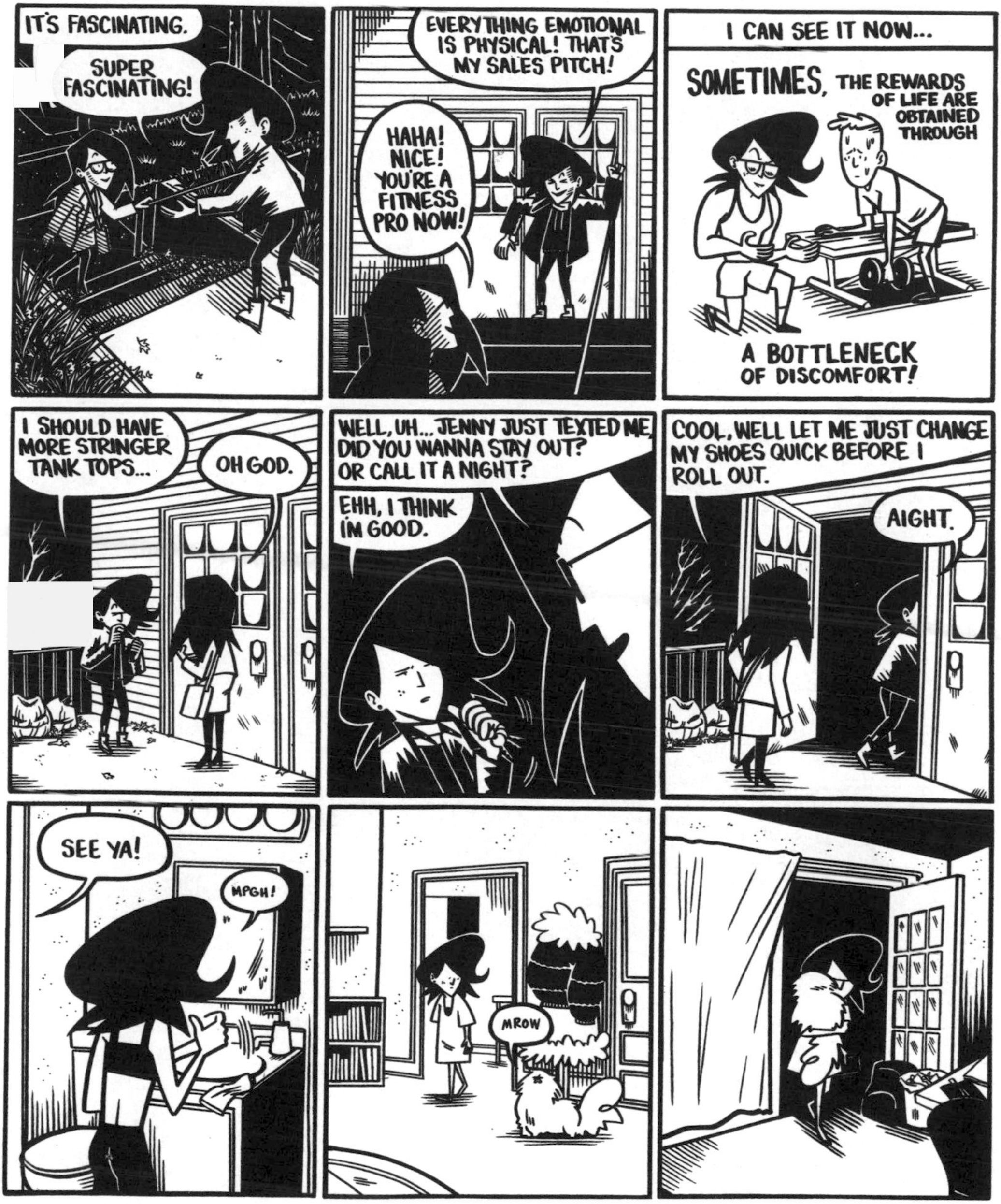
IT'S FASCINATING.
SUPER FASCINATING!
EVERYTHING EMOTIONAL IS PHYSICAL! THAT'S MY SALES PITCH!
HAHA! NICE! YOU'RE A FITNESS PRO NOW!
I CAN SEE IT NOW...
SOMETIMES, THE REWARDS OF LIFE ARE OBTAINED THROUGH
A BOTTLENECK OF DISCOMFORT!
I SHOULD HAVE MORE STRINGER TANK TOPS...
OH GOD.
WELL, UH... JENNY JUST TEXTED ME, DID YOU WANNA STAY OUT? OR CALL IT A NIGHT?
EHH, I THINK I'M GOOD.
COOL, WELL LET ME JUST CHANGE MY SHOES QUICK BEFORE I ROLL OUT.
AIGHT.
SEE YA!
MPGH!
MROW

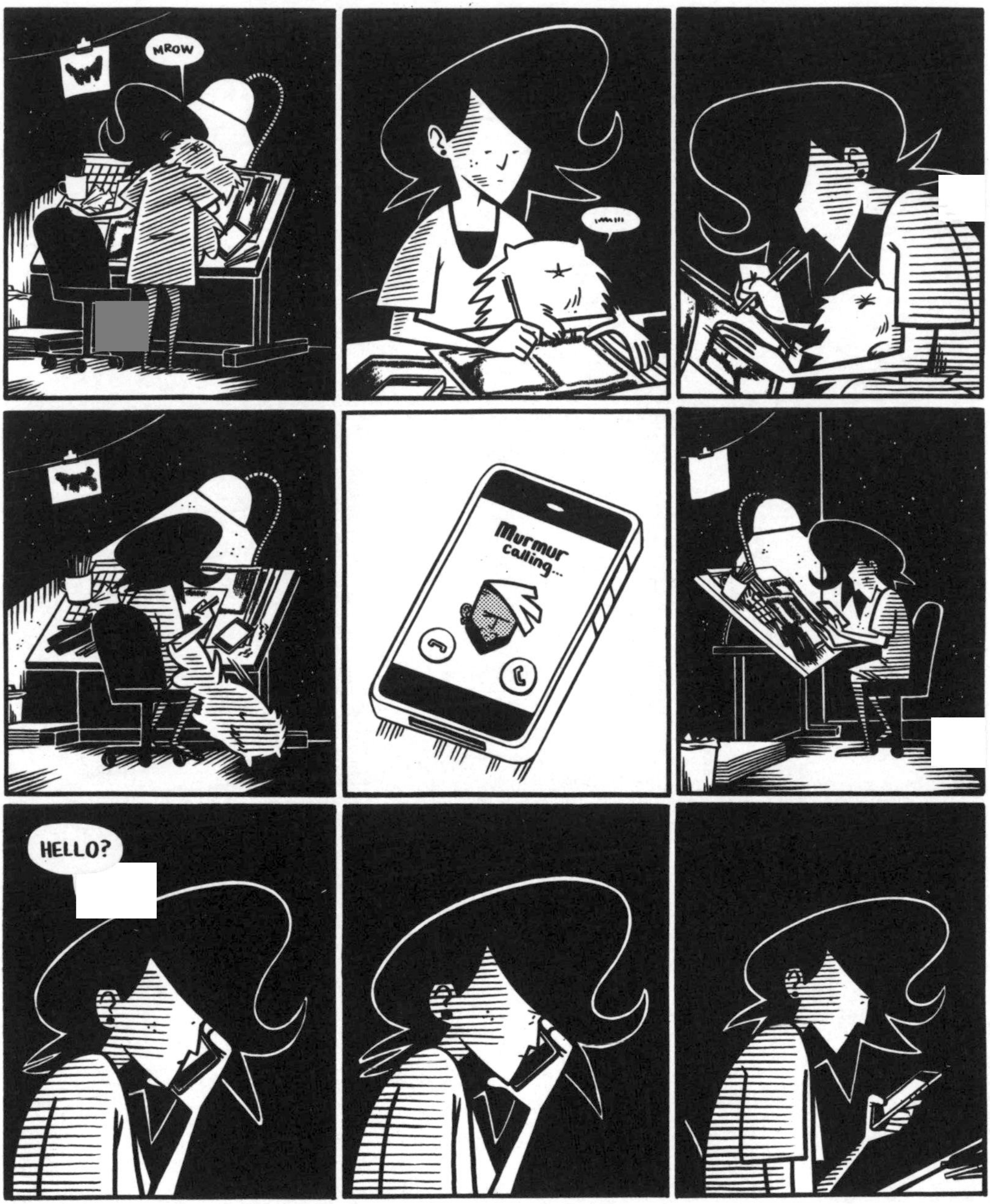
MROW
Murmur
calling...
HELLO?

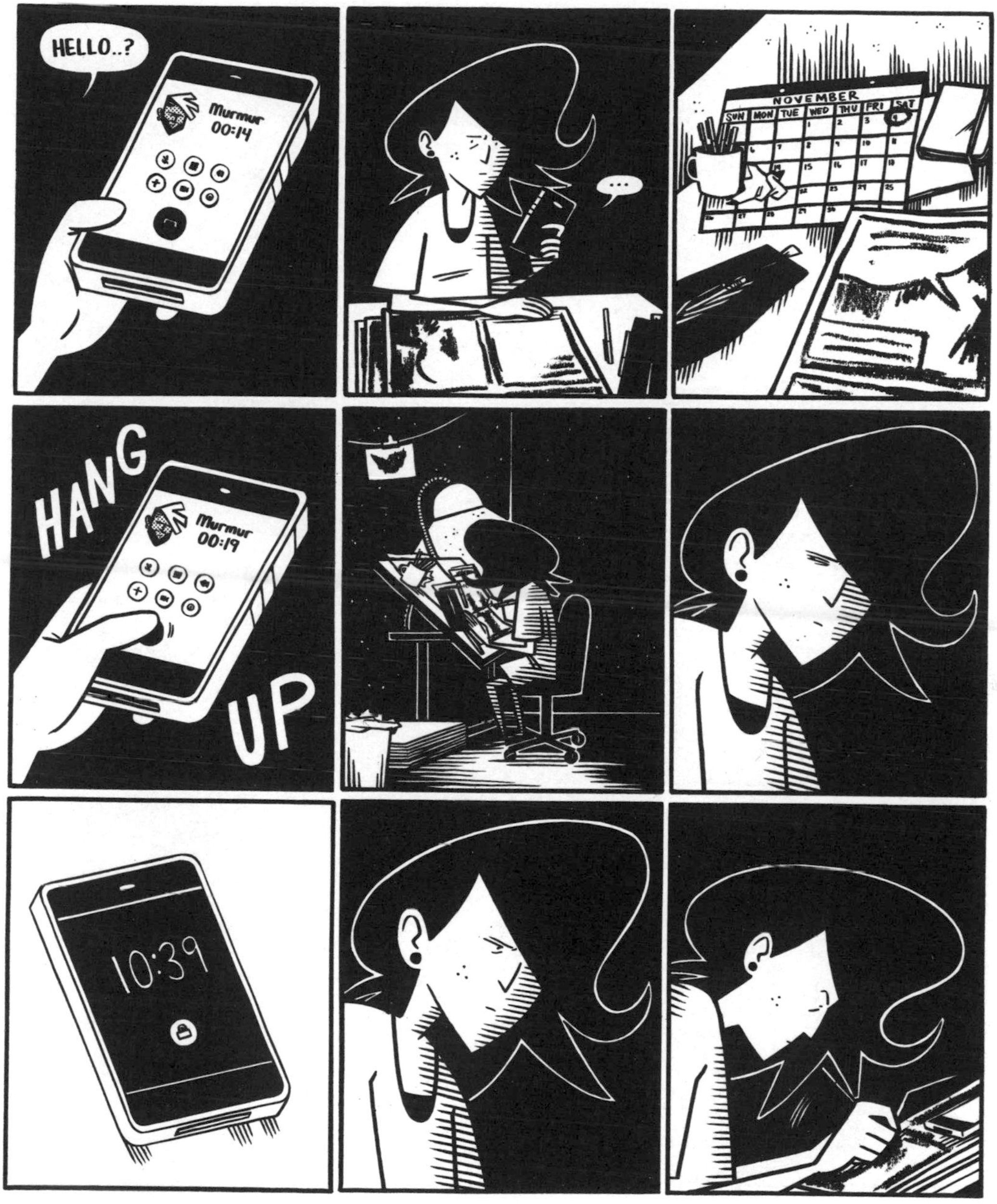
HELLO..?
Murmur
00:14
...
NOVEMBER
SUN MON TUE WED THU FRI SAT
HANG UP
Murmur
00:19
10:39

PROBABLY JUST A BUTT-DIAL, WHATEVER.

WAY TOO EASY TO BE EMOTIONAL OVER NOTHING, TO READ INTO SOMETHING TOO MUCH.

WAY TOO EASY TO ZOOM OUT AND SEE HOW POINTLESS IT ALL IS.

UP CLOSE, IT'S THIS STINGING RASH ALL OVER YOUR BODY.

SOMETHING YOU CAN'T HELP BUT SCRATCH.

FIVE MINUTES.

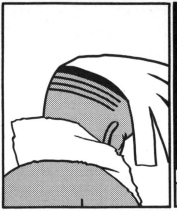

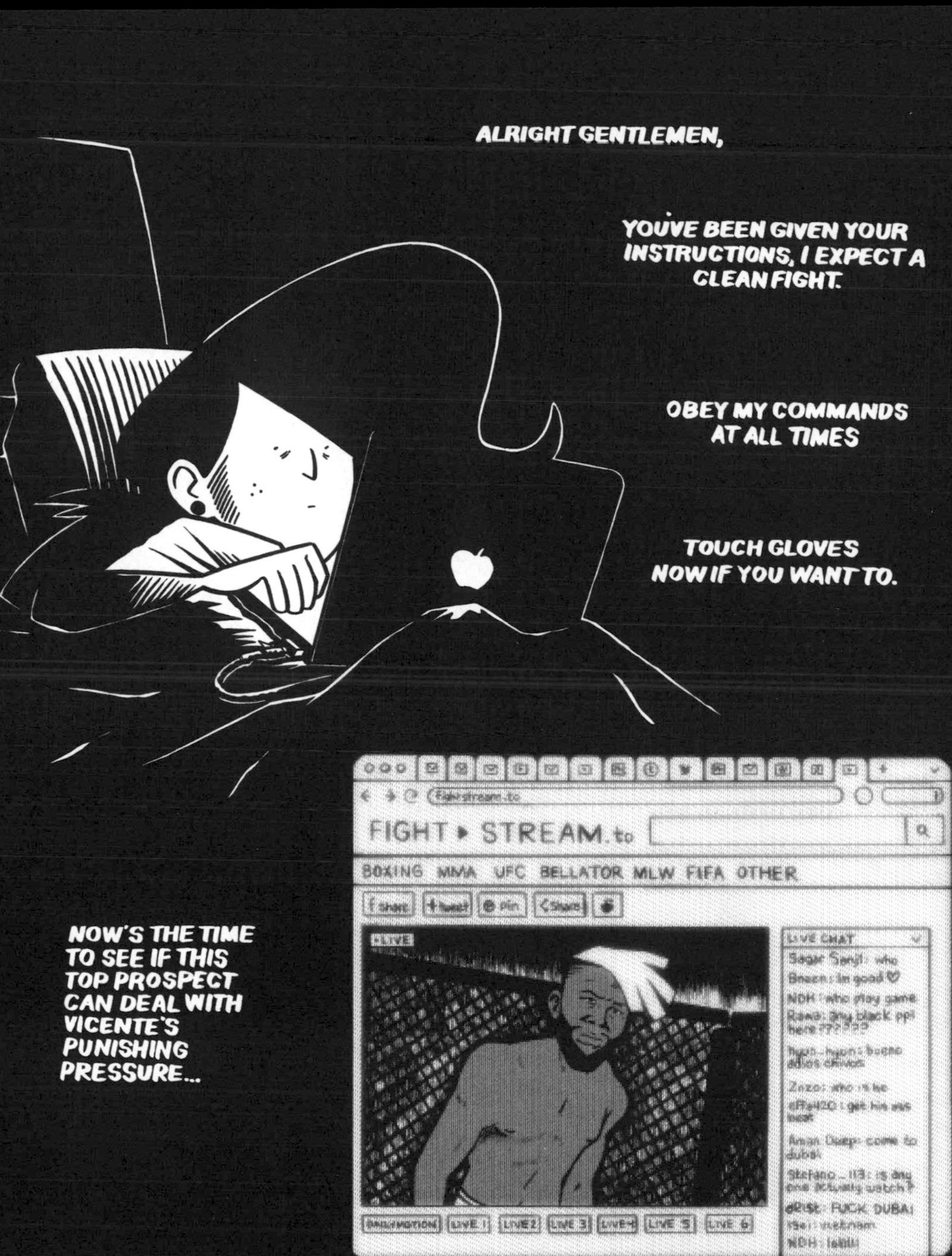
ALRIGHT GENTLEMEN,
YOU'VE BEEN GIVEN YOUR INSTRUCTIONS, I EXPECT A CLEAN FIGHT.
OBEY MY COMMANDS AT ALL TIMES
TOUCH GLOVES NOW IF YOU WANT TO.
NOW'S THE TIME TO SEE IF THIS TOP PROSPECT CAN DEAL WITH VICENTE'S PUNISHING PRESSURE...
FIGHT ▸ STREAM.to
BOXING MMA UFC BELLATOR MLW FIFA OTHER
LIVE
LIVE CHAT

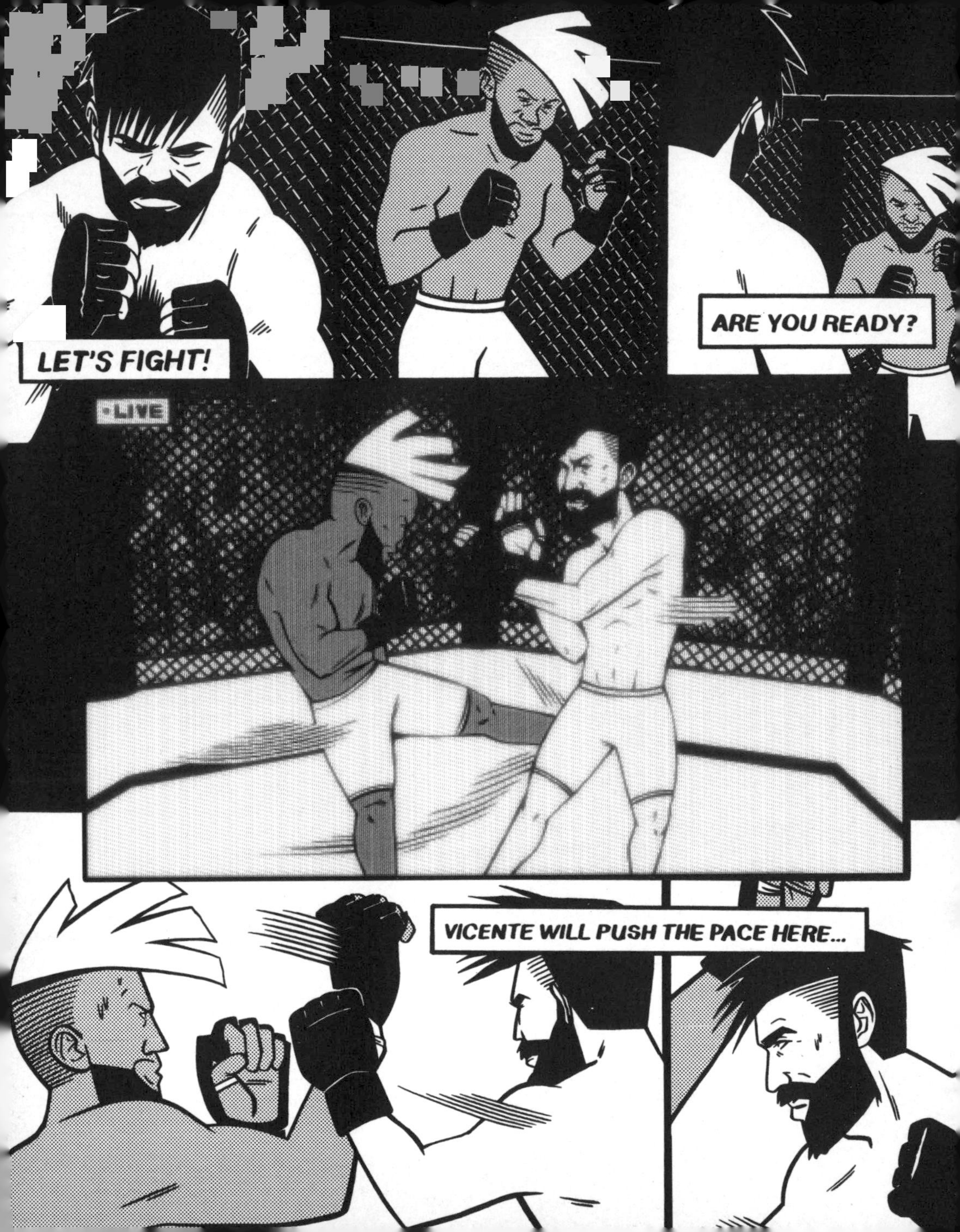
LET'S FIGHT!
ARE YOU READY?
• LIVE
VICENTE WILL PUSH THE PACE HERE...

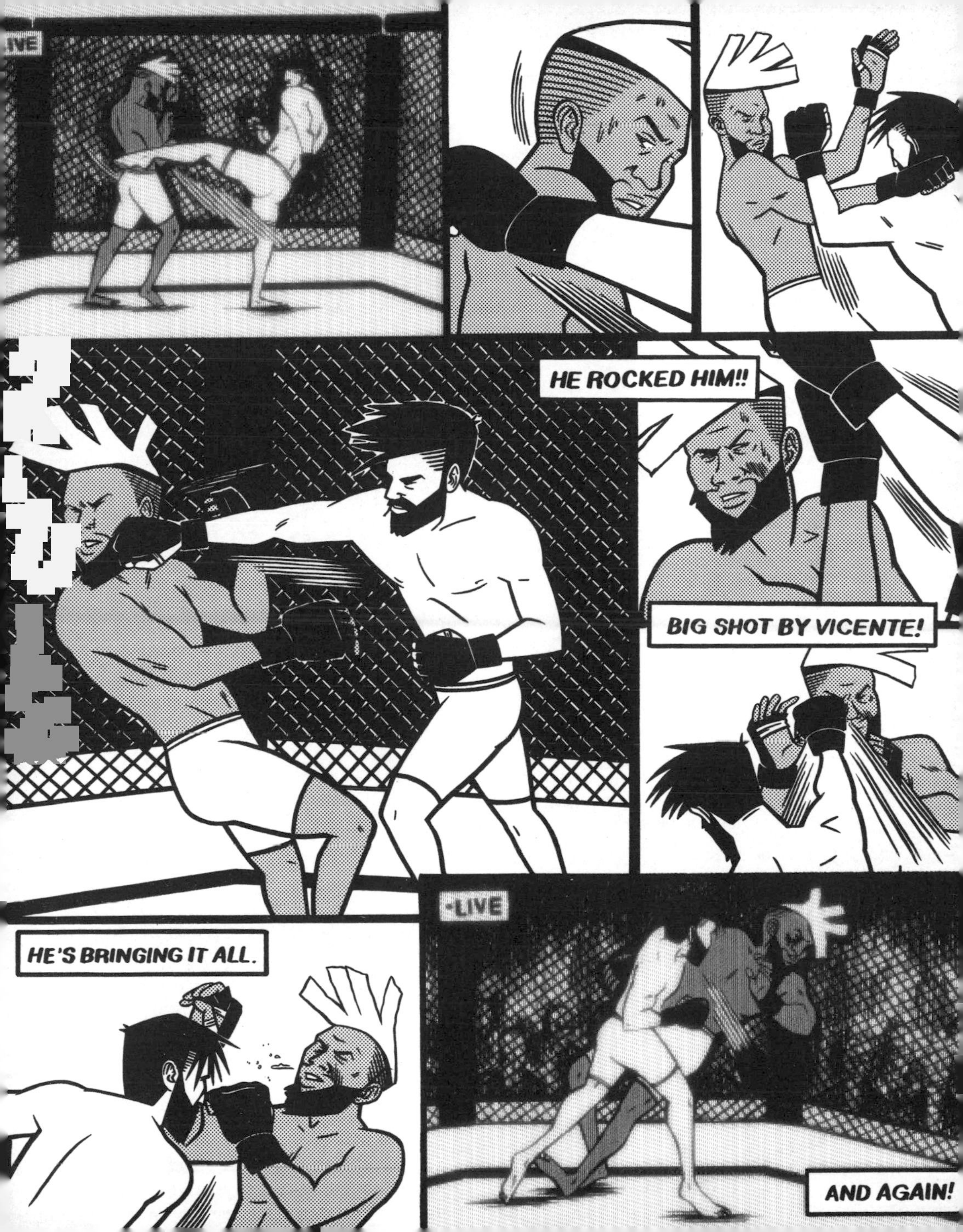
HE ROCKED HIM!!
BIG SHOT BY VICENTE!
HE'S BRINGING IT ALL.
-LIVE
AND AGAIN!

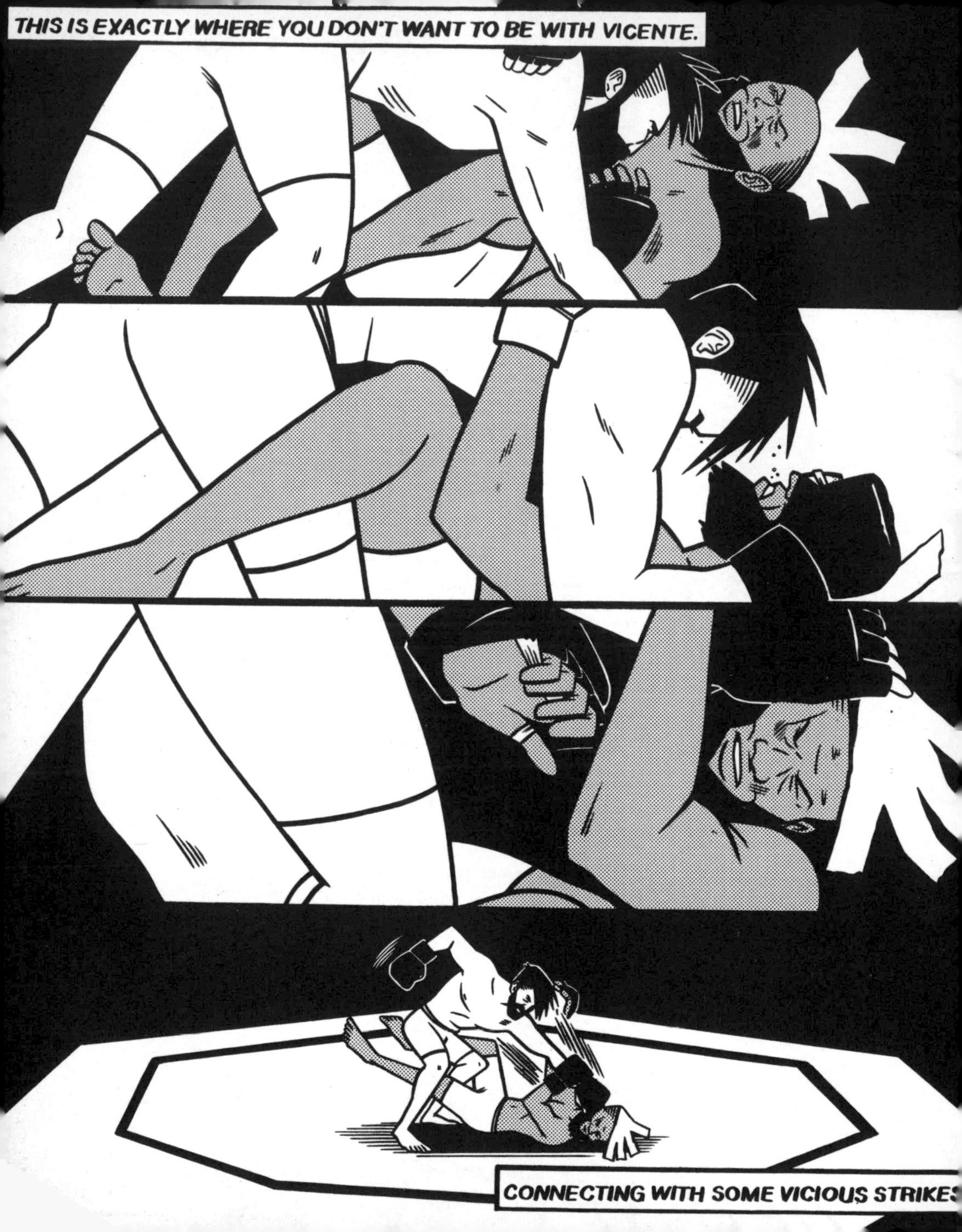
THIS IS EXACTLY WHERE YOU DON'T WANT TO BE WITH VICENTE.
CONNECTING WITH SOME VICIOUS STRIKES

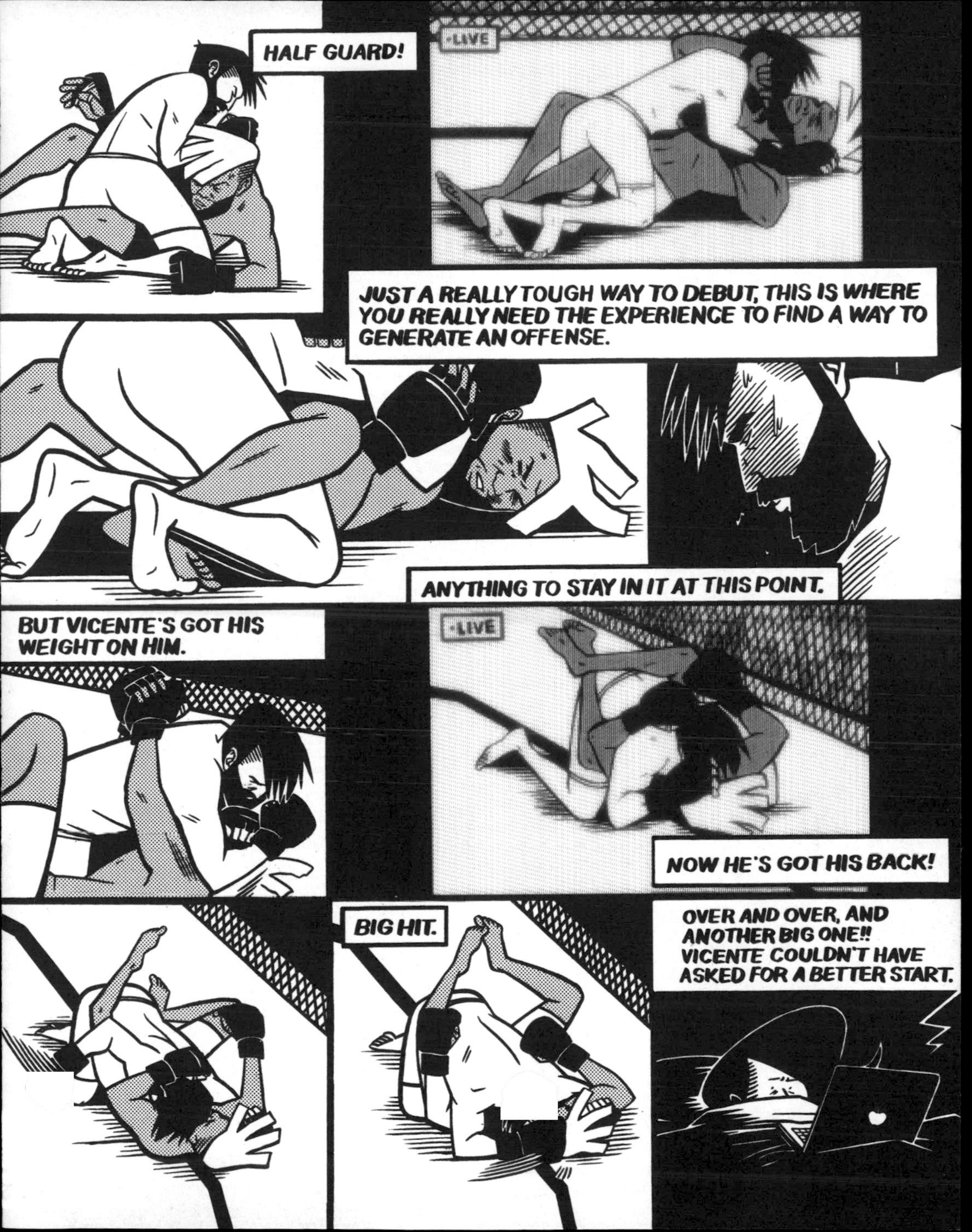
HALF GUARD!
LIVE
JUST A REALLY TOUGH WAY TO DEBUT, THIS IS WHERE YOU REALLY NEED THE EXPERIENCE TO FIND A WAY TO GENERATE AN OFFENSE.
ANYTHING TO STAY IN IT AT THIS POINT.
BUT VICENTE'S GOT HIS WEIGHT ON HIM.
LIVE
NOW HE'S GOT HIS BACK!
BIG HIT.
OVER AND OVER, AND ANOTHER BIG ONE!! VICENTE COULDN'T HAVE ASKED FOR A BETTER START.

HUGE POINTS BEING SCORED.

END OF THE FIRST ROUND.

BEEEEEEP!

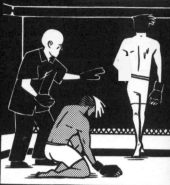

WELL, VICENTE'S GOT THAT ONE...

LOOKS LIKE SOMEWHERE IN THERE HE GOT CUT...

ABSOLUTELY BATTERED.

BUT THAT'S IT, RIGHT? HA, BIG WAKE UP TIME. NOW YOU'RE HERE.

TALK'S OVER.

TIME TO RALLY FOR ROUND TWO.

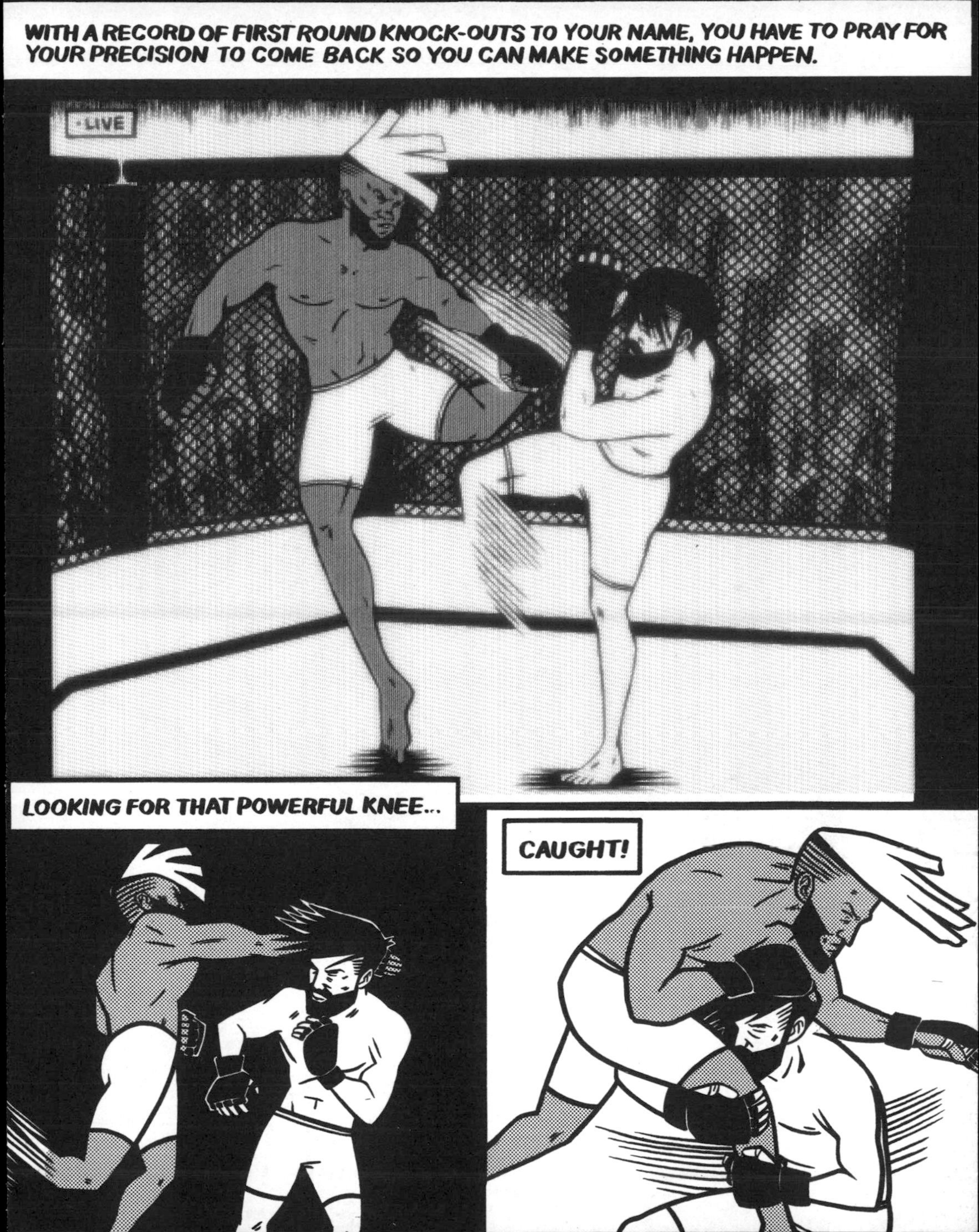
WITH A RECORD OF FIRST ROUND KNOCK-OUTS TO YOUR NAME, YOU HAVE TO PRAY FOR YOUR PRECISION TO COME BACK SO YOU CAN MAKE SOMETHING HAPPEN.
LIVE
LOOKING FOR THAT POWERFUL KNEE...
CAUGHT!

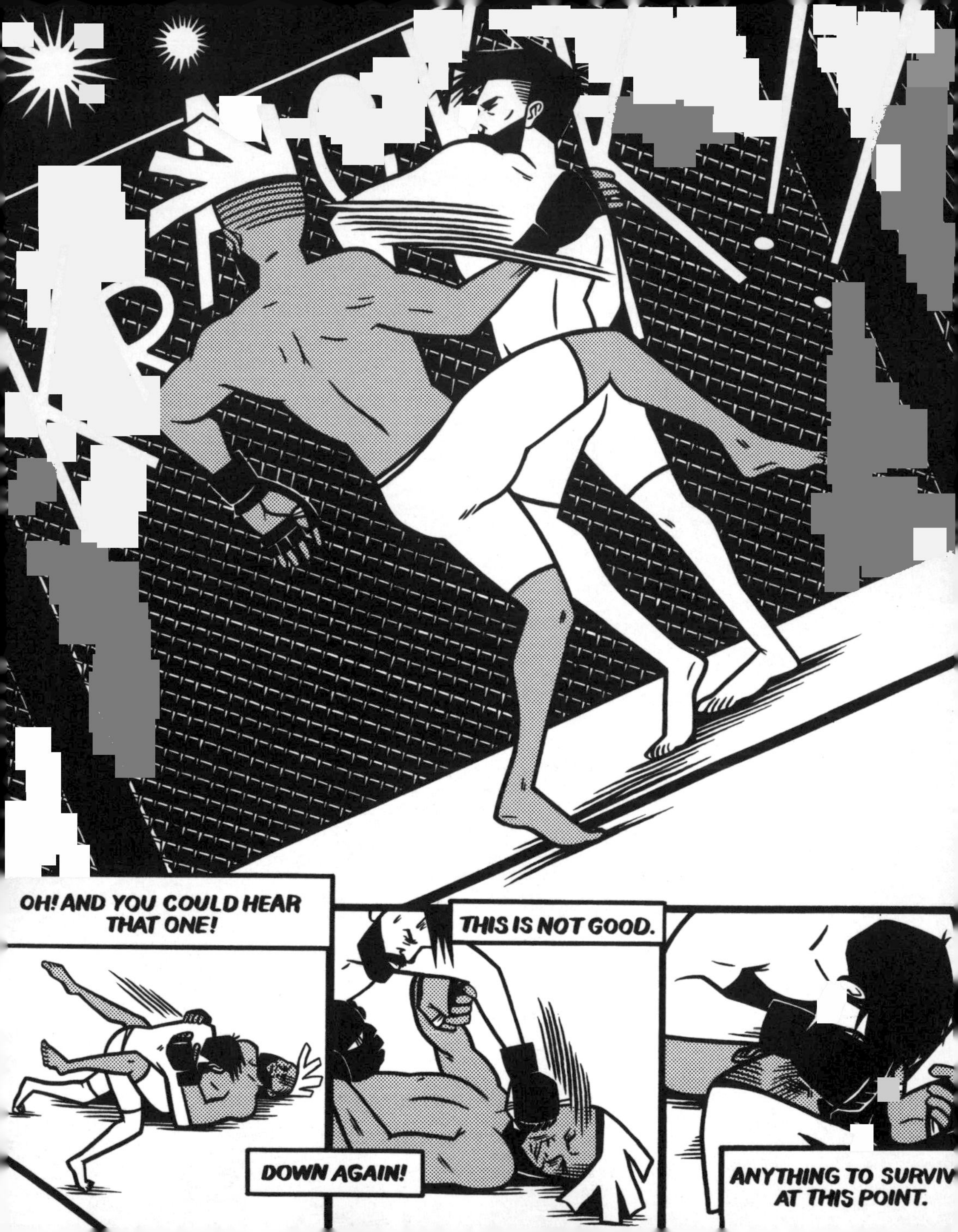
OH! AND YOU COULD HEAR THAT ONE!
DOWN AGAIN!
THIS IS NOT GOOD.
ANYTHING TO SURVIV
AT THIS POINT.

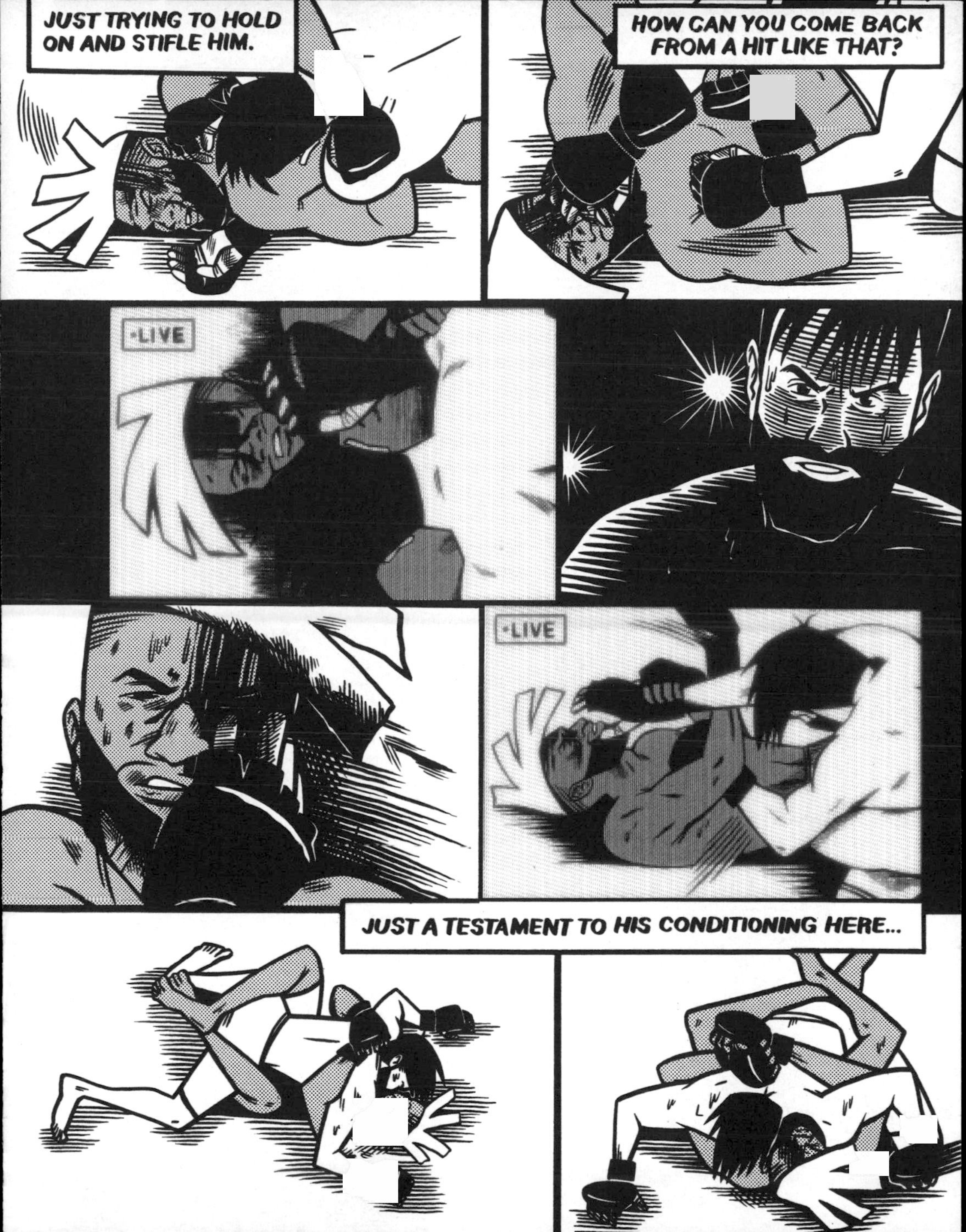
JUST TRYING TO HOLD ON AND STIFLE HIM.
HOW CAN YOU COME BACK FROM A HIT LIKE THAT?
•LIVE
•LIVE
JUST A TESTAMENT TO HIS CONDITIONING HERE...

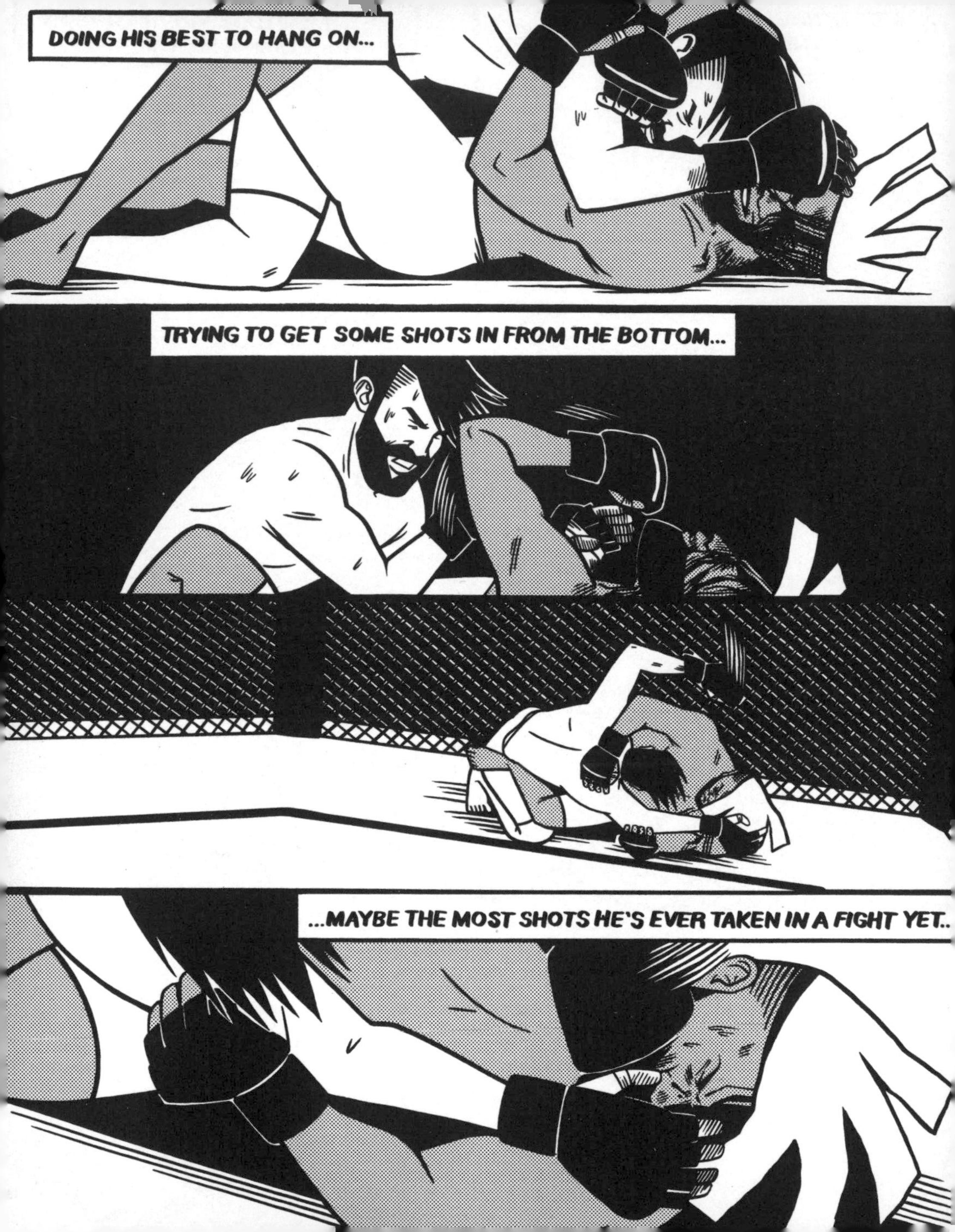
DOING HIS BEST TO HANG ON...
TRYING TO GET SOME SHOTS IN FROM THE BOTTOM...
...MAYBE THE MOST SHOTS HE'S EVER TAKEN IN A FIGHT YET..

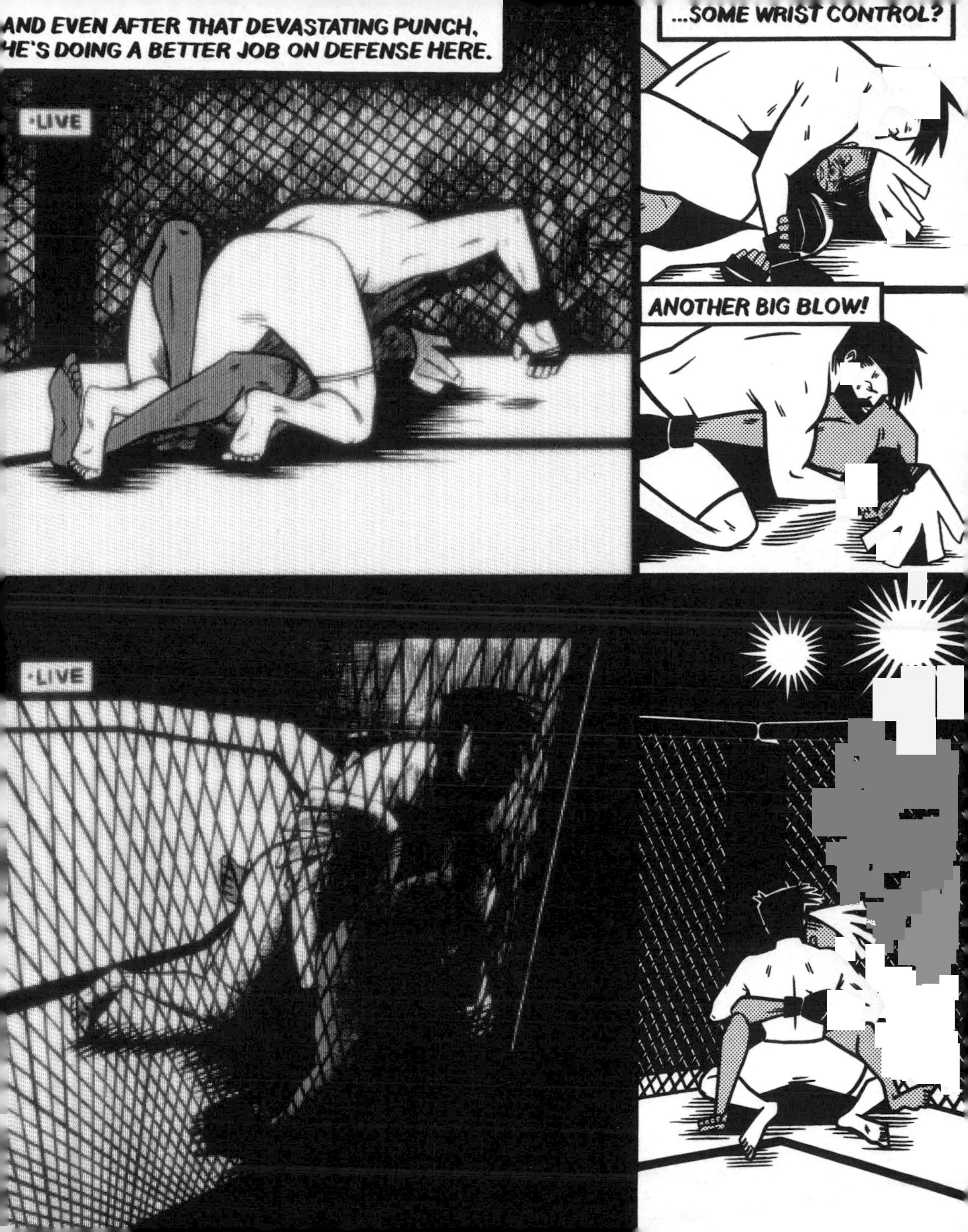

AND EVEN AFTER THAT DEVASTATING PUNCH, HE'S DOING A BETTER JOB ON DEFENSE HERE.
LIVE
...SOME WRIST CONTROL?
ANOTHER BIG BLOW!
LIVE

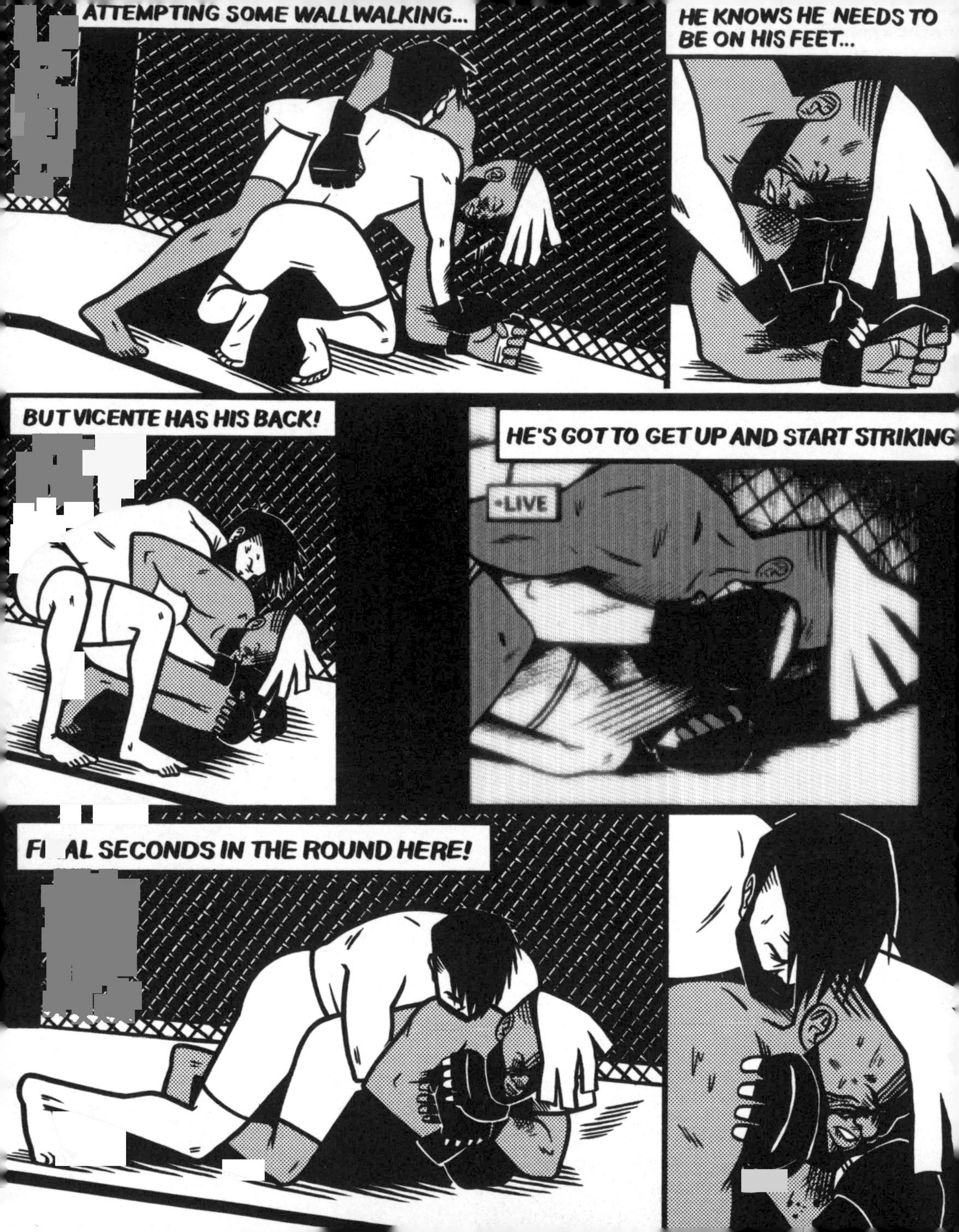
ATTEMPTING SOME WALLWALKING...
HE KNOWS HE NEEDS TO BE ON HIS FEET...
BUT VICENTE HAS HIS BACK!
HE'S GOT TO GET UP AND START STRIKING
LIVE
FI AL SECONDS IN THE ROUND HERE!

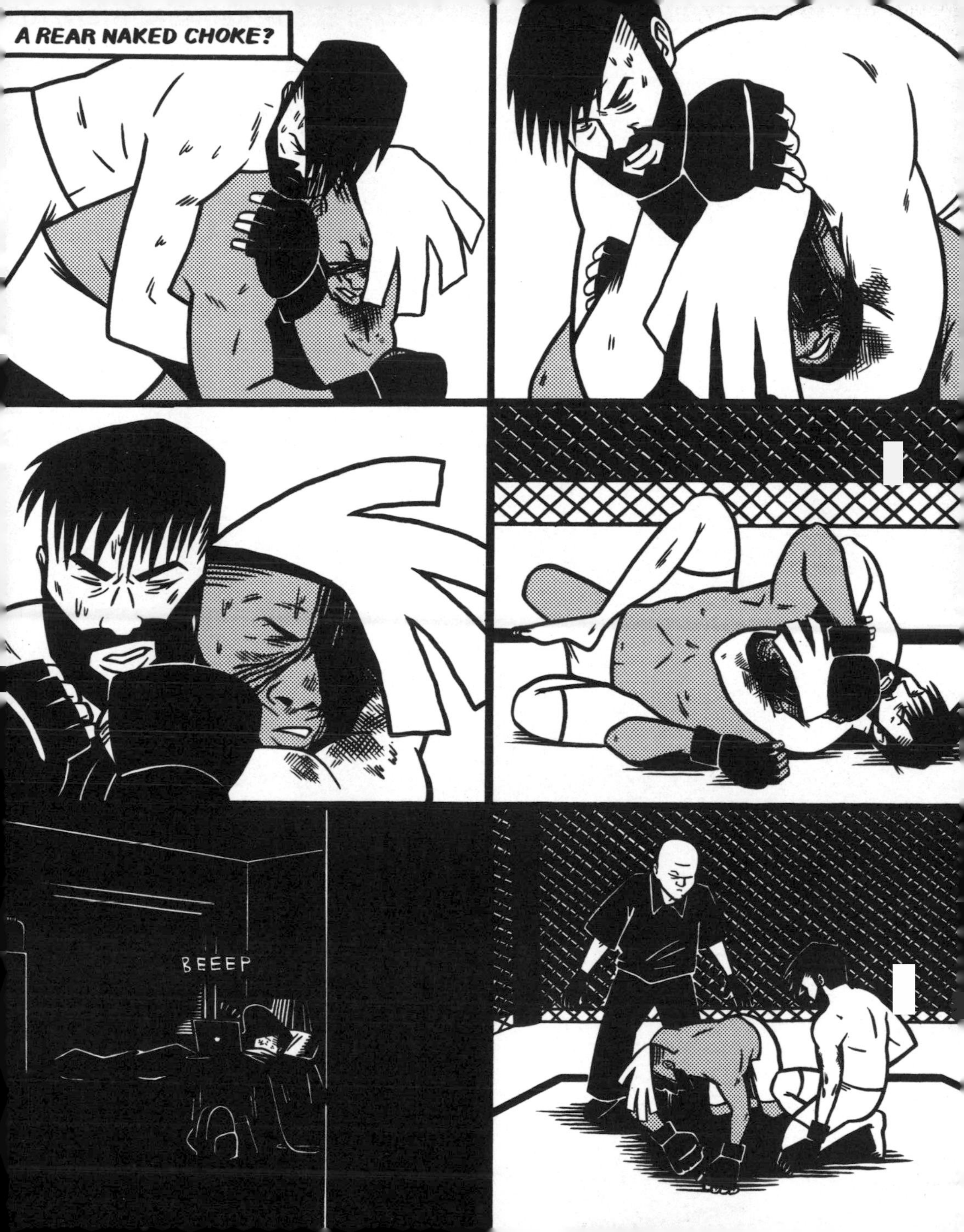
A REAR NAKED CHOKE?
BEEEP

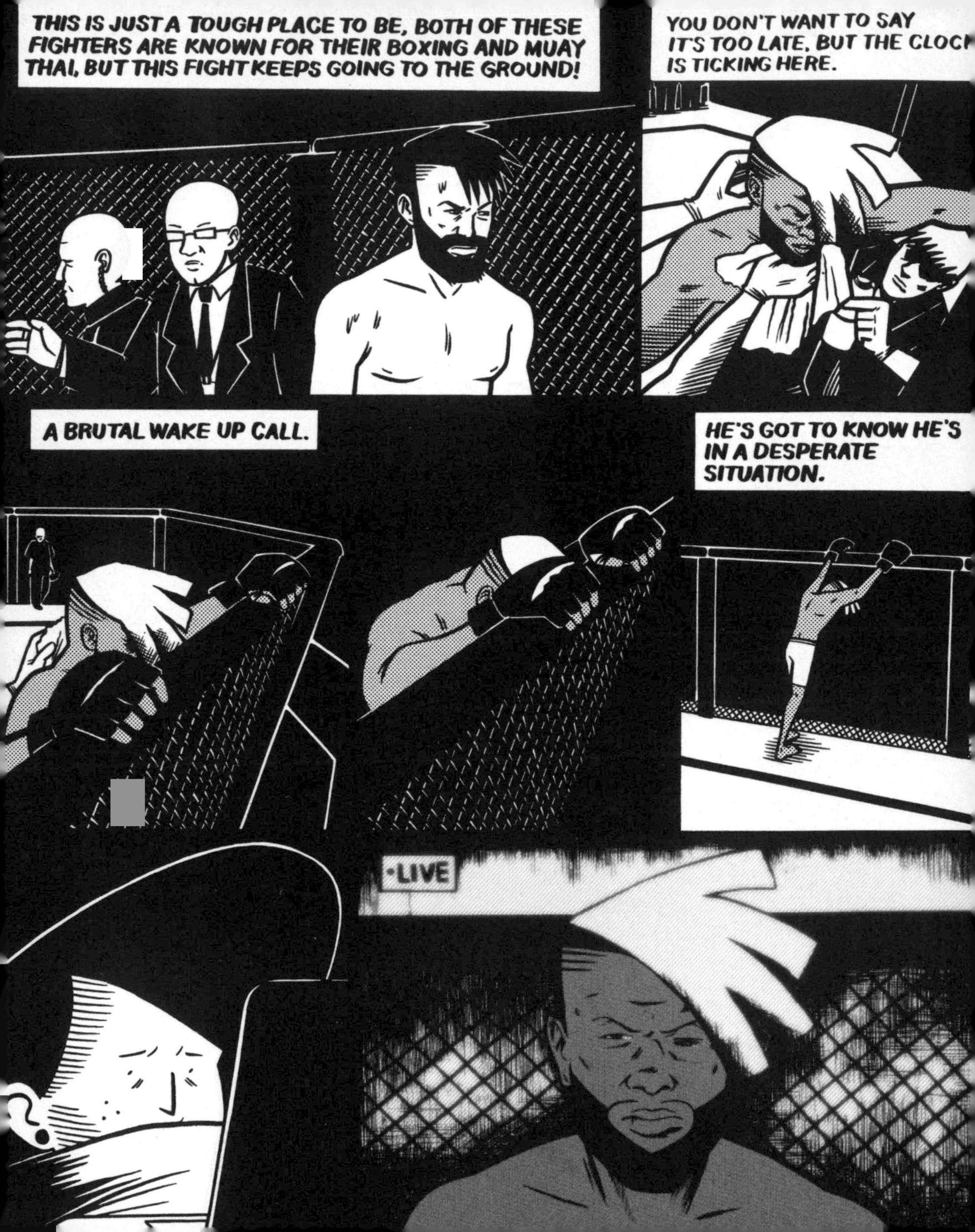
THIS IS JUST A TOUGH PLACE TO BE, BOTH OF THESE FIGHTERS ARE KNOWN FOR THEIR BOXING AND MUAY THAI, BUT THIS FIGHT KEEPS GOING TO THE GROUND!
YOU DON'T WANT TO SAY IT'S TOO LATE, BUT THE CLOCK IS TICKING HERE.
A BRUTAL WAKE UP CALL.
HE'S GOT TO KNOW HE'S IN A DESPERATE SITUATION.
•LIVE

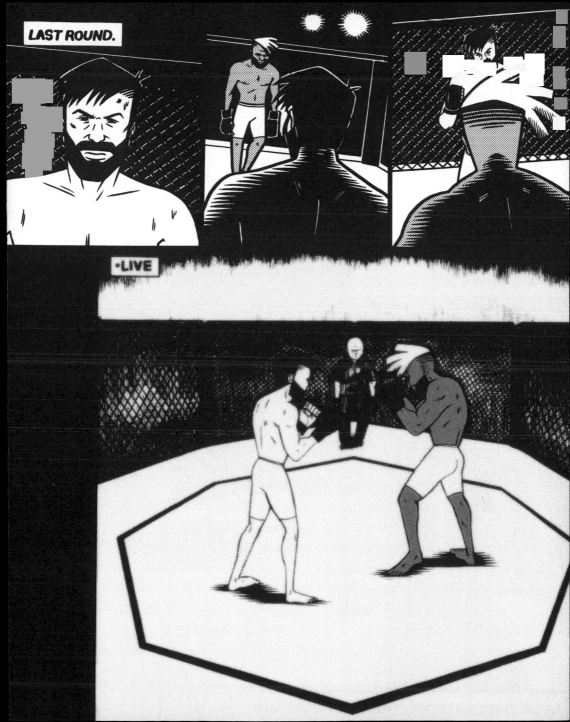

LAST ROUND.

•LIVE

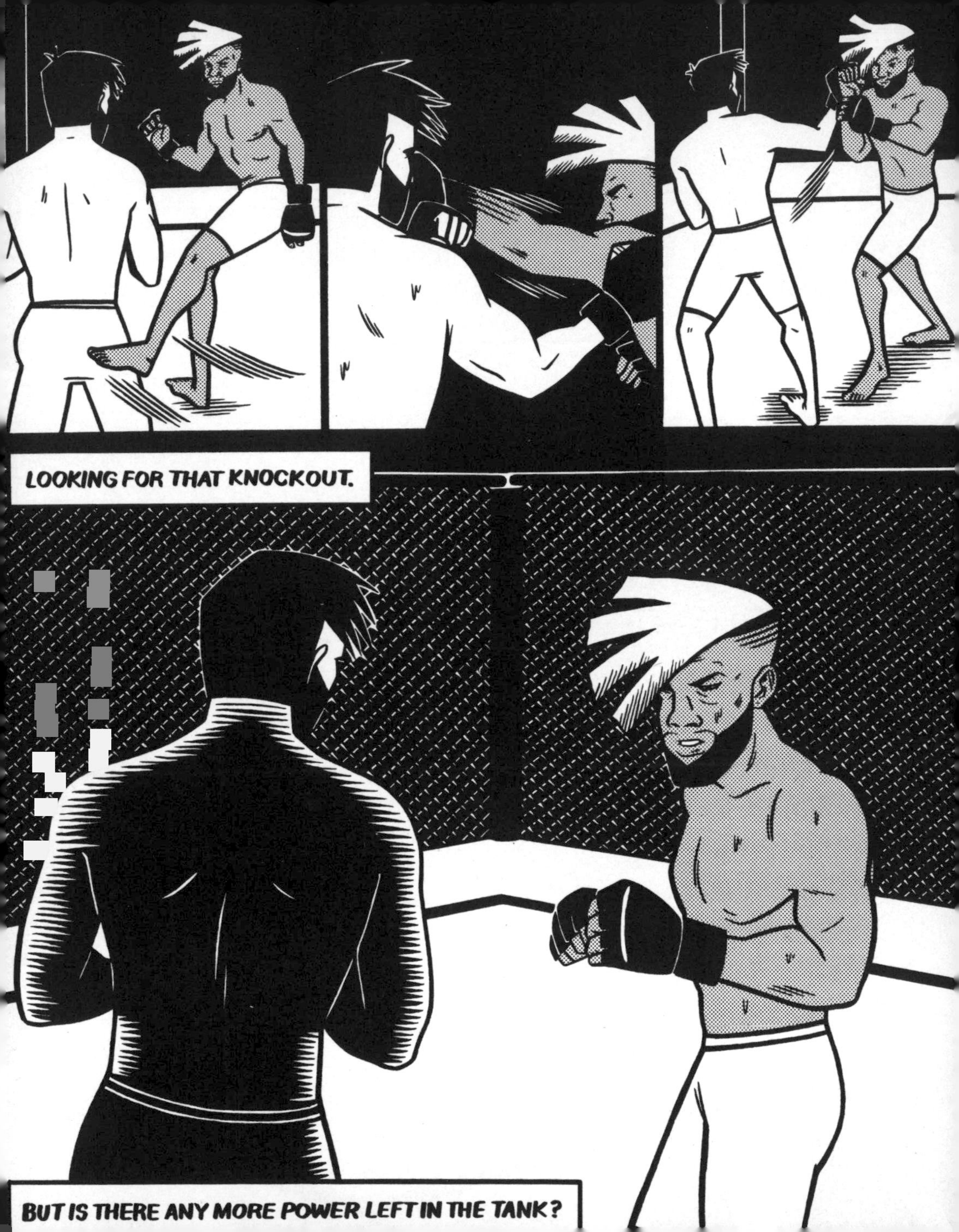
LOOKING FOR THAT KNOCKOUT.
BUT IS THERE ANY MORE POWER LEFT IN THE TANK?

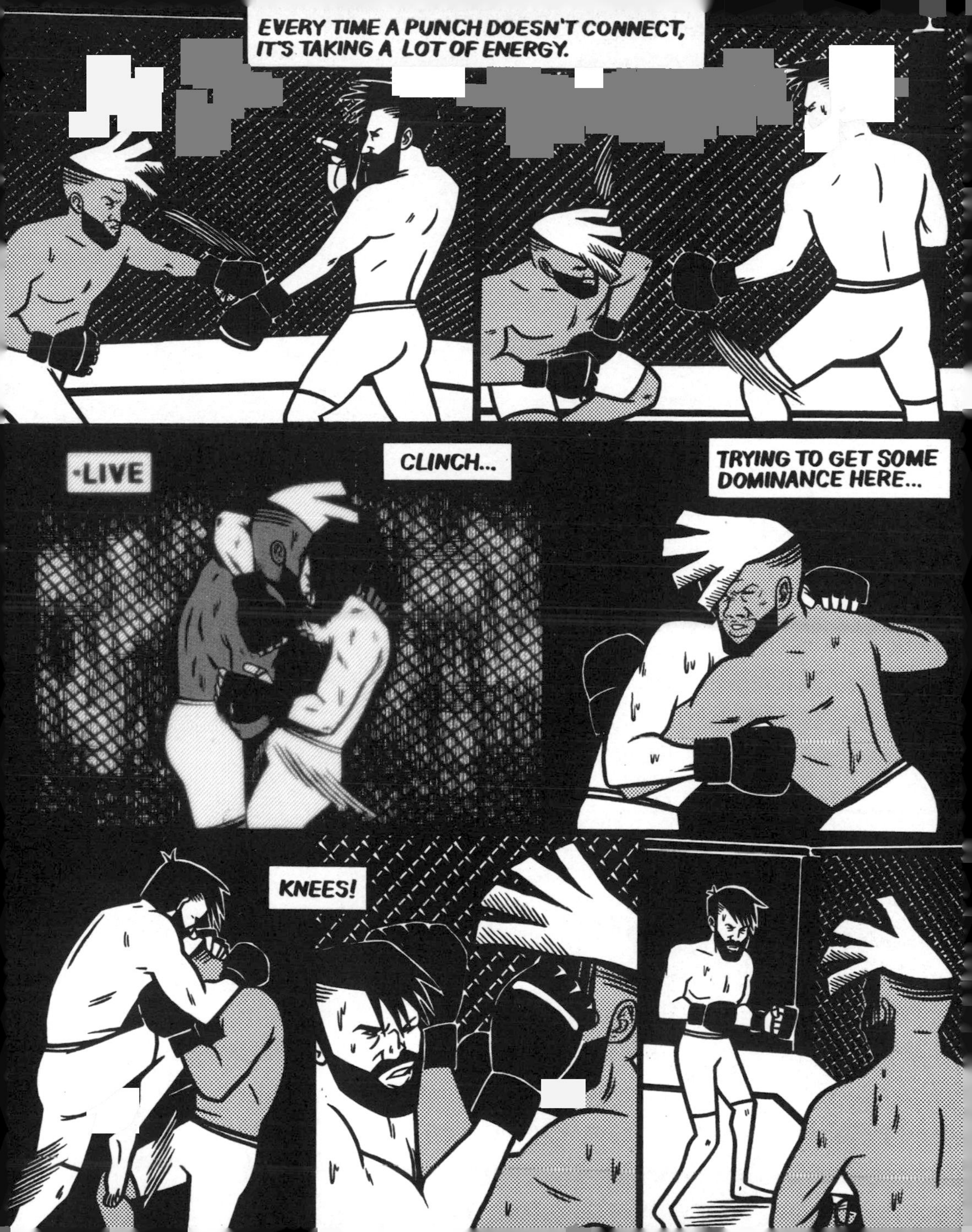
EVERY TIME A PUNCH DOESN'T CONNECT, IT'S TAKING A LOT OF ENERGY.
•LIVE
CLINCH...
TRYING TO GET SOME DOMINANCE HERE...
KNEES!

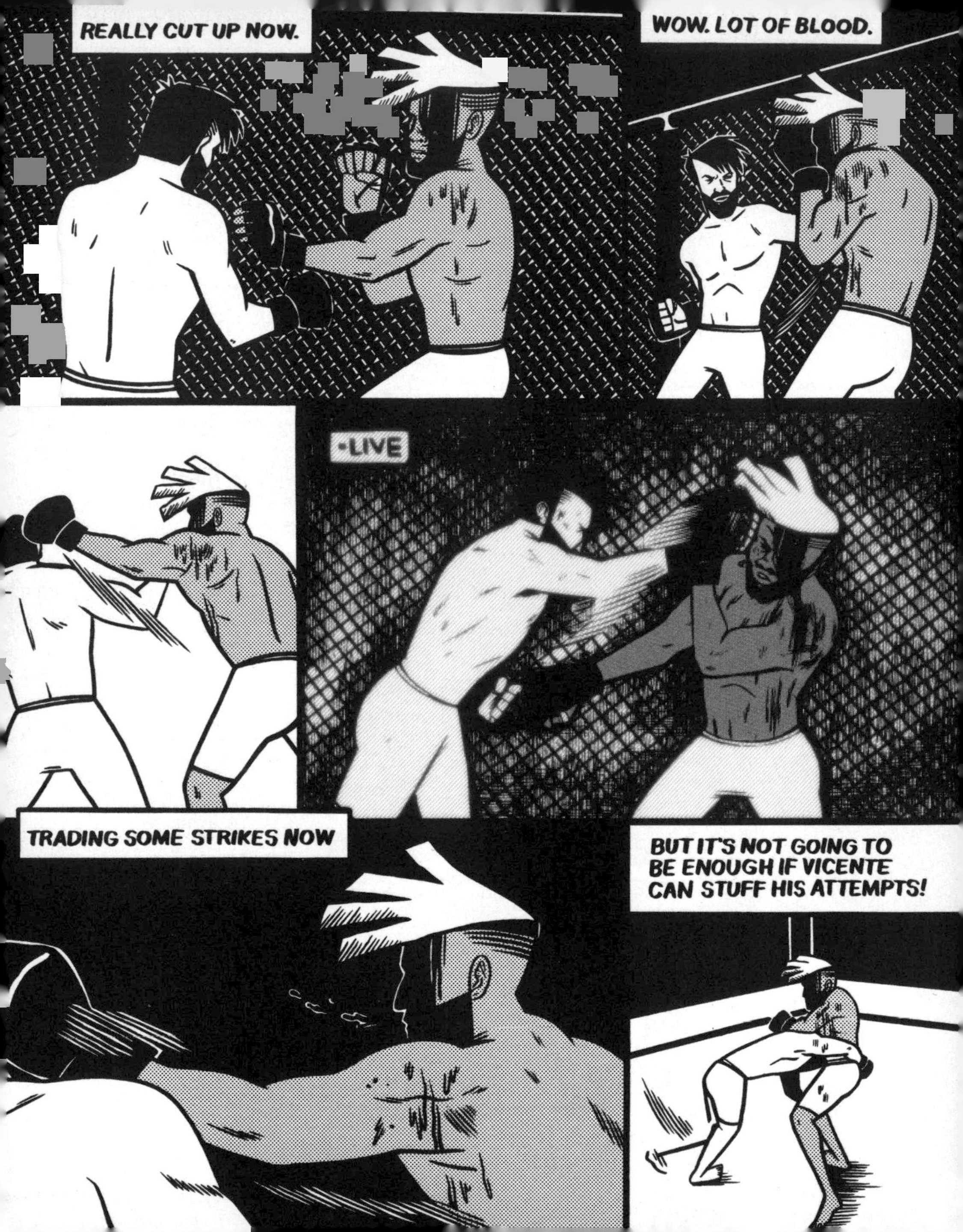
REALLY CUT UP NOW.
WOW. LOT OF BLOOD.
•LIVE
TRADING SOME STRIKES NOW
BUT IT'S NOT GOING TO BE ENOUGH IF VICENTE CAN STUFF HIS ATTEMPTS!

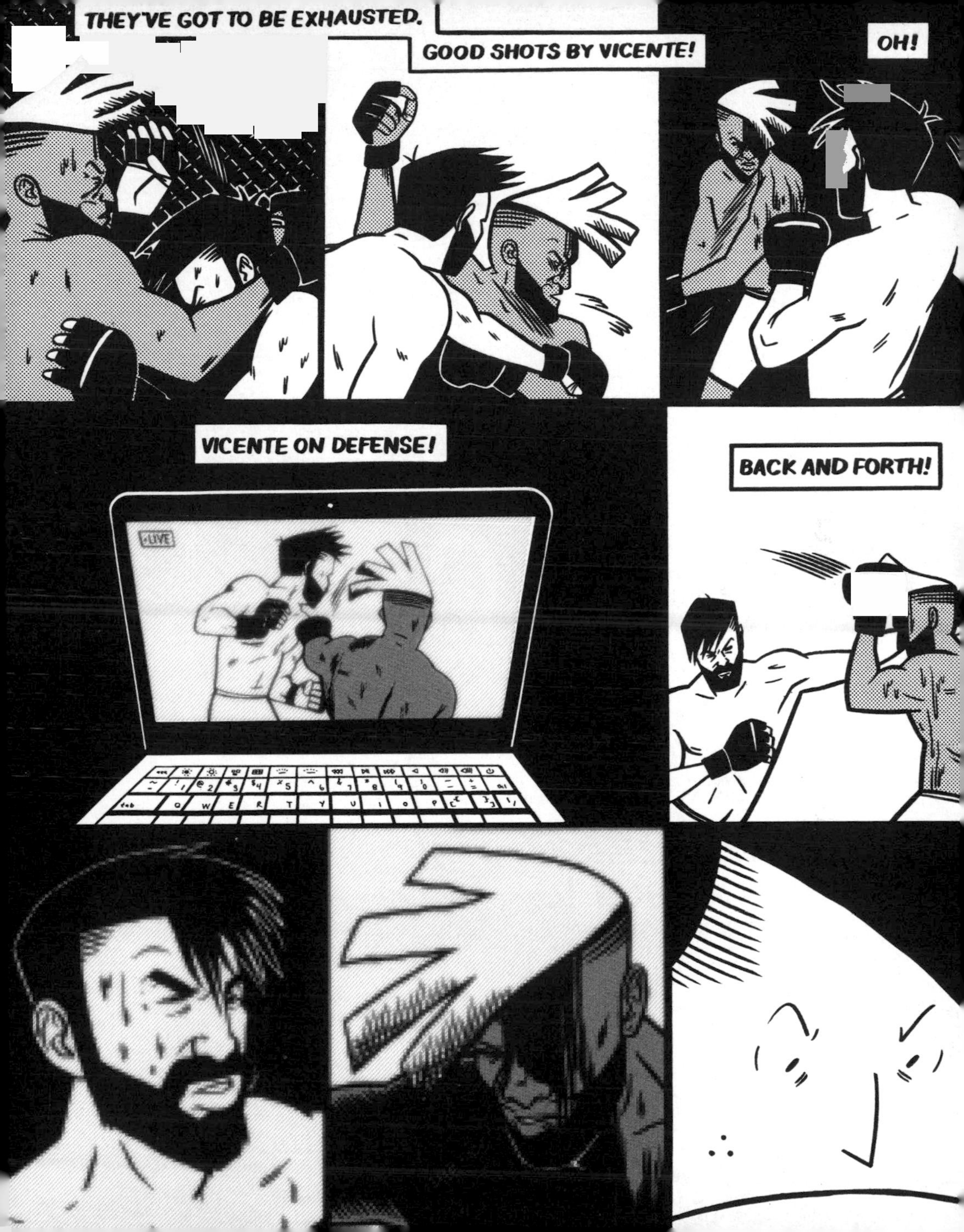
THEY'VE GOT TO BE EXHAUSTED.
GOOD SHOTS BY VICENTE!
OH!
VICENTE ON DEFENSE!
LIVE
BACK AND FORTH!

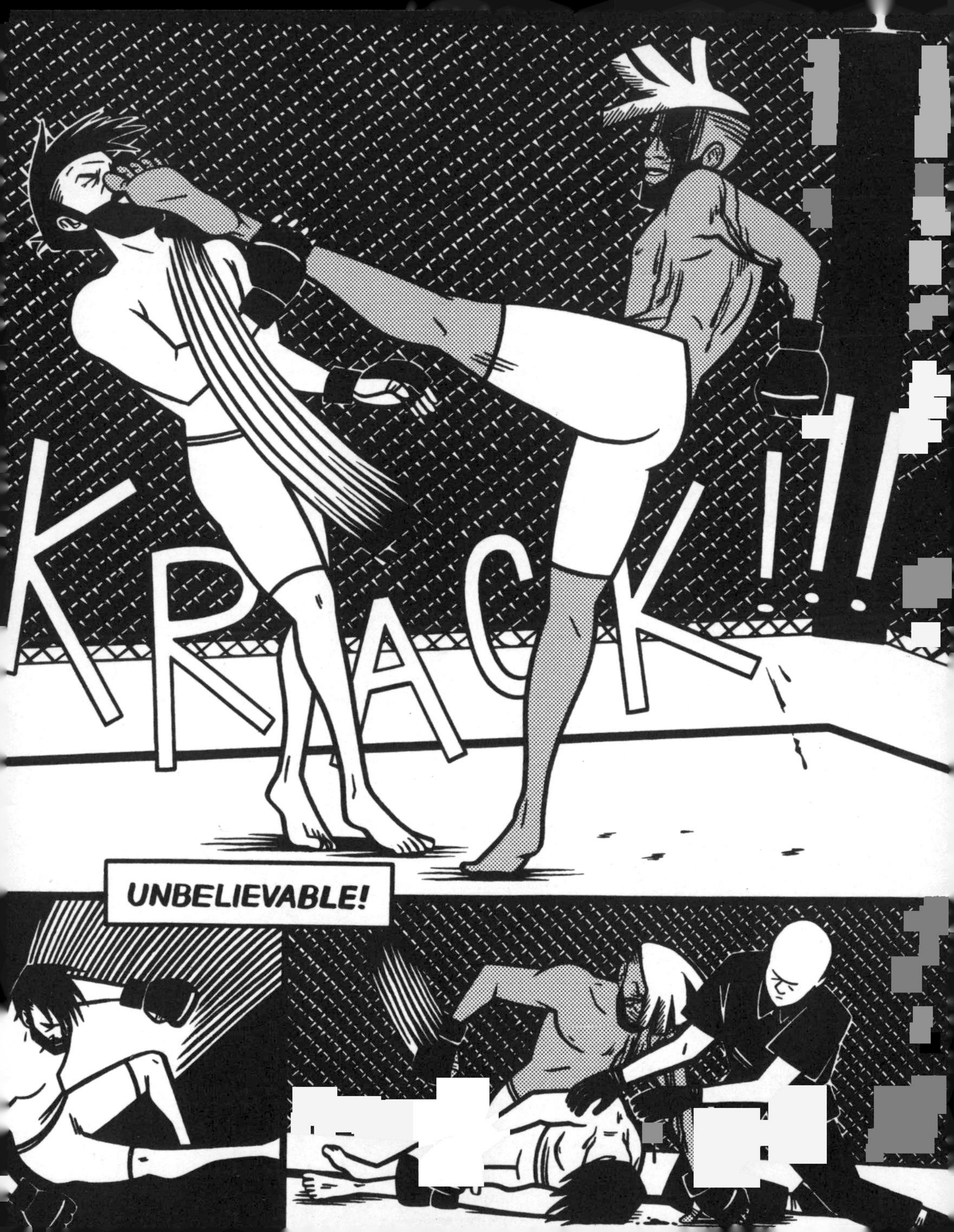
KRACK!!!
UNBELIEVABLE!

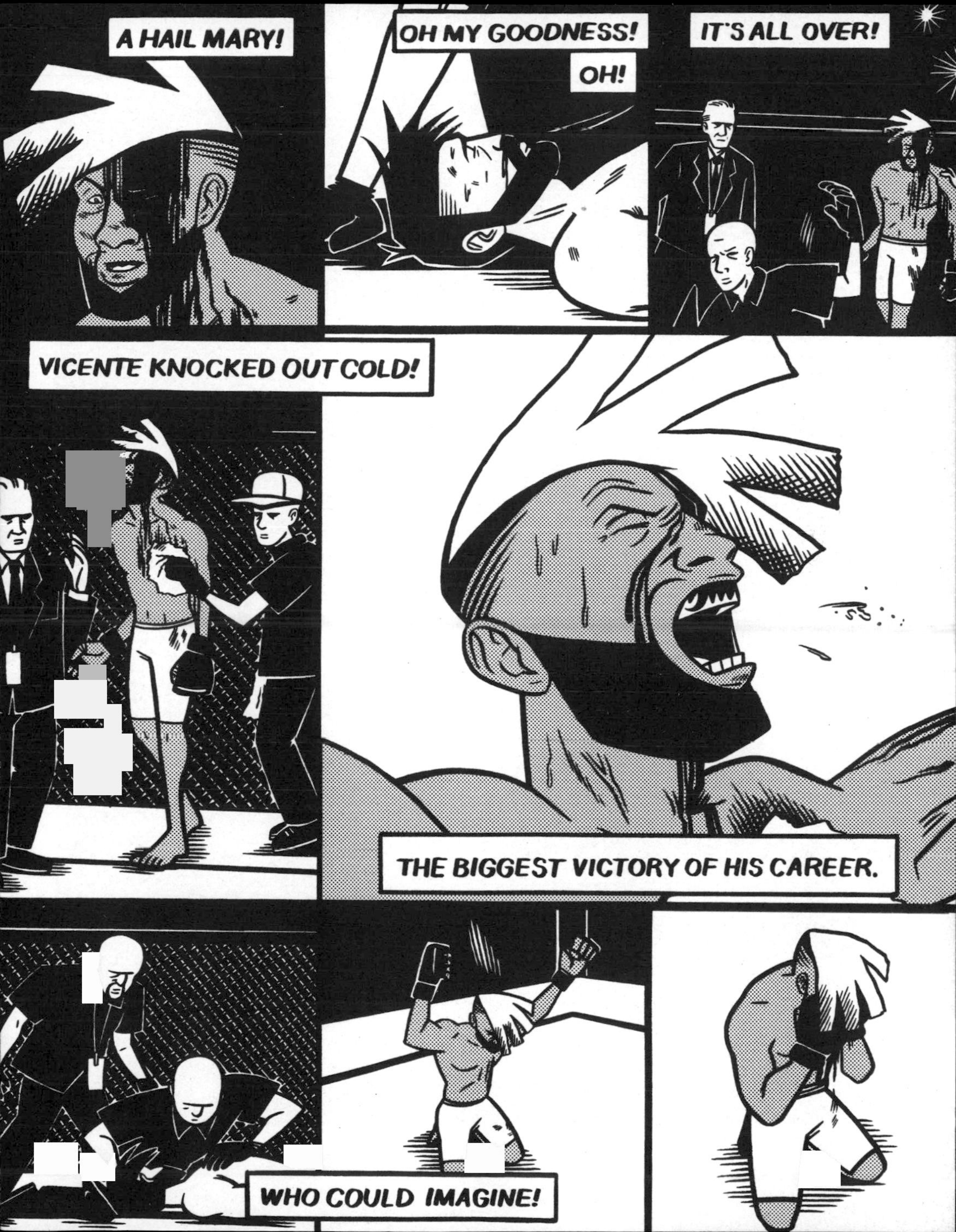
A HAIL MARY!
OH MY GOODNESS!
OH!
IT'S ALL OVER!
VICENTE KNOCKED OUT COLD!
THE BIGGEST VICTORY OF HIS CAREER.
WHO COULD IMAGINE!

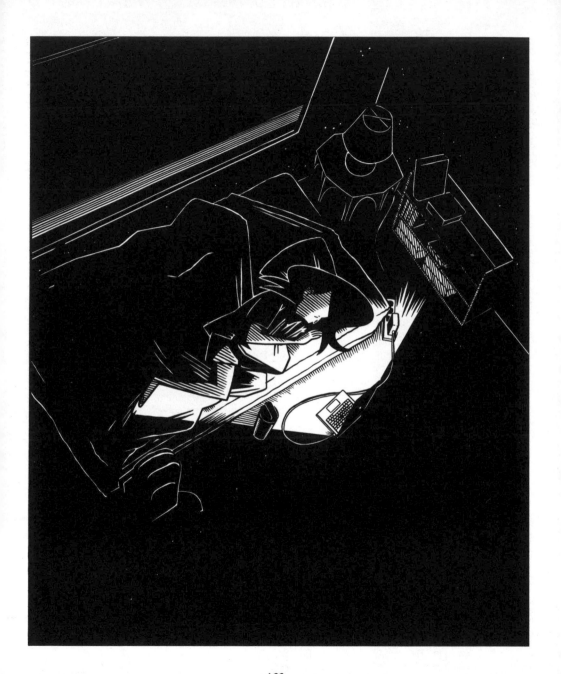

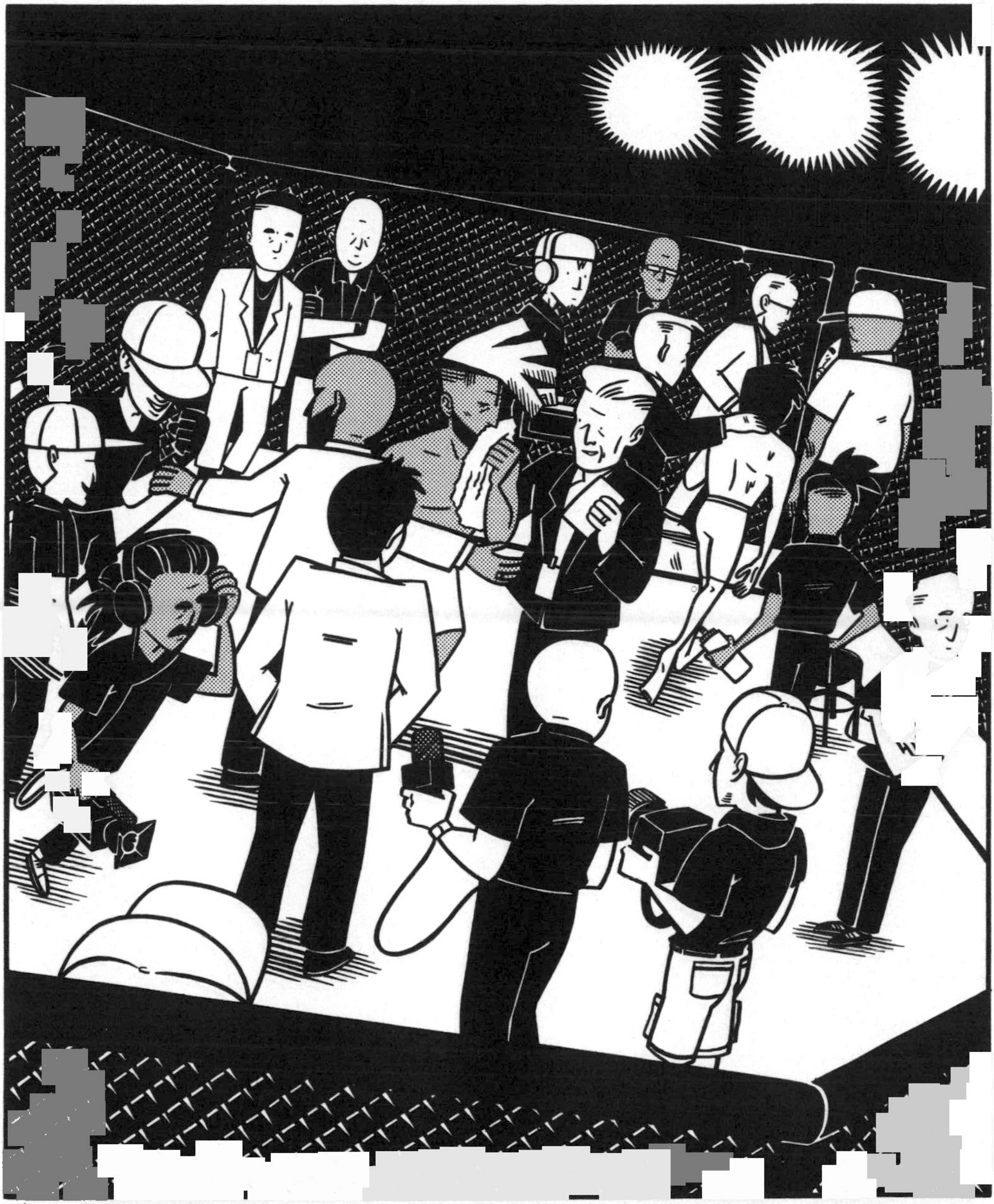

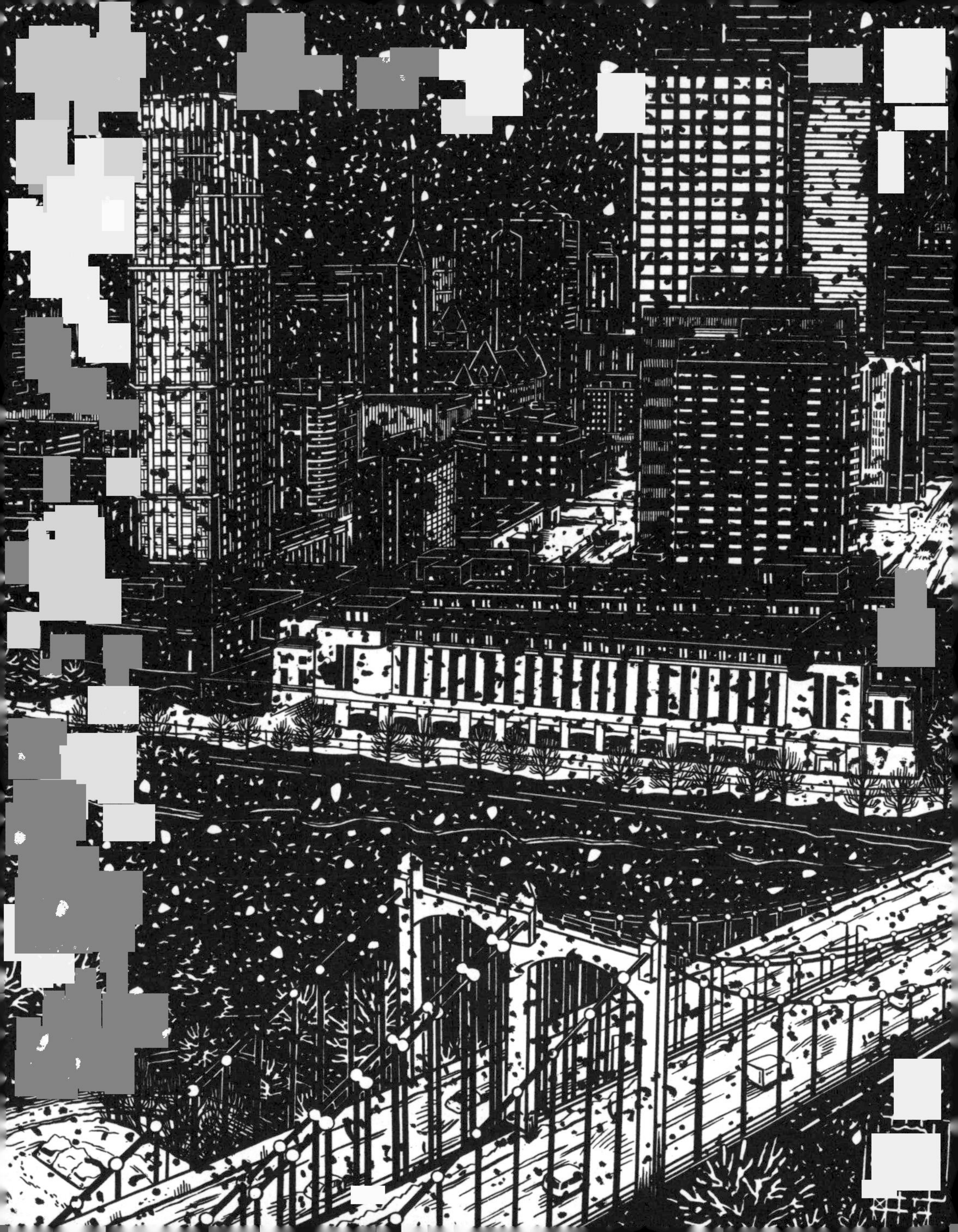

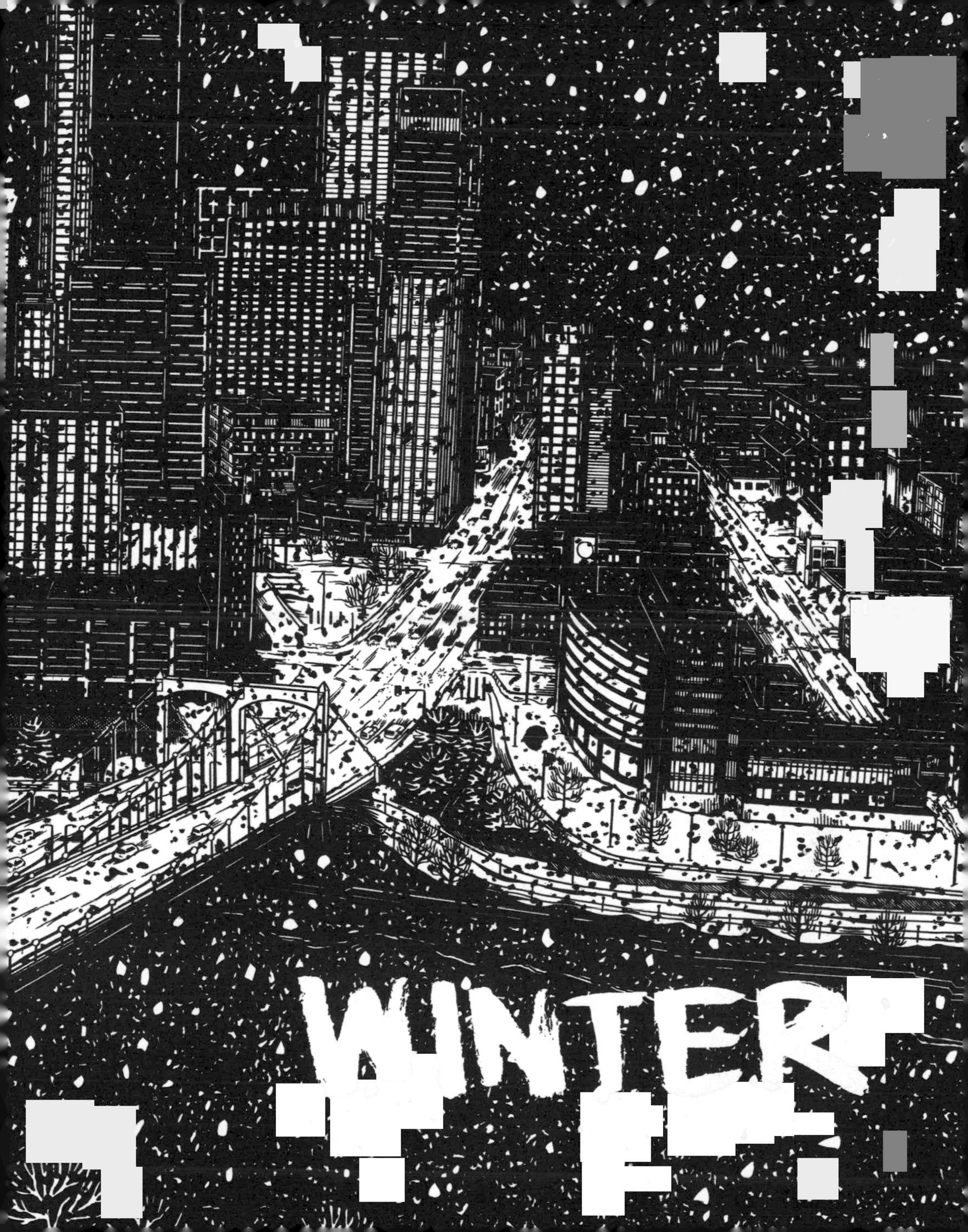
WINTER

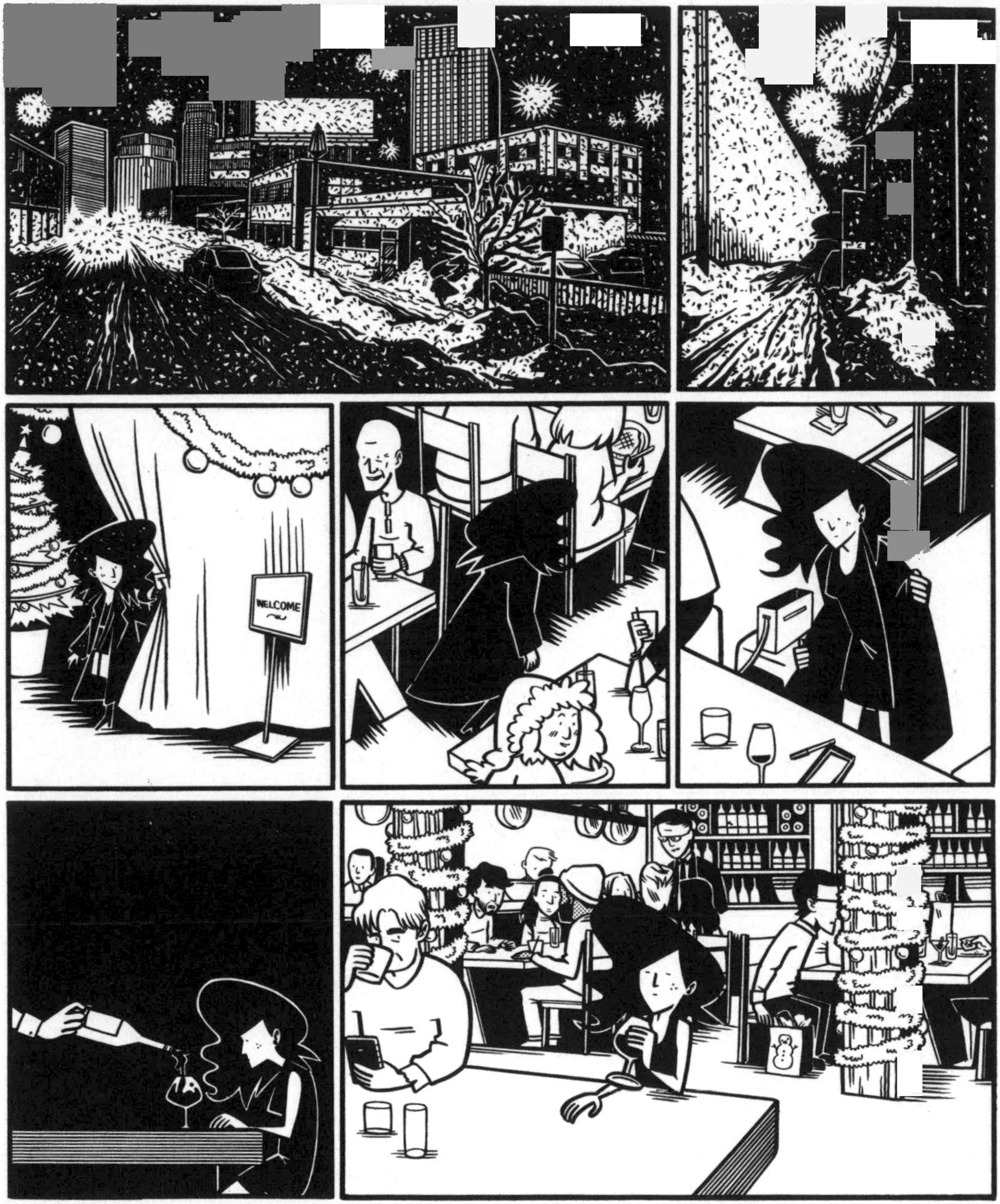
WELCOME

I PASSED THE CERTIFICATION TEST.

THERE WAS A JOB OFFER WAITING FOR ME AT THE DOWNTOWN GYM.

I WORKED OUT THERE WITH ELIS A FEW TIMES AND GOT A GOOD SENSE OF THE CLIENTELE COMING THROUGH.

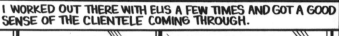

THE MANAGER HAD HEARD GOOD THINGS FROM MY BOSS AT THE POOL.

TRAINER

DID YOU GET CERTIFIED YET?

MY FIRST DAY IS NEXT WEEK.

I'LL GET YOU SET UP TO START WITH ANOTHER TRAINER I JUST HIRED.

MEANWHILE, MY BOOK WAS PRINTED AND SENT OFF TO DISTRIBUTION.

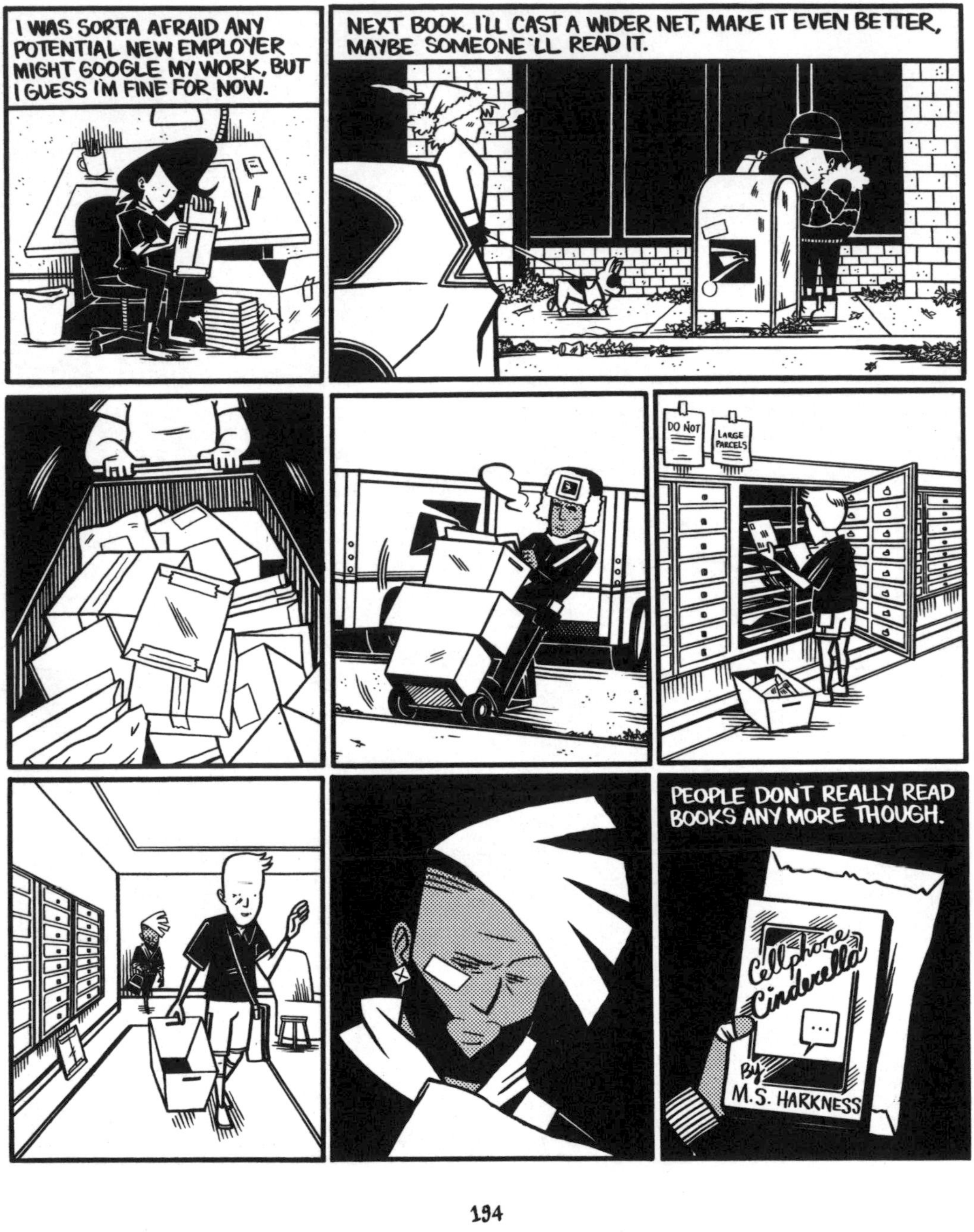
I WAS SORTA AFRAID ANY POTENTIAL NEW EMPLOYER MIGHT GOOGLE MY WORK, BUT I GUESS I'M FINE FOR NOW.
NEXT BOOK, I'LL CAST A WIDER NET, MAKE IT EVEN BETTER, MAYBE SOMEONE'LL READ IT.
DO NOT
LARGE PARCELS
PEOPLE DON'T REALLY READ BOOKS ANY MORE THOUGH.
Cellphone Cinderella
By M.S. HARKNESS

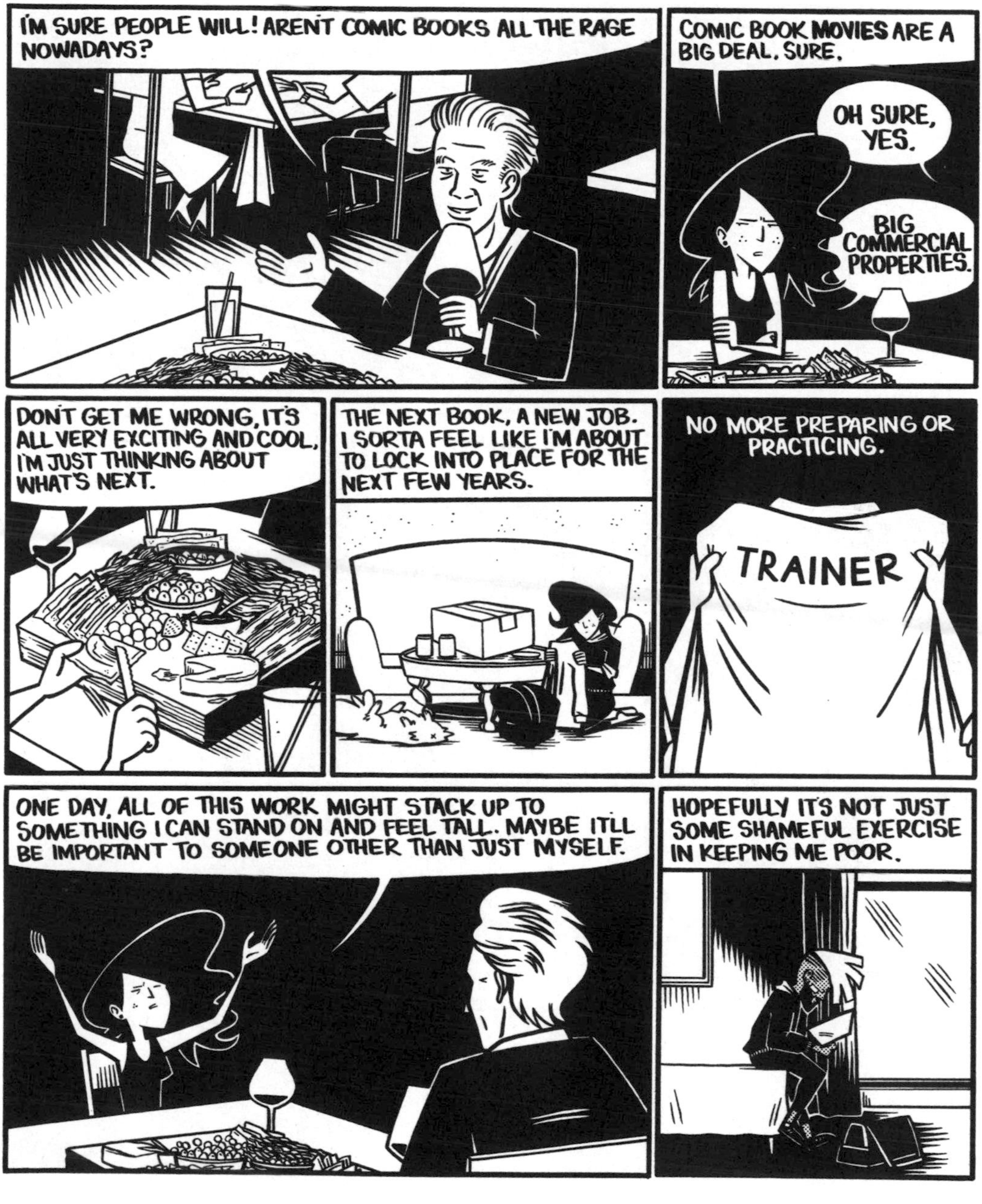
I'M SURE PEOPLE WILL! AREN'T COMIC BOOKS ALL THE RAGE NOWADAYS?
COMIC BOOK MOVIES ARE A BIG DEAL, SURE.
OH SURE, YES.
BIG COMMERCIAL PROPERTIES.
DON'T GET ME WRONG, IT'S ALL VERY EXCITING AND COOL, I'M JUST THINKING ABOUT WHAT'S NEXT.
THE NEXT BOOK, A NEW JOB. I SORTA FEEL LIKE I'M ABOUT TO LOCK INTO PLACE FOR THE NEXT FEW YEARS.
NO MORE PREPARING OR PRACTICING.
TRAINER
ONE DAY, ALL OF THIS WORK MIGHT STACK UP TO SOMETHING I CAN STAND ON AND FEEL TALL. MAYBE IT'LL BE IMPORTANT TO SOMEONE OTHER THAN JUST MYSELF.
HOPEFULLY IT'S NOT JUST SOME SHAMEFUL EXERCISE IN KEEPING ME POOR.

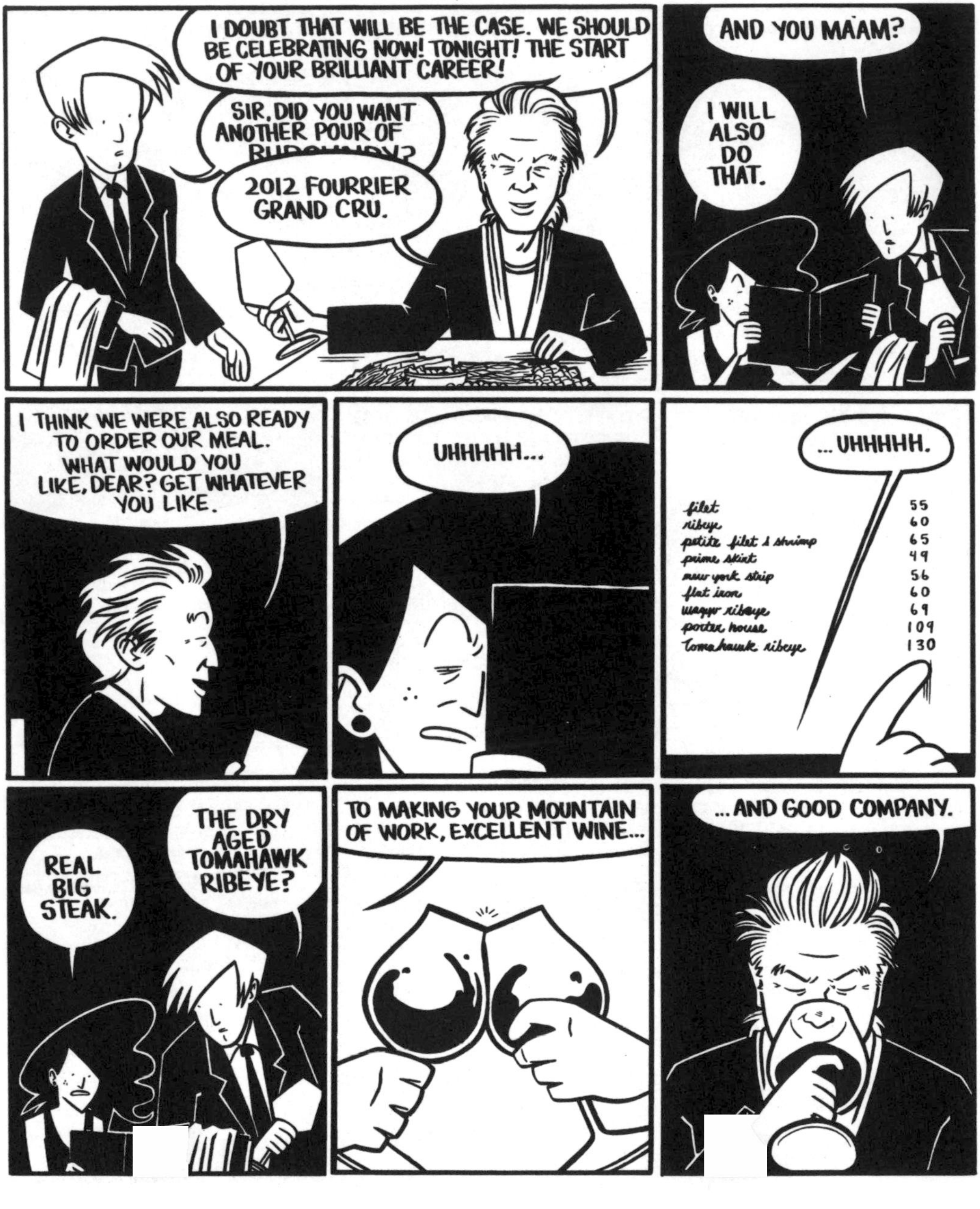
I DOUBT THAT WILL BE THE CASE. WE SHOULD BE CELEBRATING NOW! TONIGHT! THE START OF YOUR BRILLIANT CAREER!
SIR, DID YOU WANT ANOTHER POUR OF
2012 FOURRIER GRAND CRU.
AND YOU MA'AM?
I WILL ALSO DO THAT.
I THINK WE WERE ALSO READY TO ORDER OUR MEAL. WHAT WOULD YOU LIKE, DEAR? GET WHATEVER YOU LIKE.
UHHHHH...
...UHHHHH.
filet 55
ribeye 60
petite filet & shrimp 65
prime skirt 49
new york strip 56
flat iron 60
wagyu ribeye 69
porter house 109
tomahawk ribeye 130
REAL BIG STEAK.
THE DRY AGED TOMAHAWK RIBEYE?
TO MAKING YOUR MOUNTAIN OF WORK, EXCELLENT WINE...
...AND GOOD COMPANY.

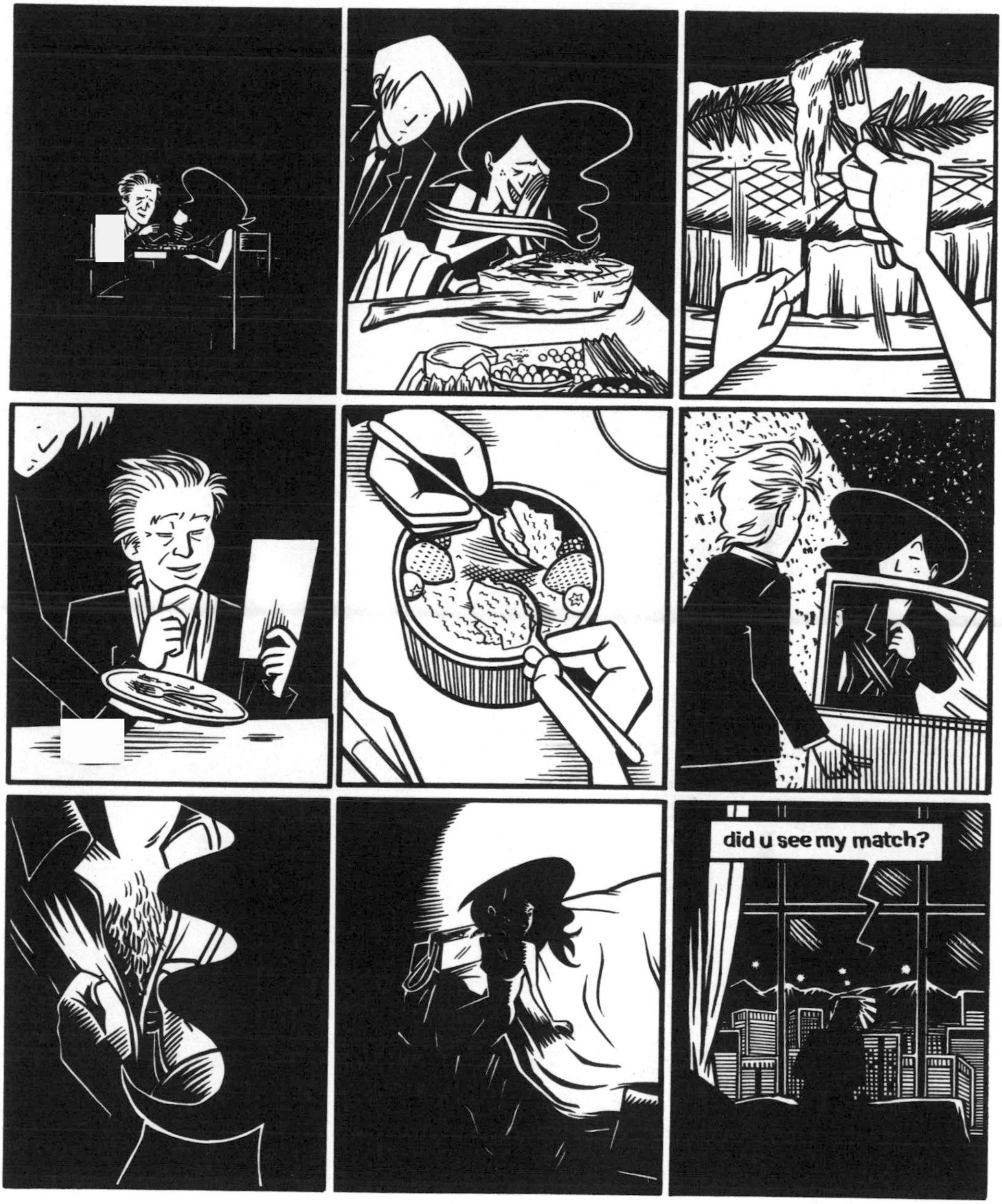
did u see my match?

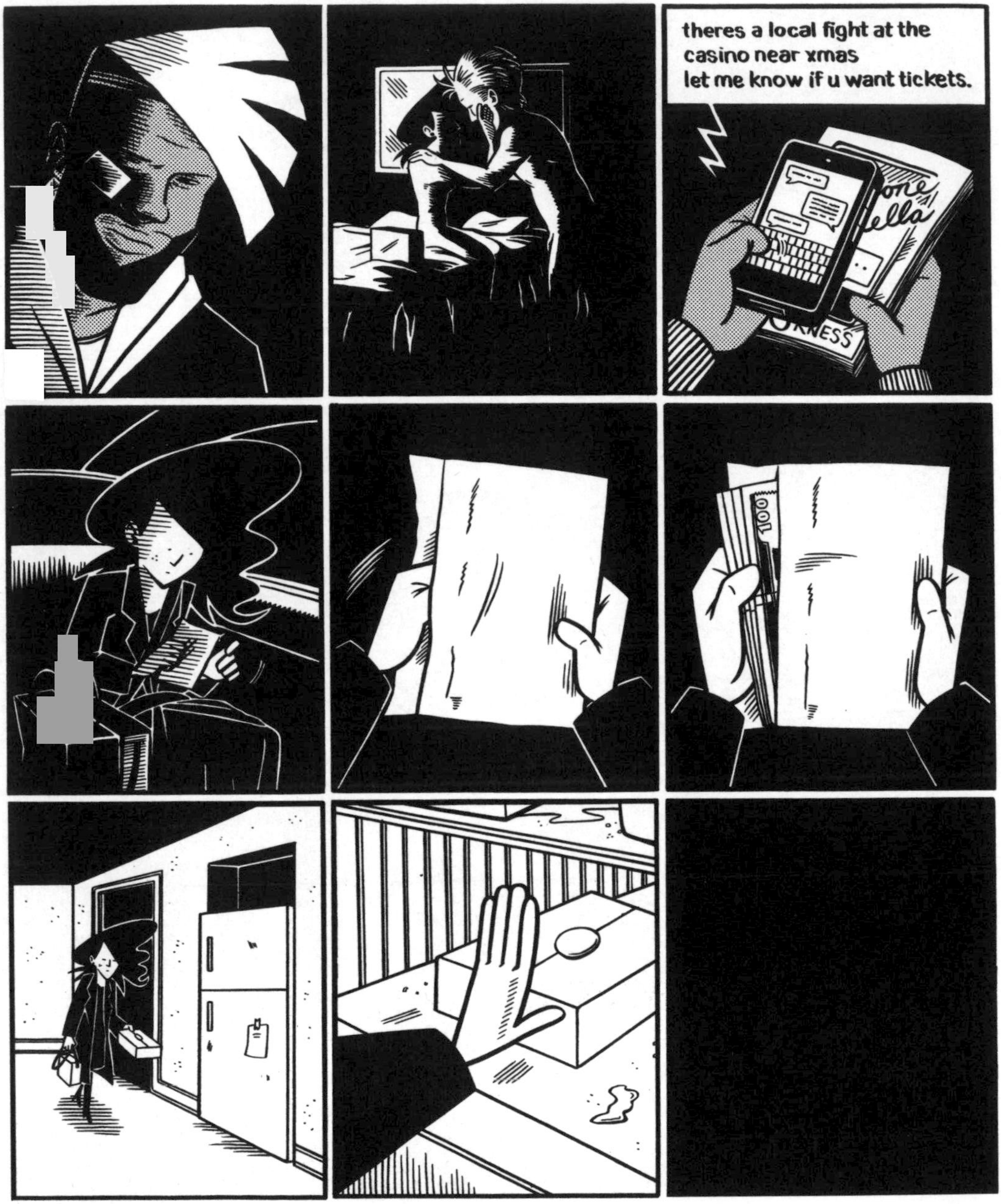
theres a local fight at the
casino near xmas
let me know if u want tickets.

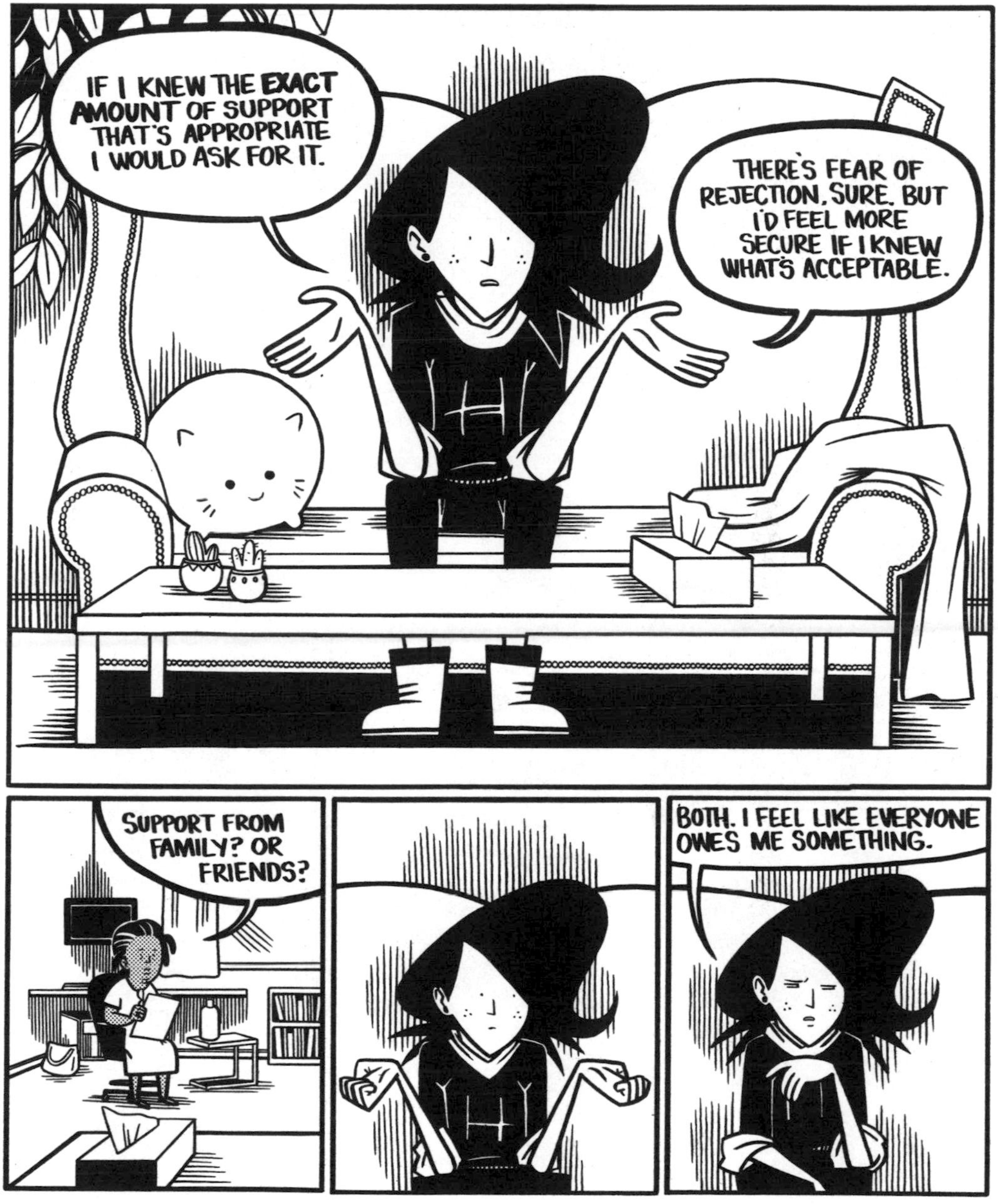
IF I KNEW THE EXACT AMOUNT OF SUPPORT THAT'S APPROPRIATE I WOULD ASK FOR IT.
THERE'S FEAR OF REJECTION, SURE. BUT I'D FEEL MORE SECURE IF I KNEW WHAT'S ACCEPTABLE.
SUPPORT FROM FAMILY? OR FRIENDS?
BOTH. I FEEL LIKE EVERYONE OWES ME SOMETHING.

ALL THE PEOPLE THAT MAKE UP MY LIFE... I DON'T KNOW WHAT'S REASONABLE TO EXPECT OF THEM.
BRYANT LAKE BOWL
CHEAP DATE NIGHT
I FEEL GUILTY ALL THE TIME, TRYING TO DETERMINE WHY I FEEL EMPTY AND DISAPPOINTED.
PIPES
OPEN
H
THESE RELATIONSHIPS NEVER FILL ME UP. I'M RAVENOUSLY HUNGRY FOR MORE TIME AND ATTENTION THAN THEY CAN GIVE.
FOR EXAMPLE,
I DON'T KNOW WHAT KIND OF RELATIONSHIP I'M SUPPOSED TO HAVE WITH MY MOTHER.

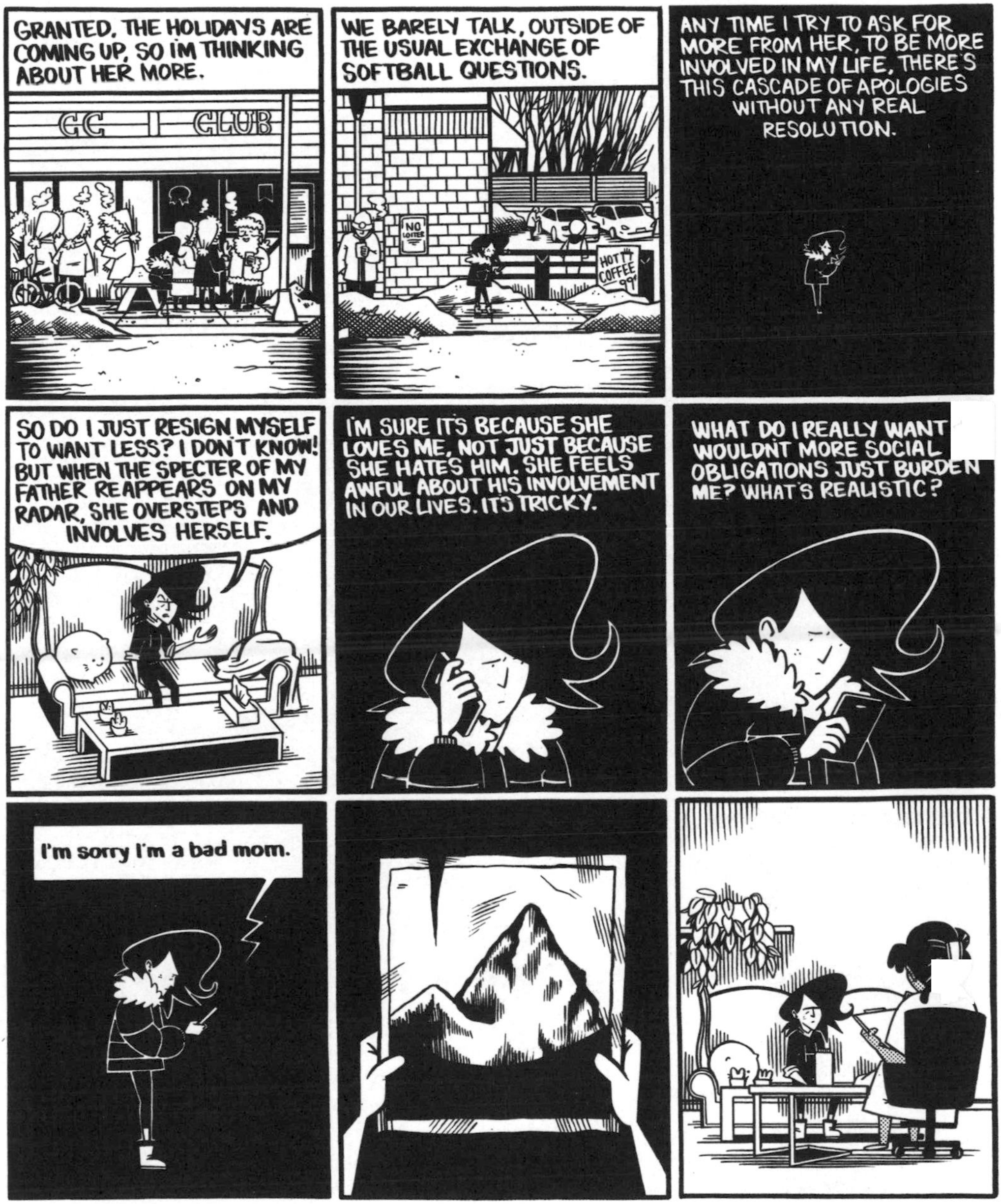
GRANTED, THE HOLIDAYS ARE COMING UP, SO I'M THINKING ABOUT HER MORE.
HOT COFFEE 99¢
WE BARELY TALK, OUTSIDE OF THE USUAL EXCHANGE OF SOFTBALL QUESTIONS.
ANY TIME I TRY TO ASK FOR MORE FROM HER, TO BE MORE INVOLVED IN MY LIFE, THERE'S THIS CASCADE OF APOLOGIES WITHOUT ANY REAL RESOLUTION.
SO DO I JUST RESIGN MYSELF TO WANT LESS? I DON'T KNOW! BUT WHEN THE SPECTER OF MY FATHER REAPPEARS ON MY RADAR, SHE OVERSTEPS AND INVOLVES HERSELF.
I'M SURE IT'S BECAUSE SHE LOVES ME, NOT JUST BECAUSE SHE HATES HIM. SHE FEELS AWFUL ABOUT HIS INVOLVEMENT IN OUR LIVES. IT'S TRICKY.
WHAT DO I REALLY WANT
WOULDN'T MORE SOCIAL OBLIGATIONS JUST BURDEN ME? WHAT'S REALISTIC?
I'm sorry I'm a bad mom.

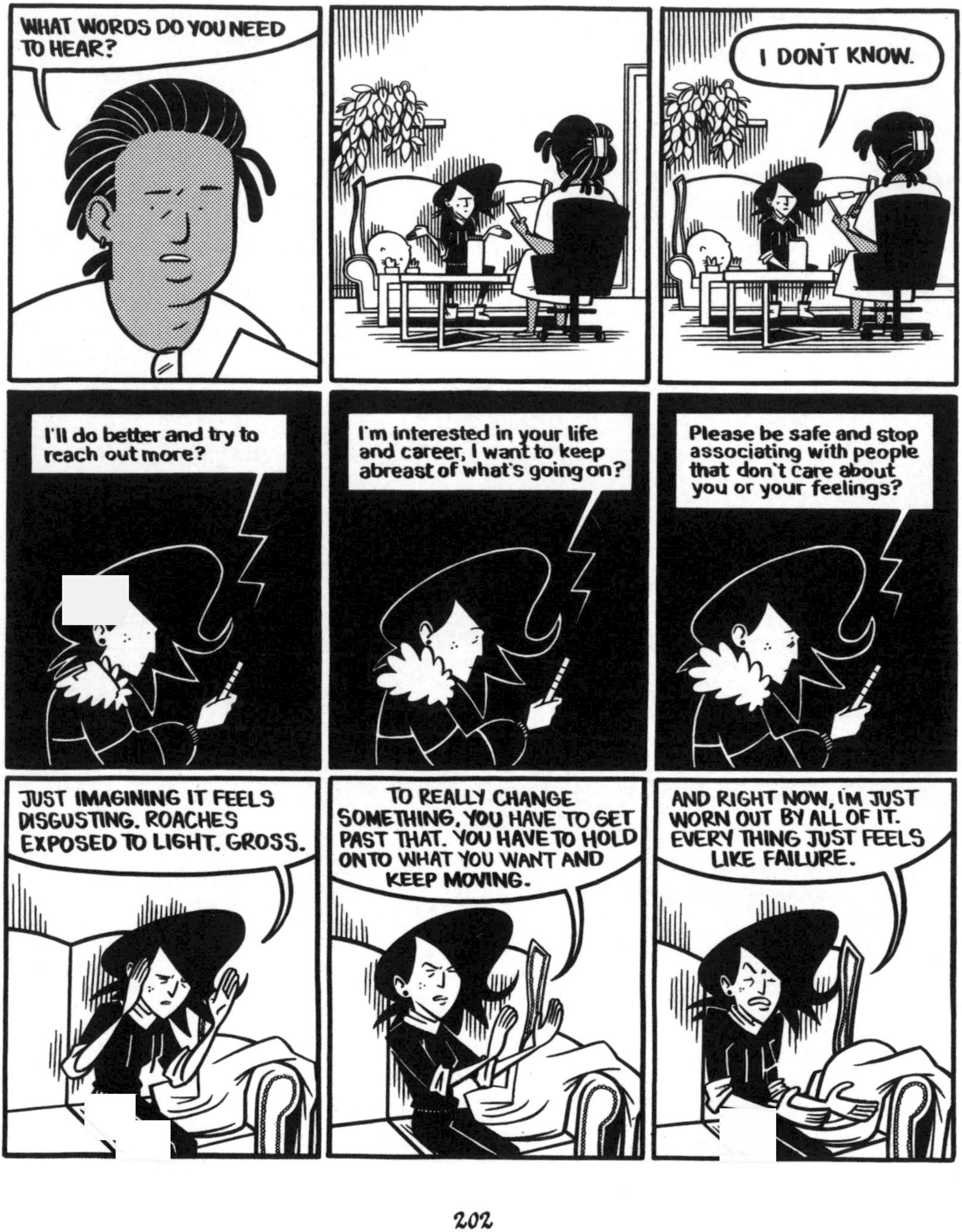
WHAT WORDS DO YOU NEED TO HEAR?
I DON'T KNOW.
I'll do better and try to reach out more?
I'm interested in your life and career, I want to keep abreast of what's going on?
Please be safe and stop associating with people that don't care about you or your feelings?
JUST IMAGINING IT FEELS DISGUSTING. ROACHES EXPOSED TO LIGHT. GROSS.
TO REALLY CHANGE SOMETHING, YOU HAVE TO GET PAST THAT. YOU HAVE TO HOLD ONTO WHAT YOU WANT AND KEEP MOVING.
AND RIGHT NOW, I'M JUST WORN OUT BY ALL OF IT. EVERY THING JUST FEELS LIKE FAILURE.

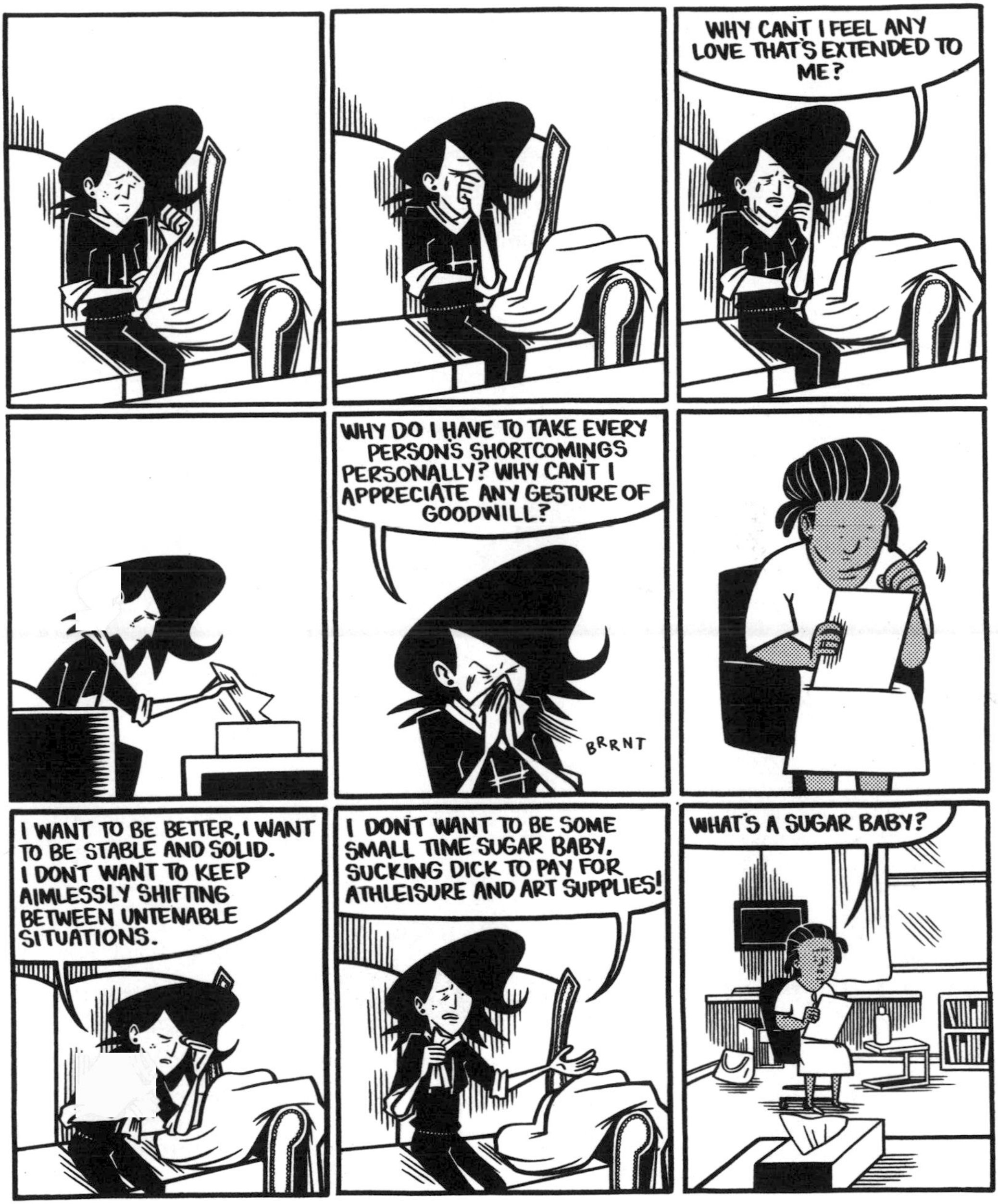
WHY CAN'T I FEEL ANY LOVE THAT'S EXTENDED TO ME?
WHY DO I HAVE TO TAKE EVERY PERSON'S SHORTCOMINGS PERSONALLY? WHY CAN'T I APPRECIATE ANY GESTURE OF GOODWILL?
BRRNT
I WANT TO BE BETTER, I WANT TO BE STABLE AND SOLID. I DON'T WANT TO KEEP AIMLESSLY SHIFTING BETWEEN UNTENABLE SITUATIONS.
I DON'T WANT TO BE SOME SMALL TIME SUGAR BABY, SUCKING DICK TO PAY FOR ATHLEISURE AND ART SUPPLIES!
WHAT'S A SUGAR BABY?

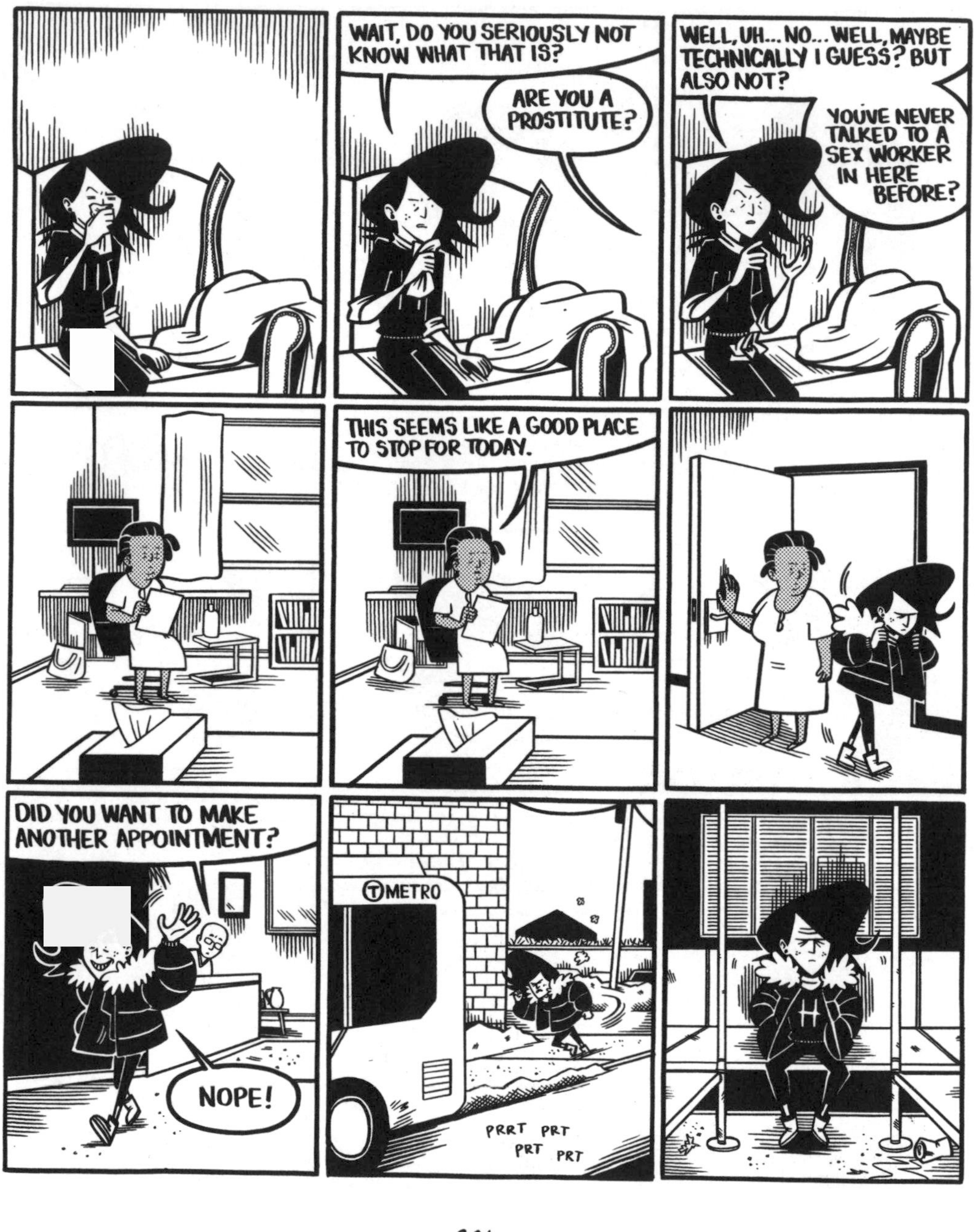
WAIT, DO YOU SERIOUSLY NOT KNOW WHAT THAT IS?
ARE YOU A PROSTITUTE?
WELL, UH... NO... WELL, MAYBE TECHNICALLY I GUESS? BUT ALSO NOT?
YOU'VE NEVER TALKED TO A SEX WORKER IN HERE BEFORE?
THIS SEEMS LIKE A GOOD PLACE TO STOP FOR TODAY.
DID YOU WANT TO MAKE ANOTHER APPOINTMENT?
NOPE!
METRO
PRRT PRT
PRT PRT

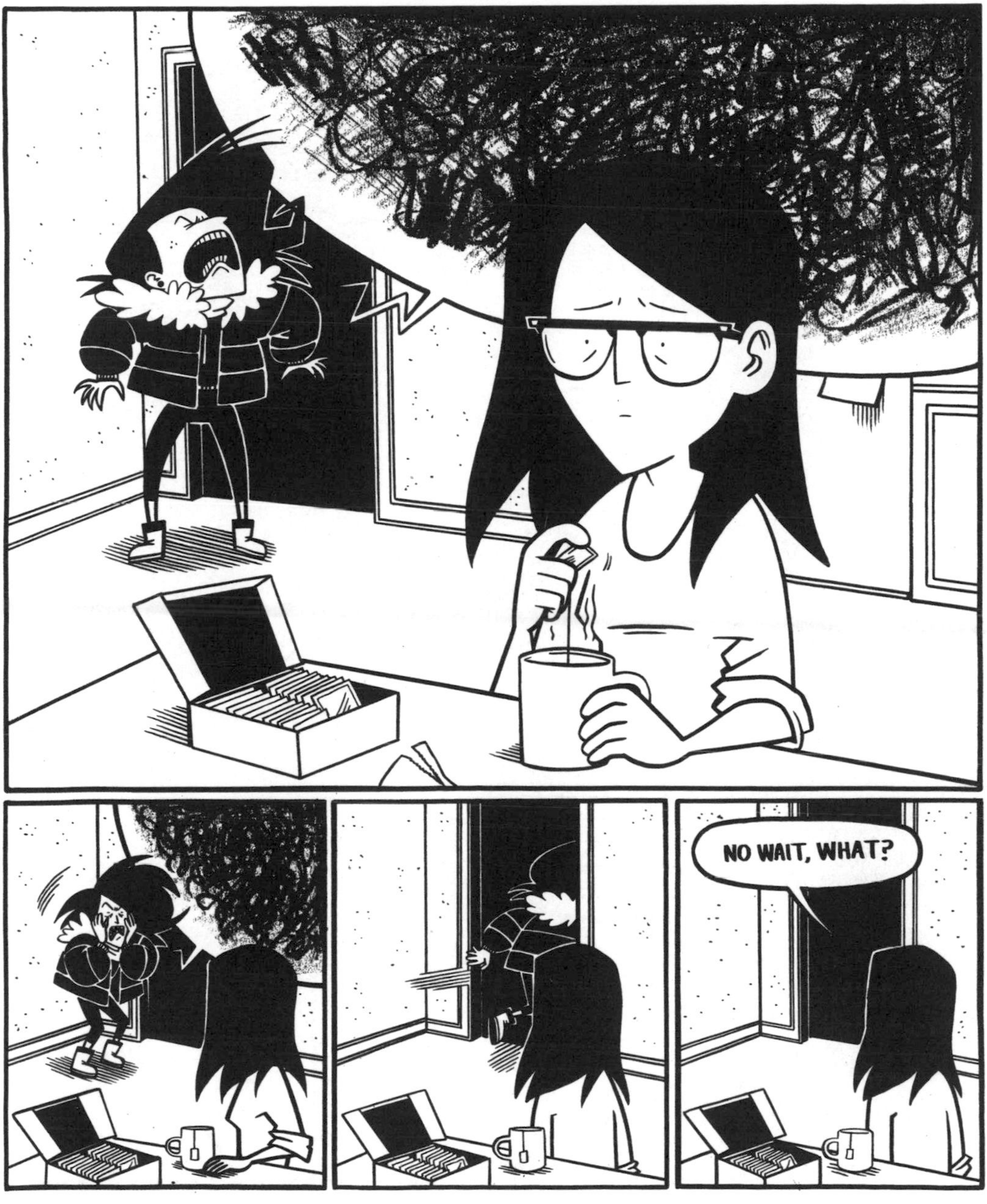
NO WAIT, WHAT?

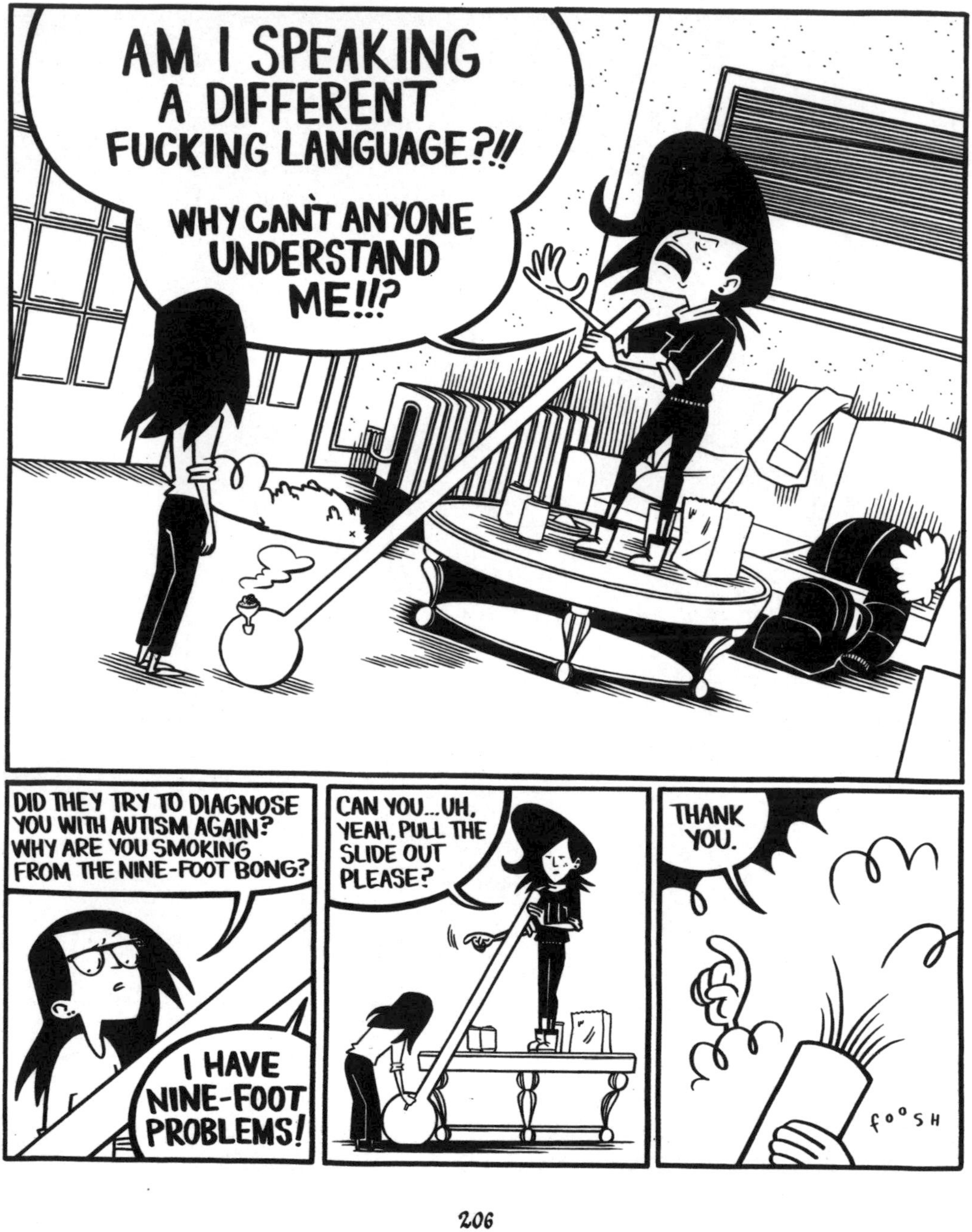
AM I SPEAKING A DIFFERENT FUCKING LANGUAGE?!!
WHY CAN'T ANYONE UNDERSTAND ME!!?
DID THEY TRY TO DIAGNOSE YOU WITH AUTISM AGAIN? WHY ARE YOU SMOKING FROM THE NINE-FOOT BONG?
I HAVE NINE-FOOT PROBLEMS!
CAN YOU...UH, YEAH, PULL THE SLIDE OUT PLEASE?
THANK YOU.
FOOSH

UH... THIRD TIMES A CHARM? TRY ANOTHER THERAPIST?

NO.

I'M SICK OF WALLOWING AROUND IN MY OWN PSYCHE, I'M TIRED OF WALKING THESE QUACKS THROUGH MY LIFE STORY WITHOUT RECEIVING ANY USEFUL ADVICE!

FAIR...

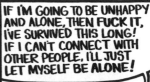

IF I'M GOING TO BE UNHAPPY AND ALONE, THEN FUCK IT, I'VE SURVIVED THIS LONG! IF I CAN'T CONNECT WITH OTHER PEOPLE, I'LL JUST LET MYSELF BE ALONE!

UMM...

EVEN IF I NEVER FEEL WARMTH OR CARE AND I KEEP LIMPING THROUGH LIFE AS A RESENTFUL CUNT, I DON'T CARE! BECAUSE I'M GUNNA FIND A WAY, GODDAMNIT!

EHHH...

I'M GOING TO TAKE THE ACID I SAVED IN THE FREEZER!!

WAIT!

I WANNA TRIP TOO.

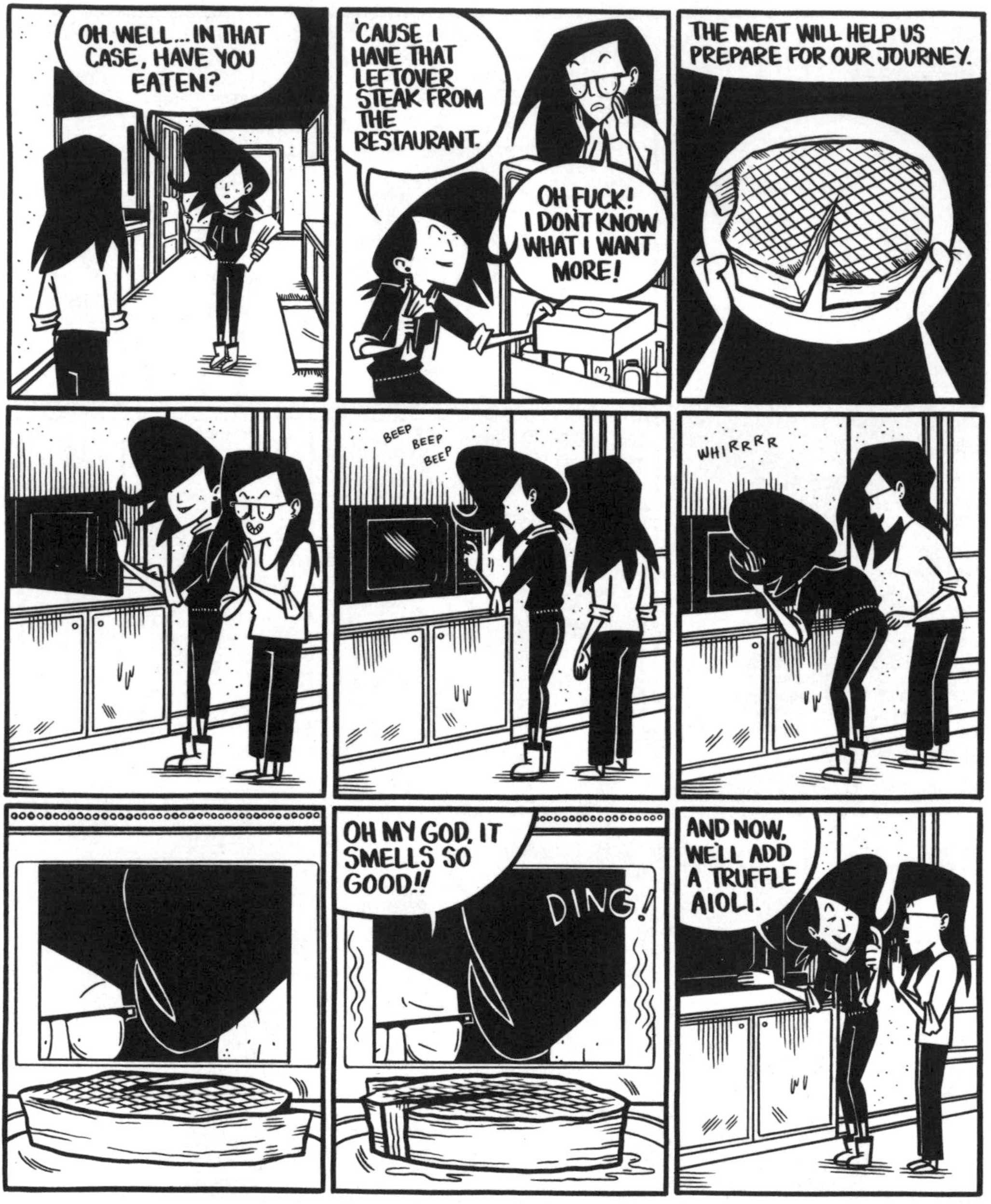
OH, WELL... IN THAT CASE, HAVE YOU EATEN?
'CAUSE I HAVE THAT LEFTOVER STEAK FROM THE RESTAURANT.
OH FUCK! I DON'T KNOW WHAT I WANT MORE!
THE MEAT WILL HELP US PREPARE FOR OUR JOURNEY.
BEEP
BEEP
BEEP
WHIRRRR
OH MY GOD, IT SMELLS SO GOOD!!
DING!
AND NOW, WE'LL ADD A TRUFFLE AIOLI.

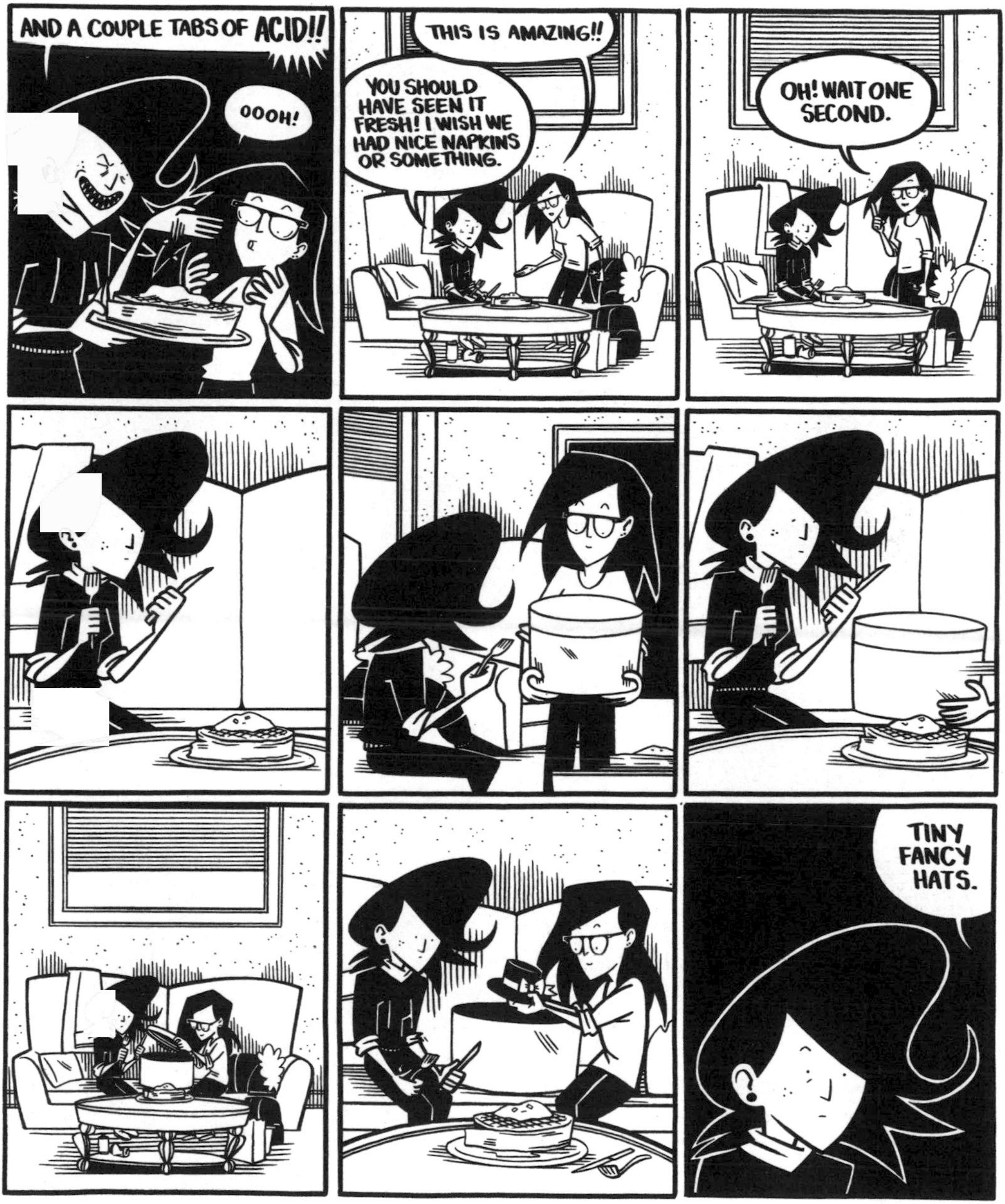
AND A COUPLE TABS OF ACID!!
OOOH!
THIS IS AMAZING!!
YOU SHOULD HAVE SEEN IT FRESH! I WISH WE HAD NICE NAPKINS OR SOMETHING.
OH! WAIT ONE SECOND.
TINY FANCY HATS.

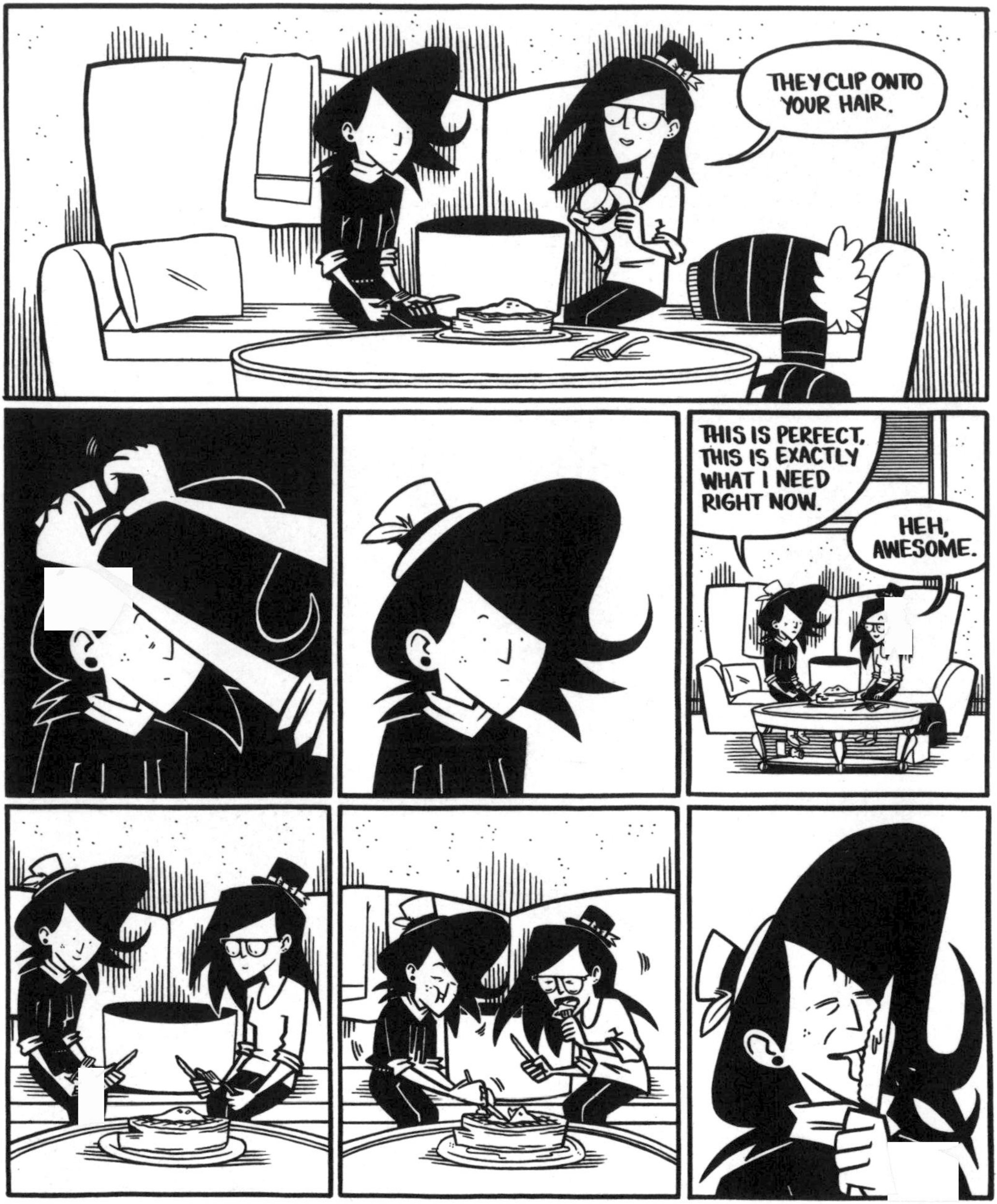
THEY CLIP ONTO YOUR HAIR.
THIS IS PERFECT, THIS IS EXACTLY WHAT I NEED RIGHT NOW.
HEH, AWESOME.

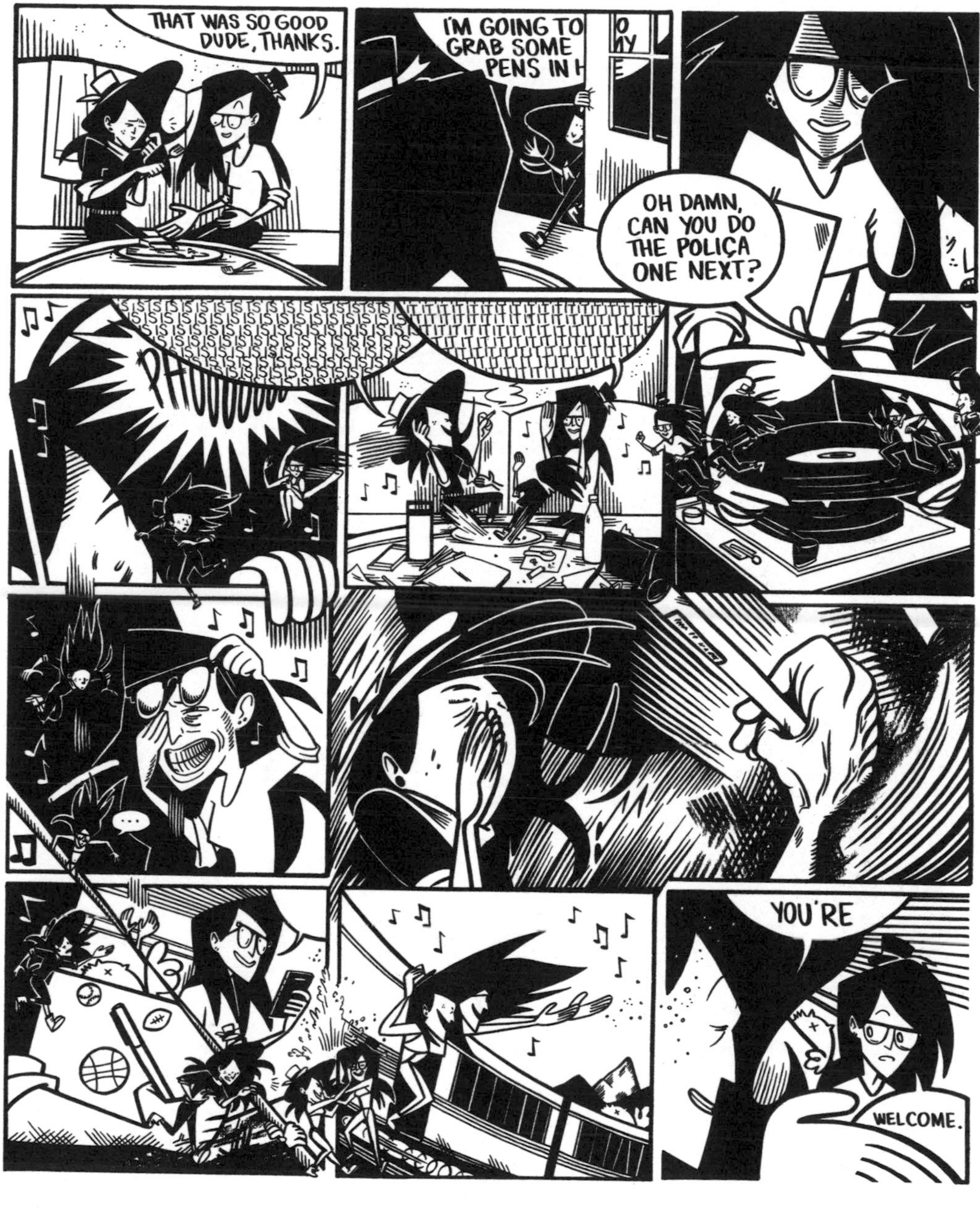
THAT WAS SO GOOD DUDE, THANKS.
I'M GOING TO GRAB SOME PENS IN H
OH DAMN, CAN YOU DO THE POLIÇA ONE NEXT?
PHOOOOOOO
...
YOU'RE
WELCOME.

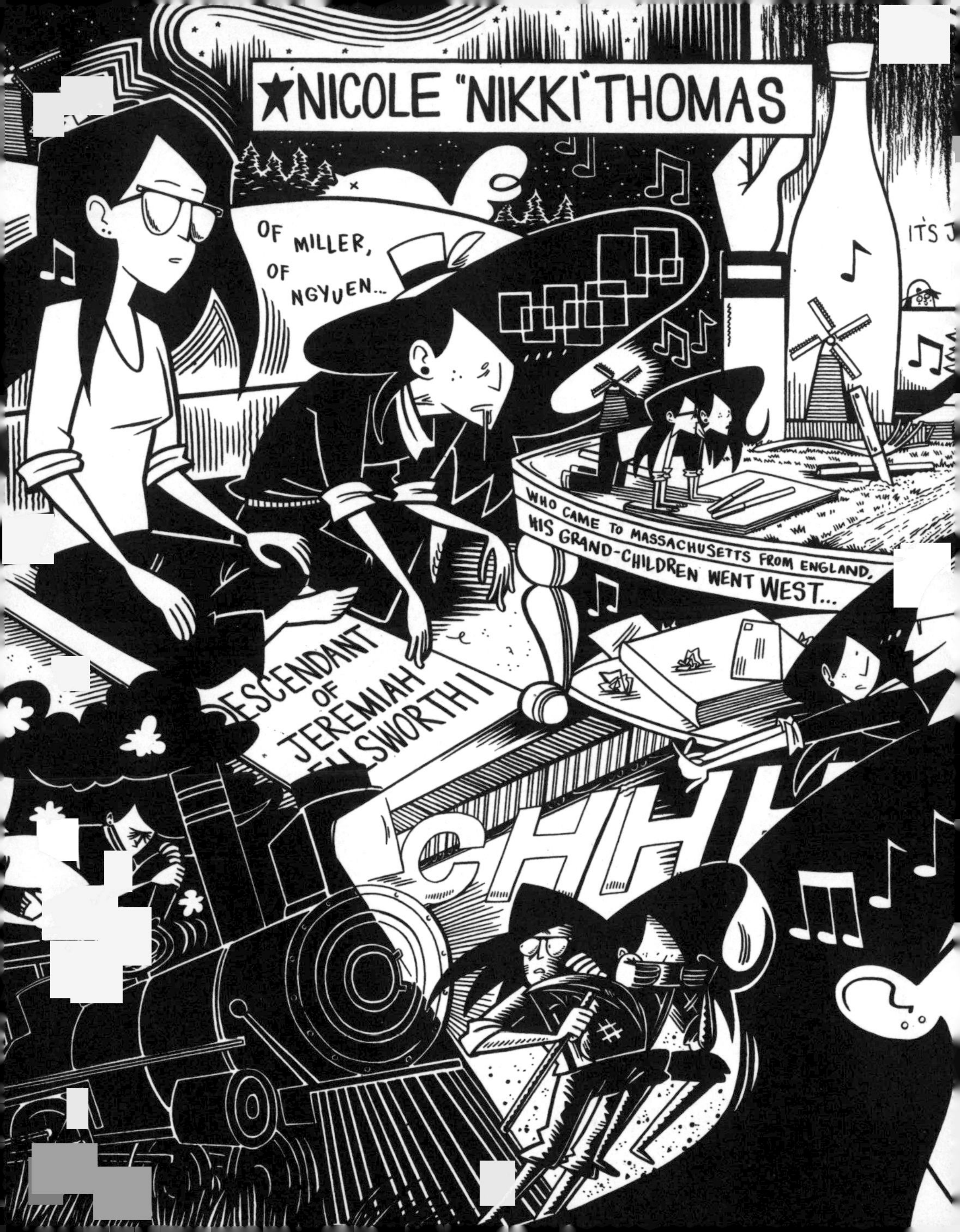
★NICOLE "NIKKI" THOMAS
OF MILLER, OF NGYUEN...
IT'S J
WHO CAME TO MASSACHUSETTS FROM ENGLAND, HIS GRAND-CHILDREN WENT WEST...
ESCENDANT OF JEREMIAH ELLSWORTH I
CHH

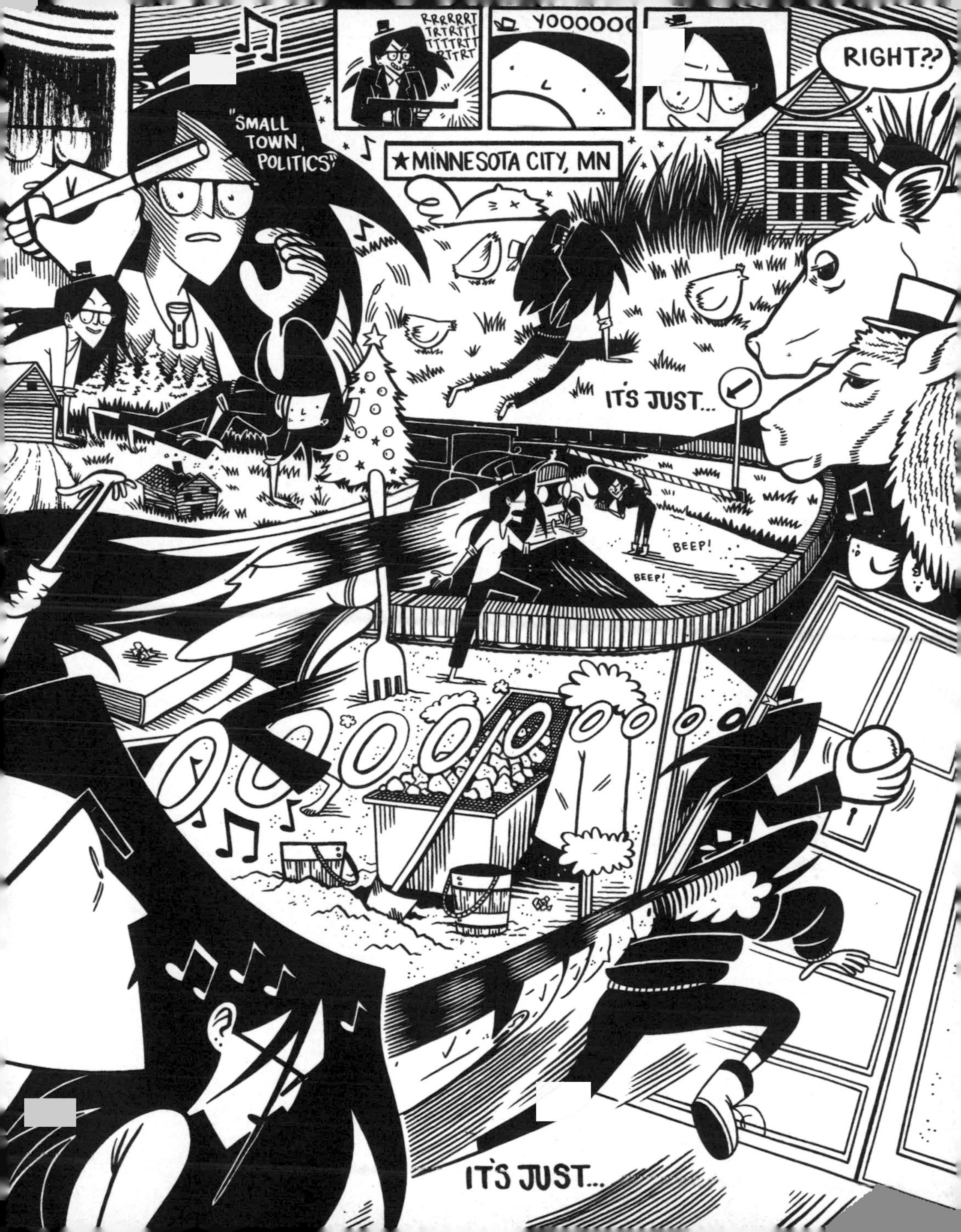

RRRRRRT TRTRTTT TTTTRTT RTTRT
YOOOOOO
RIGHT??
"SMALL TOWN POLITICS"
★MINNESOTA CITY, MN
IT'S JUST...
BEEP!
BEEP!
IT'S JUST...

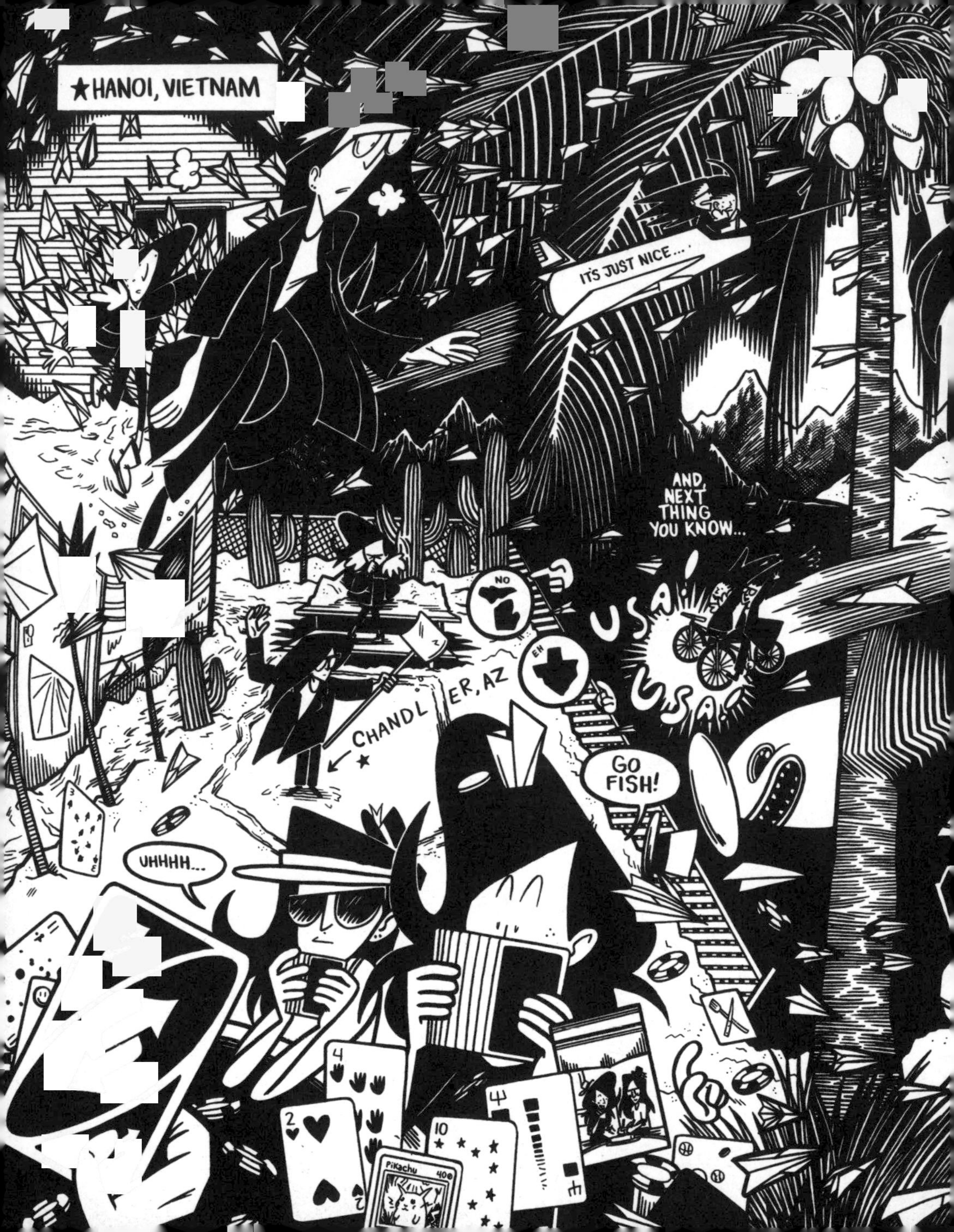
★HANOI, VIETNAM
IT'S JUST NICE...
AND, NEXT THING YOU KNOW...
NO
EH
USA!
USA!
CHANDLER, AZ
★
GO FISH!
UHHHH...
Pikachu

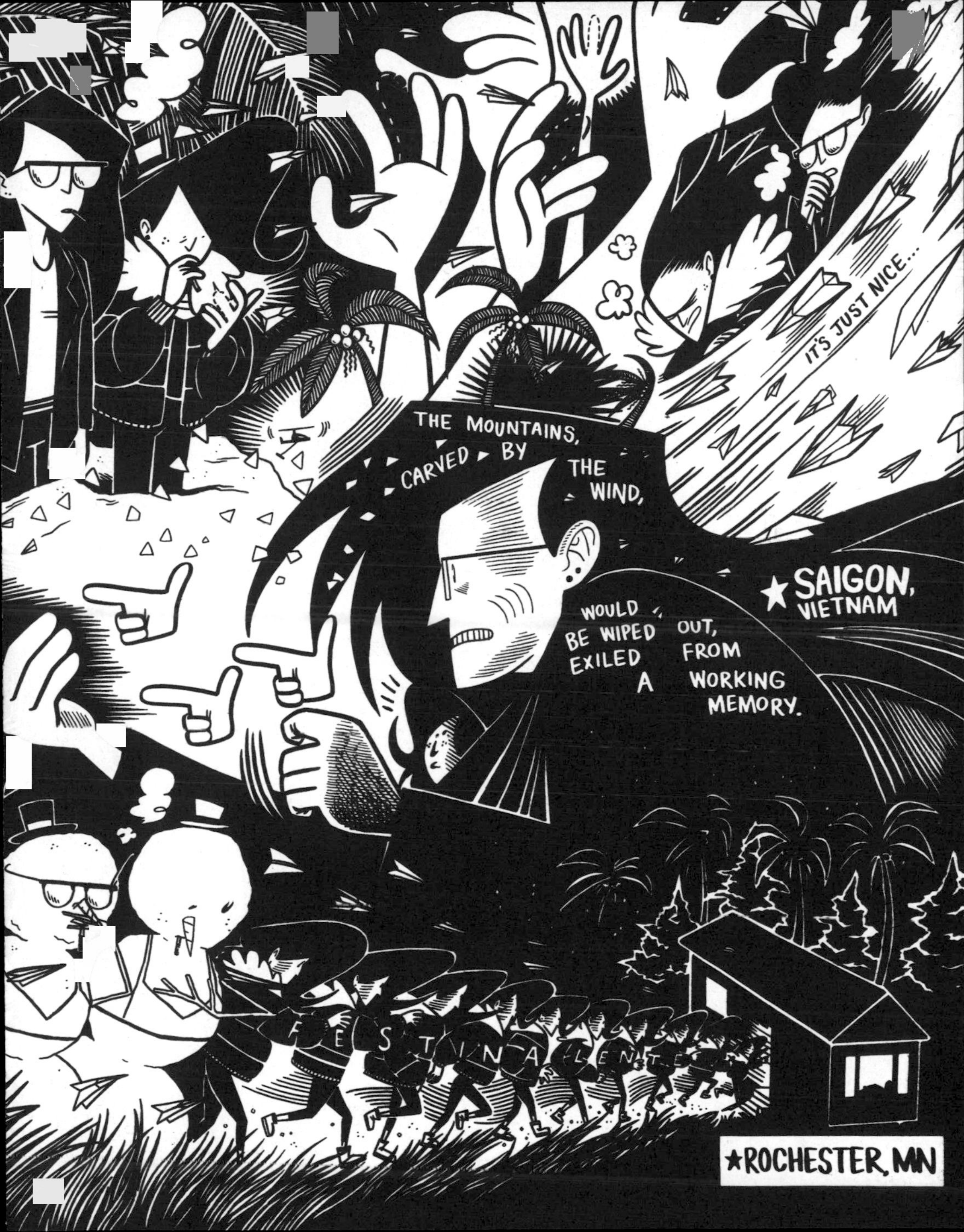
IT'S JUST NICE...
THE MOUNTAINS, CARVED BY THE WIND,
WOULD BE WIPED OUT, EXILED FROM A WORKING MEMORY.
★SAIGON, VIETNAM
FESTINA LENTE
★ROCHESTER, MN

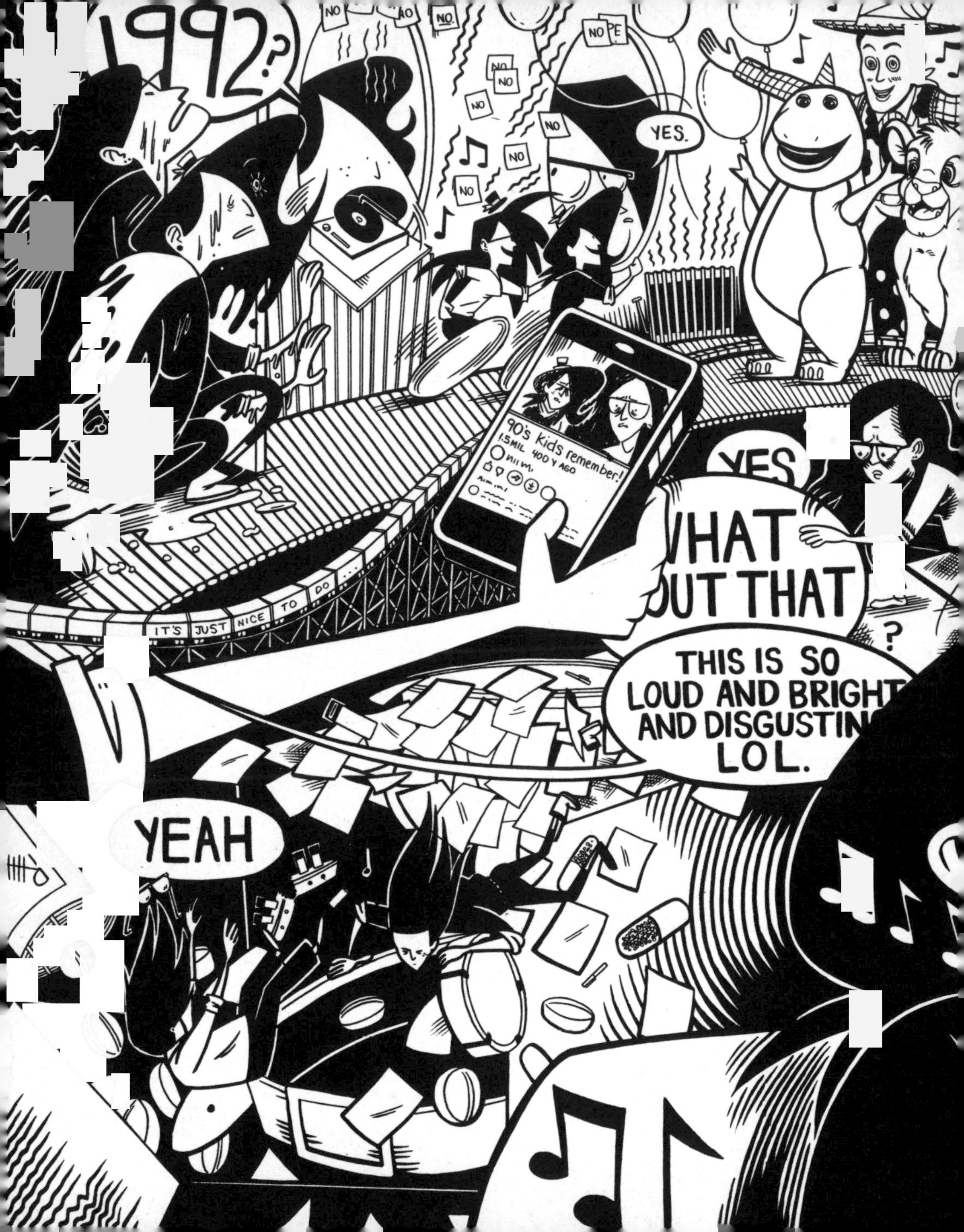
1992?
NO
NO
NO
NOPE
NO
NO
NO
NO
NO
NO
YES.
90's Kids remember!
YES
IT'S JUST NICE TO DO ...
HAT
UT THAT
?
THIS IS SO
LOUD AND BRIGHT
AND DISGUSTIN
LOL.
YEAH

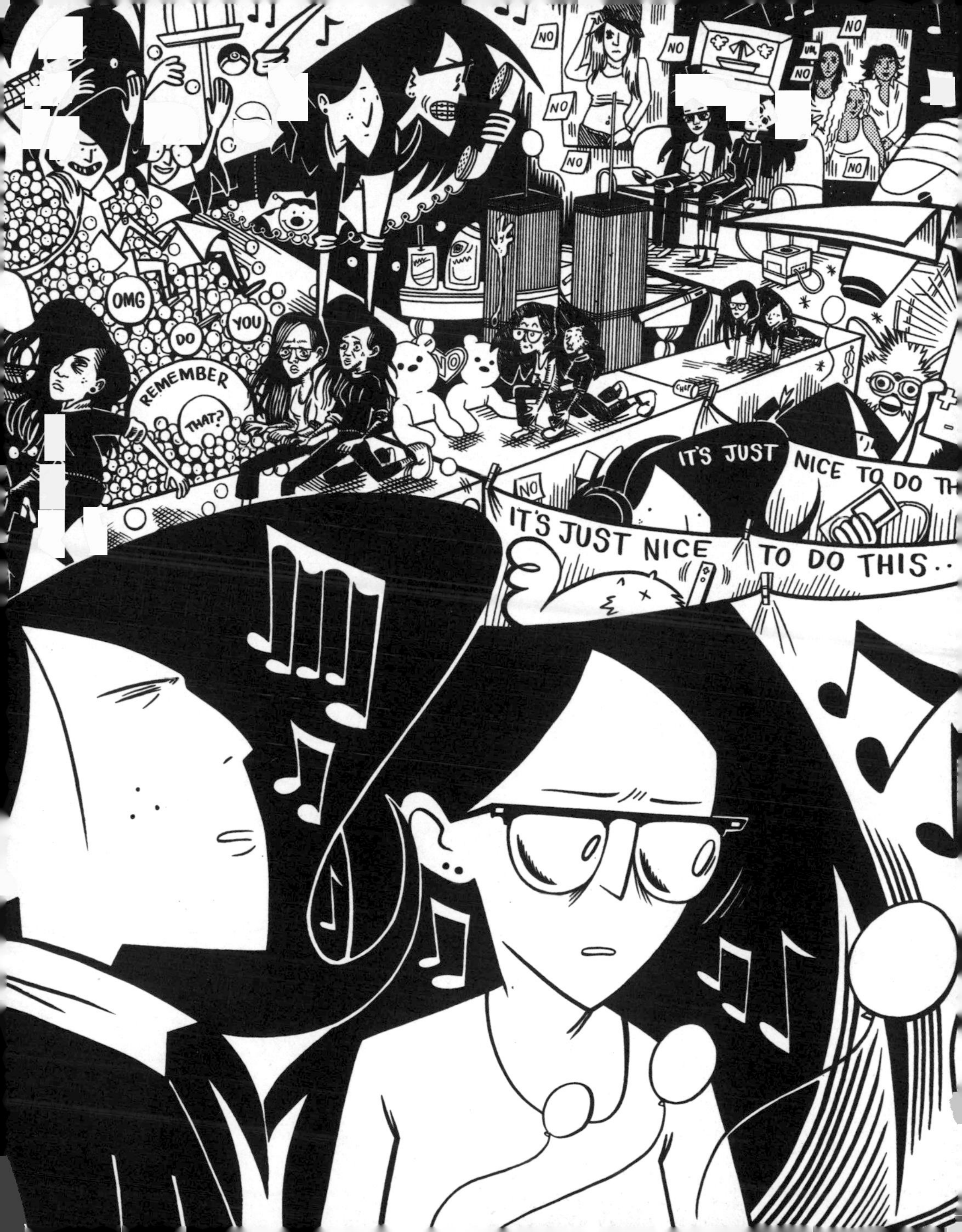
NO
NO
NO
NO
NO
NO
NO
NO
OMG
DO
YOU
REMEMBER
THAT?
IT'S JUST NICE TO DO TH
IT'S JUST NICE TO DO THIS...

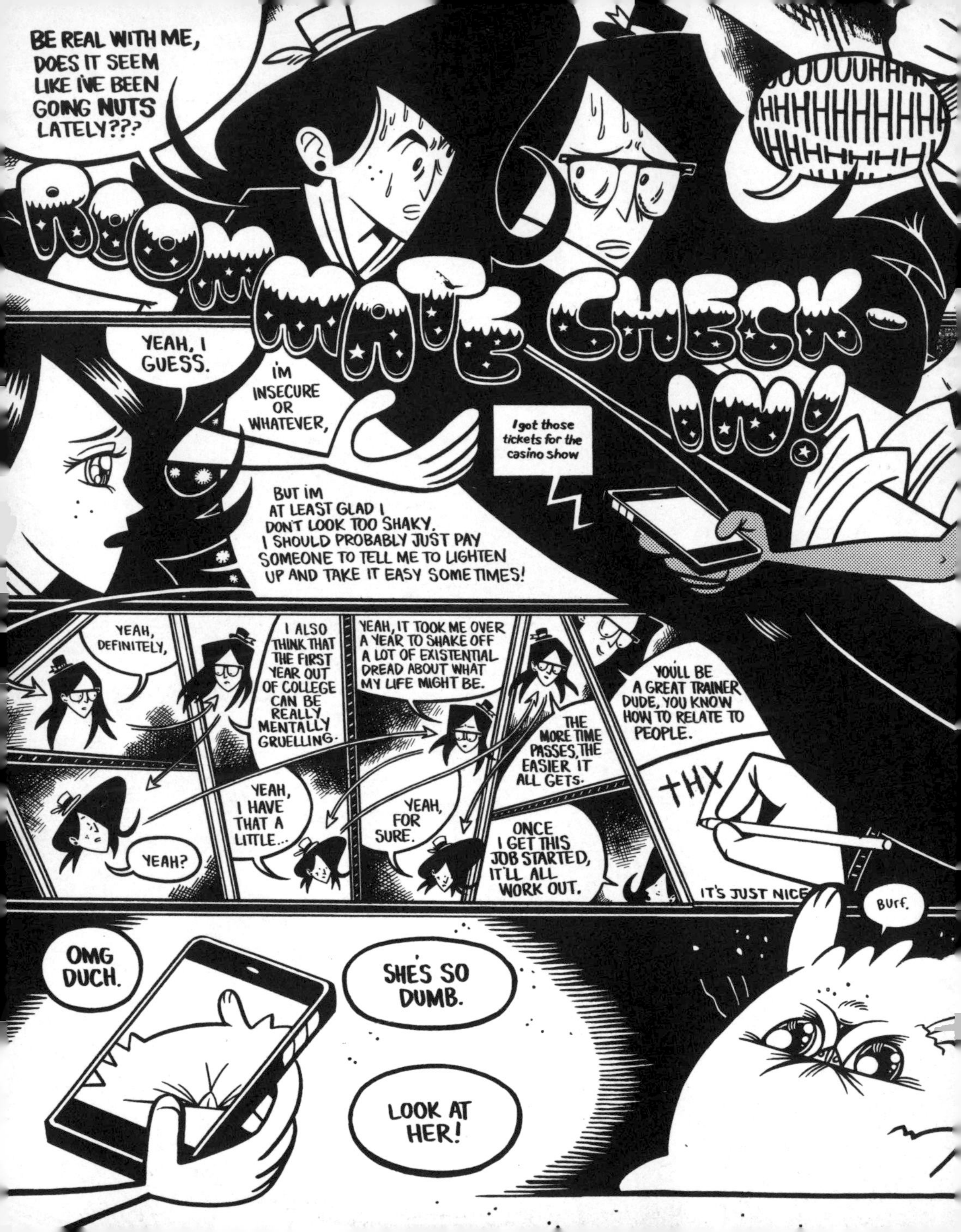

BE REAL WITH ME, DOES IT SEEM LIKE I'VE BEEN GOING NUTS LATELY???
OOOUUUUHHH HHHHHHHHHH HHHHHHHHH
ROOMMATE CHECK-IN!
YEAH, I GUESS.
I'M INSECURE OR WHATEVER,
BUT I'M AT LEAST GLAD I DON'T LOOK TOO SHAKY. I SHOULD PROBABLY JUST PAY SOMEONE TO TELL ME TO LIGHTEN UP AND TAKE IT EASY SOMETIMES!
I got those tickets for the casino show
YEAH, DEFINITELY,
I ALSO THINK THAT THE FIRST YEAR OUT OF COLLEGE CAN BE REALLY MENTALLY GRUELLING.
YEAH?
YEAH, I HAVE THAT A LITTLE...
YEAH, IT TOOK ME OVER A YEAR TO SHAKE OFF A LOT OF EXISTENTIAL DREAD ABOUT WHAT MY LIFE MIGHT BE.
YEAH, FOR SURE.
THE MORE TIME PASSES, THE EASIER IT ALL GETS.
ONCE I GET THIS JOB STARTED, IT'LL ALL WORK OUT.
YOU'LL BE A GREAT TRAINER DUDE, YOU KNOW HOW TO RELATE TO PEOPLE.
THX
IT'S JUST NICE
Burf.
OMG OUCH.
SHE'S SO DUMB.
LOOK AT HER!

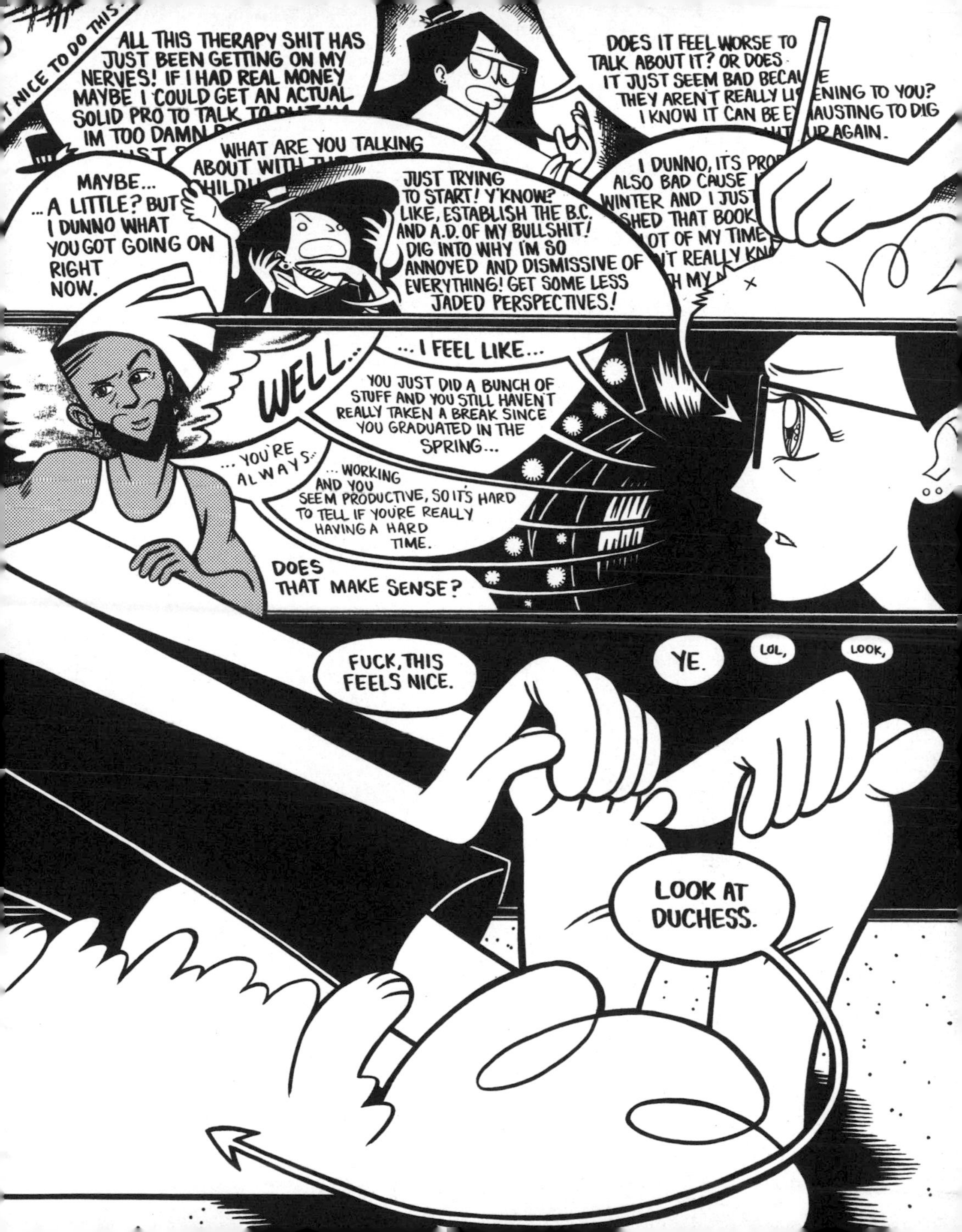

NICE TO DO THIS.
ALL THIS THERAPY SHIT HAS JUST BEEN GETTING ON MY NERVES! IF I HAD REAL MONEY MAYBE I COULD GET AN ACTUAL SOLID PRO TO TALK TO
IM TOO DAMN
DOES IT FEEL WORSE TO TALK ABOUT IT? OR DOES IT JUST SEEM BAD BECAU
THEY AREN'T REALLY LI ENING TO YOU?
I KNOW IT CAN BE E HAUSTING TO DIG
AGAIN.
WHAT ARE YOU TALKING ABOUT WITH
MAYBE... ...A LITTLE? BUT I DUNNO WHAT YOU GOT GOING ON RIGHT NOW.
JUST TRYING TO START! Y'KNOW? LIKE, ESTABLISH THE B.C. AND A.D. OF MY BULLSHIT! DIG INTO WHY I'M SO ANNOYED AND DISMISSIVE OF EVERYTHING! GET SOME LESS JADED PERSPECTIVES!
I DUNNO, IT'S PRO
ALSO BAD CAUSE
WINTER AND I JUST
SHED THAT BOOK
LOT OF MY TIME
WELL...
...I FEEL LIKE...
YOU JUST DID A BUNCH OF STUFF AND YOU STILL HAVEN'T REALLY TAKEN A BREAK SINCE YOU GRADUATED IN THE SPRING...
...YOU'RE ALWAYS...
...WORKING AND YOU SEEM PRODUCTIVE, SO IT'S HARD TO TELL IF YOU'RE REALLY HAVING A HARD TIME.
DOES THAT MAKE SENSE?
FUCK, THIS FEELS NICE.
YE.
LOL,
LOOK,
LOOK AT DUCHESS.

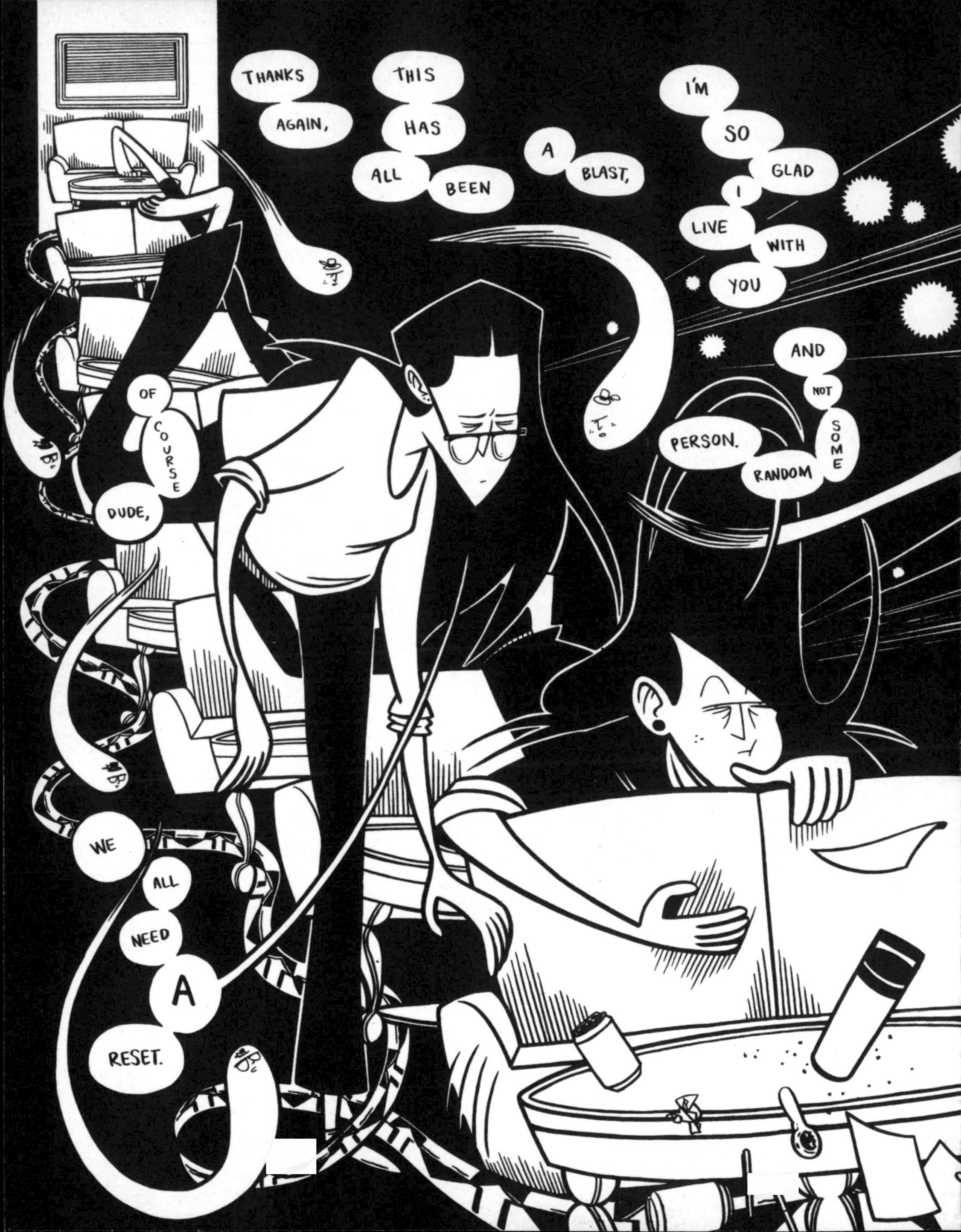
THANKS AGAIN, THIS HAS ALL BEEN A BLAST, I'M SO GLAD I LIVE WITH YOU AND NOT SOME RANDOM PERSON.
OF COURSE DUDE, WE ALL NEED A RESET.

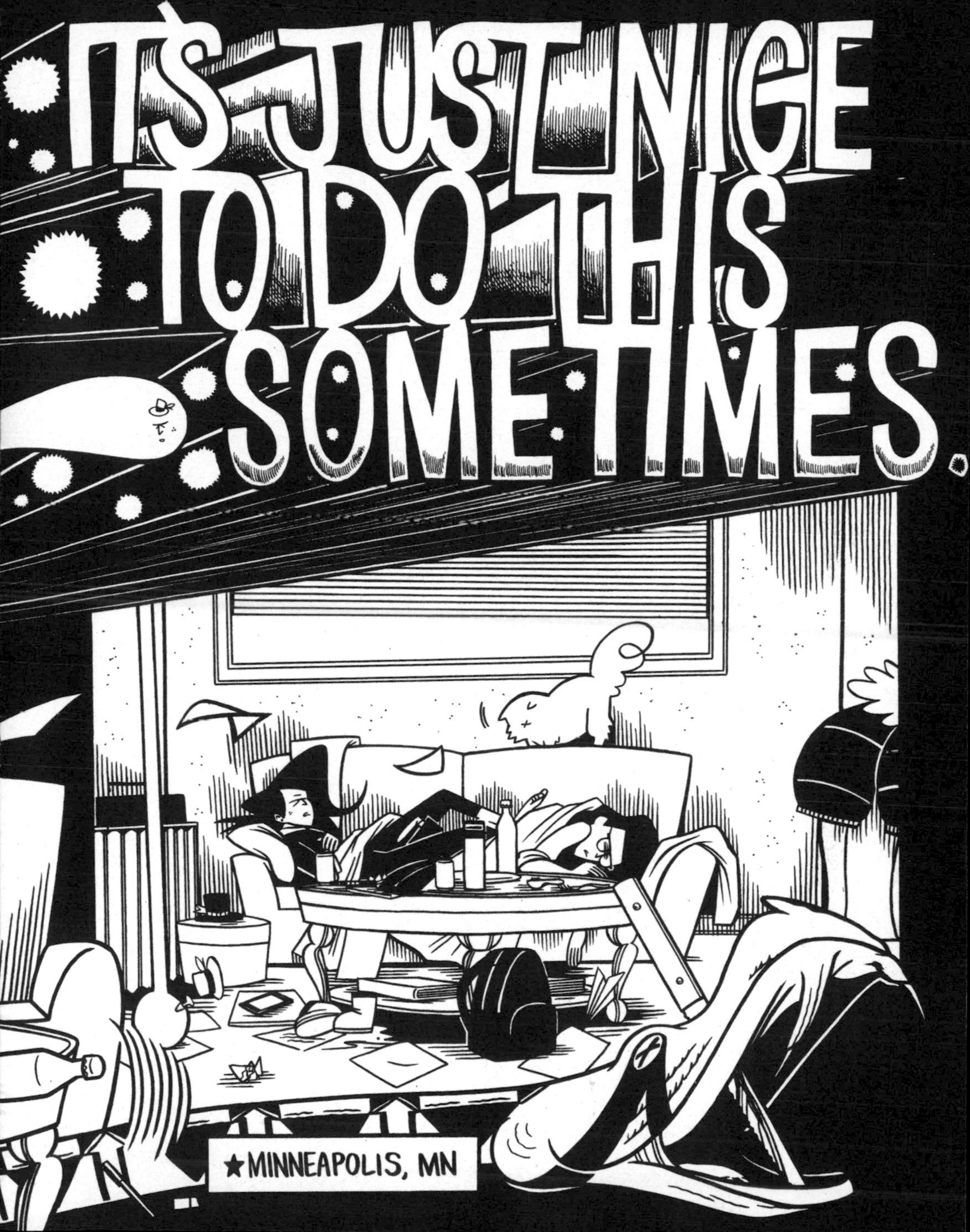
IT'S JUST NICE TO DO THIS SOMETIMES.
★MINNEAPOLIS, MN

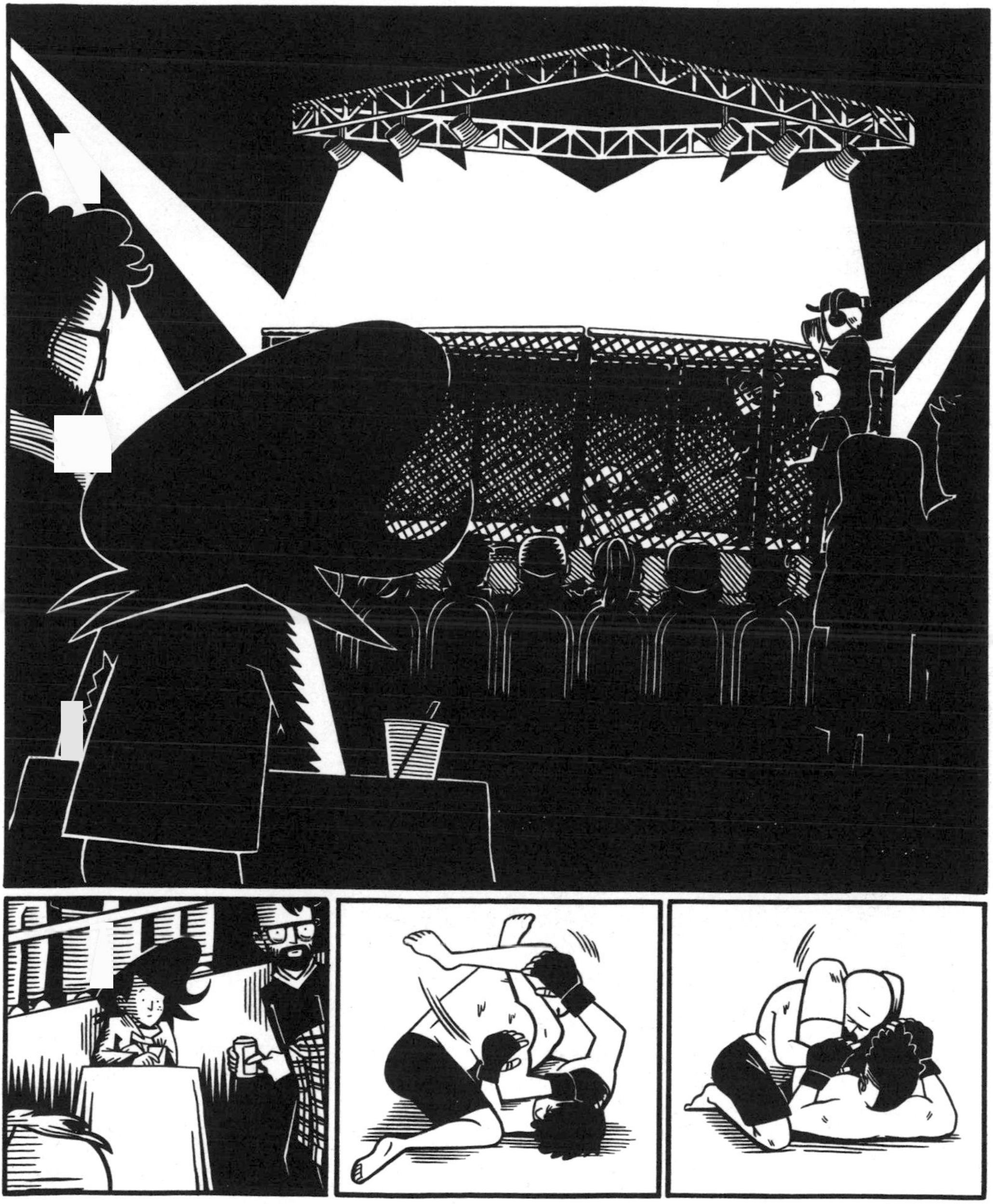

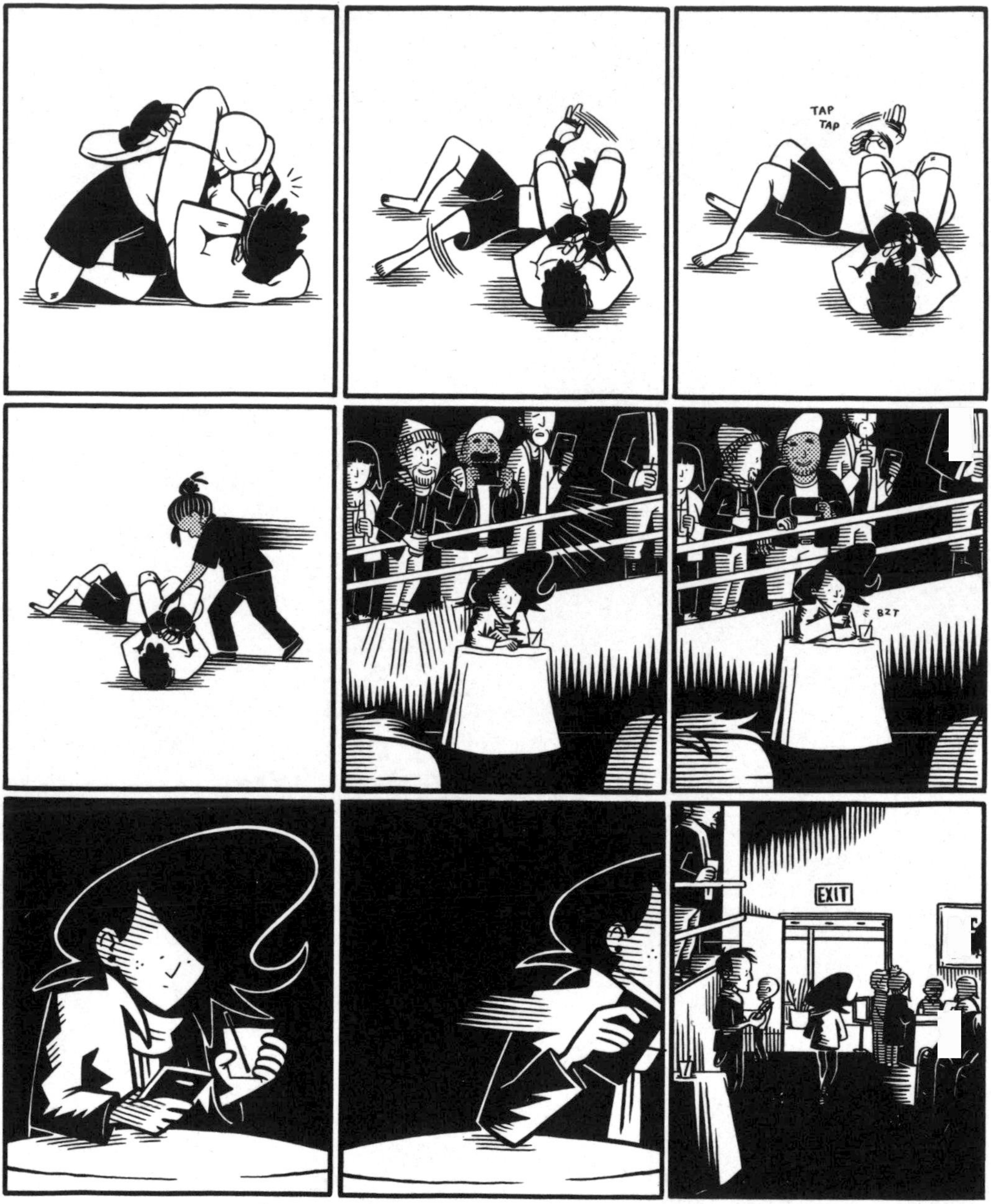
TAP
TAP
BZT
EXIT

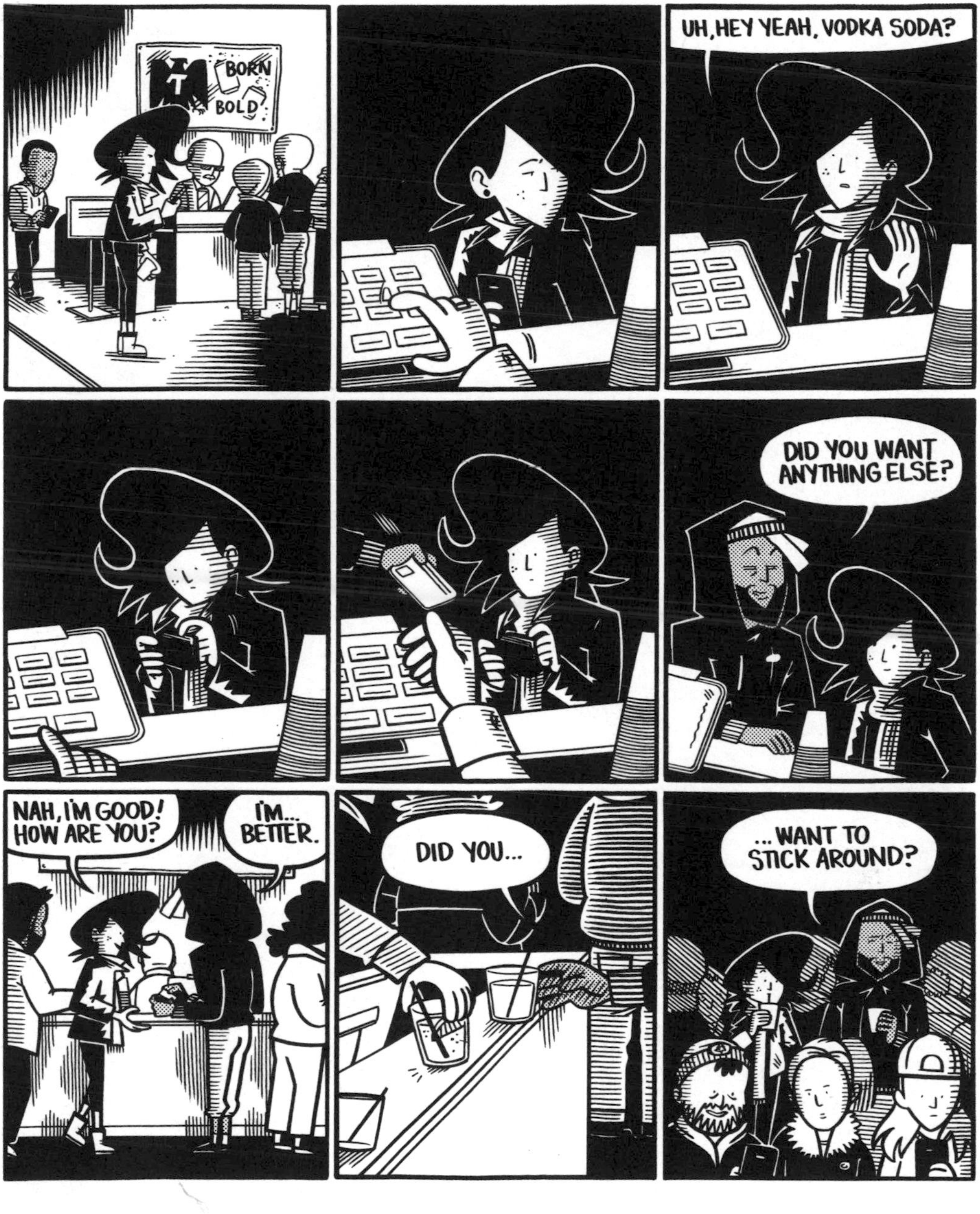
BORN
BOLD
UH, HEY YEAH, VODKA SODA?
DID YOU WANT ANYTHING ELSE?
NAH, I'M GOOD! HOW ARE YOU?
I'M... BETTER.
DID YOU...
...WANT TO STICK AROUND?

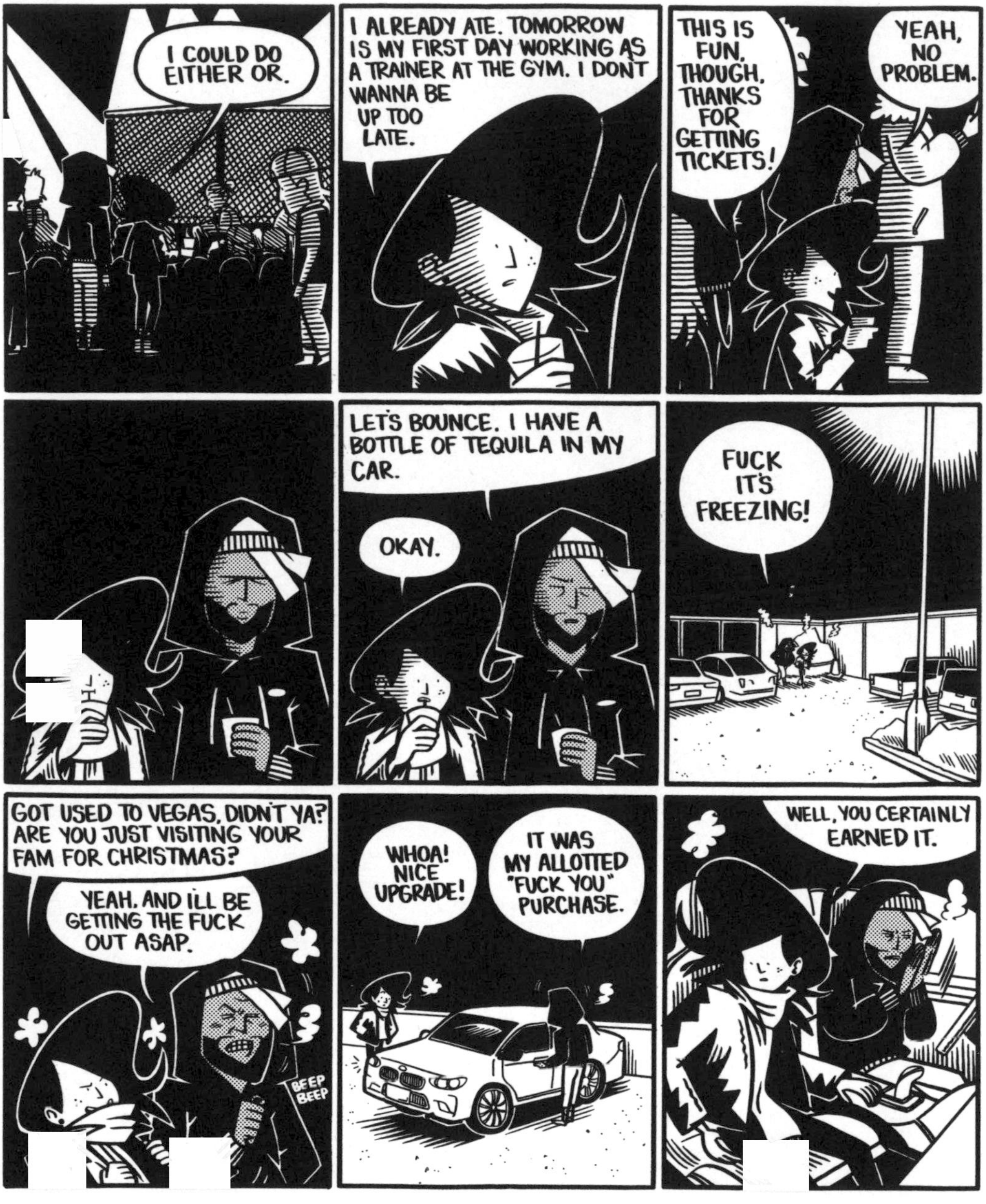
I COULD DO EITHER OR.
I ALREADY ATE. TOMORROW IS MY FIRST DAY WORKING AS A TRAINER AT THE GYM. I DON'T WANNA BE UP TOO LATE.
THIS IS FUN, THOUGH. THANKS FOR GETTING TICKETS!
YEAH, NO PROBLEM.
LET'S BOUNCE. I HAVE A BOTTLE OF TEQUILA IN MY CAR.
OKAY.
FUCK IT'S FREEZING!
GOT USED TO VEGAS, DIDN'T YA? ARE YOU JUST VISITING YOUR FAM FOR CHRISTMAS?
YEAH. AND I'LL BE GETTING THE FUCK OUT ASAP.
BEEP BEEP
WHOA! NICE UPGRADE!
IT WAS MY ALLOTTED "FUCK YOU" PURCHASE.
WELL, YOU CERTAINLY EARNED IT.

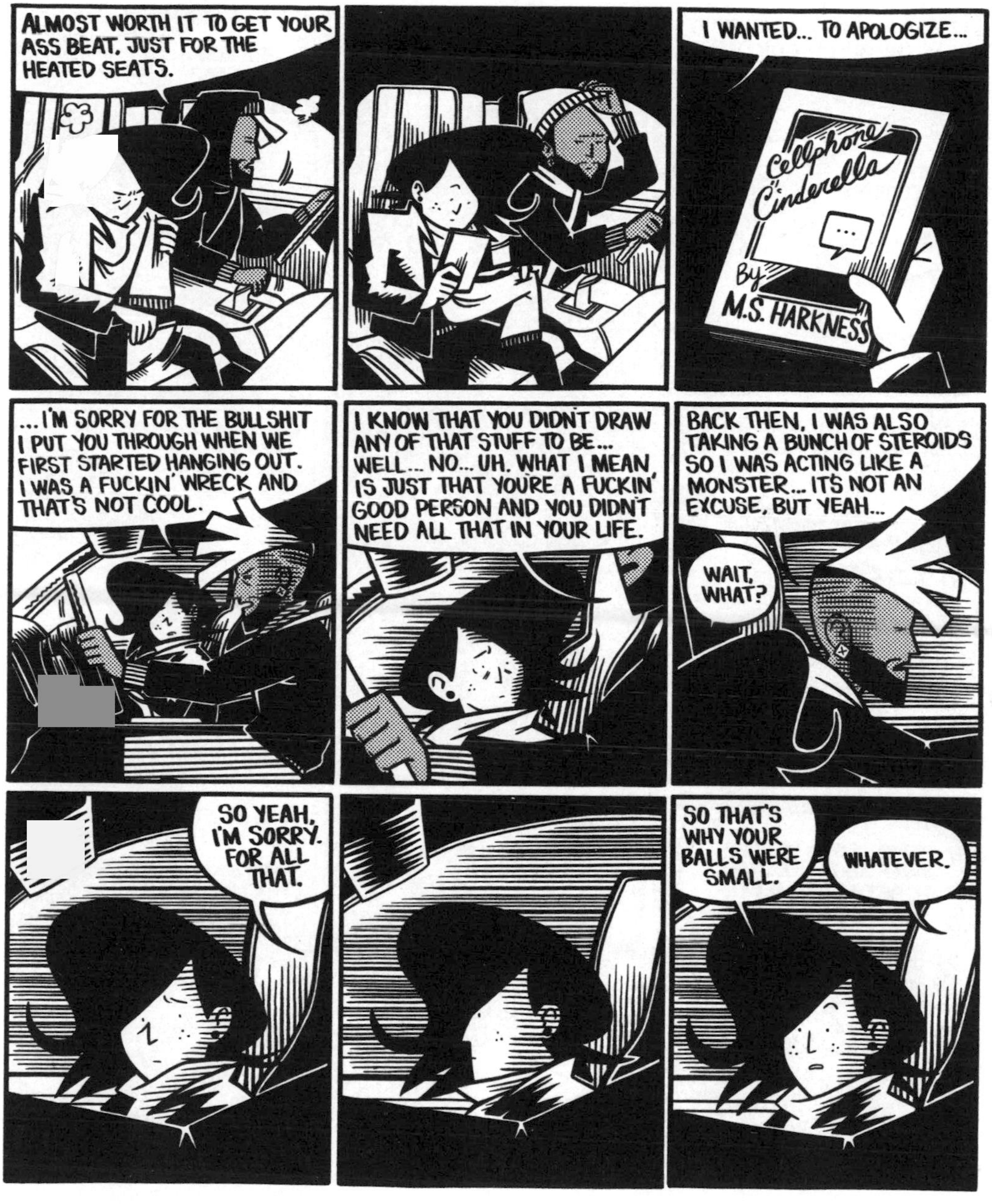
ALMOST WORTH IT TO GET YOUR ASS BEAT, JUST FOR THE HEATED SEATS.
I WANTED... TO APOLOGIZE...
Cellphone Cinderella
By M.S. HARKNESS
...I'M SORRY FOR THE BULLSHIT I PUT YOU THROUGH WHEN WE FIRST STARTED HANGING OUT. I WAS A FUCKIN' WRECK AND THAT'S NOT COOL.
I KNOW THAT YOU DIDN'T DRAW ANY OF THAT STUFF TO BE... WELL... NO... UH. WHAT I MEAN IS JUST THAT YOU'RE A FUCKIN' GOOD PERSON AND YOU DIDN'T NEED ALL THAT IN YOUR LIFE.
BACK THEN, I WAS ALSO TAKING A BUNCH OF STEROIDS SO I WAS ACTING LIKE A MONSTER... IT'S NOT AN EXCUSE, BUT YEAH...
WAIT, WHAT?
SO YEAH, I'M SORRY. FOR ALL THAT.
SO THAT'S WHY YOUR BALLS WERE SMALL.
WHATEVER.

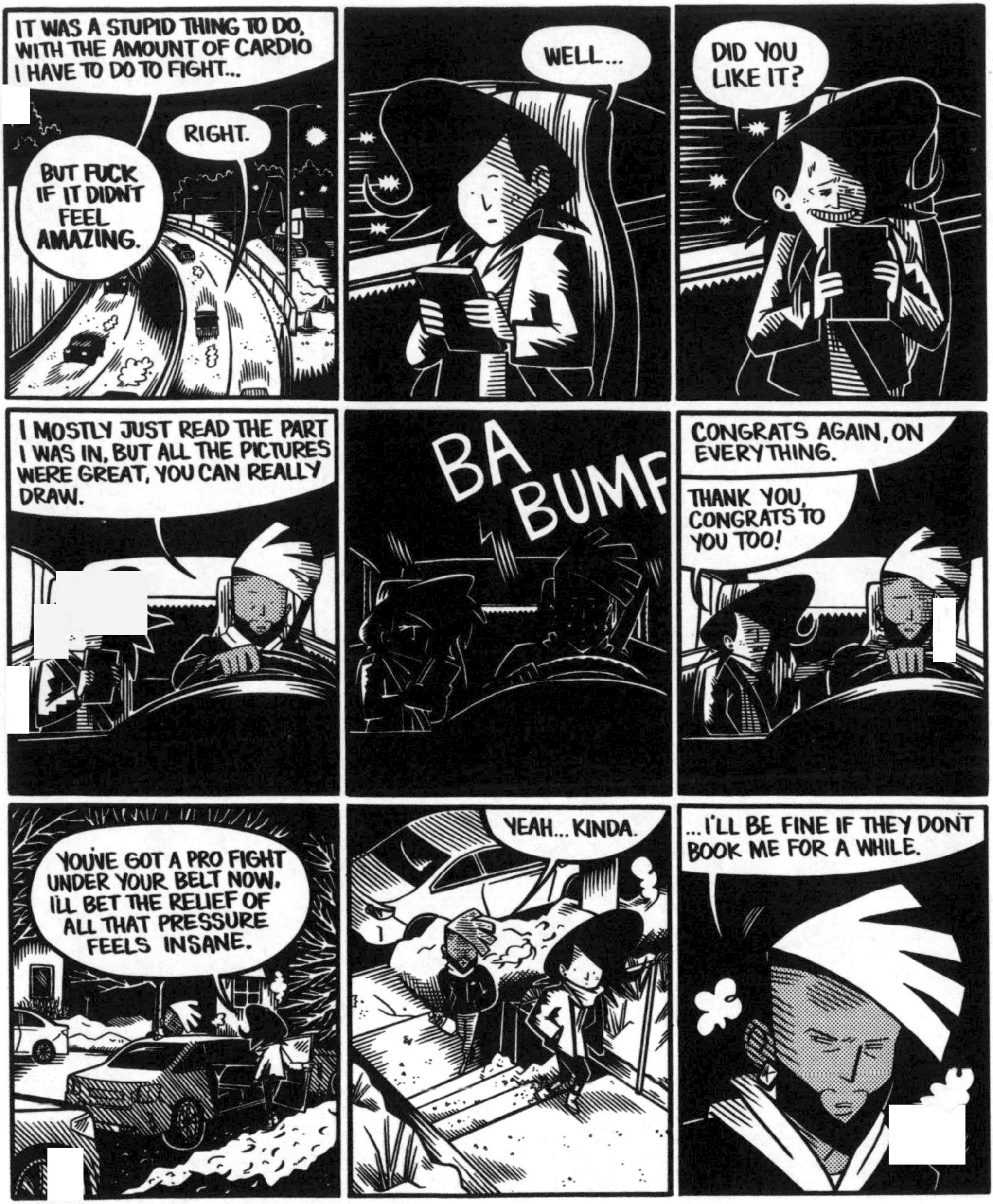
IT WAS A STUPID THING TO DO, WITH THE AMOUNT OF CARDIO I HAVE TO DO TO FIGHT...
RIGHT.
BUT FUCK IF IT DIDN'T FEEL AMAZING.
WELL...
DID YOU LIKE IT?
I MOSTLY JUST READ THE PART I WAS IN, BUT ALL THE PICTURES WERE GREAT, YOU CAN REALLY DRAW.
BA BUMP
CONGRATS AGAIN, ON EVERYTHING.
THANK YOU, CONGRATS TO YOU TOO!
YOU'VE GOT A PRO FIGHT UNDER YOUR BELT NOW, I'LL BET THE RELIEF OF ALL THAT PRESSURE FEELS INSANE.
YEAH... KINDA.
...I'LL BE FINE IF THEY DON'T BOOK ME FOR A WHILE.

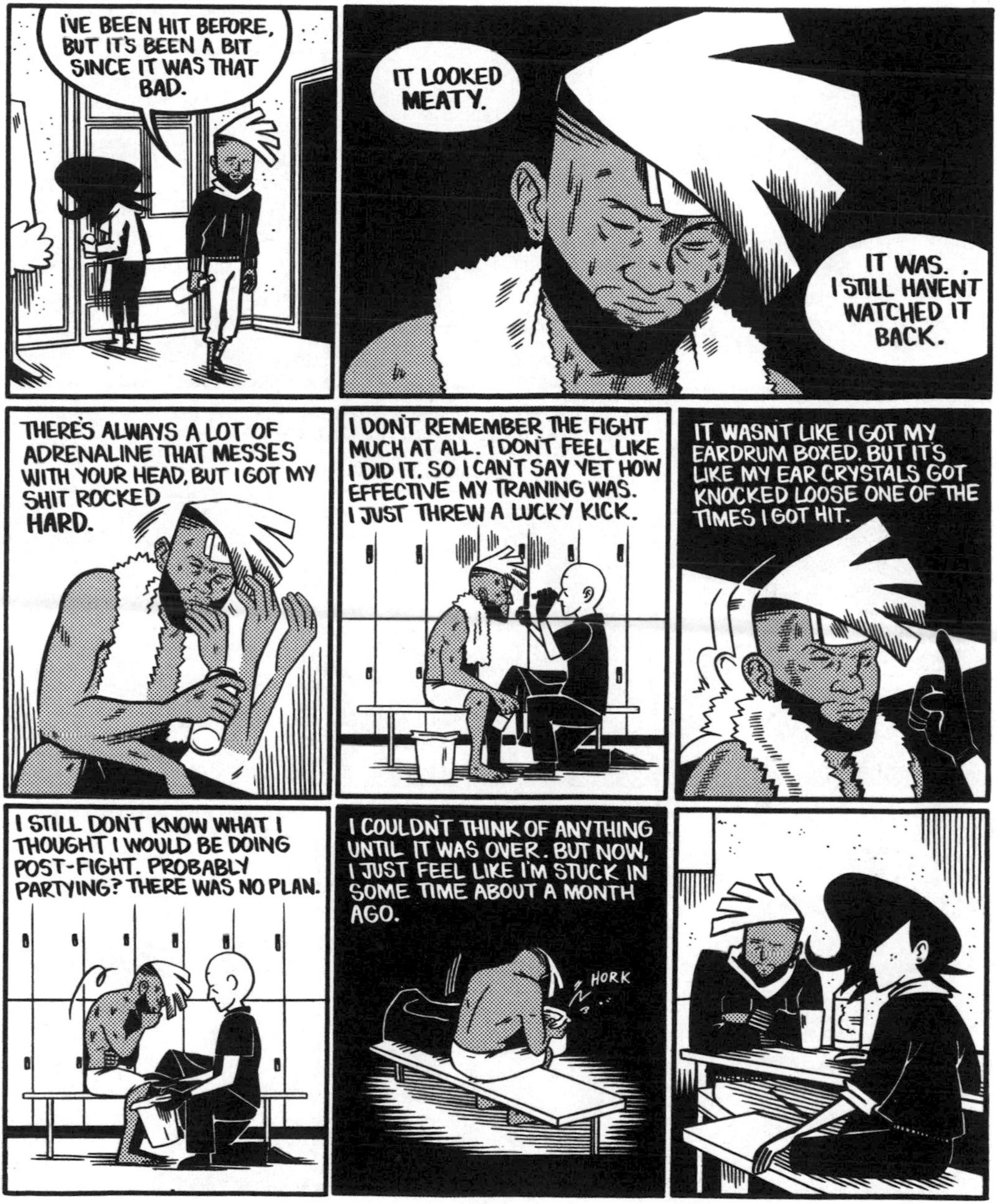
I'VE BEEN HIT BEFORE, BUT IT'S BEEN A BIT SINCE IT WAS THAT BAD.
IT LOOKED MEATY.
IT WAS. I STILL HAVEN'T WATCHED IT BACK.
THERE'S ALWAYS A LOT OF ADRENALINE THAT MESSES WITH YOUR HEAD, BUT I GOT MY SHIT ROCKED HARD.
I DON'T REMEMBER THE FIGHT MUCH AT ALL. I DON'T FEEL LIKE I DID IT. SO I CAN'T SAY YET HOW EFFECTIVE MY TRAINING WAS. I JUST THREW A LUCKY KICK.
IT WASN'T LIKE I GOT MY EARDRUM BOXED. BUT IT'S LIKE MY EAR CRYSTALS GOT KNOCKED LOOSE ONE OF THE TIMES I GOT HIT.
I STILL DON'T KNOW WHAT I THOUGHT I WOULD BE DOING POST-FIGHT. PROBABLY PARTYING? THERE WAS NO PLAN.
I COULDN'T THINK OF ANYTHING UNTIL IT WAS OVER. BUT NOW, I JUST FEEL LIKE I'M STUCK IN SOME TIME ABOUT A MONTH AGO.
HORK

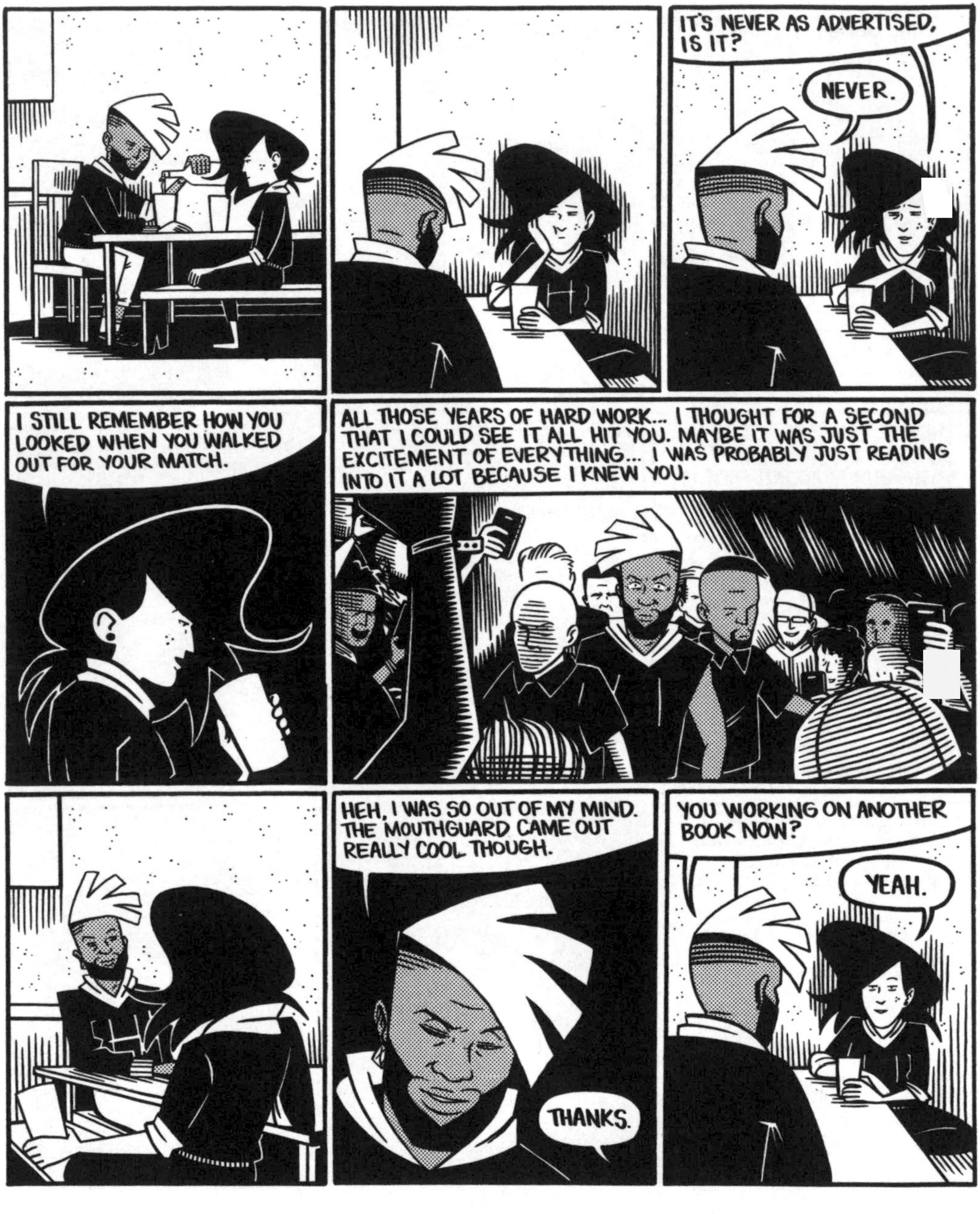
IT'S NEVER AS ADVERTISED, IS IT?
NEVER.
I STILL REMEMBER HOW YOU LOOKED WHEN YOU WALKED OUT FOR YOUR MATCH.
ALL THOSE YEARS OF HARD WORK... I THOUGHT FOR A SECOND THAT I COULD SEE IT ALL HIT YOU. MAYBE IT WAS JUST THE EXCITEMENT OF EVERYTHING... I WAS PROBABLY JUST READING INTO IT A LOT BECAUSE I KNEW YOU.
HEH, I WAS SO OUT OF MY MIND. THE MOUTHGUARD CAME OUT REALLY COOL THOUGH.
THANKS.
YOU WORKING ON ANOTHER BOOK NOW?
YEAH.

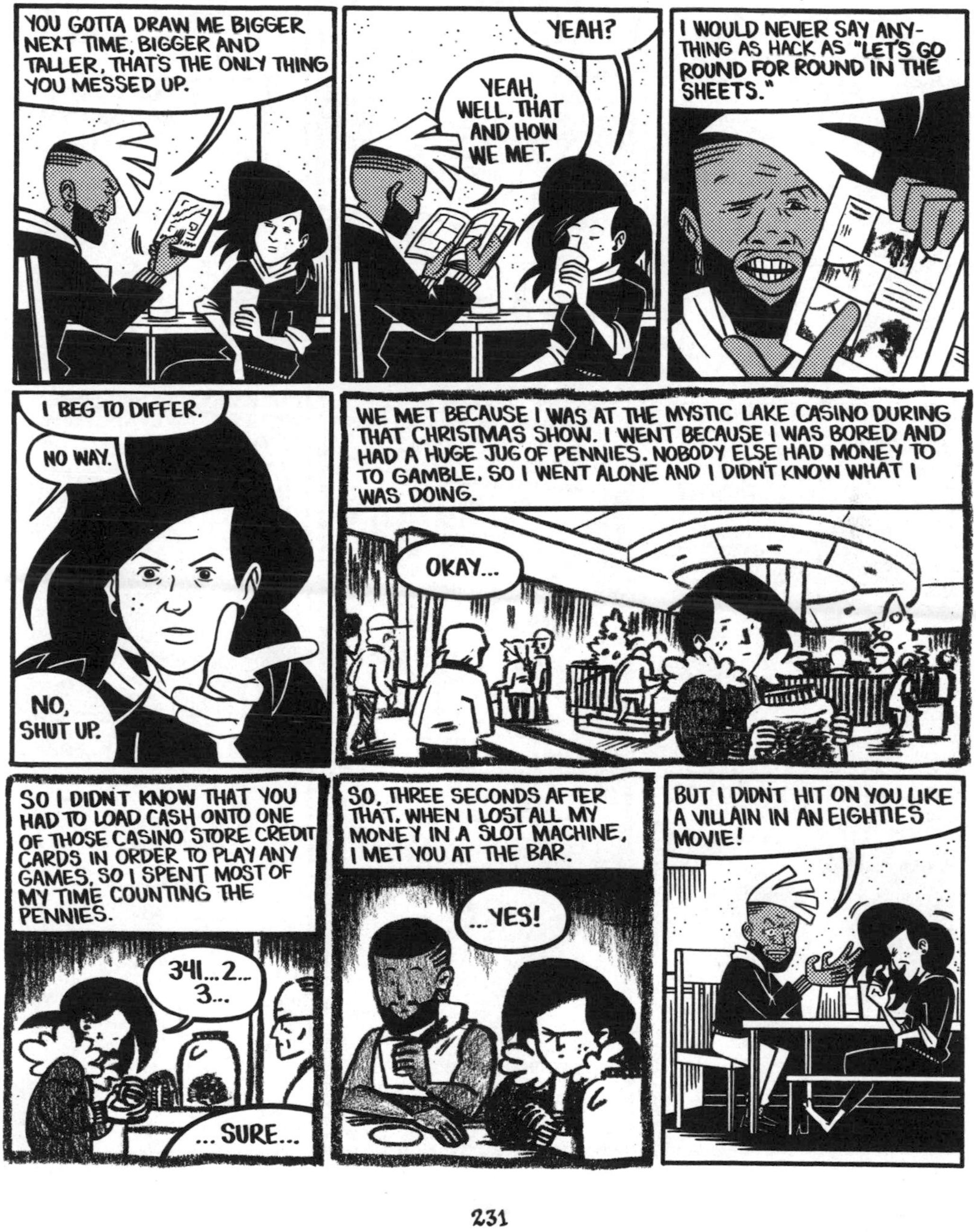
YOU GOTTA DRAW ME BIGGER NEXT TIME, BIGGER AND TALLER, THAT'S THE ONLY THING YOU MESSED UP.
YEAH?
YEAH, WELL, THAT AND HOW WE MET.
I WOULD NEVER SAY ANY-THING AS HACK AS "LET'S GO ROUND FOR ROUND IN THE SHEETS."
I BEG TO DIFFER.
NO WAY.
NO, SHUT UP.
WE MET BECAUSE I WAS AT THE MYSTIC LAKE CASINO DURING THAT CHRISTMAS SHOW. I WENT BECAUSE I WAS BORED AND HAD A HUGE JUG OF PENNIES. NOBODY ELSE HAD MONEY TO TO GAMBLE, SO I WENT ALONE AND I DIDN'T KNOW WHAT I WAS DOING.
OKAY...
SO I DIDN'T KNOW THAT YOU HAD TO LOAD CASH ONTO ONE OF THOSE CASINO STORE CREDIT CARDS IN ORDER TO PLAY ANY GAMES, SO I SPENT MOST OF MY TIME COUNTING THE PENNIES.
341...2... 3...
...SURE...
SO, THREE SECONDS AFTER THAT, WHEN I LOST ALL MY MONEY IN A SLOT MACHINE, I MET YOU AT THE BAR.
...YES!
BUT I DIDN'T HIT ON YOU LIKE A VILLAIN IN AN EIGHTIES MOVIE!

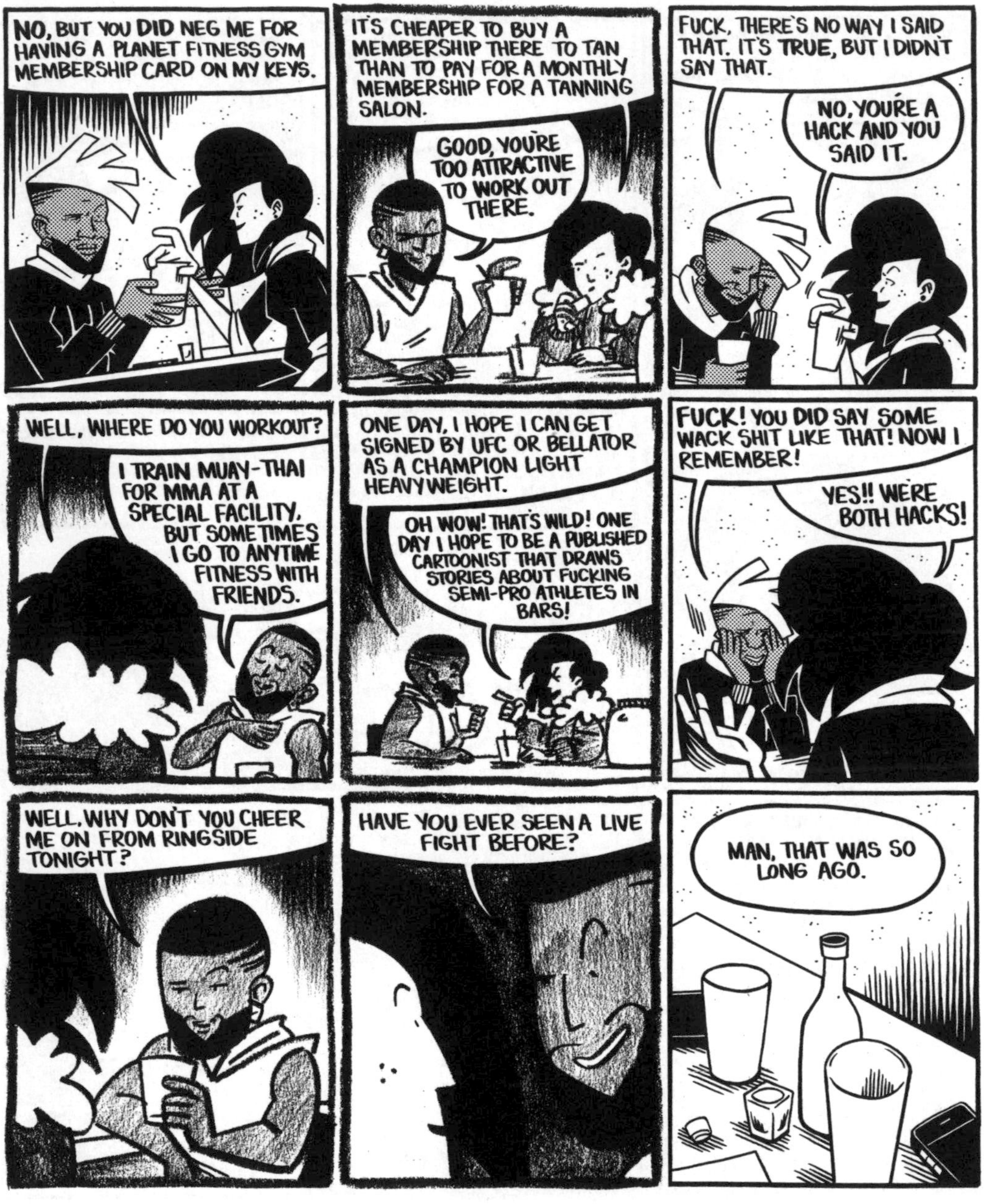
NO, BUT YOU DID NEG ME FOR HAVING A PLANET FITNESS GYM MEMBERSHIP CARD ON MY KEYS.
IT'S CHEAPER TO BUY A MEMBERSHIP THERE TO TAN THAN TO PAY FOR A MONTHLY MEMBERSHIP FOR A TANNING SALON.
GOOD, YOU'RE TOO ATTRACTIVE TO WORK OUT THERE.
FUCK, THERE'S NO WAY I SAID THAT. IT'S TRUE, BUT I DIDN'T SAY THAT.
NO, YOU'RE A HACK AND YOU SAID IT.
WELL, WHERE DO YOU WORKOUT?
I TRAIN MUAY-THAI FOR MMA AT A SPECIAL FACILITY, BUT SOMETIMES I GO TO ANYTIME FITNESS WITH FRIENDS.
ONE DAY, I HOPE I CAN GET SIGNED BY UFC OR BELLATOR AS A CHAMPION LIGHT HEAVYWEIGHT.
OH WOW! THAT'S WILD! ONE DAY I HOPE TO BE A PUBLISHED CARTOONIST THAT DRAWS STORIES ABOUT FUCKING SEMI-PRO ATHLETES IN BARS!
FUCK! YOU DID SAY SOME WACK SHIT LIKE THAT! NOW I REMEMBER!
YES!! WE'RE BOTH HACKS!
WELL, WHY DON'T YOU CHEER ME ON FROM RINGSIDE TONIGHT?
HAVE YOU EVER SEEN A LIVE FIGHT BEFORE?
MAN, THAT WAS SO LONG AGO.

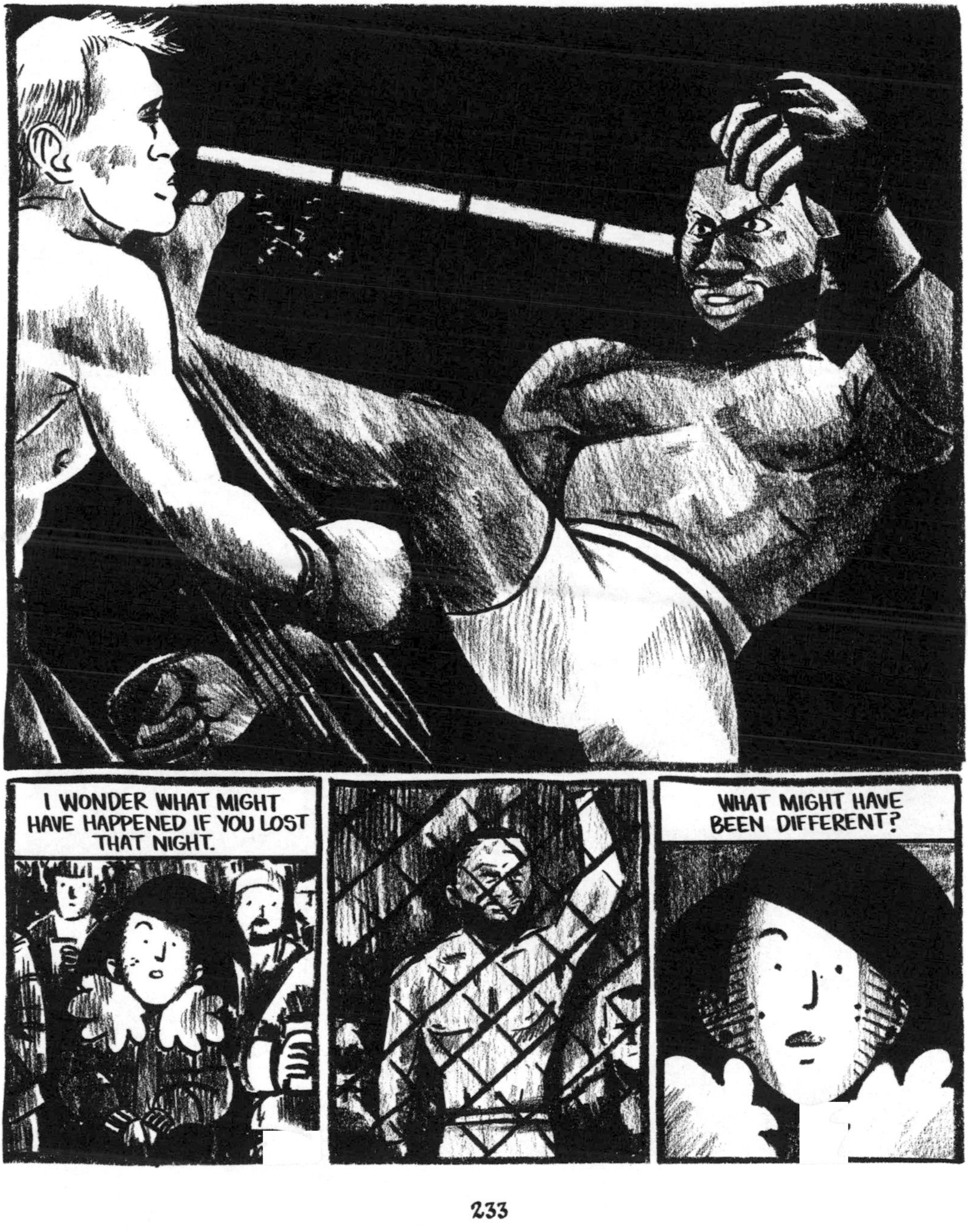
I WONDER WHAT MIGHT HAVE HAPPENED IF YOU LOST THAT NIGHT.
WHAT MIGHT HAVE BEEN DIFFERENT?

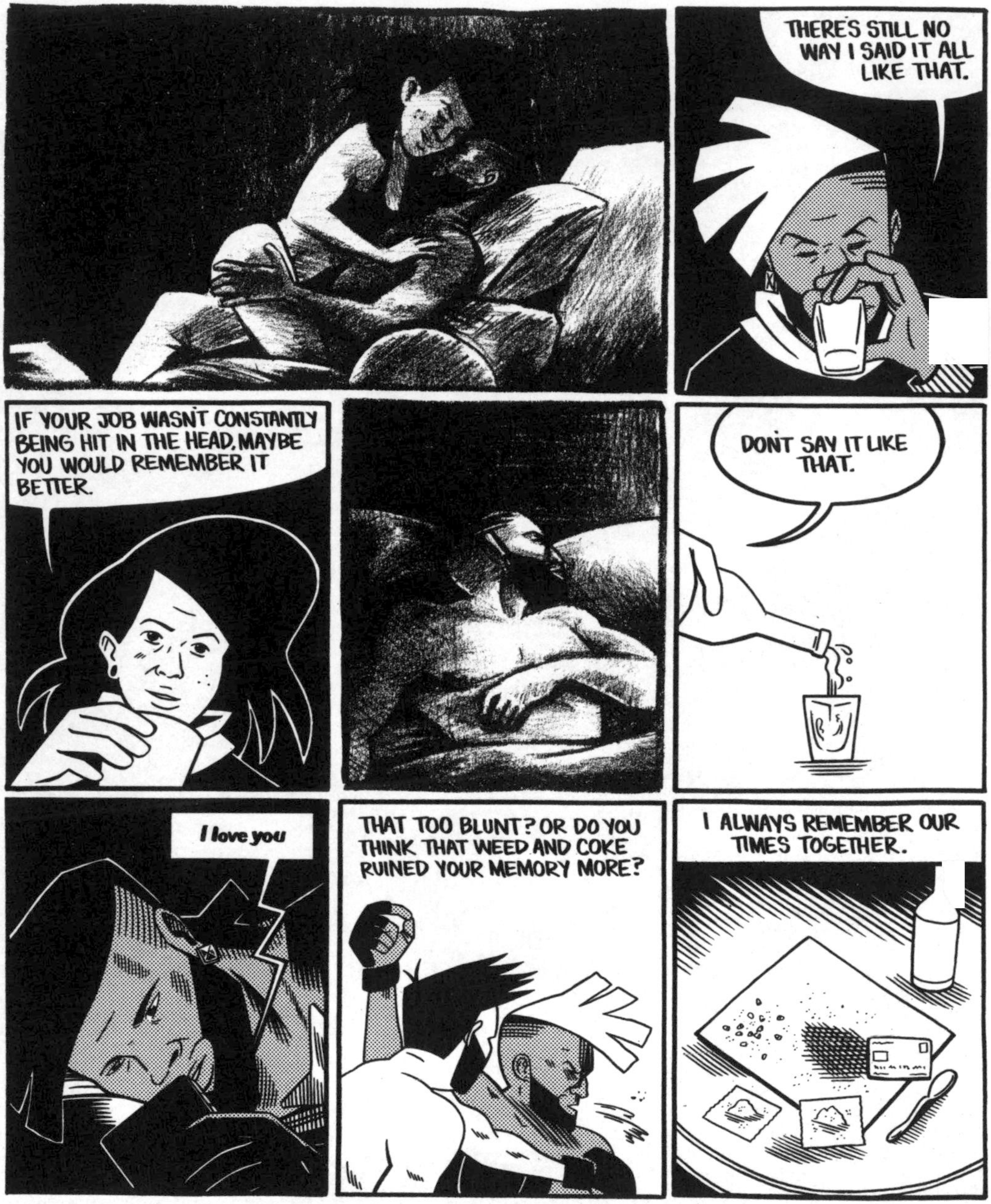
THERE'S STILL NO WAY I SAID IT ALL LIKE THAT.
IF YOUR JOB WASN'T CONSTANTLY BEING HIT IN THE HEAD, MAYBE YOU WOULD REMEMBER IT BETTER.
DON'T SAY IT LIKE THAT.
I love you
THAT TOO BLUNT? OR DO YOU THINK THAT WEED AND COKE RUINED YOUR MEMORY MORE?
I ALWAYS REMEMBER OUR TIMES TOGETHER.

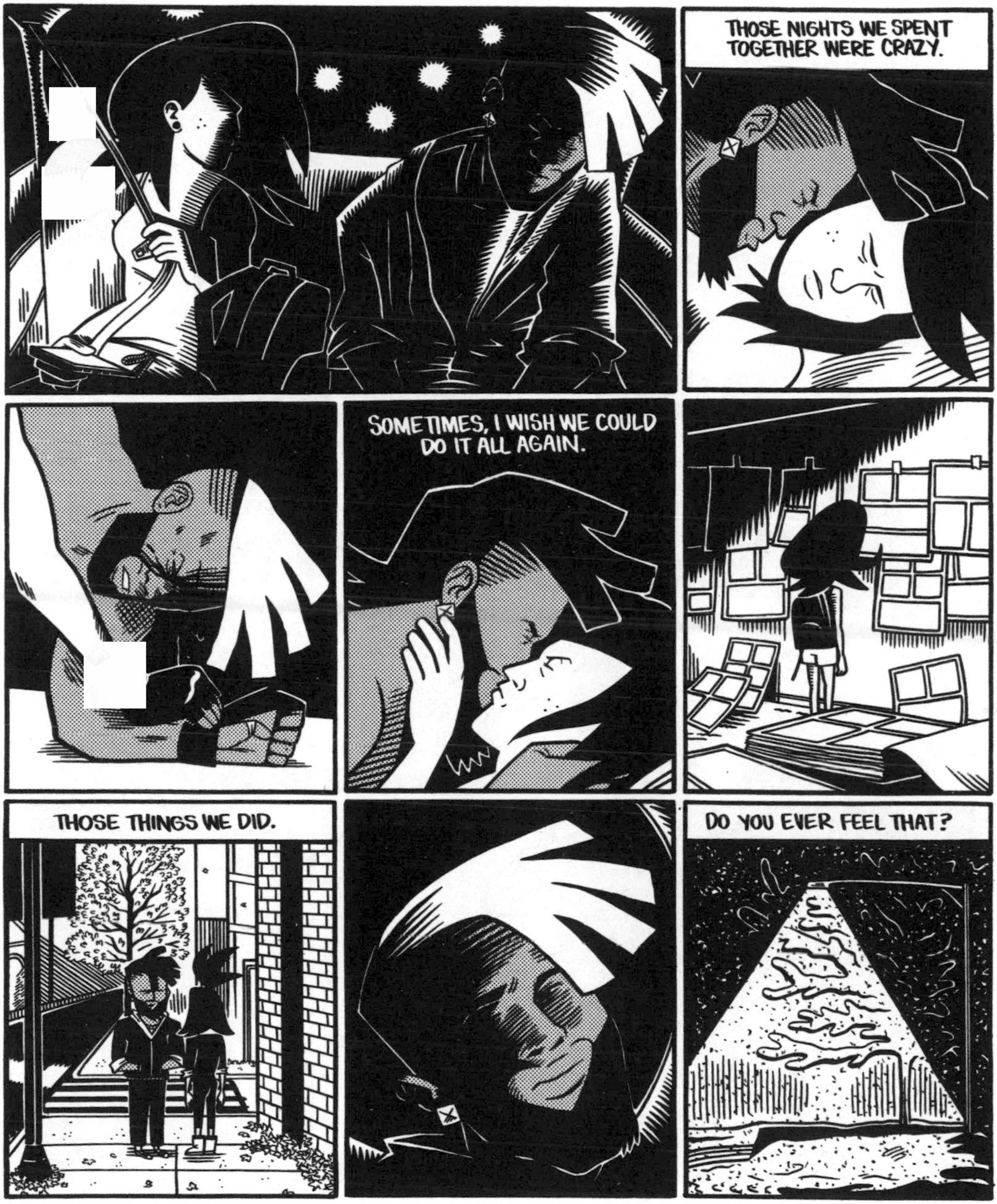
THOSE NIGHTS WE SPENT TOGETHER WERE CRAZY.
SOMETIMES, I WISH WE COULD DO IT ALL AGAIN.
THOSE THINGS WE DID.
DO YOU EVER FEEL THAT?

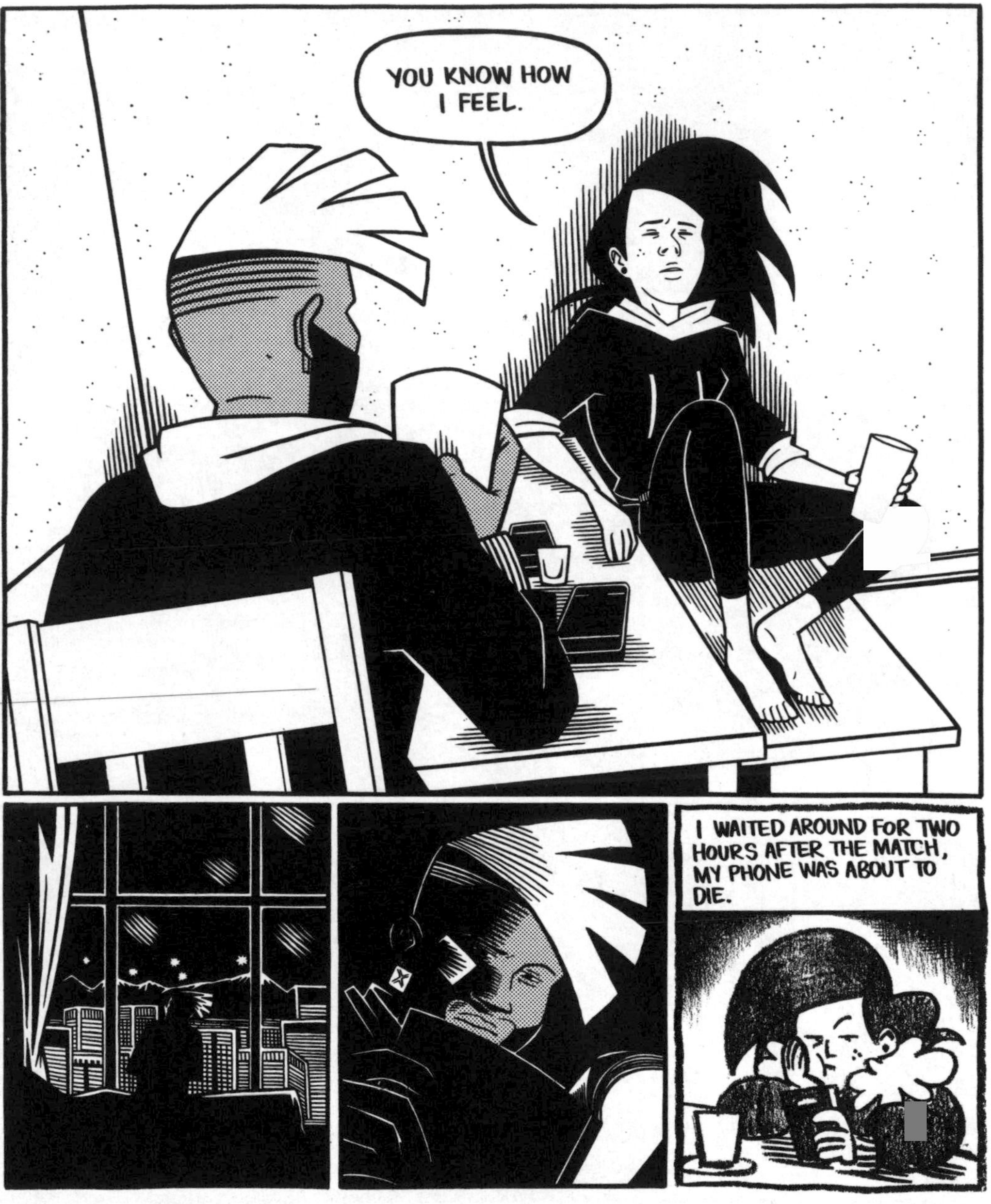
YOU KNOW HOW I FEEL.
I WAITED AROUND FOR TWO HOURS AFTER THE MATCH, MY PHONE WAS ABOUT TO DIE.

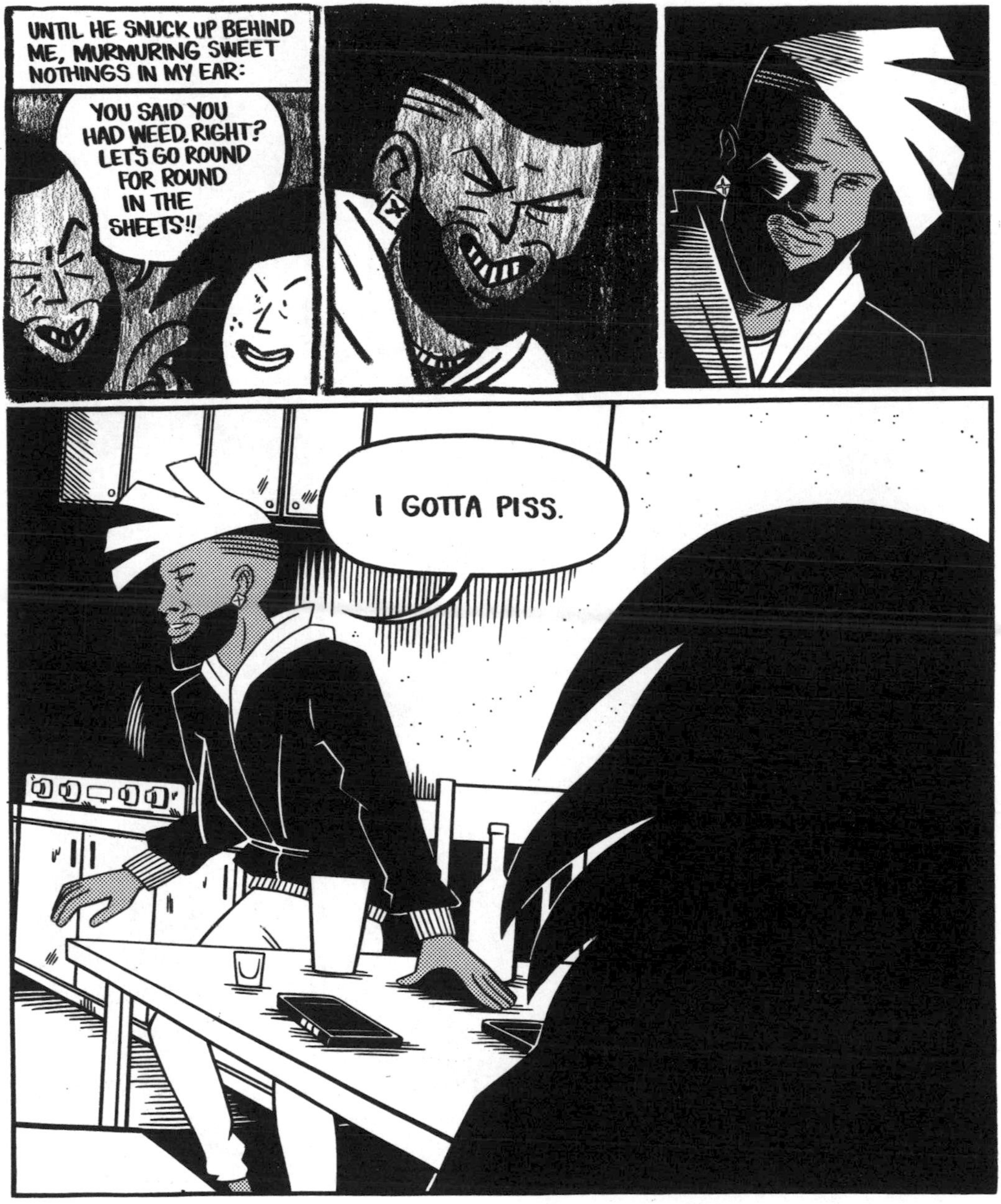
UNTIL HE SNUCK UP BEHIND ME, MURMURING SWEET NOTHINGS IN MY EAR:
YOU SAID YOU HAD WEED, RIGHT? LET'S GO ROUND FOR ROUND IN THE SHEETS!!
I GOTTA PISS.

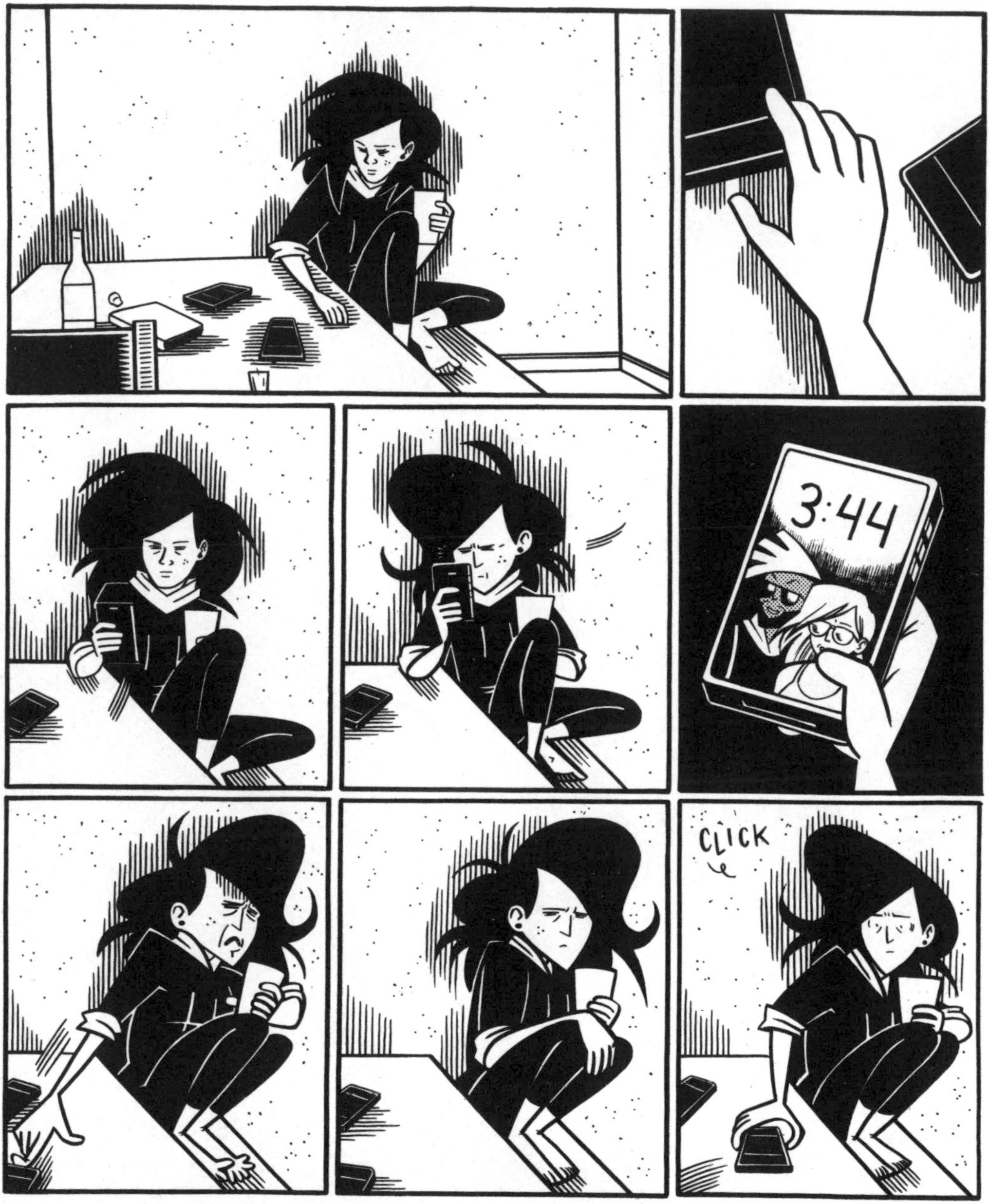
3:44
CLICK

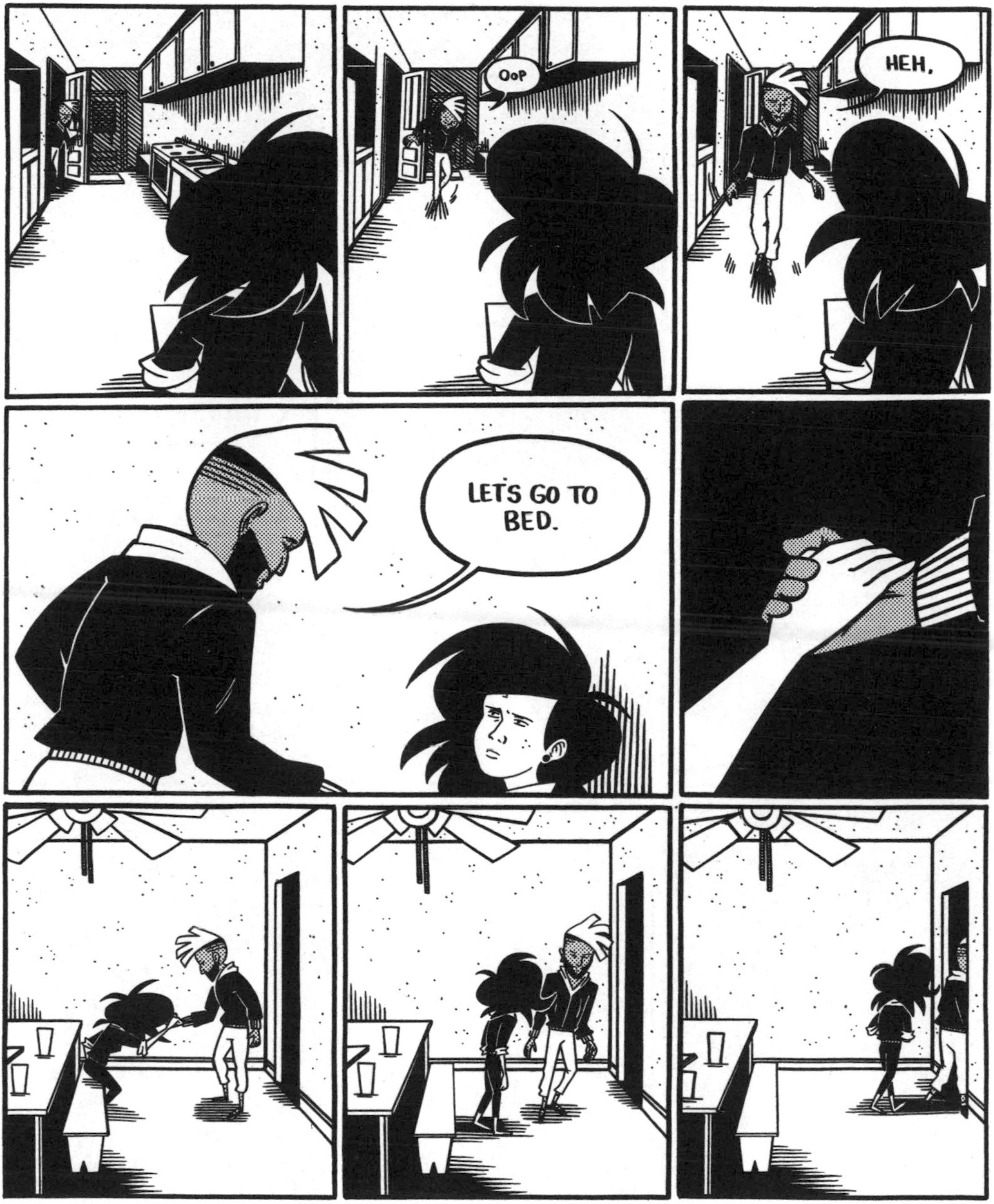
OOP
HEH.
LET'S GO TO BED.

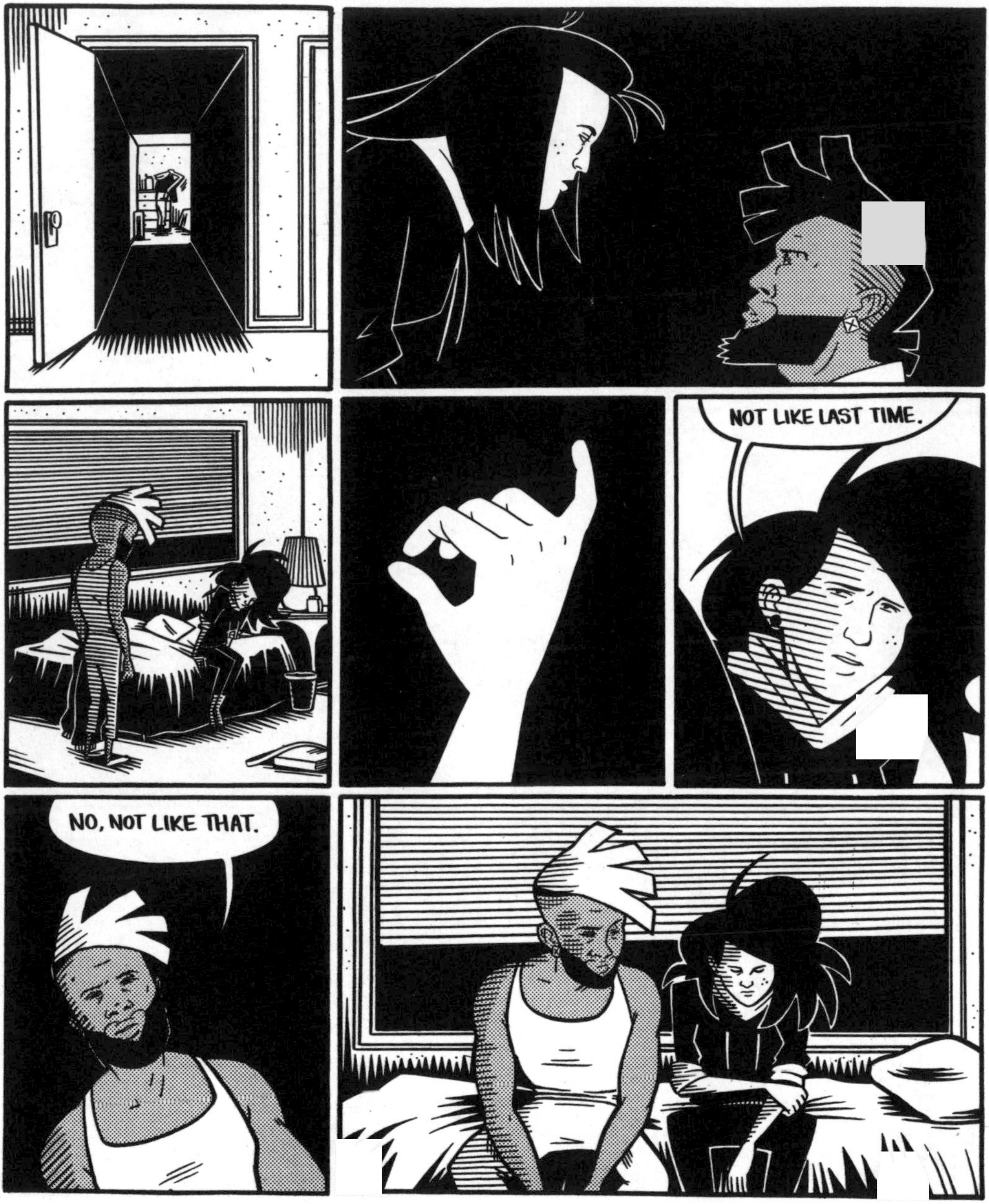
NOT LIKE LAST TIME.
NO, NOT LIKE THAT.

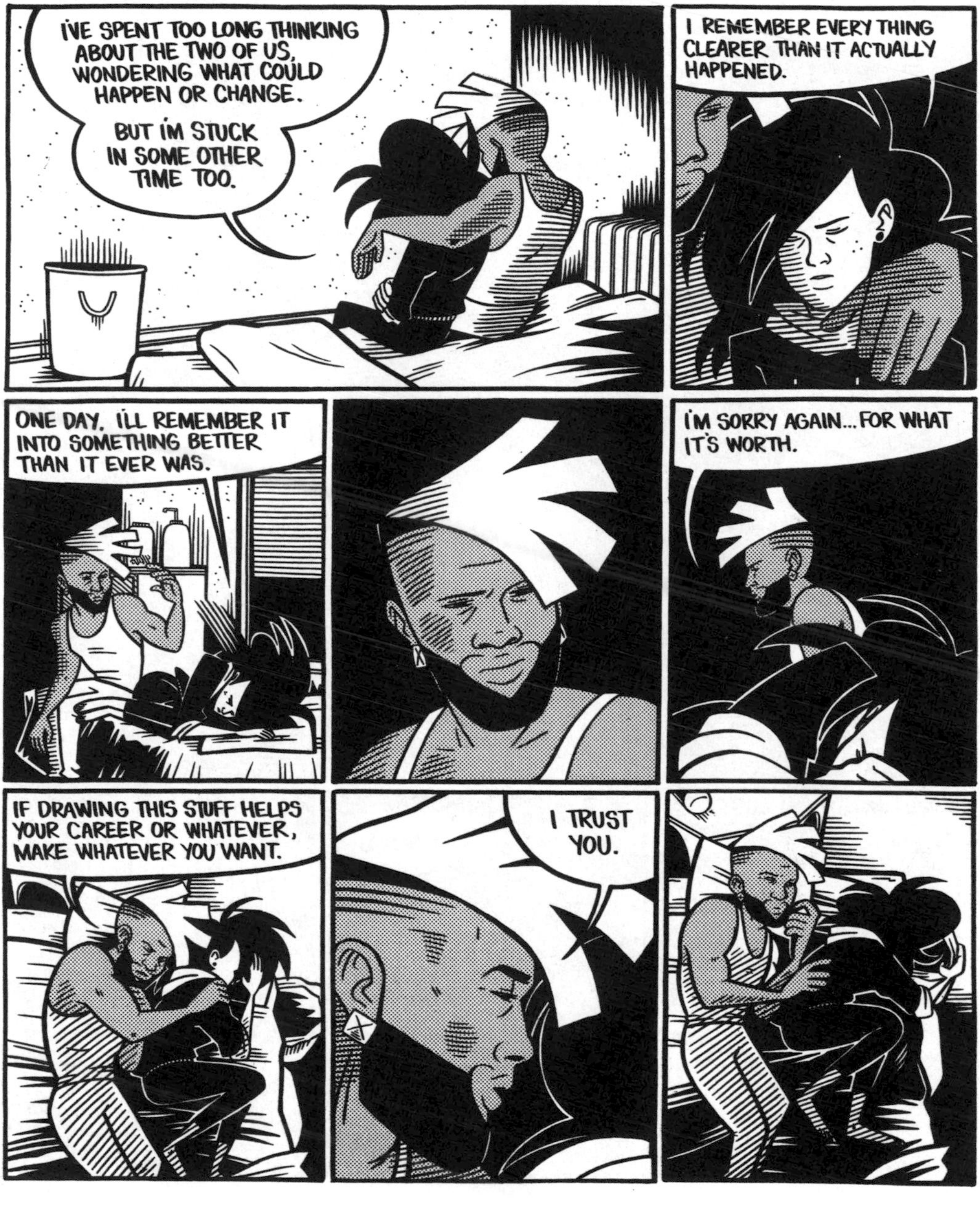
I'VE SPENT TOO LONG THINKING ABOUT THE TWO OF US, WONDERING WHAT COULD HAPPEN OR CHANGE.
BUT I'M STUCK IN SOME OTHER TIME TOO.
I REMEMBER EVERY THING CLEARER THAN IT ACTUALLY HAPPENED.
ONE DAY, I'LL REMEMBER IT INTO SOMETHING BETTER THAN IT EVER WAS.
I'M SORRY AGAIN... FOR WHAT IT'S WORTH.
IF DRAWING THIS STUFF HELPS YOUR CAREER OR WHATEVER, MAKE WHATEVER YOU WANT.
I TRUST YOU.

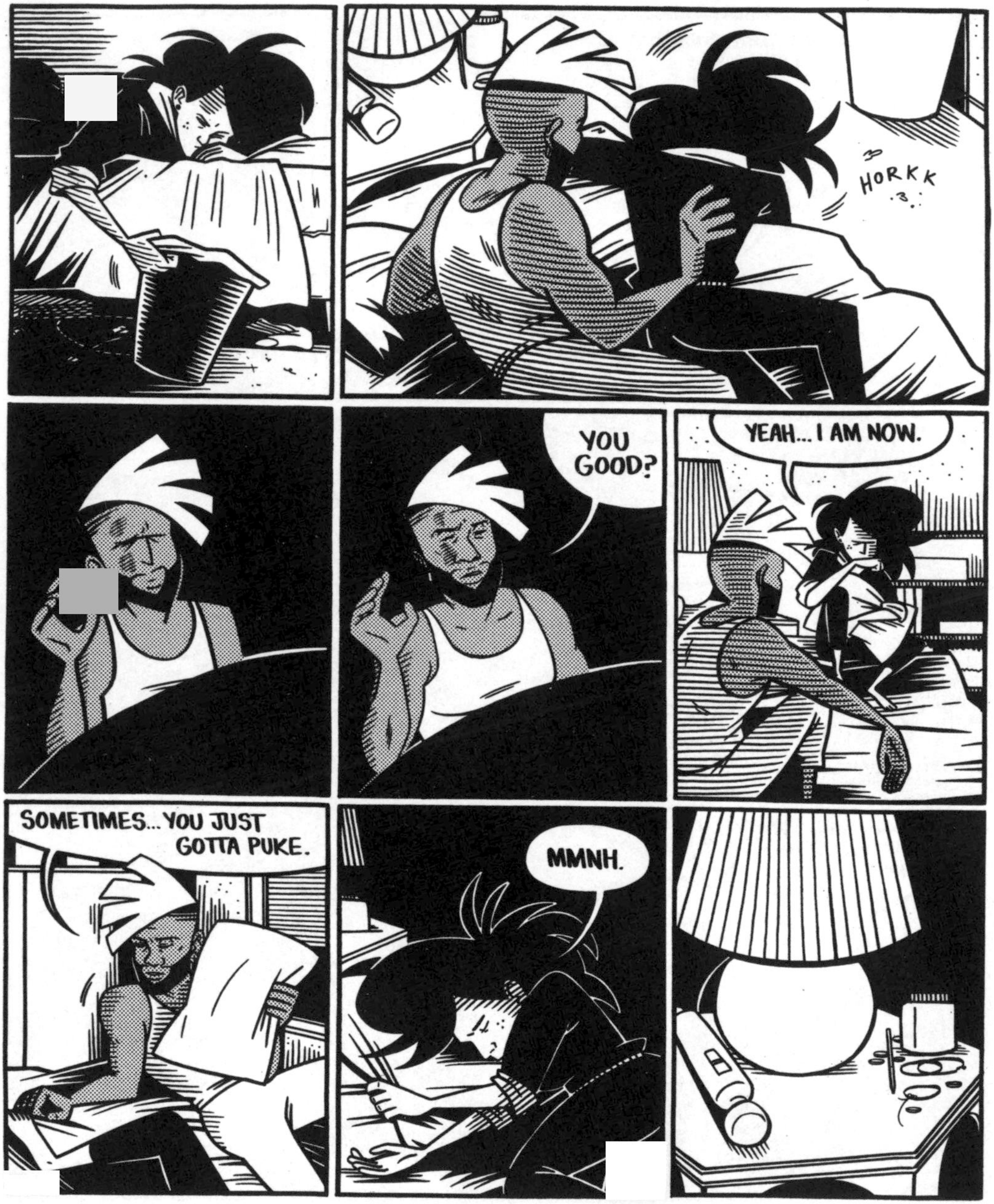
HORKK
YOU GOOD?
YEAH... I AM NOW.
SOMETIMES... YOU JUST GOTTA PUKE.
MMNH.

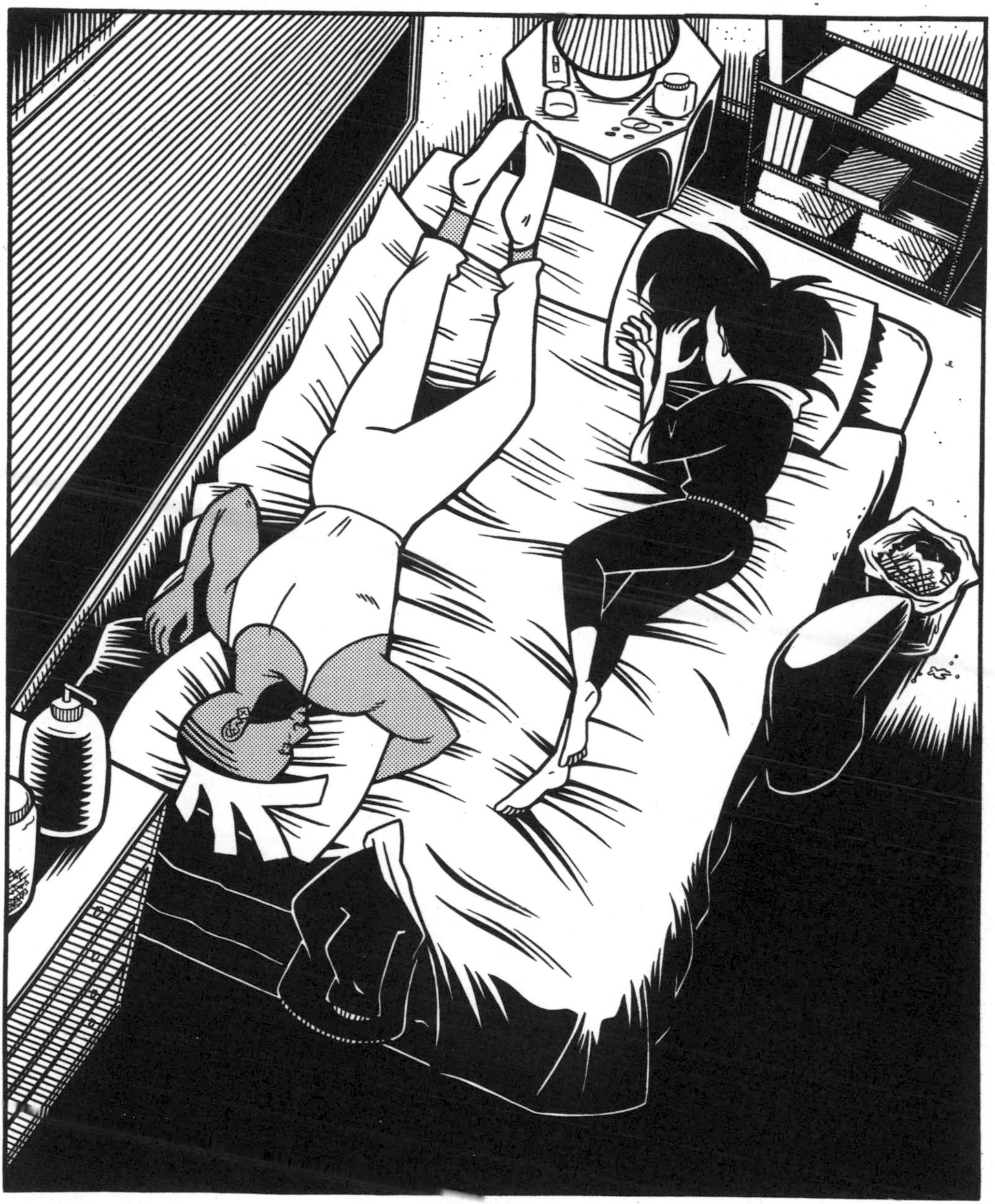

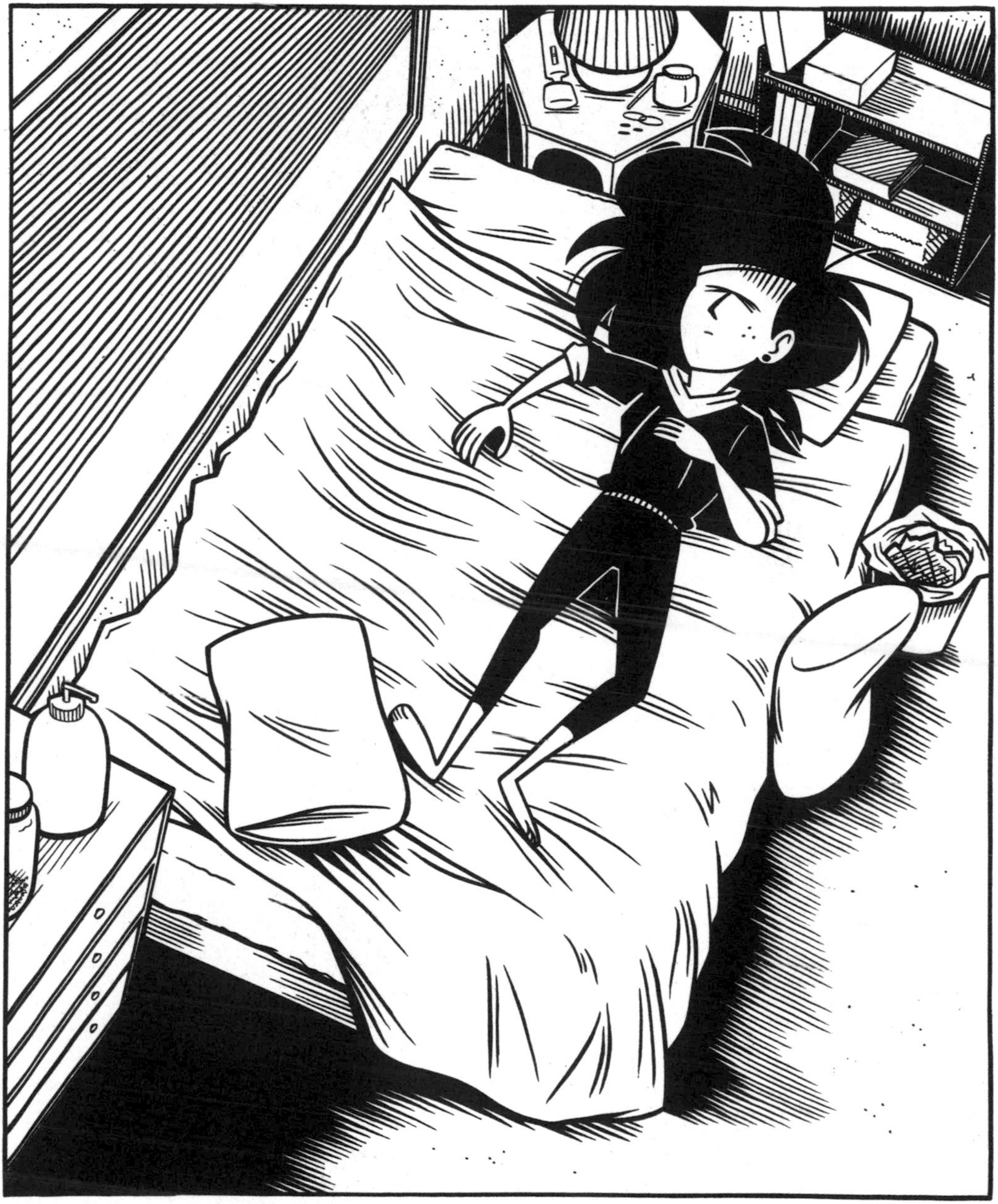

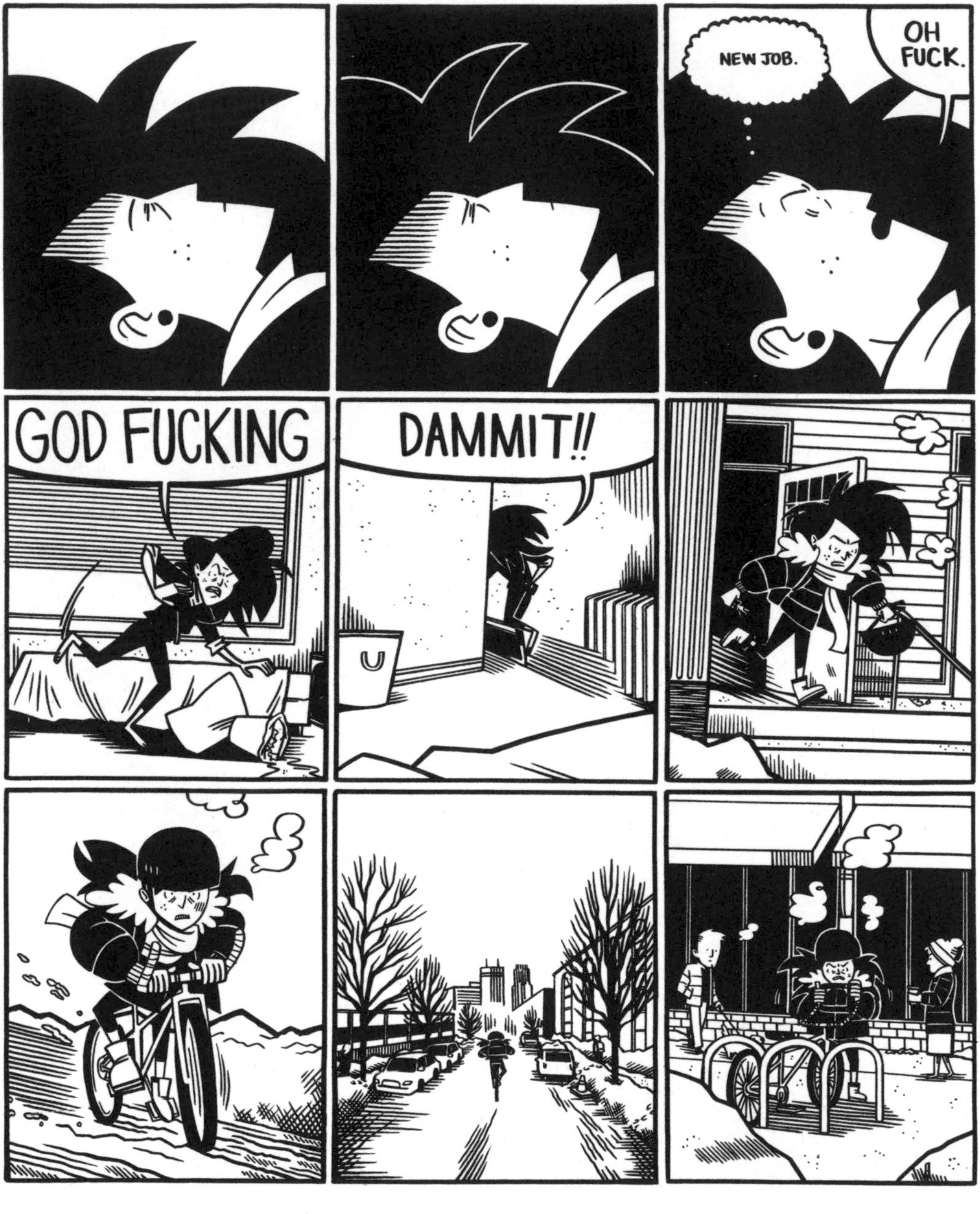
NEW JOB.
OH FUCK.
GOD FUCKING
DAMMIT!!

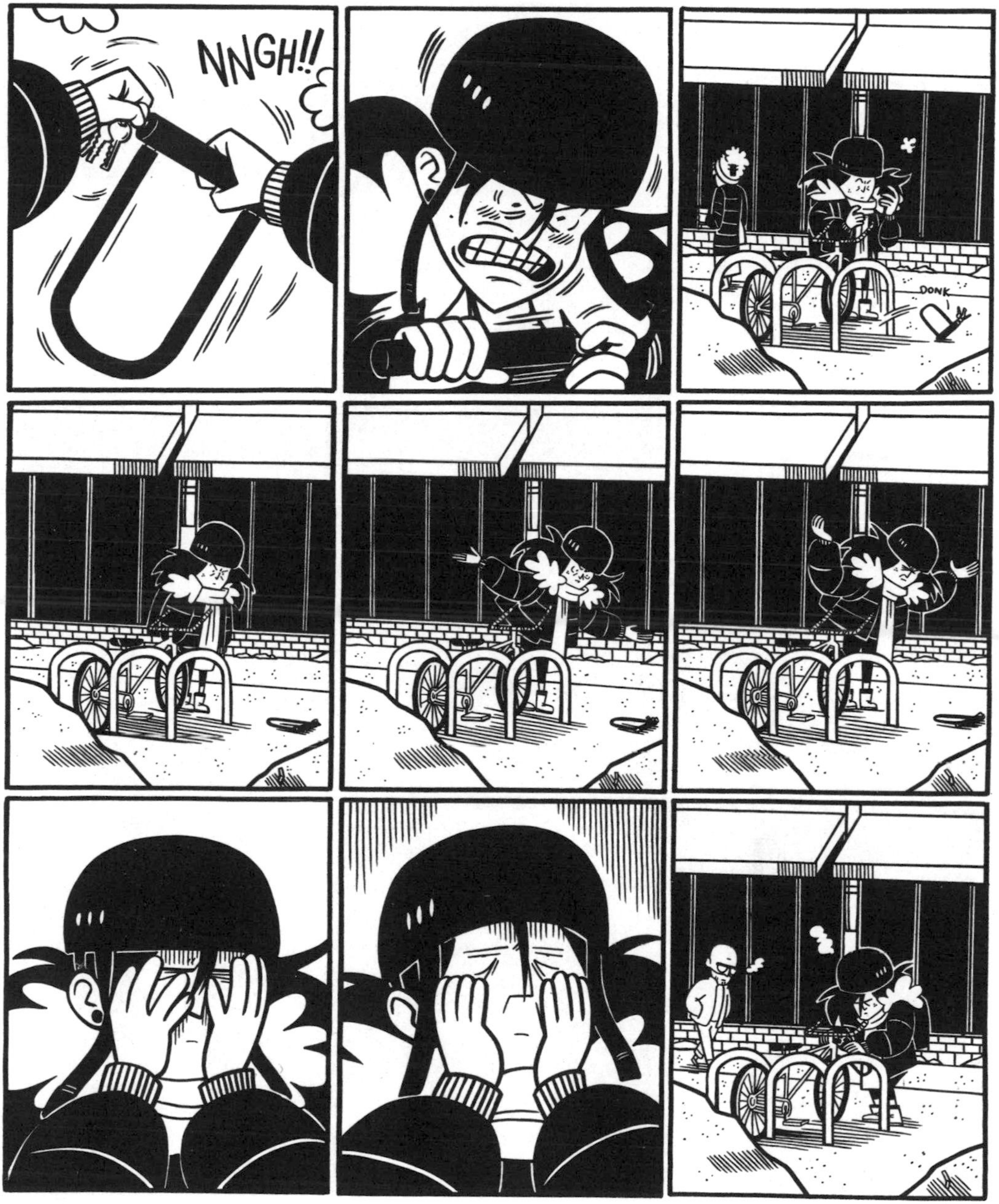
NNGH!!
DONK

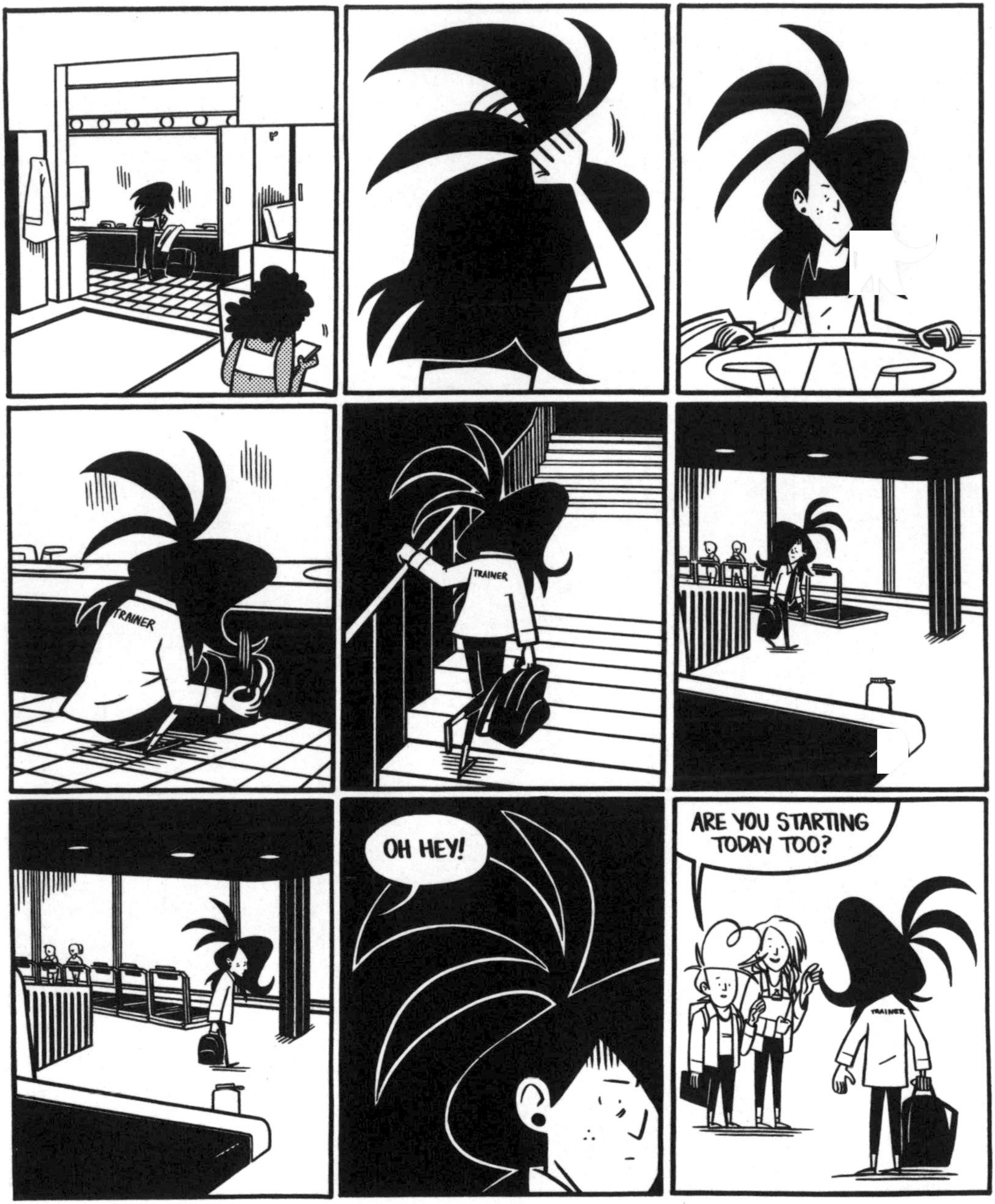
TRAINER
TRAINER
OH HEY!
ARE YOU STARTING TODAY TOO?
TRAINER

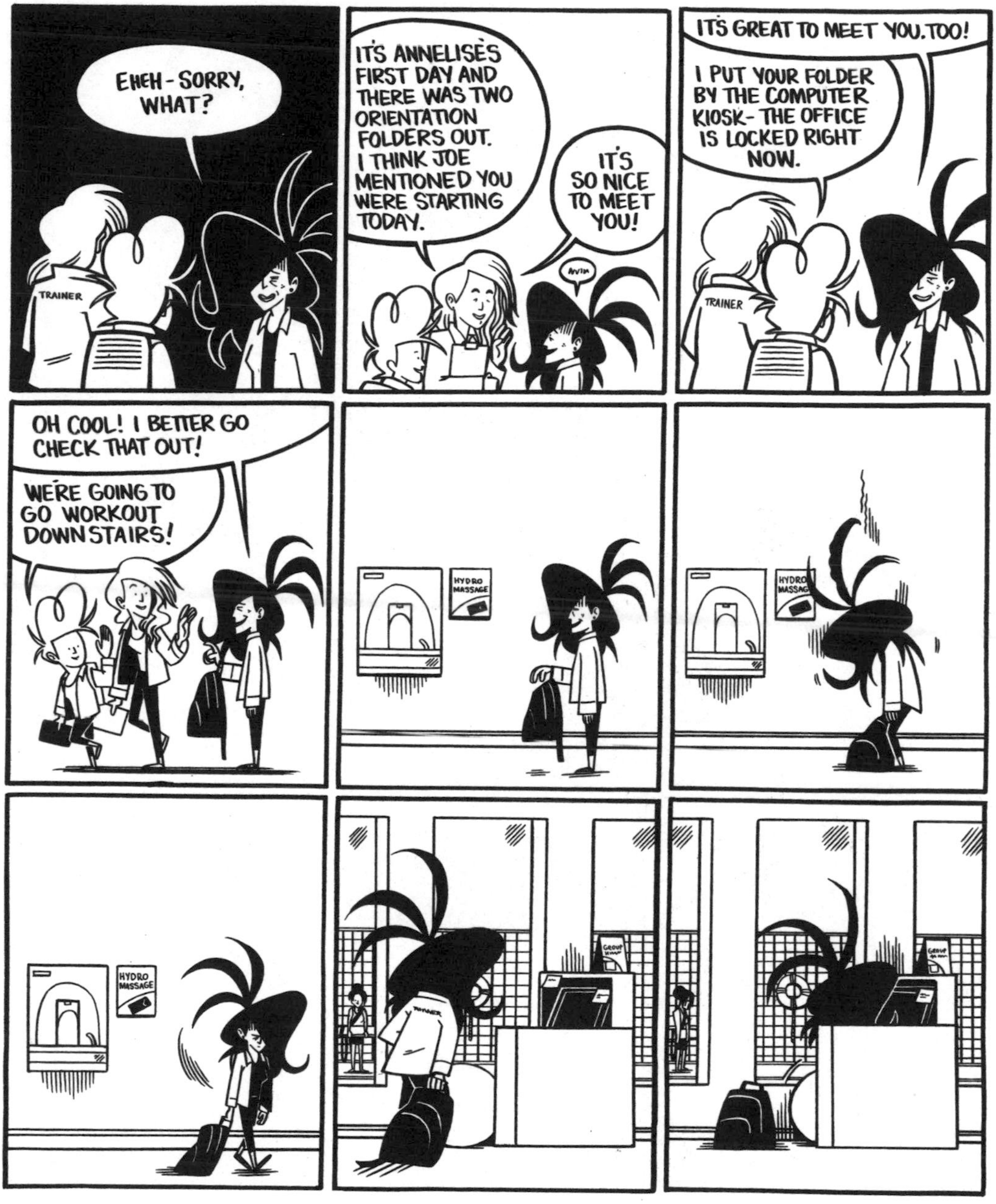
EHEH - SORRY, WHAT?
TRAINER
IT'S ANNELISE'S FIRST DAY AND THERE WAS TWO ORIENTATION FOLDERS OUT. I THINK JOE MENTIONED YOU WERE STARTING TODAY.
IT'S SO NICE TO MEET YOU!
IT'S GREAT TO MEET YOU. TOO!
I PUT YOUR FOLDER BY THE COMPUTER KIOSK- THE OFFICE IS LOCKED RIGHT NOW.
TRAINER
OH COOL! I BETTER GO CHECK THAT OUT!
WE'RE GOING TO GO WORKOUT DOWNSTAIRS!
HYDRO MASSAGE
HYDRO MASSAGE
HYDRO MASSAGE

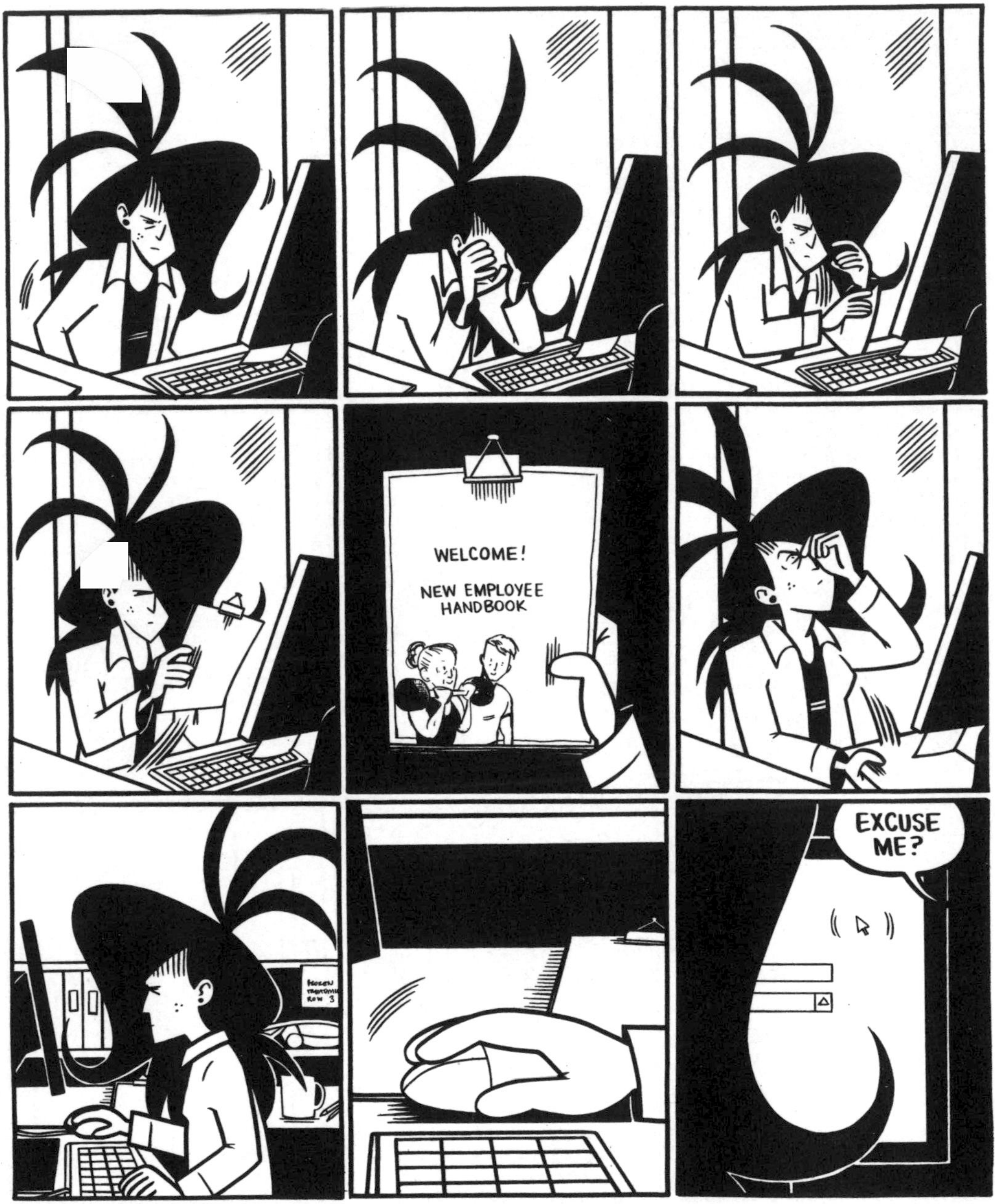
WELCOME!
NEW EMPLOYEE HANDBOOK
EXCUSE ME?

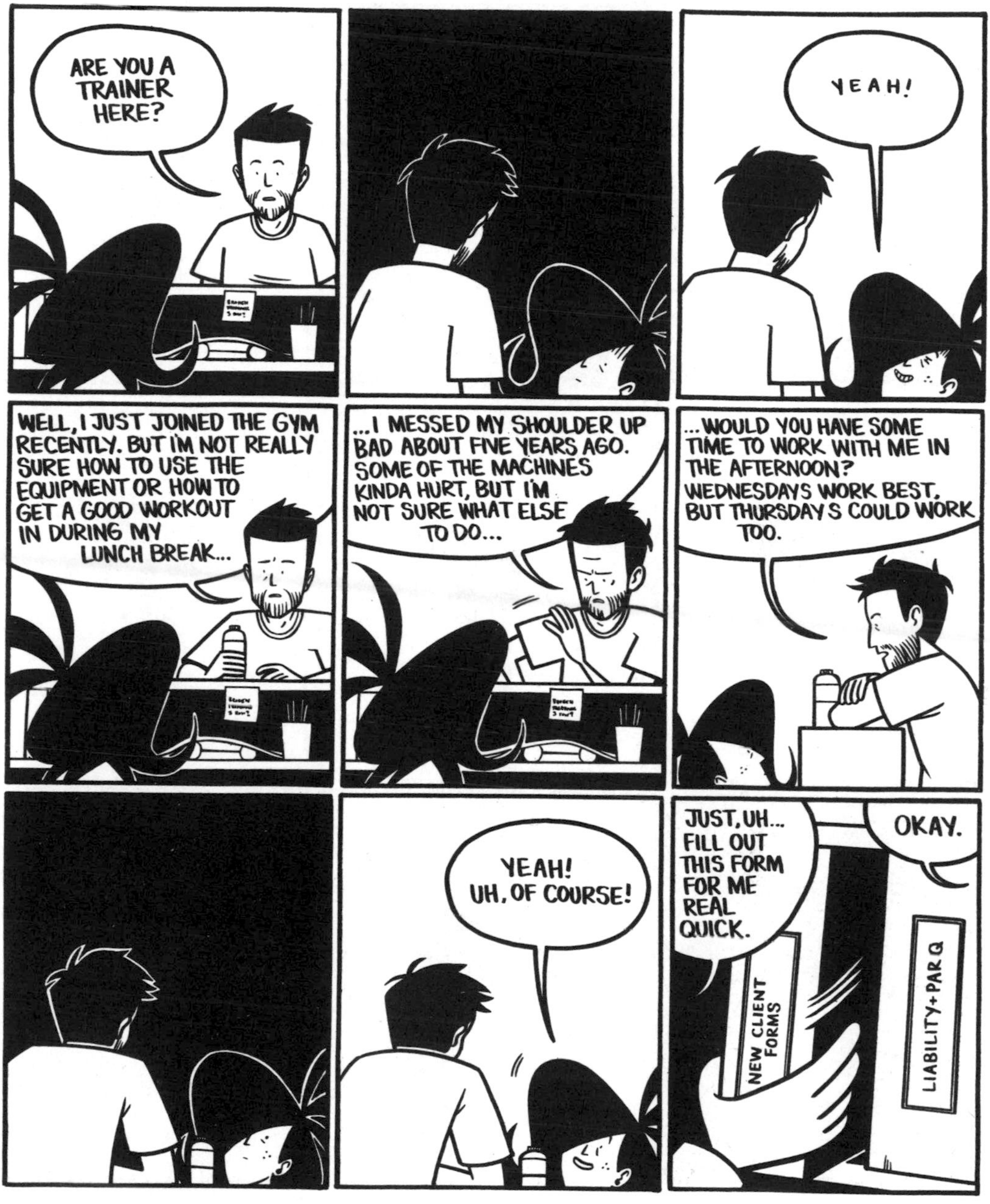
ARE YOU A TRAINER HERE?
YEAH!
WELL, I JUST JOINED THE GYM RECENTLY. BUT I'M NOT REALLY SURE HOW TO USE THE EQUIPMENT OR HOW TO GET A GOOD WORKOUT IN DURING MY LUNCH BREAK...
...I MESSED MY SHOULDER UP BAD ABOUT FIVE YEARS AGO. SOME OF THE MACHINES KINDA HURT, BUT I'M NOT SURE WHAT ELSE TO DO...
...WOULD YOU HAVE SOME TIME TO WORK WITH ME IN THE AFTERNOON? WEDNESDAYS WORK BEST, BUT THURSDAY S COULD WORK TOO.
YEAH! UH, OF COURSE!
JUST, UH... FILL OUT THIS FORM FOR ME REAL QUICK.
OKAY.
NEW CLIENT FORMS
LIABILITY + PAR Q

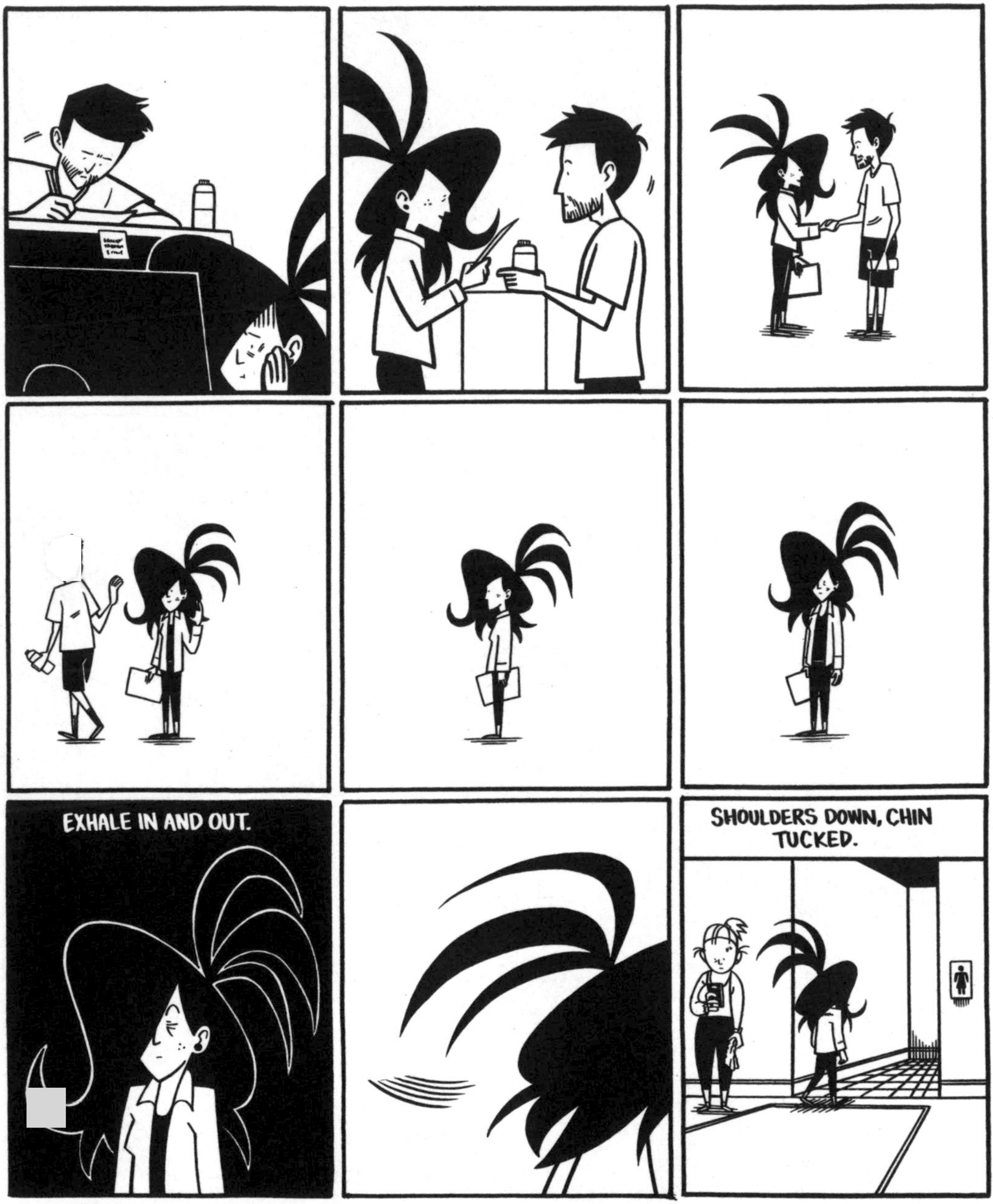
EXHALE IN AND OUT.
SHOULDERS DOWN, CHIN TUCKED.

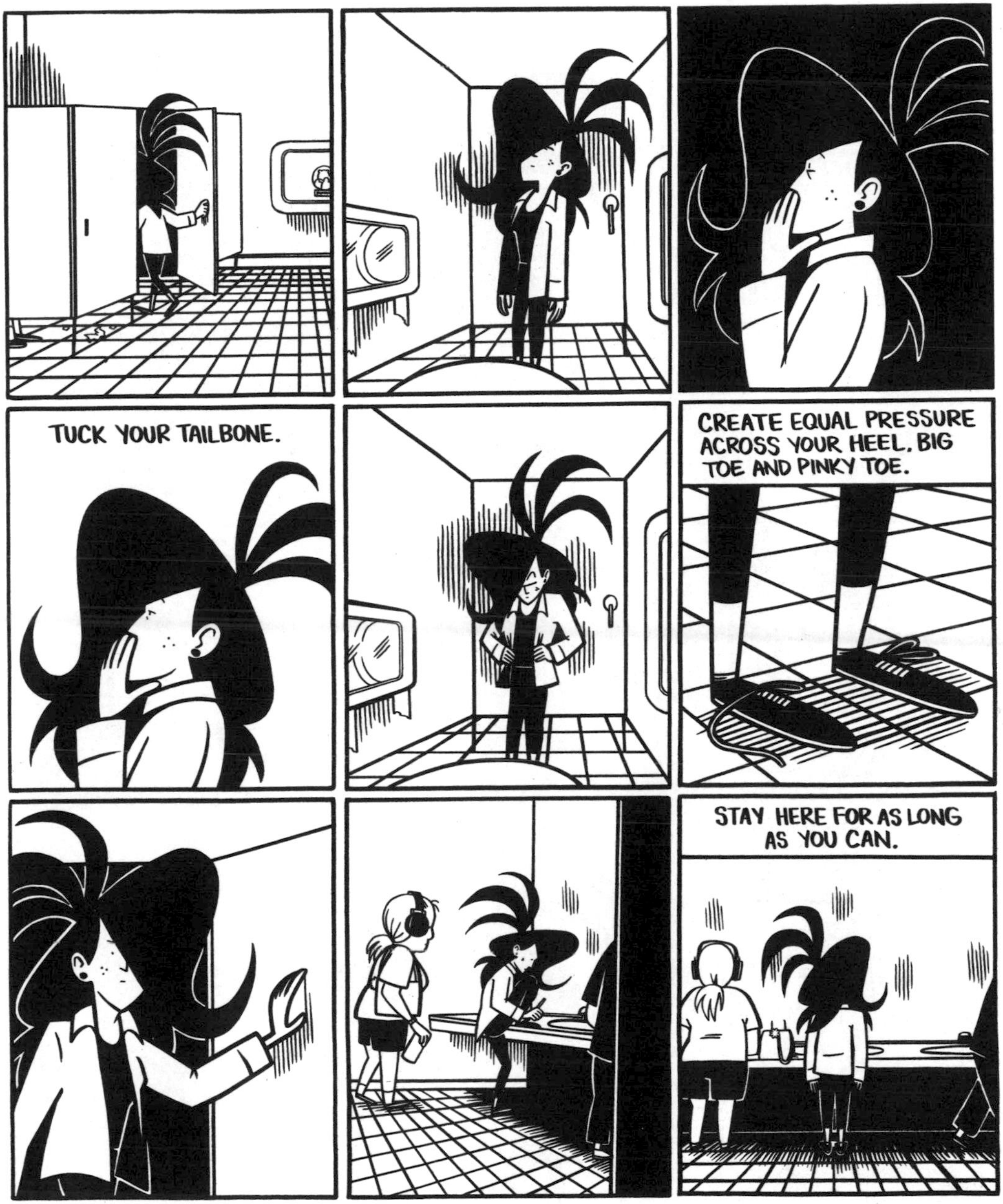
TUCK YOUR TAILBONE.
CREATE EQUAL PRESSURE ACROSS YOUR HEEL, BIG TOE AND PINKY TOE.
STAY HERE FOR AS LONG AS YOU CAN.

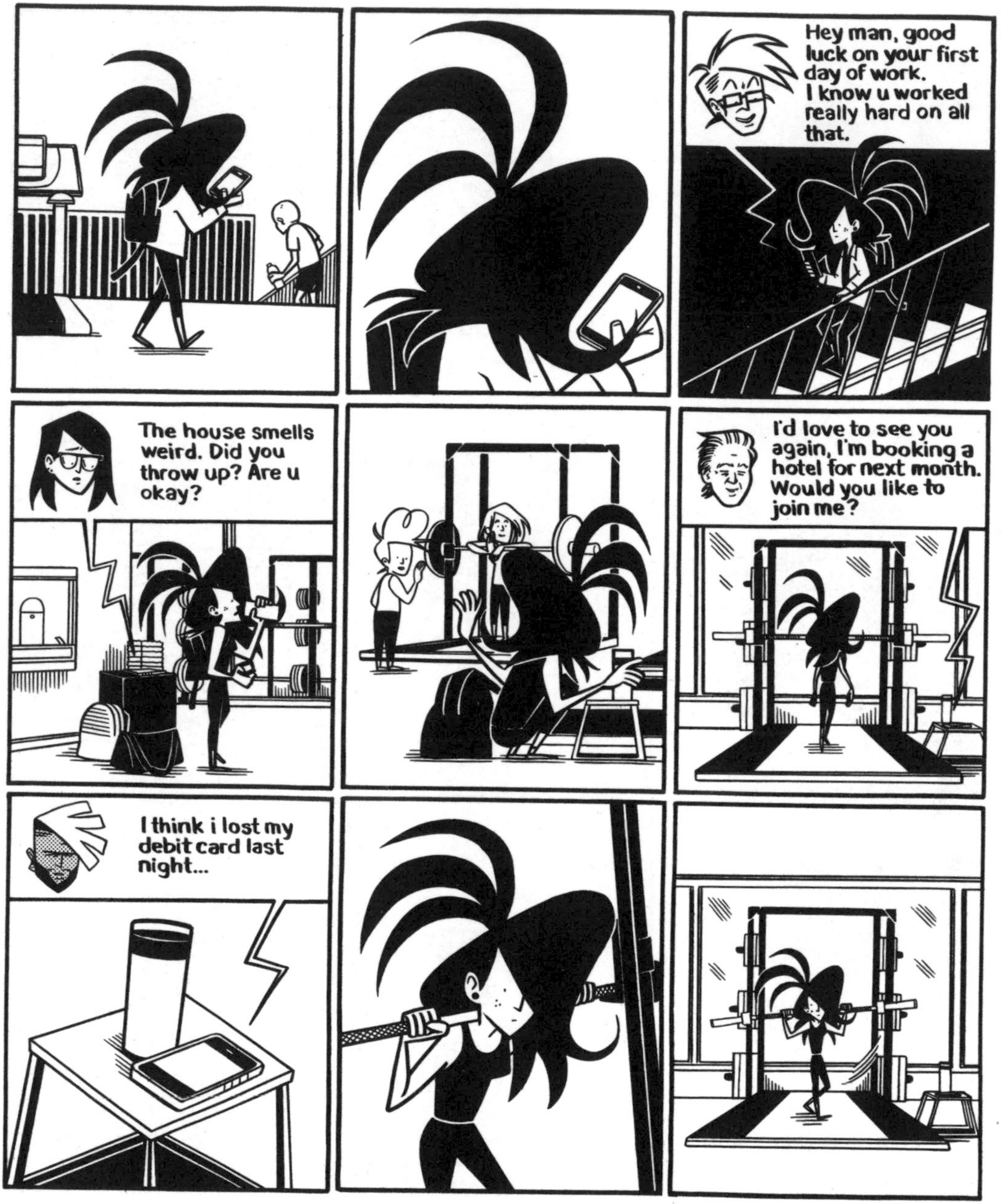
Hey man, good luck on your first day of work. I know u worked really hard on all that.
The house smells weird. Did you throw up? Are u okay?
I'd love to see you again, I'm booking a hotel for next month. Would you like to join me?
I think i lost my debit card last night...

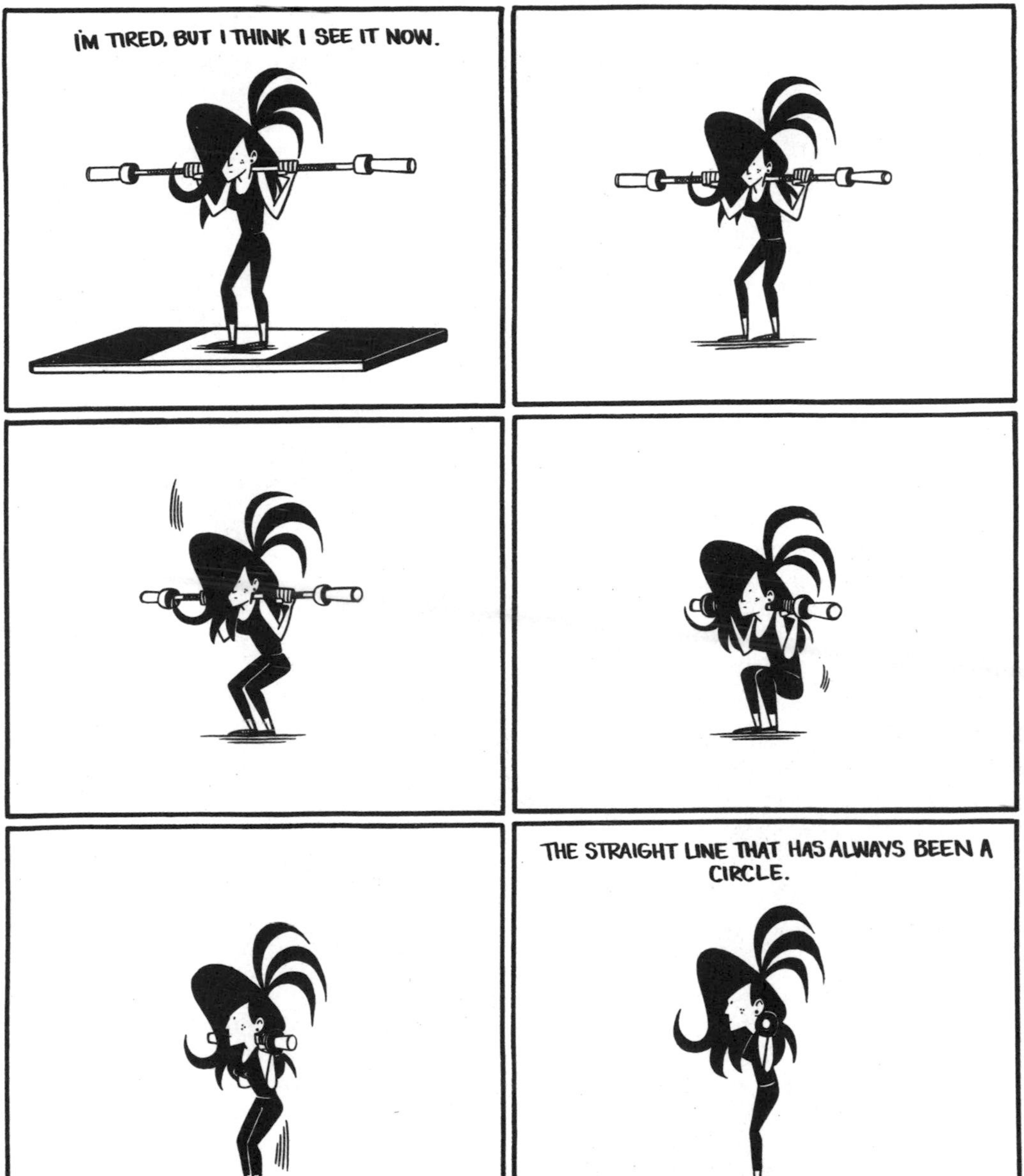
I'M TIRED, BUT I THINK I SEE IT NOW.
THE STRAIGHT LINE THAT HAS ALWAYS BEEN A CIRCLE.

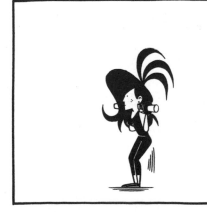

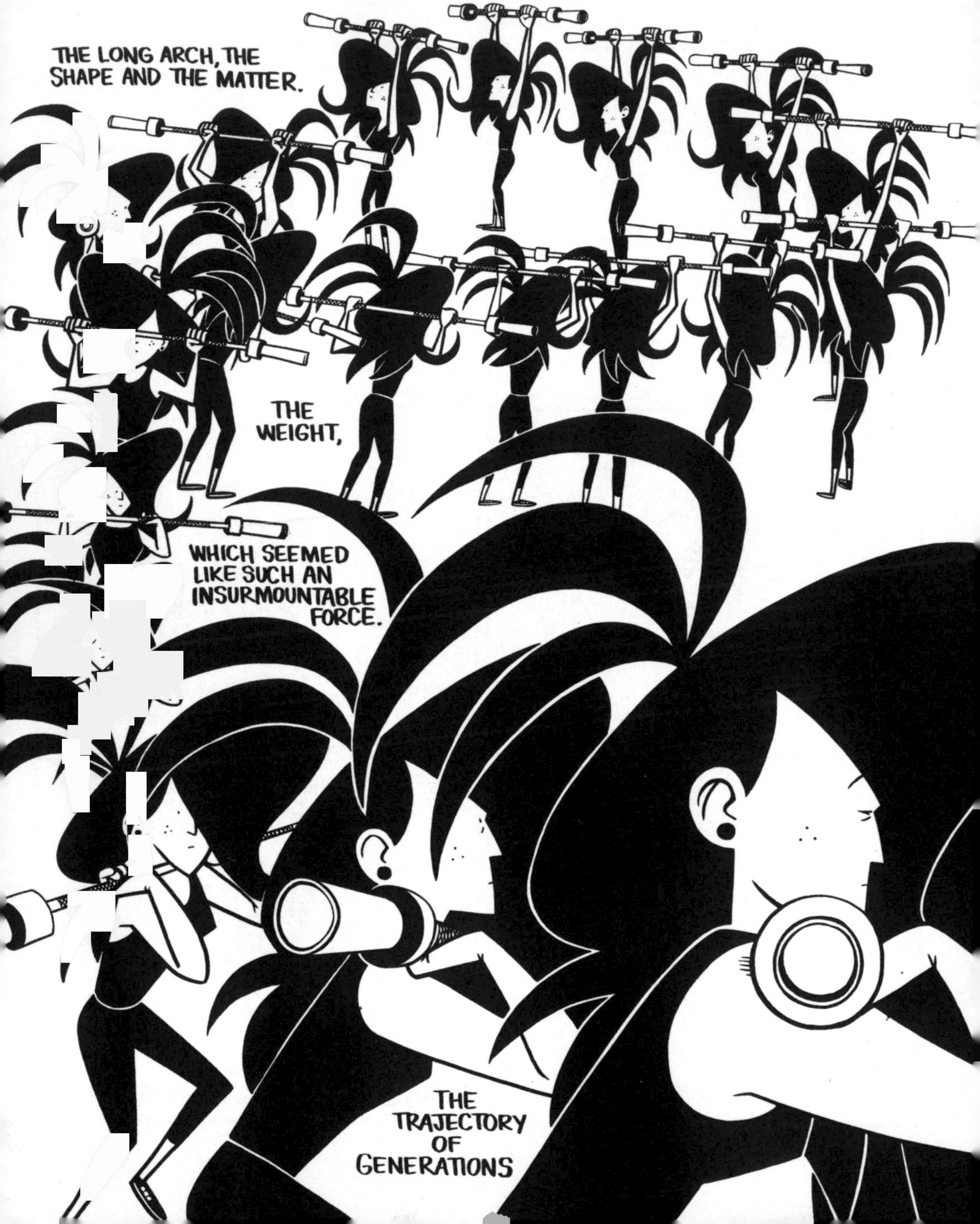
THE LONG ARCH, THE SHAPE AND THE MATTER.
THE WEIGHT,
WHICH SEEMED LIKE SUCH AN INSURMOUNTABLE FORCE.
THE TRAJECTORY OF GENERATIONS

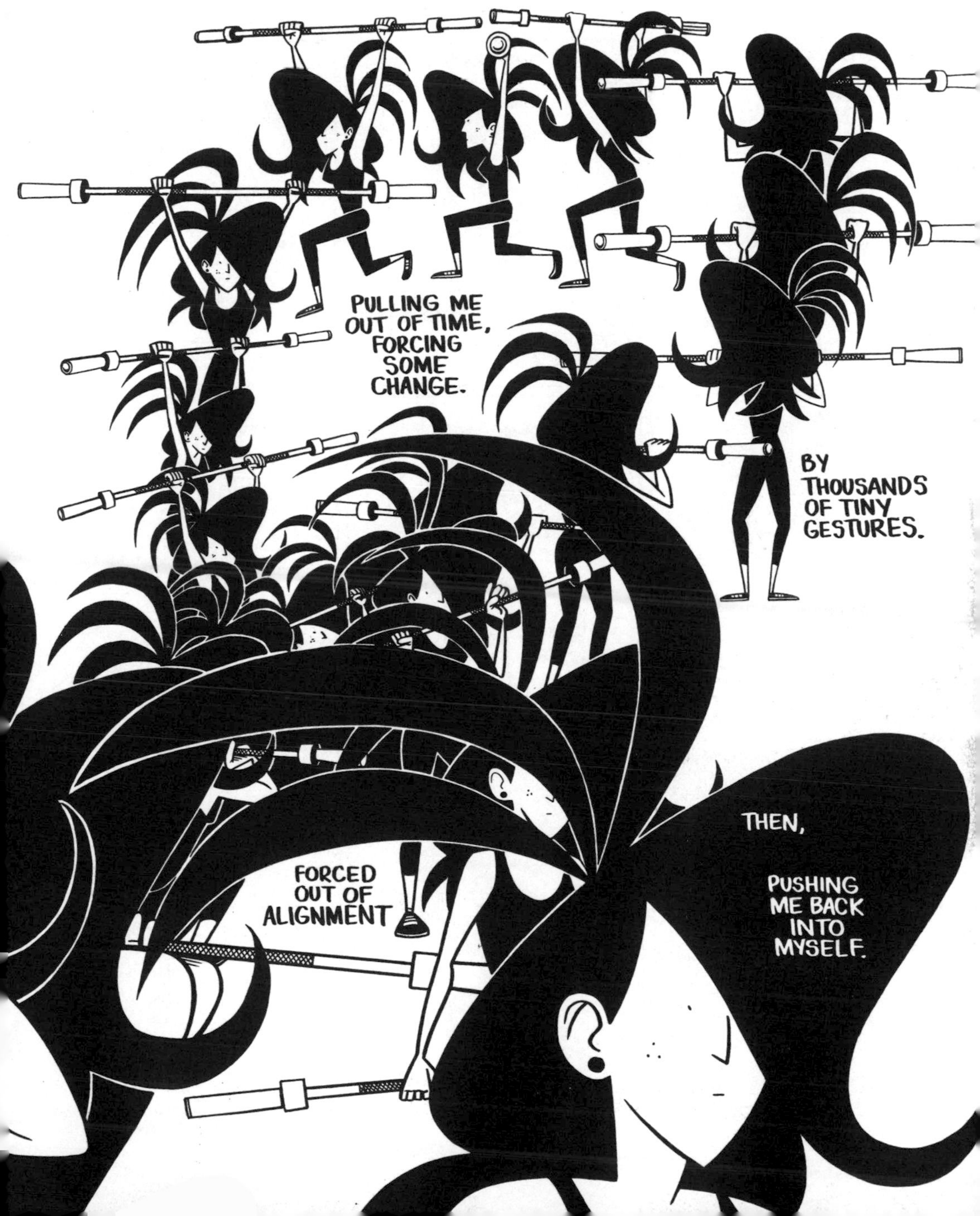
PULLING ME OUT OF TIME, FORCING SOME CHANGE.
BY THOUSANDS OF TINY GESTURES.
FORCED OUT OF ALIGNMENT
THEN,
PUSHING ME BACK INTO MYSELF.

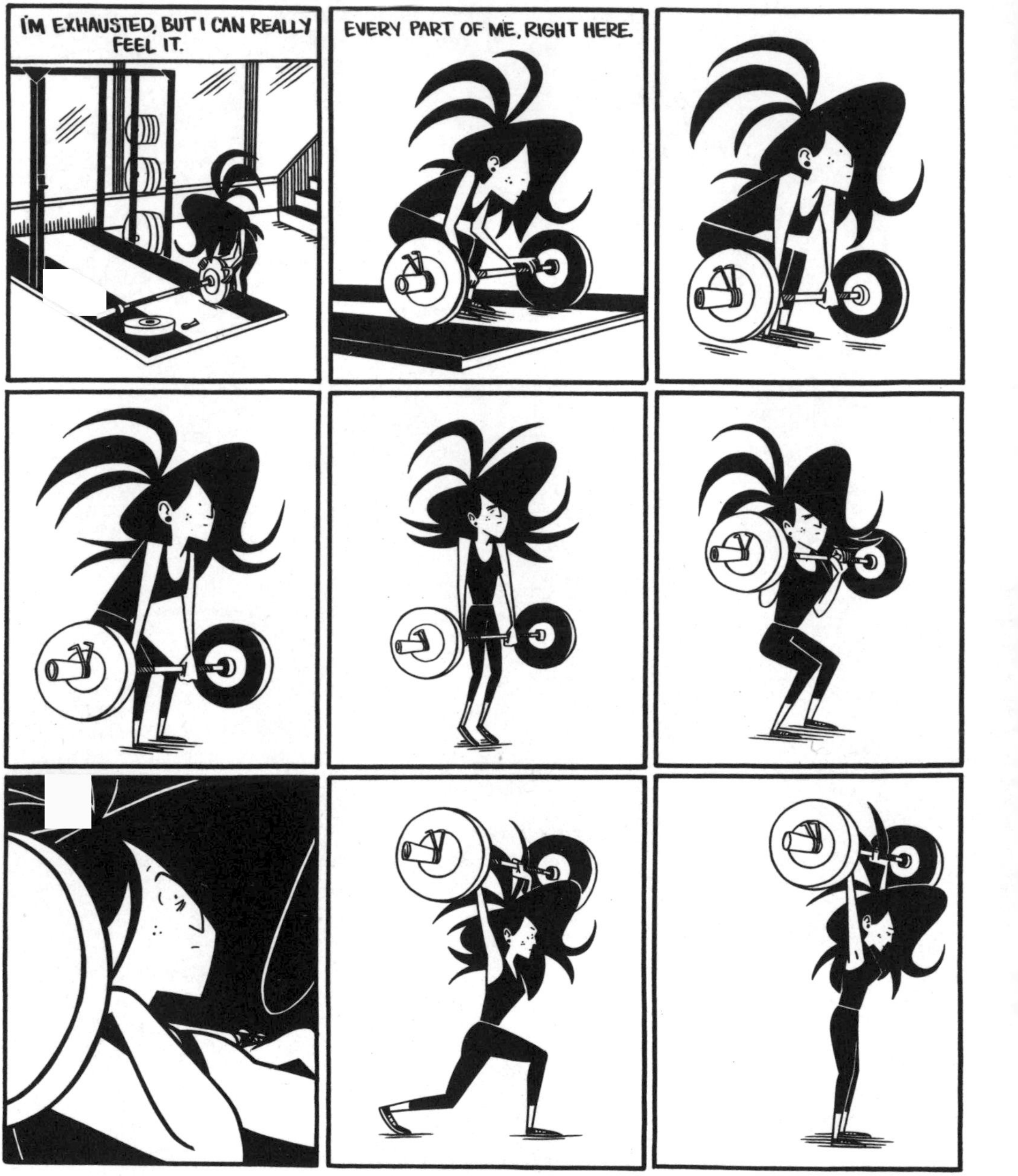
I'M EXHAUSTED, BUT I CAN REALLY FEEL IT.
EVERY PART OF ME, RIGHT HERE.

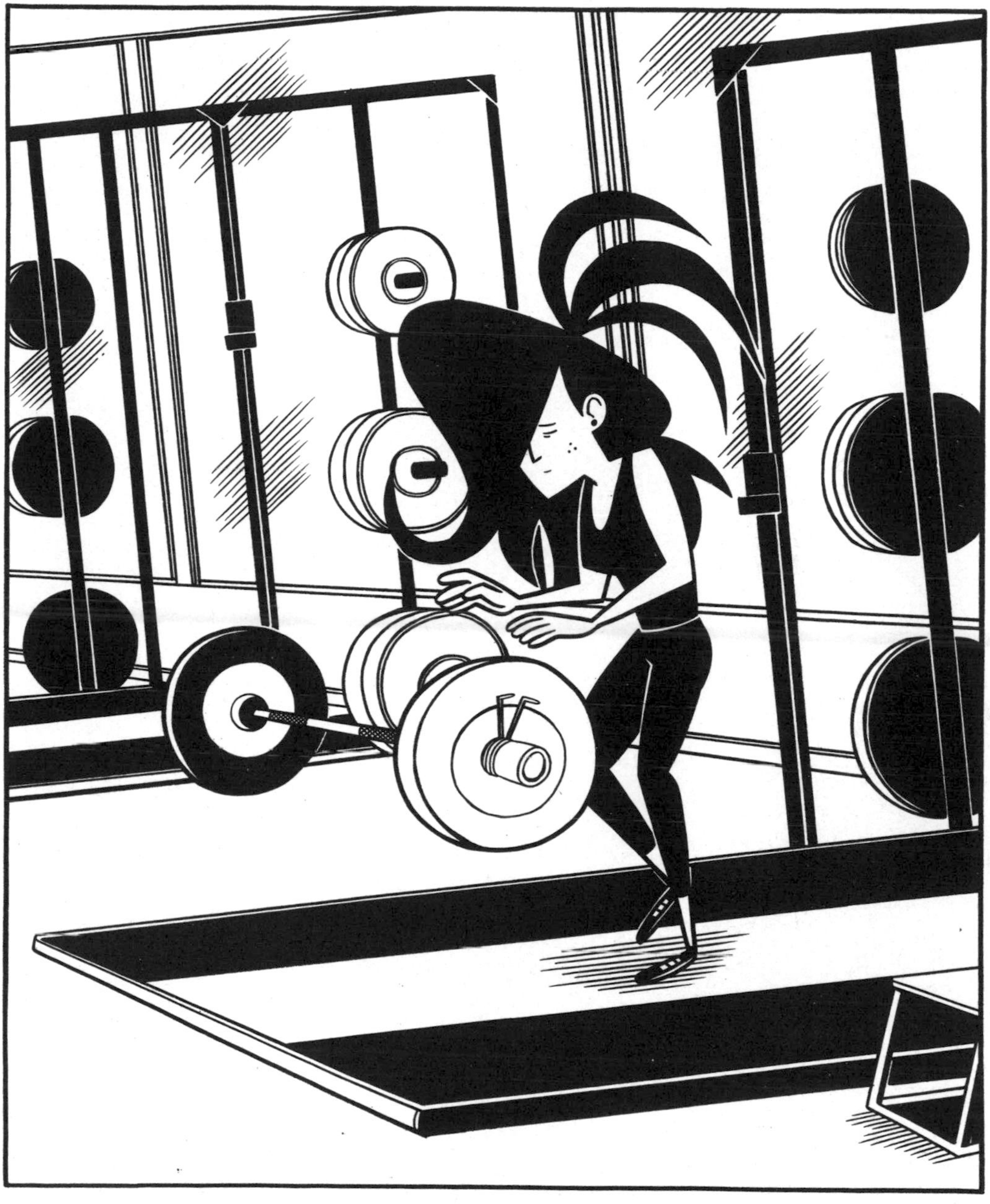

SPECIAL THANKS TO

MY DOTING FIANCE
MY MOM AND SISTER
MY PATREON SUBSCRIBERS
ARTS COMMUNITY OF COLUMBUS, OH
MINNEAPOLIS, MN
CHICAGO, IL
THE GREATER COLUMBUS ARTS COUNCIL
THE BILLY IRELAND CARTOON LIBRARY
THE FORECAST PLATFORM
ULLI LUST
CAITLIN MCGURK
ANNIE KOYAMA
HOCKING HILLS CARTOONISTS
REBECCA PERRY DAMSEN
NICOLE THOMAS
ELIS BRADSHAW
DIEGO PEREZ
NATE MCDONOUGH
VICTORIA DOUGLAS
FRANK SANTORO
SETH FERALIN
ANNELISE CHRIST
HAYDEN BUCKNER
TYRELL CANNON
ED KANERVA
LAURENN MCCUBBIN
JUNE MISSEREY
KEVIN HUIZENGA
EMI GENNIS

& THE NUMEROUS OTHERS WHO LOVED AND
SUPPORTED ME DURING THE PANDEMIC AND
THE DEVELOPMENT OF THIS BOOK.